MICRO ECONOMICS

SIXTH CANADIAN EDITION

MICRO ECONOMICS

SIXTH CANADIAN EDITION

CAMPBELL R. McCONNELL
University of Nebraska, Lincoln

STANLEY L. BRUE
Pacific Lutheran University

THOMAS P. BARBIERO
Ryerson Polytechnic University

McGraw-Hill Ryerson Limited
Toronto   Montreal   New York
Auckland   Bogotá   Caracas   Lisbon
London   Madrid   Mexico   Milan
New Delhi   Paris   San Juan
Singapore   Sydney   Tokyo

MICROECONOMICS
Sixth Canadian Edition

ISBN: 0-07-551433-8

2 3 4 5 6 7 8 9 10 RRD 2 1 0 9 8 7 6 5 4

SPONSORING EDITOR: Jennifer Mix
SUPERVISING EDITOR: Margaret Henderson
COPY EDITOR: Gail Marsden
COVER & TEXT DESIGN: Brant Cowie/ArtPlus Limited
PRINTING & BINDING: R. R. Donnelly & Sons Company

Canadian Cataloguing in Publication Data

McConnell, Campbell R.
    Microeconomics

6th Canadian ed.
Includes index.
ISBN 0-07-551433-8

1. Microeconomics. I. Brue, Stanley L., [date]-   .
II. Barbiero, Thomas Paul, [date]-   . III. title.

HB172.M24   1993 338.5   C92-095457-X

To Marta, Emilia, and Robert

About the Authors

Campbell R. McConnell earned his Ph.D. from the University of Iowa after receiving degrees from Cornell College and the University of Illinois. He taught at the University of Nebraska — Lincoln from 1953 until his retirement in 1990. He is also co-author of *Contemporary Labour Economics,* 3rd ed. (McGraw-Hill) and has edited readers for the principles and labour economics courses. He is a recipient of both the University of Nebraska Distinguished Teaching Award and the James A. Lake Academic Freedom Award, and is past-president of the Midwest Economics Association. His primary areas of interest are labour economics and economic education. He has an extensive collection of jazz recordings and enjoys reading jazz history.

Stanley L. Brue did his undergraduate work at Augustana College (S.D.) and received his Ph.D. from the University of Nebraska — Lincoln. He teaches at Pacific Lutheran University, where he has been honoured as a recipient of the Burlington Northern Faculty Achievement Award for classroom excellence and professional accomplishment. He is national President-elect and member of the International Executive Board of Omicron Delta Epsilon International Honour Society in Economics. Professor Brue is co-author of *Economic Scenes: Theory in Today's World,* 5th ed. (Prentice-Hall); *The Evolution of Economic Thought,* 4th ed. (Harcourt Brace Jovanovich); and *Contemporary Labour Economics,* 3rd ed. (McGraw-Hill). For relaxation, he enjoys boating on Puget Sound and skiing trips with his family.

Thomas P. Barbiero received his Ph.D. from the University of Toronto after completing undergraduate studies at the same university. His primary fields of interest are European economic history and economic development. He has published papers on Italian economic history, particularly on the role of agriculture in the industrial development of the North in the period 1861–1914. Professor Barbiero is presently chair of the department of economics at Ryerson Polytechnic Institute. He spends his summers with his wife and three children in Italy, where, apart from following his interest in the country's economic history, he assiduously pursues good food and drink.

Contents in Brief

Contents

Note: The global symbol ⑤ appears below in all chapter sections with substantial global content.

LIST OF KEY GRAPHS

Preface

The publication of the sixth editions of *Macroeconomics* and *Microeconomics* follows the most successful edition of this book to date. Naturally, we are pleased that sales of the Canadian and U.S. editions confirm *Economics* as the best-selling economics text in North America. Moreover, we are pleasantly surprised that the Russian translation of *Economics* will soon be the leading economics text in the former Soviet Union; Politizdat Press has taken orders for nearly 500,000 copies. This fact dramatizes how remarkable these times are for teaching and learning economics. The message of our day is clear: People who comprehend economic principles will have a great advantage functioning in, and making sense of, the emerging world. We express our sincere thanks to each of you using *Microeconomics* for granting us a modest role in your efforts to teach or learn this globally important subject.

THE REVISION

The publication of the sixth edition of *Microeconomics* marks a departure from the previous five Canadian editions of *Economics*. After careful consideration and discussion with instructors, we have decided to publish the volumes *Microeconomics* and *Macroeconomics* as independent entities, without the combined text. We believe that in today's semestered priniciples of economics curriculum, this decision will prove efficient in the use of the resources of students, instructors, and the publisher.

The sixth edition of *Microeconomics* has been thoroughly revised, polished, and updated. Many of the changes have been motivated by the comments of the many reviewers. We are grateful to these scholars and acknowledge them by name at the end of this preface.

We strive only for an overview of the changes in the sixth edition here; chapter-by-chapter details are provided in the Instructor's Manual accompanying this book.

New Topics and Analysis

Much attention has been given to applying economics to the major issues of our day. Also, this edition contains new formal economic analyses. Examples of new discussions and analyses include:

- **Economics and the environment.** Chapters 19 and 20 are new chapters on government and market failure. They discuss externalities by examining the Coase theorem, liability rules and lawsuits, markets for externality rights, and society's optimal amount of externality abatement. A case study of pollution examines the dimensions, causes, and solutions of this problem. Special attention is given to solid waste disposal and recycling.
- **Economics of information.** The idea of imperfect information in decision making is introduced *early* in the book. Box 1-1 in Chapter 1 uses the economic perspective to analyze how customers decide which fast-food line to enter. A lengthy new section of Chapter 20 looks at market failure associated with inadequate information by buyers about sellers and by sellers about buyers. Topics such as adverse selection and moral hazard

are included here. Also the discussion of advertising in Chapter 12 is completely rewritten to highlight advertising's informational role.

- **Strategic behaviour.** Game theory — specifically the prisoner's dilemma model — is presented in the discussion of oligopoly (Chapter 13).
- **Public choice and tax analysis.** A full chapter (Chapter 21) is devoted to public choice and tax analysis. Also, we have placed much more emphasis on public choice theory in our explanation of the persistence of agricultural subsidies in Chapter 22, a chapter that has been extensively revised and updated.
- **Principal–agent problem and pay-for-performance.** A new section of the chapter on wage determination (Chapter 16) explains the principal–agent problem and discusses pay-for-performance plans (piece rates, commissions and royalties, bonuses and profit sharing), seniority pay, and efficiency wages.
- **Other new discussions.** There are numerous other new discussions in the sixth edition, a few examples being: the Ricardian equivalence theorem; cross and income elasticities; rent controls; the absence of a monopoly supply curve; the Herfindahl index; and the consolidation in the airline industry.

New "Boxes"

The "Last Words" appearing in the fifth edition have been eliminated in favour of boxes positioned in strategic places within the chapter to highlight and enrich the theoretical discussion the student is reading. Some topics of the boxes provide current or historical real-world applications of economic concepts; others reveal human-interest aspects of economic concepts; and still others present economic concepts or issues in a global context.

We have selected topics for the boxes that are both highly relevant to the chapter's discussion *and* interesting to the reader. New topics are fast-food lines veiwed from the economic perspective (Chapter 1); the impact of Operation Desert Storm on Iraqi production possibilities (Chapter 2); ticket scalping (Chapter 4); the effect of supply interdiction on the price of marijuana (Chapter 6); product differentiation and nonprice competition in the market for economics textbooks (Chapter 12).

Pedagogical Improvements

The principles course had become increasingly demanding for students. Globalization of economies, developments in economic theory, and modern economic problems have added new, sometimes complex, material to the course. Concise and understandable explanations are more important than ever before. Accordingly, we have directed much effort toward improving the pedagogy of *Microeconomics*. We have "gone back to the basics," attempting to bolster what we believe to be this book's comparative advantages: Its readability and accessibility. Examples of our pedagogical changes include:

- **"Quick Reviews" within each chapter.** Two or three new reviews within the body of each chapter allow the student to pause and ponder key points. We believe these "Quick Reviews" will also help students as they study for examinations.
- **"Key Graphs."** Students often have a difficult time distinguishing which of the hundreds of graphs in economics are of fundamental importance. To direct students' attention to the essential graphs, we have designated 12 figures as "Key Graphs." These graphs are specially designed and labelled to make them easily identifiable. Figures 2-1 and 4-5 are representative. A complete listing of the Key Graphs can be found at the end of the Contents on page xvi.
- **Motivational introductions.** In many chapters new introductions are added to stimulate reader interest in the chapter's contents. These introductions relate to students' everyday experiences and observations.
- **Shorter paragraphs.** In keeping with trends in popular and academic publishing, we have shortened scores of long paragraphs.
- **Tighter sentences.** The three authors and talented McGraw-Hill editors scrutinized every sen-

tence in this edition for unnecessary verbiage. Collectively, we were able to tighten hundreds of sentences without altering the overall style of writing. In economizing on words, we were careful not to reduce the thoroughness of our explanations. Where needed, the "extra sentence of explanation" remains a distinguishing characteristic of *Microeconomics*.

- **Numbered lists and added subheads.** We have substituted numbered and labelled lists for verbal strings of "First," "Second," and "Third." The idea here is to break material into smaller parcels to help students more readily retain the content. Similarly, we have employed subheads more liberally so that the organizational structure of each chapter and topic will be clearer.
- **Footnote deletion.** We have significantly reduced the number of footnotes. Several lengthy explanatory footnotes have been deleted; a number of shorter footnotes have been integrated into the text. Footnotes suggesting additional reading have been judiciously pruned.
- **New diagrams.** All of the diagrams in the sixth edition have been redrawn; many have been reconfigured to improve their clarity. Some of the new diagrams depict fresh graphical analyses such as the economics of recycling, and a comparison of the effects of tariffs and quotas. Other new diagrams should help students visualize the interrelations of the concepts involved.
- **Added labelling in graphs.** Taking great care to avoid clutter, in a number of cases we have added labelling in figures to help guide the reader through the analysis. These labels are set so they are highly readable both within the book and on transparencies.
- **Clarified explanations of difficult subject matter.** We have continued to look for ways to explain difficult material more clearly. Even minor improvements in language or labelling of graphs can often help students better understand the material. Improvements of this sort have been made in numerous places throughout the text. Good examples are our revised discussions of efficiency (Chapter 2);

the relationship between the demand curve and total revenue (Chapter 9); the efficiency effects of oligopoly (Chapter 11); and efficiency losses of taxes (Chapter 21).

New and Enhanced Ancillaries

The ancillaries in the sixth edition package are discussed later in this Preface, but four new items are noteworthy.

- **New Instructor's Manual.** With this edition we have separated the Instructor's Manual from the Test Bank. The former now has the complete answers to the questions at the end of each chapter.
- **Augmented Test Bank.** We have added approximately 1200 questions to the Test Bank.
- **New software.** The successful *Concept Master* software introduced with the eleventh U.S. edition has been completely updated.
- **Enhanced video materials.** The power of videodisks is harnessed in this edition to provide enhanced classroom presentation of visual material. Also, there are new videotape materials that have been carefully designed for effective classroom use.

We trust that the outcome of this detailed revision is a text and package that are clearly superior to their predecessors.

FUNDAMENTAL GOALS

Although the sixth edition bears little resemblance to the first, the basic purpose remains the same — to introduce the beginning economics student to those principles essential to an understanding of the fundamental economic problems and the policy alternatives available for dealing with these problems. We hope that the ability to reason accurately and objectively about economic matters and the development of a lasting interest in economics will be two valuable by-products of this basic objective. Our intention remains to present the principles and problems of economics in a straightforward, logical fashion. To this end, we continue to put great stress on clarity of presentation and on logical organization.

DISTINGUISHING FEATURES

This text embraces a number of features that perhaps distinguish it from other books in the field.

- **Comprehensive explanations at an appropriate level.** We have attempted to craft a comprehensive, analytical text that is challenging to better students, yet accessible — with appropriate hard work — to average students. We think the thoroughness and accessibility of *Microeconomics* enables the instructor to select topics for special classroom emphasis with confidence that students can independently read and comprehend other assigned material in the book.
- **Comprehensive definition of economics.** The principles course sometimes fails to provide students with a comprehensive and meaningful definition of economics. To avoid this shortcoming, all of Chapter 2 is devoted to a careful statement and development of the economizing problem and an exploration of its implications. This foundation should help put the many particular subject areas of economics in proper perspective.
- **Emphasis on the theory of the firm**. We have purposely given much attention to microeconomics in general and to the theory of the firm in particular, for two reasons: First, the concepts of microeconomics are difficult for most beginning students. Short expositions usually compound these difficulties by raising more questions than they answer. Second, we have coupled analysis of the various market structures with a discussion of the impact of each market arrangement on price, output levels, resource allocation, and the rate of technological advance.
- **Chapters on economic issues.** As most students see it, Part 5 on micro-oriented problems is where the action is. We have sought to guide the action along logical lines through the application of appropriate analytical tools. Our bias in these parts is in favour of inclusiveness; each instructor can effectively counter this bias by omitting those chapters

felt to be less relevant for a particular group of students.

ORGANIZATION AND CONCEPT

We believe that the basic prerequisite of an understandable economics text is the logical arrangement and clear exposition of subject matter. This book has been organized so that the exposition of each particular topic and concept is directly related to the level of difficulty, which, in our experience, the average student is likely to encounter. For this reason, the relationship between production analysis and cost curves, price–output decisions of firms, and analysis of resource markets are given comprehensive and careful treatment. Simplicity here is correlated with comprehensiveness, not brevity.

Furthermore, our experience suggests that in the treatment of each basic topic — for example, the theory of the firm — it is desirable to couple analysis with policy. A three-step development of basic analytical tools is employed: (1) verbal descriptions and illustrations; (2) numerical examples; and (3) graphical presentation based on these numerical illustrations.

ORGANIZATIONAL ALTERNATIVES

Although economics instructors generally agree as to the basic content of a principles of microeconomics course, there are differences of opinion on what particular arrangement of material is best. The structure of this book provides considerable organizational flexibility. Users of prior editions tells us they accomplished substantial rearrangements of chapters with little sacrifice of continuity.

Those interested in the one-semester principles course will be able to discern several possible groups of chapters from *Microeconomics* and *Macroeconomics* that will be appropriate to such a course. Tentative outlines for three one-semester courses, emphasizing microeconomics, macroeconomics, or a survey of micro and macro theory, are included following the preface in the Instructor's Manual.

ASSISTANCE FOR STUDENTS

Microeconomics is highly student oriented.

1 Students who are comfortable with graphical analysis and a few related quantitative concepts are in an advantageous position to understand principles of economics. To help students in this regard, an appendix to Chapter 1 carefully reviews graphing, line slopes, and linear equations.

2 The introductory paragraphs of each chapter state objectives, present an organizational overview of the chapter, and relate the chapter to what has been covered before and what will follow.

3 Because a significant portion of any introductory course is devoted to terminology, terms are given special emphasis. In particular, each important term is in **boldface type** where it first appears in each chapter. We have tried to make all definitions clear and succinct. At the end of each chapter all new terms are listed in the "Terms and Concepts" section. Finally, at the end of the book a comprehensive glossary of almost 1000 terms is found. This glossary is also contained in the Study Guide.

4 As we noted earlier, each chapter contains two or three "Quick Reviews" at appropriate places in the chapter to reinforce key points for students and help them study for examinations.

5 Figures worthy of intensive study are designated as "Key Graphs" by a key symbol.

6 The legends accompanying all diagrams are written as self-contained analyses of the relevant concepts shown. This is a strategic means of reinforcing student comprehension.

7 Much thought has gone into the end-of-chapter questions. Though purposely intermixed, the questions are of three general types. Some are designed to highlight the main points of each chapter. Others are "open-end" discussion, debate, or thought questions. Wherever pertinent, numerical problems that require the student to derive and manipulate key concepts and relationships are employed. Numerical problems are stressed in those chapters that deal with analytical material. Some optional "advanced analysis" questions accompany certain theory chapters. These problems usually involve the stating and manipulation of certain basic concepts in equation form.

8 Many of the end-of-chapter questions deal with subject matter that is reinforced by the excellent computerized tutorial *Concept Master II,* which accompanies the text. A floppy disk symbol ▨ appears in conjunction with questions whose underlying content correlates to a lesson in the tutorial program.

SUPPLEMENTS FOR STUDENTS

The sixth edition of *Microeconomics* is accompanied by supplements that we feel equal or surpass competing texts in terms of both quality and quantity.

Study Guide

Professor Cyril Grant has prepared the sixth edition of the Study Guide that many students find to be an indispensable aid. It contains for each chapter an introductory statement, a checklist of behavioural objectives, an outline, a list of important terms, fill-in questions, problems and projects, objective questions, and discussion questions. Answers to all odd-numbered problems in the text are found at the end of the Study Guide. The glossary found at the end of *Microeconomics* also appears in the Study Guide.

The Guide comprises, in our opinion, a superb "portable tutor" for the principles student.

Economic Concepts

Economic Concepts, by the late Robert C. Bingham and Professor W.H. Pope, provides carefully designed programmed materials for all the key analytical areas of the principals course.

Instructor's Manual

The sixth edition of the Instructor's Manual has been greatly improved. Along with chapter summaries, listings of "what's new" in each chapter, teaching suggestions, learning objectives, data and visual aid sources, and questions and problems, the new manual now includes answers to all the end-of-chapter questions in *Microeconomics* and *Macroeconomics*. We think instructors will find this manual useful and time-saving.

The Test Bank

The *Test Bank* now comprises some 4800 questions, all written by the text authors; approximately 3600 are carried over from the previous edition and over 1200 have been prepared by the authors for the new edition. The new questions are identified with the letter "N."

Adopters of the text will be able to use this sizable number of questions with maximum flexibility. The fact that the text authors have prepared all the text items will assure the fullest possible correlation with the context of the text.

Additional Supplements

Computerized testing. The Test Bank is available in computerized versions, as well as print. Available for IBM-PCs and compatibles, the computerized test generation system includes the capability to produce high-quality graphs from the test bank. The system also features the ability to generate multiple tests, with versions "scrambled" to be distinctive, and has many other useful features that meet the various needs of the widest spectrum of computer users.

Colour transparencies. Over 200 new full-colour transparencies for overhead projectors are available for use with the sixth edition. Sets are available on request to adopters.

Student software. For users of IBM-PCs and compatibles, a student software package, *Concept Master II,* has been prepared by Professor William Gunther, of the University of Alabama, and Irene Gunther. The previous version of this software was widely praised by the users, and it has been improved to provide even more flexibility. The software program includes over twenty graphics-based tutorial programs to which text questions with a floppy disk symbol relate; 1600 multiple-choice quiz questions with answers; and several other useful features. Wherever possible, they include a global perspective.

For users of MacIntosh computers, there are two new and exciting Hypercard-based programs, *VizEcon* and *Discoverecon.*

Videodisks. New to this edition are videodisks designed to harness this exciting new technology for classroom presentation. These videodisks offer an array of graphical illustrations of key economic concepts to further student understanding.

Videos. New videotape materials have been assembled for this edition to illustrate fundamental concepts and economic issues in a manner that will be equally effective in classroom settings or media resource centres. Among these materials is the new "MacNeil/Lehrer Quarterly Report on Economics," a new series of excerpts from the acclaimed U.S. Public Broadcasting System news program, "The MacNeil/Lehrer Newshour." Your local McGraw-Hill Ryerson representative can provide details on all new video ancillaries for the text.

ACKNOWLEDGEMENTS

The publication of this sixth edition will extend the life of *Microeconomics* well into its second decade. The acceptance of the parent text, *Economics,* which was generous from the outset, has expanded with each edition. This gracious reception has no doubt been fostered by the many teachers and students who have been kind enough to provide their suggestions and criticisms.

Our colleagues at the University of Nebraska-Lincoln, Pacific Lutheran University, and Ryerson Polytechnical Institute have generously shared knowledge of their specialties with us and have provided encouragement. We are especially indebted to Ryerson professors Dagmar Rajagopal, Donald Wheaton, John Hughes, and Mark Lovewell, who have been most helpful in offsetting our comparative ignorance in their areas of specialty.

As indicated, the sixth edition has benefitted from a number of perceptive reviews. In both quality and quantity, they provided the richest possible source of suggestions for this revision. We wish to thank the following instructors who participated in the formal review process:

M. Benarroch	University of Winnipeg
K. Dawson	Conestoga College
S. Dodaro	St. Francis Xavier University
S. Fefferman	NAIT
P. Fortura	Algonquin College
E. Jacobson	NAIT
S. Kamp	University of Alberta
V. Nallainayagam	Mount Royal College
A. Nimarko	Vanier College
L. Smith	University of Waterloo

We also owe a debt of gratitude to all those instructors who contributed in an informal manner their comments and suggestions to authors, editors, and McGraw-Hill Ryerson representatives over the life of the fifth edition.

We are greatly indebted to the many professionals at McGraw-Hill Ryerson — and in particular to Margaret Henderson and Ann Byford — for their expertise in the production and distribution of the book. Gail Marsden's editing has been absolutely invaluable. Without her constant vigilance, such a major revision of *Economics* would undoubtedly have had many mistakes. Whatever errors or omissions remain are certainly due to our own oversight. Our greatest debt is to Jennifer Mix for her conscientious supervision of this revision. Her patience and many positive contributions are gratefully acknowledged.

CAMPBELL R. MCCONNELL
STANLEY L. BRUE
THOMAS P. BARBIERO

An Introduction to Economics

1

The Nature and Method of Economics

Human beings, unfortunate creatures, are plagued with many material wants. The improvement of their material well-being is one of the main concerns of economics. We want to use the available resources — labour and managerial talents, tools and machinery, land and mineral deposits — to produce goods and services that satisfy people's material wants. And this is precisely what is done through the organizational mechanism we call the *economic system*.

The fact is, however, that the total of all our material wants is beyond the productive capacity of all available resources. Thus, absolute material abundance is not possible. This unyielding fact is the basis of our definition of economics: **Economics *is concerned with the efficient use (or management) of limited productive resources for the purpose of attaining the maximum satisfaction of human material wants.*** Though it may not be self-evident, all of the headline-grabbing issues of the day — inflation, unemployment, the federal budget deficit, poverty and inequality, pollution, government regulation of business, and the rest — have their roots in the issue of using scarce resources efficiently.

In this chapter, however, we must resist the temptation to plunge into the problem and issues of the moment. Our immediate concern is with some basic preliminary questions:

1. Of what importance or consequence is the study of economics?

2. How should we study economics — what are the proper procedures? What methods do economists use?

3. What specific problems, limitations, and pitfalls might we encounter in studying economics?

THE AGE OF THE ECONOMIST

Is economics a discipline of consequence? Is the study of economics an endeavour worthy of your time and effort? Half a century ago John Maynard Keynes (1883–1946) — one of the most influential economists of this century — offered a telling response:

> The ideas of economists and political philosophers, both when they are right and when they are wrong, are more powerful than is commonly understood. Indeed the world is ruled by little else. Practical men, who believe themselves to be quite exempt from any intellectual influences, are usually the slaves of some defunct economist.

The ideologies of the modern world that compete for people's minds have often been shaped in substantial measure by the great economists of the past — for example, Adam Smith, David Ricardo, John Stuart Mill, Karl Marx, and John Maynard Keynes.[1] And it is currently commonplace for world leaders to receive and invoke the advice and policy prescriptions of economists. The Government of Canada has more than a thousand economists in its various ministries and agencies — and the advice of this army of economists is considered essential to the functioning of modern government.

[1] Any of the following three volumes — Robert Heilbroner, *The Worldly Philosophers*, 6th ed. (New York: Simon and Schuster, Inc., 1986), Daniel R. Fusfeld, *The Age of the Economist*, 5th ed. (Chicago: Scott, Foresman and Company, 1986), or E. Ray Canterbery, *The Making of Economics*, 3rd ed. (Belmont, Calif.: Wadsworth Publishing Company, 1987) — will provide the reader with a fascinating introduction to the historical development of economic ideas.

Economics for Citizenship

A basic understanding of economics is essential if we are to be well-informed citizens. Many of the problems of the day have important economic aspects, and as informed voters we can influence the decisions of our political leaders in these matters. What are the causes and consequences of the federal budget deficit that is often in the news? What of the depressing stories of homeless street people? Are mergers of corporations good or bad? Why is inflation undesirable? What can be done to reduce unemployment? Are existing welfare programs effective and justifiable? Should we continue to subsidize farmers? Do we need further reform of our tax system? Will Canada-United States free trade help or hurt our industries, employment, and incomes? Has the deregulation of the airlines and banking industries been a boon or a bane to society?

Since the answers to such questions are determined in large measure by our elected officials, intelligence at the polls requires that we have a basic working knowledge of economics. Needless to say, a sound grasp of economics is more than helpful to politicians themselves!

Personal Applications

Economics is also an important discipline for more down-to-earth and immediate reasons. Economics is of practical value in business. An understanding of the overall operation of the economic system puts the business executive in a better position to decide on policies. The executive who understands the causes and consequences of inflation is better equipped, during inflationary periods, to make more intelligent business decisions. Indeed, more and more economists are appearing on the payrolls of large corporations. Their job is to gather and interpret economic information on which rational business decisions can be made.

Economics also gives the individual as consumer and worker some insights as to how to make wiser buying and employment decisions. How should one decide what to buy and in what amounts? How can one "hedge" against the reduction in the purchasing power of the dollar that accompanies inflation? Similarly, an individual who understands, for example, the relationship between budget deficits and security (stock and bond) values will be able to make more enlightened personal financial investment decisions.

METHODOLOGY

What do economists do? What are their goals? What procedures do they employ? Economists formulate economic *principles* that are useful in establishing *policies* designed to solve economic *problems*.

The procedures employed by economists are summarized in Figure 1-1.

1. Economists gather facts relevant to a specific economic problem. This task is called **descriptive** or **empirical economics**.

2. From the facts a general principle or **theory** is derived about the way individuals and institutions behave.

As Figure 1-1 shows, economists are as likely to move from theory to facts in studying economic behaviour as they are from facts to theory. Stated more formally, economists use both deductive and inductive methods. **Induction** involves the distilling of general principles or theories from facts. We begin with an accumulation of facts, which are then arranged systematically and analysed so as to permit the derivation of a generalization or principle. Induction moves from facts to theory, from the particular to the general. The inductive method is suggested by the left upward arrow from box 1 to box 2 in the figure.

Economists frequently set about their task by beginning at the level of theory and proceeding to the verification or rejection of this theory by an appeal to the facts. This is **deduction** or the hypothetical method. Thus economists may draw on casual observation, insight, logic, or intuition to frame a tentative, untested principle called a **hypothesis**. For example, they may conjecture that it is rational for consumers to buy more of a product when its price is low than when its price is high. The validity of this hypothesis must then be tested by repeated examination of relevant facts. The deductive method goes from the general to the particular, from theory to facts. This method is implicit in the right-side downward arrow from box 2 to box 1 in Figure 1-1.

Deduction and induction are complementary, rather than opposing, techniques of investigation. Hypotheses formulated by deduction provide guidelines for economists as they gather and systematize empirical data. Conversely, some understanding of factual evidence — of the "real world" — is prerequisite to the formulation of meaningful hypotheses.

The general knowledge of economic behaviour that economic principles provide can then be used in formulating policies for correcting or avoiding the problem under scrutiny. This aspect of the field is sometimes called "applied economics" or **policy economics** (box 3).

Continuing to use Figure 1-1 as a point of reference, let us now examine the economist's methodology in more detail.

Descriptive Economics

All sciences are empirical. That means all sciences are based on observable and verifiable behaviour of certain data or subject matter. In the physical sciences, the factual data are inorganic. As a social science, economics is concerned with the behaviour of individuals and institutions engaged in the production, exchange, and consumption of goods and services.

The gathering of economic data can be an infinitely complex task. Because the world of reality is cluttered with a multitude of interrelated facts, the economist must use discretion in gathering them.

FIGURE 1-1   The relationship between facts, principles, and policies in economics

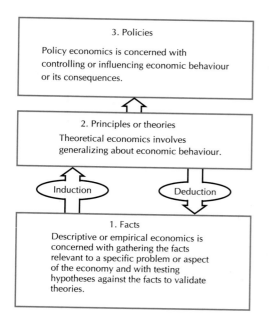

In analysing problems or aspects of the economy, economists may use the inductive method, whereby they gather, systematically arrange, and generalize upon facts. Alternatively, the deductive method entails the development of hypotheses that are then tested against facts. Generalizations derived from either method of inquiry are useful not only in explaining economic behaviour, but also as a basis for formulating economic policies.

One must distinguish economic from noneconomic facts and then determine which economic facts are relevant and which are irrelevant for the particular problem under consideration. But even when this sorting process has been completed, the relevant economic facts may appear diverse and unrelated. Economic data by themselves simply describe economic phenomena and are often referred to as *descriptive economics*.

Economic Theory

The task of economic theory or analysis is to systematically arrange, interpret, and generalize upon economic data or facts. **Principles** and theories bring order and meaning to facts by tying them together, putting them in correct relationship to one another, and generalizing upon them. But facts in turn serve as a constant check on the validity of principles already established. Facts — how individuals and institutions actually behave in producing, exchanging, and consuming goods and services may change with time. This makes it essential that economists continuously check existing theories against the changing economic environment.

Terminology   A word on terminology is essential at this point. Economists talk about "laws," "principles," "theories," and "models." These terms all mean essentially the same thing: generalizations, or statements of regularity, concerning the economic behaviour of individuals and institutions. Some people incorrectly associate the term "theory" with idle pipe dreams and ivory-tower hallucinations, divorced from the facts and realities of the world. In truth, theory helps us to understand the facts and realities of the world. In this book the four terms (laws, principles, theories, and models) will be used synonymously. The choice of terms in labelling any particular generalization will be governed by custom or convenience. Hence the relationship between the price of a product and the quantity consumers purchase will be called the "law" of demand, rather than the theory or principle of demand, because this is the customary designation.

Several other points regarding the character and derivation of economic principles are in order.

Generalizations   Economic principles are **generalizations**. They are frequently stated in terms of averages or statistical probabilities. For example, when economists say that the average family earned an income of $52,000 in 1991, they are generalizing. It is recognized that some families earned much more and many Canadian families earned less. Yet this generalization, properly handled and interpreted, can be very meaningful and useful. Similarly, economic generalizations are often stated in terms of probabilities. For example, a researcher may tell us that there is a 95% probability that every $1.00 reduction in personal income taxes will result in a $0.90 increase in consumer spending.

"Other Things Equal" Assumption   Like other scientists, economists make use of the **ceteris paribus**, or **other things being equal**, assumption in constructing their generalizations. They assume that all other variables, except those under immediate consideration, are held constant. This technique simplifies the reasoning process by isolating the relationship under consideration. To illustrate: In considering the relationship between the price of Pepsi and the amount purchased, it is helpful to assume that of all factors that might influence the amount of Pepsi purchased (for example, the prices of other goods, such as Coke, and consumer incomes and tastes), only the price of Pepsi varies. The economist is then able to focus on the "price of Pepsi–purchases of Pepsi" relationship without reasoning being blurred or confused by the intrusion of other variables.

In the natural sciences, controlled experiments usually can be performed where "all other things" are in fact held constant, or virtually so. Thus the scientist can test the assumed relationship between two variables with great precision. But economics is not a laboratory science. The economist's process of empirical verification is based on "real world" data generated by the actual operation of the economy. In this rather bewildering environment, "other things" *do* change. Despite the development of rather complex statistical techniques designed to hold other things equal, such controls are less than perfect. As a result, economic theories are sometimes less certain and less precise in application than those of the laboratory sciences.

Abstractions   Economic principles, or theories, are necessarily abstractions. The very process of sorting out noneconomic and irrelevant facts in the fact-gathering process involves abstracting from reality. Unfortunately, the abstractness of economic theory prompts the uninformed to identify theory as something that is impractical and unrealistic. This is nonsense!

Economic theories are practical for the simple reason that they are abstractions. Economists theorize in order to give meaning to a maze of facts that would otherwise be confusing and useless, and to put facts into a more usable, practical form. Thus, to generalize is to abstract or purposely simplify; generalization for this purpose is practical, and therefore so is abstraction. An economic theory is a model — a simplified picture or map — for some segment of the economy. This model enables us to better understand reality *because* it avoids confusing details. Theories — *good* theories — are grounded on facts and therefore are realistic. Theories that do not fit the facts are simply not good theories.

Macro and Micro There are two levels of analysis at which the economist can derive laws concerning economic behaviour. The level of **macroeconomics** is concerned either with the economy as a whole or with the basic subdivisions or aggregates — such as the household, business, government, and foreign trade sectors — that make up the economy. An aggregate is a collection of specific economic units that are treated *as though* they were one unit. Thus we might find it convenient to lump together the many businesses in our economy and treat them as though they were one huge unit. Macroeconomics is concerned with obtaining an overview, or general outline, of the structure of the economy and the relationships between the major aggregates that constitute the economy. It is concerned with such magnitudes as *total* output, the *total* level of employment, *total* income, *aggregate* expenditures, and the *general* level of prices, in analysing various economic problems. In short, macroeconomics examines the forest, not the trees. It gives us a bird's-eye view of the economy.

On the other hand, **microeconomics** is concerned with *specific* economic units and a *detailed* consideration of the behaviour of these individual units. Here we analyse an individual industry, firm, or household and concentrate on such magnitudes as the output or price of a *specific* product, the number of workers employed by a single firm, the revenue or income of a particular firm or household, and the expenditures of a given firm or family. In microeconomics we examine the trees, not the forest.

Many topics and subdivisions of economics are rooted in both "micro" and "macro." Indeed, there has been a convergence of macro and micro in important areas in recent years. For example, while the problem of unemployment was treated primarily as a macroeconomic topic ("unemployment depends on *aggregate* spending"), economists now recognize that decisions made by *individual* workers in searching for jobs and the manner in which product and labour markets function are also critical in determining the unemployment rate.

Graphic Expression Many of the economic models or principles presented in this book will be expressed graphically. You are strongly urged to read the appendix to this chapter to refresh your memory on graphing and other relevant quantitative relationships.

QUICK REVIEW (1-1)

1. **Economics is concerned with the efficient management of scarce resources.**
2. **Economists use facts to formulate (induction) and test (deduction) economic theories.**
3. **Economic theories ("laws," "principles," or "models") are generalizations concerning the economic behaviour of individuals and institutions.**
4. **Macroeconomics is concerned with the economy as a whole; microeconomics focuses on specific units that comprise the economy.**

Policy Economics: Positive and Normative

As we move from the fact and principles levels (boxes 1 and 2) of Figure 1-1 to the policy level (box 3) we are making a critical leap from positive to normative economics.

Positive economics attempts to set forth scientific statements about economic behaviour devoid of value judgments. In contrast, **normative economics** embodies someone's value judgments. Positive economics is concerned with *what is*, while normative economics embodies subjective feelings about *what ought to be*. Positive economics is concerned with what the economy is actually like; normative economics has to do with whether certain conditions or aspects of the economy are desirable or not. Consider the following examples. Positive statement: "Unemployment is 7% of the labour force." Normative statement: "Unemployment ought to be reduced." Positive statement: "Other things being the same, if tuition is increased, enrolment at Informed University (IU) will fall." Normative statement: "Tuition should be lowered at IU so that more students can obtain an education." Indeed, whenever such words as "ought" or "should" appear in a sentence, there is a strong chance that you are dealing with a normative statement. However, it is worth noting that the choice of what positive statement to make may, in itself, be a normative statement.

Most of the apparent disagreement among economists involves normative, value-based, policy questions. To be sure, various economists present and support different theories or models of the economy and its component parts. But by far most economic controversy reflects differing value judgments as to what our society should be like. There is greater agreement about the actual distribution of income in our society than there is about how income should be distributed.

Economic Goals A number of **economic goals** or value judgments are widely, though not universally, accepted in our society. These goals are as follows:

1. ECONOMIC GROWTH The production of more and better goods and services, for the purpose of attaining a higher standard of living, is desired.

2. FULL EMPLOYMENT Suitable jobs should be available for all who are willing and able to work.

3. PRICE LEVEL STABILITY Sizable upswings or downswings in the general price level, that is, inflation and deflation, should be avoided.

4. AN EQUITABLE DISTRIBUTION OF INCOME No group of citizens should face stark poverty while other citizens enjoy extreme luxury.

5. BALANCE OF TRADE We seek a reasonable balance in our international trade and financial transactions.

This list of widely accepted goals provides the basis for several significant points.

1. *Interpretation* Note that this or any other statement of basic economic goals inevitably entails problems of interpretation. What, for example, is an "equitable" distribution of income? On the other hand, most of us might accept the above goals, but might disagree as to the types of policies needed to attain these goals.

2. *Complementary* Certain of these goals are complementary in that when one goal is achieved, some other goal or goals will also tend to be realized. For example, growth (goal 1) will help achieve full employment (goal 2).

3. *Conflicting* Some goals *may* be conflicting or mutually exclusive. Some economists argue that those forces that further the attainment of economic growth and full employment may be the very same forces that cause inflation. In fact, the possible conflict between goals 2 and 3 has been at the forefront of economic research and debate in recent years. Goals 1 and 4 may also be in conflict. Some economists point out that efforts to achieve greater equality in the distribution of income may weaken incentives

to work, invest, innovate, and take business risks, all of which promote rapid economic growth.

4. *Priorities* When basic goals do conflict, society is forced to develop a system of priorities for the objectives it seeks. To illustrate: If full employment is accompanied by some inflation *and* price stability entails some unemployment, society must decide on the relative importance of these two goals. There is clearly ample room for disagreement here.

Formulating Economic Policy The creation of specific policies designed to achieve the broad economic goals of our society is no simple matter. The following is a brief examination of the basic steps in policy formulation.

1. *Stating Goals* Make a clear statement of goals. If we say that we want "full employment," do we mean that everyone between, say, sixteen and sixty-five years of age should have a job? Or do we mean that everyone who wants to work should have a job? Should we allow for some "normal" unemployment caused by workers voluntarily changing jobs?

2. *Policy Options* We must state and recognize the possible effects of alternative policies designed to achieve the goal. This entails a clear-cut understanding of the economic impact, benefits, costs, and political feasibility of alternative programs.

3. *Evaluation* We are obligated to both ourselves and future generations to look back on our experiences with chosen policies and evaluate their effectiveness; it is only through this type of evaluation that we can hope to improve policy applications.

QUICK REVIEW (1-2)

1. **Positive economics is concerned with factual statements ("what is"), while normative economics embodies value judgments ("what ought to be").**

2. **Some of society's economic goals are complementary while others are conflicting.**

PITFALLS TO STRAIGHT THINKING

Our discussion of the economist's procedure has up to this point skirted some of the problems and pitfalls frequently encountered in thinking straight about economic problems. The following obstacles often impede valid economic reasoning.

Bias

In contrast to neophyte physicists or chemists, budding economists often launch into their field of study with a bundle of biases and preconceptions. For example, one might be suspicious of business profits or feel that deficit spending is invariably evil. Needless to say, biases may cloud our thinking and interfere with objective analysis. Students beginning their studies in economics must be willing to shed biases and preconceptions that are not warranted by facts.

Loaded Terminology

The economic terminology to which we are exposed in newspapers and popular magazines is sometimes emotionally loaded. The writer — or, more frequently, the particular interest group represented — may have a cause to further or an axe to grind, and the terms will be slanted to solicit the support of the reader. A governmental flood-control project in the Prairies may be called "creeping socialism" by its opponents and "protecting the national interest" by its proponents. We must be prepared to discount such terminology in achieving objectivity in the understanding of important economic issues.

Definitions

No scientist is obligated to use immediately understandable definitions of terms. The economists may find it convenient and essential to define terms in such a way that they are clearly at odds with the definitions held by most people in everyday speech. So long as the economist is explicit and consistent in these definitions, he or she is on safe ground. A typical example: The term "investment" to John Q. Citizen is associated with the buying of bonds and stocks in the securities market. How often have we heard someone talk of investing in Bell Canada stock or government bonds? But to the economist, "investment" means the purchase of real capital assets such as machinery and equipment, or the construction of a new factory building.

Fallacy of Composition

Another pitfall in economic thinking is to assume that "what is true for the individual or part of a group is *necessarily* also true for the group or whole." This is a logical **fallacy of composition**; it is *not* correct. For example, a wage increase for Smith is desirable because, given constant product prices, it increases Smith's purchasing power and standard of living. But if everyone gets a wage increase, product prices will likely rise; that is, inflation will occur. Thus Smith's standard of living may be unchanged as higher prices offset this larger salary. Second illustration: An *individual* farmer who is fortunate enough to realize a bumper crop is likely to realize a sharp increase in income. But this generalization does not apply to farmers as a *group*. An individual farmer's bumper crop will not influence crop prices because it is such a negligible fraction of the total farm output, but for farmers as a group prices vary inversely with total output. Thus if *all* farmers realize bumper crops, the total output of farm products rises, thereby depressing crop prices. If price declines are relatively greater than the increased output, farm incomes will *fall*.

Cause and Effect: *Post Hoc* Fallacy

Still another hazard in economic thinking is to assume that simply because one event precedes another, the first is necessarily the cause of the second. This kind of faulty reasoning is known as the **post hoc, ergo propter hoc**, or **"after this, therefore because of this" fallacy**. The rooster crows before dawn, but this doesn't mean the rooster is responsible for the sunrise!

It is especially important in analysing various sets of empirical data *not* to confuse **correlation** with **causation**. Correlation is a technical term that indicates that two sets of data are associated in some systematic and dependable way. For example, we may find that when X increases, Y also increases. But this does not necessarily mean that the increase in X is the cause of the increase in Y. The relationship could be purely coincidental or determined by some other factor, Z, not included in the analysis.

Example: Economists have found a positive correlation between education and income. In general, people with more education earn higher incomes than do people with less education. Common sense prompts us to label education as the cause and higher incomes as the effect; more education suggests a more productive worker and such workers receive larger monetary rewards. But on second thought, might not causation run the other way? Do people with higher incomes buy more education, just as they buy more automobiles and more steaks? Or is the relationship explainable in terms of still other factors? Are education and income positively correlated because the bundle of characteristics — ability, motivation, personal habits — required to succeed in education are the same characteristics required to be a productive and highly paid worker? On reflection, seemingly simple cause–effect relationships — "more education results in more income" — may prove to be suspect or perhaps flatly incorrect.

THE ECONOMIC PERSPECTIVE

The methodology used by economists is common to all of the natural and social sciences. All scholars try to avoid the reasoning errors just discussed. Hence,

economists do *not* think in a special way. But they *do* think about things from a special perspective. (See Box 1-1.) Economists have developed a keen alertness to certain aspects of everyday conduct and situations. They look for *rationality* or *purposefulness* in

Box 1-1

FAST-FOOD LINES: AN ECONOMIC PERSPECTIVE

How might the economic perspective help us understand the behaviour of fast-food consumers?

When you enter a fast-food restaurant, which line do you select? What do you do when you are in a long line in the restaurant and a new station opens? Have you ever gone to a fast-food restaurant, only to see long lines, and then leave? Have you ever had someone in front of you in a fast-food line place an order that takes a long time to fill?

The economic perspective is useful in analysing the behaviour of fast-food customers. These customers are at the restaurant because they expect the benefit or satisfaction from the food they buy to match or exceed its cost. When customers enter the restaurant they scurry to the *shortest* line — lest someone else beats them there — in the belief that the shortest line will reduce their time cost of obtaining their food. They are acting purposefully; time is limited and most people would prefer using it in some way other than standing in line.

All lines in the fast-food establishment normally are of roughly equal lengths. If one line is temporarily shorter than other lines, some people will move toward that line. These movers apparently view the time saving associated with the shorter line to exceed the cost of moving from their present line. Line changing normally results in an equilibrium line length. No further movement of customers between lines will occur once all lines are of equal length.

Fast-food customers face another cost–benefit decision when a clerk opens a new station at the counter. Should customers move to the new station or stay put? Those who do shift to the new line decide that the benefit of the time savings from the move exceeds the extra cost of physically moving. In so deciding, customers must also consider just how quickly they can get to the new station compared to others who may be contemplating the same move. (Those who hesitate in this situation are lost!)

Customers at the fast-food establishment select lines without having perfect information. For example, they do not first survey those in the lines to determine what they are ordering before deciding on which line to enter. There are two reasons. First, most customers would tell them "It is none of your business," and therefore no information would be forthcoming. Second, even if they could obtain the information, the amount of time necessary to get it (cost) would most likely exceed any time saving associated with finding the best line (benefit). Because information is costly to obtain, fast-food patrons select lines on the basis of imperfect information. Thus, not all decisions turn out to be as expected. For example, some people may enter a line in which the person in front of them is ordering hamburgers and fries for the 40 people in the Greyhound bus parked out back! Nevertheless, at the time the customer made the decision, he or she thought that it was optimal.

Imperfect information also explains why some people who arrive at a fast-food restaurant and observe long lines decide to leave. These people conclude that the total cost (monetary plus time costs) of obtaining the fast food is too large relative to the benefit. They would not have come to the restaurant in the first place had they known the lines were so long. But, getting that information by, say, employing an advance scout with a cellular phone, would cost more than the perceived benefit.

Finally, customers must decide what to order when they arrive at the counter. In making these choices they again compare costs and benefits in attempting to obtain the greatest personal well-being.

Economists believe that what is true for the behaviour of customers at fast-food restaurants is true for economic behaviour in general. Faced with an array of choices, consumers, workers, and businesses rationally compare costs and benefits in making decisions.

human actions and economic institutions. This purposefulness implies that people, individually and collectively, make choices by comparing costs and benefits. It therefore might be said that the **economic perspective** is a *cost–benefit perspective.*

Because people make economic choices from a wide array of alternatives, all choices entail sacrifices or costs. To buy a new VCR may mean not being able to afford a new personal computer. Taking a course in economics may preclude taking a course in accounting, political science, or computer science. A decision by government to provide improved pensions for the elderly may mean less publicly-financed daycare for children. Alas, costs are everywhere!

Economic actions of workers, producers, and consumers also produce personal economic benefits. For example, workers receive wages, producers garner profits, and consumers obtain satisfaction. People *compare* these benefits with costs in deciding how to spend their time, which products to buy, whether or not to work, which goods to produce and sell, and so forth. If the added benefits associated with a given course of action exceed the added costs, then it is rational to take that action. But if added costs are greater than added benefits, that action is not rational and should not be undertaken. Furthermore, when costs or benefits *change*, people *alter* their behaviour accordingly. Economists look carefully at costs and benefits to understand the everyday activities of people and institutions in the economy. This economic perspective will become increasingly evident as you advance through the book.

QUICK REVIEW (1-3)

1. **Beware of reasoning errors such as the fallacy of composition and the *post hoc* fallacy when engaging in economic reasoning.**

2. **The economic perspective is a cost-benefit perspective; it helps us analyse the economic behaviour of individuals and institutions.**

CHAPTER SUMMARY

1. Economics is concerned with the efficient use of scarce resources in the production of goods and services to satisfy material wants.

2. Economics is studied for several reasons: *a.* it provides valuable knowledge concerning our social environment and behaviour; *b.* it helps to equip a democratic citizenry to render decisions intelligently; *c.* economics may provide the business executive or consumer with valuable information.

3. The tasks of descriptive or empirical economics are *a.* the gathering of those economic facts that are relevant to a particular problem or specific segment of the economy and *b.* the testing of hypotheses against facts to validate theories.

4. The generalizations stated by economists are called "principles," "theories," "laws," or "models." The derivation of these principles is the task of economic theory.

5. Induction entails the distilling of theories from facts; deduction involves stating a hypothesis and then gathering facts to determine whether the hypothesis is valid.

6. Some economic principles are concerned with macroeconomics (the economy as a whole or major aggregates), while others pertain to microeconomics (specific economic units or institutions).

7. Economic principles are particularly valuable in understanding how an economy and its component parts work; they are the bases for economic predictions and for the formation of economic policy designed to solve problems and control undesirable economic events.

8. Positive statements embody facts ("what is"), while normative statements encompass value judgments ("what ought to be").

9. Full employment, economic growth, price stability, a viable balance of payments, and equity in the distribution of incomes are all widely accepted economic goals in our society. Some of these goals are complementary; others may be mutually exclusive.

10. In studying economics there are numerous pitfalls that the beginner may encounter. Some of the more important are *a.* biases and preconceptions; *b.* terminological difficulties; *c.* the fallacy of composition; and *d.* the difficulty of establishing clear cause–effect relationships.

11. The economic perspective envisions individuals and institutions making rational decisions based on costs and benefits.

TERMS AND CONCEPTS

ceteris paribus or "other things being equal" assumption (p. 6)
correlation and causation (p. 9)
descriptive economics (p. 5)
economics (p. 3)
economic goals (p. 8)
economic perspective (p. 11)
economic theory (p. 6)
fallacy of composition (p. 9)

hypothesis (p. 5)
induction and deduction (p. 5)
macroeconomics and microeconomics (p. 7)
policy economics (p. 5)
positive and normative economics (p. 7)
post hoc, ergo propter hoc or "after this, therefore because of this" fallacy (p. 9)
principles or generalizations (p. 6)

QUESTIONS AND STUDY SUGGESTIONS

1. Explain in detail the interrelationships between economic facts, theory, and policy. Critically evaluate: "The trouble with economics is that it is not practical. It has too much to say about theory and not enough to say about facts."

2. Analyse and explain the following quotation:

   Facts are seldom simple and usually complicated; theoretical analysis is needed to unravel the complications and interpret the facts before we can understand them . . . the opposition of facts and theory is a false one; the true relationship is complementary. We cannot in practice consider a fact without relating it to other facts, and the relation is a theory. Facts by themselves are dumb; before they will tell us anything we have to arrange them, and the arrangement is a theory. Theory is simply the unavoidable arrangement and interpretation of facts, which gives us generalizations on which we can argue and act, in the place of a mass of disjointed particulars.[2]

3. Of what significance is the fact that economics is not a laboratory science? What problems may be involved in deriving and applying economic principles?

4. Explain each of the following statements:

   a. "Like all scientific laws, economic laws are established in order to make successful prediction of the outcome of human actions."

---

[2] Henry Clay, *Economics for the General Reader* (New York: The Macmillan Company, 1925), pp. 10–11.

b. "Abstraction . . . is the inevitable price of generality . . . indeed abstraction and generality are virtually synonyms."

c. "Numbers serve to discipline rhetoric."

5. Indicate whether each of the following statements pertains to microeconomics or macroeconomics:

a. The unemployment rate in Canada was 10.3% in 1991.

b. The Alpo dogfood plant in Bowser, Alberta, laid off fifteen workers last month.

c. An unexpected freeze in central Florida reduced the citrus crop and caused the price of oranges to rise.

d. Our domestic output, adjusted for inflation, dropped by 1.5% in 1991.

e. Last week the Bank of Montreal lowered its interest rate on business loans by one-half of a percentage point.

f. The consumer price index rose by more than 5% in 1991.

6. Identify each of the following as either a positive or a normative statement:

a. The high temperature today was 33°C.

b. It was too hot today.

c. The general price level rose by 4.4% last year.

d. Inflation greatly eroded living standards last year and should be reduced by government policies.

7. To what extent would you accept the five economic goals stated and described in this chapter? What priorities would you assign to them? It has been said that we seek simply four goals: progress, stability, justice, and freedom. Is this list of goals compatible with that given in the chapter?

8. Analyse each of the following specific goals in terms of the five general goals stated in this chapter, and note points of conflict and compatibility: *a.* conservation of natural resources and the lessening of environmental pollution; *b.* increasing leisure; *c.* protection of Canadian producers from foreign competition. Indicate which of these specific goals you favour and justify your position.

9. Explain and give an illustration of *a.* the fallacy of composition; *b.* the "after this, therefore, because of this" fallacy. Why are cause-and-effect relationships difficult to isolate in the social sciences?

10. "Economists should never be popular; men who afflict the comfortable serve equally as those who comfort the afflicted and one cannot suppose that . . . capitalism would prosper without the critics its leaders find such a profound source of annoyance."[3] Interpret and evaluate.

11. Use the economic perspective to explain why someone who normally is a light eater at a standard restaurant may become somewhat of a glutton at a buffet-style restaurant that charges a single price for all you can eat.

---

[3] John Kenneth Galbraith, *American Capitalism*, rev. ed. (Boston: Houghton Mifflin Company, 1956), p. 49.

Appendix to Chapter 1

GRAPHS AND THEIR MEANING

If you glance quickly through the pages of this text, you will find many graphs. Some will appear to be relatively simple while others appear more formidable. Graphs are employed to help students visualize and understand important economic relationships. They are a way for economists to express their theories or models. Physicists and chemists sometimes illustrate their theories by building arrangements of multicoloured wooden balls that represent protons, neutrons, and so forth, held in proper relation to one another by wires or sticks. Economists often use graphs to illustrate their models, and by understanding these "pictures" students can more readily understand these models.

Most of our models will explain the relationship between just two sets of economic facts, and therefore two-dimensional graphs are a convenient way of visualizing and manipulating these relationships.

Constructing a Graph

A graph is a visual representation of the relationship between two variables. Table A1-1 provides a hypothetical illustration that shows the relationship between income and consumption. Without ever having studied economics, one would intuitively expect that high-income people consume more than

low-income people. Thus we are not surprised to find in Table A1-1 that consumption increases as income increases.

How can the information in Table A1-1 be expressed graphically? Glance at the graph shown in Figure A1-1. Now look back at the information in Table A1-1 and we will explain how to represent that information in a meaningful way by constructing the graph you just examined.

What we are trying to visually show is how consumption changes as income changes. Since income is the determining factor, we represent it on the horizontal axis of the graph as is customary. And, because consumption is dependent on income, we

TABLE A1-1   The relationship between income and consumption

Income (per week)	Consumption (per week)	Point
$ 0	$ 50	a
100	100	b
200	150	c
300	200	d
400	250	e

FIGURE A1-1   Graphing the direct relationship between consumption and income

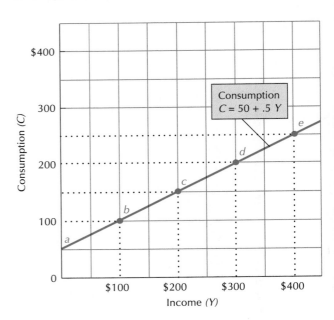

Consumption
C = 50 + .5 Y

Two sets of data that are positively or directly related, such as consumption and income, graph as an upsloping line. In this case the vertical intercept is $50 and the slope of the line is +½.

represent it on the vertical axis of the graph, as is also customary. What we are doing is representing the independent variable on the **horizontal axis** and the dependent variable on the **vertical axis**.

Now arrange the vertical and horizontal scales of the graph so that they reflect the range of values of consumption and income. As you can see, the ranges in the graph cover the ranges of values in Table A1-1. The increments on both scales are $100 for each 1.5 cm.

Next, we locate for each consumption value and the income value a single point that reflects the same information graphically. Our five income–consumption combinations are plotted by drawing perpendiculars from the appropriate points on the two axes. For example, in plotting point c — the $200 income–$150 consumption point — perpendiculars must be drawn up from the horizontal (income) axis at $200 and across from the vertical (consumption) axis at $150. Where these perpendiculars intersect at point c locates this particular income–consumption combination. The other income–consumption combinations shown in Table A1-1 have also been located in Figure A1-1. A line or curve can now be drawn to connect these points.

Using Figure A1-1 as a benchmark, we can make a number of additional observations.

Direct and Inverse Relationships

Our upsloping line tells us that there is a direct relationship between income and consumption. By a positive or **direct relationship**, we mean that the two variables change in the *same* direction. An increase in consumption is associated with an increase in income; conversely, a decrease in consumption is associated with a decrease in income. When two sets of data are positively or directly related, they will always graph as an *upsloping* line as in Figure A1-1.

In contrast, two sets of data may be inversely related. Consider Table A1-2, which shows the relationship between the price of hockey tickets and game attendance at Informed University (IU). We observe a negative or **inverse relationship** between ticket prices and attendance; these two variables change in *opposite* directions. When ticket prices decrease, attendance increases. Conversely, when ticket prices increase, attendance decreases. In Figure A1-2 we have plotted the six data points of Table A1-2 following the same procedure outlined above. Observe that an inverse relationship will always graph as a *downsloping* line.

TABLE A1-2 **The relationship between ticket prices and attendance**

Ticket price	Attendance (thousands)	Point
$25	0	a
20	4	b
15	8	c
10	12	d
5	16	e
0	20	f

Dependent and Independent Variables

Although the task is sometimes formidable, economists seek to determine which variable is "cause" and which is "effect," or, more formally, the independent and the dependent variables. By definition, the **dependent variable** is the "effect" or outcome; it changes as a consequence of a change in some other (independent) variable. The **independent variable** is the "cause"; it causes the change in the dependent variable. In our income–consumption

FIGURE A1-2 **Graphing the inverse relationship between ticket prices and game attendance**

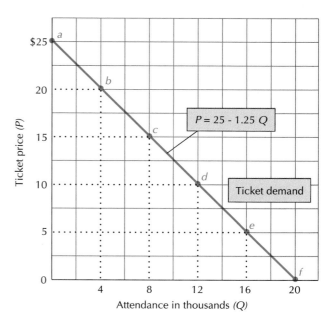

Two sets of data that are negatively or inversely related, such as ticket price and the attendance at basketball games, graph as a downsloping line. The slope of this line is $-1\frac{1}{4}$.

example, income is the independent variable and consumption is the dependent variable. Income causes consumption to be what it is rather than the other way around. Similarly, ticket prices determine attendance at IU hockey games; attendance does not determine ticket prices. Ticket price is the independent variable, and the quantity purchased is the dependent variable.

You may recall from your high school courses that mathematicians always put the independent variable (cause) on the horizontal axis and the dependent variable (effect) on the vertical axis. Economists are less tidy; their graphing of independent and dependent variables is more arbitrary. Thus their conventional graphing of the income–consumption relationship is consistent with mathematical presentation. But economists put price and cost data on the vertical axis. Hence, the economist's graphing of IU's ticket price–attendance data conflicts with mathematical procedure.

Other Variables Held Constant

Our simple two-variable graphs ignore a variety of other factors that might affect the amount of consumption that occurs at each income level or the number of people that attend IU hockey games at each possible ticket price. When we plot the relationship between any two variables, we invoke the *ceteris paribus* or "other things being equal" assumption, discussed in the body of this chapter. Thus in Figure A1-1 all other factors (that is, all factors other than income) that might affect the amount of consumption are presumed to be constant or unchanged. Similarly, in Figure A1-2 all factors other than ticket price that might influence attendance at IU hockey games are assumed constant. In reality, we know that "other things" often change, and when they do, the specific relationships presented in our two tables and graphs may change. Specifically, we would expect the lines we have plotted to shift to new locations.

For example, what might happen to the income–consumption relationship if there occurred a stock market crash such as that of October 1987? The expected impact of this dramatic fall in the value of stocks would be to make people feel less wealthy and therefore less willing to consume at each income level. Thus, we would anticipate a downward shift of the consumption line in Figure A1-1. You should plot a new consumption line based on the assumption that consumption is, say, $20 less at each income level. Note that the relationship remains direct, but the line has merely shifted to reflect less consumer spending at each level of income.

Similarly, a variety of factors other than ticket prices might affect IU game attendance. For example, if the provincial government were to abandon its program of student loans, IU enrolment and hence attendance at games might be less at each ticket price. You are urged to redraw Figure A1-2 on the assumption that 2,000 fewer students attend IU games at each ticket price. Question 2 at the end of this appendix introduces other variables that might cause the relationship shown in Figure A1-2 to shift to another position.

Slope of a Line

Lines can be described in terms of their slopes. The **slope of a straight line** between any two points is defined as the ratio of the vertical change (the rise or fall) to the horizontal change (the run) involved in moving between those points. For example, moving from point *b* to point *c* in Figure A1-1 we find that the rise or vertical change (the change in consumption) is + $50 and the run or horizontal change (the change in income) is + $100. Therefore:

$$\text{Slope} = \frac{\text{vertical change}}{\text{horizontal change}} = \frac{+50}{+100} = +\frac{1}{2}$$

Note that our slope of ½ is positive because consumption and income change in the same direction, that is, consumption and income are directly or positively related.

A slope of + ½ indicates that there will be a $1 increase in consumption for every $2 increase in income. It also indicates that for every $2 decrease in income there will be a $1 decrease in consumption.

For our ticket price–attendance data, the relationship is negative or inverse, with the result that the slope of Figure A1-2's line is negative. In particular, the vertical change or fall is 5 and the horizontal change or run is 4. Therefore:

$$\text{Slope} = \frac{\text{vertical change}}{\text{horizontal change}} = \frac{-5}{+4} = -1\frac{1}{4}$$

This slope of $\frac{-5}{+4}$ or $-1\frac{1}{4}$ means that lowering the price of a ticket by $5 will increase attendance by 4,000 people. Or, alternatively stated, it implies that a $1 price reduction will increase attendance by 800 persons.

In addition to its slope, the other information needed in locating a line is the vertical intercept. By definition, the **vertical intercept** is the point at which the line meets the vertical axis. For Figure A1-1 the intercept is $50. This means that, if current income was zero, consumers would still spend $50.

How might they manage to consume when they have no current income? Answer: By borrowing or by selling off some of their assets. The vertical intercept in Figure A1-2 shows us that at a $25 ticket price IU's hockey team would be playing their games in an empty arena.

Given the intercept and the slope, our consumption line can be succinctly described in equation form. In general, a linear equation is written as $y = a + bx$, where y is the dependent variable, a is the vertical intercept, b is the slope of the line, and x is the independent variable. For our income–consumption example, if we let C represent consumption (the dependent variable) and Y represent income (the independent variable), we can write $C = a + bY$. By substituting the values of the intercept and the slope for our specific data, we have $C = 50 + 0.5Y$. This equation allows us to determine consumption at *any* level of income. For example, at the $300 income level (point d in Figure A1-1), our equation predicts that consumption will be $200 = $[50 + (0.5 × $300)]. You should confirm that at the $250 income level consumption will be $175.

When economists reverse mathematical convention by putting the independent variable on the vertical axis and the dependent variable on the horizontal axis, in a sense the standard linear equation solves for the independent, rather than the dependent, variable. We noted earlier that this case is relevant for IU ticket price–attendance data. If we let P represent the ticket price and Q represent attendance, our relevant equation is $P = 25 - 1.25Q$, where the vertical intercept is 25 and the slope is $-1\frac{1}{4}$ or -1.25. But knowing the value for P enables us to solve for Q, which is actually our dependent variable. For example, if $P = 15$, then the values in our equation become: $15 = 25 - 1.25(Q)$, or $1.25Q = 10$, or $Q = 8$. Check this answer against Figure A1-2, and use this equation to predict IU ticket sales when the price is $7.50.

Slope of a Nonlinear Curve

Let us now move from the simple world of linear relationships (straight lines) to the slightly more complex world of nonlinear relationships (curves). By definition, the slope of a straight line is constant

FIGURE A1-3   Determining the slopes of curves

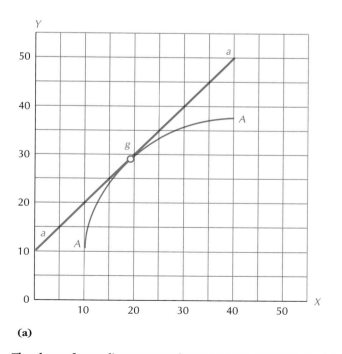

(a)

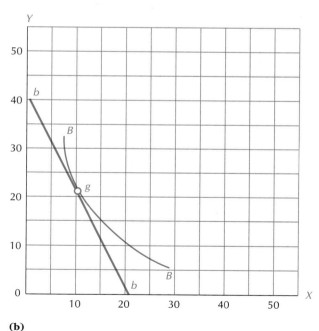

(b)

The slope of a nonlinear curve changes as one moves from point to point on the curve. The slope at any point can be determined by drawing a straight line tangent to that point and calculating the slope of that line.

throughout. In contrast the slope of a curve changes as we move from one point to another on the curve. For example, consider the curve *AA* in Figure A1-3(a). Although its slope is positive throughout, we observe that the slope diminishes or flattens as we move northeast along the curve. Given that the slope is constantly changing, we can only measure the slope at some particular point on the curve.

This is done by drawing a straight line that is tangent to the curve at that point where we want to measure its slope. By definition, a line is **tangent** at that point where it touches, but does not intersect, the curve. Thus line *aa* is tangent to curve *AA* at point *g* in Figure A1-3. Having drawn this tangent, we can measure the slope of *AA* at point *g* by measuring the slope of the straight tangent line *aa*. In Figure A1-3(a) we see that, when the vertical change (rise) in *aa* is $+10$, the horizontal change (run) is also $+10$. Thus the slope of the tangent *aa* line is $+10/+10$ or $+1$, and therefore the slope of *AA* at *g* is also $+1$.

Now consider the downsloping curve *BB* in Figure A1-3(b). In this case the slope of *BB* is negative and the slope diminishes as we move down the curve. To find the slope at point *g* we draw line *bb*, which is tangent to curve *BB* at *g*. In this case we see that when the vertical change (fall) in *bb* is -10, the horizontal change is only $+5$. Thus the slope of *BB* at point *g* is $-10/+5$ or -2. Question 6 at the end of this appendix is relevant.

APPENDIX SUMMARY

1. Graphs are a convenient and revealing means of presenting economic relationships or principles.

2. Two variables are positively or directly related when their values change in the same direction. Two variables directly related will plot as an up-sloping line on a graph.

3. Two variables are negatively or inversely related when their values change in opposite directions. Two variables inversely related will graph as a downsloping line.

4. The value of the dependent variable ("effect") is determined by the value of the independent variable ("cause").

5. When "other factors" that might affect a two-variable relationship are allowed to change, we can expect the plotted relationship to shift to a new location.

6. The slope of a straight line is the ratio of the vertical change to the horizontal change in moving between any two points. The slope of an upsloping line is positive, while that of a downsloping line is negative.

7. The vertical (or horizontal) intercept and the slope of a line establish its location and are used in expressing the relationship between two variables as an equation.

8. The slope of a curve at any point is determined by calculating the slope of a straight line drawn tangent to that point.

APPENDIX TERMS AND CONCEPTS

dependent and independent variables (p. 15)
direct and inverse relationships (p. 15)
slope of a straight line (p. 16)
tangent (p. 18)
vertical and horizontal axes (p. 15)
vertical intercept (p. 16)

APPENDIX QUESTIONS AND STUDY SUGGESTIONS

1. Briefly explain the use of graphs as a means of presenting economic principles. What is an inverse relationship? How does it graph? What is a direct relationship? How does it graph? Graph and explain the relationships one would expect to find between *a.* the number of centimetres of rainfall per month and the sale of umbrellas; *b.* the amount of tuition and the level of enrolment at a university; *c.* the size of an NHL club's budget for player salaries and the number of games won. In each case, cite and explain how considerations other than those specifically mentioned might upset the expected relationship. Is your second generalization consistent with the fact that historically enrolments and tuition have both increased? If not, explain any difference.

2. Indicate how each of the following might affect the data shown in Table A1-2 and Figure A1-2 of this appendix: *a.* IU's athletic director schedules higher quality opponents; *b.* IU's fighting aard-varks experience three losing seasons; *c.* IU contracts to have all of its home games televised.

3. The following table contains data on the relation-ship between saving and income. Rearrange

these data as required, and graph the data on the accompanying grid. What is the slope of the line? The vertical intercept? Interpret the meaning of both the slope and the intercept. Write the equation that represents this line. What would you predict saving to be at the $12,500 level of income?

Income (per year)	Saving (per year)
$15,000	$1,000
0	− 500
10,000	500
5,000	0
20,000	1,500

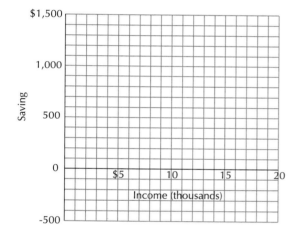

4. Construct a table from the data shown on the accompanying graph. Which is the dependent and which the independent variable? Summarize the data in equation form.

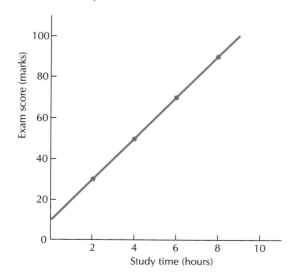

5. Suppose that when the interest rate that must be paid to borrow funds is 16%, businesses find that it is unprofitable to invest in machinery and equipment. However, when the interest rate is 14%, $5 billion worth of investment is profitable. At 12%, a total of $10 billion of investment is profitable. Similarly, total investment increases by $5 billion for each successive 2 percentage point decline in the interest rate. Indicate the relevant relationship between the interest rate and investment verbally, tabularly, graphically, and as an equation. Put the interest rate on the vertical axis and investment on the horizontal axis. In your equation use the form $i = a - bI$, where i is the interest rate, a is the vertical intercept, b is the slope of the line, and I is the level of investment. Comment upon the advantages and disadvantages of each of these four forms of presentation.

6. The accompanying diagram shows curve XX and three tangents at points A, B, and C. Calculate the slope of the curve at these three points.

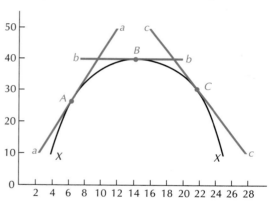

7. In the accompanying diagram is the slope of curve AA' positive or negative? Does the slope increase or decrease as we move from A to A'? Answer the same two questions for curve BB'.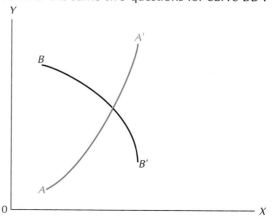

2 The Economizing Problem

The essence of the economizing problem is demonstrated in decisions you make every day. For example, suppose you have $30 and want to spend it. Many choices will confront you. Should you buy a pair of blue jeans? A couple of compact discs? A ticket for a rock concert?

Similarly, what to do with the time between 3 and 6 p.m. on Thursday. You have a number of options. You could work on a term project, prepare for the upcoming economics test, watch TV, or take a nap.

Money and time are both scarce given our unlimited wants and, thus, choices must be made. But choices imply forgone opportunities. If you choose the jeans, the cost is that you forgo the CDs or the concert. If you nap or watch TV, the cost will likely be a low grade on the economics test. Scarcity, choices, and costs — these underly the economizing problem, further analysed in this chapter.

The primary objective of this chapter is to explore what constitutes the foundation of economic science. We want to expand on the definition of economics introduced in Chapter 1 and explore the essence of the economizing problem. To this end, we will extend our definition of economics by the use of production possibilities tables and curves. We will also survey briefly the different ways in which institutionally and ideologically diverse economies go about "solving" or responding to the economizing problem.

THE FOUNDATION OF ECONOMICS

Two fundamental facts provide the foundation for economics and comprise the **economizing problem**. You must fully understand these two facts, because everything that follows in our study of economics depends directly or indirectly on them: *1. Society's material wants are virtually unlimited. 2. Economic resources — the means for producing goods and services — are limited or scarce.*

Unlimited Wants

In the first statement, what do we mean by "material wants"? We mean, first, the desires of consumers to obtain and use various *goods and services* that provide **utility**, the economist's term for pleasure or satisfaction.[1] An amazingly wide range of products fills the bill in this respect: houses, automobiles, toothpaste, compact-disc players, pizzas, sweaters, and the like. Innumerable products, which we sometimes classify as *necessities* (food, shelter, clothing) and *luxuries* (perfumes, yachts, mink coats), are all capable of satisfying human wants. Needless to say, what is a luxury to Smith may be a necessity to Jones, and what is a commonplace necessity today may have been a luxury a few short years ago.

But services satisfy our wants as much as do tangible products. A repair job on our car, the removal of our appendix, a haircut, and legal advice also satisfy human wants. We buy many goods — such as automobiles and washing machines — for the services they render. The differences between goods and services are often less than they seem to be at first.

Material wants also include those that businesses and governments seek to satisfy. Businesses want factory buildings, machinery, trucks, warehouses, communication systems, and so forth, to assist them in realizing their production goals. Government, reflecting the collective wants of its citizenry or goals of its own, seeks highways, schools, hospitals, and military equipment.

As a group, these material wants are for practical purposes *unlimited*. This means that material wants for goods and services are incapable of being completely satisfied. Our wants for a *particular* good or service can be satisfied. For example, over a short period of time we can get sufficient amounts of toothpaste or beer. Certainly one appendicitis operation is par for the course. But goods *in general* are another story. Here we do not, and presumably cannot, get enough. A simple experiment will help to verify this point. Suppose we are asked to list those goods and services we want. If we take time to ponder our unfilled material wants, chances are our list will be impressive.

Furthermore, over a period of time, our wants multiply so that as we fill some of the wants on the list, at the same time we add new ones. Material wants, like rabbits, have a high reproduction rate. The rapid introduction of new products whets our appetites and extensive advertising tries to persuade us that we need countless items we might not otherwise consider buying. Not too many years ago, the desire for personal computers, light beer, video cassette recorders, fax machines, and compact discs was nonexistent. Furthermore, we often cannot stop with simple satisfaction: the acquisition of an Escort or Firefly has been known to whet the appetite for a Porsche or Jaguar.

Let us emphatically add that the overall objective of all economic activity is the attempt to satisfy these diverse material wants.

Scarce Resources

Consider the second fundamental fact: *Economic resources are limited or scarce*. What do we mean by "economic resources"? In general, we are referring to all the natural, human, and manufactured resources that go into the production of goods and services. This covers a lot of ground: factory and farm buildings and all sorts of equipment, tools, and machinery used in the production of manufactured goods and agricultural products; a variety of transportation and communication facilities; innumerable types of labour, and land and mineral resources of all kinds.

Resource Categories   Let us divide these various resources into categories.

Land   **Land** refers to all natural resources or raw materials — all "gifts of nature" — that are usable in the productive process. Resources such as arable land, forests, mineral and oil deposits, and water resources come under this general classification.

---

[1] This definition leaves a variety of wants — recognition, status, love, and so forth — for the other social sciences to worry about.

Capital   **Capital**, or investment goods, refers to all manufactured aids to production; that is, all tools, machinery, equipment, and factory, storage, transportation, and distribution facilities used in producing goods and services and getting them to the consumer. The process of producing and purchasing capital goods is known as **investment**.

Two other points are pertinent. First, *capital goods* ("tools") differ from *consumer goods* in that the latter satisfy wants directly, whereas capital goods do so indirectly by facilitating the production of consumable goods. Second, the term "capital" does *not* refer to money. Business executives and economists often do talk of "money capital," meaning money that is available for use in the purchase of machinery, equipment, and other productive facilities. But money, as such, produces nothing, and therefore is not an economic resource. To re-emphasize, *real capital* — tools, machinery, and other productive equipment — is an economic resource; *money* or *financial capital* is not.

Labour   **Labour** is a broad term the economist uses in referring to all the human physical and mental talents usable in producing goods and services (with the exception of a special set of human talents — entrepreneurial ability — which, because of their special significance in a market economy, we choose to consider separately). Thus, the services of a logger, retail clerk, machinist, teacher, professional football player, and nuclear physicist all fall under the general heading of labour.

Entrepreneurial Ability   The final category is **entrepreneurial ability**, or, more simply, *enterprise*. The entrepreneur has four related functions:

1. The entrepreneur takes the initiative in combining the resources of land, capital, and labour in the production of a good or service. The entrepreneur is at once the driving force behind production and the agent that combines the other resources in what is hoped will be a profitable venture.

2. The entrepreneur undertakes basic business-policy decisions — that is, those nonroutine decisions that set the course of a business enterprise.

3. The entrepreneur is an innovator — the person who attempts to introduce on a commercial basis new products, new productive techniques, or new forms of business organization.

4. The entrepreneur is a risk taker. This is apparent from a close examination of the other three entrepreneurial functions. The entrepreneur in a market economy has no guarantee of profit. The reward for

his or her time, efforts, and abilities may be large profits *or* losses and eventual bankruptcy.

Resource Payments   These resources are provided to business institutions in exchange for money income. The income received from supplying property resources — raw materials and capital equipment — is called **rental** and **interest income**. The income to those who supply labour is called **wages** and includes salaries and various wage and salary supplements, such as bonuses, commissions, and royalties. Entrepreneurial income is called **profits** (which may be a negative figure — losses).

These four broad categories of economic resources, or **factors of production** as they are often called, leave room for debate when it comes to classifying specific resources. For example, is a dividend on some newly issued Canadian Pacific stock you may own an interest return for the capital equipment the company was able to buy with the money you provided, or a profit that compensates you for the risks involved in purchasing corporate stock? But, although we might quibble about classifying a given flow of income as wages, rent, interest, or profits, all income can be listed without too much arbitrariness under one of the general headings.

Relative Scarcity   All economic resources, or factors of production, have one fundamental characteristic in common: ***They are scarce or limited in supply given our unlimited wants***. Our "spaceship earth" contains only limited amounts of resources that can be put to use in the production of goods and services. Quantities of arable land, mineral deposits, capital equipment, and labour (time) are all limited. The scarcity of productive resources and the constraint this scarcity puts on productive activity means output will necessarily be limited. Society will *not* be able to produce and consume all of the goods and services it might want.

ECONOMICS AND EFFICIENCY

We have arrived once again at the basic definition of economics first stated at the beginning of Chapter 1. ***Economics is the social science concerned with the problem of using or allocating scarce resources (the means of producing) so as to attain the greatest or maximum fulfilment of society's unlimited wants (the goal of producing)***. Economics is concerned with "doing the best with what we have." If our wants are virtually unlimited and our resources are scarce, we cannot conceivably satisfy all society's material wants. The next best thing is to achieve the greatest possible satisfaction of these wants. Economics is a science of efficiency — efficiency in the use of scarce resources.

Efficiency as economists use the term means something similar to the term "efficiency" as used in engineering. The mechanical engineer tells us that a steam locomotive is only "15% efficient" because a large part — some 85% — of the energy in its fuel is not transformed into useful power but is wasted through friction and heat loss.

Economic efficiency is also concerned with **inputs** and **outputs**. Specifically, it is concerned with the relationship between the units of scarce resources that are put into the process of production and the resulting output of some wanted product. More output from a given quantity of inputs means an increase in efficiency.

Full Employment and Full Production

Society wants to use its limited resources efficiently; that is, it wants to get the maximum amount of useful goods and services produced with its available resources. To achieve this it must achieve both full employment and full production.

Full Employment   By **full employment** we mean that all available resources are employed. No workers are involuntarily out of work; the economy provides employment for all who are willing and able to work. Nor will capital equipment or arable land sit idle.

Full Production   But the employment of all available resources is insufficient to achieve efficiency. Full production must also be realized. **Full production** occurs when all employed resources are used so as to make the most valued contributions to domestic output. If we fail to achieve full production, our resources are *underemployed*.

Full production implies that two kinds of efficiency — allocative and productive efficiency — are achieved. **Allocative efficiency** means that resources are devoted to those goods most wanted by society. For example, we want resources allocated to the production of compact discs and cassettes, not to 78 rpm or to long-play records.

Productive efficiency means that the least costly production techniques are used in the production of wanted goods and services. Efficiency requires that Tauruses and Grand Ams be produced with computerized and roboticized assembly techniques rather than primitive assembly lines of 1920 Henry Ford vintage. Nor do we want our farmers harvesting wheat

with scythes or picking corn by hand when elaborate harvesting equipment will do the job at a much lower cost per bushel.

QUICK REVIEW (2-1)

1. **Human material wants are virtually unlimited.**
2. **Economic resources — land, capital, labour, and entrepreneurial ability — are scarce or limited.**
3. **Economics is concerned with the efficient management of these scarce resources to achieve the maximum fulfilment of our material wants.**
4. **Economic efficiency entails full employment and full production.**

Production Possibilities Table

The nature of the economizing problem can be brought into clearer focus by the use of a **production possibilities table**. This device reveals the core of the economizing problem: *Because resources are scarce, a full-employment, full-production economy cannot have an unlimited output of goods and services. As a result, choices must be made about which goods and services to produce and which to forgo.*

Assumptions   We make several assumptions to set the stage for our illustration.

1 Efficiency   The economy is operating at full employment and achieving full production.

2 Fixed Resources   The available supplies of the factors of production are fixed in both quantity and quality. But they can be shifted or reallocated, within limits, among different uses; for example, a relatively unskilled labourer can work on a farm, at a fast-food restaurant, or in a gas station.

3 Fixed Technology   Technology does not change during the course of our analysis.

The second and third assumptions are another way of saying that we are looking at our economy at some specific point in time. Over a relatively long period technological advances are possible and resource supplies can vary.

4 Two Products   To simplify our illustration further, let us suppose that our economy is producing just two products — industrial robots and pizza — instead of the innumerable goods and services actually produced. Pizza is symbolic of **consumer**

goods, those goods and services that directly satisfy our wants; industrial robots are symbolic of **capital goods**, those goods that satisfy our wants *indirectly*, by permitting more efficient production of consumer goods.

Necessity of Choice   It is evident from our assumptions that a choice must be made among alternatives since the available resources are limited. Thus the total amounts of robots and pizza that our economy is capable of producing are limited. *Limited resources mean a limited output.* Since resources are limited in supply and fully employed, any increase in the production of robots will necessitate the shifting of resources away from the production of pizza. And the reverse holds true: if we choose to step up the production of pizza, needed resources must come at the expense of robot production.

Let us note, in Table 2-1, some alternative combinations of robots and pizza that our economy might choose. Though the data in this and ensuing production possibility tables are hypothetical, the points illustrated are of great practical significance. At alternative *A*, our economy would be devoting all its resources to the production of robots, (capital goods), At alternative *E*, all available resources would be devoted to the production of pizza (consumer goods).

Both these alternatives are unrealistic extremes: any economy typically strikes a balance in dividing its total output between capital and consumer goods. As we move from alternative *A* to alternative *E*, we step up the production of consumer goods (pizza) by shifting resources away from capital goods production.

Since consumer goods directly satisfy our wants, any movement toward alternative *E* looks tempting. In making this move, society increases the current satisfaction of its wants. But there is a cost involved. This shift of resources catches up with society over time as its stock of capital goods dwindles — or at

least ceases to expand at the current rate — with the result that the potential for greater future production is impaired. In moving from alternative *A* toward alternative *E*, society is in effect choosing "more now" at the expense of "much more later."

In moving from *E* toward *A*, society is choosing to forgo current consumption. This sacrifice of current consumption frees resources that can now be used to increase the production of capital goods. By building up its stock of capital, society can anticipate greater production and therefore greater consumption in the future.

Production Possibilities Curve

To ensure our understanding of the production possibilities table, let us view these data graphically. We employ a two-dimensional graph, arbitrarily putting the output of robots (capital goods) on the vertical axis and the output of pizza (consumer goods) on the horizontal axis, as in Figure 2-1. Following the plotting procedure discussed in the appendix to Chapter 1, we can locate the "production possibilities" curve, as shown in **Figure 2-1 (Key Graph)**.

FIGURE 2-1   The production possibilities curve

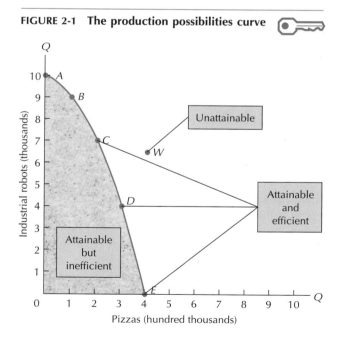

Each point on the production possibilities curve or frontier represents some maximum output of any two products. Society must choose which product mix it desires: more robots means less pizza, and vice versa. Limited supplies of human and property resources make any combination of robots and pizza lying outside the production possibilities frontier, such as *W*, unattainable.

TABLE 2-1   Production possibilities of pizza and robots with full employment, 1993 (*hypothetical data*)

Type of product	Production alternatives				
	A	*B*	*C*	*D*	*E*
Pizza (in hundred thousands)	0	1	2	3	4
Robots (in thousands)	10	9	7	4	0

Each point on the production possibilities curve represents some maximum output of the two products. Thus the curve is, in effect, a frontier. To realize the various combinations of pizza and robots that fall on the production possibilities curve, society must achieve full employment and full production. All combinations of pizza and robots *on* the frontier represent maximum quantities attainable as the result of the most efficient use of all available resources. Points lying *inside* the curve are also attainable, but not as desirable as points on the curve.

Points lying *outside* the production possibilities frontier, like point W, would be superior to any point on the curve; but such points are unattainable, given the current supplies of resources and technology. The production barrier of limited resources prohibits the production of any combination of capital and consumer goods lying outside the production possibilities frontier.

Optimal Product-Mix

If all outputs on the production possibilities curve reflect full employment and full production, which combination will society prefer? Consider, for example, points C and D in Figure 2-1. Which output mix is superior or "best"? This is a normative matter; it reflects the values of society as expressed by its electorate, the citizenry, the individual institutions, or some combination thereof.

What the economist can say is that if a society's production possibilities are as in Table 2-1 *and* if that society seeks the product mix indicated by, say, alternative C, it is not using its resources efficiently if it realizes a total output comprised only of 6 units of robots and 1 unit of pizza. And the economist can also say that the society cannot hope to achieve a national output of 8 units of robots and 3 units of pizza with its available resources. These are quantitative, objective, positive statements. But although he or she may have opinions as an individual, the economist as a social scientist cannot say that combination C is "better" or "worse" than combination D. This is a qualitative or normative matter.

Law of Increasing Opportunity Costs

The amount of other products that must be forgone or sacrificed to obtain some amount of any given product is called the opportunity cost of that good. In our case the amount of Y (robots) that must be forgone or given up to get another unit of X (pizza) is the **opportunity cost** of that unit of X. In moving from possibility A to B in Table 2-1, we find that the cost of 1 unit of pizza is 1 unit of robots. But as we now pursue the concept of cost through the additional production possibilities — B to C, C to D, and so forth — the sacrifice or cost of robots involved in getting each additional unit of pizza *increases*. This is called the **law of increasing opportunity costs**. In moving from A to B, just 1 unit of robots is sacrificed for 1 more unit of pizza; but going from B to C involves the sacrifice of 2 units of robots for 1 more of pizza; then 3 of robots for 1 of pizza; and finally 4 to 1. Conversely, you should confirm that in moving from E to A the cost of an additional robot is $\frac{1}{4}$, $\frac{1}{3}$, $\frac{1}{2}$, and 1 unit of pizza respectively for each of the four shifts.

Observe that this discussion of opportunity cost is couched in terms of *added* or *marginal* unit of a good rather than *total*, or cumulative, opportunity cost. For example, the opportunity cost of the third unit of pizza in Table 2-1 is 3 units of robots ($= 7 - 4$). But the total opportunity cost of 3 units of pizza is 6 units of robots ($= 10 - 4$, or $1 + 2 + 3$).

Concavity   Graphically, the law of increasing opportunity costs is reflected in the shape of the production possibilities curve. The curve is *concave*, or bowed out from the origin, because, when the economy moves from A toward E, it must give up successively larger amounts of robots (1, 2, 3, 4) to acquire equal increments of pizza (1,1,1,1). This means that the slope of the production possibilities curve becomes steeper as we move from A to E. Such a curve, by definition, is concave as viewed from the origin.

Rationale   The rationale for the law of increasing opportunity costs is: *Economic resources are not completely adaptable to alternative uses.* As we attempt to step up pizza production, resources less and less adaptable to this use must be induced, or "pushed," into this line of production. As we move from B to C, C to D, and so on, those resources that are highly productive of pizza become increasingly scarce. To get more pizza, resources whose productivity in robots is great in relation to their productivity in pizza will be needed. It will take more and more of such resources — and hence an increasingly great sacrifice of robots — to achieve a given increase of 1 unit in the production of pizza. This lack of perfect flexibility, or interchangeability, is behind the law of increasing opportunity costs.

The production possibilities curve illustrates four basic concepts.

1. **The scarcity of resources is implicit in that all combinations of output lying outside the production possibilities curve are unobtainable.**

2. **Choice is reflected in the need for society to select among the various attainable combinations of goods lying on (or within) the curve.**

3. **The downward slope of the curve implies the notion of opportunity cost.**

4. **The concavity of the curve reveals increasing opportunity costs.**

UNEMPLOYMENT, GROWTH, AND THE FUTURE

It is important to understand what happens when the first three assumptions underlying the production possibilities curve are released.

Unemployment and Underemployment

The first assumption was that our economy is characterized by full employment and full production. With *un*employment or *under*employment, the economy would be producing less than each alternative shown in Table 2-1.

Graphically, a situation of unemployment or underemployment can be illustrated by a point *inside* the original production possibilities frontier, such as point *U* in Figure 2-2. Here the economy is falling short of the various maximum combinations of pizza and robots reflected by all the points *on* the production possibilities frontier. The broken arrows in Figure 2-2 indicate three of the possible paths back to full employment and full production. A movement towards full employment and full production will mean a greater output of one or both products.

A Growing Economy

When we drop the remaining assumptions that the quantity and quality of resources and technology are fixed, the production possibilities curve will shift position and the potential total output of the economy will change. An expanding economy will shift the frontier rightward, while an economy whose potential total output declines will shift the production possibility curve leftward. What are the factors

FIGURE 2-2   **Unemployment and the production possibilities curve**

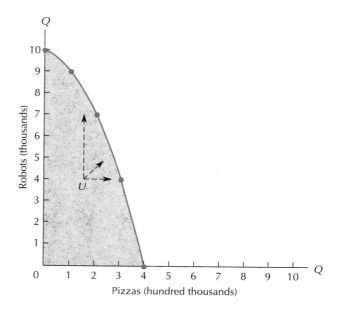

Any point inside the production possibilities curve or frontier, such as *U*, indicates unemployment or underemployment. By moving toward full employment and full production, the economy can produce more of either or both of the two products, as the arrows indicate.

that can change the potential total output of an economy?

Expanding Resource Supplies

Let's now abandon the simplifying assumption that our total supplies of land, labour, capital, and entrepreneurial ability are fixed in both quantity and quality. Common sense tells us that over a period of time, a nation's growing population will bring about increases in the supplies of labour and entrepreneurial ability.[2] Also, the quality of labour improves over time. For example, the percentage of community college and university age Canadians enrolled in these institutions rose from 11% in 1970–71 to 29% by 1989–90.

The stock of capital will affect the potential output capacity of an economy. Those nations that devote a large proportion of their outputs to the production of

_____
[2] This is not to say that population growth as such is always desirable. Overpopulation can be a constant drag on the living standards of many less-developed countries. In advanced countries, overpopulation can have adverse effects on the environment and the quality of life.

capital goods achieve high rates of economic growth. And although we are depleting some of our energy and mineral resources, new sources are constantly being discovered. Assuming continuous full employment and full production, the net result of these increased supplies of the factors of production will be the ability to produce more of both robots and pizza.

Thus in, say, the year 2013, the production possibilities of Table 2-1 (for 1993) may be obsolete, having given way to those shown in Table 2-2. Observe that the greater abundance of resources results in a greater potential output of one or both products at each alternative. But note such a favourable shift in the production possibilities frontier does not guarantee that the economy will actually operate at a point on that new frontier. The economy might fail to realize fully its new potentialities.

Technological Advance   An advancing technology entails new and better goods *and* improved ways of producing these goods. For the moment, let us think of technological advance as comprising improvements in capital facilities — more efficient machinery and equipment. Such technological advance alters our earlier discussion of the economizing problem by improving productive efficiency, and allowing society to produce more goods with a fixed amount of resources. As with increases in resource supplies, technological advance permits the production of more robots *and* more pizza.

When the supplies of resources increase or an improvement in technology occurs the frontier shifts outward and to the right, as illustrated by the thin curve in Figure 2-3. **Economic growth** — *the ability to produce a larger total output — is reflected in a rightward shift of the production possibilities frontier; it is the result of increases in resource supplies, improvements in resource quality, and technological progress.* The consequence of growth is that our full-employment economy can enjoy a greater output of both pizza and robots.

FIGURE 2-3   **Economic growth and the production possibilities curve**

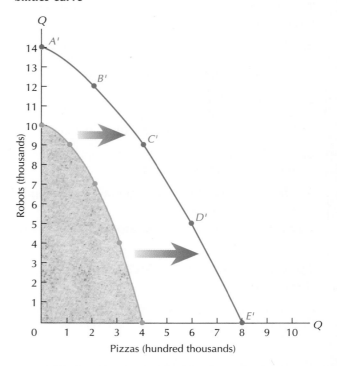

The expanding resource supplies and technological advances that characterize a growing economy move the production possibilities curve or frontier outward and to the right. This permits the economy to enjoy larger quantities of both types of goods.

Economic growth does *not* typically entail proportionate increases in a nation's capacity to produce various products. Note in Figure 2-3 that, while the economy is able to produce twice as much pizza, the increase in robot production is only 40%. On Figure 2-3 you should pencil in two new production possibilities curves: one to show the situation where a better technique for producing robots has been developed, the technology for producing pizza being unchanged, and the other to illustrate an improved technology for pizza, the technology for producing robots being constant.

Present Choices and Future Possibilities

An economy's current choice on its production possibilities frontier is a basic determinant of the future location of that curve. To illustrate this notion, let us designate the two axes of the production possibilities frontier as "goods for the future" and "goods for the present," as in Figures 2-4(a) and (b). By "goods for the future" we refer to such things as capital goods,

TABLE 2-2   **Production possibilities of pizza and robots with full employment, 2013 (*hypothetical data*)**

Type of product	Production alternatives				
	A'	B'	C'	D'	E'
Pizza (in hundred thousands)	0	2	4	6	8
Robots (in thousands)	14	12	9	5	0

FIGURE 2-4   An economy's present choice of position on its production possibilities curve helps determine the curve's future location

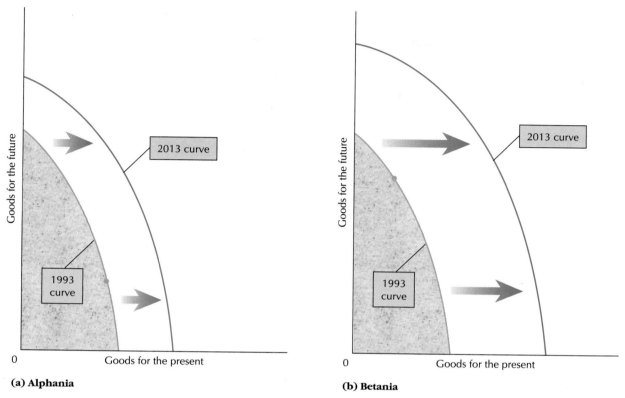

(a) Alphania

(b) Betania

A current choice favouring "present goods," as rendered by Alphania in (a), will cause a modest rightward shift of the frontier. A current choice favouring "future goods," as rendered by Betania in (b), will result in a greater rightward shift of the frontier.

research and education, and preventive medicine, which increase the quantity and quality of resources, enlarge the stock of technological information, and improve the quality of human resources. It is "goods for the future" that are the ingredients of economic growth. By "goods for the present" we mean pure consumer goods in the form of foodstuffs, clothing, automobiles, power mowers, boats, and so forth.

Now suppose there are two economies, Alphania and Betania, which are identical in every respect except that Alphania's current (1993) choice of position on its production possibilities frontier strongly favours "present goods" as opposed to "future goods." The dot in Figure 2-4(a) indicates this choice. Betania, on the other hand, renders a current (1993) choice that stresses large amounts of "future goods" and lesser amounts of "present goods" (Figure 2-4(b)). All other things being the same, we can expect the future (2013) production possibilities frontier of Betania to be farther to the right than that of Alphania. By currently choosing an output that is more conducive

to technological advance and to increases in the quantity and quality of resources, Betania will achieve greater economic growth than will Alphania. In terms of capital goods, Betania is choosing to make larger current additions to its "national factory" — that is, to invest more of its current output — than is Alphania. The payoff or benefit from this choice is more rapid growth — greater future productivity capacity — for Betania. The opportunity cost is fewer consumer goods in the present.

QUICK REVIEW (2-3)

1. **Unemployment and underemployment (the inefficient use of employed resources) cause the economy to operate at a point inside its production possibilities curve.**

2. **Expanding resource supplies, improvements in resource quality, and technological progress cause economic growth — an outward shift of the production possibilities curve.**

Box 2-1

DIFFICULT CHOICES IN THE SOVIET UNION'S WANING YEARS

The scarce resources–unlimited wants dilemma underscores the difficult choices made in the Soviet Union before its breakup.

On coming to power in 1985, Soviet leader Mikhail Gorbachev moved vigorously to revitalize a lagging economy. The Soviet economy had fared badly in the previous fifteen years or so. Economic growth had declined, production methods had become increasingly obsolete in comparison to other industrialized nations, and manufactured goods were shoddy by western standards.

A basic feature of Gorbachev's program of "restructuring" or reforming the economy was to invest heavily in technologically advanced machinery and equipment to update the Soviet Union's "national factory." How could this be done? From what alternative uses might the needed resources be obtained?

The most obvious option was to reduce consumption. But consumption levels were already low in the Soviet Union. Per capita consumption was only about one-third that of Canada and many basic consumer goods were in chronic short supply. Indeed, a basic objective of reform was to provide the Soviet population with long-promised increases in their standard of living.

Another option was to reallocate resources from the military sector to investment. It was estimated that before the country's breakup, Soviet military spending was about equal to that of the United States. Given that the Soviet domestic output was only about one-half that of the United States, their military burden was roughly twice as great.

Another option was to increase efficiency. That is, instead of freeing up resources from alternative uses, could existing resources somehow be made capable of producing more output? One means of doing this is to enhance the incentives of workers and managers to produce. The Gorbachev reforms included modest steps to permit for-profit production outside of the central planning system and farmers were permitted to lease land from the government to produce crops for profits. Another way of increasing productivity is to obtain the superior technologies and managerial skills of other industrialized nations. Thus the Gorbachev regime showed a greater interest in joint ventures with firms from the West.

Unfortunately, the Gorbachev reforms did not bring about the desired results quickly enough, and the country disintegrated into various republics, the largest of which is Russia. Many of these republics have speeded up reforms to convert to a market economy. It is clear that the scarce resources–unlimited wants problem is very much in evidence in the overall character of those reforms.

3. **An economy's present choice of output — particularly of capital and consumer goods — helps determine the future location of its production possibilities curve.**

Applications

Let us consider several of many possible applications of the production possibilities curve that highlight the concepts of scarcity, choice, and opportunity cost.

1 Budgeting Individuals have limited money incomes. A limited budget means choices or trade-offs in buying goods and services. The purchase of a pair of blue jeans may entail the opportunity cost of dinner and a rock concert. Many students are faced with the problem of allocating a fixed amount of time between studying and working to finance their education. The implied production possibilities type of trade-off is that more hours spent working mean more income, but also less study time and a lower grade average.

2 Going to War An historical illustration: In beginning to produce war goods for World War II, Canada found itself with considerable unemployment. Hence our economy was able to accomplish the production of a large quantity of war goods and at the same time increase the volume of consumer goods output[3] (Figure 2-2). The Soviet Union, on the other hand, entered World War II operating close to full employment. Therefore, its military preparations

---

[3] There did occur, however, rather acute shortages of specific types of consumer goods.

Box 2-2

OPERATION DESERT STORM AND IRAQ'S PRODUCTION POSSIBILITIES

War can seriously diminish a nation's production possibilities.

The quick and decisive military victory of the United States and its allies (including Canada) in Operation Desert Storm has had a devastating economic impact upon Iraq. Forty-three days of intensive allied bombing inflicted great physical damage to Iraq's productive facilities and infrastructure. Civilian factories, roads, bridges, railroads, power plants, water purification plants, and communication facilities were all severely impaired. Commerce and communications have been greatly disrupted. Furthermore, despite its greatly diminished productive potential, the United Nations has ordered Iraq to pay up to 30% of its future oil revenues as war reparations to Kuwait and others harmed by the war. This means that a significant portion of Iraq's future domestic output will be unavailable for either its consumers or to rebuild its productive facilities.

Devastation to Iraq's human resources was also severe. One estimate suggests that as many as 100,000 to 120,000 Iraqi troups plus 5,000 to 20,000 civilians were killed in the war. Another 20,000 lost their lives in the post-war rebellion against Saddam Hussein. Finally, an estimated 15,000 to 30,000 Kurds and other displaced people have died in camps and on the road. A Harvard medical team has predicted that 170,000 Iraqi children will die because of delayed effects of the Gulf war. In particular, typhoid, cholera, diarrhea, malnutrition, and other health problems will cause the death rate of children under age five to be two or three times higher than before the war. Without electrical power, water treatment plans are silent; sewage cannot be pumped or treated. Backed-up pipes now drain into rivers and canals from which people have no choice but to bathe and drink. Further, there is no power to run irrigation pumps and little gasoline is available for harvesting machines. Food harvests are in doubt and refrigeration is no longer available to store existing food supplies.

In short, Iraq invaded Kuwait to bring Kuwait's oil resources under its control and by so doing increase Iraq's production possibilities. Instead, Iraq's resources — and hence its production possibilities — have been seriously diminished by Operation Desert Storm.

entailed a considerable shifting of resources away from the production of civilian goods and a concomitant drop in the standard of living.

3 Discrimination   Discrimination based on race, sex, age, or ethnic background is an obstacle to the efficient allocation or employment of human resources and thereby keeps the economy operating at some point inside the production possibilities frontier. Discrimination prevents racial minorities, women, and others from obtaining jobs wherein society can efficiently utilize their skills and talents. The elimination of discrimination would therefore help to move the economy from some point inside the production possibilities curve outwards towards the frontier.

4 Productivity Slowdown   During the 1970s and early 1980s, Canada experienced a decline in the growth of output per worker hour. Some economists believe a major cause of this decline was that the rate of increase in the mechanization of labour slowed because of insufficient investment in manufacturing. The proposed remedy was an increase in investment as compared with consumption. That is, a *D* to *C*

type of shift in Figure 2-1. Special tax incentives to make business investment more profitable would be an appropriate policy to facilitate such a shift. The restoration of a more rapid rate of productivity growth would accelerate the growth of the economy and shift of the production possibilities frontier rightward.

During the mid-1980s the growth of output per hour recovered somewhat. While the reasons for the partial recovery of productivity are complex and controversial, the increase in investment contributed to the improvement.

5 International Trade Aspects   The simple message of the production possibilities curve is that a nation cannot live beyond its means or production potential. When the possibility of international trade is taken into account, this statement must be modified in two ways.

a. We will discover in later chapters that through international specialization and trade a nation can circumvent the output constraint imposed by its domestic production possibilities curve. That is, international specialization and trade have the same impact as having more and better resources or discovering improved production techniques. Both have the effect of increasing the quantities of both capital and consumer goods available to society. International specialization and trade are the equivalent of economic growth.

b. Within the context of international trade, a nation can achieve a combination of goods outside of its domestic production possibilities curve (such as point *W* in Figure 2-1) by incurring a **trade deficit**, that is, by buying and receiving an amount of imported goods from the rest of the world that exceeds the amount of goods exported to the rest of the world.

This looks like a very favourable state of affairs. Unfortunately, there is a catch. To finance its deficit — to pay for its excess of imports over exports — a nation must go into debt to its international trading partners *or* it must give up ownership of some of its assets to those other nations. Analogy: How can you live beyond your current income? Answer: Borrow from your parents, the sellers of goods, or a financial institution. Or, alternatively, sell some of your real assets (your car or stereo) or financial assets (stocks or bonds) that you own.

We would find that a major consequence of large and persistent trade deficits is that foreign nationals hold larger portions of our private and public debt and own larger amounts of our business corporations, agricultural land, and real estate. To pay for debts and to repurchase those assets would mean living well *within* a nation's means. A **trade surplus** is required to pay off world debts and reacquire ownership of those assets.

6 Growth The growth impact of a nation's decision on how to divide its domestic output is vividly illustrated by comparing the growth performance of a few advanced industrialized nations. In recent years Japan has been investing over 25% of its domestic output in productive machinery and equipment. Not surprisingly Japan has had impressive output growth during the last few decades. The United States, on the other hand, has invested only about 10% of its domestic output and, thus, has had a lower growth rate in recent years compared to Japan. In the 1980s Canada invested about 20% of its domestic output, which translated into healthy economic growth between 1983–1990.

7 Famine in Africa In modern industrial societies we tend to take economic growth — more-or-less continuous rightward shifts of the production possibilities frontier — for granted. But as the recent cata-strophic famine in Ethiopia, Chad, Sudan, and other African nations indicates, in some circumstances the production possibilities frontier may shift leftward. An important cause of the African famine is ecological degradation or, more simply, poor land-use practices. Land has been deforested, over-farmed, and overgrazed, causing the production possibilities of these highly agriculturally oriented countries to diminish. Combined with rapid population growth, the leftward-shifting production possibilities frontiers have resulted in malnourishment and famine. In fact, the per capita domestic output of most of these nations declined in the 1980s.

THE "ISMS"

A variety of different institutional arrangements and coordinating mechanisms may be used by a society in responding to the economizing problem. Generally speaking, the industrially advanced economies of the world differ essentially on two grounds: (1) the ownership of the means of production, and (2) the method by which economic activity is coordinated and directed. Let's briefly examine the main characteristics of the two "polar" types of economic systems.

Pure Capitalism

Pure, or **laissez-faire, capitalism** is characterized by the private ownership of resources and the use of a system of markets and prices to coordinate and direct economic activity. In such a system each participant is motivated by his or her own self-interests. The market system functions as a mechanism through which individual decisions and preferences are communicated and coordinated. The fact that goods and services are produced and resources are supplied under competitive conditions means there are many independent buyers and sellers of each product and resource. As a result, economic power is widely dispersed. Advocates of pure capitalism argue that such an economy is conducive to efficiency in the use of resources, output and employment stability, and rapid economic growth. Hence, there is little or no need for government planning, control, or intervention. Indeed, the term *laissez-faire* roughly translates as "let it be": keep the government from interfering with the economy. Interference will disturb the efficiency with which the market system functions. Government's role is therefore limited to the protection of private property and establishing an appropriate legal framework to facilitate the functioning of free markets.

The Command Economy

The polar alternative to pure capitalism is the **command economy** or **communism**, characterized by public ownership of virtually all property resources and the rendering of economic decisions through central economic planning. All major decisions concerning the level of resource use, the composition and distribution of output, and the organization of production are determined by a central planning board. Business firms are government owned and produce according to state directives. Production targets are determined by the planning board for each enterprise and the plan specifies the amounts of resources to be allocated to each enterprise so that it might realize its production goals. The division of output between capital and consumer goods is centrally decided and capital goods are allocated among industries in terms of the central planning board's long-term priorities.

Mixed Systems

Most economies are arrayed between the extremes of pure capitalism and the command economy. The Canadian economy leans toward pure capitalism, but with important differences. Government plays an active role in our economy in promoting economic stability and growth, in providing certain goods and services that would be underproduced or not produced at all by the market system, in modifying the distribution of income, and so forth. In contrast to the wide dispersion of economic power among many small units that characterizes pure capitalism, Canadian capitalism has spawned powerful economic organizations in the form of large corporations and strong labour unions. The ability of these power blocs to manipulate and distort the functioning of the market system to their advantage provides a further reason for governmental involvement in the economy. While China historically has approximated the command economy, it relies to some extent upon market-determined prices and has some vestiges of private ownership. Recent reforms in China and most of the Eastern European nations are designed to move these command economies toward more market-oriented systems.

But it must be emphasized that private ownership and reliance on the market system do not always go together, nor do public ownership and central planning. For example, the *fascism* of Hitler's Nazi Germany has been dubbed **authoritarian capitalism** because the economy was subject to a high degree of governmental control and direction, but property was privately owned. In contrast, the Yugoslavian economy of **market socialism** was characterized by public ownership of resources coupled with increasing reliance on free markets to organize and coordinate economic activity. The Swedish economy is also a hybrid system. Although over 90% of business activity is in private hands, government is deeply involved in achieving economic stability and in redistributing income. Similarly, the market oriented Japanese economy entails a great deal of planning and "coordination" between government and the business sector. Table 2-3 summarizes the various ways economic systems can be categorized on the basis of the two criteria we are using. Keep in mind that the real-world examples we have plugged into this framework are no more than rough approximations.

The Traditional Economy

Table 2-3 is couched in terms of industrially advanced or at least semideveloped economies. Many of the less developed countries of the world have **traditional** or **customary economies**. Production methods, exchange, and the distribution of income are all sanctioned by custom. Heredity and caste circumscribe the economic roles of individuals and socioeconomic immobility is pronounced. Technological change and innovation may be closely constrained because they clash with tradition and threaten the social fabric. Economic activity is often secondary to religious and cultural values and society's desire to perpetuate the status quo. In making the decision to pursue economic development, traditional economies must face the question as to which model in Table 2-3 will result in growth and simultaneously be the least incompatible with other economic and noneconomic goals valued by that society.

The basic point to be emphasized is that there is no unique or universally accepted way to respond to the economizing problem. Various societies, having

TABLE 2-3 Comparative economic systems

		Coordinating mechanism	
		Market system	Central planning
Ownership of resources	Private	United States	Nazi Germany
	Public	Yugoslavia	China

different cultural and historical backgrounds, different mores and customs, and contrasting ideological frameworks — not to mention resources that differ both quantitatively and qualitatively — use different institutions in dealing with the reality of relative scarcity. Canada, China, the United States, and Great Britain, for example, are all — in terms of their accepted

goals, ideology, technologies, resources, and culture — attempting to achieve efficiency in the use of their respective resources. The best method for responding to the unlimited wants–scarce resources dilemma in one economy may be inappropriate for another economic system.

CHAPTER SUMMARY

1. Economics centres on two basic facts: first, human material wants are virtually unlimited; second, economic resources are scarce.

2. Economic resources may be classified as land, capital, labour, and entrepreneurial ability.

3. Economics is concerned with the problem of administering scarce resources in the production of goods and services for the fulfilment of the material wants of society. Both the full employment and the full production of available resources are essential if this administration is to be efficient.

4. At any point in time a full-employment, full-production economy must sacrifice the output of some types of goods and services to achieve increased production of others. Because resources are not equally productive in all possible uses, the shifting of resources from one use to another gives rise to the law of increasing opportunity costs; that is, the production of additional units of product X entails the sacrifice of increasing amounts of product Y.

5. Over time, technological advance and increases in the quantity and quality of resources permit the economy to produce more of all goods and services. Society's choice as to the composition of current output is a determinant of the future location of the production possibilities curve.

6. The various economic systems of the world differ in their ideologies and also in their responses to the economizing problem. Critical differences centre on a. private versus public ownership of resources, and b. the use of the market system versus central planning as a coordinating mechanism.

TERMS AND CONCEPTS

allocative efficiency (p. 24)
authoritarian capitalism (p. 33)
capital goods (p. 24)
command economy or communism (p. 33)
consumer goods (p. 24)
economic growth (p. 28)
economizing problem (p. 22)
full employment (p. 24)
full production (p. 24)
investment (p. 23)

land, capital, labour, and entrepreneurial ability (pp. 22–23)
law of increasing opportunity costs (p. 26)
market socialism (p. 33)
production possibilities table (curve) (pp. 24, 25)
productive efficiency (p. 24)
pure or laissez-faire capitalism (p. 32)
traditional or customary economies (p. 33)
utility (p. 22)

QUESTIONS AND STUDY SUGGESTIONS

1. "Economics is the study of the principles governing the allocation of scarce means among competing ends when the objective of the allocation is to maximize the attainment of the ends." Explain. Why is the problem of unemployment a part of the subject matter of economics?

2. Critically analyse: "Wants aren't insatiable. I can prove it. I get all the coffee I want to drink every morning at breakfast." Explain: "Goods and services are scarce because resources are scarce." Analyse: "It is the nature of all economic problems that absolute solutions are denied us."

3. What are economic resources? What are the major functions of the entrepreneur? "Economics is . . . neither capitalist nor socialist: it applies to every society. Economics would disappear only in a world so rich that no wants were unfulfilled for lack of resources. Such a world is not imminent and may be impossible, for time is always limited." Carefully evaluate and explain these statements. Do you agree that time is an economic resource?

4. Distinguish between allocative efficiency and productive efficiency. Give an illustration of *a.* achieving allocative, but not productive efficiency, and *b.* achieving productive, but not allocative, efficiency.

5. Comment on the following statement from a newspaper article: "Our junior high school serves a splendid hot meal for $1 without costing the taxpayers anything, thanks in part to a government subsidy."

6. The following is a production possibilities table for war goods and civilian goods:

Type of production	Production alternatives				
	A	B	C	D	E
Automobiles (in millions)	0	2	4	6	8
Guided missiles (in thousands)	30	27	21	12	0

a. Show these production possibilities data graphically. What do the points on the curve indicate? How does the curve reflect the law of increasing opportunity costs? Explain. If the economy is currently at point C, what is the cost of 1 million more automobiles? Of 1000 more guided missiles?

b. Label point G inside the curve. What does it indicate? Label point H outside the curve. What does this point indicate? What must occur before the economy can attain the level of production indicated by point H?

c. On what specific assumptions is the production possibilities curve based? What happens when each of these assumptions is released?

d. Suppose improvement occurs in the technology of producing guided missiles but not in the production of automobiles. Draw the new production possibilities curve. Now assume that a technological advance occurs in producing automobiles but not in producing guided missiles. Draw the new production possibilities curve. Finally, draw a production possibilities curve that reflects technological improvement in the production of both products.

7. What is the opportunity cost of attending university?

8. Suppose that you arrive at a store expecting to pay $100 for an item, but learn that a store three kilometres away is charging $50 for the identical good. Would you drive to the second store? How does your decision benefit you? What is the opportunity cost of your decision? Now suppose that you arrive at a store expecting to pay $6000 for an item, but learn that the second store has the identical good priced at $5950. Do you make the same decision as before? Perhaps surprisingly, you should! Explain why.

9. "The present choice of position on the production possibilities curve is a major factor in economic growth." Explain.

10. Contrast the means by which pure capitalism, market socialism, and a command economy attempt to cope with economic scarcity.

11. Explain how an international trade deficit may permit an economy to acquire a combination of goods in excess of its domestic production potential. Explain why nations try to avoid having trade deficits.

3

Overview of the Market System and the Circular Flow

In the past few years the media have inundated us with stories of how the centrally planned economies are trying to alter their systems in the direction of capitalism, otherwise referred to as the market system or market economy. Precisely what are the features and institutions of a market system that these nations are trying to emulate?

You have virtually nothing whatsoever to do with the production of the vast majority of goods and services you consume. Why is it that production is so specialized in modern economies?

Nearly every day you have the experience of exchanging paper dollars — whose intrinsic value is virtually nil — for a wide variety of products of considerable value. Why do such seemingly irrational monetary transactions occur?

The foregoing questions are but some of those we will address in the pages that follow. Our initial task is to describe and explain how pure, or laissez-faire, capitalism would function.

Strictly speaking, a pure market system has never existed. Why, then, do we bother to consider the operation of such an economy?

Because it provides us with a useful first approximation of how the economies of Canada and many other industrially advanced nations function. And approximations or models, when properly handled, can be very useful. In other words, a pure market system constitutes a simplified model that we will then modify and adjust in later chapters to correspond more closely to the reality of these modern economies.

The Market System

Unfortunately, there is no neat and universally accepted definition of capitalism. We must examine in some detail the basic tenets of the market economy to acquire a comprehensive understanding of what it entails. The framework of the market system embodies the following institutions and assumptions: (1) private property, (2) freedom of enterprise and choice, (3) self-interest as the dominant motive, (4) competition, (5) reliance on self-regulating markets, and (6) a limited role for government.

Private Property

In a pure market system, resources are owned by private individuals and private institutions rather than by government. **Private property**, coupled with the freedom to negotiate binding legal contracts, permits private persons or businesses to obtain, control, employ, and dispose of resources as they see fit. The institution of private property is sustained over time by the right of a property owner to designate the recipient of this property at the time of death.

There are broad legal limits to this right to private ownership. For example, the use of one's resources for the production of illicit drugs is prohibited. Nor is public ownership nonexistent. Even in a pure market system, public ownership of certain "natural monopolies" may be essential to the achievement of efficiency in the use of resources.

Freedom of Enterprise and Choice

Closely related to private ownership of property is freedom of enterprise and choice. The market system charges its component economic units with the responsibility of making certain choices.

Freedom of enterprise means that private business enterprises are free to obtain economic resources, to organize these resources in the production of a good or service of the firm's own choosing, and to sell it in the markets of their choice. No artificial obstacles or restrictions imposed by government or other producers block an entrepreneur's choice to enter or leave a particular industry.

Freedom of choice means that owners of resources can employ or dispose of them as they see fit. It also means that workers are free to enter any of those lines of work for which they are qualified. It also means that consumers are at liberty, within the limits of their money incomes, to buy goods and services that they feel satisfy their wants.

Freedom of *consumer* choice may well be the most profound of these freedoms. The consumer is in a particularly strategic position in a market economy; in a sense, the consumer is sovereign. The range of free choices for suppliers of resources is circumscribed by the choices of consumers. The consumer ultimately decides what the economy should produce and resource suppliers must make their choices within the constraints delineated. Resource suppliers and businesses are not "free" to produce goods and services consumers do not desire.

Again, broad legal limitations prevail in the expression of all these free choices.

Role of Self-Interest

The primary driving force of a market economy is **self-interest**; each economic unit attempts to do what is best for itself. Hence entrepreneurs aim at the maximization of their firms' profits, and owners of resources attempt to achieve the highest price or rent from these resources. Those who supply labour resources will also attempt to obtain the highest possible incomes from their employment. Consumers, in purchasing a given product, will seek to obtain it at the lowest price. Consumers also apportion their expenditures to maximize their satisfaction. In short, a market economy presumes self-interest as the fundamental method of operation for the various economic units as they express their free choices.

It is worth noting that the pursuit of economic self-interest should not be confused with selfishness. The stockholder who receives corporate dividends may contribute a portion to the United Way or leave bequests to grandchildren. Similarly, a church official will carefully compare price and quality among various brands in buying new pews for the church.

Competition

Freedom of choice exercised in terms of promoting one's own monetary returns provides the basis for

competition, or economic rivalry, as a fundamental feature of a market economy. Competition entails:

1. The presence of large numbers of independently acting buyers and sellers operating in the market for any particular product or resource.

2. The freedom of buyers and sellers to enter or leave particular markets.

Markets and Prices

The basic coordinating mechanism of a capitalist economy is the market. *Capitalism is a* **market economy**. The decisions of buyers and sellers of products and resources are coordinated through a system of markets. The preferences of sellers and buyers are registered on the supply and demand sides of various markets, and the outcome of these choices is a system of product and resource prices. These prices are guideposts on which resource owners, entrepreneurs, and consumers make and revise their free choices in furthering their self-interests.

Just as competition is the controlling mechanism, so a system of markets and prices is a basic organizing force. The market system is an elaborate communication system through which innumerable individual free choices are recorded, summarized, and balanced against one another. Those who obey the dictates of the market system are rewarded, those who ignore it are penalized.

Through this communication system, society decides what the economy should produce, how production can be efficiently organized, and how the fruits of productive endeavour are to be distributed among the individual economic units.

Limited Government

A competitive market economy promotes a high degree of efficiency in the use of its resources. Hence there is allegedly little real need for government interference in the operation of an economy beyond its role of imposing broad legal limits on the exercise of individual choices and use of private property. The concept of a pure market system as a self-regulating and self-adjusting economy precludes any significant economic role for government.

OTHER CHARACTERISTICS

Private property, freedom of enterprise and choice, self-interest as a motivating force, competition, and reliance on a market system are all institutions and assumptions that are more or less exclusively associated with pure capitalism. In addition, there are certain institutions and practices characteristic of all modern economies: (1) the use of an advanced technology and large amounts of capital goods, (2) specialization, and (3) the use of money. Specialization and an advanced technology are prerequisites to the efficient employment of any economy's resources. The use of money is a permissive characteristic that allows society more easily to practise and reap the benefits of specialization and of the employment of advanced productive techniques.

Extensive Use of Capital Goods

All modern economies are based on advanced technology and the extensive use of capital goods. In a market economy it is competition that brings about technological advance. The market is highly effective in harnessing incentives to develop new products and improved techniques of production because the monetary rewards accrue directly to the innovator. A market economy therefore presupposes the extensive use and relatively rapid development of complex capital goods: tools, machinery, large-scale factories, and facilities for storage, transportation, and marketing.

The existence of an advanced technology and the extensive use of capital goods is important because the most direct method of producing a product is usually the least efficient. Even Robinson Crusoe avoided the inefficiencies of direct production in favour of **roundabout production**. It would be ridiculous for a farmer — even a backyard farmer — to go at production with bare hands. It pays huge dividends to fashion tools of production, that is, capital equipment, to aid in the productive process. There is a better way of getting water out of a well than to dive in after it!

But there is a catch. Recall our discussion of the production possibilities curve and the basic nature of the economizing problem. With full employment and full production, resources must be diverted from the production of consumer goods in order to be used in the production of capital goods. We must currently tighten our belts as consumers in order to free resources for the production of capital goods that will increase productive efficiency and allow a greater output of consumer goods at some future date.

QUICK REVIEW (3-1)

1. **A pure market system is predicated on the private ownership of property and freedom of enterprise and choice.**

2. **Economic actors — businesses, resource suppliers, and consumers — seek to further their own self-interests.**

3. **The coordinating mechanism of capitalism is a competitive system of markets.**

4. **The efficient function of the market system allegedly precludes significant government intervention.**

5. **Advanced economies achieve greater efficiency in production through the use of large quantities of capital goods.**

THE COMPETITIVE MARKET SYSTEM

There are two primary *decision makers* in a market economy: **households** (consumers) and **firms** (businesses). Households are the ultimate suppliers of all economic resources and simultaneously the major spending group in the economy. Firms provide goods and services to the economy.

Consumers are at liberty to buy what they choose; firms to produce and sell what they choose; and resource suppliers, to make their resources available in whatever occupations they choose. On reflection, we might wonder why such an economy does not collapse in chaos. If consumers want breakfast cereal, businesses choose to produce aerobic shoes, and resource suppliers want to offer their services in manufacturing computer software, production would seem to be deadlocked because of the apparent inconsistency of these free choices.

In reality, the millions of decisions made by households and firms are highly consistent with one another. Firms do produce those particular goods and services that consumers want. Households provide the kinds of labour that businesses want to hire. What we want to explain is how a competitive market system constitutes a coordinating mechanism that overcomes the potential chaos suggested by freedom of enterprise and choice. The competitive market system is a mechanism both for communicating the decisions of consumers, producers, and resource suppliers to one another and for synchronizing those decisions toward consistent production objectives.

THE FIVE FUNDAMENTAL QUESTIONS

To understand the operation of a market economy we must recognize that there are **Five Fundamental Questions** to which *every* economy must respond:

1. *How much* is to be produced? At what level — to what degree — should available resources be employed or utilized in the production process?

2. *What* is to be produced? What collection of goods and services will best satisfy society's material wants?

3. *How* is that output to be produced? How should production be organized? What firms should do the producing and what productive techniques should they use?

4. *Who* is to receive the output? In particular, how should the output of the economy be shared by consumers?

5. Can the system *adapt* to change? Can the system negotiate appropriate adjustments when changes in consumer wants, resource supplies, and technology occur?

Two points are relevant at the outset. First, we will defer the "how much" question for the moment. Macroeconomics deals in detail with the complex question of the level of resource employment.

Second, the Five Fundamental Questions are merely an elaboration of the choices underlying Chapter 2's production possibilities curve. These questions would be irrelevant were it not for the economizing problem.

THE MARKET SYSTEM AT WORK

Determining What Is To Be Produced

Given the product and resource prices established by competing buyers and sellers in both the product and resource markets, how would a market economy decide the types and quantities of goods to be produced? Remembering that businesses seek profits and want to avoid losses, we can generalize that those goods and services that can be produced at a profit will be produced and those whose production entails a loss will not. Those industries that are profitable usually expand, those that incur losses usually contract.

Organizing Production

How is production to be organized in a market economy? This Fundamental Question is composed of three subquestions:

1. How should resources be allocated among specific industries?

2. What specific firms should do the producing in each industry?

3. What combinations of resources — what technology — should each firm employ?

The market system steers resources to those industries whose products consumers want badly enough to make their production profitable. It simultaneously deprives unprofitable industries of scarce resources. If all firms had sufficient time to enter prosperous industries and to leave unprosperous industries, the output of each industry would be large enough for the firms to make normal profits (Chapter 9).

The second and third subquestions are closely intertwined. In a competitive market economy, the firms that do the producing are those that are willing and able to employ the economically most efficient technique of production. And what determines the most efficient technique? Economic efficiency depends on:

1. Available technology, that is, the alternative combinations of resources or inputs that will produce the desired output.

2. The prices at which the needed resources can be obtained.

Distributing Total Output

The market system enters the picture in two ways in solving the problem of distributing total output. Generally speaking, any given product will be distributed to consumers on the basis of their ability and willingness to pay the existing market price for it. This is the rationing function of equilibrium prices.

The size of one's money income determines a consumer's ability to pay the equilibrium price for X and other available products. And money income depends upon the quantities of the various resources that the income receiver supplies and the prices that they command in the resource market. Thus, resource prices play a key role in determining the size of each household's income claim against the total output of society. Within the limits of a consumer's money income, his or her willingness to pay the equilibrium price for X determines whether or not some of this product is distributed to that person. And this willingness to buy X will depend upon one's preference for X in comparison with available close substitutes for X and their relative prices. Thus, product prices play a key role in determining the expenditure patterns of consumers.

There is nothing particularly ethical about the market system as a mechanism for distributing output. Households that accumulate large amounts of property by inheritance, through hard work and frugality, through business acumen, or by crook will receive large incomes and thus command large shares of the economy's total output. Others, offering unskilled and relatively unproductive labour resources that elicit low wages, will receive meager money incomes and small portions of total output.

Accommodating Change

Industrial societies are dynamic: Consumer preferences, technology, and resource supplies all change. This means that the particular allocation of resources that is *now* the most efficient for a *given* pattern of consumer tastes, for a *given* range of technological alternatives, and for *given* supplies of resources can be expected to become obsolete and inefficient as consumer preferences change, new techniques of production are discovered, and resource supplies alter over time. The market economy negotiates adjustments to these changes so that resources are still used efficiently.

Competition and Control: The "Invisible Hand"

The market mechanism of supply and demand communicates the wants of consumers (society) to businesses and through businesses to resource suppliers. It is competition, however, that forces businesses and resource suppliers to make appropriate responses. But competition does more than guarantee responses appropriate to the wishes of society. It also forces firms to adopt the most efficient productive techniques. In a competitive market, the failure of some firms to use the least costly production technique means their eventual elimination by more efficient firms. Finally, competition provides an environment conducive to technological advance.

The operation and the adjustments of a competitive market system create a curious and important identity — the identity of private and social interests. Firms and resource suppliers, seeking to further their own self-interest and operating within the framework of a highly competitive market system, will simultaneously, as though guided by an "**invisible hand**," promote the public or social interest. For example, in a competitive environment, business firms use the least costly combination of resources in producing a given output because it is in their private self-interest to do so. To act otherwise would be to forgo profits or even to risk bankruptcy. But, at the same time, it is clearly also in the social interest to use scarce resources in the least costly, that is, most efficient, manner. Not to do so would be to produce a given output at a greater cost or sacrifice of alternative goods than is necessary. It is self-interest, awakened and guided by the competitive market system, that induces responses appropriate to the assumed change in society's wants. Businesses seeking to make higher profits and to avoid losses, on the one hand, and resource suppliers pursuing greater monetary rewards, on the other, negotiate the changes in the allocation of resources and therefore the composition of output that society demands. The force of competition controls or guides the self-interest motive in such a way that it automatically, and quite unintentionally, furthers the best interests of society. The "invisible hand" tells us that when firms maximize their profits, society's domestic output is also maximized.

QUICK REVIEW (3–2)

1. **The output mix of the competitive market system is determined by profits. Profits cause industries to expand; losses cause them to contract.**

2. **Competition forces firms to use the least costly (most efficient) production methods.**

3. **The distribution of output in a market economy is determined by consumer incomes and product prices.**

4. **Competitive markets reallocate resources in response to changes in consumer tastes, technological progress, and changes in resource supplies.**

SPECIALIZATION AND EFFICIENCY

The extent to which society relies on **specialization** is astounding. The vast majority of consumers produce virtually none of the goods and services they consume. The machine-shop worker who spends a lifetime stamping out parts for jet engines may never "consume" an airline trip. The assembly-line worker who devotes eight hours a day to the installation of windows in Chevrolets may own a Honda.

Few households seriously consider any extensive production of their own food, shelter, and clothing. Many farmers sell their milk to the local dairy and then buy margarine at the nearest supermarket. Society learned long ago that self-sufficiency breeds inefficiency. The jack-of-all-trades may be a very colourful individual, but is certainly not efficient.

Division of Labour

In what ways might specialization — the **division of labour** — enhance productive efficiency?

1. Specialization permits individuals to take advantage of existing differences in their abilities and skills. If caveman A is strong, swift afoot, and accurate with a spear, and caveman B is weak and slow, but patient, this distribution of talents can be most efficiently used by making A a hunter and B a fisherman.

2. Even if the abilities of A and B are identical, specialization may be advantageous. By devoting all one's time to a single task, the doer is more likely to develop the appropriate skills and to discover improved techniques than when apportioning time among a number of diverse tasks. One learns to be a good hunter by hunting!

3. Specialization — devoting all one's time to a single task — also avoids the loss of time shifting from one job to another. For all these reasons, the division of labour results in greater productive efficiency in the use of resources.

Geographic Specialization   Specialization is also desirable on a regional and international basis. Apples could be grown in Saskatchewan, but because of the unsuitability of the land, rainfall, and temperature, the cost involved would be exceedingly high. The Okanagan Valley could achieve some success in the production of wheat, but for similar reasons such production would be relatively costly. As a result, Saskatchewan produces those products — wheat in particular — for which its resources are best adapted and the Okanagan does the same, producing apples and other fruit.

In so doing, both produce surpluses of their specialities. Then Saskatchewan and the Okanagan swap some of their surpluses. Specialization permits each area to turn out those goods its resources can most efficiently produce. In this way, both Saskatchewan and the Okanagan can enjoy a larger amount of both wheat and applies than would otherwise be the case.

Similarly, on an international basis we find Canada specializing in such items as the Dash-8 aircraft and communication equipment that it sells abroad in exchange for video cassette recorders from Japan, bananas from Honduras, shoes from Italy, and coffee from Brazil. In short, *specialization is essential to achieve efficiency in the use of resources.*

Disadvantages   Despite these efficiency advantages, specialization does have certain drawbacks.

1. The potential monotony and drudgery of specialized work are well known. Imagine the boredom of our previously mentioned assembly-line worker, who is still putting windows in Chevrolets.

2. Specialization and mutual interdependence vary directly with one another. For example, developments in the Persian Gulf could threaten the economic stability of those nations dependent on imported oil. The less each of us produces for ourselves, the more we are dependent on the output of others. A railway or truckers' strike may very quickly result in product shortages.

3. A third problem centres on the exchange of the surpluses. An examination of this problem leads us into a discussion of the use of money in the domestic and world economies.

Use of Money

Virtually all economies, advanced or primitive, use money. Money performs a variety of functions, but first and foremost it is a **medium of exchange**.

In our Saskatchewan–Okanagan example, Saskatchewan must trade or exchange wheat for the Okanagan's apples if both regions are to share in the benefits of specialization. Because consumers want a wide variety of products, in the absence of trade, they would tend to devote their resources to many diverse types of production. If exchange could not occur or was very inconvenient, Saskatchewan and the Okanagan would be forced to be self-sufficient, and the advantages of specialization would not occur. *In short, a convenient means of exchanging goods is a prerequisite of specialization.*

Exchange can, and sometimes does, occur on the basis of **bartering**, that is, swapping goods for goods. But bartering as a means of exchange can pose serious problems for the economy. Exchange by barter requires a **coincidence of wants** between the two transactors. In our example, we assumed that Saskatchewan had excess wheat to trade and that it wanted to obtain apples. We also assumed the Okanagan had excess apples to swap and that it wanted to acquire wheat. So exchange occurred. But if this

coincidence of wants did not exist, trade would not occur. Let us examine this.

Suppose Saskatchewan does not want any of the Okanagan's apples but is interested in buying potatoes from New Brunswick. Ironically, New Brunswick wants the Okanagan's apples but not Saskatchewan's wheat. And to complicate matters, suppose that the Okanagan wants some of Saskatchewan's wheat but none of New Brunswick's potatoes. The situation is summarized in Figure 3–1.

In no case do we find a coincidence of wants. Trade by barter would be difficult. To overcome such a stalemate, modern economies use **money**, which is a convenient social invention for facilitating the exchange of goods and services. Historically cattle, cigarettes, skins, liquor, playing cards, shells, stones, pieces of metal, and many other diverse commodities have been used with varying degrees of success as a medium for facilitating exchange. To be money, an item needs to pass only one test: *it must be generally acceptable by buyers and sellers in exchange.* Money is socially defined; whatever society accepts as a medium of exchange is money. Most modern econ-

FIGURE 3-1   Money facilitates trade where wants do not coincide

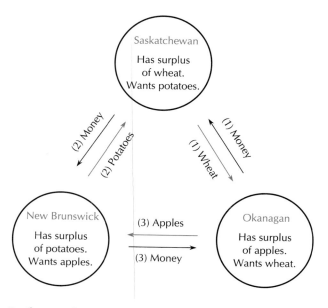

By the use of money as a medium of exchange, trade can be accomplished, as indicated by the arrows, despite a noncoincidence of wants. By facilitating exchange, the use of money permits an economy to realize the efficiencies of specialization.

omies, for reasons made clear in macroeconomics, find it convenient to use paper as money. We will assume that this is the case with the Saskatchewan–Okanagan–New Brunswick economy; they use pieces of paper, which they call "dollars," as money. Can the use of paper dollars as a medium of exchange overcome the stalemate we have posed?

Indeed it can, with trade occurring as shown in Figure 3–1:

1. The Okanagan can exchange money for some of Saskatchewan's wheat.

2. Saskatchewan can take the money realized from the sale of wheat and exchange it for some of New Brunswick's potatoes.

3. New Brunswick can then exchange the money received from the sale of potatoes for some of the Okanagan's surplus apples.

The willingness to accept paper money (or any other kind of money) as a medium of exchange has permitted a three-way trade, which allows each region to specialize in one product and obtain the other product(s) its residents desire, despite the absence of a coincidence of wants between any two of the parties. Barter, resting as it does on a coincidence of wants, would have impeded this exchange. In so doing it would have induced the three regions not to specialize. The efficiencies of specialization would then have been lost to those regions.

QUICK REVIEW (3–3)

1. Specialization enhances efficiency and brings about surpluses.

2. The use of money is necessary to facilitate the exchange of goods that specialization entails.

THE CIRCULAR FLOW MODEL

Our discussion of specialization and the need for a monetary system to facilitate exchange puts us in a position to re-emphasize the role of markets and prices in a market economy. The remainder of this chapter is devoted to an overview of the market system for the purpose of pinpointing the two basic types of markets.

Resource and Product Markets

Figure 3-2 (Key Graph) provides the simple overview we seek. Here we find the two groups of *deci-*

sion makers — households and businesses. The *coordinating mechanism* that brings the decisions of households and businesses into consistency with one another is the market system, in particular resource and product markets.

The upper half of the diagram portrays the **resource market**. Here, households, which directly or indirectly (through their ownership of business corporations) own all economic resources, *supply* these resources to business. Businesses will *demand* resources because they are needed to produce goods and services. The interaction of demand and supply for the immense variety of resources establishes the price of each. Payments businesses make to obtain resources are costs to them, but also constitute flows of wage, rent, interest, and profit income to the households supplying these resources.

Now consider the **product market** shown in the bottom half of the diagram. The money income received by households from the sale of resources does not have real value. Consumers cannot eat or wear coins and paper money. Hence through the expenditure of money income, households express their *demand* for a vast array of goods and services. Simultaneously, businesses combine the resources they have obtained to produce and *supply* goods and services in these same markets. The interaction of these demand and supply decisions determines product prices.

The **circular flow model** shows the interrelated web of decision-making and economic activity. Note that households and businesses participate in both markets, but on different sides of each market. Businesses are on the buying or demand side of the resource markets and households, as resource owners and suppliers, are on the selling or supply side. In the product market, these positions are reversed. The net result is a counter-clockwise *real* flow of economic resources and finished goods and services and a clockwise *money* flow of income and consumption expenditures.

Limitations

Our model is simplified in many ways. Intrahousehold and intrabusiness transactions are concealed. Government, private not-for-profit agencies, and the "rest of the world" are ignored. The model subtly implies constant flows of output and income, while in fact these flows are unstable over time.

FIGURE 3-2   The circular flow of output and income

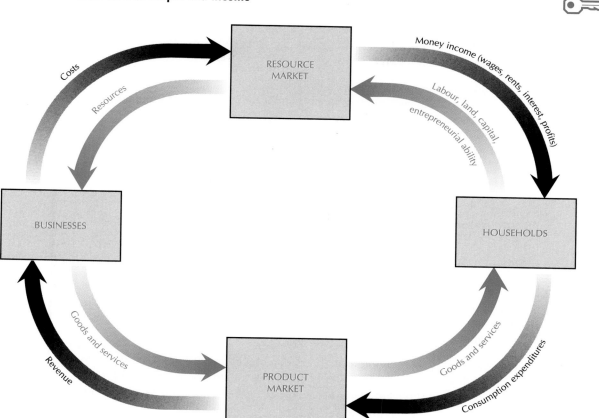

The prices paid for the use of land, labour, capital, and entrepreneurial ability are determined in the resource market shown in the upper loop. Businesses are on the demand side and households on the supply side of this market. The prices of finished goods and services are determined in the product market located in the lower loop. Households are on the demand side and businesses on the supply side of this market.

CHAPTER SUMMARY

1. The capitalist, or market, system is characterized by private ownership of resources and the freedom of individuals to engage in the economic activities of their choice as a means for advancing their material well-being. Self-interest is the driving force of such an economy, and competition functions as a regulatory or control mechanism.

2. Capitalist production is not organized in terms of a government plan, but rather features the market system as a means of organizing and making effective the many individual decisions that determine what is produced, the methods of production, and the sharing of output. A pure capitalist system envisions government playing a minor and relatively passive economic role.

3. Every economy is confronted with Five Fundamental Questions: *a.* At what level should available resources be employed? *b.* What goods and services are to be produced? *c.* How is that output to be produced? *d.* To whom should the output be distributed? *e.* Can the system adapt to changes in consumer tastes, resource supplies, and technology?

4. The competitive market system can communicate changes in consumer tastes to resource suppliers and entrepreneurs, thereby prompting appropriate adjustments in the allocation of the economy's resources. The competitive market system also provides an environment conducive to technological advance and capital accumulation.

5. Competition, the primary mechanism of control in the market economy, will foster an identity of private and social interests; as though directed by an "invisible hand," competition harnesses the self-interest motives of businesses and resource suppliers so as to simultaneously further the social interest in using scarce resources efficiently.

6. Specialization and an advanced technology based on the extensive use of capital goods are features common to all modern economies.

7. Functioning as a medium of exchange, money circumvents problems entailed in bartering and thereby permits greater specialization both domestically and internationally.

8. An overview of the operation of the market system can be gained through the circular flow of income. This simplified model locates the product and resource markets and presents the major income-expenditure flows and resources-output flows.

TERMS AND CONCEPTS

bartering (p. 43)
circular flow model (p. 44)
coincidence of wants (p. 43)
competition (p. 39)
firms (p. 40)
Five Fundamental Questions (p. 40)
freedom of choice (p. 38)
freedom of enterprise (p. 38)
households (p. 40)

"invisible hand" (p. 41)
market economy (p. 39)
medium of exchange (p. 43)
money (p. 43)
private property (p. 38)
resource and product markets (p. 44)
roundabout production (p. 39)
self-interest (p. 38)
specialization and division of labour (p. 42)

QUESTIONS AND STUDY SUGGESTIONS

1. "Capitalism may be characterized as an automatic self-regulating system motivated by the self-interest of individuals and regulated by competition." Explain and evaluate.

2. Explain how the market system is a means of communicating and implementing decisions concerning allocation of the economy's resources.

3. What advantages result from "roundabout" production? What problem is involved in increasing a full-employment, full-production economy's stock of capital goods? Illustrate this problem in terms of the production possibilities curve. Does an economy with unemployed resources face the same problem?

4. Describe in detail how the market system answers the Fundamental Questions. Why must economic choices be made? Explain: "The capitalist system is a profit and loss economy."

5. Evaluate and explain the following statements:

   a. "The most important feature of capitalism is the absence of a central economic plan."

   b. "Competition is the indispensable disciplinarian of the market economy."

   c. "Production methods that are inferior in the engineering sense may be the most efficient methods in the economic sense."

6. What are the advantages of specialization in the use of resources? The disadvantages? Explain: "Exchange is the necessary consequence of specialization."

7. What problems does barter entail? Indicate the economic significance of money as a medium of exchange. "Money is the only commodity that is good for nothing but to be gotten rid of. It will not feed you, clothe you, shelter you, or amuse you unless you spend or invest it. It imparts value only in parting." Explain this statement.

8. Describe the operation of pure capitalism as portrayed by the circular flow model. Locate resource and product markets and emphasize the fact of scarcity throughout your discussion. Specify the limitations of the circular flow model.

4

Understanding Individual Markets: Demand and Supply

"**T**each a parrot to say, 'Demand and supply,' and you have an economist!" There is a strong element of truth in this quip. The simple tools of demand and supply can take one far in understanding not only specific economic issues, but also the operation of the entire economic system.

The goal of this chapter is to understand the nature of markets and how prices and outputs are determined. Our circular flow model of Chapter 3 identified the participants in both product and resource markets. But we assumed product and resource prices were "given"; no attempt was made to explain how prices are "set" or determined. Let's build on the circular flow model by discussing more fully the concept of a market.

MARKETS DEFINED

A **market** is *an institution or mechanism that brings together buyers ("demanders") and sellers ("suppliers") of particular goods and services.* Markets exist in many forms. The corner gas station, the fast-food outlet, the local record shop, a farmer's roadside stand, are all familiar markets. The Toronto Stock Exchange and the Chicago Board of Trade are highly organized markets where buyers and sellers of stocks and bonds and farm commodities, respectively, are brought into contact with one another. Similarly, auctioneers bring together potential buyers and sellers of art, livestock, used farm equipment, and sometimes real estate. The professional hockey player and his agent bargain with the owner of an NHL team. A graduating engineer interviews with Canadian Pacific and Petro-Canada at the university placement office.

All of these situations that link potential buyers with potential sellers constitute markets. Some markets are local while others are national or international in scope. Some are highly personal, involving face-to-face contact between demander and supplier; others are impersonal in that buyer and seller never see or know one another.

This chapter is concerned with the functioning of *purely competitive markets.* Such markets presume large numbers of independently acting buyers and sellers exchanging a standardized product. The kind of market we have in mind is not the record shop or corner gas station, where products have price tags on them, but such competitive markets as a central grain exchange, a stock market, or a market for foreign currencies, where the equilibrium price is "discovered" by the interacting decisions of buyers and sellers.

We also seek to find how prices are established in resource markets by the demand decisions of competing businesses and the supply decisions of competing households (Figure 3-2). We will concentrate on the product market, and then shift our attention later in the chapter to the resource market. Our goal is to explain the mechanics of prices.

DEMAND

Demand *is defined as a schedule that shows the various amounts of a product consumers are willing and able to purchase at each specific price during some specified period of time, all other things being equal.* [1]

---
[1] In adjusting this definition to the resource market, substitute the word "resource" for "product" and "businesses" for "consumers."

We usually view demand from the vantage point of price. We read demand as showing the amounts consumers will buy at various possible prices. Table 4-1 is a hypothetical **demand schedule** for a single consumer purchasing bushels of oats.

This demand curve reflects the relationship between the price of oats and the quantity that our hypothetical consumer would be willing and able to purchase at each of these prices. Note that we say willing and *able,* because willingness alone will not suffice. I may be willing to buy a Porsche, but if this willingness is not backed by the ability to buy, it will not be effective and therefore not be reflected in the market. In Table 4-1, if the price of oats in the market happened to be $5 per bushel, our consumer would buy 10 bushels per week; if it were $4, the consumer would buy 20 bushels per week, and so forth.

The demand schedule does not tell us which of the five possible prices will actually exist in the oats market. This depends on demand *and supply.* Demand is simply a statement of a buyer's plans or intentions, with respect to the purchase of a product.

To be meaningful the quantities demanded at each price must relate to some specific time period — a day, a week, a month, and so forth. To say "a consumer will buy 10 bushels of oats at $5 per bushel" is vague and meaningless. In the absence of a specific time period we would be unable to tell whether the demand for a product was large or small.

Law of Demand

A fundamental characteristic of demand is this: All else being constant, as price falls, the quantity demanded rises. Or, other things being equal, as price increases, the quantity demanded falls. In short, there is an *inverse* relationship between price and quantity demanded. Economists call this inverse relationship the **law of demand**.

The "other things being constant" assumption is critical here. Many factors other than the price of the product under consideration can affect the amount purchased. For example, the quantity of Nikes pur-

TABLE 4-1 An individual buyer's demand for oats (hypothetical data)

Price per bushel	Quantity demanded per week
$5	10
4	20
3	35
2	55
1	80

chased will depend not only on the price of Nikes, but also on the prices of such substitute shoes as Reeboks, Addidas, and L.A. Gear. The law of demand in this case says that fewer pairs of Nikes will be purchased if the price of Nikes rises *and the prices of Reeboks, Addidas, and L.A. Gear all remain constant*. Thus, if the *relative price* of Nikes increases, fewer Nikes will be bought.

On what foundation does the law of demand rest? There are several levels of analysis on which the case can be argued.

1. Common sense and simple observation are consistent with the law of demand. People ordinarily *do* buy more of a given product at a low price than they do at a high price. Price is an obstacle that deters consumers from buying. The fact that businesses have "sales" is concrete evidence of their belief in the law of demand. "Bargain days" are based on the law of demand. Businesses reduce their inventories by lowering prices, not by raising them!

2. In any given time period, each buyer of a product will derive less satisfaction or utility from each successive unit of a product. The second hamburger will yield less satisfaction than the first; the third still less than the second, and so forth. Hence because consumption is subject to **diminishing marginal utility** — successive units of a particular product yield less and less extra satisfaction — consumers will only buy additional units if price is reduced.

3. The law of demand can be explained in terms of substitution effects and income effects. The **substitution effect** suggests that at a lower price, you have the incentive to substitute the cheaper good for similar goods that are now relatively more expensive. The **income effect** indicates that at a lower price, you can afford more of the good without giving up other goods. A decline in the price of a product will increase the purchasing power of your money income, enabling you to buy more of the product than before.

A higher price will have the opposite effect. To illustrate: At a lower price, beef is relatively more attractive and it is substituted for pork, lamb, chicken, and fish (the substitution effect). A decline in the price of beef will increase the purchasing power of consumer incomes, enabling them to buy more beef (the income effect). The substitution and income effects combine to make consumers able and willing to buy more of a product at a low price than at a high price.

The Demand Curve

This inverse relationship between product price and quantity demanded can be represented on a simple two-dimensional graph, measuring quantity demanded on the horizontal axis and price on the vertical axis. The process involves locating on the graph those five price–quantity possibilities shown in Table 4-1. Assuming the same inverse relationship between price and quantity demanded at all points between the ones graphed, we can generalize on the inverse relationship between price and quantity demanded by drawing a curve to represent *all* price–quantity-demanded possibilities within the limits shown on the graph. The resulting curve is called a **demand curve** and is labelled *D* in Figure 4-1. It slopes downward and to the right because the relationship it portrays between price and quantity demanded is negative or inverse. The law of demand is reflected in the downward slope of the demand curve.

What is the advantage of graphing our demand schedule? After all, Table 4-1 and Figure 4-1 contain exactly the same data and reflect the same relationship between price and quantity demanded. The advantage of graphing is that it permits us to represent clearly a given relationship — in this case, the law of demand — in a much simpler way. A single curve on a graph, if understood, is simpler to state *and to manipulate* than tables and lengthy verbal presentations would be. Graphs are invaluable tools in economic analysis. They permit clear expression and handling of often complex relationships.

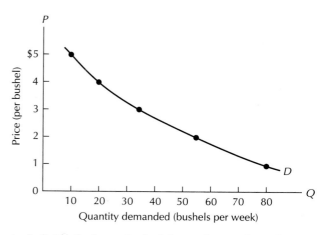

FIGURE 4-1   An individual buyer's demand curve for oats

An individual's demand schedule graphs as a downsloping curve such as *D*, because price and quantity demanded are inversely related. Specifically, the law of demand generalizes that consumers will buy more of a product as its price declines.

Individual and Market Demand

Until now we have been dealing in terms of just one consumer. The transition from an *individual* to a *market* demand schedule can be accomplished easily by the process of summing the quantities demanded by each consumer at the various possible prices. If there were just three buyers in the market, as shown in Table 4-2, it would be easy to determine the total quantities demanded at each price. Figure 4-2 shows the same summing procedure graphically, using only the $3 price to illustrate the adding-up process. Note that we are simply summing the three individual demand curves *horizontally* to derive the total demand curve.

Competition entails many more than three buyers of a product. To avoid a lengthy addition process, let us suppose there are 200 buyers of oats in the market, each of whom chooses to buy the same amount at each of the various prices as our original consumer does. We can determine total or market demand by multiplying the quantity demanded data of Table 4-1 by 200, as in Table 4-3. Curve D_0 in Figure 4-3 indicates this market demand curve for the 200 buyers.

Determinants of Demand

Constructing a demand curve such as D_0 in Figure 4-3, assumes that price is the most important determinant of the amount of any product purchased. But factors other than price can and do affect purchases. Thus in locating a given demand curve such as D_0, it must also be assumed that other *determinants* of the amount demanded are constant. When these determinants of demand do change, the location of the demand curve will shift to some new position to the right or left of D_0. For this reason these determinants are also referred to as "demand shifters."

The major determinants of market demand are: (1) the tastes or preferences of consumers, (2) the number of consumers in the market, (3) the money incomes of consumers, (4) the prices of related goods, and (5) consumer expectations with respect to future prices and incomes.

Changes in Demand

A change in one or more of the determinants will change the demand schedule data in Table 4-3, and therefore the location of the demand curve in Figure 4-3. A change in the demand schedule data or, graphically, a shift in the location of the demand curve, is called a **change in demand**.

If consumers buy more of this particular good at each possible price than is reflected in column 4 of Table 4-3, the result will be an *increase in demand*. In Figure 4-3, this increase in demand is reflected in a shift of the demand curve to the right from D_0 to D_1. Conversely, a *decrease in demand* occurs when, because of a change in one or more of the determinants, consumers buy less of the product at each possible price than is indicated in column 4 of Table 4-3. Graphically, a decrease in demand is shown as a shift of the demand curve to the left, from D_0 to D_2 in Figure 4-3.

Let's now examine how changes in each of the determinants affects demand.

1 Tastes   A change in consumer tastes or preferences favourable to a product — possibly prompted by advertising or fashion changes — will result in more being demanded at each price; that is, demand will increase. An unfavourable change in consumer preferences will cause demand to decrease, shifting the curve to the left. Note that technological change in the form of new products may prompt a revision of consumer tastes. The introduction of compact discs has tended to decrease the demand for long-playing records. The demand for oat bran has

TABLE 4-2   Market demand for oats, three buyers (*hypothetical data*)

Price per bushel	Quantity demanded, first buyer		Quantity demanded, second buyer		Quantity demanded, third buyer		Total quantity demanded per week
$5	10	+	12	+	8	=	30
4	20	+	23	+	17	=	60
3	35	+	39	+	26	=	100
2	55	+	60	+	39	=	154
1	80	+	87	+	54	=	221

FIGURE 4-2   **The market demand curve is the sum of the individual demand curves**

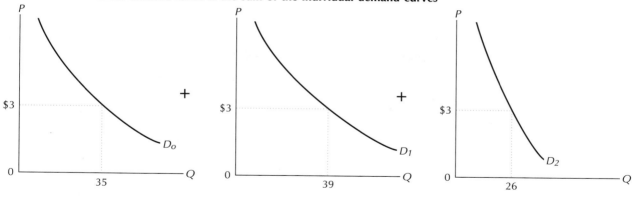

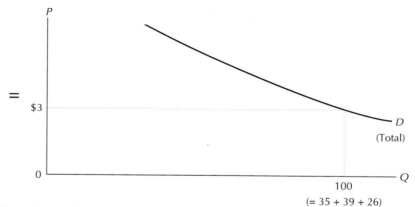

Graphically, the market demand curve (*D* total) is found by summing horizontally the individual demand curves (*D*₀, *D*₁, and *D*₂) of all consumers in the market.

increased because of studies linking it to lower cholesterol levels.

2 Number of Buyers   An increase in the number of consumers in a market — brought about perhaps by improvements in transportation or by population growth — will increase demand. Fewer consumers will result in a decrease in demand. Examples: Dramatic improvements in communications have made financial markets international in scope, increasing the demand for stocks, bonds, and other financial instruments. The "baby boom" of the post–World War II period increased the demand for diapers and baby lotion, not to mention the services of obstetricians. When the "baby boom" generation reached their twenties in the 1970s, the demand for housing greatly increased. Conversely, the aging of the baby boomers in the late 1980s and 1990s has been an important factor in the recent "slump" in housing demand. Increasing life expectancy has increased the

demands for medical care, retirement communities, and nursing homes.

TABLE 4-3   **Market demand for oats, 200 buyers (*hypothetical data*)**

(1) Price per bushel	(2) Quantity demanded per week, single buyer		(3) Number of buyers in the market		(4) Total quantity demanded per week
$5	10	×	200	=	2,000
4	20	×	200	=	4,000
3	35	×	200	=	7,000
2	55	×	200	=	11,000
1	80	×	200	=	16,000

FIGURE 4-3 Changes in the demand for oats

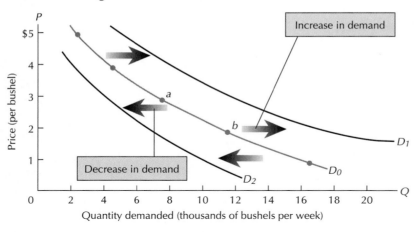

Quantity demanded (thousands of bushels per week)

A change in one or more of the determinants of demand — consumer tastes, the number of buyers in the market, money incomes, the prices of other goods, or consumer expectations — will cause a change in demand. An increase in demand shifts the demand curve to the right, as from D_0 to D_1. A decrease in demand shifts the demand curve to the left, as from D_0 to D_2. A change in the quantity demanded involves a movement, caused by a change in the price of the product under consideration, from one point to another — as from a to b — on a fixed demand curve.

3 Income For most commodities, a rise in income will cause an increase in demand. Consumers typically buy more shoes, steaks, sunscreen, and stereos, as their incomes increase. Conversely, the demand for such products will decline in response to a fall in incomes. Commodities whose demand varies *directly* with money income are called **superior** or **normal goods**.

Although most products are normal goods, there are a few exceptions. Examples: As incomes increase beyond some point, the amounts of bread or potatoes or cabbages purchased at each price may diminish because higher incomes now allow consumers to buy more high-protein foods, such as dairy products and meat. Rising incomes may also decrease the demands for used clothing and third-hand automobiles. Rising incomes may cause the demands for hamburger to decline, as wealthier consumers switch to T-bone steak. Goods whose demand varies *inversely* with a change in money income are called **inferior goods**.

4 Prices of Related Goods Whether a given change in the price of a related good will increase or decrease the demand for the product under consideration will depend on whether the related good is a substitute for, or a complement to, the product. A substitute good is one that can be used in place of another good. A complementary good is one that is used in conjunction with another good. For example, butter and margarine are **substitute goods** to consumers not worried about cholesterol. When the price of butter rises, consumers will purchase a smaller amount of butter, and this will cause the

demand for margarine to increase.[2] Conversely, as the price of butter falls, consumers will buy larger quantities of butter, causing the demand for margarine to decrease. *To generalize: When two products are substitutes, the price of one good and the demand for the other are directly related.* So it is with sugar and Nutrasweet, Toyotas and Hondas, Coke and Pepsi, and tea and coffee.

But other pairs of products are **complementary goods**; they "go together" in that they are jointly-demanded. If the price of gasoline falls you drive your car more, and this extra driving will increase your demand for motor oil. Conversely, an increase in the price of gasoline will diminish the demand for motor oil.[3] Thus gas and oil are jointly demanded; they are complements. And so it is with ham and eggs, university courses and textbooks, VCRs and video cassettes, golf clubs and golf balls, cameras and rolls of film. *When two commodities are complements, the price of one good and the demand for the other are inversely related.*

Many pairs of goods are not related at all — they are *independent* goods. For such pairs of commodi-

---

[2] Note that the consumer is moving up a stable demand curve for butter. But the demand curve for margarine shifts to the right. Given the supply of margarine, this rightward shift in demand means that more margarine will be purchased and that its price will also rise.

[3] Again, note that while the buyer is moving up a stable demand curve for gasoline, the demand for motor oil shifts to the left (decreases). Given the supply of motor oil, this decline in demand for motor oil will decrease both the amount purchased and its price.

ties as, for example, butter and golf balls, potatoes and automobiles, bananas and wristwatches, we expect that a change in the price of one would have little or no impact on the demand for the other.

5 Expectations Consumer expectations about future product prices, product availability, and future income can shift demand. Consumer expectations of higher future prices may prompt them to buy now to "beat" the anticipated price rises. The expectation of rising incomes may induce consumers to be less tight-fisted in their current spending. For example, if freezing weather destroys a substantial portion of Florida's citrus crop, consumers may reason that forthcoming shortages of frozen orange juice will escalate its price. Hence they purchase large quantities now. Several years ago Johnny Carson jokingly predicted a toilet paper shortage. Many of his fans took his comment seriously, and within a few days toilet paper was not to be found on the shelves of many supermarkets. A first-round NHL draft choice might splurge on a new Mercedes in anticipation of a lucrative professional hockey contract.

Table 4-4 provides a convenient listing of the determinants of demand along with additional illustrations.

Changes in Quantity Demanded

A "change in demand" must not be confused with a "change in the quantity demanded." A **change in demand** refers to a shift in the entire demand curve either to the right (an increase in demand) or to the left (a decrease in demand). As used by economists, the term "demand" refers to a schedule or curve; therefore, a "change in demand" must mean that the entire schedule has changed, and that graphically, the curve has shifted its position.

In contrast, a **change in the quantity demanded** designates the movement from one point to another on a fixed demand curve. The cause of a change in the quantity demanded is a change in the price of the product under consideration. In Table 4-3, a decline in the price asked by suppliers of oats from $5 to $4 will increase the quantity of oats demanded from 2,000 to 4,000 bushels.

The distinction between a change in demand and a change in the quantity demanded can be seen in Figure 4-3. The shifts of the demand curve D_0 to either D_1 or D_2 are each a "change in demand." But the movement from point a to point b on curve D_0 is a "change in the quantity demanded."

You should decide whether a change in demand or a change in the quantity demanded is involved in each of the following illustrations:

TABLE 4-4 Determinants of demand: factors that shift the demand curve

1. *Change in buyer tastes* Example: Physical fitness increases in popularity, increasing the demands for jogging shoes and bicycles.
2. *Change in number of buyers* Examples: Japanese reduce import restrictions on Canadian telecommunications equipment, thereby increasing the demand for such equipment; a decline in the birthrate reduces the demand for education.
3. *Change in income* Examples: An increase in incomes increases the demand for such normal goods as butter, lobster, and filet mignon, while reducing the demand for such inferior goods as cabbage, turnips, retreaded tires, and used clothing.
4. *Change in the prices of related goods* Examples: An increase in air fares because of increased concentration of ownership (mergers) increases the demand for bus transportation (substitute goods); a decline in the price of compact disc players increases the demand for compact discs (complementary goods).
5. *Change in expectations* Example: Inclement weather in South America causes the expectation of higher future coffee prices, thereby increasing the current demand for coffee.

1. Consumer incomes rise, with the result that more jewellery is purchased.

2. A barber raises the price of haircuts and finds that the volume of business declines.

3. The price of Toyotas goes up and, as a consequence, the sales of Chevrolets increase.

QUICK REVIEW (4-1)

1. **A market is any arrangement that facilitates the purchase and sale of goods, services, or resources.**

2. **The law of demand indicates that, other things being constant, the quantity of a good purchased will vary inversely with its price.**

3. **The demand curve will shift as a consequence of changes in (a) consumer tastes, (b) the number of buyers in the market, (c) incomes, (d) the prices of substitute or complementary goods, and (e) expectations.**

4. **A "change in the quantity demanded" refers to a movement from one point to another on a stable demand curve; a "change in demand" designates a shift in the entire demand curve.**

SUPPLY

Supply *is a schedule that shows the various amounts of a product that a producer is willing and able to produce and make available for sale at each specific price during some specified time period, all other things being equal.*[4] This **supply schedule** portrays a series of alternative possibilities, such as those shown in Table 4-5 for a single producer.

Suppose in this case that our producer is a farmer producing oats, the demand for which we have just considered. Our definition of supply indicates that supply is usually viewed from the vantage point of price. That is, we read supply as showing the amounts producers will offer at various possible prices.

Law of Supply

Table 4-5 shows a positive or *direct* relationship between price and quantity supplied. As price rises, the corresponding quantity supplied rises; as price falls, the quantity supplied also falls. This relationship is called the *law of supply*. It tells us that producers are willing to produce and offer for sale more of their product at a high price than they are at a low price.

Price is a deterrent from the consumer's standpoint. The higher the price, the less the consumer buys. To a supplier, price is revenue per unit and therefore an incentive to produce and sell a product. Given production costs, a higher product price will result in larger profits for the supplier and thus an incentive to increase the quantity supplied.

Consider a farmer who can shift resources among alternative products. As price moves up in Table 4-5, the farmer will find it profitable to take land out of wheat, rye, and barley production and put it into oats. Higher oat prices will make it possible for the farmer to cover the costs associated with more intensive cultivation and the use of larger quantities of fertilizers and pesticides. These efforts result in more output of oats.

Also, as output increases producers generally find that costs rise. They rise because certain productive resources — in particular, the firm's plant and

TABLE 4-5   **An individual producer's supply of oats (hypothetical data)**

Price per bushel	Quantity demanded per week
$5	60
4	50
3	35
2	20
1	5

machinery — cannot be expanded in a short period of time. Hence, as the firm increases the amounts of more readily variable resources such as labour, materials, and component parts, the fixed plant will at some point become crowded or congested, with the result that productive efficiency declines and the cost of successive units of output increases. Producers must receive a higher price to produce these more costly units.

The Supply Curve

As with demand, it is convenient to present graphically the concept of supply. Our axes in Figure 4-4 are the same as those in Figure 4-3, except for the change of "quantity demanded" to "quantity supplied" on the horizontal axis. The graphing procedure is the same as that previously explained, but the quantity data and relationship involved are different. The market supply data graphed in Figure 4-4 as S_0 are shown in Table 4-6, which assumes there are 200 suppliers in the market having the same supply schedules as the producer previously portrayed in Table 4-5.

Determinants of Supply

In constructing a supply curve, we assume that price is the most significant determinant of the quantity supplied of any product. But as with the demand curve, the supply curve is anchored on the "other things are equal" assumption. The supply curve is drawn assuming that certain determinants of the amount supplied are given and do not change. If any of these determinants of supply do in fact change, the location of the supply curve will shift.

The basic determinants of supply are (1) the technique of production, (2) resource prices, (3) taxes and subsidies, (4) prices of other goods, (5) price

---

[4] In discussing the resource market, our definition of supply reads: A schedule that shows the various amounts of a resource that its owners are willing to supply in the market at each possible price during some specified time, all other things being equal.

expectations, and (6) the number of sellers in the market.

A change in any one or more of these determinants or "supply shifters" will cause the supply curve for a product to move to either the right or the left. A shift to the *right*, from S_0 to S_1 in Figure 4-4, designates an *increase in supply*: producers are now supplying larger quantities of the product at each possible price. A shift to the *left*, S_0 to S_2 in Figure 4-4, indicates a *decrease in supply*: suppliers are offering less at each price.

Changes in Supply

Let us consider how changes in each of these determinants affect supply.

1 Resource Prices The relationship between production costs and supply is a close one. A firm must receive higher prices for additional units of output because those extra units are more costly to produce. It follows that a decrease in resource prices will lower production costs and increase supply (shift the supply curve to the right). Example: If the prices of oat seed and fertilizer decrease, we can expect the supply of oats to increase. Conversely, an increase in input prices will raise production costs and reduce supply (shift the supply curve to the left). Example: Increases in the prices of iron ore and coke will increase the cost of producing steel and reduce its supply.

2 Technology A technological improvement means producing a unit of output with fewer

TABLE 4-6 Market supply of oats, 200 producers (*hypothetical data*)

(1) Price per bushel	(2) Quantity supplied per week, single producer		(3) Number of sellers in the market		(4) Total quantity supplied per week
$5	60	×	200	=	12,000
4	50	×	200	=	10,000
3	35	×	200	=	7,000
2	20	×	200	=	4,000
1	5	×	200	=	1,000

resources. Given the prices of these resources, this will lower production costs and increase supply. Example: Currently about 30% of electric power is lost when transmitted by copper cable. Recent breakthroughs in the area of superconductivity point to the possibility of transporting electrical power with little or no loss. The consequence is significant cost reductions and supply increases may occur in a wide range of products in which energy is an important input.

3 Taxes and Subsidies An increase in taxes on business will increase costs and reduce supply. Conversely, subsidies are "taxes in reverse." If government subsidizes the production of some good, it in effect lowers costs and increases supply.

FIGURE 4-4 Changes in the supply of oats

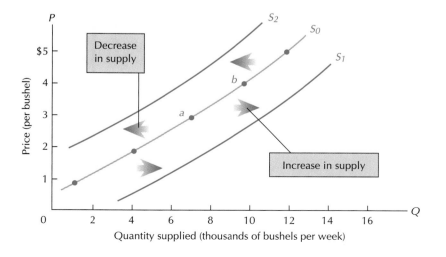

Quantity supplied (thousands of bushels per week)

A change in one or more of the determinants of supply — productive techniques, resource prices, taxes and subsidies, the prices of other goods, price expectations, or the number of sellers in the market — will cause a change in supply. An increase in supply shifts the supply curve to the right, as from S_0 to S_1. A decrease in supply is shown graphically as a movement of the curve to the left, as from S_0 to S_2. A change in the quantity supplied involves a movement, caused by a change in the price of the product under consideration, from one point to another — as from *a* to *b* — on a fixed supply curve.

4 Prices of Other Goods   Changes in the prices of other goods can also shift the supply curve of a product. A decline in the price of wheat may cause a farmer to produce and offer more oats at each possible price. A firm manufacturing sports equipment might reduce its supply of basketballs in response to a rise in the price of soccer balls.

5 Expectations   Expectations concerning the future price of a product can affect a producer's current willingness to supply that product. It is difficult, however, to generalize about how the expectations will affect the present supply curve of a product. Farmers might withhold some of their current harvest of oats from the market, anticipating a higher price of oats in the future. This will cause a decrease in the current supply of oats. On the other hand, in many types of manufacturing, expected price increases may induce firms to expand production immediately, causing supply to increase.

6 Number of Sellers   Generally, the larger the number of suppliers, the greater will be market supply. As more firms enter an industry, the supply curve will shift to the right. As firms leave an industry, the supply curve shifts to the left.

Table 4-7 provides a checklist of the determinants of supply; the accompanying illustrations deserve careful study.

Changes in Quantity Supplied

The distinction between a "change in supply" and a "change in the quantity supplied" parallels that between a change in demand and a change in the quantity demanded. A **change in supply** means the entire supply curve shifts. The cause of a change in supply is a change in one or more of the determinants of supply. The term "supply" refers to a schedule or curve.

A **change in the quantity supplied**, on the other hand, refers to the movement from one point to another point on a supply curve. The cause of such a movement is a change in the price of the product under consideration. In Table 4-6, a decline in the price of oats from $5 to $4 decreases the quantity of oats supplied from 12,000 to 10,000 bushels.

Shifting the supply curve from S_0 to S_1 or S_2 in Figure 4-4 each entails a "change in supply." The movement from point *a* to point *b* on S_0, however, is a "change in the quantity supplied."

You should determine which of the following involves a change in supply and which entails a change in the quantity supplied.

TABLE 4-7   Determinants of supply: factors that shift the supply curve

1. *Change in technology*   Example: The development of a more effective insecticide for corn rootworm increases the supply of corn.
2. *Change in resource prices*   Examples: A decline in the price of bauxite increases the supply of aluminum; an increase in the price of irrigation equipment reduces the supply of corn.
3. *Changes in taxes and subsidies*   Examples: An increase in the excise tax on cigarettes reduces the supply of cigarettes; a decline in provincial grants to universities reduces the supply of higher education.
4. *Changes in prices of other goods*   Example: A decline in the prices of mutton and pork increases the supply of beef cattle.
5. *Change in expectations*   Example: Expectations of substantial declines in future oil prices cause oil companies to increase current supply.
6. *Change in number of suppliers*   Example: An increase in the number of firms producing personal computers increases the supply of personal computers; formation of a new American professional football league increases the supply of professional football games on Canadian TV.

---

1. Because production costs decline, producers sell more automobiles.

2. The price of wheat declines, causing the number of bushels of oats sold per month to increase.

3. Fewer apples are offered for sale because their price has decreased in retail markets.

4. The federal government doubles its excise tax on the production of liquor.

QUICK REVIEW (4-2)

1. **The law of supply states that, other things being unchanged, the quantity of a good supplied varies directly with its price.**

2. **The supply curve will shift because of changes in (a) resource prices, (b) technology, (c) taxes or subsidies, (d) expectations regarding future product prices, and (e) the number of suppliers.**

3. **A "change in supply" means a shift in the supply curve; a "change in the quantity supplied" designates the movement from one point to another point on a given supply curve.**

SUPPLY AND DEMAND: MARKET EQUILIBRIUM

Let's now bring the concepts of supply and demand together to see how the interaction of the buying decisions of households and the selling decisions of producers will determine the price of a product and the quantity that is actually bought and sold in the market. In Table 4-8, columns 1 and 2 reproduce the market supply schedule for oats (from Table 4-6), and columns 2 and 3 show the market demand schedule for oats (from Table 4-3). Note that in column 2 we are using a common set of prices. We assume competition — a large number of buyers and sellers.

TABLE 4-8 Market supply and demand for oats (hypothetical data)

(1) Total quantity supplied per week	(2) Price per bushel	(3) Total quantity demanded per week	(4) Surplus (+) or shortage (−) (arrows indicate effect on price)
12,000	$5	2,000	+10,000↓
10,000	4	4,000	+6,000↓
7,000	3	7,000	0
4,000	2	11,000	−7,000↑
1,000	1	16,000	−15,000↑

Box 4-1

TICKET SCALPING: SIN AND THEOLOGY

While commonly condemned, ticket scalping entails a voluntary market transaction that benefits both buyer and seller.

It is sometimes difficult to keep straight the distinction between sin and sanctity in the realm of the market.

"Scalping" is usually defined as the exchange of a good — typically tickets to sports events — at any price greater than that the original seller listed. There are definitional variations: New York prohibits any resale of tickets for more than 25 percent above their face value. Twenty-five percent sin is reputable; 26 percent sin is damnable. Oh, morality *is* a subtle thing.

But if scalping is a sin, just what is the nature of the inherent evil? The pejorative term suggests the extortion of wealth, with the extortioner's gain being the victim's loss. In actuality, there is no redistributional compulsion — no coerced shift of wealth — when tickets are bought, even when the price exceeds the face value.

Ticket scalping is voluntary exchange in which both exchangers gain. The buyer obtains a ticket worth more to him than the money paid; the seller obtains money he values more than the ticket sold. Indeed, if both did not benefit, the exchange would not take place. The reason why voluntary exchange occurs is because goods are not initially owned by those who most value them. Ticket scalping — like all uncoerced trade — is a way of shifting assets to those who value them most.

Scalpers are middlemen who bid tickets away from those who value them less in order to sell them to people who value them more. The middleman is productive: he creates wealth by facilitating desired redistribution of tickets. The scalper's motive is personal gain, but that can be obtained only by sharing the mutual gains of exchange which arise from moving tickets to uses most valued. Scalping enables community preferences to be satisfied more efficiently.

[We are told] that scalping is "deleterious, not only to the event and the promoter, but to the people involved in it." This is fascinating doctrine. If the promoter is injured, it is because he initially underpriced his tickets, not because the tickets are later resold. If the people involved are hurt, it is because they are mysteriously made worse off by making themselves better off. And if the event suffers, it is because it is a bad thing to have an audience composed of those who most want to be there.

William R. Allen, *Midnight Economist: Broadcast Essays IV* (Los Angeles: International Institute for Economic Research, 1982), pp. 36–37, abridged. Reprinted by permission.

Of the five possible prices at which oats might sell in this market, which will actually prevail as the market price for oats? Could $5 be the prevailing market price for oats? The answer is no because producers are willing to produce and offer in the market some 12,000 bushels of oats, while buyers are willing to take only 2,000 bushels at this price. The relatively high price of $5 encourages farmers to produce a great deal of oats, but discourages most consumers from buying the product. Other products appear as better buys when oats are high priced. The result, in this case, is a 10,000-bushel **surplus** or *excess supply* of oats in the market. This surplus, shown in column 4, is the excess of quantity supplied over quantity demanded at the price of $5. Oat farmers would find themselves with unwanted inventories of output. Thus, the price of $5 could not persist over a period of time.

Let us now jump to the other end of our price column and examine $1 as the possible market price for oats. Observe in column 4 that at this price quantity demanded is in excess of quantity supplied by 15,000 units. This relatively low price discourages farmers from devoting their resources to oats production and encourages consumers to attempt to buy more oats than would otherwise be the case. The result is a 15,000-bushel **shortage** of, or *excess demand* for, oats. This price of $1 cannot persist as

the market price. Competition among buyers will bid up the price to something greater than $1.

At a price of $3, *and only at this price*, the quantity of oats farmers are willing to produce and supply in the market is identical with the amount consumers are willing and able to buy. There is neither a shortage nor a surplus of oats at this price. A surplus causes price to decline and a shortage causes price to rise.

With neither a shortage nor a surplus at $3, there is no reason for the actual price of oats to move away from this price. This price is the *market clearing* or **equilibrium price**, equilibrium meaning "in balance" or "at rest." At $3, quantity supplied and quantity demanded are in balance, and thus **equilibrium quantity** is 7,000 bushels. Hence $3 is the only stable price of oats under the supply and demand conditions shown in Table 4-8.

Figure 4-5 (Key Graph) puts the market supply and market demand curves for oats on the same graph. At any price above the equilibrium price of $3, quantity supplied will exceed quantity demanded. This surplus will cause a competitive bidding down of price by sellers eager to rid themselves of their surplus. The falling price will cause less oats to be offered and will simultaneously encourage consumers to buy more. These adjustments are shown in Figure 4-5 by the arrows pointing down the supply and demand curves.

FIGURE 4-5   The equilibrium price and quantity for oats as determined by market demand and supply

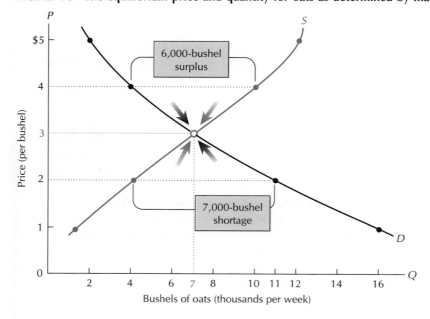

The intersection of the downsloping demand curve *D* and the upsloping supply curve *S* indicates the equilibrium price and quantity, $3 and 7,000 bushels in this instance. The shortages of oats that would exist at below-equilibrium prices, for example, 7,000 bushels at $2, drive price up and in so doing increase the quantity supplied and reduce the quantity demanded until equilibrium is achieved. The surpluses that above-equilibrium prices would entail, for example 6,000 bushels at $4, push price down and thereby increase the quantity demanded and reduce the quantity supplied until equilibrium is achieved.

Any price below the equilibrium price will entail a shortage; that is, quantity demanded will exceed quantity supplied. Competitive bidding by buyers will push the price up toward the equilibrium level. This rising price will simultaneously cause producers to increase the quantity supplied and buyers to want less, thereby causing the shortage to vanish. These adjustments are shown in Figure 4-5 by the arrows pointing up the supply and demand curves. *The intersection of the supply curve and the demand curve for the product will indicate the equilibrium point.* In this case, equilibrium price and quantity are $3 and 7,000 bushels.

Rationing Function of Prices

The ability of the competitive forces of supply and demand to establish a price where selling and buying decisions are synchronized is called the **rationing function of prices**. In this case, the equilibrium price of $3 clears the market, leaving no burdensome surplus for the sellers and no inconvenient shortage for buyers. Freely made individual buying and selling decisions sets this price that clears the market. The market mechanism of supply and demand dictates that any buyer who is willing and able to pay $3 for a

bushel of oats will be able to acquire one. Similarly, any seller who is willing and able to produce bushels of oats and offer them for sale at a price of $3 will be able to do so successfully. Were it not that competitive prices automatically bring supply and demand decisions into consistency with one another, some type of administrative control by government would be necessary to avoid or control the shortages or surpluses that might otherwise occur.

Changes in Supply and Demand

We know that demand might change because of fluctuations in consumer tastes or incomes, changes in consumer expectations, or variations in the prices of related goods. Supply might vary in response to changes in technology, resource prices, or taxes. Our analysis would be incomplete if we did not stop to consider the effect of changes in supply and demand upon equilibrium price.

Changing Demand   Let us first analyse the effects of a change in demand, assuming supply is constant. Suppose that demand increases, as shown in Figure 4-6(a). What is the effect upon price? The new intersection of the supply and demand curves is at a higher point on both the price and quantity axes.

Box 4-2

In the Media

The following article clearly shows the law of supply and demand at work. An increasing supply and a shrinking world demand translates into lower steel prices.

STEEL MAKERS FACE SOFTENING PRICES AND GROWING GLUT

HAMILTON (CP) — Another stormy year awaits steel makers as their market is flooded by production capacity and their profits are eroded by low prices.

Stelco Inc. chairman Fred Telmer offers a blunt forecast.

"I'm looking forward to a very gloomy winter," said Telmer in an interview from his company's downtown Stelco Tower headquarters.

"There's a lot of nervousness in the marketplace and prices are being held down. We're expecting a continuation of difficult conditions in 1992."

Dofasco chairman Paul Phoenix offers a similar assessment from his headquarters in Hamilton's industrialized northeast end.

"There's no pricing relief that we can see," Phoenix said. "And we're looking at ongoing poor market conditions."

Phoenix said a worldwide oversupply of steel and shrinking demand continue to drive down steel prices despite rising production costs.

The Toronto Star, Jan. 2, 1992. By permission of The Canadian Press.

FIGURE 4-6   Changes in demand and supply and the effects on price and quantity

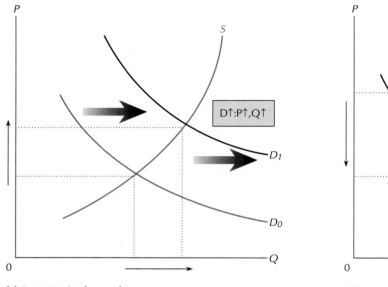

(a) Increase in demand

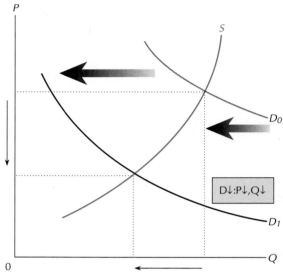

(b) Decrease in demand

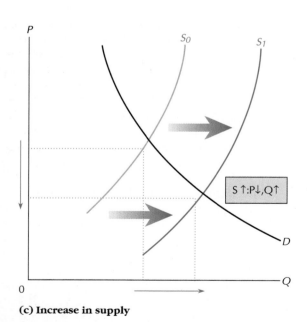

(c) Increase in supply

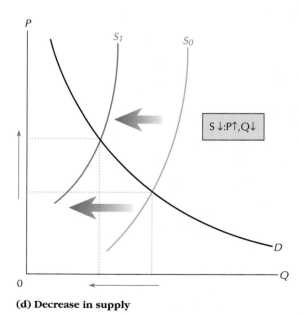

(d) Decrease in supply

The increase in demand of (a) and the decrease in demand of (b) indicates a direct relationship between a change in demand and the resulting changes in equilibrium price and quantity. The increase in supply of (c) and the decrease in supply of (d) shown an inverse relationship between a change in supply and the resulting change in equilibrium price, but a direct relationship between a change in supply and the accompanying change in equilibrium quantity.

Thus, an increase in demand, other things (supply) being equal, will have a *price-increasing effect* and a *quantity-increasing effect*. A decrease in demand, as illustrated in Figure 4-6(b), reveals a *price-decreasing effect* and a *quantity-decreasing effect*. Price falls and quantity also declines. *In brief, we find a direct relationship between a change in demand and the resulting changes in both equilibrium price and quantity.*

Changing Supply Let us analyse the effect of a change in supply on price, assuming that demand is constant. If supply increases, as in Figure 4-6(c), the new intersection of supply and demand is at a lower equilibrium price. Equilibrium quantity, however, increases. If supply decreases, product price will rise. Figure 4-6(d) illustrates this situation. Here, price increases but quantity declines. In short, an increase in supply has a *price-decreasing* and a *quantity-increasing effect*. A decrease in supply has a *price-increasing* and a *quantity-decreasing effect. There is an inverse relationship between a change in supply and the resulting change in equilibrium price, but the relationship between a change in supply and the resulting change in equilibrium quantity is direct.*

The Resource Market

What about the shape of the supply and demand curves in the resource market? As in the product market, resource supply curves are typically upsloping and resource demand curves are downsloping because they reflect a *direct* relationship between resource price and quantity supplied. It is in the interests of resource owners to supply more of a particular resource at a high price than at a low price. High-income payments in a particular occupation or industry encourage households to supply more of their resources. Low-income payments do the opposite.

On the demand side, businesses buy less of a given resource as its price rises and they substitute other, relatively low-priced, resources for it. More of a particular resource will be demanded at a low price than at a high price as entrepreneurs try to minimize costs. The result is a downsloping demand curve for the various resources.

"Other Things Equal" Revisited

Recall from Chapter 1 that as a substitute for their inability to conduct controlled experiments, econo-

mists invoke the "other things being equal" assumption in their analyses. We have seen in the present chapter that a number of forces bear on both supply and demand. Hence in locating specific supply and demand curves such as D_0 and S in Figure 4-6(a), economists are isolating the impact of what they judge to be the most important determinant of the amounts supplied and demanded — that is, the price of the specific product under consideration. In thus representing the laws of demand and supply by downsloping and upsloping curves respectively, we assume that all determinants of demand (incomes, tastes, and so forth) and supply (resource prices, technology, and other factors) are constant. That is, price and quantity demanded are inversely related, *other things being equal*. And price and quantity supplied are directly related, *other things being equal*.

If you forget the "other things equal" assumption you can encounter confusing situations that *seem* to be in conflict with these laws. For example: Suppose General Motors of Canada sells 100,000 Cutlasses in 1992 at $21,000; 150,000 at $22,000 in 1993; and 200,000 in 1994 at $23,000. Price and the number purchased vary *directly*, and these real-world data seem to be at odds with the law of demand.

These data do *not* refute the law of demand. The catch is that the law of demand's "other things equal" assumption has been violated over the three years in the example. Because of, for example, growing incomes, population growth, and relatively high gasoline prices that increase the attractiveness of intermediate and compact cars, the demand curve for Cutlasses has increased over the years — shifted to the right as from D_0 to D_1 in Figure 4-6(a) — causing price to rise and, simultaneously, a larger quantity to be purchased.

Conversely, consider Figure 4-6(d). Comparing the original S_0D and the new S_1D equilibrium positions, we note that *less* of the product is being sold or supplied at a higher price. Price and quantity supplied seem to be *inversely* related, rather than *directly* related as the law of supply indicates. The catch, again, is that the "other things equal" assumption underlying the upsloping supply curve has been violated. Perhaps production costs have gone up or a specific tax has been levied on this product, shifting the supply curve from S_0 to S_1. These examples also emphasize the importance of our earlier distinction between a "change in the quantity demanded (or supplied)" and a "change in demand (supply)."

QUICK REVIEW (4-3)

1. In competitive markets, price adjusts to the equilibrium level at which quantity demanded equals quantity supplied.

2. A change in demand alters both equilibrium price and equilibrium quantity in the same direction as the change in demand.

3. A change in supply causes equilibrium price to change in the opposite direction, but equilibrium quantity to change in the same direction, as the change in supply.

4. Over time, equilibrium price and quantity may change in directions that seem at odds with the laws of demand and supply because the "other things equal" assumption is violated.

CHAPTER SUMMARY

1. A market is any institution or arrangement that brings buyers and sellers of some product or service together.

2. Demand refers to a schedule that summarizes the willingness of buyers to purchase a given product during a specific time period at each of the various prices at which it might be sold. According to the law of demand, consumers will ordinarily buy more of a product at a low price than they will at a high price. Other things being equal, the relationship between price and quantity demanded is negative or inverse and demand graphs as a downsloping curve.

3. Changes in one or more of the basic determinants of demand — consumer tastes, the number of buyers in the market, the money incomes of consumers, the prices of related goods, and consumer expectations — will cause the market demand curve to shift. A shift to the right is an increase in demand; a shift to the left, a decrease in demand. A "change in demand" is distinguished from a "change in the quantity demanded," the latter involving the movement from one point to another point on a fixed demand curve because of a change in the price of the product under consideration.

4. Supply is a schedule showing the amounts of a product producers would be willing to offer in the market during a given time period at each possible price at which the commodity might be sold. The law of supply says that producers, other things being equal, will offer more of a product at a higher price than they will at a low price. The relationship between price and quantity supplied is a positive or direct one, and the supply curve is upsloping.

5. A change in production techniques, resource prices, taxes or subsidies, the prices of other goods, price expectations, or the number of sellers in the market will cause the supply curve of a product to shift. A shift to the right is an increase in supply; a shift to the left, a decrease in supply. In contrast, a change in the price of the product under consideration will result in a change in the quantity supplied, a movement from one point to another on a given supply curve.

6. Under competition, the interaction of market demand and market supply will adjust price to that point at which the quantity demanded and the quantity supplied are equal. This is the equilibrium price. The corresponding quantity is the equilibrium quantity.

7. The ability of market forces to synchronize selling and buying decisions so as to eliminate potential surpluses or shortages is termed the "rationing function" of prices.

8. A change in either demand or supply will cause equilibrium price and quantity to change. There is a direct relationship between a change in demand and the resulting changes in equilibrium price and quantity. Though the relationship between a change in supply and the resulting change in equilibrium price is inverse, the relationship between a change in supply and equilibrium quantity is direct.

9. The concepts of supply and demand are also applicable to the resource market.

TERMS AND CONCEPTS

change in demand (supply) versus change in the quantity demanded (supplied) (p. 55, 58)

complementary goods (p. 54)

demand (p. 50)

demand schedule (p. 50)

diminishing marginal utility (p. 51)

equilibrium price and quantity (p. 60)

income and substitution effects (p. 51)

inferior goods (p. 54)

law of demand (p. 50)

law of supply (p. 56)

market (p. 50)

normal (superior) goods (p. 54)

rationing function of prices (p. 61)

shortage (p. 60)

substitute goods (p. 54)

supply (p. 56)

supply schedule (curve) (p. 56)

surplus (p. 60)

QUESTIONS AND STUDY SUGGESTIONS

1. Explain the law of demand. Why does a demand curve slope downward? What are the determinants of demand? What happens to the demand curve when each of these determinants changes? Distinguish between a change in demand and a change in the quantity demanded, noting the cause(s) of each.

2. Critically evaluate: "In comparing the two equilibrium positions in Figure 4-6(a), I note that a larger amount is actually purchased at a higher price. This obviously refutes the law of demand."

3. Explain the law of supply. Why does the supply curve slope upward? What are the determinants of supply? What happens to the supply curve when each of these determinants changes? Distinguish between a change in supply and a change in the quantity supplied, noting the cause(s) of each.

4. Explain the following news dispatch from Hull, England: "The fish market here slumped today to what local commentators called 'a disastrous level' — all because of a shortage of potatoes. The potatoes are one of the main ingredients in a dish that figures on almost every café menu — fish and chips."

5. Suppose the total demand for eggs (Grade A large) and the total supply of eggs (Grade A large) per month in the Halifax market are as follows:

Thousands of dozens demanded	Price per dozen	Thousands of dozens supplied	Surplus (+) or shortage (−)
85	$1.25	72	_____
80	1.30	73	_____
75	1.35	75	_____
70	1.40	77	_____
65	1.45	79	_____
60	1.50	81	_____

a. What will be the market or equilibrium price? What is the equilibrium quantity? Using the surplus-shortage column, explain why your answers are correct.

b. Using the above data, graph the demand for eggs and the supply of eggs. Be sure to label the axes of your graph correctly. Label equilibrium price "*P*" and equilibrium quantity "*Q*".

c. Why will $1.25 not be the equilibrium price in this market? Why not $1.50? "Surpluses drive prices up; shortages drive them down." Do you agree?

d. Now suppose that the government establishes a ceiling price of, say, $1.30 for these eggs. Explain carefully the effects of this ceiling price. Demonstrate your answers graphically. What might prompt government to establish a ceiling price?

e. "Government fixed prices strip the price mechanism of its rationing function." Explain this statement in terms of your answers to 5d.

6. Given supply, what effect will each of the following have upon the demand for, and equilibrium price and quantity of, product B?

a. Product B becomes more fashionable.

b. The price of product C, a good substitute for B, goes down.

c. Consumers anticipate declining prices and falling incomes.

d. There is a rapid upsurge in population growth.

7. Given demand, what effect will each of the following have upon the supply and equilibrium price and quantity of product B?

a. A technological advance in the methods of producing B.

b. A decline in the number of firms in industry B.

c. An increase in the prices of resources required in the production of B.

d. The expectation that the equilibrium price of B will be lower in the future than it is currently.

e. A decline in the price of product A, a good whose production requires substantially the same techniques and resources as does the production of B.

8. Explain and illustrate graphically the effect of:

a. An increase in income upon the demand curve of an inferior good.

b. A drop in the price of product S upon the demand for substitute product T.

c. A decline in income upon the demand curve of a normal good.

d. An increase in the price of product J upon the demand for complementary good K.

9. "In the oats market, demand often exceeds supply and supply sometimes exceeds demand." "The price of oats rises and falls in response to changes in supply and demand." In which of these two statements are the terms "supply" and "demand" used correctly? Explain.

10. How will each of the following changes in demand and/or supply affect equilibrium price and equilibrium quantity in a competitive market; that is, do price and quantity *rise, fall, remain unchanged,* or are the answers *indeterminate,* depending upon the magnitudes of the shifts in supply and demand? You should rely on a supply and demand diagram to verify answers.

a. Supply decreases and demand remains constant.

b. Demand decreases and supply remains constant.

c. Supply increases and demand is constant.

d. Demand increases and supply increases.

e. Demand increases and supply is constant.

f. Supply increases and demand decreases.

g. Demand increases and supply decreases.

h. Demand decreases and supply decreases.

11. "Prices are the automatic regulator that tends to keep production and consumption in line with each other." Explain.

12. Explain: "Even though parking meters may yield little or no net revenue, they should nevertheless be retained because of the rationing function they perform."

13. *Advanced analysis*: Assume that the demand for a commodity is represented by the equation $P = 10 - 0.2Q_d$ and supply by the equation $P = 2 + 0.2Q_s$, where Q_d and Q_s are quantity demanded and quantity supplied respectively and P is price. Using the equilibrium condition $Q_s = Q_d$ solve the equations to determine equilibrium price. Then determine equilibrium quantity. Graph the two equations to substantiate your answers.

5

Elasticity

Demand and supply analysis is a powerful tool with which to explain prices. But is not the demand for insulin by a diabetic very different from the demand for perfume or after-shave lotion? Would a diabetic consumer change the quantity demanded of insulin and perfume by the same amount if their prices both doubled? The answer to this question can be arrived at by using the concept of elasticity.

In this chapter we will extend our understanding of demand and supply. Specifically, we will:

1. Examine the concept of price elasticity as it applies to both demand and supply;

2. Generalize the elasticity concept by looking at cross and income elasticity of demand.

PRICE ELASTICITY OF DEMAND

The law of demand tells us that consumers will respond to a price decline by buying more of a product. But the degree of consumer responsiveness to a price change may vary considerably from product to product. We will also find that consumer responsiveness typically varies substantially between different price ranges for the same product.

The responsiveness or sensitivity of consumers to a change in the price of a product is measured by the concept of **price elasticity of demand**. Demand for some products is such that consumers are relatively responsive to price changes: modest price changes give rise to considerable changes in the quantity purchased. The demand for such products is said to be *relatively elastic* or simply *elastic*. For other products, consumers are relatively unresponsive to price changes: substantial price changes result in modest changes in the amount purchased. In such cases demand is *relatively inelastic* or simply *inelastic*.

The Price Elasticity Formula

Economists measure the degree of elasticity by the *elasticity coefficient*, or E_d, in the *price elasticity formula*:

$$E_d = \frac{\text{percentage change in quantity demanded of product X}}{\text{percentage change in price of product X}}$$

These *percentage* changes are calculated by dividing the change in price by the original price and the consequent change in quantity demanded by the original quantity demanded. Thus we can restate our formula as:

$$E_d = \frac{\dfrac{\text{change in quantity demanded of product X}}{\text{original quantity demanded of product X}}}{\div \dfrac{\text{change in price of product X}}{\text{original price of product X}}}$$

Use of Percentages   But why use percentages rather than absolute amounts in measuring consumer responsiveness? The answer is two-fold.

1. If we use absolute changes, our impression of buyer responsiveness will be arbitrarily affected by the choice of units. If the price of product X falls from $3 to $2 and consumers, as a result, increase their purchases from 60 to 100 kilograms, we get the impression that consumers are quite sensitive to price changes and therefore that demand is elastic. After all, a price change of "one" has caused a change in the amount demanded of "forty." But by changing the monetary unit from dollars to cents (why not?),

we find that a price change of "one hundred" causes a quantity change of "forty," giving the impression that demand is inelastic. The use of percentage changes avoids this problem. The given price decline is 33% whether measured in terms of dollars ($1/$3) or cents (100 cents/300 cents).

2. The other reason for using percentages is that we can more meaningfully compare consumer responsiveness to changes in the prices of different products. It makes little sense to compare the effects on quantity demanded of a $1 increase in the price of a $10,000 auto with a $1 increase in the price of a $1 can of beer. Here the price of the auto is rising by .0001 percent while the beer price is up by 100 percent! If we increase the price of both products by 1 percent — $100 for the car and 1¢ for the beer — we obtain a sensible comparison of consumer sensitivity to the price changes.

Ignore Minus Sign   We know from the downsloping demand curve that price and quantity demanded are inversely related. This means that the price elasticity coefficient of demand will always yield a *negative* number. For example, if price declines, then quantity demanded will increase. This means that the numerator in our formula will be negative and the denominator positive, yielding a negative coefficient. We usually ignore the minus sign and simply present the *absolute value* of the elasticity coefficient to avoid an ambiguity that might otherwise arise.

Interpretations   Now let's interpret our formula. Demand is **elastic** if a given percentage change in price results in a *larger* percentage change in quantity demanded. If a 2% decline in price results in a 4% increase in quantity demanded, demand is elastic. Where demand is elastic, the elasticity coefficient will be greater than 1; in this case it is 2.

If a given percentage change in price is accompanied by a relatively *smaller* change in quantity demanded, demand is **inelastic**. If a 3% decline in price leads to only a 1% increase in the amount demanded, demand is inelastic. Specifically, the elasticity coefficient is .33 in this instance. The elasticity coefficient will always be less than 1 when demand is inelastic. The borderline case that separates elastic and inelastic demands occurs where a percentage change in price and the accompanying percentage change in quantity demanded are equal. For example, if a 1% drop in price causes a 1% increase in the amount sold. This special case is termed *unit elasticity*, because the elasticity coefficient is exactly 1, or unity.

The term **perfectly inelastic demand** refers to the extreme situation wherein a change in price results in no change whatsoever in the quantity demanded. Approximate examples: An acute diabetic's demand for insulin or an addict's demand for heroin. A demand curve parallel to the vertical axis — such as D_0 in Figure 5-1 — shows this graphically. In the extreme situation where a small price reduction would cause buyers to increase their purchases from zero to all they could obtain, we say that demand is **perfectly elastic**. A perfectly elastic demand curve is a line parallel to the horizontal axis, such as D_1 in Figure 5-1.

Refinement: Midpoints Formula

The hypothetical demand data shown in Table 5-1 are useful in explaining an annoying problem that arises in applying the price elasticity formula. In calculating the elasticity coefficient for the $5–$4 price range, should we use the $5–4 units price–quantity combination or the $4–5 units combination as a point of reference in calculating the percentage changes in price and quantity the elasticity formula requires? Our choice will influence the outcome.

FIGURE 5-1   Perfectly inelastic and elastic demand

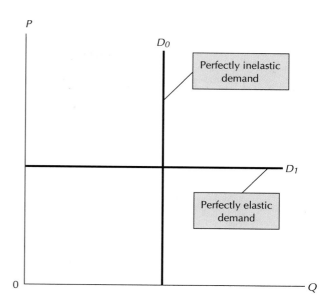

A perfectly inelastic demand curve, D_0, graphs as a line parallel to the vertical axis; a perfectly elastic demand curve, D_1, is drawn parallel to the horizontal axis.

TABLE 5-1   Price elasticity of demand as measured by the elasticity coefficient and the total revenue test (hypothetical data)

(1) Total quantity demanded per week	(2) Price per unit	(3) Elasticity coefficient, E_d	(4) Total revenue (1) × (2)	(5) Total revenue test
1	$8		$ 8	
		5.00		Elastic
2	7		14	
		2.60		Elastic
3	6		18	
		1.57		Elastic
4	5		20	
		1.00		Unit elastic
5	4		20	
		0.64		Inelastic
6	3		18	
		0.38		Inelastic
7	2		14	
		0.20		Inelastic
8	1		8	

Using the $5–4 unit reference point, the percentage decrease in price is 20% and the percentage increase in quantity is 25%. Substituting in the formula, the elasticity coefficient is 25/20 or 1.25, indicating the demand is somewhat elastic. But using the $4–5 unit bushel reference point, the percentage increase in price is 25% and the percentage decline in quantity is 20%. The elasticity coefficient is therefore 20/25, or .80, meaning demand is slightly inelastic. Which is it? Is demand elastic or inelastic?

A workable solution to this problem is achieved by using the *averages* of two prices and the two quantities under consideration for reference points. In the $5–$4 price range case, the price reference is $4.50 and the quantity reference 4.5 units. The percentage change in price is now about 22% and the percentage change in quantity is also about 22%, giving us an elasticity of 1. Instead of gauging elasticity at either one of the extremes of this price–quantity range, this solution estimates elasticity at the midpoint of the $5–$4 price range. We can refine our earlier statement of the elasticity formula to read

$$E_d = \frac{\text{change in quantity}}{\text{sum of quantities}/2} \div \frac{\text{change in price}}{\text{sum of prices}/2}$$

Substituting data for the $5–$4 price range, we get

$$E_d = \frac{1}{9/2} \div \frac{1}{9/2} = 1$$

This indicates that *at* the $4.50–4.5 price–quantity point the price elasticity of demand is unity. A 1% price change would result in a 1% change in quantity demanded.

In column 3 you should verify the elasticity calculations for the $1–$2 and $7–$8 price ranges. The interpretation of the coefficient for the $1–$2 range is that a 1% change in price will change quantity demanded by 5%. For the $7–$8 range a 1% change in price will change quantity demanded by only 0.2%.

Graphic Analysis

In Figure 5-2(a) we have plotted our demand curve from Table 5-1. This portrayal brings two points into focus.

Elasticity and Price Range   First, elasticity typically varies over the different price ranges of the same demand schedule or curve. For all straight-line and most demand curves, demand is more elastic in the upper-left portion ($5–$8 price range) than in the lower-right portion ($4–$1 price range). This is a con-

FIGURE 5-2   Price elasticity of demand and its relation to total revenue

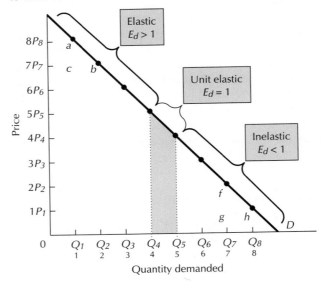

(a) Demand curve

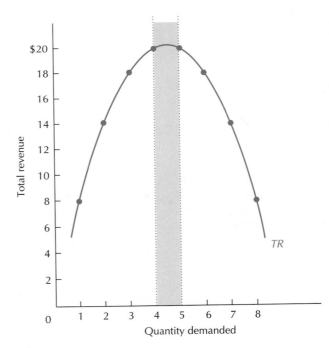

(b) Total revenue curve

As shown in (a), the typical demand curve is elastic in high price ranges and inelastic in lower price ranges. In (b) we observe that total revenue rises in the elastic range as price is reduced. Where demand elasticity is unity, a change in price will not change total revenue. In this range total revenue is maximized. Price reductions in the inelastic range of the demand curve cause total revenue to fall.

sequence of the arithmetic properties of the elasticity measure.

Specifically, in the upper-left portion, the percentage change in quantity is large because the original quantity from which the percentage quantity change is derived is small. In this portion the percentage change in price is small because the original price from which the percentage price change is calculated is large. The relatively large percentage change in quantity divided by the relatively small change in price yields an elastic demand.

The reverse holds true for the lower-right portion of the demand curve. Here the percentage change in quantity is small, because the original quantity from which the percentage change is determined is large. Similarly, the percentage change in price is large, because the original price from which the relative price change is calculated is small. The relatively small percentage change in quantity divided by the relatively large change in price results in an inelastic demand.

Assignment: Draw two linear demand curves that are parallel to one another. Demonstrate that for any given price change demand is more elastic on the curve closer to the origin.

Elasticity versus Slope The second point is that the graphic appearance, that is, the slope, of a demand curve is *not* a sound basis for judging its elasticity. The catch is that the slope — the flatness or steepness — of a demand curve is based on *absolute* changes in price and quantity, while elasticity involves *relative* or *percentage* changes in price and quantity.

Observe in Figure 5-2(a) that our demand curve is linear, which, by definition, means the slope is constant throughout. But we have already demonstrated that such a curve is elastic in its high-price ($8–$5) range and inelastic in its low-price ($4–$1) range.

QUICK REVIEW (5-1)

1. **Price elasticity of demand measures the extent to which consumers alter the quantity of a product purchased when its price changes.**

2. **Price elasticity of demand is the ratio of the percentage change in quantity demanded to the percentage change in price. The average of the prices and quantities are used in calculating the percentage changes.**

3. **When price elasticity is greater than 1, demand is elastic; when less than 1, it is inelastic. When equal to 1, demand is of unit elasticity.**

4. **Demand is typically elastic in the high-price (low-quantity) range and inelastic in the low-price (high-quantity) range of the demand curve.**

The Total-Revenue Test

Perhaps the easiest way to infer whether demand is elastic or inelastic is to note what happens to total revenue when product price changes.

1 Elastic Demand If demand is *elastic*, a *decrease* in price will result in an *increase* in total revenue. Even though a lower price is being received per unit, enough additional units are now being sold to more than make up for the lower price. This is shown in Figure 5-2(a) for the $8–$7 price range of our demand curve from Table 5-1. (Ignore Figure 5-2(b) for the moment.) Total revenue is price times quantity. Total revenue is $8 when price is $8 and quantity demanded is 1 unit. When price declines to $7, causing the quantity demanded to increase to 2 units, total revenue changes to $14, which is clearly larger than $8. It is larger because the *loss* in revenue due to the lower price per unit is *less* than the *gain* in revenue due to the larger sales that accompany the lower price.

This reasoning is reversible: If demand is elastic, a price *increase* will cause total revenue to *decrease*. The *gain* in total revenue caused by the higher unit price is *less* than the *loss* in revenue associated with the accompanying fall in sales. ***If demand is elastic, a price change will cause total revenue to change in the opposite direction.***

2 Inelastic Demand If demand is *inelastic*, a price *decrease* will cause total revenue to *decrease*. The modest increase in sales that occurs will be insufficient to offset the decline in revenue per unit, and the net result is that total revenue declines. This situation exists for the $2–$1 price range of our demand curve, as shown in Figure 5-2(a). Initially total revenue is $14 when price is $2 and quantity demanded is 7 units.

If we reduce price to $1, quantity demanded will increase to 8 units. Total revenue will change to $8, which is clearly less than $14. It is smaller because the loss in revenue due to the lower unit price is larger than the *gain* in revenue due to the accompanying increase in sales.

Again, our analysis is reversible: if demand is inelastic, a price increase will increase total revenue. ***If*** *demand is inelastic, a price change will cause total revenue to change in the same direction*.

3 Unit Elasticity In the special case of **unit elasticity**, an increase or decrease in price will leave total revenue unchanged. Loss in revenue due to a lower unit price will be exactly offset by the gain in revenue from the accompanying increase in sales.

In Figure 5-2(a) we find that at the $5 price 4 units will be sold to yield total revenue of $20. At $4 a total of 5 units will be sold, again resulting in $20 of total revenue. The $1 price reduction causes the loss of $4 in revenue on the 4 units that could have been sold for $5 each. This is exactly offset by a $4 revenue gain that results from the sale of 1 more unit at the lower $4 price.

Graphic Portrayal The relationship between price elasticity of demand and total revenue can be demonstrated graphically by comparing Figures 5-2(a) and 5-2(b). In Figure 5-2(b) we have graphed the eight total revenue–quantity demanded points from columns 1 and 4 of Table 5-1.

Lowering price over the $8–$5 price range increases total revenue. We know from the elasticity coefficient calculations in Table 5-1 that demand is *elastic* in this range so any given percentage decline in price results in a larger percentage increase in quantity demanded. The lower price per unit is more than offset by the increase in sales and, consequently, total revenue rises.

The $5–$4 price range is characterized by *unit* elasticity. Here the percentage decline in price causes an equal percentage increase in quantity demanded. The price cut is exactly offset by increased purchases so total revenue is unchanged.

Finally, our coefficient calculations tell us that in the $4–$1 price range demand is *inelastic*, which means that any given percentage decline in price will be accompanied by a smaller percentage increase in sales, causing total revenue to diminish. Question 2 at the end of this chapter is recommended at this point.

Our logic is reversible. A price *increase* in the elastic $8–$5 price range will reduce total revenue. Similarly, a price *increase* in the inelastic $4–$1 range causes total revenue to increase.

Reprise Table 5-2 provides a convenient summary of the characteristics of price elasticity of demand and merits careful study.

Determinants of Price Elasticity of Demand

There are no iron-clad generalizations about the determinants of the elasticity of demand. The following points, however, are helpful.

1 Substitutability Usually the larger the number of good substitute products available, the greater the elasticity of demand. Also, the elasticity of demand for a product depends on how narrowly the product is defined. The demand for Petro-Canada motor oil is more elastic than is the overall demand for motor oil. A number of other brands are readily substitutable

TABLE 5-2 Price elasticity of demand: a summary

Absolute value of elasticity coefficient	Terminology	Description	Impact on total revenue (expenditures) of a price: Increase	Decrease
Greater than 1 ($E_d > 1$)	Elastic or relatively elastic	Quantity demanded changes by a larger percentage than does price	Total revenue decreases	Total revenue increases
Equal to 1 ($E_d = 1$)	Unit or unitary elastic	Quantity demanded changes by the same percentage as does price	Total revenue is unchanged	Total revenue is unchanged
Less than 1 ($E_d < 1$)	Inelastic or relatively inelastic	Quantity demanded changes by a smaller percentage than does price	Total revenue increases	Total revenue decreases

for Petro-Canada's oil, but there is no good substitute for motor oil per se.

2 Proportion of Income Other things being equal, the larger a service or product is in one's budget, the greater will be the elasticity of demand for it. A 10% increase in the price of pencils or chewing gum will amount to a few pennies and elicit little response in terms of amount demanded. A 10% increase in the price of automobiles or housing means price increases of perhaps $1,500 and $15,000, respectively. These latter increases are significant fractions of the annual incomes of many families, and quantities purchased could be expected to diminish significantly.

3 Luxuries versus Necessities The demand for necessities tends to be inelastic; for luxuries, it is elastic. Bread and electricity are generally regarded as necessities. A price increase will not significantly reduce the amount of bread consumed or the amount of lighting and power used in a household. Note the low price elasticity of the latter in Table 5-3 (page 76). A more extreme case: One does not decline an operation for acute appendicitis on being told the physician has found a way to extra-bill!

French cognac and emeralds, on the other hand, are luxuries that can be forgone without undue inconvenience. If the price of cognac or emeralds rises, one need not purchase them.

The demand for salt is highly inelastic on several counts. It is a necessity, and there are no good substitutes available. Moreover, salt is a negligible item in the family budget.

4 Time Usually, the demand for a product is more elastic the longer the time period under consideration. When the price of a product rises, it takes time to seek out and experiment with other products to see if they are acceptable. Consumers may not immediately reduce purchases very much when the price of beef rises by 10%. But in time they might switch to chicken or fish. Another consideration is product durability. Studies show that short-run demand for gasoline is more inelastic at 0.3 than is long-run demand at 0.8. In the long run, large gas-guzzling automobiles wear out and, with rising gasoline prices, are replaced by smaller, more fuel-efficient, cars.

An empirical study of commuter rail transportation in the Philadelphia area estimates that the long-run elasticity of demand is almost three times as great as the short-run elasticity. Short-run commuter responses (defined as occurring immediately at the time of a fare change) are inelastic at 0.68. In contrast, the long-run response (defined as occurring over a four-year period) is elastic at 1.84. The greater long-run elasticity occurs over time because potential rail commuters can make choices concerning automobile purchases, car pooling, and the locations of residences and employment. These different elasticities led to the prediction that the commuter system, with about one hundred thousand riders, could immediately *increase* daily revenues by $8,000 by raising the price of a one-way ticket by 25¢ or about 9%, since short-run demand is inelastic. But, in the long-run, the same 9% fare increase is estimated to *reduce* total revenue per day by over $19,000 because demand is elastic. The implication is that a fare increase that is profitable in the short run may lead to financial difficulties in the long run.[1]

Table 5-3 shows price elasticities of demand for a variety of products. Use the elasticity determinants just discussed to explain or rationalize each of these elasticity coefficients.

QUICK REVIEW (5-2)

1. **A price change will cause total revenue to vary in the opposite direction when demand is elastic and in the same direction when demand is inelastic.**

2. **Price elasticity of demand is greater (a) the larger the number of substitutes available; (b) the larger the product is in one's budget; (c) the greater the extent to which the product is a luxury; and (d) the longer the time period involved.**

Applications

The concept of price elasticity of demand is of great practical significance, as the following examples make evident.

1 Bumper Crops Studies indicate that demand for most farm products is highly inelastic, perhaps 0.20 or 0.25. As a result, increases in the output of farm products, due to a good growing season or productivity increases, depress both the price of farm products and total revenues (incomes) of farmers. For farmers as a group, the inelastic nature of

---

[1] Richard Voith, "Commuter Rail Ridership: The Long and the Short Haul," *Business Review* (Federal Reserve Bank of Philadelphia), November–December 1987, pp. 13–23.

TABLE 5-3   Selected price elasticities of demand

Product or service	Price elasticity of demand	
Housing	.01	
Electricity (household)	.13	
Bread	.15	
Telephone service	.26	
Medical care	.31	
Eggs	.32	
Legal services	.37	inelastic
Automobile repair	.40	
Clothing	.49	
Milk	.63	
Household appliances	.63	
Movies	.87	
Beer	.90	
Shoes	.91	
Motor vehicles	1.14	
China, glassware, tableware	1.54	elastic
Restaurant meals	2.27	
Lamb and mutton	2.65	

Main sources: H. S. Houthakker and Lester D. Taylor, *Consumer Demand in the United States: Analyses and Projections*, 2d ed. (Cambridge, Mass.: Harvard University Press, 1970); P. S. George and G. A. King, *Consumer Demand for Food Commodities in the United States with Projections for 1980* (Berkeley: University of California, 1971); and Ahsan Mansur and John Whalley, "Numerical Specification of Applied General Equilibrium Models: Estimation, Calibration, and Data," in Herbert E. Scarf and John B. Shoven, *Applied General Equilibrium Analysis* (New York: Cambridge University Press, 1984).

demand for their products means that a bumper crop may be undesirable. For policy makers it means that higher total farm income depends on the restriction of farm output.

2 Automation   The impact of automation on the level of employment depends in part on the elasticity of demand for the product being manufactured. Suppose a firm installs new labour-saving machinery, resulting in the technological unemployment of five hundred workers. Suppose also that part of the cost reduction resulting from this technological advance is passed on to consumers in the form of reduced product prices. The effect of this price reduction on the firm's sales, and therefore the quantity of labour it needs, will depend on the elasticity of product demand. An elastic demand might increase sales to the extent that some of, all, or even more than, the five hundred displaced workers are reabsorbed by the firm. An inelastic demand will mean that few, if any, of the displaced workers will be re-employed, because the increase in the volume of the firm's sales and output will be small.

3 Excise Taxes   Government pays attention to the elasticity of demand when selecting goods and services upon which to levy excise taxes. Assume a $1 tax is currently levied on some product, and 10,000 units are sold. Tax revenue is $10,000. If the tax is now raised to $1.50 and the consequent higher price causes sales to decline to 5,000, tax revenue will *decline* to $7,500. A higher tax on a product for which demand is elastic will bring in less tax revenue. Hence legislatures will seek out products for which demand is inelastic — for example, liquor, gasoline, and cigarettes — when levying excises.

4 Heroin and Street Crime   The fact that the demand for heroin by addicts is highly inelastic poses some awkward trade-offs in law enforcement. The approach typically used in attempting to reduce heroin addiction is to restrict supply by cracking down on its shipment into Canada. But if this policy is successful, given the highly inelastic demand, the street price to addicts will rise sharply while the amount purchased will decrease only slightly. For the drug dealers this means increased revenues and profits. For the addicts it means greater total expenditures on heroin. Because much of the income that addicts spend on heroin comes from crime — shoplifting, burglary, prostitution, and muggings — these kinds of crimes will increase as addicts increase their total expenditures for heroin. Thus, the effort of law-enforcement authorities to control the spread of drug addiction may increase the amount of crime committed by addicts.

In recent years the controversial proposal to legalize drugs has been widely debated. Proponents contend that drugs should be treated like alcohol. Drugs should be made legal for adults and regulated for purity and potency. The current war on drugs, it is argued, has been unsuccessful and the associated costs — including enlarged police forces, an overburdened court system, and untold human costs — have increased markedly. Legalization would allegedly reduce drug trafficking greatly by taking the profit out of it. Heroin, for example, is cheap to produce and could be sold at a low price in a legal market. Because the demand of addicts is highly inelastic, the amount consumed at the lower price will only increase modestly. Total expenditures for heroin by addicts will decline and so will the street crime that finances these expenditures.

Opponents of legalization take the position that, in addition to the addict's inelastic demand, there is another segment of the market where demand may be more elastic. This is the segment populated by occasional users or "dabblers." Dabblers will use heroin when its price is low, but abstain or substitute, say, alcohol when heroin's price is high. For this group the lower price of heroin associated with legalization will increase consumption by dabblers and in time turn many of them into addicts. This will increase street crime and enlarge all of the social costs associated with drug use.

Price Elasticity of Supply

The concept of price elasticity also applies to supply. If producers are responsive to price changes, supply is elastic. If they are relatively insensitive to price changes, supply is inelastic.

The elasticity formula is pertinent in determining the degree of elasticity of supply. The only alteration is the substitution of "percentage change in quantity *supplied*" for "percentage change in quantity *demanded*."

$$E_s = \frac{\text{percentage change in quantity supplied of product X}}{\text{percentage change in price of product X}}$$

For reasons explained earlier, the midpoints of the changes in quantity supplied and price are used in calculations. Suppose price were to increase from $4 to $6, causing quantity supplied to rise from 8 to 12. The percentage change in quantity supplied would be 4/10 or 40% and the percentage change in price would be 2/5 or 40%. Substituting in our formula, we determine elasticity of supply to be 40/40 or +1. Note that, because price and quantity supplied are directly related, the coefficient will always be positive.

The main determinant of the **elasticity of supply** is the amount of *time* a producer has to respond to a given change in product price. We can expect a greater output response — and therefore greater elasticity of supply — the longer the amount of time a producer has to adjust to a given price change. A producer's response to an increase in the price of product X depends on the ability to shift resources from the production of other products (whose prices we assume remain constant) to the production of X. The shifting of resources takes time.

In analysing the impact of time upon the elasticity of supply, economists distinguish between the immediate market period, the short run, and the long run.

1 The Market Period The immediate **market period** is so short a time that producers cannot respond to a change in demand and price. Suppose a small farmer brings an entire season's output of tomatoes — one truckload — to market. The supply curve will be perfectly inelastic. The farmer will sell the truckload whether the price is high or low because he/she cannot offer more tomatoes than the one truckload if the price of tomatoes should be higher than anticipated. It will take another full growing season to respond to a higher-than-expected price by producing more than one truckload. Similarly, because the product is perishable, the farmer cannot withhold it from the market. If the price is lower than anticipated, the farmer will still sell the entire truckload. Even though the price of tomatoes may fall far short of production costs, the farmer will sell out to avoid a total loss through spoilage.

Figure 5-3(a) illustrates the truck farmer's perfectly inelastic supply curve in the market period. Note that truck farmers cannot respond to an assumed increase in demand since they do not have time to increase the amount supplied. The price increase from P_o to P_m rations a fixed supply to buyers, but elicits no increase in output.[2]

2 The Short Run In the **short run**, the plant capacity of individual producers and the industry is presumed fixed. But firms *do* have time to use their plants more or less intensively. Thus in the short run, our truck farmer's plant, comprised of land and farm machinery, is fixed. But the farmer does have time, in the short run, to cultivate tomatoes more intensively by applying more labour and more fertilizer and pesticides to the crop. The result is a greater output response to the presumed increase in demand. This greater output response is reflected in a more elastic supply of tomatoes as shown by S_s in Figure 5-3(b). Note that the increase in demand is met by a larger quantity adjustment (Q_o to Q_s) and a smaller price adjustment (P_o to P_s) than in the market period: price is therefore lower than in the market period.

---

[2] The supply curve need not be perfectly inelastic (vertical) in the market period. If the product is not perishable, producers may choose, at low current prices, to store some of their product for future sale. This will cause the market period supply curve to have some positive slope.

FIGURE 5-3 Time and the elasticity of supply

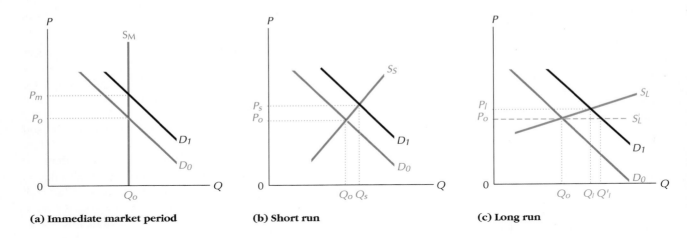

(a) Immediate market period   (b) Short run   (c) Long run

The greater the amount of time producers have to adjust to a change in demand, the greater will be their output response. In the immediate market period (a) there is insufficient time to change output, and so supply is perfectly inelastic. In the short run (b) plant capacity is fixed, but output can be altered by changing the intensity of its use; supply is therefore more elastic. In the long run (c) all desired adjustments — including changes in plant capacity — can be made, and supply becomes still more elastic.

3 The Long Run The **long run** is a time period long enough that firms can make all desired resource adjustments. Individual firms can expand (or contract) their plant capacities, and new firms can enter (or existing firms can leave) the industry. In the "tomato industry," the truck farmer can acquire additional land and buy more machinery and equipment. More farmers may be attracted to tomato production by the increased demand and higher price. These adjustments mean an even greater supply response, that is, an even more elastic supply curve S_L. The result, shown in Figure 5-3(c), is a small price effect (P_o to P_l) and a large output effect (Q_o to Q_l) in response to the assumed increase in demand.

CROSS AND INCOME ELASTICITY OF DEMAND

In addition to price elasticity, two other elasticity concepts are significant.

Cross Elasticity of Demand

We have seen that *price elasticity of demand* measures the effect of a change in a product's price on the quantity of *that* product demanded. The concept of **cross elasticity of demand** measures how sensitive consumer purchases of *one* product (X) are to a change in the price of some *other* product (Y). Our formula for the coefficient of cross elasticity of demand is similar to simple price elasticity except that we are relating the percentage change in the consumption of X to a percentage change in the price of Y:

$$E_{xy} = \frac{\text{percentage change}}{\text{percentage change in price of Y}}$$

This elasticity concept allows us to quantify and more fully understand substitute and complementary goods as introduced in Chapter 4.

If cross elasticity of demand is *positive* — the quantity demanded of X varies directly with a change in the price of Y — then X and Y are *substitute goods*. For example, an increase in the price of butter (Y) will cause consumers to buy more margarine (X). The larger the positive coefficient, the greater the substitutability between the two products.

When cross elasticity is *negative*, then we know that X and Y "go together" and are *complementary goods*. Thus an increase in the price of cameras will decrease the amount of film purchased. The larger the negative coefficient, the greater the complementarity between the two goods.

A zero or near-zero coefficient suggests that the two products are unrelated or *independent goods*.

For example, we would not expect a change in the price of butter to have any significant impact on the purchases of film.

Income Elasticity of Demand

The **income elasticity of demand** measures the percentage change in the quantity of a product demanded that results from some percentage change in consumer incomes:

$$E_i = \frac{\text{percentage change in quantity demanded}}{\text{percentage change in income}}$$

For most goods the income elasticity coefficient will be *positive*. Those products of which more is purchased as incomes increase are called *normal* or *superior goods*. But the positive elasticity coefficient varies greatly among products. For example, the income elasticity of demand for automobiles has been estimated to be about $+3.00$, while for most farm products it is only about $+0.20$.

A *negative* income elasticity coefficient designates an *inferior good*. Retreaded tires, potatoes, cabbage, and used clothing are likely candidates. Consumers *decrease* their purchases of such products as incomes *increase*.

Income elasticity coefficients help us predict which industries are likely to be expanding industries and which will probably be declining industries. Other things being equal, a high positive income elasticity implies that that industry will share more than proportionately in the overall income growth of the economy. A small positive or, worse yet, a negative coefficient implies a declining industry. For example, the indicated high positive income elasticity of demand for automobiles portends a greater likelihood of long-run prosperity for that industry in comparison to agriculture's low coefficient, which suggests chronic problems.

QUICK REVIEW (5-3)

1. **Price elasticity of supply is the ratio of the percentage change in quantity supplied to the percentage change in price. The elasticity of supply varies directly with the amount of time producers have to respond to the price change.**

2. **Cross elasticity of demand is the percentage change in the quantity demanded of one product divided by the percentage change in the price of another product. If the cross elasticity coefficient is positive, the two products are substitutes; if negative, they are complements.**

3. **Income elasticity is the percentage change in quantity demanded divided by the percentage change in income. A positive coefficient indicates a normal or superior good. The coefficient is negative for an inferior good.**

CHAPTER SUMMARY

1. Price elasticity of demand measures the responsiveness of consumers to price changes. If consumers are relatively sensitive to price changes, demand is elastic. If consumers are relatively unresponsive to price changes, demand is inelastic.

2. The price elasticity formula measures the degree of elasticity or inelasticity of demand. The formula is

$$E_d = \frac{\text{percentage change in quantity demanded of X}}{\text{percentage change in price of X}}$$

The averages of the prices and quantities under consideration are used as reference points in determining the percentage changes in price and quantity. If E_d is greater than 1, demand is elastic. If E_d is less than 1, demand is inelastic. Unit elasticity is the special case in which E_d equals 1. A perfectly inelastic demand curve is portrayed by a line parallel to the vertical axis. A perfectly elastic demand curve is shown by a line above and parallel to the horizontal axis.

3. Elasticity varies at different price ranges on a demand curve, tending to be elastic in the northwest segment and inelastic in the southeast segment. Elasticity cannot be judged by the steepness or flatness of a demand curve on a graph.

4. Price elasticity of demand can be determined by observing the effect of a price change upon total revenue from the sale of the product. If price and total revenue move in opposite directions, demand is elastic. If price and total revenue move in the same direction, demand is inelastic. In the case where demand is of unit elasticity, a change in price will leave total revenue unchanged.

5. The number of available substitutes, the size of an item in one's budget, whether the product is a luxury or necessity, and the time period involved are all determinants of elasticity of demand.

6. The elasticity concept also applies to supply. Elasticity of supply depends upon the shiftability of resources between alternative employments. This shiftability varies with the time producers have to adjust to a given price change.

7. Cross elasticity gauges how sensitive the purchases of one product are to changes in the price of another product. It is measured by the percentage change in the quantity demanded of product X divided by the percentage change in the price of product Y.

8. Income elasticity indicates the responsiveness of consumer purchases to a change in income. It is measured by the percentage change in the quantity demanded of the product divided by the percentage change in income.

TERMS AND CONCEPTS

cross elasticity of demand (p. 78)
elastic versus inelastic demand (p. 70)
income elasticity of demand (p. 79)
market period (p. 77)
perfectly elastic demand (p. 71)
perfectly inelastic demand (p. 71)

price elasticity of demand (p. 70)
price elasticity of supply (p. 76)
short run and long run (p. 77, 78)
total-revenue test (p. 73)
unit elasticity (p. 74)

QUESTIONS AND STUDY SUGGESTIONS

1. In some industries — for example, the petroleum industry — producers justify their reluctance to lower prices by arguing that demand for their products is inelastic. Explain.

2. How will the following changes in price affect total revenue (expenditures); that is, will total revenue *increase, decline, or remain unchanged*?

   a. Price falls and demand is inelastic.

   b. Price rises and demand is elastic.

   c. Price rises and supply is elastic.

   d. Price rises and supply is inelastic.

   e. Price rises and demand is inelastic.

   f. Price falls and demand is elastic.

   g. Price falls and demand is of unit elasticity.

3. Determine the elasticity of demand and supply for the following demand and supply schedules. Use the total-revenue test to check the answers given by the E_d formula.

E_s	Quantity supplied	Product price	Quantity demanded	Total revenue	E_d
_____	28,000	$10	10,000	$ _____	_____
_____	22,500	9	13,000	_____	_____
_____	17,000	8	17,000	_____	_____
_____	13,000	7	22,000	_____	_____
_____	11,000	6	25,000	_____	_____

4. What are the major determinants of price elasticity of demand? Use these determinants in judging whether the demand for the following products is elastic or inelastic: *a.* oranges; *b.* cigarettes; *c.* Export cigarettes; *d.* gasoline; *e.* butter; *f.* salt; *g.* automobiles; *h.* football games; *i.* diamond bracelets; and *j.* this textbook.

5. Why is it difficult to judge elasticity of demand or supply by simply observing the appearance of a demand or supply curve on a graph?

6. Empirical estimates suggest the following demand elasticities: 0.6 for physicians' services; 4.0 for foreign travel; 1.2 for radio and television receivers. Use the generalizations for the determinants of elasticity developed in this chapter to explain each of these figures.

7. What effect may a rule that university students live in university dormitories have upon the elasticity of demand for dormitory space? What impact might this in turn have on room rates?

8. You are sponsoring an outdoor rock concert. Your major costs — for the band, land rent, and security — are largely independent of attendance. Use the concept of price elasticity of demand to explain how you might establish ticket prices to maximize profits.

9. What is the elasticity of the supply of Rembrandt paintings? Can you relate your answer to the extremely high prices paid for classical art at auctions?

10. Graph the accompanying demand data and then use either the elasticity coefficient or the total-revenue test to determine price elasticity of demand for each possible price change. What can you conclude about the relationship between the slope of a curve and its elasticity? Explain in a nontechnical way *why* demand tends to be elastic in the northwest segment of the demand curve and inelastic in the southeast segment. Graph the total-revenue data below the demand curve (see Figure 5-2) and generalize upon the relationship between price elasticity and total revenue.

Product price	Quantity demanded
$5	1
4	2
3	3
2	4
1	5

11. How would you expect the elasticity of supply of product X to differ in a situation of full employment in industry X, on the one hand, and of considerable unemployment in the industry, on the other? Explain.

12. "If the demand for farm products is highly price inelastic, a bumper crop may reduce farm incomes." Evaluate and illustrate graphically.

13. In the 1950s the local Boy Scout troop in Jackson, Wyoming, decided to gather and sell at auction elk antlers shed by thousands of elk wintering in the area. Buyers were mainly local artisans that used the antlers to make belt buckles, buttons, and tie clasps. Price per pound was 6¢, and the troop took in $500 annually. In the 1970s a fad developed in Asia that involved grinding antlers into powder to sprinkle on food for purported aphrodisiac benefits. In 1979 the price per pound of elk antlers in the Jackson auction was $6 per pound and the Boy Scouts earned $51,000! Show graphically and explain these dramatic increases in price and total revenue. Assuming no shift in the supply curve of elk antlers, use the midpoints formula to calculate the coefficient for the elasticity of supply.

14. In May of 1990 Vincent van Gogh's painting "Portrait of Dr. Gachet" sold at auction for $82.5 million. Portray this sale in a demand and supply diagram and comment upon the elasticity of supply.

15. In the 1970s the Organization of Petroleum Exporting Countries (OPEC) became operational as a cartel that reduced the world supply of oil, greatly increasing OPEC's revenues and profits. What can you infer regarding the elasticity of demand for oil? Would you expect countries exporting bananas or pineapples to be able to emulate OPEC? Explain.

16. In 1987 the average price of a home rose from $97,000 in April to $106,800 in May. During the same period home sales fell from 724,000 to 616,000 units. If we assume that mortgage interest rates and all other factors affecting home sales are constant, what do these figures suggest about the elasticity of demand for housing?

17. Suppose the cross elasticity of demand for products A and B is +3.6 and for products C and D is −5.4. What can you conclude about how products A and B and products C and D are related?

18. The income elasticities of demand for movies, dental services, and clothing have been estimated to be +3.4, +1.0, and +0.5 respectively. Interpret these coefficients. What does it mean if the income elasticity coefficient is negative?

6

The Market System at Work

Supply and demand analysis and the concept of elasticity are powerful tools that help to explain how markets function and how prices are determined. An even better understanding of markets and prices can be had sometimes by investigating cases where markets are not allowed to clear. In this chapter we analyse government imposed price ceilings and floors, and the particular cases of price controls, rent controls, and credit card interest ceilings. We end with a discussion of the foreign exchange market, and how the forces of supply and demand determine the value of the Canadian dollar vis-à-vis other currencies.

INTERVENING WITH SUPPLY AND DEMAND: PRICE CEILINGS AND FLOORS

Supply and demand analysis and the elasticity concept will be applied repeatedly in the remainder of this book. Let us strengthen our understanding of these analytical tools and their significance by examining two important applications: (1) prices fixed by law and (2) the foreign exchange market.

Prices Fixed by Law

On occasion the general public and government feel that the forces of supply and demand result in prices that are either unfairly high to buyers or unfairly low to sellers. In such instances government may intervene by limiting by law how high or low the price may go. Let's examine what happens to the functioning of the market when government price-fixing occurs.

Price Ceilings and Shortages   A **price ceiling** *is the maximum lawful price that a seller may charge for a product or service.* The rationale for price ceilings on specific products is that they purportedly enable consumers to obtain some "essential" good or service they could not afford at the equilibrium price. Rent controls and usury laws (which specify maximum interest rates that may be charged to borrowers) are examples. On a more general basis, price ceilings or general price controls have been used in attempting to restrain the overall rate of inflation in the economy. Wage and price controls were invoked during World War II, as well as from 1975 to 1979.

World War II Price Controls   Let's turn back the clock to World War II and analyse the effects of a price ceiling on butter. The booming wartime prosperity of the early 1940s was shifting demand for butter to the right so that, as in Figure 6-1, the equilibrium or market price P_o was, say, $1.20 per pound. The rapidly rising price of butter made it difficult to get for those families whose money incomes were not keeping pace with the increasing cost of living. To help stop inflation and to keep butter on the tables of the poor, government imposed a price ceiling P_c of, say, $0.90 per pound. Note that to be effective a ceiling price must be *below* equilibrium price. A price ceiling of $1.50 would have no immediate impact on the butter market.

What will be the effects of this price ceiling? The rationing ability of the competitive market will be rendered ineffective. At the price ceiling, there will

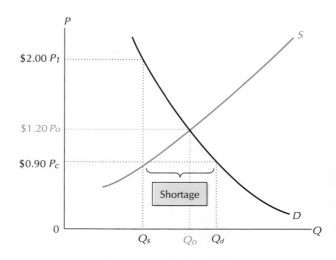

FIGURE 6-1   Price ceilings result in persistent shortages

Because the imposition of a price ceiling, such as P_c, results in a persistent product shortage (as indicated by the distance Q_sQ_d), government must undertake the job of rationing the product in order to achieve an equitable distribution.

be a persistent shortage of butter. The quantity of butter demanded at P_c is Q_d and the quantity supply is only Q_s, hence, a persistent excess demand or shortage in the amount $Q_s Q_d$ occurs. The size of this shortage varies directly with the price elasticities of supply and demand. The important point is that the fixed price P_c prevents the usual market adjustment, where competition among buyers would bid up price, thereby inducing more production and rationing some buyers out of the market until the shortage disappears at the equilibrium price and quantity, P_o and Q_o.

By preventing market-clearing adjustments from occurring, the price ceiling poses problems born of the market disequilibrium.

1. How is the available quantity supplied, Q_s, to be apportioned among buyers who want amount Q_d? Should the amount be distributed on a first-come, first-served basis? Or should the grocer distribute butter on the basis of favouritism? An unregulated shortage is hardly conducive to the equitable distribution of butter. To avoid a haphazard distribution of butter, the government must establish some formal system of rationing it to consumers. This was accomplished during World War II by issuing ration coupons to individuals on an equitable basis. An effective rationing system entails the printing of ration coupons equal to Q_s pounds of butter and their equitable distribution among consumers so that the rich family of four and the poor family of four will both get the same number of coupons.

2. But the use of ration coupons does not prevent a second problem from arising. The demand curve in Figure 6-1 tells us there are many buyers who are willing to pay more than the ceiling price. And of course it is more profitable for grocers to sell above the ceiling price. Thus, despite the sizable enforcement bureaucracy that accompanied World War II price controls, illegal *black markets* — markets where products were bought and sold at prices above the legal limits — flourished for many goods. Counterfeiting of ration coupons was also a problem. As Figure 6-1 indicates, there is a shortage (or excess quantity demanded) of butter at the ceiling price of $0.90. Since only quantity Q_s, is available, a black market price of P_1 ($2.00) would come about. The black market would be given impetus by coupon holders willing to forgo part of their ration to get $2.00 cash for each pound of butter they would be willing to part with.

Rent Controls   Rent controls are another example of attempts to intervene in the functioning of the market to achieve a well-intentioned social goal. Rent control legislation has been fairly common in Canada in the past few decades as provincial governments have attempted to maintain existing stocks of "affordable" rental housing. In several provinces these laws have since been phased out, although controls are still in force in Ontario.

When controls are first imposed they usually restrict increases in rents above current levels. The short-run supply curve for rental accommodation is almost completely inelastic because it takes landlords some time to react to price changes. Most tenants benefit, since the quantity of rental accommodation currently on the market or under construction is not significantly affected. Hence the program appears to be successful. Figure 6-2 portrays a market for rental accommodation with rents fixed at r_c.

If overtime demand increases, a shortage of rental accommodation will appear. As Figure 6-2 shows, at the controlled rent r_c quantity demanded becomes q_1 even if only q_2 is available, leading to shortages. Quantity supplied may continually decline as construction of new units decreases and landlords try to convert existing units to other uses or allow them to deteriorate. The supply curve therefore becomes more elastic in the long run as shown by S_L in Figure 6-2, making the shortage worse.

FIGURE 6-2   Rent controls

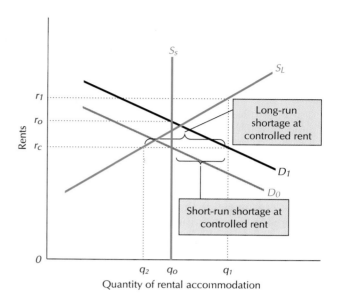

In the short run, supply is completely inelastic. If rents are fixed at r_c, an increase in demand from D_0 to D_1 will create a shortage q_0q_1. In the long run, supply becomes more elastic as landlords are able to add or withdraw units from the market. In the long run the shortage q_0q_1 will worsen to q_2q_1 if rent controls remain unaltered. On the black market rents of r_1 will be charged.

The gradually worsening shortage in the long run leads to several related problems. As in the case of controls on food prices, a black market will emerge. The black market in rental accommodation is characterized by the charging of "key money." Prospective tenants will often be forced to bribe a landlord or a subletting tenant in order to acquire a particular rental unit. The acceptance of key money is illegal in most jurisdictions that have rent controls, but the practice is difficult to stamp out because it is to the advantage of both parties involved to engage in such transactions. Those desperate for rental accommodation will have to pay the black market rate of r_1, shown in Figure 6-2.

Another problem that results from controls is the emergence of a dual rental market if new buildings coming on the market are exempt from controls. Apartment units whose rents are substantially below market levels are almost always rented informally or with some form of key money attached. The units that have recently come on the market will be offered at rents above the levels that would exist without controls as landlords attempt to compensate for future restrictions on rent increases. Because of discrimination by landlords and the ability to pay key money, middle-class tenants will often find it easier to secure units in the controlled market, while the poor will often be forced to seek units in the uncontrolled market. Perversely, tenants with higher incomes can be the major beneficiaries of the program.[1]

Because of these problems most economists are opposed to rent controls. Landlord groups and right-wing commentators view the shortage of affordable housing as being primarily income-related. They contend the problem can best be addressed by directly subsidizing income while allowing market forces to function freely. Tenant groups and left-wing observers maintain that the shortage results from underlying flaws in the private market rather than from rent controls. They contend that affordable housing can only be guaranteed through publicly financed housing schemes or through subsidies and tax incentives for private suppliers.

In brief, rent controls distort market signals so that resources are misallocated: too few resources are allocated to rental housing, too many to alternative uses. Ironically, although rent controls are often legislated to mitigate the effects of perceived housing shortages, in fact controls are an important source of such shortages.

Credit Card Interest Ceilings   In 1988, attempts were made in Parliament by private members to have a nationwide interest-rate ceiling imposed on credit card accounts. In fact, in the United States several states now have such laws and others have legislation under consideration. The rationale for interest-rate ceilings is that the banks and retail stores issuing such cards are presumably "gouging" users, particularly lower-income users.

What are the likely responses to the imposition by law of below-equilibrium interest rates on credit cards? According to a study by the United States' central bank, the Federal Reserve,[2] profits on bank-issued credit cards have been low, while retail store cards have generally entailed losses for their issuers.

Hence, lower interest income associated with an interest ceiling set by law would require adjustments by issuers to reduce costs or enhance revenues. What forms might these responses take?

1. Card issuers might tighten credit standards so as to reduce nonpayment losses and collection costs. In particular, low-income people and young people who have not yet established their credit-worthiness would find it more difficult to obtain credit cards.

2. The annual fee charge to card holders might be increased, as might the fee charged to merchants for processing credit card sales. Card users might also be charged a fee for every transaction.

3. Card users have a "grace period" in which the credit provided is interest-free. This period could be shortened or eliminated.

4. Retail stores that issue cards might increase their merchandise prices to help offset the decline of interest income. This would mean that customers who pay cash would in effect be subsidizing customers who use credit cards.

Empirical studies of American states that now have ceilings on credit card interest rates have confirmed our first and fourth predictions.

Rock Concerts   Below-equilibrium pricing should not be associated solely with government policies. Superstars such as Madonna or Michael Jackson frequently price their concert tickets below the market-clearing price. Tickets are usually rationed on a first-come, first-served basis, and black market "scalping" is common. Why should rock stars want to subsidize their fans — at least those who are fortunate enough to obtain tickets — with below-equilibrium prices? Why not set ticket prices at a higher, market-clearing level and realize more income from a tour? The answer is that long lines of fans waiting hours or days for bargain-priced tickets catch the attention of the press, as does an occasional attempt by those who do not get tickets to crash a sold-out concert. The millions of dollars worth of free publicity undoubtedly stimulates record and CD sales, from which a major portion of any rock star's income is derived. Thus, the "gift" of below-equilibrium ticket prices a rock star gives to fans also benefits the star. The gift also imposes costs upon fans — the opportunity cost of the time spent waiting in line to buy tickets.

Price Floors and Surpluses   Price floors — *minimum prices fixed by government that are above equilibrium prices* — have generally been invoked when society has felt that the free functioning of the market system has not provided a sufficient income for certain groups of resource suppliers or

---

[1] For example, a recent study of Ontario rent controls suggests that middle-class tenants benefited most from the provincial program in the early 1980s. See W.T. Stanbury and Ilan B. Vertinsky, *Rent Regulation: Design Characteristics and Effects*, Research Study 18, Commission of Inquiry into Residential Tenancies, Toronto, 1986.

[2] Glenn B. Canner and James T. Fergus, "The Economic Effects of Proposed Ceilings on Credit Card Interest Rates," *Federal Reserve Bulletin*, January 1987, pp. 1–13.

Box 6-1

In the Media

The commodity market, in which futures are traded, is one in which an individual can see the laws of supply and demand functioning on an hourly basis! In anticipation of lower supply, future wheat and corn prices rise. Conversely, in anticipation of ample soybean stocks, prices fall.

TIGHT WHEAT SUPPLY BOOSTS FUTURES PRICES

Corn recovers from profit-taking

Associated Press

NEW YORK — Wheat traders sent futures prices sharply higher yesterday on the Chicago Board of Trade in response to reports of dwindling U.S. supplies.

Corn futures also firmed, while soybean prices retreated on news of ample stocks.

For wheat, it was the second session in a row of strong price moves as traders received a double dose of bullish supply data from the U.S. Department of Agriculture.

On Friday, they learned that farmers had planted 7 per cent fewer acres to winter wheat than a year earlier. This was far below what the market had expected.

Then, on Monday, the USDA pegged the supply of wheat at the end of the 1991–92 crop year at 390 million bushels, down from its December estimate of 414 million and far below last season's carryover of 866 million.

"The ending stocks registered the largest drop on record from one year to the next," said William Biedermann, research director of Allendale Inc. in Crystal Lake, Ill.

Corn futures suffered from some profit-taking during the session, but prices firmed near the close.

The USDA put the year-ending stocks of corn at 1.08 billion bushels, down from 1.52 billion a year earlier.

With wheat in short supply, users would normally look to corn as a substitute.

"But how can you switch over to corn when corn's not there," Mr. Biedermann said.

Soybean futures declined. The USDA said year-ending soybeans would total 325 million bushels, 10 million more than the market was expecting.

The Globe and Mail, Jan. 15, 1992. By permission of AP-Associated Press.

producers. Minimum-wage legislation and the support of agricultural prices are the two most widely discussed examples of government price floors. Let's examine price floors as applied to a specific farm commodity.

Suppose the going market price for oats is $2 per bushel, and as a result of this price, many farmers realize extremely low incomes. Government decides to lend a helping hand by establishing a price fixed by law of $3 per bushel.

What will be the effects? At any price above the equilibrium price, quantity supplied will exceed quantity demanded. There will be a persistent excess supply or surplus of the product. Farmers will be willing to produce and offer for sale more than private buyers are willing to purchase at the price floor. The size of this surplus will vary directly with the

elasticity of demand and supply. The greater the elasticity of demand and supply, the greater the resulting surplus. As is the case with a ceiling price, the rationing ability of the free market has been disrupted by imposing a legal price.

Figure 6-3 illustrates the effect of a price floor. Let S and D be the supply and demand curves for corn. Equilibrium price and quantity are P and Q, respectively. If government imposes a price floor of P_f, farmers will produce Q_s, but private buyers will only take Q_d off the market at that price. The surplus is measured by the excess of Q_s over Q_d.

Government may cope with the surplus a price floor entails in two basic ways.

1. It might restrict supply (for example, allotments by which farmers agree to take a certain amount of land out of production) or increase demand (for

FIGURE 6-3   Price floors result in persistent surpluses

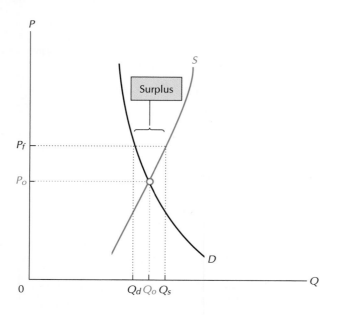

A price floor such as P_f gives rise to a persistent product surplus as indicated by the distance Q_dQ_s. Government must either purchase these surpluses or take measures to eliminate them by restricting product supply or increasing product demand.

example, researching new uses for agricultural products). In these ways the difference between the equilibrium price and the price floor and thereby the size of the resulting surplus might be reduced.

2. If these efforts are not wholly successful, then government must purchase the surplus output (thereby subsidizing farmers) and store or otherwise dispose of it.

Price ceilings and price floors rob the free-market forces of supply and demand of their ability to bring the supply decisions of producers and the demand decisions of buyers into accord with one another. Freely determined prices automatically ration products to buyers, prices fixed by law do not. Therefore, government must accept the administrative problem of rationing that stems from price ceilings and the problem of buying or eliminating surpluses that price floors entail. Prices fixed by law bring about controversial trade-offs. Alleged benefits of price ceilings and floors to consumers and producers respectively must be set against costs associated with consequent shortages and surpluses.

Our discussions of World War II price controls, rent controls, and interest-rate ceilings on credit

cards indicate that governmental interference with the market can have unintended side effects. Rent controls are likely to discourage housing construction and repair. Instead of protecting low-income families from high interest charges, interest-rate ceilings may simply make credit unavailable to them.

QUICK REVIEW (6-1)

1. **Price ceilings and floors negate the rationing function of prices and have unintended side effects. Price ceilings lead to shortages, price floors lead to surpluses.**

2. **Rent controls are attempts to make rents "affordable," but the unintended side effects are shortages of rental accommodations, key money, and black markets where desperate tenants pay rents above those specified by law.**

3. **Credit card interest ceilings can have the unintended effect of making it more difficult to get a credit card (especially for those with low incomes), and the price of merchandise may rise to offset the decline in interest income.**

SUPPLY AND DEMAND: THE FOREIGN EXCHANGE MARKET[3]

We close this chapter by applying our understanding of demand and supply to the **foreign exchange market**, the market where various national currencies are exchanged for one another. At the outset two points merit emphasis.

1. Real-world foreign exchange markets conform closely to the kinds of markets we have studied. These are competitive markets characterized by large numbers of buyers and sellers dealing in a standardized "product" such as the Canadian dollar, the German mark, the British pound, or the Japanese yen.

2. The price or exchange value of a nation's currency is an unusual price in that it links *all* domestic (Canadian) prices with *all* foreign (say, Japanese or German) prices. Exchange rates enable consumers in one country to translate the prices of foreign goods into units of their own currency by multiplying the foreign product price by the exchange rate. For example, if the dollar/yen exchange rate is $1.00 for 100 yen (or 1 cent per yen), a Sony cassette player priced at 20,000 yen will cost a Canadian $200 (= 20,000 × $.01). But if the exchange rate is $2.00 for

---
[3] Some instructors may choose to skip this section.

Box 6-2

THE HIGH PRICE OF MARIJUANA

In late 1990 and early 1991 the Drug Enforcement Agency in the U.S. reported that the price of marijuana reached historic highs.

At the start of this decade the price of a "lid" (an ounce) of marijuana ranged from $200 to $400 in the United States. In comparison an ounce of gold was selling for $370.

Simple supply and demand explains this "reefer madness." On the demand side marijuana is by far the most commonly used illegal drug. It is esimated that about one-third of all American adults — some 66 million people — have used pot at least once during their lives. However, the demand for marijuana is declining. In 1979 over 35% of all young adults (aged 18–25) used pot at least once a month. By 1990 this figure had declined to less than 13%. Stated differently, over 22 million people smoked marijuana in 1979 compared to slightly over 10 million in 1990. Other things the same, a declining demand should mean lower, not higher, pot prices.

But other things have not been the same. For a variety of reasons substantial reductions in marijuana supply have occurred. First, law enforcement in Mexico — a major exporter of pot to both Canada and the United States — has improved. Second, many pot producers have shifted their resources to alternative drugs. In particular, Colombia's incredibly profitable cocaine industry has expanded and attracted resources from marijuana. It is also cheaper and easier to smuggle small quantities of cocaine compared to bulky truck- and planeloads of marijuana. Third, the interdiction of pot smugglers has improved; less marijuana is coming over our borders. Finally, within Canada and the United States efforts to apprehend marijuana growers and destroy their crops have been increasingly effective.

How to explain the high price of pot? Quite simply: Supply has fallen much more dramatically than has demand.

---

100 yen (or 2 cents per yen), the Sony will cost a Canadian $400 (= 20,000 × $.02). All other Japanese products will double in price to Canadian buyers. As we shall see, a change in exchange rates can have important implications for a nation's levels of domestic production and employment.

The Dollar–Yen Market

Skirting technical details, we now examine how the foreign exchange market for, say, dollars and yen might work. When nations trade, they need to exchange their currencies. For example, Canadian exporters who sell to Japan want to be paid in dollars, not yen; but Japanese importers of Canadian goods possess yen, not dollars. This problem is resolved by Japanese offering or supplying yen in exchange for dollars. Conversely, Canadian importers need to pay Japanese exporters with yen, not dollars. To do so they go to the foreign exchange market as demanders of yen. We can think of Japanese importers as suppliers of yen and Canadian importers as demanders of yen. The interaction of the demand for yen and the supply of yen will establish the dollar price of yen. Suppose the equilibrium dollar price of

yen — the dollar–yen exchange rate — is $1 = ¥100. That is, a dollar will buy 100 yen (the "dollar price" of 1 yen is 1 cent) and therefore 100 yen worth of Japanese goods. Conversely, 100 yen will buy $1 worth of Canadian goods.

Changing Rates: Depreciation and Appreciation

What might cause this exchange rate to change? The determinants of the demand for and the supply of yen are quite similar to those we have already discussed. From the vantage point of Canada, a number of things might occur to increase the demand for — and therefore the dollar price — of yen. (An increase in demand is depicted by D_1 in Figure 6-4.) For example, incomes might rise in Canada, causing Canadians to buy not only more domestic goods, but also more Sony televisions, more Nikon cameras, and more Nissan automobiles from Japan. To do this Canadians need to obtain more yen, so the demand for yen increases. Or there may occur a change in Canadian tastes that enhances our preferences for Japanese goods. For instance, when gasoline prices soared in the 1970s, many Canadian auto buyers

FIGURE 6-4   The foreign exchange market

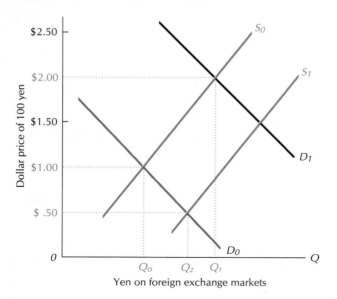

Exchange rates enable consumers in one country to translate the price of foreign goods into units of their own currency. If the demand for Japanese yen increases, the dollar will depreciate against the yen.

shifted their demands from large, gas-guzzling domestic cars to gas-efficient Japanese compact cars. In so doing the demand for yen increased.

The critical point is that an increase in the Canadian demand for Japanese goods will increase the demand for yen and raise the dollar price of yen. This situation is shown graphically in Figure 6-4 by a shift of demand to D_1. Let us suppose the dollar price of yen rises from $1 = ¥100 (or 1¢ = ¥1) to $2 = ¥100 (or 2¢ = ¥1).

When the dollar price of yen *increases*, a **depreciation** of the dollar relative to the yen has occurred. Dollar depreciation means that it takes more dollars (pennies in this case) to buy a single unit of a foreign currency (the yen). A dollar is worth less because it will buy fewer yen and therefore a smaller quantity of Japanese goods.

If events opposite to those we have presumed had occurred — that is, if incomes rose in Japan and Japanese preferences for Canadian goods strengthened — then the *supply* of yen in foreign exchange markets would increase. This increase in the supply of

yen relative to demand would *decrease* the equilibrium dollar price of yen. For example, supply might increase to the extent that the dollar price of yen declines from the original $1 = ¥100, or 1¢ = ¥1, to $.50 = ¥100 or ½¢ = ¥1. Such a situation is depicted by a rightward shift of the supply curve to S_1 in Figure 6-4.

This *decrease* in the dollar price of yen means there has been an **appreciation** of the dollar relative to the yen. Appreciation means it takes fewer dollars (pennies) to buy a single yen than previously. The dollar is worth more because it is capable of purchasing more yen and therefore more Japanese goods.

Economic Consequences

The consequences of changes in exchange rates are easily perceived. Suppose Canada is operating at a point inside its production possibilities curve and the dollar depreciates, that is, the dollar price of yen rises from 1¢ = ¥1 to 2¢ = ¥1. This means that the yen and therefore *all* Japanese goods are now more expensive to Canadians. So what happens? Canadian consumers shift their expenditures from Japanese to domestic goods. For example, the Chevy Corsica is now relatively more attractive than the Honda Accord to Canadian consumers. Canadian industries in general are stimulated by this shift in expenditures and their production and employment both rise. Conversely, Japanese export industries find the sales of their products diminishing, so output and employment both tend to decline. The depreciation of the dollar has led to an increase of domestic output in Canada.

With the economic stakes potentially high, it is easy to understand why governments are tempted to interfere with otherwise "free" foreign exchange markets. Thus, the Bank of Canada might attempt to depreciate the dollar in the short term when our economy is at less than full employment. The problem, however, is that the consequent shift in Canadian expenditures from foreign goods to domestic goods will lower Japanese exports and tend to depress *their* economy. The Japanese government may well be interested in offsetting the depreciation of the dollar that the Canadians desire, leading to retaliatory actions. Thus, in the final analysis both Canada and Japan may be worse off if one of them attempts to get the upper hand by depreciating its currency.

CHAPTER SUMMARY

1. Prices fixed by law upset the rationing function of equilibrium prices. Effective price ceilings result in persistent product shortages and, if an equitable distribution of the product is sought, government will have to ration the product to consumers. Price floors lead to product surpluses; government must purchase these surpluses *or* eliminate them by imposing restrictions on production or by increasing private demand.

2. The foreign exchange market is an important application of demand and supply analysis. Foreign importers are suppliers of their currencies and Canadian importers are demanders of foreign currencies. The resulting equilibrium exchange rates link the price levels of all nations. Depreciation of the dollar reduces our imports and stimulates our domestic economy; appreciation of the dollar increases our imports and depresses our domestic economy.

TERMS AND CONCEPTS

depreciation and appreciation of the dollar (p. 89)
foreign exchange market (p. 88)
price ceiling (p. 84)

price floor (p. 86)
rent controls (p. 85)
shortage (p. 84)
surplus (p. 86)

QUESTIONS AND STUDY SUGGESTIONS

1. Why is it desirable for price ceilings to be accompanied by government rationing? And for price floors to be accompanied by surplus-purchasing or output-restricting or demand-increasing programs? Show graphically why price ceilings entail shortages and price floors result in surpluses. What effect, if any, does elasticity of demand and supply have upon the size of these shortages and surpluses? Explain.

2. Toronto has had rent controls since the 1970s. What effect do you think they have had on the amount of housing demanded? On the construction of new rental housing? Explain: "Rent controls are a kind of self-fulfiling prophecy. They are designed to cope with housing shortages, but instead create such shortages." Can you predict the economic consequences of usury laws? Show diagrammatically the expected effect of the minimum wage on employment of low-wage workers.

3. Use two market diagrams to explain how an increase in provincial funding of the public school system might affect tuition and enrolments in both public and private schools.

4. What effects would Canadian import quotas on Japanese automobiles have upon the Canadian price of Japanese cars *and* upon the demand for, and price of, North American–made cars?

5. Many countries have usury laws that stipulate the maximum interest rate that lenders (commercial banks, credit unions, and so forth) can charge borrowers.

Indicate in some detail what would happen in the loan market during those periods when the equilibrium interest rate exceeds the stipulated maximum. On the basis of your analysis, do you favour usury laws?

6. "Our imports create a demand for foreign monies; foreign imports of our goods generate supplies of foreign monies." Do you agree? Other things being equal, would a decline in Canadian incomes or a weakening of Canadian preferences for foreign products cause the dollar to depreciate or appreciate? What would be the effects of that depreciation or appreciation upon production and employment domestically and abroad?

2

The Economics of Consumption, Production, and Cost

7

Consumer Behaviour and Utility Maximization[1]

Every day you shop. You might buy textbooks, office supplies, shoes, food, etc. But there are thousands of items to choose from. How do you decide whether to buy two pairs of shoes, or a single pair and a shirt, or the many other possible combinations?

Why is it that when you attend a party, food and drink often run out; whereas at a nightclub or restaurant it is much less likely to happen? At parties, where food and drink is "free," it is not uncommon to find people opening a bottle, taking a few sips, and leaving the rest. The likelihood of such an occurrence when one pays for a soft drink or beer is small.

In this chapter our focus is on explaining consumer behaviour, which will lead to a better understanding of the law of demand and the shape of the demand curve.

---

[1] Some instructors may choose to omit this chapter. This can be done without impairing the continuity and meaning of ensuing chapters.

TWO EXPLANATIONS OF THE LAW OF DEMAND

The law of demand may be treated as a common-sense notion. A high price discourages consumers from buying, while a low price encourages them to buy. We now explore two complementary explanations of the downsloping demand curve. (A third explanation, based on indifference curves, is summarized in the appendix of this chapter.)

Income and Substitution Effects

In Chapter 4, we saw that the law of demand — the downsloping demand curve — can be explained in terms of the income and substitution effects. Whenever a product's price decreases, two things happen to cause the amount demanded to increase.

1 Income Effect The **income effect** is the impact of a change in the price of a product on the real income of a consumer and, thus, on the quantity demanded. If the price of a product — say, steak — declines, the real income or purchasing power of anyone buying that product will increase. This increase in real income will result in increased purchases of many products, including steak. For example, with a constant money income of $40 per week you can purchase 5 kilograms of steak at a price of $8 per kilogram. But if the price of steak falls to $4 per kilogram and you buy 5 kilograms, $20 per week is freed to buy more of this and other commodities. A decline in the price of steak increases the real income of the consumer, enabling him or her to purchase more steak.[2]

2 Substitution Effect The **substitution effect** is the impact of a change in the price of a product on the relative cost of that product, thus on the quantity demanded. The lower price of a product means it is now cheaper relative to all other products. Consumers will substitute the less expensive product for other products that are now relatively more expensive. In our example, as the price of steak falls — the prices of other products remaining unchanged — steak will become more attractive to the buyer. At $4 per kilogram it is a better buy than at $8 per kilogram. Steak may well be substituted for pork, chicken, veal, fish, and a variety of other foods.

The substitution and income effects combine to make a consumer able and willing to buy more of a specific good at a low price than at a high price.

---

[2] We assume here that steak is a *normal* or *superior* good.

Law of Diminishing Marginal Utility

A second explanation is that the more of a specific product consumers obtain, the less willing they are to get additional units of the same product. This can be most readily seen for durable goods. A consumer's want for an automobile, when he or she has none, may be very strong; the desire for a second car is much less intense; for a third or fourth, very weak. Even the wealthiest families rarely have more than a half-dozen cars, although their incomes would allow them to purchase a whole fleet of them.

The falling satisfaction derived from one more unit of a product is referred to as the **law of diminishing marginal utility**. Recall from Chapter 4 that **utility** is the benefit or satisfaction one gets from consuming a good or service. Two characteristics of this concept must be emphasized.

1. "Utility" and "usefulness" are *not* synonymous. Paintings by Picasso may be useless in the functional sense and yet be of tremendous utility to art connoisseurs.

2. Utility is a subjective notion. The utility of a specific product will vary widely from person to person. A bottle of cheap wine may yield substantial utility to the destitute alcoholic, but zero or negative utility to a nondrinker. Eyeglasses have great utility to someone that is extremely far- or near-sighted, but no utility to a person with 20–20 vision.

By *marginal* utility we mean the extra utility, or satisfaction, a consumer gets from one additional unit of a specific product. In any relatively short time wherein the consumer's tastes can be assumed not to change, the marginal utility derived from successive units of a given product will decline. A consumer will eventually become relatively saturated, or "filled up," with that particular product.

Because it is a subjective concept, utility is not susceptible to precise quantitative measurement. But for purposes of illustration, assume we can measure satisfaction with units we will call "utils." This hypothetical unit of satisfaction is a convenient device that will allow us to quantify consumer behaviour. Thus in Table 7-1 we can illustrate the relationship between the quantity obtained of a product — say, fast-food hamburgers — and the accompanying extra utility derived from each successive unit. We assume that the law of diminishing marginal utility sets in with the first hamburger consumed. Each successive hamburger yields less extra utility than the previous one as the consumer's want for hamburgers comes closer and closer to fulfilment. *Total utility* can be found by adding up the marginal-utility figures. For

TABLE 7-1 The law of diminishing marginal utility as applied to hamburgers (*hypothetical data*)

Unit of hamburger	Marginal utility, in utils	Total utility, in utils
First	10	10
Second	6	16
Third	2	18
Fourth	0	18
Fifth	−5	13

example, three hamburgers yield a total utility of 18 utils (= 10 + 6 + 2). Note that marginal utility becomes zero for the fourth hamburger and negative for the fifth.

Relation to Demand and Elasticity How does the law of diminishing marginal utility explain why the demand curve for a specific product is downsloping? If successive units of a good yield smaller and smaller amounts of marginal, or extra, utility, then the consumer will buy additional units of a product only if its price falls. The consumer for whom these utility data are relevant may buy two hamburgers at a price of $1. But owing to diminishing marginal utility from additional hamburgers, a consumer will choose *not* to buy more at this price, because giving up money really means giving up other goods, that is, alternative ways of getting utility. Therefore, additional hamburgers are not worth it unless the price (sacrifice of other goods) declines. (When marginal utility becomes negative, McDonalds or Burger King would have to pay *you* to eat another hamburger!)

The amount by which marginal utility declines as more units of a product are consumed will determine its price elasticity of demand. Other things being equal, if marginal utility falls sharply as successive units are consumed, we would expect demand to be inelastic. Conversely, modest declines in marginal utility as consumption increases imply an elastic demand.

THEORY OF CONSUMER BEHAVIOUR

In addition to providing a basis for explaining the law of demand, the idea of diminishing marginal utility is critical in explaining how consumers allocate their money income among the many goods and services available to them.

Consumer Choice and Budget Constraint

The typical consumer has the following attributes and constraints:

1 Rational Behaviour The average consumer is a rational person attempting to dispose of money income so as to derive the greatest amount of satisfaction, or utility, from it. Consumers want to get the most for their money or, more technically, to maximize total utility.

2 Preferences The consumer has rather clear-cut preferences for various goods and services available in the market. We assume buyers have a good idea of how much marginal utility they will get from successive units of the various products they might choose to purchase.

3 Budget Constraint Since a consumer's money income is limited, all consumers are subject to a *budget constraint.*

4 Prices If a consumer has a limited income, he or she will be able to purchase only a limited amount of goods. The consumer cannot buy everything wanted when each purchase exhausts a portion of a limited money income. The consumer must make choices among alternative goods to obtain, with limited money resources, the most satisfying collection of goods and services.

Utility-Maximizing Rule

The **utility-maximizing rule** assumes that *the consumer's money income is allocated so that the last* *dollar spent on each product purchased yields the same amount of extra (marginal) utility.* When the consumer is "balancing margins" in accordance with this rule, the consumer will be in *equilibrium* and, barring a change in tastes, income, or the prices of the various goods, will be worse off — total utility will decline — by any alteration in the collection of goods purchased.

Numerical Example An illustration will help explain this rule. For simplicity's sake, we limit our discussion to just two products. Keep in mind that the analysis can readily be extended to any number of goods. Suppose that consumer Brooks is trying to decide which combination of two products — A and B — she should purchase with her limited daily income of $10. Brooks's preferences for these two products and their prices will be basic data determining the combination of A and B that will maximize her satisfactions.

Table 7-2 summarizes Brooks's preferences for products A and B. Column 2a shows the amount of marginal utility she will derive from each successive unit of A. Column 3a reflects her preferences for product B.

Marginal Utility per Dollar Before we can apply the utility-maximizing rule to these data, we must put the marginal-utility information of columns 2a and 3a on a per-dollar-spent basis. A consumer's choices will be influenced not only by the extra utility successive units of product A will yield, but also by how many dollars (and therefore how many units of alternative good B) she must give up to obtain those added units of A. The rational consumer will compare the extra utility from each product with its cost.

Suppose you prefer a pizza whose marginal utility is 36 utils to a movie whose marginal utility is just 24 utils. But if the pizza's price is $12 and to go to a movie only $6, the choice would be for the movie rather than the pizza. Why? Because the *marginal utility per dollar spent* would be 4 utils for the movie (4 = 24 ÷ $6) as compared with only 3 utils for the pizza (3 = 36 ÷ 12). You could go to two movies for $12 and, assuming the marginal utility of the second movie is 16 utils, your total utility would be 40 utils. Forty units of satisfaction from two movies is obviously superior to 36 utils derived from the same $12 expenditure on one pizza.

To make the amounts of extra utility derived from differently priced goods comparable, marginal utility must be put on a per-dollar-spent basis. This is done in columns 2b and 3b. These figures are obtained by dividing the marginal-utility data of columns 2a and 3a by the assumed prices of A and B — $1 and $2, respectively.

TABLE 7-2   The utility-maximizing combination of products A and B obtainable with an income of $10* (*hypothetical data*)

(1) Unit of product	(2) Product A: price = $1		(3) Product B: price = $2	
	(a) Marginal utility, utils	(b) Marginal utility per dollar (MU/price)	(a) Marginal utility, utils	(b) Marginal utility per dollar (MU/price)
First	10	10	24	12
Second	8	8	20	10
Third	7	7	18	9
Fourth	6	6	16	8
Fifth	5	5	12	6
Sixth	4	4	6	3
Seventh	3	3	4	2

*It is assumed in this table that the amount of marginal utility received from additional units of each of the two products is independent of the quantity of the other product. For example, the marginal-utility schedule for product A is independent of the amount of B obtained by the consumer.

Box 7-1

THE WATER-DIAMOND PARADOX

Water is clearly one of the most useful products in the world; our very survival depends upon it. Yet water is very cheap. In contrast, diamonds — which are merely decorative and have little practical value — are very expensive. Why do prices apparently fail to measure the usefulness of goods? Our theory of consumer behaviour and the distinction between total and marginal utility help resolve this paradox.

The explanation of the water-diamond paradox lies in two related considerations. First, the supplies of the two products are much different. Water is plentiful and, as a consequence, its price is low and we therefore consume large quantities of it. In doing so we extend our use of water to uses wherein the utility from the last unit of water — water's marginal utility — is very low. For example, we water our lawns, make ice cubes, and wash our cars. In contrast, diamonds are rare and costly to mine, cut, and polish. Therefore, their supply is restricted and they are available only at a high price. The marginal utility of diamonds is therefore very large.

The second consideration relates back to the utility-maximizing rule, which states that consumers should purchase any good until the ratio of its marginal utility to price is the same as that for all other goods. Although the *marginal* utility of water may be low because it is plentiful and its price is low, the *total* utility derived from its consumption is exceedingly large because of the great quantity consumed. Conversely, the total utility derived from diamonds is low because the very high price that reflects the scarcity of diamonds causes consumers to purchase relatively few of them. In short, the total utility derived from water is relatively great and the total utility derived from diamonds is relatively small, but it is *marginal* utility that is relevant to the price people are willing to pay for a good. Water yields much more total utility to us than do diamonds, even though the utility of an additional litre of water is much less than the utility of an additional diamond. Society would gladly give up *all* of the diamonds in the world if that were necessary to obtain *all* of the water in the world. But society would rather have an *additional* diamond than an *additional* litre of water, given the abundant stock of water available.

Decision-Making Process Now we have Brooks's preferences — on unit and per dollar basis — and the price tags of A and B before us. Brooks stands patiently with $10 to spend on A and B. In what order should she allocate her dollars on units of A and B to achieve the highest degree of utility within the limits imposed by her money income? What specific combination of A and B will she have obtained at the time that she exhausts her $10?

Concentrating on columns 2b and 3b of Table 7-2, we find that Brooks should first spend $2 on the first unit of B because its marginal utility per dollar of 12 utils is higher than A's. But now Brooks finds herself indifferent about whether she should buy a second unit of B or the first unit of A, because the marginal utility per dollar of both is 10, so she buys both of them. Brooks now has 1 unit of A and 2 of B.

With this combination of goods, the last dollar spent on each yields the same amount of extra utility. Does this combination of A and B therefore represent the maximum amount of utility Brooks can obtain?

The answer is no. This collection of goods only costs $5 [= (1 × $1) + (2 × $2)]; Brooks has $5 remaining, which she can spend to achieve a still higher level of total utility.

Examining columns 2b and 3b again, we find Brooks should spend the next $2 on a third unit of B because marginal utility per dollar for the third unit of B is 9, compared with 8 for the second unit of A. But now with 1 unit of A and 3 of B, we find she is again indifferent to a second unit of A and a fourth unit of B. So again Brooks purchases one more unit of each. Marginal utility per dollar is now the same at 8 utils for the last dollar spent on each product, *and* Brooks's money income of $10 is exhausted [(2 × $1) + (4 × $2)]. *The utility-maximizing combination of goods attainable by Brooks is 2 units of A and 4 of B.*[3]

---

[3] To simplify, we assume in this example that Brooks spends her entire income; she neither borrows nor saves. Saving can be regarded as a utility-yielding commodity and incorporated in our analysis. It is treated thus in question 5 at the end of the chapter.

By summing the marginal utility information of columns 2a and 3a we find that Brooks is realizing 18(= 10 + 8) utils of satisfaction from the 2 units of A and 78 (= 24 + 20 + 18 + 16) utils of satisfaction from the 4 units of B. Her $10 income, optimally spent, yields 96 (= 18 + 78) utils of satisfaction. Table 7-3 summarizes this step-by-step process for maximizing consumer utility and merits careful study.

Inferior Options   There are other combinations of A and B obtainable with $10. But none will yield a level of total utility as high as 2 units of A and 4 of B. For example, 4 units of A and 3 of B can be obtained for $10. However, this combination violates the utility-maximizing rule; total utility here is only 93 utils, clearly inferior to the 96 utils yielded by 2 of A and 4 of B. Furthermore, there are other combinations of A and B (such as 4 of A and 5 of B *or* 1 of A and 2 of B) wherein the marginal utility of the last dollar spent is the same for both A and B. But such combinations are either unobtainable with Brooks's limited money income (as 4 of A and 5 of B) or fail to exhaust her money income (as 1 of A and 2 of B) and therefore do not yield her the maximum utility attainable.

Problem: Suppose that Brooks's money income was $14 rather than $10. What now would be the utility-maximizing combination of A and B? Are A and B normal or inferior goods?

Algebraic Restatement

Our rule says that a consumer will maximize satisfaction when he or she allocates money income so that the last dollar spent on product A, the last on product B, and so forth, yield equal amounts of marginal utility.

The marginal utility per dollar spent on A is indicated by MU of product A/price of A (column 2b of Table 7-2) and the marginal utility per dollar spent on B by MU of product B/price of B (column 3b of Table 7-2). Our utility-maximizing rule merely requires that these ratios be equal. That is,

$$\frac{\text{MU of product A}}{\text{price of A}} = \frac{\text{MU of product B}}{\text{price of B}}$$

The consumer must exhaust any available income. Our illustration has shown us that the combination of 2 units of A and 4 of B fulfils these conditions in that

$$\frac{8}{1} = \frac{16}{2}$$

and the consumer's $10 income is spent.

If the equation is not fulfilled, there will be some reallocation of the consumer's expenditures between A and B, from the low to the high marginal-utility-per-dollar product, that will increase the consumer's total utility. For example, if the consumer spent $10 on 4 of A and 3 of B, we would find that

$$\frac{\text{MU of A: 6 utils}}{\text{price of A: \$1}} < \frac{\text{MU of B: 18 utils}}{\text{price of B: \$2}}$$

The last dollar spent on A provides only 6 utils of satisfaction, and the last dollar spent on B provides 9 (= 18 ÷ $2). On a per dollar basis, units of B provide more extra satisfaction than units of A. The consumer will increase his or her total satisfaction by purchasing more of B and less of A. As dollars are reallocated

---

TABLE 7-3   **Sequence of purchases in achieving consumer equilibrium**

Potential choice		Marginal utility per dollar	Purchase decision	Income remaining
1.	First unit of A First unit of B	10 12	First unit of B for $2	$8 = $10 − $2
2.	First unit of A Second unit of B	10 10	First unit of A for $1 and second unit of B for $2	$5 = $8 − $3
3.	Second unit of A Third unit of B	8 9	Third unit of B for $2	$3 = $5 − $2
4.	Second unit of A Fourth unit of B	8 8	Second unit of A for $1 and fourth unit of B for $2	$0 = $3 − $3

from A to B, the marginal utility from additional units of B will decline as the result of moving *down* the diminishing marginal-utility schedule for B, and the marginal utility of A will rise as the consumer moves *up* the diminishing marginal-utility schedule for A. At some new combination of A and B — specifically, 2 of A and 4 of B — the equality of the two ratios, and therefore consumer equilibrium, will be achieved. As we already know, the net gain in utility is 3 utils (= 96 − 93).

MARGINAL UTILITY AND THE DEMAND CURVE

It is a simple step from the utility-maximizing rule to the construction of an individual's downsloping demand curve. Recall that the basic determinants of an individual's demand curve for a specific product are (1) preferences or tastes, (2) money income, and (3) the prices of other goods. The utility data of Table 7-2 reflect our consumer's preferences. We continue to suppose that money income is given at $10. And, concentrating on the construction of a simple demand curve for product B, we assume that the price of A — representing "other goods" — is at $1.

Deriving the Demand Curve We can now derive a simple demand schedule for B by considering alternative prices at which B might be sold and by determining the quantity our consumer will purchase. We have already determined one such price–quantity combination in explaining the utility-maximizing rule: given tastes, income, and prices of other goods, the rational consumer will purchase 4 units of B at $2. Now assume the price of B falls to $1. The marginal-utility-per-dollar data of column 3b will double, because the price of B has been halved; the new data for column 3b in Table 7-2 are in fact identical to those in column 3a. The purchase of 2 units of A and 4 of B is no longer an equilibrium combination. By applying the same reasoning used to develop the utility-maximizing rule, we now find Brooks's utility-maximizing position is 4 units of A and 6 of B. We can sketch Brooks's demand curve for B as in Table 7-4, confirming the downsloping demand curve.

Income and Substitution Effects Revisited At the beginning of this chapter we indicated that increased purchases of a good whose price had fallen could be understood in terms of the substitution and income effects. Although our analysis does not permit us to sort out these two effects, quantita-

TABLE 7-4 The demand schedule for product B

Price per unit of B	Quantity demanded
$2	4
1	6

tively, we can see intuitively how each is involved in the increased purchase of product B.

The *substitution effect* can be understood by referring back to our utility-maximizing rule. Before the price of B declined, Brooks was in equilibrium in that $MU_A(8)/P_A(\$1) = MU_B(16)/P_B(\$2)$ when purchasing 2 units of A and 4 units of B. But after B's price falls from $2 to $1, $MU_A(8)/P_A(\$1) < MU_B(16)/P_B(\$1)$ or, simply stated, the last dollar spent on B now yields more utility (16 utils) than does the last dollar spent on A (8 utils). This indicates that a switching of expenditures from A to B is needed to restore equilibrium. A *substitution* of now cheaper B for A will occur in the bundle of goods that Brooks purchases.

What about the *income effect?* The assumed decline in the price of B from $2 to $1 increases Brooks's real income. Before the price decline, Brooks was in equilibrium when buying 2 of A and 4 of B. But at the lower $1 price for B, Brooks would have to spend only $6 rather than $10 on this same combination of goods. She has $4 left over to spend on more of A, more of B, or more of both products. The decline in the price of B has caused Brooks's *real* income to increase so that she can now obtain larger amounts of A and B with the same $10 *money* income. The portion of the 2 unit increase in her purchase of B that is due to this increase in real income is the income effect.

QUICK REVIEW (7-2)

1. The theory of consumer behaviour assumes that, within a context of limited money incomes and given product prices, consumers make rational choices on the basis of well-defined preferences.

2. A consumer maximizes utility by allocating money income so that the marginal utility per dollar spent is the same for every good purchased.

3. A downsloping demand curve can be derived by changing the price of one product in the consumer-behaviour model.

THE TIME DIMENSION

The theory of consumer behaviour has been generalized to take the economic value of *time* into account. Both consumption and production activities take time. And time is a valuable economic resource; by working — by using an hour in productive activity — one may earn $6, $10, or $50, depending upon one's education, skills, and so forth. By using that hour for leisure or in consumption activities, one incurs the opportunity cost of forgone income; you sacrifice the $6, $10, or $50 you could have earned by working.

The Value of Time

In the marginal utility theory of consumer behaviour, we have assumed that consumption is an instantaneous act. However, it is logical to argue that "prices" of consumer goods should include not merely the market price, but also the value of the time required in the consumption of the good. In other words, the denominators of our earlier marginal-utility/price ratios are incomplete because they do not reflect the "full price" — market price *plus* the value of consumption time — of the product.

Imagine a consumer who is considering the purchase of a round of golf and a concert. The market price of the golf game is $10 and the concert is $16. But the golf game is more time-intensive than the concert. Suppose you will spend four hours on the golf course, but only two hours at the concert. If your time is worth $10 per hour then we must recognize that the "full price" of the golf game is $50 (the $10 market price *plus* $40 worth of time). Similarly, the "full price" of the concert is $36 (the $16 market price *plus* $20 worth of time). We find that contrary to what market prices alone would indicate, the "full price" of the concert is really *less* than the "full price" of the golf game.

If we assume that the marginal utility derived from successive golf games and concerts is identical, traditional theory would indicate that one should consume more golf games than concerts, because the market price of the former is lower ($10) than the latter ($16). But when time is taken into account, the situation is reversed and golf games are more expensive ($50) than are concerts ($36). Hence it is rational to consume more concerts than golf games.

Some Implications

By taking time into account, we can explain certain observable phenomena. It may be rational for the unskilled worker or retiree, whose time has little or no market value, to ride a bus from Winnipeg to Edmonton. But the corporate executive, whose time is valuable, will find it cheaper to fly, even though bus fare is only a fraction of plane fare. It is sensible for the retiree, living on a modest pension and having ample time, to spend many hours shopping for bargains. It is equally rational for the highly paid physician, working fifty-five hours a week, to patronize the hospital cafeteria and to buy a new television set over the phone.

Affluent North Americans are "wasteful" of food and other material goods, but "overly economical" in the use of time. North Americans who visit less-developed countries might perceive that time is used casually or "squandered," while material goods are highly prized and carefully used. These differences are not a paradox or a case of radically different temperaments. The differences are a rational reflection of the fact that the high labour productivity that is characteristic of an advanced society gives time a high market value, whereas the opposite is true in a less-developed country.

A final point: As labour productivity has historically increased with the growth of our economy, time has become more valuable in the labour market. Or, stated differently, time used on pure leisure and various consumer activities has become more expensive. Thus, we make a great effort to use nonwork time more "productively." Where possible, we try to increase the pleasure or utility yield per hour by consuming more per unit of time. In some cases, this means making consumption more goods-intensive. For example, by buying or renting a motorized golf cart, the time required for a round of golf can be reduced. Watching the news on television takes less time than reading the newspaper. In other instances, we consume two or more items simultaneously.

But the yield from certain uses of time — pure idleness, cultural pursuits, and the "cultivation of mind and spirit" — cannot be readily increased. Hence time tends to be shifted from these uses to areas where the yield is greater. This helps explain why, although economic development may bring affluence in the form of goods, it also increases the relative scarcity of time and creates a more hectic lifestyle. Economic growth, it is argued, cannot produce abundance in all respects. Total affluence — an abundance of *both* goods and time — is a logical fallacy. Advanced economies are goods rich and time poor, while less-developed countries are time rich and goods poor.

CHAPTER SUMMARY

1. The law of demand can be explained in terms of the substitution and income effects or the law of diminishing marginal utility.

2. The substitution effect points out that a lower price will make a product relatively more attractive and therefore increase the consumer's willingness to substitute it for other products. The income effect says that a decline in the price of a product will enable the consumer to buy more of it with a fixed money income.

3. The law of diminishing marginal utility states that beyond some point, additional units of a specific good will yield ever-declining amounts of extra satisfaction to a consumer.

4. We may assume that the typical consumer is rational and acts on the basis of rather well-defined preferences. Because income is limited and goods have prices on them, consumers cannot purchase all the goods and services they might like to have. They therefore select that attainable combination of goods that will maximize their utility or satisfaction.

5. The consumer's utility will be maximized when income is allocated so that the last dollar spent on each product purchased yields the same amount of extra satisfaction. Algebraically, the utility-maximizing rule is fulfilled when

$$\frac{\text{MU of product A}}{\text{price of A}} = \frac{\text{MU of product B}}{\text{price of B}}$$

and the consumer's income is spent.

6. The utility-maximizing rule and the downsloping demand curve are logically consistent. Since marginal utility declines, a lower price is needed to induce consumers to increase their purchases.

7. The theory of consumer choice has been generalized by taking into account the value of the time required in the consumption of various goods and services.

TERMS AND CONCEPTS

budget constraint (p. 97)
income effect (p. 96)
law of diminishing marginal utility (p. 96)

substitution effect (p. 96)
utility (p. 96)
utility-maximizing rule (p. 97)

QUESTIONS AND STUDY SUGGESTIONS

1. Explain the law of demand through the substitution and income effects, using a price increase as a point of departure for your discussion. Explain the law of demand in terms of diminishing marginal utility.

2. Mr. Peterson buys loaves of bread and litres of milk each week at prices of $1.20 and $1.00 respectively. At present, he is buying these two products in amounts such that the marginal utilities from the last units purchased of the two products are 120 and 110 units, respectively. Is Peterson currently buying the utility-maximizing combination of bread and milk? If not, in what manner should he reallocate his expenditures between the two goods?

3. You are choosing between two goods, X and Y, and your marginal utility from each is as shown below. If your income is $9 and the prices of X and Y are $2 and $1 respectively, what quantities of each will you purchase in maximizing utility? Specify the amount of total utility you will realize. Assume that, other things remaining unchanged, the price of X falls to $1. What quantities of X and Y will you now purchase? Using the two prices and quantities you have derived for X, graph your demand curve for X.

Units of X	MU_x	Units of Y	MU_y
1	10	1	8
2	8	2	7
3	6	3	6
4	4	4	5
5	3	5	4
6	2	6	3

4. "Nothing is more useful than water: but it will purchase scarce any thing; scarce any thing can be had in exchange for it. A diamond, on the contrary, has scarce any value in use; but a very great quantity of other goods may frequently be had in exchange for it." Explain.

5. Columns 1 to 4 of the following table show the marginal utility, measured in terms of utils, that Mrs. Black would get by purchasing various amounts of products A, B, C, and D. Column 5 shows the marginal utility Black gets from saving. Assume that the prices of A, B, C, and D are $18, $6, $4 and $24, respectively, and that Black has a money income of $106.

Column 1		Column 2		Column 3		Column 4		Column 5	
Units of A	MU	Units of B	MU	Units of C	MU	Units of D	MU	No. of dollars saved	MU
1	72	1	24	1	15	1	36	1	5
2	54	2	15	2	12	2	30	2	4
3	45	3	12	3	8	3	24	3	3
4	36	4	9	4	7	4	18	4	2
5	27	5	7	5	5	5	13	5	1
6	18	6	5	6	4	6	7	6	$\frac{1}{2}$
7	15	7	2	7	$3\frac{1}{2}$	7	4	7	$\frac{1}{4}$
8	12	8	1	8	3	8	2	8	$\frac{1}{8}$

a. What quantities of A, B, C, and D will Black purchase to maximize satisfactions?

b. How many dollars will Black choose to save?

c. Check your answers by substituting in the algebraic statement of the utility-maximizing rule.

6. "In the long run it may be irrational to purchase goods on the basis of habit, but in the short run habitual buying may prove to be a very sensible means of allocating income." Do you agree? Explain.

7. How can time be incorporated into the theory of consumer behaviour? Foreigners frequently point out that Canadians are very wasteful of food and other material goods and very conscious of, and overly economical in, their use of time. Can you explain this observation?

8. Explain:

   a. "Before economic growth, there were too few goods; after growth, there is too little time."

   b. "It is irrational for an individual to take the time to be completely rational in economic decision-making."

9. In the last decade or so there has been a dramatic expansion of small retail convenience stores — such as Mac's Milk and Beckers — although their prices are generally much higher than those in the large supermarkets. Can you explain the success of the convenience stores?

10. *Advanced analysis.* Let $MU_a = z = 10 - x$ and $MU_b = z = 21 - 2y$, where z is marginal utility measured in utils, x is the amount spent on product A, and y is the amount spent on product B. Assume the consumer has $10 to spend on A and B; that is, $x + y = 10$. How is this $10 best allocated between A and B? How much utility will the marginal dollar yield?

Appendix to Chapter 7

INDIFFERENCE CURVE ANALYSIS

Another explanation of consumer behaviour and consumer equilibrium is based upon (1) budget lines and (2) indifference curves.

The Budget Line: What Is Attainable

*A budget line **shows various combinations of two products that can be purchased with a given money income**.* If the price of product A is $1.50 and the price of B $1.00, the consumer could purchase all of the combinations of A and B shown in Table A7-1 with $12 of money income. At one extreme the consumer might spend all of his or her income on 8 units of A and have nothing left to spend on B. Or, by giving up 2 units of A, the consumer could have 6 units of A and 3 of B. And so on to the other extreme, at which the consumer could buy 12 units of B at $1.00 each.

Figure A7-1 shows the budget line graphically. The slope of the budget line measures the ratio of the price of B to the price of A. The absolute value of the slope is $P_B/P_A = \$1.00/\$1.50 = 2/3$. This is the mathematical way of saying that the consumer must forgo 2 units of A (measured on the vertical axis) at $1.50 each to have $3 to spend on 3 units of B (measured on the horizontal axis). In moving down the budget

FIGURE A7-1   A consumer's budget line

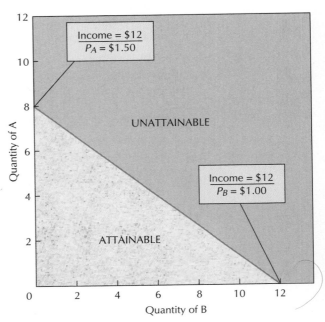

The budget line shows all of the various combinations of any two products that can be purchased, given the prices of the products and the consumer's money income.

line, 2 of A (at $1.50 each) must be given up to obtain 3 of B (at $1.00 each). This yields a slope of 2/3.

Two other characteristics of the budget line merit comment.

1 Income Changes   The location of the budget line varies with money income. An *increase* in money income will shift the budget line to the *right*; a *decrease* in money income will move it to the *left*. To verify, simply recalculate Table A7-1 on the assumption that money income is (a) $24 and (b) $6, and plot the new budget lines in Figure A7-1.

2 Price Changes   A change in product prices will also shift the budget line. A decline in the prices of

TABLE A7-1   The budget line: combinations of A and B obtainable with income of $12 (*hypothetical data*)

Units of A (Price = $1.50)	Units of B (Price = $1.00)	Total expenditures
8	0	$12 (= $12 + $0)
6	3	$12 (= $9 + $3)
4	6	$12 (= $6 + $6)
2	9	$12 (= $3 + $9)
0	12	$12 (= $0 + $12)

both products — the equivalent of a real income increase — will shift the curve to the right. You can verify this by recalculating Table A7-1 and replotting Figure A7-1 assuming that P_A = $0.75 and P_B = $0.50. Conversely, an increase in the prices of A and B will shift the curve to the left. Assume P_A = $3 and P_B = $2 and rework Table A7-1 and Figure A7-1 to substantiate this statement.

Note also what happens if we change P_B while holding P_A (and money income) constant. If we lower P_B from $1.00 to $0.50, the budget line will fan outward to the right. Conversely, by increasing P_B from $1.00 to $1.50, the line will fan inward to the left. In both instances, the line remains "anchored" at 8 units on the vertical axis because P_A has not changed.

Indifference Curves: What Is Preferred

Budget lines reflect "objective" market data involving income and prices. The budget line reveals the combinations of A and B that are obtainable, given money income and prices. Indifference curves, on the other hand, embody "subjective" information about consumer preferences for A and B. *An indifference curve shows all combinations of products A and B that will yield the same level of satisfaction or utility to the consumer.*

Table A7-2 and Figure A7-2 present a hypothetical indifference curve involving products A and B. The consumer's preferences are such that he or she will realize the same total utility from each combination of A and B shown in the table or curve. Thus, the consumer will be indifferent as to which combination is obtained.

It is essential to understand several characteristics of indifference curves.

1 Downsloping Indifference curves are downsloping because both product A and product B yield utility to the consumer. Moving from combination *j* to combination *k*, the consumer is obtaining more of

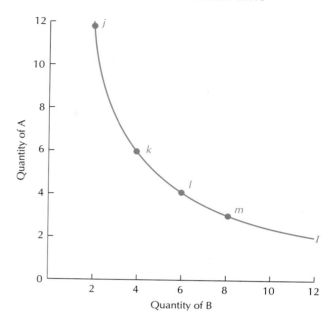

FIGURE A7-2 A consumer's indifference curve

Every point on an indifference curve represents some combination of products A and B that is equally satisfactory to the consumer; that is, each combination of A and B embodies the same level of total utility.

B and less of A but total utility remains the same. More of A necessitates less of B, so that the quantities of A and B are inversely related. Any curve that reflects inversely related variables is downsloping.

2 Convex to Origin Viewed from the origin, a downsloping curve can be concave (bowed outward) or convex (bowed inward). A concave curve has an increasing (steeper) slope as one moves down the curve, while a convex curve has a diminishing (flatter) slope as one moves down it.

We note in Figure A7-2 that *the indifference curve is convex viewed from the origin*. The slope diminishes or becomes flatter as we move down the curve. Technically, the slope of the indifference curve measures the **marginal rate of substitution (MRS)** because it shows the rate, at the margin, at which the consumer will substitute one good for the other (B for A) to remain equally satisfied. The diminishing slope of the indifference curve means the willingness to substitute B for A *diminishes* as one moves down the curve.

The rationale for this convexity, that is, for a diminishing MRS, is that a consumer's willingness to substitute B for A (or vice versa) will depend on the

TABLE A7-2 An indifference schedule (*hypothetical data*)

Combination	Units of A	Units of B
j	12	2
k	6	4
l	4	6
m	3	8

amounts of B and A he or she has to begin with. Consider Table A7-2 and Figure A7-2 once again, beginning at point *j*. Here, in relative terms, the consumer has a substantial amount of A and very little of B. This means that, "at the margin," B is very valuable (its marginal utility is high), while A is less valuable at the margin (its marginal utility is low). The consumer will be willing to give up a substantial amount of A to get a few more units of B. In this particular case the consumer is willing to forgo 6 units of A to get 2 more units of B. Thus the MRS is 6/2 or 3.

In general, as the amount of B *increases*, the marginal utility of additional units of B *decreases*. Similarly, as the quantity of A *decreases*, its marginal utility *increases*. In Figure A7-2 we see that in moving down the curve the consumer will be willing to give up smaller and smaller amounts of A to offset acquiring each additional unit of B. The result is a curve with a diminishing slope, one that is convex when viewed from the origin. The MRS declines as one moves southeast along the indifference curve.

3 Indifference Map   The single indifference curve of Figure A7-2 reflects some constant (but unspecified) level of total utility or satisfaction. It is possible — and useful for our analysis — to sketch a whole series of indifference curves, an **indifference map** as shown in Figure A7-3. Each curve reflects a different level of total utility. Each curve to the *right* of our original curve (labelled I_2 in Figure A7-3) reflects combinations of A and B that yield *more* utility than I_2. Each curve to the *left* of I_2 reflects *less* total utility than I_2. *As we move out from the origin each successive indifference curve entails a higher level of utility.* This can be demonstrated by drawing a line in a northeasterly direction from the origin. Note that its points of intersection with each successive curve entail larger amounts of *both* A and B, and therefore a higher level of total utility.

Equilibrium at Tangency

We can now determine the consumer's **equilibrium position** by combining the budget line and the indifference map, as shown in Figure A7-4. By definition, the budget line indicates all combinations of A and B that the consumer can attain, given his or her money income and the prices of A and B. Of these attainable combinations, the consumer will most prefer the combination that yields the greatest satisfaction or utility. *The utility-maximizing combination will be the one lying on the highest attainable indifference curve.* In terms of Figure A7-4, the consumer's utility-

FIGURE A7-3   An indifference map

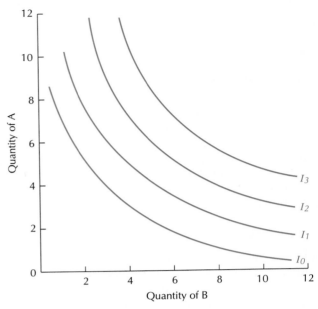

An indifference map is comprised of a set of indifference curves. Each successive curve further from the origin indicates a higher level of total utility. That is, any combination of products A and B shown by a point on I_3 is superior to any combination of A and B shown by a point on I_2, I_1, or I_0.

maximizing or equilibrium combination of A and B is at point *x*, where the budget line is *tangent* to I_2.

But why not point *y*? Because *y* is on a lower indifference curve, I_1. By trading "down" the budget line — by shifting dollars from purchases of A to purchases of B — the consumer can get on an indifference curve further from the origin and thereby increase total utility from the same income.

How about point *w* on indifference curve I_3? While it is true that *w* entails a higher level of total utility than does *x*, point *w* is beyond (outside of) the budget line and hence *not* attainable to the consumer.

Point *x* is the best or optimum *attainable* combination of products A and B. At this point, by definition of tangency, we note that the slope of the highest obtainable indifference curve equals the slope of the budget line. Because the slope of the indifference curve reflects the MRS and the slope of the budget line is P_B/P_A, the optimum or equilibrium position is where

$$\text{MRS} = P_B/P_A$$

FIGURE A7-4   The consumer's equilibrium position

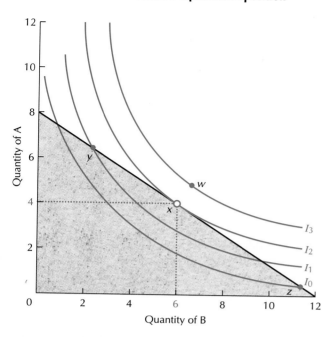

The consumer's equilibrium position is at point *x*, where the budget line is tangent to the highest attainable indifference curve, I_2. In this case, the consumer will buy 4 units of A at $1.50 per unit and 6 of B at $1 per unit with a $12 money income. Points *z* and *y* also represent attainable combinations of A and B, but yield less total utility, as is evidenced by the fact that they are on lower indifference curves. While *w* would entail more utility than *x*, it is outside of the budget line and therefore unattainable.

Digression: The Measurement of Utility

There is an important difference between the marginal utility theory and the indifference curve theory of consumer demand. The marginal utility theory assumes the utility is *numerically* measurable. The consumer is assumed to be able to say *how much* extra utility he or she derives from an extra unit of A or B. Given the prices of A and B, the consumer must be able to measure the marginal utility derived from successive units of A and B in order to realize the utility-maximizing (equilibrium) position, as previously indicated by

$$\frac{\text{Marginal utility of A}}{\text{Price of A}} = \frac{\text{Marginal utility of B}}{\text{Price of B}}$$

The indifference curve approach poses a less stringent requirement for the consumer: he or she need only be able to specify whether a given combination

of A and B yields more, less, or the same amount of utility than some other combinations of A and B. The consumer need only say, for example, that 6 of A and 7 of B yield more (or less) satisfaction than 4 of A and 9 of B. Indifference curve analysis does *not* require the consumer to specify *how much* more (or less) satisfaction will be realized.

When the equilibrium situations in the two approaches are compared we find that (1) in the indifference curve analysis the MRS equals P_B/P_A; (2) in the marginal utility approach the ratio of marginal utilities also equals P_B/P_A. We therefore deduce that the MRS is equivalent in the marginal utility approach to the ratio of marginal utilities of the two goods.[1]

Deriving the Demand Curve

Earlier we noted that given the price of A, an increase in the price of B will cause the budget line to fan inward to the left. This can now be used to derive a demand curve for product B. In Figure A7-5(a) we have simply reproduced Figure A7-4, showing our initial consumer equilibrium at point *x*. The budget line involved in determining this equilibrium position assumes that the money income is $12 and that $P_A = \$1.50$ and $P_B = \$1.00$. Let us examine what happens to the equilibrium position if we increase P_B to $1.50, holding money income and the price of A constant.

The result is shown in Figure A7-5(a). The budget line fans to the left, yielding a new equilibrium point of tangency with indifference curve I_1 at point *x'*. At *x'*, the consumer is buying 3 units of B and 5 of A (compared to 4 of A and 6 of B at *x*). We now have sufficient information to locate the demand curve for product B. We know that, at equilibrium point *x*, the price of B is $1.00 and 6 units are purchased; at equilibrium point *x'*, the price of B is $1.50 and 3 units are purchased.

These data are shown graphically as a demand curve for B in Figure A7-5(a). Note that the horizontal axes of Figures A7-5(a) and A7-5(b) are identical; both measure the quantity demanded of B. Hence, we can drop dashed perpendiculars from Figure A7-5(a) down to the horizontal axis of Figure A7-5(b). On the vertical axis of Figure A7-5(b), we locate the two chosen prices of B. Connecting these prices with

---

[1] If we begin with the utility-maximizing rule, $MU_A/P_A = MU_B/P_B$, then multiply through by P_B and divide through by MU_A, we obtain $P_B/P_A = MU_B/MU_A$. In indifference curve analysis we know that the optimum or equilibrium position is where MRS $= P_B/P_A$. Hence, MRS also equals MU_B/MU_A.

FIGURE A7-5   Deriving the demand curve

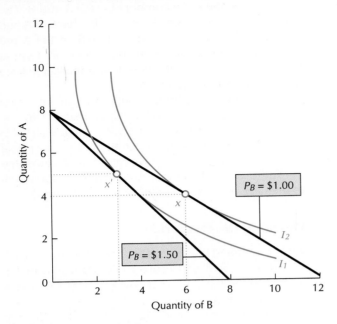

(a) Two equilibrium positions

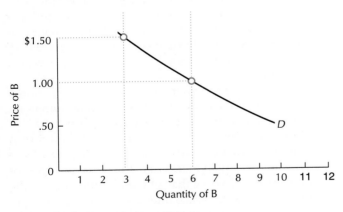

(b) The demand curve for product B

When the price of B is increased from $1.00 to $1.50 in (a), the equilibrium position moves from *x* to *x'*, decreasing the quantity demanded from 6 to 3 units. The demand curve for B is determined in (b) by plotting the $1.00–6 units and the $1.50–3 units price–quantity combinations for B.

the relevant quantities demanded, we locate two points on the demand curve for B.

By simple manipulation of the price of B in an indifference curve-budget line context, a down-sloping demand curve for B can be derived. We have derived the law of demand under the correct assumption of "other things being equal" since *only* the price of B has been changed. The price of A as well as the consumer's income and tastes have remained constant when deriving the consumer's demand curve for product B.

APPENDIX SUMMARY

1. The indifference curve approach to consumer behaviour is based upon the consumer's budget line and indifference curves.

2. The budget line shows all combinations of two products the consumer can purchase, given money income and product prices.

3. A change in product prices or money income will shift the budget line.

4. An indifference curve shows all combinations of two products that will yield the same level of total utility to the consumer. Indifference curves are downsloping and convex to the origin.

5. An indifference map consists of a number of indifference curves; the further from the origin, the higher the level of utility associated with each curve.

6. The consumer will select that point on the budget line that puts him or her on the highest attainable indifference curve.

7. Changing the price of one product shifts the budget line and determines a new equilibrium position. A downsloping demand curve can be determined by plotting the price–quantity combinations associated with the old and new equilibrium positions.

TERMS AND CONCEPTS

budget line (p. 106)
equilibrium position (p. 108)
indifference curve (p. 107)
indifference map (p. 108)
marginal rate of substitution (p. 107)

APPENDIX QUESTIONS AND STUDY SUGGESTIONS

1. What information is embodied in a budget line? What shifts will occur in the budget line as money income *a.* increases, and *b.* decreases? What shifts will occur in the budget line as the product price shown on the horizontal axis *a.* increases and *b.* decreases?

2. What information is contained in an indifference curve? Why are such curves *a.* downsloping and *b.* convex to the origin? Why does total utility increase as the consumer moves to indifference curves further from the origin? Why can't indifference curves intersect?

3. Using Figure A7-4, explain why the point of *tangency* of the budget line with an indifference curve is the consumer's equilibrium position. Explain why any point where the budget line *intersects* an indifference curve will *not* be equilibrium. Explain: "The consumer is in equilibrium where MRS $= P_B/P_A$."

4. Assume that the data in the accompanying table is an indifference curve for Ms. Chen. Graph this curve, putting A on the vertical and B on the horizontal axis. Assuming the prices of A and B are $1.50 and $1.00 respectively and that Ms. Chen has $24 to spend, add the resulting budget line to your graph. What combination of A and B will Ms. Chen purchase? Does your answer meet the MRS $= P_B/P_A$ rule for equilibrium?

Units of A	Units of B
16	6
12	8
8	12
4	24

5. Explain graphically how indifference curve analysis can be used to derive a demand curve.

6. *Advanced analysis.* Demonstrate that the equilibrium condition MRS $= P_B/P_A$ is the equivalent of the utility-maximizing rule $MU_A/P_A = MU_B/P_B$.

8

The Organization of Production

If you pick up the business section of any newspaper, you will read about the various types of firms that exist in a market economy — corporations, partnerships, sole proprietorships — and the continuous changes that they undergo due to takeovers or reorganization. In a healthy market economy such changes are to be expected as some sectors expand and others contract.

In Chapter 7 we analysed how households make decisions regarding what they consume. In the next several chapters we focus our attention on how firms make decisions. Before we do that, we need to know how firms are organized. This chapter sets out the different forms of business organization and the strengths and weaknesses of each. The second part of this chapter looks at industrial organization in Canada.

THE NEED FOR FIRMS

Businesses, or firms, constitute one of the two major aggregates of the private sector, the other being the household — or consumption — sector.

As will be discussed shortly, there are many ways to organize a firm. But why is there a need for the firm in a market economy? Could we not have people working in their own homes? While this could be possible, it would greatly decrease the efficiency of an economy. Production and distribution could be much more efficiently carried out at a centralized location. The task of organizing production and distribution at a centralized location would be easier and less costly.

The Main Goal of the Firm

It cannot be emphasized enough that the main goal of a firm is to maximize profits. (More details about the nature of profits will be investigated in the next chapter.) The firm may have many objectives — behaving in a socially responsible manner, giving to charities, offering scholarships, etc. — but the over-riding goal is to maximize profit.

THE BUSINESS SECTOR

Plants, Firms, and Industries

To avoid any possible confusion, we preface our discussion of sector with some comments concerning terminology: we must distinguish between a plant, a firm, and an industry.

1. A **plant** is a physical establishment, in the form of a factory, farm, mine, retail or wholesale store, or warehouse, that performs one or more specific functions in the fabrication and distribution of goods and services.

2. A business **firm** is the organization that owns and operates these plants. Although most firms operate only one plant, many firms own and operate many plants. Multi-plant firms may be "horizontal," "vertical," or "conglomerate" combinations.

Both of the large steel firms of our economy — Dominion Foundries and Steel (Dofasco) and the Steel Company of Canada (Stelco) — are **vertical combinations** of plants. Both firms own plants at various stages of the production process. Each steelmaker owns ore and coal mines, limestone quarries, coke ovens, blast furnaces, rolling mills, forge shops, foundries, and, in some cases, fabricating shops.

The large chain stores in the retail field — Eaton's, the Bay, Loblaws — are **horizontal combinations**: each plant is at the same stage of production.

Other firms are **conglomerates**: they comprise plants that operate across many different markets and industries. For example, Canadian Pacific, apart from the railway, is involved through subsidiaries in such diverse fields as aviation, trucking, hotels, real estate, mining, shipping, and telecommunications.

3. An **industry** is a group of firms producing the same, or at least similar, products. Though an apparently uncomplicated concept, industries are usually difficult to identify in practice. For example, how are we to identify the automobile industry? And what about trucks? Certainly, small pick-up trucks are similar in some respects to station wagons. Is it better to speak of the "motor-vehicle industry" rather than of the automobile industry?

Delineating an industry becomes more difficult when it is recognized that most enterprises are multi-product firms. The Canadian subsidiaries of the American automobile manufacturers also produce such diverse products as diesel-electric locomotives, transit coaches, off-highway haulers, front-end loaders, earth-moving equipment, buses, pleasurecraft motors, and boats. Thus, industry classifications are rarely clearcut and are always somewhat arbitrary.

LEGAL FORMS OF BUSINESS ENTERPRISES

The business population is extremely diverse, ranging from giant corporations like Bell Canada Enterprises, Inc. to neighbourhood speciality shops and "mom and pop" groceries with one or two employees. This diversity makes it desirable to classify business firms by some criterion such as legal structure, industry, or size.

The present emphasis, however, is on the basic legal forms of businesses: (1) the sole proprietorship, (2) the partnership, and (3) the corporation. Let's define and outline the advantages and disadvantages associated with each.

Sole Proprietorship

A **sole proprietorship** is an individual in business for himself or herself. The proprietor owns or obtains the materials and capital equipment needed by the business and personally runs it.

Advantages This simple type of business organization has certain advantages:

1. A sole proprietorship is easy to organize.

2. The proprietor is his or her own boss and has very substantial freedom of action. Since the proprietor's profit income depends on the enterprise's success, there is a strong incentive to manage the business affairs efficiently.

Disadvantages But the disadvantages of this form of business organization are great.

1. With rare exceptions, the financial resources of a sole proprietorship are insufficient to permit the firm to grow into a large-scale enterprise. Finances are usually limited to what the proprietor has in his or her bank account and to what he or she is able to borrow. Since proprietorships often fail, banks are not eager to extend much — or often, any — credit to them.

2. Complete control of an enterprise forces the proprietor to carry out all basic management functions. A proprietor must make all basic decisions concerning, for example, buying, selling, the acquisition and hiring and training of personnel, and producing, advertising, and distributing the product. Thus, the potential benefits of specialization in business management are usually inaccessible to the typical small-scale proprietorship.

3. Most important of all, the proprietor is subject to **unlimited liability**. This means that individuals in business for themselves risk not only the assets of their firm but also their personal assets. If the assets of an unsuccessful proprietorship are insufficient to satisfy the claims of creditors, those creditors can file claims against the proprietor's personal property.

Partnership

The **partnership** is more or less a natural outgrowth of the sole proprietorship. Partnerships were developed to overcome some of the major shortcomings of proprietorships. A partnership is a form of business organization in which two or more individuals agree to own and operate a business. Usually they pool their financial resources and their business expertise. They also share the risks and the profits or losses that may accrue to them.

Advantages The advantages of a partnership arrangement are:

1. It is easy to organize. Although a written agreement is almost invariably involved, legal red tape is not great.

2. Greater specialization in management is possible because there are more participants.

3. Financial resources of a partnership will be less limited than those of a sole proprietorship. Partners can pool their money capital, and they are usually better risks in the eyes of bankers.

Disadvantages The partnership raises some new potential problems the sole proprietorship does not.

1. Whenever there are several people participating in management, this division of authority can lead to inconsistent, divided policies or to inaction when action is required. Worse, partners may flatly disagree on basic policy. For all these reasons, management in a partnership may be unwieldy and cumbersome.

2. The finances of partnerships are still limited, although generally superior to those of a sole proprietorship. The financial resources of partners may be insufficient, and severely restrict the potential growth of a successful enterprise.

3. The continuity of a partnership is very precarious. The withdrawal or death of a partner often means the dissolution and complete reorganization of the firm, potentially disrupting its operations.

4. Finally, unlimited liability plagues a partnership, just as it does a proprietorship. In fact, each partner is liable for all business debts incurred, not only as a result of his or her own management decisions, but also as a consequence of the actions of any other partner. A wealthy partner risks money on the prudence of less affluent partners.

Corporation

Corporations are legal entities, distinct and separate from the individuals who own them. As such, these governmentally designated "legal persons" can acquire resources, own assets, produce and sell products, incur debts, extend credit, sue and be sued, and carry on all those functions any other type of enterprise performs.

Advantages The advantages of the corporate form of business enterprise have brought this type of firm into a dominant position in the modern market economy. Although corporations are relatively small in number, they are frequently large in size and scale of operations. In fact, they account for over 70% of the output of all private businesses.

1. The corporation is by far the most effective form of business organization for raising money capital. The corporation sells stocks and bonds, thus allowing the firm to tap the savings of untold thousands of households. Through the securities market (stock and bond market), corporations can pool the financial resources of extremely large numbers of people. Financing by the sale of securities also has advantages from the viewpoint of purchasers of these securities.

First, households can now participate in enterprise and share the expected monetary reward without having to assume an active part in management. In addition, an individual can spread risk by buying the securities of a variety of corporations. Finally, it is usually easy for the holder of corporate securities to dispose of them. Organized stock exchanges facilitate the transfer of securities among buyers and sellers. This increases the willingness of savers to buy corporate securities. Furthermore, corporations ordinarily have easier access to bank credit than do other types of business organizations. Corporations are better risks and are more likely to provide banks with profitable accounts.

2. Corporations have the distinct advantage of **limited liability**. The owners (stockholders) of a corporation risk *only* what they paid for the stock purchased. Their personal assets are not at stake if the corporation becomes bankrupt. Creditors can sue the corporation as a legal person, but not the owners of that corporation as individuals. Limited liability clearly eases the corporation's task in acquiring money capital.

3. Because of their advantage in attracting money capital, successful corporations find it easier to expand the size and scope of their operations and to realize associated advantages. In particular, corporations may be able to take advantage of mass-production technologies. Similarly, size permits greater specialization in the use of resources, particularly labour. While a sole proprietor may be forced to share time between production, accounting, and marketing functions, a larger corporation can hire specialized personnel in each of these areas and achieve greater efficiency.

4. As a legal entity, the corporation has a life independent of its owners and, for that matter, of its individual officials. Proprietorships are subject to sudden and unpredictable demise but, legally at least, corporations are immortal. The transfer of corporate ownership through the sale of stock will not disrupt the continuity of the corporation. In short, corporations have a certain permanence, lacking in other forms of business organizations, that is conducive to long-range planning and growth.

5. Incorporation yields a tax advantage to an enterprise. The federal corporate tax rate facing a corporation is presently 28%, compared to a maximum 29% rate of the federal personal income tax. Provinces

also levy a corporate tax, but their marginal tax rates are generally higher.[1]

Disadvantages   The corporation's advantages are of tremendous significance, yet the drawbacks of the corporate form of organization merit mentioning.

1. Red tape and legal expenses are involved in obtaining a corporate charter.

2. From the social point of view, it must be noted that the corporate form of enterprise lends itself to certain abuses. Because the corporation is a legal entity, unscrupulous business owners sometimes can avoid personal responsibility for questionable business activities by adopting the corporate form of enterprise. And despite legislation to the contrary, the corporate form of organization often facilitates the issue and sale of worthless securities. Note, however, that these are potential abuses of the corporate form, not inherent defects.

3. A further possible disadvantage of corporations has to do with the **double taxation** of corporate income. That part of corporate income that is paid out as dividends to stockholders is taxed twice — once as a part of corporation profits and again as a part of the stockholders' personal incomes.[2] This disadvantage must be weighed against the previously noted fact that the maximum tax rates on corporate enterprises are less than those that may apply to unincorporated firms.

4. In the sole proprietorship and partnership forms, those who own the real and financial assets of the firm also directly manage or control those assets. Most observers agree that this is as it should be. But in larger corporations where the ownership of common stock is widely diffused over tens or hundreds of thousands of stockholders, a fundamental **separation of ownership and control** will arise. Most stockholders do not exercise their voting rights or, if they do, merely sign these rights over by proxy to the corporation's present officers. And why not? Average stockholders know little or nothing about the efficiency with which their corporation is being managed. Because the typical stockholder may own only one thousand of fifteen million shares of common stock outstanding, his or her vote "really doesn't make a bit of difference"! Not voting, or the automatic signing over of one's proxy to current corpo-

---

[1] The maximum varies by province.
[2] However, a "dividend tax credit" of 13⅓% of the taxable amount of dividends from taxable Canadian corporations reduces this double taxation.

Box 8-1

THE FINANCING OF CORPORATE ACTIVITY

One of the main advantages of corporations is their ability to finance their operations through the sale of stocks and bonds. It is informative to examine the nature of corporate finance in more detail.

Generally speaking, corporations finance their activities in three different ways. First, a very large proportion of a corporation's activity is financed internally out of undistributed corporate profits. Second, like individuals or unincorporated businesses, corporations may borrow from financial institutions. For example, a small corporation that wants to build a new plant or warehouse may obtain the funds from a chartered bank, a trust company, or an insurance company. Also, unique to corporations, common stocks and bonds can be issued.

A common stock is an ownership share. The purchaser of a stock certificate has the right to vote in the selection of corporate officers and to share in any declared dividends. If you own 1000 of the 100,000 shares issued by Specific Motors, Inc. (hereafter SM), then you own 1% of the company, are entitled to 1% of any dividends declared by the board of directors, and control 1% of the votes in the annual election of corporate officials. In contrast, a bond is not an ownership share. A bond purchaser is simply lending money to a corporation. A bond is merely an IOU, in acknowledgement of a loan, whereby the corporation promises to pay the holder a fixed amount at some specified future date and other fixed amounts (interest payments) every year up to the bond's maturity date. For example, one might purchase a ten-year SM bond with a face value of $1000 with a 10% stated rate of interest. This means that in exchange for your $1000 SM guarantees you a $100 interest payment for each of the next ten years and then to repay your $1000 principal at the end of that period.

There are clearly important differences between stocks and bonds. First, as noted, the bondholder is not an owner of the company, but is only a lender. Second, bonds are considered to be less risky than stocks for two reasons. On the one hand, bondholders have a "legally prior claim" on a corporation's earnings. Dividends cannot be paid to stockholders until all interest payments due to bondholders have been paid. Moreover, holders of SM stock do not know how much their dividends will be or how much they might obtain for their stock if they decide to sell. If Specific Motors falls upon hard times, stockholders may receive no dividends at all and the value of their stock may plummet. Provided the corporation does not go bankrupt, the holder of an SM bond is guaranteed a $100 interest payment each year and the return of his or her $1000 at the end of ten years.

But this is not to imply that the purchase of corporate bonds is riskless. The market value of your SM bond may vary over time in accordance with the financial health of the corporation. If SM encounters economic misfortunes that raise questions about its financial integrity, the market value of your bond may fall. Should you sell the bond prior to maturity you may receive only $600 or $700 for it (rather than $1000) and thereby incur a capital loss.

Changes in interest rates also affect the market prices of bonds. Specifically, increases in interest rates cause bond prices to fall and vice versa. Assume you purchase a $1000 ten-year SM bond this year (1993) when the going interest rate is 10%. This means that your bond provides a $100 fixed interest payment each year. But now suppose that by next year the interest rate has jumped to 15% and SM must now guarantee a $150 fixed annual payment on its new 1994 $1000 ten-year bonds. Clearly, no sensible person will pay you $1000 for your bond that pays only $100 of interest income per year when new bonds can be purchased for $1000 that pay the holder $150 per year. Hence, if you sell your 1993 bond before maturity, you will suffer a capital loss.

Bondholders face another element of risk due to inflation. If substantial inflation occurs over the ten-year period you hold a SM bond, the $100 principal repaid to you at the end of that period will represent substantially less purchasing power than the $1000 you loaned to SM ten years earlier. You will have lent "dear" dollars, but will be repaid in "cheap" dollars.

"In the unlikely event of bankruptcy, a leveraged buy out, or other chaos from deregulation, bus tickets will automatically drop from the overhead compartment."

rate officials, has the effect of making those officials self-perpetuating.

The separation of ownership and control is of no fundamental consequence so long as the action of the control (management) group and the wishes of the ownership (stockholder) group are in accord. The catch lies in the fact that the interests of the two groups are not always identical. For example, management, seeking the power and prestige that goes along with control of a *large* enterprise, may favour unprofitable expansion of the firm's operations. Or a conflict of interest can easily develop with respect to current dividend policies. What portion of corporate earnings after taxes should be paid out as dividends, and what amount should be retained by the firm as undistributed profits? More obviously, corporation officials may vote themselves large salaries, pensions, and bonuses out of corporate earnings that might otherwise be used for increased dividend payments. In short, the separation of ownership and control raises important and intriguing questions about the distribution of power and authority, the accountability of corporate managers, and the possibility of conflicts between managers and shareholders.

Incorporate or Not?

What determines whether or not a firm incorporates? As our discussion of the corporate form implies, the need for money capital is a critical determinant. The money capital required to establish and operate a barber shop, a shoeshine stand, or a small gift shop is modest, making incorporation unnecessary. In contrast, modern technology makes incorporation imperative in many lines of production. For example, in most branches of manufacturing — automobiles, steel, fabricated metal products, electrical equipment, household appliances, and so forth — very substantial money requirements for investment in fixed assets and for working capital are involved. Given these circumstances, there is no choice but to incorporate.

QUICK REVIEW (8-1)

1. **Business firms are either sole proprietorships, partnerships, or corporations.**

2. **Although relatively small in number, corporations dominate our economy because of their superior ability to raise money capital.**

THE STRUCTURE OF THE CANADIAN ECONOMY AND ITS EVOLUTION OVER TIME

Table 8-1 sets out the contribution to domestic output (GDP) by each sector and industry. The major sectors of any economy are: **primary, secondary**, and **tertiary** (which is more commonly referred to as the service sector). Table 8-1 also breaks each sector into sub-sectors or industries.

The service sector has come to dominate in terms of its contributing share to domestic output, followed by the secondary sector in which manufacturing dominates. The primary sector has experienced an

TABLE 8-1   Production shares by sector, selected years 1870–1986

	% of Gross Domestic Product at Factor Cost						
	1870	1911	1926	1960	1970	1980	1986
PRIMARY	46.2	39.4	23.4	10.4	8.3	11.2	10.0
Agriculture	34.3	30.8	18.1	4.9	3.3	3.3	3.3
Forestry	9.9	4.6	1.3	1.3	0.8	0.9	0.7
Fishing and trapping	1.1	1.5	0.8	0.2	0.2	0.2	0.2
Mining, quarrying, oil wells	0.9	2.5	3.2	4.0	4.0	6.8	5.8
SECONDARY	22.6	29.7	38.7	44.8	41.4	38.3	36.7
Manufacturing	na	18.8	21.7	26.4	23.3	20.6	19.5
Construction	na	10.3	4.1	6.0	6.3	5.9	7.0
Transportation and communication	na	na	} 12.9	9.6	8.9	8.3	7.3
Electric power, gas, and water utilities	na	0.6		2.8	2.9	3.5	2.9
TERTIARY	31.2[a]	30.8[a]	37.9	44.8	50.2	50.5	53.3
Trade (wholesale, retail)	na	na	11.6	12.8	12.4	11.0	11.7
Finance, insurance, real estate	na	na	10.0	11.6	11.3	11.3	14.1
Public administration, defence	na	na	3.4	6.9	7.3	7.4	7.2
Service	na	na	12.9	13.5	19.2	20.8	20.3
Total	100.0	100.0	100.0	100.0	100.0	100.0	100.0

[a]Includes income generated by the railway and telephone industries.

Source: C. Green, *Canadian Industrial Organization and Policy* (Toronto: McGraw-Hill Ryerson Ltd., 1990), p. 4.

almost continuous decline in terms of GDP share over the last century.

Table 8-2, which shows employment shares by each sector and industry in broad terms, reflects contribution to domestic output. For example, agriculture's employment share fell from about a quarter of the workforce in 1947 to a mere 4% in 1987. Manufacturing has also experienced a decline in employment share, but a much less steep decline. The service sector, on the other hand, has almost doubled its employment share of the economy.

We noted in Chapter 3 that industries expand and contract on their profitability. Within the context of this chapter, you must keep in mind that the intersectoral shifts are due to a number of factors, of which technological improvements and accompanying productivity increases are dominant. For example, while there has been a continuous decline in agriculture's employment share, it has come about because of large labour (and land) productivity improvements. While this may at first seem odd, a large labour productivity improvement means that you now need fewer people in that sector, unless there is an accompanying increase in the demand for foodstuffs. Since there is a limit to our capacity to increase our food intake, the excess labour had to find work elsewhere. Throughout the 19th and early 20th century excess agricultural workers found jobs in the secondary sector, primarily in manufacturing.

Since about the time of the Second World War the secondary sector has been contracting in terms of employment share as productivity in that sector rose. Manufacturing in particular has seen a significant drop in its employment share. However, note in Table 8-1 that manufacturing's GDP share has dropped somewhat from a high of 26% in 1960, but it remained at about a fifth of domestic output in 1986.

Note that while it is true that natural resources are important to Canada's economy, the output and

TABLE 8-2　Employment shares (%) by economic sector and industry

	1891[a]	1921[a]	1947	1960	1970	1975	1980	1987
PRIMARY	49	36	27.5	14.3	9.3	7.8	7.3	6.4
Agriculture			24.1	11.3	6.5	5.2	4.5	4.0
Forestry			1.2	1.1	0.9	0.9	0.7	0.6
Fishing and trapping			0.7	0.4	0.3	0.3	0.3	0.3
Mining, quarrying, oil wells			1.5	1.5	1.6	1.4	1.8	1.5
SECONDARY	31	34	40.3	40.7	37.5	37.3	34.0	30.4
Manufacturing			26.7	24.9	22.7	22.1	19.7	17.1
Construction			5.2	7.2	6.0	6.5	5.8	5.7
Transportation and communication			7.7	7.5	7.7	7.6	7.3	6.6
Public utilities			0.7	1.1	1.1	1.1	1.2	1.0
TERTIARY	20	30	32.1	45.0	53.2	54.9	58.7	63.2
Trade (wholesale, retail)			12.3	16.2	16.7	17.2	17.2	17.7
Finance, insurance, real estate			2.7	3.8	4.6	4.9	5.7	5.8
Community, business, personal services (including health, education)			17.1	25.0	25.7	26.1	28.9	32.9
Public administration					6.2	6.7	6.9	6.8
Total	100.0	100.0	100.0	100.0	100.0	100.0	100.0	100.0

[a] Based on occupational data in which all clerical workers are allocated to the tertiary sector and all nonprimary sector labourers are allocated to the secondary sector.
Source: Green, *op. cit.,* p. 6.

TABLE 8-3　Foreign ownership and control of Canadian industry

Industrial division	Percentage of capital employed	
	Foreign-owned in 1987	Foreign-controlled in 1991
Manufacturing	48%	56%
Petroleum and natural gas	35	41
Mining and smelting	40	36
Railways	40	0
Other utilities	27	2
Total of above specified industries, merchandising and construction	31%	26%

Source: Statistics Canada, Canada's International Investment Position, 1991 (Ottawa, March 1992).

employment share of the primary sector continues to fall. Only the mining, quarrying, and oil wells category has maintained a steady employment share, but a decreasing GDP share.

There is good evidence to suggest that some Canadian industries are highly concentrated in terms of market power. More will be said about this topic in Chapter 13. For now it will suffice to say that compared with the U.S. economy, many of our industries are dominated by a few firms that control a significant percentage of the market.

Foreign Ownership

Another distinguishing characteristic of our economy is that a high percentage is foreign owned, particularly by Americans. Table 8-3 shows the extent of **foreign ownership** in a number of industries. The term "foreign owned" generally connotes outright ownership of a firm or at least owning 51% of the stocks, which means control of a firm.

Foreign ownership has costs and benefits. These have been extensively debated. Given the difficulties of measuring costs and benefits, it is not surprising that the issue of foreign ownership often arouses the strongest of emotions. Perhaps the most serious accusation against foreign ownership is that it jeopardizes Canada's political autonomy. However, such an accusation is difficult to prove or disprove.

There are various explanations of the high incidence of foreign direct investment in Canada. Some attribute it to the relatively high Canadian tariffs instituted in 1879 with the formation of the National Policy. Since foreign firms, particularly American firms, couldn't compete by exporting here, they decided to establish production facilities. Our patent laws in the past, which allowed no protection to their foreign owner, also helped to stimulate foreign ownership as firms not wishing to have their technologies imitated quickly established themselves in Canada. The fact that our country shares a border with the U.S. also has stimulated foreign ownership, as firms often viewed Canada as an extension of their American domestic market.

All these explanations have some merit. However, all that can be said with certainty is that if firms decided to establish productive capacities in Canada, it must have been because it was the most profitable alternative.

CHAPTER SUMMARY

1. The firm is the most efficient form of organizing production and distribution. The main goal of a firm is to maximize profit.

2. Sole proprietorships, partnerships, and corporations are the major legal forms that business enterprises may assume. Though proprietorships dominate numerically, the bulk of total output is produced by corporations. Corporations have grown to their position of dominance in the business sector primarily because they are *a.* characterized by limited liability and *b.* in a superior position to acquire money capital for expansion.

3. In terms of both employment share and contribution to domestic production, the service sector dominates in the Canadian economy.

4. Compared to the U.S. economy, many of our industries are highly concentrated; a relatively few firms represent a high percentage of output and sales. A high proportion of our industries are foreign owned.

TERMS AND CONCEPTS

conglomerates (p. 114)
corporation (p. 115)
double taxation (p. 116)

firm (p. 114)
foreign ownership (p. 120)
horizontal and vertical combinations (p. 114)

industry (p. 114)
limited liability (p. 116)
partnership (p. 115)
plant (p. 114)
primary sector (p. 118)

secondary sector (p. 118)
separation of ownership and control (p. 116)
sole proprietorship (p. 114)
tertiary sector (p. 118)
unlimited liability (p. 115)

Questions and study suggestions

1. Why are firms necessary?

2. Distinguish clearly between a plant, a firm, and an industry. Why is an industry often difficult to define in practice?

3. What are the major legal forms of business organization? Briefly state the advantages and disadvantages of each. How do you account for the dominant role of corporations in our economy? Explain and evaluate the separation of ownership and control that characterizes the corporate form of business enterprise. What are the major industries in the Canadian economy in terms of the percentage contribution to production?

4. Distinguish between the primary, secondary, and tertiary sectors.

5. Give one explanation of why some sectors have expanded over the last century while others have contracted. Be sure to include in your discussion the case of agriculture, manufacturing, and the service sector.

6. Give some explanation as to why so many Canadian industries are foreign owned.

CHAPTER 9

The Costs of Production

Product prices are determined by the interaction of demand and supply. In preceding chapters we focused our attention on factors underlying demand. As observed in Chapter 4, the basic factor underlying the ability and willingness of firms to supply a product or service in the market is the cost of production. Production of a good requires economic resources that, because of their relative scarcity, have a price. The amount of any product a firm is willing to supply depends on the prices (costs), the productivity of the resources needed to produce it, and the price the product will bring on the market.

This chapter is concerned with the general nature of production costs. Product prices are introduced in the following four chapters, and supply decisions of producers are then explained.

ECONOMIC COSTS

Costs exist because resources are scarce and have alternative uses. To use a bundle of resources in producing some particular good means that certain alternative production opportunities have been forgone. ***Costs deal with forgoing the opportunity to produce alternative goods and services.*** The **opportunity cost** of any resource in producing a good is its value in its best alternative use.

This concept of costs is embodied in the production possibilities curve of Chapter 2. Note, for example, that at point *C* in Table 2-1 the opportunity cost of producing 100,000 *more* pizzas is the 3,000 industrial robots that must be forgone. If an assembly-line worker can produce automobiles or washing machines, then the cost to society in employing that worker in an automobile plant is the contribution the worker could have made in producing washing machines. The cost to you in reading this chapter is the alternative uses of your time — studying for a biology exam or going to a movie — that you must forgo.

Explicit and Implicit Costs

Consider costs from the viewpoint of an individual firm. Given the notion of opportunity costs, we can say that ***economic costs are payments a firm must make to resource suppliers to attract these resources away from alternative production opportunities***. These payments may be either explicit or implicit.

The monetary payments — the out-of-pocket or cash expenditures a firm makes to those "outsiders" who supply labour services, materials, fuel, transportation services, and power — are called **explicit costs**.

But, in addition, a firm may use certain resources the firm itself owns. Our concept of opportunity costs tells us that regardless of whether a resource is owned or hired by an enterprise, there is a cost involved in using that resource in a specific employment. The costs of such self-owned, self-employed resources are **implicit costs** — the money payments the self-employed resources could have earned in their best alternative uses. The best alternative uses refer to those that have the highest money payments.

Example: Suppose Jones operates a corner grocery as a sole proprietor. She owns the store building outright and supplies all her own labour and money capital. Though her enterprise has no explicit rental or wage costs, implicit costs are incurred. By using her own building for a grocery, Jones sacrifices the $1,000 monthly rental income she could have earned by renting it to someone else. Similarly, by using her money capital and labour in her own enterprise, Jones sacrifices the interest and wage incomes she could have earned by supplying these resources in their best alternative uses.

Normal Profits as a Cost

The minimum payment required to keep Jones's entrepreneurial talents engaged in this enterprise is called a **normal profit**. As is true of implicit rent or implicit wages, the normal return for performing entrepreneurial functions is an implicit cost. If this minimum, or normal, return is not realized, the entrepreneur will withdraw his or her efforts from this line of production and reallocate them to a more profitable line of production. Or the individual may cease being an entrepreneur in favour of becoming a wage or salary earner.

The economist includes as costs all payments — explicit and implicit, the latter including a normal profit — required to attract and retain resources in a given line of production.

Economic Profits

Economists and accountants use the term "profits" differently. *Accounting profits are the firm's total revenue less its explicit costs.* But to economists, **economic profits** *are total revenue less all costs (explicit and implicit, the latter including a normal profit to the entrepreneur)*. Therefore, when an economist says that a firm is just covering its costs, it is meant that all explicit and implicit costs are being met and that the entrepreneur is receiving a return just large enough to retain his or her talents in the present line of production.

If a firm's total receipts exceed all its economic costs, any residual accrues to the entrepreneur. This residual is called ***economic profit***:

$$\text{Economic profits} = \text{total revenue} \\ - \text{opportunity cost of} \\ \text{all inputs}$$

An economic profit is a return in excess of the normal profit required to retain the entrepreneur in this particular line of production.

Figure 9-1 shows the relationships between various cost and profit concepts and merits close examination. You should also consider question 2 at the end of this chapter.

FIGURE 9-1   Economic and accounting profits

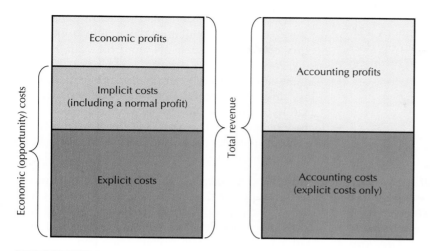

Economic profits are equal to total revenue less opportunity costs. Economic or opportunity costs are the sum of explicit and implicit costs, the latter including a normal profit to the entrepreneur. Accounting profits are equal to total revenue less accounting (explicit) costs.

Short Run and Long Run

The costs a firm incurs in producing any given output will depend on the types of adjustments it can make in the amounts of the various resources it employs. The quantities employed of many resources — most labour, raw materials, fuel, and power — can be varied easily and quickly. Other resources require more time for adjustment. The capacity of a manufacturing plant — the size of the factory building and the amount of machinery and equipment in it — can only be varied over a considerable period of time. In some heavy industries, it may take several years to alter plant capacity.

Short Run: Fixed Plant   These differences in the time necessary to vary quantities of various resources used in the productive process make it essential to distinguish between the short run and the long run. The **short run** is a period of time too brief for an enterprise to alter its plant capacity. The firm's plant capacity is fixed in the short run, but output can be varied by applying larger or smaller amounts of labour, materials, and other resources to that plant. Existing plant capacity can be used more or less intensively in the short run.

Long Run: Variable Plant   The **long run** refers to a period of time extensive enough to allow firms to change the quantities of *all* resources employed, including plant capacity. The long run also encompasses enough time for existing firms to dissolve and leave the industry and for new firms to be created

and to enter the industry. *While the short run is a "fixed-plant" time period, the long run is a "variable-plant" time period.*

Illustrations   If a Northern Telecom plant hired one hundred extra workers or added an entire shift of workers, these would be short-run adjustments. If the same Northern Telecom plant added a new wing to its building and installed more equipment, this would be a long-run adjustment.

Note that the short run and long run are *conceptual* rather than specific calendar time periods. In light manufacturing industries, changes in plant capacity may be negotiated almost overnight. A small T-shirt firm can increase its plant capacity in a few days or less by ordering and installing new cutting tables and several extra sewing machines. But heavy industry is a different story. It may take Petro-Canada several years to construct a new oil refinery.

QUICK REVIEW (9-1)

1. **Explicit costs are money payments a firm makes to outside suppliers of resources; implicit costs are the opportunity costs associated with a firm's use of resources it owns.**

2. **Economic profits are total revenue less all explicit and implicit costs, including a normal profit.**

3. **In the short run a firm's plant capacity is fixed; in the long run a firm can vary its plant size.**

PRODUCTION COSTS IN THE SHORT RUN

In the short run, a firm can change its output by adding variable resources to a fixed plant. But how does output change as more and more variable resources are added to the firm's fixed resources?

Law of Diminishing Returns

The answer is provided in general terms by the **law of diminishing returns** also called the "law of diminishing marginal product" and the "law of variable proportions." This law states that *as successive units of a variable resource are added to a fixed resource, beyond some point the extra, or marginal, output attributable to each additional unit of the variable resource will decline.* For example, if additional workers are applied to a given amount of capital equipment, eventually output will rise by smaller and smaller amounts as more workers are employed.

Rationale   Consider a small manufacturer of wood furniture frames. The firm has a given amount of equipment in the form of lathes, planers, saws, sanders, and so forth. If this firm hired just one or two workers, total output and productivity (output per worker) would be very low. These workers would have a number of different jobs to perform, and the advantages of specialization would be lost. Time would also be lost in switching from one job operation to another, and the machines would stand idle much of the time. Production would be inefficient because there is too much capital relative to labour.

These difficulties would disappear as more workers were added. Equipment would be more fully utilized, and workers could now specialize on a single job. Time would no longer be lost as a result of job-switching. Thus as more workers are hired by the initially understaffed plant, the extra or marginal product of each will rise as a result of more efficient production. But this cannot go on indefinitely. As still more workers are added, problems of overcrowding arise. Workers must wait in line to use the machinery, so now *workers* are underutilized. Total output increases at a diminishing rate because, given the fixed plant size, each worker will have less capital equipment to work with as more and more labour is hired. The marginal product of additional workers declines because the plant is overstaffed. There is too much labour in proportion to the fixed amount of capital equipment. In the extreme case, the continuous addition of labour to the plant would use up all standing room, and production would be brought to a standstill.

It is to be emphasized that the law of diminishing returns assumes that all units of variable inputs are of equal quality. In the case of labour, for example, each successive worker is presumed to have the same innate ability, motor coordination, education, training, and work experience. Marginal product ultimately diminishes, not because successive workers are qualitatively inferior, but because too many workers are being used relative to the amount of capital equipment available.

Numerical Example   Table 9-1 presents a numerical illustration of the law of diminishing returns. Column 2 indicates the **total product** resulting from combining each level of labour input in column 1 with a fixed amount of capital equipment.

Column 3, **marginal product**, shows the *change* in total output associated with each additional input of labour. Note that with no labour inputs, total product is zero; a plant with no workers will yield no output. The first two workers reflect increasing returns, their marginal products being 10 and 15 units of output respectively. But then, beginning with the third worker, marginal product diminishes continuously, and actually becomes zero with the eighth worker and negative with the ninth. **Average product** or output per worker (also called "labour productivity") is shown in column 4. It is calculated by dividing total product (column 2) by the corresponding number of workers (column 1).

Graphic Portrayal   Figures 9-2(a) and **(b) (Key Graphs)** on page 128 show the law of diminishing returns graphically and will help to explain more fully the relationships between total, marginal, and average product. Note first that total product goes through three phases; it rises initially at an increasing rate; then it increases, but at a decreasing rate; and finally it reaches a maximum and declines.

Geometrically, marginal product is the slope of the total product curve. Marginal product measures the rate of change in total product associated with each successive worker. Hence, the three phases of total product are also reflected in marginal product. Where total product is increasing at an increasing rate, marginal product is necessarily rising. Here extra workers are adding larger and larger amounts to total product. Where total product is increasing but at a decreasing rate, marginal product is positive but falling. Each additional worker adds less to total product than did preceding workers. When total product is at a maximum, marginal product is zero.

TABLE 9-1 The law of diminishing returns (hypothetical data)

(1) Inputs of the variable resource (labour L)	(2) Total product (TP)	(3) Marginal product $\left(\dfrac{\triangle TP}{\triangle L}\right)^*$		(4) Average product ($2 \div 1$)
0	0			—
1	10	10	Increasing marginal returns	10
2	25	15		$12\frac{1}{2}$
3	37	12		$12\frac{1}{3}$
4	47	10		$11\frac{3}{4}$
5	55	8	Diminishing marginal returns	11
6	60	5		10
7	63	3		9
8	63	0		$7\frac{7}{8}$
9	62	−1	Negative marginal returns	$6\frac{8}{9}$

*The Greek capital letter Delta, whose symbol is △, denotes difference or change.

When total product declines, marginal product becomes negative.

Average product also reflects the same general "increasing-maximum-diminishing" relationship between variable inputs of labour and output as does marginal product. But note the relationship between marginal product and average product: where marginal product exceeds average product, the latter must rise. And wherever marginal product is less than average product, then average product must be declining. It follows that marginal product intersects average product where the average product is at a maximum.

For example, you raise your average course grade only when your score on an additional (marginal) examination is greater than the average of all your past scores. If your grade on an additional exam is below your current average, your average will be pulled down.

In our production example, so long as the amount an additional worker adds to total product exceeds the average product of all workers already employed, average product will rise. Conversely, when an extra worker adds an amount to total product that is less than the present average product, then that worker will lower average product.

The law of diminishing returns is embodied in the shapes of all three curves. But, as our earlier definition of the law of diminishing returns indicates, we are most concerned with marginal product. The stages of increasing, diminishing, and negative marginal product (returns) are shown in Figure 9-2. Glancing back at columns 1 and 3 of Table 9-1, we observe increasing returns for the first two workers, decreasing returns for workers 3 to 7, zero returns for the eighth worker, and negative returns for the ninth.

Fixed, Variable, and Total Costs

The production data described by the law of diminishing returns must be coupled with resource prices to determine the total and per unit costs of producing various levels of output. We have already emphasized that in the short run, some resources — those associated with the firm's plant — are fixed. Others are variable. This means that in the short run, costs can be classified as either fixed or variable.

Fixed Costs Fixed costs *are those costs that do not vary with changes in output.* Fixed costs are associated with the very existence of a firm's plant and must be paid even if the firm's output is zero. Such costs as interest on a firm's debt, rental payments, insurance premiums, and the salaries of top management and key personnel are generally fixed costs. In column 2 of Table 9-2 (page 129) we assume that the firm's total fixed costs are $100. By definition, this fixed-cost figure prevails at all levels of output, including zero.

FIGURE 9-2   **The law of diminishing returns**

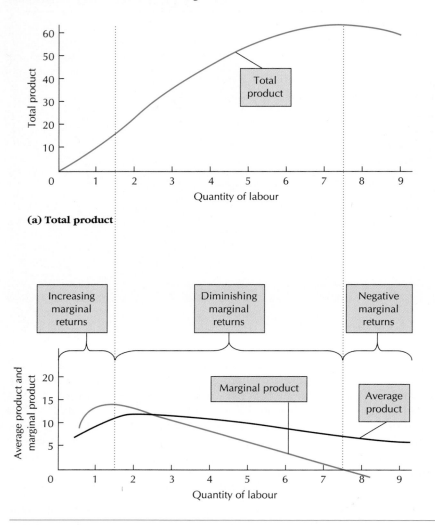

As a variable resource (labour) is added to fixed amounts of other resources (land, capital), the resulting total product will eventually increase by diminishing amounts, reach a maximum, and then decline as in (a). Marginal product in (b) reflects the changes in total product associated with each input of labour. Average product is simply output per worker. Note that marginal product intersects average product at the maximum average product.

Variable Costs   Variable costs *are those costs that change with the level of output.* They include payments for materials, fuel, power, transportation services, most labour, and similar variable resources. In column 3 of Table 9-2, we find that the total of variable costs changes directly with output. But note that *the increases in variable costs associated with each one-unit increase in output are not constant.* As production begins, variable costs will, for a time, increase by a *decreasing* amount; this is true up to the fourth unit of output. Beyond the fourth unit, however, variable costs rise by *increasing* amounts for each successive unit of output. Variable costs act in this way because of the law of diminishing returns. At first, because of *increasing* marginal product, smaller and smaller increases in

the amounts of variable resources will be needed to get each successive unit of output produced. Because all units of the variable resources have the same price, total variable costs will increase by decreasing amounts. But when marginal product begins to decline as diminishing returns set in, larger and larger additional amounts of variable resources are needed to produce each successive unit of output. Total variable costs will therefore increase by increasing amounts.

Total Cost   Total cost *is the sum of fixed and variable costs at each level of output.* It is shown in column 4 of Table 9-2. At zero units of output, total cost is equal to the firm's fixed costs. Then for each unit of production — 1 to 10 — total cost increases by the same amounts as variable cost.

TABLE 9-2   Total- and average-cost schedules for an individual firm in the short run (*hypothetical data*)

Total-cost data, per week				Average-cost data, per week			
(1)	(2)	(3)	(4)	(5)	(6)	(7)	(8)
Total product	Total fixed cost	Total variable cost	Total cost	Average fixed cost	Average variable cost	Average total cost	Marginal cost
(Q)	(TFC)	(TVC)	(TC)	(AFC)	(AVC)	(ATC)	(MC)
			$TC = TFC + TVC$	$AFC = \dfrac{TFC}{Q}$	$AVC = \dfrac{TVC}{Q}$	$ATC = \dfrac{TC}{Q}$	$MC = \dfrac{\text{change in TC}}{\text{change in } Q}$
0	$100	$ 0	$ 100				
1	100	90	190	$100.00	$90.00	$190.00	$ 90
2	100	170	270	50.00	85.00	135.00	80
3	100	240	340	33.33	80.00	113.33	70
4	100	300	400	25.00	75.00	100.00	60
5	100	370	470	20.00	74.00	94.00	70
6	100	450	550	16.67	75.00	91.67	80
7	100	540	640	14.29	77.14	91.43	90
8	100	650	750	12.50	81.25	93.75	110
9	100	780	880	11.11	86.67	97.78	130
10	100	930	1,030	10.00	93.00	103.00	150

Figure 9-3 shows graphically the fixed-cost, variable-cost, and total-cost data of Table 9-2.

The distinction between fixed and variable costs is very significant to the business manager. Variable costs are those costs businesses can control or alter in the short run by changing production levels. In contrast, fixed costs are beyond the business executive's control; they are incurred in the short run and must be paid regardless of output level.

Per Unit, or Average, Costs

Producers are certainly interested in their total costs, but they are equally concerned with *per unit*, or *average*, costs. Average-cost data are better for making comparisons with product price, which is always stated on a per-unit basis. Average fixed cost, average variable cost, and average total cost are shown in columns 5 to 7 of Table 9-2. We want to know how these unit-cost figures are derived and how they vary as output changes.

1 AFC   Average fixed cost (AFC) is found by dividing total fixed cost (TFC) by the corresponding output (Q):

$$AFC = \frac{TFC}{Q}$$

FIGURE 9-3   Total cost is the sum of fixed and variable costs

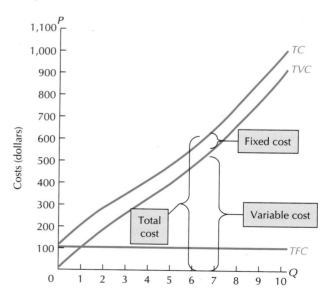

Total variable costs (*TVC*) change with output. Fixed costs are independent of the level of output. The total cost (*TC*) of any output is the vertical sum of the fixed and variable costs of that output.

While total fixed costs are, by definition, independent of output, AFC will decline as output increases. As output increases, a given total fixed cost of $100 is being spread over a larger and larger output. When output is just 1 unit, total fixed costs and AFC are equal at $100. But at 2 units of output, total fixed costs of $100 become $50 worth of fixed costs per unit; then $33.33, as $100 is spread over 3 units; and $25, when spread over 4 units. This is commonly referred to as "spreading the overhead." We find, in Figure 9-4, that AFC graphs as a continually declining figure as total output is increased.

2 AVC   Average variable cost (AVC) is calculated by dividing total variable cost (TVC) by the corresponding output (Q):

$$AVC = \frac{TVC}{Q}$$

AVC declines initially, reaches a minimum, and then increases again. Graphically, this provides us with a U-shaped AVC curve, as shown in Figure 9-4.

Because total variable cost reflects the law of diminishing returns, so must the AVC figures, which are derived from total variable cost. Due to increasing returns, it takes fewer and fewer additional variable resources to produce each of the first 4 units of output. As a result, variable cost per unit will decline. AVC hits a minimum with the fifth unit of output, and, beyond this point, AVC rises as diminishing returns require more and more variable resources to produce each additional unit of output.

You can verify the U shape of the AVC curve by returning to Table 9-1. Assume the price of labour is $10 per unit. By dividing average product (output per worker) into $10 (price per worker), labour cost per unit of output can be determined. Because we have assumed labour to be the only variable input, labour cost per unit of output *is* variable cost per unit of output, or AVC. When average product is initially low, AVC will be high. As workers are added, average product rises and AVC falls. When average product is at its maximum, AVC will be at its minimum. As still more workers are added and average product declines, AVC will rise. The "hump" of the average product curve is reflected in the U-shaped AVC curve. A glance ahead at Figure 9-6 will confirm this graphically.

3 ATC   Average total cost (ATC) is found by dividing total cost (TC) by total output (Q) or by adding AFC and AVC for each of the ten levels of output:

FIGURE 9-4   The average-cost curves

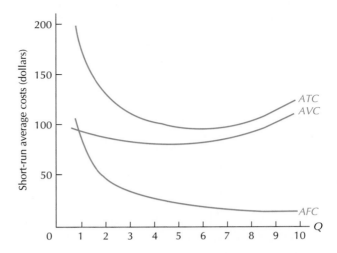

Average total cost (*ATC*) is the vertical sum of average variable cost (*AVC*) and average fixed cost (*AFC*). *AFC* necessarily falls as a given amount of fixed costs is apportioned over a larger and larger output. *AVC* initially falls because of increasing returns but then rises because of diminishing returns.

$$ATC = \frac{TC}{Q} = AFC + AVC$$

These data are shown in column 7 of Table 9-2.

Marginal Cost

One final and very crucial cost concept remains — marginal cost. **Marginal cost (MC)** *is the additional cost of producing one more unit of output.* MC can be calculated as follows:

$$MC = \frac{\text{change in TC}}{\text{change in } Q}$$

Our data are structured so that the "change in Q" is always "1," so we have defined MC as the cost of *one* more unit of output.

Calculations   In Table 9-2, production of the first unit of output increases total cost from $100 to $190. Therefore, the additional, or marginal, cost of that first unit is $90. The marginal cost of the second unit is $80 ($270 − $190); the MC of the third is $70 ($340 − $270); and so forth. MC for each of the 10 units of output is shown in column 8 of Table 9-2.

MC can also be calculated from the total-variable-cost column because the only difference between total cost and total variable cost is the constant amount of fixed costs ($100). Thus, the *change* in total cost and the *change* in total variable cost associated with each additional unit of output are always the same.

Marginal Decisions   Marginal cost is a strategic concept because it designates those costs over which the firm has direct control. Specifically, MC indicates those costs incurred in the production of the last unit of output and, simultaneously, the cost that can be "saved" by reducing total output by the last unit. A firm's decisions as to what output level to produce are typically marginal decisions, that is, decisions to produce a few more or a few less units.

Graphic Portrayal   Marginal cost is shown graphically in **Figure 9-5 (Key Graph)**. Note that marginal cost declines sharply, reaches a minimum, and then rises rather sharply. This mirrors the fact that variable cost, and therefore total cost, increases first by decreasing amounts and then by increasing amounts (see Figure 9-3 and columns 3 and 4 of Table 9-2).

MC and Marginal Product   The shape of the marginal-cost curve is a reflection of, and the consequence of, the law of diminishing returns. The relationship between marginal product and marginal cost can be seen in Table 9-1. If each successive unit of a variable resource (labour) is hired at a constant price, the marginal cost of each extra unit of output will *fall* so long as the marginal product of each additional worker is *rising*. This is so because marginal cost is the (constant) price or cost of an extra worker divided by his or her marginal product. Hence in Table 9-1, suppose each worker can be hired for $10. Because the first worker's marginal product is 10 and the hire of this worker increases the firm's costs by $10, the marginal cost of each of these 10 extra units of output will be $1 (= $10 ÷ 10). The second worker also increases costs by $10, but the marginal product is 15, so that the marginal cost of each of these 15 extra units of output is $0.67 (= $10 ÷ 15). In general, so long as marginal product is rising, marginal cost will be falling.

But as diminishing returns set in — in this case, with the third worker — marginal cost will begin to rise. Thus for the third worker, marginal cost is $0.83 (= $10 ÷ 12); $1.00 for the fourth worker; $1.25 for the fifth; and so on. ***Given the price (cost) of the variable resource, increasing returns will be reflected in a declining marginal cost and diminishing returns in a rising marginal cost.*** The MC curve is a mirror reflection of the marginal product curve.

FIGURE 9-5   The relationship of marginal cost to average total cost and average variable cost

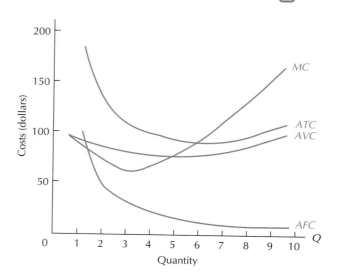

Marginal cost (*MC*) cuts both *ATC* and *AVC* at their minimum points. This is so because whenever the extra or marginal amount added to total cost (or variable cost) is less than the average of that cost, the average will necessarily fall. Conversely, whenever the marginal amount added to total (or variable) cost is greater than the average of that cost, the average must rise.

As Figure 9-6 shows, when marginal product is rising, marginal cost is necessarily falling. When marginal product is at its maximum, marginal cost is at its minimum. And when marginal product is falling, marginal cost is rising.

Relation of MC to AVC and ATC   The marginal cost curve intersects both the AVC and ATC curves at their minimum points. Why is this so?

When the amount added to total cost (marginal cost) is less than the average of total cost, ATC will fall. Conversely, when marginal cost exceeds ATC, ATC will rise. This means, in Figure 9-5, that so long as MC lies below ATC, the latter will fall, and where MC is above ATC, ATC will rise. Therefore at the point of intersection where MC equals ATC, ATC has just ceased to fall but has not yet begun to rise. This, by definition, is the minimum point on the ATC curve. ***The marginal cost curve intersects the average total cost curve at its minimum point.***

Because MC can be defined as the addition either to total cost or to total variable cost resulting from one more unit of output, this same rationale explains why the MC curve also crosses the AVC curve at its minimum point.

FIGURE 9-6 The relationship between productivity curves and cost curves

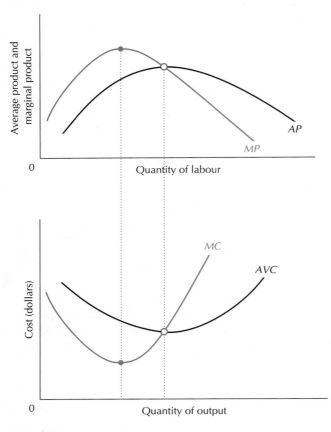

The marginal cost (*MC*) and average variable cost (*AVC*) curves are mirror images of the marginal product (*MP*) and average product (*AP*) curves respectively. Assuming labour is the only variable input and that its price (the wage rate) is constant, *MC* is found by dividing the wage rate by *MP*. Hence when *MP* is rising, *MC* is falling; when *MP* reaches its maximum, *MC* is at its minimum; and when *MP* is diminishing, *MC* is rising. A similar relationship holds between *AP* and *AVC*.

variable input rose, the AVC, ATC, and MC curves would all shift upward but the position of AFC would remain unchanged. Reductions in the prices of fixed or variable resources will entail cost curve shifts exactly opposite to those just described.

If a more efficient technology were discovered, then the productivity of all inputs would increase, and the cost figures in Table 9-1 would all be lower. To illustrate, if labour is the only variable input and wages are $10 per hour and average product is 10 units, then AVC would be $1. But if a technological improvement increases the average product of labour to 20 units, then AVC will decline to $0.50. More generally, an upshift in the productivity curves shown in the top portion of Figure 9-6 will mean a downshift in the cost curves portrayed in the bottom portion of that diagram.

QUICK REVIEW (9-2)

1. **The law of diminishing returns indicates that, beyond some point, output will increase by diminishing amounts as a variable resource (labour) is added to a fixed resource (capital).**

2. **In the short run the total cost of any level of output is the sum of fixed and variable costs (TC = TFC + TVC).**

3. **Average fixed, average variable, and average total costs refer to cost per unit of output; marginal cost is the cost of producing one more unit of output.**

4. **Average fixed cost declines continuously as output increases; average variable cost and average total cost are U-shaped, reflecting increasing and then diminishing returns; marginal cost falls but then rises, intersecting both average variable and average total cost at their minimum points.**

Shifting the Cost Curves

Changes in either resource prices or technology will cause cost curves to shift. If fixed costs had been higher — say, $200 rather than the $100 we assumed in Table 9-2 — then the AFC curve in Figure 9-5 would shift upward. The ATC curve would also be at a higher position because AFC is a component of ATC. But the positions of the AVC and MC curves would be unaltered because their locations are based on the prices of variable rather than fixed resources. Thus, if the price (wage) of labour or some other

PRODUCTION COSTS IN THE LONG RUN

In the long run, an industry and individual firms can undertake all desired resource adjustments. The firm can alter its plant capacity; it can build a larger plant or revert to a smaller plant than assumed in Table 9-2. The long run is also sufficient time for new firms to enter or existing firms to leave an industry. The impact of the entry and exodus of firms from an industry will be discussed in the next chapter; here we are concerned only with changes in plant capacity made by a single firm. We will couch our analysis in terms of ATC, making no distinction between fixed and variable costs because all resources, and therefore all costs, are variable in the long run.

Firm Size and Costs

Suppose a single-plant manufacturing enterprise starts out on a small scale and then, as the result of successful operations, expands to successively larger plant sizes. For a time, successively larger plants will bring lower average total costs. However, eventually the building of a still larger plant may cause ATC to rise.

Figure 9-7 illustrates this situation for five possible plant sizes. ATC-1 is the average-total-cost curve for the smallest of the five plants, and ATC-5 for the largest. Constructing a larger plant will mean lower minimum per unit costs to plant size 3. But beyond this point, a larger plant will mean a higher level of minimum average total costs.

The Long-Run Cost Curve

The dotted lines indicate those outputs at which the firm should change plant size in order to realize the lowest attainable per-unit costs of production. In Figure 9-7, for all outputs up to 20 units, the lowest per unit costs are attainable with plant size 1. However, if the firm expands to some level greater than 20 but less than 30 units, it can achieve lower per unit costs by constructing a larger plant — plant size 2. Although *total* cost will be higher at the greater levels of production, the cost *per unit* of output will be less than before. For any output between 30 and 50 units,

plant size 3 will yield the lowest per-unit cost. For the 50- to 60-unit range of output, plant size 4 must be built to achieve the lowest unit costs. Lowest per unit costs for any output over 60 units demand the construction of the still larger plant size 5.

Tracing these adjustments, we can conclude that the long-run ATC curve for the enterprise will comprise segments of the short-run ATC curves for the various plant sizes that can be constructed. ***The long-run ATC curve shows the least per-unit cost at which any output can be produced after the firm has had time to make all appropriate adjustments in its plant size.*** In Figure 9-7, the heavy curve is the firm's long-run ATC curve or, as it is often called, the firm's planning curve.

In most lines of production, the choice of plant sizes is much wider than that assumed in our illustration. In fact, in many industries the number of possible plant sizes is virtually unlimited and, in time, quite small changes in the volume of output will lead to changes in plant size.

Graphically, this implies an unlimited number of short-run ATC curves, as suggested by **Figure 9-8 (Key Graph)**. The minimum ATC of producing each possible level of output is shown by the long-run ATC curve. Rather than being comprised of *segments* of short-run ATC curves, as in Figure 9-7, the long-run ATC curve is made up of all the *points of tangency* of the short-run ATC curves from which the long-run ATC curve is derived.

Economies and Diseconomies of Scale

We have accepted the contention that for a time, a larger and larger plant size will translate into lower

---

FIGURE 9-7   The long-run average-cost curve:five possible plant sizes

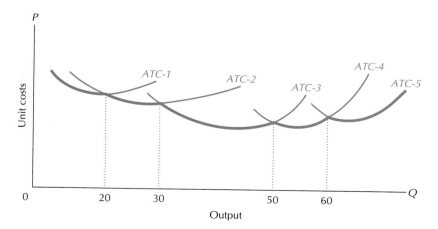

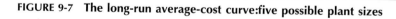

The long-run average-cost curve is made up of segments of the short-run cost curves (*ATC*-1, *ATC*-2, etc.) of the various-sized plants from which the firm might choose. Each point on the bumpy planning curve shows the least unit cost attainable for any output when the firm has had time to make all desired changes in its plant size.

FIGURE 9-8   **The long-run average-cost curve: unlimited number of plant sizes**

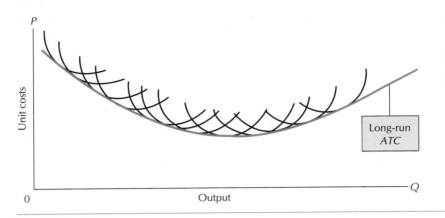

If the number of possible plant sizes is very large, the long-run average-cost curve approximates a smooth curve. Economies of scale, followed by diseconomies of scale, cause the curve to be U-shaped.

unit costs but that beyond some point, successively larger plants will mean higher average total costs. Exactly why is the long-run ATC curve U-shaped? Note, first, that **the law of diminishing returns does not apply here**, because the long run assumes that all resources are variable. Furthermore, our discussion assumes resource prices are constant. We can explain the U-shaped long-run average-cost curve in terms of **economies** and **diseconomies** of large-scale production.

Economies of Scale   Economies of scale or, more commonly, economies of mass production, explain the downsloping part of the long-run ATC curve. As plant size increases, a number of factors will lead to lower average costs of production.

1 Labour Specialization   Increased labour specialization is feasible as a plant increases in size. The hiring of more workers means that jobs can be divided and subdivided. Each worker may now have just one task to perform instead of five or six. Workers can be used full-time on those particular operations at which they have — or can develop — special skills. Greater specialization also eliminates the loss of time that accompanies the shifting of workers from one job to another. Such specialization will reduce costs.

2 Managerial Specialization   Large-scale production means better utilization of, and greater specialization in, management. A supervisor who can handle twenty workers will be underutilized in a small plant with only ten people. The production

staff can be doubled with no increase in administrative costs. Nor will small firms be able to use management specialists to best advantage. In a small plant, a sales specialist may have to divide his or her time between several executive functions — for example, marketing, personnel, and finance. A larger scale of operations will mean that the marketing expert can supervise sales and product distribution full time, while appropriate specialists perform other managerial functions. Greater efficiency and lower unit costs are the net result.

3 Efficient Capital   Small firms often cannot employ the most technologically efficient productive equipment. In many lines of production, the most efficient machinery is available only in very large and extremely expensive units. Furthermore, effective utilization of this equipment demands a high volume of production, so only large-scale producers can afford and efficiently operate the best available equipment.

In the automobile industry, for example, the most efficient fabrication method employs robotics and elaborate assembly-line equipment. The efficient use of this equipment demands an annual output of an estimated 200,000 to 400,000 automobiles. Only very large-scale producers can afford to purchase and use this equipment efficiently.

4 By-products   The large-scale producer can more intensely use by-products than can a small firm. The large meat-packing plant makes glue, fertilizer, pharmaceuticals, and a host of other products from animal remnants that would be discarded by smaller producers.

All these technological considerations — greater specialization in labour and management, the ability to use the most efficient equipment, and effective use of by-products — will contribute to lower unit costs for the firm able to expand its scale of operation.

Another way of thinking about economies of scale is that an increase in *all* resources of, say, 10% will cause a more-than-proportionate increase in output of, say, 20%. The result will be a decline in the long-run ATC.

Diseconomies of Scale But in time, the expansion of a firm *may* lead to diseconomies and therefore higher per-unit costs.

The main factor causing **diseconomies of scale** lies with managerial problems in efficiently controlling and coordinating a firm's operations as it becomes a large-scale producer. In a small plant, a single key executive may make all the basic decisions for the plant's operation. The executive is close to the production line and can readily understand the firm's operations, easily digest information gained from subordinates, and make clear and efficient decisions.

However, as a firm grows, the many echelons between the executive suite and the assembly line keep top management far removed from the actual production operations of the plant. One person cannot assemble, understand, and digest all the information essential to rational decision making in a large-scale enterprise. Authority must be delegated to innumerable vice-presidents, second vice-presidents, and so forth. This expansion in depth and width of the management hierarchy leads to problems of communication, coordination, and bureaucratic red tape, and the possibility that the decisions of various subordinates will fail to mesh. The result is impaired efficiency and rising average costs.

Another way of thinking about diseconomies of scale is that an increase in *all* resources of, say, 10% will cause a less-than-proportionate increase in output of, say, 5%. As a consequence, ATC will increase. Diseconomies of scale are illustrated by the rising portion of the long-run ATC.

Constant Returns to Scale In some instances there may exist a rather wide range of output between the output level at which economies of scale are exhausted and the point at which diseconomies of scale are encountered. That is, there will exist a range of **constant returns to scale** over which long-run average cost is constant. The q_0q_1 output range of Figure 9-9(a) is relevant. Here a given percentage increase in *all* inputs of, say, 10% will

FIGURE 9-9 **Various possible long-run average-cost curves**

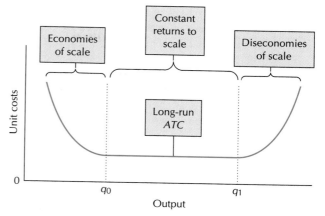

(a)

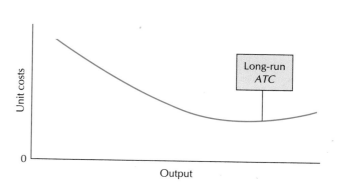

(b)

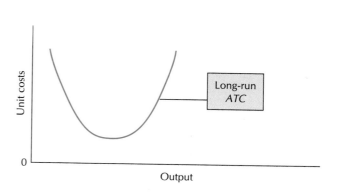

(c)

(a) Where economies of scale are rather rapidly exhausted and diseconomies not encountered until a considerably larger scale of output has been achieved, long-run average costs will be constant over a wide range of output. **(b)** When economies of scale are extensive and diseconomies remote, the *ATC* will fall over a wide range of production. **(c)** If economies of scale are exhausted quickly, followed immediately by diseconomies, minimum unit costs will be encountered at a relatively low output.

cause a proportionate 10% increase in output. Thus the long-run ATC does not change.

Relevance In many Canadian manufacturing industries economies of scale have been of great significance. Firms that have expanded their scale of operations to realize economies of mass production have survived and flourished. Those unable to achieve this expansion have found themselves in the unenviable position of being high-cost producers, doomed to a marginal existence or ultimate insolvency.

There is some difference of opinion among economists as to the relevance of diseconomies of scale. Some believe that the existence and past growth of such gigantic corporations as General Motors, AT&T, Exxon, and Prudential Life Insurance seem to cast doubt on the concept. In practice, computerized information and communication systems have often been developed and applied to forestall the decision-making problems embodied in the notion of diseconomies of scale. Where these efforts are successful, the long-run average-cost curve would fall and then become more or less constant as economies of scale are exhausted.

But there is case-study and anecdotal evidence to suggest that diseconomies of scale are a fact and, when encountered, can be significant. Large firms often design their organizational structures in the hope of avoiding diseconomies of scale. For example, among its many subdivisions, General Motors has established five automobile-producing divisions (Chevrolet, Buick, Oldsmobile, Pontiac, and Cadillac), each of which is largely autonomous and competing. GM's recent Saturn automobile project even entailed the creation of a separate company. A degree of decentralization has been sought that will allow full realization of economies of scale, yet help to avoid diseconomies of scale.

MES and Industry Structure

Economies and diseconomies of scale are an important determinant of an industry's structure. To understand this, it is helpful to introduce the concept of **minimum efficient scale (MES)**, which is the smallest level of output at which a firm can minimize long-run average costs. In Figure 9-9(a) this occurs at $0q_0$ units of output. Because of the extended range of constant returns to scale, firms producing substan-

tially larger outputs could also realize the minimum attainable average costs. Specifically, firms would be equally efficient within the q_0q_1 range. An industry with such costs conditions is populated by firms of quite different sizes. The meat-packing, furniture, wood products, and small-appliance industries provide approximate examples. With an extended range of constant returns to scale, relatively large and relatively small firms could coexist in an industry and be equally viable.

Compare this with Figure 9-9(b), where economies of scale are extensive and diseconomies are remote. Here the long-run average-cost curve will decline over a long range of output, as is the case in the automobile, aluminum, steel, and other heavy industries. Given consumer demand, efficient production will be achieved only with a small number of industrial giants. Small firms cannot realize the minimum efficient scale and will not be viable. In the extreme, economies of scale might extend beyond the market's size, resulting in what is termed a natural monopoly. A **natural monopoly** is a market situation where unit costs are minimized by having a single firm produce the particular good or service.

Where economies of scale are exhausted quickly, followed immediately by diseconomies, minimum efficient size occurs at a small level of output as shown in Figure 9-9(c). In such industries, a given level of consumer demand will support a large number of relatively small producers. Many retail trades, some types of farming, and certain types of light manufacturing, such as the baking, clothing, and shoe industries, fall into this category. Fairly small firms are as efficient as, or more efficient than, large-scale producers in such industries.

The point is that the shape of the long-run average-cost curve, as determined by economies and diseconomies of scale, can be significant in determining the structure and competitiveness of an industry. Whether an industry is "competitive" — populated by a relatively large number of small firms — or "concentrated" — dominated by a few large producers — is sometimes a reflection of an industry's technology and the resulting shape of its long-run average-cost curve.

But we must be cautious in making this statement, because industry structure does not depend on cost conditions alone. Government policies, the geographic size of a market, managerial ability, and a variety of other factors must be considered in explaining the structure of a given industry.

1. Most firms have U-shaped long-run average-cost curves, reflecting economies and then diseconomies of scale.

2. Economies of scale are the consequence of greater specialization of labour and management, more efficient capital equipment, and the use of by-products.

3. Diseconomies of scale are caused by problems of coordination and communication that arise in large firms.

4. Minimum efficient scale is the lowest level of output at which a firm's long-run average costs are at a minimum.

CHAPTER SUMMARY

1. Economic costs include all payments that must be received by resource owners to assure continued supply of these resources in a particular line of production. This definition includes explicit costs, which flow to resource suppliers separate from a given enterprise, and also implicit costs, the remuneration of self-owned and self-employed resources. One of the implicit cost payments is a normal profit to the entrepreneur for functions performed.

2. In the short run, a firm's plant capacity is fixed. The firm can use its plant more or less intensively by adding or subtracting units of variable resources, but the firm does not have sufficient time to alter plant size.

3. The law of diminishing returns describes what happens to output as a fixed plant is used more intensively. The law states that as successive units of a variable resource such as labour are added to a fixed plant, beyond some point the resulting marginal product associated with each additional worker will decline.

4. Because some resources are variable and others fixed, costs can be classified as variable or fixed in the short run. Fixed costs are independent of the level of output. Variable costs vary with output. The total cost of any output is the sum of fixed and variable costs at that output.

5. Average fixed, average variable, and average total costs are fixed, variable, and total costs per unit of output. Average fixed costs decline continuously as output increases, because a fixed sum is being spread over a larger and larger number of units of production. Average variable costs are U-shaped, reflecting the law of diminishing returns. Average total cost is the sum of average fixed and average variable cost; it, too, is U-shaped.

6. Marginal cost is the extra, or additional, cost of producing one more unit of output. Graphically, the marginal cost curve intersects the ATC and AVC curves at their minimum points.

7. Lower resource prices shift cost curves downward, as does technological progress. Higher input prices shift cost curves upward.

8. The long run is a period of time sufficiently long for a firm to vary the amounts of all resources used, including plant size. In the long run all costs are variable. The long-run ATC, or planning, curve is composed of segments of the short-run ATC curves, representing the various plant sizes a firm can construct in the long run.

9. The long-run ATC curve is generally U-shaped. Economies of scale are first encountered as a small firm expands. A number of considerations — particularly greater specialization in the use of labour and management, ability to use the most efficient equipment, and more complete utilization of by-products — contribute to these economies of scale. Diseconomies of scale stem from the managerial complexities that accompany large-scale production. The relative importance of economies and diseconomies of scale in an industry is often an important determinant of the structure of that industry.

TERMS AND CONCEPTS

average fixed cost (p. 129)

average total cost (p. 130)

average variable cost (p. 130)

constant returns to scale (p. 135)

economic (opportunity) cost (p. 124)

economies and diseconomies of scale
   (p. 133)

explicit and implicit costs (p. 124)

fixed costs (p. 127)

law of diminishing returns (p. 126)

marginal cost (p. 130)

minimum efficient scale (p. 136)

natural monopoly (p. 136)

normal and economic profits (p. 124)

short run and long run (p. 125)

total cost (p. 128)

total, marginal, and average product (p. 126)

variable costs (p. 128)

QUESTIONS AND STUDY SUGGESTIONS

1. Distinguish between explicit and implicit costs, giving examples of each. What are the explicit and implicit costs of going to university? Why does the economist classify normal profits as a cost? Are economic profits a cost of production?

2. Bozzelli runs a small firm that makes pottery. He hires one helper at $12,000 a year, pays annual rent of $5,000 for his shop, and materials cost $20,000 per year. Bozzelli has $40,000 of his own funds invested in equipment (pottery wheels, kilns, and so forth) that could earn him $4,000 a year if alternatively invested. Bozzelli has been offered $15,000 a year to work as a potter for a competitor. He estimates his entrepreneurial talents are worth $3,000 a year. Total annual revenue from pottery sales is $72,000. Calculate accounting profits and economic profits for Bozzelli's pottery.

3. Which of the following are short-run and which are long-run adjustments? *a.* Petro-Canada builds a new oil refinery; *b.* Dofasco hires 200 more workers; *c.* a farmer increases the amount of fertilizer used on the corn crop; *d.* an Alcan plant adds a third shift of workers.

4. Why can the distinction between fixed and variable costs be made in the short run? Classify the following as fixed or variable costs: advertising expenditures, fuel, interest on company-issued bonds, shipping charges, payments for raw materials, real estate taxes, executive salaries, insurance premiums, wage payments, depreciation and obsolescence charges, sales taxes, and rental payments on leased office machinery. "There are no fixed costs in the long run; all costs are variable." Explain.

5. List the fixed and variable costs associated with owning and operating an automobile. Suppose you are considering whether to drive your car or fly one thousand kilometres to a ski resort for spring break. Which costs — fixed, variable,

or both — would you take into account in making your decision? Would any implicit costs be relevant? Explain.

6. Use the following data to calculate marginal product and average product. Plot total, marginal, and average product and explain in detail the relationship between each pair of curves. Explain why marginal product first rises, then declines, and ultimately becomes negative.

Inputs of labour	Total product	Marginal product	Average product
1	15		_____
2	34	_____	_____
3	51	_____	_____
4	65	_____	_____
5	74	_____	_____
6	80	_____	_____
7	83	_____	_____
8	82	_____	_____

What bearing does the law of diminishing returns have on short-run costs? Be specific. "When marginal product is rising, marginal cost is falling. And when marginal product is diminishing, marginal cost is rising." Illustrate and explain graphically and through a numerical example.

7. A firm has fixed costs of $60 and variable costs as indicated in the table below. Complete the table. When finished, check your calculations by referring to question 6 at the end of Chapter 10.

Total product	Total fixed cost	Total variable cost	Total cost	Average fixed cost	Average variable cost	Average total cost	Marginal cost
0	$_____	$ 0	$_____	$_____	$_____	$_____	
1	_____	45	_____	_____	_____	_____	$_____
2	_____	85	_____	_____	_____	_____	_____
3	_____	120	_____	_____	_____	_____	_____
4	_____	150	_____	_____	_____	_____	_____
5	_____	185	_____	_____	_____	_____	_____
6	_____	225	_____	_____	_____	_____	_____
7	_____	270	_____	_____	_____	_____	_____
8	_____	325	_____	_____	_____	_____	_____
9	_____	390	_____	_____	_____	_____	_____
10	_____	465	_____	_____	_____	_____	_____

a. Graph fixed cost, variable cost, and total cost. Explain how the law of diminishing returns influences the shapes of the variable-cost and total-cost curves.

b. Graph AFC, AVC, ATC, and MC. Explain the derivation and shape of each of these four curves and the relationships they bear to one another. Specifically, explain in nontechnical terms why the MC curve intersects both the AVC and ATC curves at their minimum points.

c. Explain how the locations of each of the four curves graphed in question 7b would be altered if (1) total fixed cost had been $100 rather than $60 and (2) total variable cost had been $10 less at each level of output.

8. Indicate how each of the following would shift the (a) marginal cost curve, (b) average variable cost curve, (c) average fixed cost curve, and (d) average total cost curve of a manufacturing firm. In each case specify the direction of the shift.

   a. A reduction in business property taxes.

   b. An increase in the nominal wages of production workers.

   c. A decrease in the price of electricity.

   d. An increase in insurance rates on plant and equipment.

   e. An increase in transportation costs.

9. Suppose a firm has only three possible firm size options as shown in the accompanying figure. What plant size will the firm choose in producing a. 50, b. 130, c. 160, and d. 250 units of output? Draw the firm's long-run average-cost curve on the diagram and define this curve.

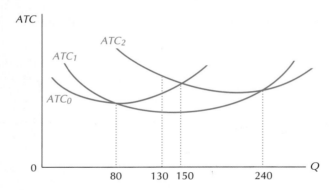

10. Use the concepts of economies and diseconomies of scale to explain the shape of a firm's long-run ATC curve. What is the concept of minimum efficient scale? What bearing may the exact shape of the long-run ATC curve have on the structure of an industry?

Markets, Prices, and Resource Allocation

10

Price and Output Determination: Pure Competition

We now have the basic tools of analysis for understanding how product price and output are determined. But a firm's decisions concerning price and production will vary depending on the character of the industry in which it is operating. There is no such thing as an "average" or "typical" industry. The business sector of our economy has a number of different market structures. At one extreme we find a single producer dominating a market; at the other we discover thousands of firms, each supplying a minute fraction of market output. In this chapter we first introduce the four basic market structures, and then focus in on the first of these — pure competition.

FOUR BASIC MARKET STRUCTURES

Any attempt to examine each specific industry is an impossible task. We seek a more realistic objective — to define and discuss several basic market structures, or models. We will acquaint ourselves with the *general* way in which price and output are determined in most of the market types that characterize our economy.

There are four relatively distinct market structures. These are (1) pure competition, (2) pure monopoly, (3) monopolistic competition, and (4) oligopoly. These four market models differ in terms of the number of firms in the industry, whether the product is standardized or differentiated, and how easy or difficult it is for new firms to enter the industry.

Table 10-1 indicates the main characteristics of these four models. A more detailed analysis of each will follow in the next three chapters.

1. In **pure competition** there are a very large number of firms producing a standardized product (for example, wheat or corn). New firms can enter the industry very easily.

2. At the other extreme **pure monopoly** (Chapter 11) is a market in which one firm is the sole seller of a product or service (a local electric company). Entry of additional firms is blocked so that the firm *is* the industry. Because there is only one product, there is no product differentiation.

3. **Monopolistic competition** (Chapter 12) is characterized by a relatively large number of sellers

TABLE 10-1   Characteristics of the four basic market models

Characteristic	Market Model			
	Pure competition	Monopolistic competition	Oligopoly	Pure monopoly
Number of firms	A very large number	Many	Few	One
Type of product	Standardized	Differentiated	Standardized or differentiated	Unique; no close substitutes
Control over price	None, price taker	Some, but within rather narrow limits	Circumscribed by mutual interdependence; considerable with collusion	Considerable, price maker
Conditions of entry	Very easy, no obstacles	Relatively easy	Significant obstacles present	Blocked
Nonprice competition	None	Considerable emphasis on advertising, brand names, trademarks, and so on	Typically a great deal, particularly with product differentiation	Mostly public relations advertising ("goodwill")
Examples	Agriculture	Retail trade, dresses, shoes	Steel, automobiles, farm implements, many household appliances	Bell Canada, local utilities

producing differentiated products (women's clothing, furniture, books). Differentiation is the basis for product promotion and development. Entry to a monopolistically competitive industry is quite easy.

4. Finally, in **oligopoly** (Chapter 13) there are a few sellers, and this "fewness" means that pricing and output decisions are interdependent. Each firm is affected by the decisions of rivals and must take these decisions into account in determining its own price–output behaviour. Products may be standardized (such as steel or aluminum) or differentiated (automobiles). Generally, entry into oligopolistic industries is very difficult. These definitions and the characteristics outlined in Table 10-1 will come into sharper focus as we examine each market structure in detail.

We will find it convenient to occasionally distinguish between the characteristics of a purely competitive market and those of all other basic market structures — pure monopoly, monopolistic competition, and oligopoly. To facilitate such comparisons, we will employ **imperfect competition** as a generic term to designate all those market structures deviating from the purely competitive market model.

The Importance of Market Structure

The market structure in which a firm exists will be an important determinant of what price is charged for its output and the quantity produced. We already know that the overriding goal of a firm is to maximize profits. But how a firm pursues that goal, and whether it can make normal or economic profit, is to a large degree determined by the market structure it is in. A monopolist's output and price behaviour can be expected to diverge significantly from a firm's in pure competition, where there are many firms selling a homogeneous product. In a pure competitive industry a firm has to be on the alert to *adapt to* constantly changing market conditions, whereas a monopolist can to an extent *influence* market conditions.

But no matter what market structure prevails, as the firm attempts to maximize its profits it must continuously look over its shoulder since other and potentially new firms are trying to do the same. Even a monopolist, unless protected by entry barriers, is under a constant threat as potential competitors enviously eye its healthy (economic) profits. On the other hand, firms will naturally attempt to outdo their competitors with lower prices, unique products and services, or erection of entry barriers of different types. This is the dynamics of the supply side in a market economy.

PURE COMPETITION: CONCEPT AND OCCURRENCE

A purely competitive market has several distinct characteristics that distinguish it from other market structures.

1 Very Large Numbers A basic feature of a purely competitive market is the presence of a large number of independently acting sellers, offering their products in an organized market. Markets for farm commodities (in the absence of marketing boards), stock markets, and the foreign-exchange market are sometimes cited as close approximations in our economy.

2 Standardized Product Competitive firms produce a standardized, or homogeneous, product. Given price, the consumer is indifferent as to the firm from which a purchase is made. Because of product standardization, there is no reason for **nonprice competition**, — competition based on differences in product quality, advertising, or sales promotion.

3 "Price Taker" In a purely competitive market, *individual firms* exert no significant control over product price. This characteristic follows from the preceding two. Under pure competition, each firm produces such a small fraction of total output that increasing or decreasing its output will not perceptibly influence total supply or product price.

For example, assume there are 10,000 competing firms, each currently producing 100 units of output. Total supply is 1,000,000. Now suppose one of these firms cuts its output to 50 units. This will not affect price because this restriction of output by a single firm has almost no impact on total supply. The total quantity supplied declines from 1,000,000 to 999,950. This is not enough of a change in total supply to noticeably affect product price. Thus, the individual competitive firm is a *price taker*, it cannot adjust market price, but can only adjust to it.

4 Free Entry and Exit New firms can freely enter and existing firms can freely leave purely competitive industries. No significant obstacles — legal, technical, financial, or other — exist to prohibit new firms from coming into being and selling their outputs in competitive markets.

Relevance Pure competition is quite rare in practice. This does not mean, however, that an analysis of how competitive markets work is useless and irrelevant.

1. A few industries more closely approximate the competitive model than they do any other market structure. For example, much can be learned about

Canadian agriculture by understanding the functioning of competitive markets.

2. Pure competition provides the simplest context in which to apply the revenue and cost concepts developed in the previous chapter. Pure competition is a clear and meaningful starting point for any discussion of price and output determination.

3. In the concluding section of this chapter, we will discover that the operation of a purely competitive economy provides us with a standard against which the efficiency of the real-world economy can be compared and evaluated.

Our analysis of pure competition has four major objectives: First, we will examine demand from the competitive seller's viewpoint. Second, we seek how a competitive producer adjusts to market price in the short run. Third, the nature of long-run adjustments in a competitive industry is explored. Finally, we wish to evaluate the efficiency of competitive industries from the standpoint of society.

DEMAND AND A COMPETITIVE FIRM

Because each competitive firm offers a negligible fraction of total supply, the individual firm cannot perceptibly influence the market price. Rather, the firm can merely *adjust* to the market price, which it must regard as a given determined by the market. The competitive seller is a *price taker*, rather than a *price maker*.

Perfectly Elastic Demand

Thus, ***the demand curve facing the individual competitive firm is perfectly elastic.*** Columns 1 and 2 of Table 10-2 reflect a perfectly elastic demand curve, where market price is assumed to be $131. Note that the firm cannot obtain a higher price by restricting output; nor need it lower price to increase its sales volume.

We are *not* saying that the *market* demand curve is perfectly elastic in a competitive market. Instead, it is typically a downsloping curve, as a glance ahead at Figure 10-7(b) indicates. However, the demand schedule faced by the *individual firm* in a purely competitive industry is perfectly elastic.

The distinction comes about in this way. For the industry a larger sales volume can be realized only by accepting a lower product price. All firms, acting independently but simultaneously, can and do affect total supply and therefore market price. But not so for the individual firm. If a *single* producer increases or decreases output, the outputs of all other compet-

ing firms being constant, the effect on total supply and market price is negligible. The single firm's demand or sales schedule is therefore perfectly elastic, as shown in Figures 10-1 and 10-7(a). This is an instance in which the fallacy of composition is worth remembering. What is true for the group of firms (a downsloping, less than perfectly elastic demand curve), is *not* true for the individual firm (a perfectly elastic demand curve).

Average, Total, and Marginal Revenue

The firm's demand schedule is simultaneously a revenue schedule. What appears in column 1 of Table 10-2 as price per unit to the purchaser is revenue per unit, or **average revenue**, to the seller. To say that a buyer must pay $131 per unit is to say that the revenue per unit, or average revenue, received by the seller is $131. Price and average revenue are the same thing seen from different viewpoints.

Total revenue for each sales level can be determined by multiplying price by the corresponding quantity the firm can sell. Multiply column 1 by column 2, and the result is column 3. In this case, total

---

FIGURE 10-1   Demand, marginal revenue, and total revenue of a purely competitive firm

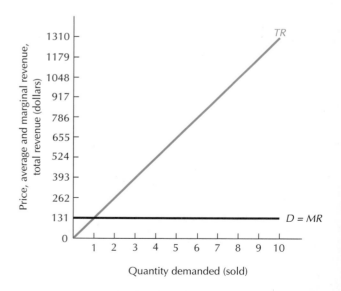

Quantity demanded (sold)

Because it can sell additional units of output at a constant price, the marginal-revenue curve (*MR*) of a purely competitive firm coincides with its perfectly elastic demand curve (*D*). The firm's total-revenue curve (*TR*) is a straight upsloping line.

TABLE 10-2   The demand and revenue schedules for an individual purely competitive firm (*hypothetical data*)

Firm's demand or average-revenue schedule		Revenue data	
(1) Product price (average revenue)	(2) Quantity demanded (sold)	(3) Total revenue	(4) Marginal revenue
$131	0	$ 0	$131
131	1	131	131
131	2	262	131
131	3	393	131
131	4	524	131
131	5	655	131
131	6	786	131
131	7	917	131
131	8	1048	131
131	9	1179	131
131	10	1310	131

receipts increase by a constant amount, $131, for each additional unit of sales. Each unit sold adds exactly its price to total revenue.

When a firm is pondering a change in its output, it will consider how its revenue will *change* as a result of that shift in output. What will be the additional revenue from selling another unit of output? **Marginal revenue** is the change in total revenue, that is, the extra revenue that results from selling one more unit of output. In column 3 of Table 10-2 total revenue is zero when zero units are being sold. The first unit of output sold increases total revenue from zero to $131, marginal revenue is therefore $131. The second unit sold increases total revenue from $131 to $262, so marginal revenue is again $131. Note in column 4 that marginal revenue is a constant figure of $131, because total revenue increases by a constant amount with every extra unit sold.

Under purely competitive conditions, product price is constant to the individual firm; added units, therefore, can be sold without lowering product price. This means that each additional unit of sales adds exactly its price — $131, in this case — to total revenue. And marginal revenue *is* this increase in total revenue. Marginal revenue is constant under pure competition, because additional units can be sold at a constant price.

Graphic Portrayal

The competitive firm's demand curve and total- and marginal-revenue curves are shown graphically in Figure 10-1. The demand or average-revenue curve is perfectly elastic. The marginal-revenue curve coincides with the demand curve because product price is constant to the competitive firm. Each extra unit of sales increases total revenue by $131. Total revenue is a straight line up to the right. Its slope is constant — it is a straight line — because marginal revenue is constant.

QUICK REVIEW (10-1)

1. **In a purely competitive industry there are a large number of firms producing a homogeneous product and no significant entry barriers.**

2. **The competitive firm's demand curve is perfectly elastic at the market price.**

3. **Marginal and average revenue coincide with the firm's demand curve; total revenue rises by the amount of product price for each additional unit sold.**

PROFIT MAXIMIZATION IN THE SHORT RUN: TWO APPROACHES

In the short run, the competitive firm has a fixed plant and maximizes its profits or minimizes its losses by adjusting its output through changes in the amounts of variable resources (materials, labour, and so forth) it employs. The economic profits it seeks are the difference between total revenue and total costs. Indeed, this is the direction of our analysis. The revenue data of the previous section and the cost data of Chapter 9 must be brought together so that the profit-maximizing output for the firm can be determined.

There are two complementary approaches to determining the level of output at which a competitive firm will realize maximum profits or minimum losses. The first compares total revenue and total costs; the second, compares marginal revenue and marginal cost. Both approaches apply not only to a purely competitive firm but also to firms operating in any of the other three basic market structures. To understand output determination under pure competition, we will use both approaches, emphasizing the marginal approach. Furthermore, hypothetical data will be employed to clarify the two approaches.

Total-Revenue–Total-Cost Approach

Given the market price of its product, the competitive producer is faced with three related questions: (1) Should we produce? (2) If so, what amount? (3) What profit (or loss) will be realized?

At first, the answer to question one seems obvious: "You should produce if it is profitable to do so." But the situation is more complex than this. In the short run, part of the firm's total costs is variable costs, and the remainder is fixed costs. The latter have to be paid "out of pocket" even when the firm is closed down. In the short run, a firm takes a loss equal to its fixed costs when it produces zero units of output. This means that although there may be no level of output at which the firm can realize a profit, the firm might still produce if it can realize a loss less than the fixed-cost loss it will face in closing down. Thus, the correct answer to the "Should we produce?" question is: *The firm should produce in the short run if it can realize either (1) a profit or (2) a loss that is less than its fixed costs.*

Assuming the firm *will* produce, the second question is: "How much should be produced?" The answer here is evident: *In the short run, the firm should produce that output at which it maximizes profits or minimizes losses.*

We now examine three cases demonstrating the validity of these two generalizations and answer our third query by indicating how profits and losses can be calculated. In the first case, the firm will maximize its profits by producing. In the second case, it will minimize its losses by producing. In the third case, the firm will minimize its losses by closing down. We will assume the same short-run cost data from Table 10-2 for all three cases and explore the firm's production decisions when faced with three different product prices.

Profit-Maximizing Case   Columns 3 through 5 of Table 10-3 repeat the fixed-cost, variable-cost, and total-cost data developed in Table 9-2. Assuming that market price is $131, we derive total revenue for each output level by multiplying output by price, as we did in Table 10-2. These data are presented in column 2. Then in column 6, the profit or loss encountered at each output is found by subtracting total cost from total revenue. Now we have all the data needed to answer the three questions.

Should the firm produce? Yes, because it can realize a profit by doing so. How much? Nine units, because column 6 tells us this is the output at which total economic profits will be at a maximum. The size of that profit is $299.

Figure 10-2(a) graphically compares total revenue and total cost. Total revenue is a straight line because under pure competition each additional unit adds the same amount to total revenue (Table 10-2).

Total costs increase with output; more production requires more resources. But the rate of increase in total costs varies with the relative efficiency of the firm. The cost data reflect the law of diminishing returns (Chapter 9). For a time the rate of increase in total cost diminishes as the firm uses its fixed resources more efficiently. Then after a time, total cost begins to rise by ever-increasing amounts because of the inefficiencies accompanying more intensive use of the firm's plant. Comparing total cost with total revenue in Figure 10-2(a), note that a **break-even point** occurs at 2 units of output. If our data were extended beyond 10 units of output, another such point would be incurred where total cost would catch up with total revenue, as is shown in Figure 10-2(a). Any output outside of these points will entail losses. Any output within these break-even points will produce an economic profit. Maximum profit is achieved where the vertical difference between total revenue and total cost is greatest. For our data, this is at 9 units of output and the resulting maximum profit is $299.

FIGURE 10-2   The (a) profit-maximizing (b) loss-minimizing, and close-down cases as shown by the total-revenue– total-cost approach

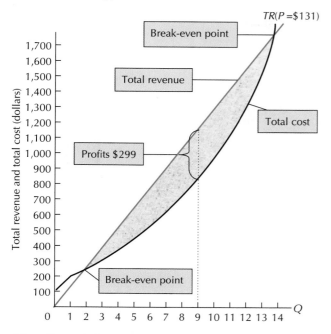

(a) Profit-maximizing case

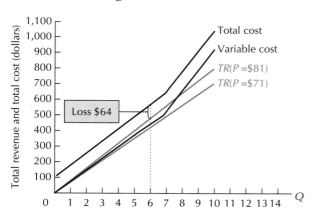

(b) Loss-minimizing and close-down cases

In (a), a firm's profits are maximized at that output at which total revenue exceeds total cost by the maximum amount. In (b), a firm will minimize its losses by producing at that output at which total cost exceeds total revenue by the smallest amount. However, if there is no output at which total revenue exceeds variable costs, the firm will minimize losses in the short run by closing down.

Loss-Minimizing Case   Assuming no change in costs, the firm may not realize economic profits if the market yields a price considerably below $131. Sup-

pose the market price is $81. As column 6 of Table 10-4 indicates, at this price all levels of output will lead to losses. But the firm will *not* close down because, by producing, it realizes a loss considerably less than the $100 fixed-cost loss it would incur by closing down. The firm will minimize its losses by producing 6 units of output. The resulting $64 loss is clearly preferable to the $100 loss that closing down would involve. By producing 6 units the firm earns a total revenue of $486, sufficient to pay all the firm's variable cost ($450) and also a substantial portion — $36 worth — of the firm's $100 of fixed costs.

In general terms, whenever total revenue exceeds total *variable* costs, the firm will produce because all variable costs as well as some portion of total fixed costs can be paid out of revenue. If the firm closed down, all of its total fixed costs would have to be paid out of the entrepreneur's pocket. By producing, some amount less than total fixed costs will have to be paid out of pocket.

Note that there are several other outputs that entail a loss less than the firm's $100 fixed costs, but at 6 units of output the loss is minimized.

Close-Down Case   Assume that the market price is $71. Given short-run costs, column 9 of Table 10-4 indicates that at all levels of output, losses will exceed the $100 fixed-cost loss the firm will incur by closing down. It follows that the firm will minimize its losses by closing down.

Figure 10-2(b) demonstrates the loss-minimizing and close-down cases graphically. In the loss-minimizing case, the total-revenue line TR ($P = 81) exceeds total variable cost by the maximum amount at 6 units of output. Here total revenue is $486, and the firm recovers all its $450 of variable costs and also $36 worth of fixed costs. The firm's minimum loss is $64, superior to the $100 fixed-cost loss involved in closing down. In the close-down case, the total-revenue line TR ($P = 71) lies below the total-variable-cost curve at all points; there is no output at which variable costs can be recovered. By producing, the firm would incur losses exceeding its fixed costs. The firm's best choice is to close down and pay its $100 fixed-cost loss out of pocket.

TABLE 10-3   The profit-maximizing output for a purely competitive firm: total-revenue–total-cost approach (price = $131) (*hypothetical data*)

(1) Total product	(2) Total revenue	(3) Total fixed cost	(4) Total variable cost	(5) Total cost	(6) Total economic profit (+) or loss (−), = (2) − (5)
0	$ 0	$100	$ 0	$ 100	$ − 100
1	131	100	90	190	− 59
2	262	100	170	270	− 8
3	393	100	240	340	+ 53
4	524	100	300	400	+ 124
5	655	100	370	470	+ 185
6	786	100	450	550	+ 236
7	917	100	540	640	+ 277
8	1,048	100	650	750	+ 298
9	1,179	100	780	880	+ 299
10	1,310	100	930	1,030	+ 280

TABLE 10-4   The loss-minimizing outputs for a purely competitive firm: total-revenue–total-cost approach (prices = $81 and $71) (*hypothetical data*)

	Product price = $81					Product price = $71		
(1) Total product	(2) Total revenue	(3) Total fixed cost	(4) Total variable cost	(5) Total cost	(6) Total economic profit (+) or loss (−), = (2) − (5)	(7) Total revenue	(8) Total cost	(9) Total economic profit (+) or loss (−), = (7) − (8)
0	$ 0	$100	$ 0	$ 100	$ − 100	$ 0	$ 100	$ − 100
1	81	100	90	190	− 109	71	190	− 119
2	162	100	170	270	− 108	142	270	− 128
3	243	100	240	340	− 97	213	340	− 127
4	324	100	300	400	− 76	284	400	− 116
5	405	100	370	470	− 65	355	470	− 115
6	486	100	450	550	− 64	426	550	− 124
7	567	100	540	640	− 73	497	640	− 143
8	648	100	650	750	− 102	568	750	− 182
9	729	100	780	880	− 151	639	880	− 241
10	810	100	930	1,030	− 220	710	1,030	− 320

QUICK REVIEW (10-2)

1. In the short run a firm should produce if it can realize profit or a loss that is smaller than its total fixed costs.

2. Profits are maximized where the excess of total revenue over total cost is greatest.

3. Losses are minimized where the excess of total cost over total revenue is smallest and is some amount less than total fixed costs.

4. If losses at all levels of output exceed total fixed costs, the firm should close down in the short run.

Marginal-Revenue–Marginal-Cost Approach

An alternative means for determining the amounts a competitive firm would produce at each possible price is for the firm to determine and compare the amounts that each *additional* unit of output will add to total revenue on the one hand, and to total cost on the other. The firm should compare the *marginal revenue* (MR) and the *marginal cost* (MC) of each successive unit of output. Any unit whose marginal revenue exceeds its marginal cost should be produced because, on each such unit, the firm gains more in revenue from its sale than it adds to costs producing the unit.

MR = MC Rule   At relatively low levels of output, marginal revenue will usually (but not always) exceed marginal cost. It is therefore profitable to produce through this range of output. But as output increases, marginal cost will exceed marginal revenue. To maximize profits, the firm must not produce in this range.

Separating these two production ranges will be a unique point at which marginal revenue equals marginal cost. This point is the key to the output-determining rule: *The firm will maximize profits or minimize losses by producing at the point where marginal revenue equals marginal cost.* For convenience, we call this profit-maximizing guide the **MR = MC** rule. For most sets of MR and MC data, there will not be a nonfractional level of output at which MR and MC are precisely equal. In such instances, the firm should produce the last complete unit of output whose MR *exceeds* its MC.

Three Characteristics   Three features of this MR = MC rule merit comment.

1. The rule presumes that the firm will choose to produce rather than close down. Shortly, we will note that marginal revenue must be equal to, or must exceed, average variable cost, or the firm will find it preferable to close down rather than produce the MR = MC output.

2. The MR = MC rule is an accurate guide to profit maximization for all firms, be they purely competitive, monopolistic, monopolistically competitive, or oligopolistic.

3. The MR = MC rule can be conveniently restated in a slightly different form when being applied to a purely competitive firm. Product price is determined by the market forces of supply and demand and, although the competitive firm can sell as much or as little as it chooses at that price, the firm cannot manipulate the price itself. The demand schedule faced by a competitive seller is perfectly elastic at the going market price. The result is that product price and marginal revenue are equal; each extra unit sold adds precisely its price to total revenue, as shown in Figure 10-1.

Thus under pure competition — and *only* under pure competition — we may substitute price for marginal revenue in the rule, so that it reads as follows: *To maximize profits or minimize losses, the competitive firms should produce at that point where price equals marginal cost (P = MC).* This P = MC rule is simply a special case of the MR = MC rule.

Profit-Maximizing Case   Table 10-5 reproduces the unit- and marginal-cost data derived in Table 9-2. It is, of course, the marginal-cost data of column 5 in Table 10-5 that we wish to compare with price (equal to marginal revenue) for each unit of output. Suppose first that market price, and therefore marginal revenue, is $131, as shown in column 6.

What is the profit-maximizing output? We see that each and every unit of output up to and including the ninth adds more to total revenue than to total cost, thus marginal revenue exceeds marginal cost on all of the first 9 units of output. Each unit therefore adds to the firm's profits and should be produced. The tenth unit however, will not be produced, because it would add more to costs ($150) than to revenue ($131).

Profit Calculations   The level of economic profits realized by the firm can be calculated from the unit-cost data. Multiplying price ($131) times output (9), we find total revenue to be $1,179. Total cost of $880 is found by multiplying average total cost ($97.78) by output (9).[1] The difference of $299 (= $1,179 − $880) is economic profits.

An alternative means of calculating economic profits is to determine profit *per unit* by subtracting average total cost ($97.78) from product price ($131) and multiplying the difference (per unit profits of $33.22) by the level of output (9).

---

[1] In most instances, the unit-cost data are rounded figures. Therefore, economic profits calculated from them will typically vary by a few cents from the profits determined in the total-revenue–total-cost approach. We here ignore the few cents differentials and make our answers consistent with the results of the total-revenue–total-cost approach.

TABLE 10-5 The profit-maximizing output for a purely competitive firm: marginal-revenue-equals-marginal-cost approach (price = $131) (*hypothetical data*)

(1) Total product	(2) Average fixed cost	(3) Average variable cost	(4) Average total cost	(5) Marginal cost	(6) Price = marginal revenue	(7) Total economic profit (+) or loss −
0						$ −100
				$ 90	$131	
1	$100.00	$90.00	$190.00			− 59
				80	131	
2	50.00	85.00	135.00			− 8
				70	131	
3	33.33	80.00	113.33			− 53
				60	131	
4	25.00	75.00	100.00			+124
				70	131	
5	20.00	74.00	94.00			+185
				80	131	
6	16.67	75.00	91.67			+236
				90	131	
7	14.29	77.14	91.43			+277
				110	131	
8	12.50	81.25	93.75			+298
				130	131	
9	11.11	86.67	97.78			+299
				150	131	
10	10.00	93.00	103.00			+280

***Graphic Portrayal* Figure 10-3 (Key Graph)** compares price and marginal cost graphically. Here per unit economic profit is indicated by the distance *AP*. When multiplied by the profit-maximizing output, the total economic profit is shown by the shaded rectangular area.

It should be noted that the firm is seeking to maximize its *total* profits, not its *per unit* profits. Per unit profits are largest at 7 units of output, where price exceeds average total cost by $39.57 ($131 minus $91.43). But by producing only 7 units, the firm would be forgoing the production of two additional units of output that would clearly contribute to total profits. The firm is happy to accept lower per-unit profits if the resulting extra units of sales more than compensate for the lower per-unit profits.

Loss-Minimizing Case Now assume that market price is $81 rather than $131. Should the firm produce? If so, how much? And what will the resulting profits or losses be? The answers are, respectively, yes, six units, and a loss of $64.

Column 6 of Table 10-6 shows the new price (equal to marginal revenue) alongside the same unit- and marginal-cost data presented in Table 10-5. Comparing columns 5 and 6, we find that the first unit of output adds $90 to total cost but only $81 to total revenue. One might conclude, "Don't produce — close down!" But this would be hasty. Remember that at very low levels of production, marginal product is

"*Actually, Lou, I think it was more than just my being in the right place at the right time. I think it was my being the right race, the right religion, the right sex, the right socioeconomic group, having the right accent, the right clothes, going to the right schools . . .*"

FIGURE 10-3   The short-run profit-maximizing position of a purely competitive firm

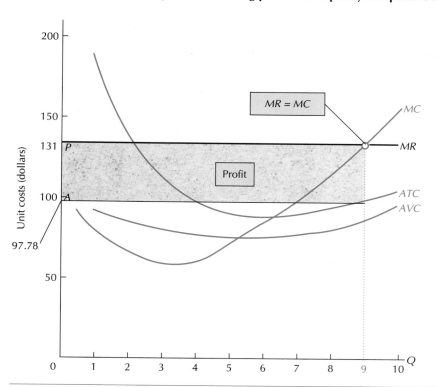

The $P = MC$ output allows the competitive producer to maximize profits or minimize losses. In this case, price exceeds average total cost at the $P = MC$ output of 9 units. Economic profits per unit of AP are realized; total economic profits are indicated by the shaded rectangle.

low, making marginal cost unusually high. The price–marginal-cost relationship might improve with increased production. And it does.

On the next 5 units — 2 through 6 — price exceeds marginal cost. Each of these 5 units adds more to revenue than to cost, more than compensating for the "loss" taken on the first unit. Beyond 6 units, however, MC exceeds MR ($=P$). The firm

TABLE 10-6   The loss-minimizing outputs for a purely competitive firm: marginal-revenue-equals-marginal-cost approach (prices = $81 and $71) (*hypothetical data*)

(1)	(2)	(3)	(4)	(5)	(6)	(7)	(8)	(9)
	Average	Average	Average		$81 price =	Profit (+)	$71 price =	Profit (+)
Total	fixed	variable	total	Marginal	marginal	or loss (−),	marginal	or loss (−),
product	cost	cost	cost	cost	revenue	$81 price	revenue	$71 price
0						$ −100		$ −100
1	$100.00	$90.00	$190.00	$ 90	$81	−109	$71	−119
2	50.00	85.00	135.00	80	81	−108	71	−128
3	33.33	80.00	113.33	70	81	− 97	71	−127
4	25.00	75.00	100.00	60	81	− 76	71	−116
5	20.00	74.00	94.00	70	81	− 65	71	−115
6	16.67	75.00	91.67	80	81	− 64	71	−124
7	14.29	77.14	91.43	90	81	− 73	71	−143
8	12.50	81.25	93.75	110	81	−102	71	−182
9	11.11	86.67	97.78	130	81	−151	71	−241
10	10.00	93.00	103.00	150	81	−220	71	−320

should therefore produce at 6 units. In general, the profit-seeking firm should always compare marginal revenue (or price under pure competition) with the *rising* portion of its marginal-cost schedule or curve.

Loss Determination Will production be profitable? No, because at 6 units of output, average total costs of $91.67 exceed price of $81 by $10.67 per unit. Multiply by the 6 units of output, and we find the firm's total loss is $64. Then why produce? Because this loss is less than the firm's $100 worth of fixed costs — the $100 loss the firm would incur in the short run by closing down. The firm receives enough revenue per unit ($81) to cover its variable cost of $75 and also provide $6 per unit, or a total of $36, to apply against fixed costs. Therefore, the firm's loss is only $64 ($100 − $36), rather than $100.

Graphic Portrayal This case is shown in Figure 10-4. Whenever price exceeds the minimum average variable cost but falls short of average total cost, the firm can pay part of, but not all, its fixed costs by producing. In this instance, total variable costs are shown by the area $0VGF$. Total revenue, however, is $0PEF$, greater than total variable costs by $VPEG$. This excess of revenue over variable costs can be applied against total fixed costs, represented by area $VACG$. By producing 6 units, the firm's loss is only area $PACE$; by closing down, its loss would be its fixed costs shown by the larger area $VACG$.

Close-Down Case Suppose now that the market yields a price of only $71. It will now pay the firm to close down because there is no output at which the firm can cover its average variable costs, much less its average total cost. In other words, the smallest loss it can realize by producing is greater than the $100 worth of fixed costs it will lose by closing down.

This can be verified by comparing columns 3 and 8 of Table 10-6 and can be seen in Figure 10-5. Price comes closest to covering average variable costs at the MR ($=P$) = MC output of 5 units. But even here, price or revenue per unit would fall short of average variable cost by $3 (= $74 minus $71). By producing at the MR ($=P$) = MC output, the firm would lose its $100 worth of fixed costs, *plus* $15 ($3 on each of the five units) worth of variable costs, for a total loss of $115. This clearly compares unfavourably with the $100 fixed-cost loss the firm would incur by closing down. In short, it will pay the firm to close down rather than operate at a $71 price or, for that matter, at any price less than minimum average variable cost of $74.

The close-down case obligates us to modify our MR ($=P$) = MC rule for profit maximization or loss minimization: ***A competitive firm will maximize profits or minimize losses in the short run by producing at that output at which MR ($=P$) = MC, provided that price exceeds minimum average-variable-cost.***

FIGURE 10-4 The short-run loss-minimizing position of a purely competitive firm

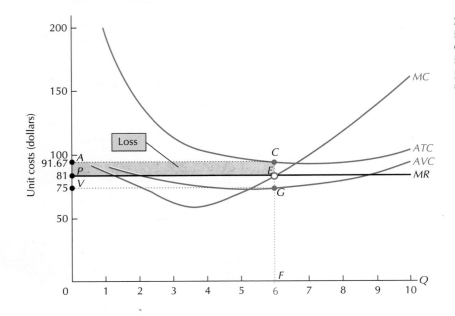

If price exceeds the minimum *AVC* but is less than *ATC*, the *P* = *MC* output of 6 units will permit the firm to minimize its losses. In this instance, losses are *AP* per unit; total losses are shown by the area *PACE*.

FIGURE 10-5   The short-run close-down position of a purely competitive firm

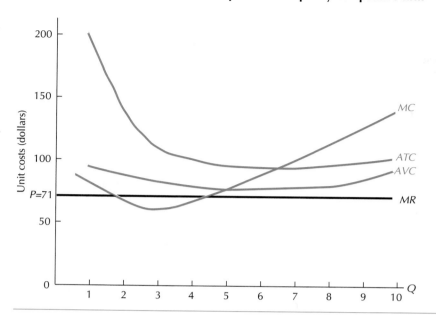

If price falls short of minimum *AVC*, the competitive firm will minimize its losses in the short run by closing down. There is no level of output at which the firm can produce and realize a loss smaller than its fixed costs.

Marginal Cost and the Short-Run Supply Curve

You will recognize that we have simply selected three different prices and asked how much the profit-seeking competitive firm, faced with certain costs, would choose to supply in the market at each of these prices. This information — price and corresponding quantity supplied — constitutes the supply schedule for the competitive firm.

Table 10-7 summarizes the supply-schedule data for the three prices chosen — $131, $81, and $71. You are urged to apply the MR $(=P)$ = MC rule (modified by the close-down case) to verify the quantity-supplied data for the $151, $111, $91, and $61 prices and calculate the corresponding profits or losses. We confirm that the supply schedule is up-sloping. Here price must be $74 (equal to minimum average variable cost) or greater before any output is supplied. And because the marginal cost of successive units of output is increasing, the firm must get successively higher prices for it to be profitable to produce these additional units of output.

Figure 10-6 (Key Graph) generalizes on our application of the MR $(=P)$ = MC rule. We have drawn the appropriate cost curves and from the vertical axis have extended a series of marginal-revenue lines from some possible prices the market might set

for the firm. The crucial prices are P_1 and P_3. Our close-down case reminds us that at any price *below* P_1 — the price that is equal to the minimum average variable cost — the firm should close down.

P_3 is strategic because it is the price at which the firm will just break even by producing Q_3 units of output, as indicated by the MR $(=P)$ = MC rule. Here, total revenue will just cover total costs (including a normal profit).

At P_2 the firm supplies Q_2 units of output and minimizes its losses. At any other price between P_1 and

TABLE 10-7   The supply schedule of a competitive firm confronted with the cost data of Table 10-5 (hypothetical data)

Price	Quantity supplied	Maximum profit (+) or minimum loss (−)
$151	10	$ _____
131	9	+299
111	8	_____
91	7	_____
81	6	−64
71	0	−100
61	0	_____

FIGURE 10-6   The $P = MC$ rule and the competitive firm's short-run supply curve

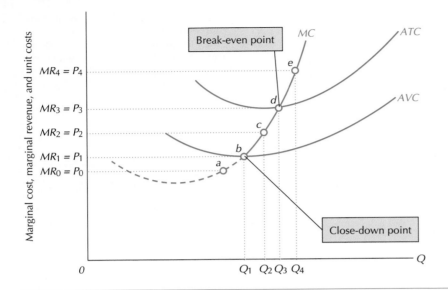

Application of the $P = MC$ rule, as modified by the close-down case, reveals that the (solid) segment of the firm's MC curve that lies above AVC is the firm's short-run supply curve. More specifically, at price P_0, $P = MC$ at point a, but the firm will produce no output because P_0 is less than minimum AVC. At price P_1 the firm is in equilibrium at point b, where it produces Q_1 units and incurs a loss equal to its fixed costs. At P_2 equilibrium is at point c, where output is Q_2 and losses are less than fixed costs. Equilibrium is at point d if price is P_3, in this case the firm breaks even because at output Q_3 price equals ATC. At price P_4 the firm reaches an equilibrium at point e and maximizes its economic profit by producing Q_4 units.

P_3, the firm will minimize its losses by producing to the point where MR $(-P) = MC$.

At any price above P_3, the firm will maximize its economic profits by producing to the point where MR $(=P) = MC$. Thus at P_4 the firm will realize the greatest profits by supplying Q_4 units of output.

The basic point is that each of the various MR $(=P) = MC$ intersection points shown as b, c, d, and e in Figure 10-6 indicates a possible product price (on the vertical axis) and the corresponding quantity the profit-seeking firm would supply at that price (on the horizontal axis). These points by definition locate the supply curve of the competitive firm. We can conclude that *the portion of the firm's marginal-cost curve that lies above its average-variable-cost curve is its* **short-run supply curve.** The heavy segment of the marginal-cost curve is the short-run supply curve in Figure 10-6.

In Chapter 9 we saw that changes in such factors as the prices of variable inputs or in technology will shift the marginal-cost or short-run supply curve to a new location. For example, a wage increase would shift the supply curve upward, constituting a decrease in supply. Technological progress that increases the productivity of labour would shift the marginal cost or supply curve downward, representing an increase in supply. You should determine how (1) a specific tax on the product and (2) a per unit subsidy on this product would shift the supply curve.

Table 10-8 provides a convenient check on the total-revenue–total-cost and MR = MC approaches

to determining the competitive firm's profit-maximizing output. This table warrants careful study by the reader.

QUICK REVIEW (10-3)

1. **Profits are maximized or losses minimized at that output at which marginal revenue or price equals marginal cost.**

2. **At any price below minimum average variable cost the firm will minimize losses by closing down.**

3. **The segment of the firm's marginal cost curve that lies above average variable cost is its short-run supply curve.**

Firm and Industry: Equilibrium Price

We must now determine which of the various price possibilities will actually be the equilibrium price. From Chapter 4, we know that in a purely competitive market, equilibrium price is determined by *total* supply and total demand. To derive total supply, the sales schedules or curves of the individual competitive firms must be summed. Thus in Table 10-9, columns 1 and 3 repeat the individual competitive firm's supply schedule just derived in Table 10-7. We now

TABLE 10-8   Summary of competitive output determination in the short run

	Total-revenue–total-cost approach	Marginal-revenue–marginal-cost approach
Should the firm produce?	Yes, if TR exceeds TC or if TC exceeds TR by some amount less than total fixed costs.	Yes, if price is equal to, or greater than, minimum average variable cost.
What quantity should be produced to maximize profits?	Produce where the excess of TR over TC is a maximum or where the excess of TC over TR is a minimum (and less than total fixed costs).	Produce where MR or price equals MC.
Will production result in an economic profit?	Yes, if TR exceeds TC. No, if TC exceeds TR.	Yes, if price exceeds average total cost. No, if average total cost exceeds price.

assume that there are a total of 1,000 competitive firms in this industry, each having the same total and unit costs as the single firm we have discussed. This lets us calculate the total- or market-supply schedule (columns 2 and 3) by multiplying the quantity-supplied figures of the single firm (column 1) by 1,000.

Market Price and Profits   To determine equilibrium price and output, this total-supply data must be compared with total-demand data. For purposes of illustration, let's assume total-demand data are as shown in columns 3 and 4 of Table 10-9. Comparing the total quantity supplied and total quantity demanded at the seven possible prices, we determine that equilibrium price is $111 and equilibrium quantity 8,000 units for the industry, and 8 units for each of the 1,000 identical firms.

Will these conditions of market supply and demand make this a prosperous industry? Multiplying product price ($111) by output (8), we find the total revenue of each firm is $888. Total cost is $750, found by multiplying average total cost of $93.75 by 8, or simply by looking at column 5 of Table 10-3. The $138 difference is the economic profit of each firm. For the industry, total economic profit is $138,000. This is a prosperous industry.

Graphic Portrayal   Figures 10-7(a) and (b) show this analysis graphically. The individual supply curves of each of the 1,000 identical firms — one of which is shown as *s* in Figure 10-7(a) — are summed horizontally to get the total-supply curve *S* of Figure 10-7(b). Given total demand *D*, equilibrium price is $111, and equilibrium quantity for the industry is

TABLE 10-9   Firm and market supply and market demand (*hypothetical data*)

(1) Quantity supplied, single firm	(2) Total quantity supplied, 1,000 firms	(3) Product price	(4) Total quantity demanded
10	10,000	$151	4,000
9	9,000	131	6,000
8	8,000	111	8,000
7	7,000	91	9,000
6	6,000	81	11,000
0	0	71	13,000
0	0	61	16,000

FIGURE 10-7   Short-run competitive equilibrium for (a) a representative firm and (b) the industry

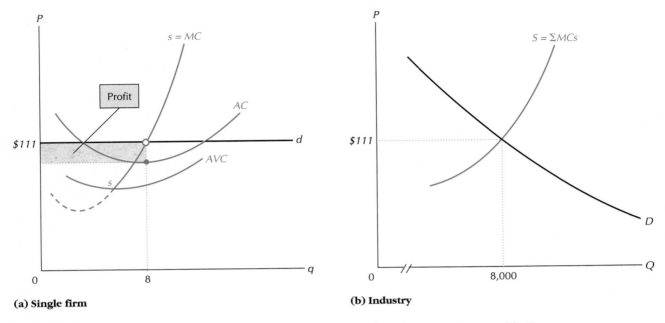

(a) Single firm

(b) Industry

The horizontal sum of the 1,000 firms' supply curves (s) determines the industry supply curve (S). Given industry demand (D), the short-run equilibrium price and output for the industry are $111 and 8,000 units. Taking the equilibrium price as given datum, the representative firm establishes its profit-maximizing output at 8 units and, in this case, realizes the economic profit shown by the colour area.

8,000 units. This equilibrium price is given and unalterable to the individual firm; that is, each firm's demand curve is perfectly elastic at the equilibrium price, indicated by d. Because price is given and constant to the individual firm, the marginal-revenue curve coincides with the demand curve. This $111 price exceeds average total cost at the firm's equilibrium MR ($=P$) = MC output, resulting in a situation of economic profits similar to that already portrayed in Figure 10-3.

Assuming no changes in costs or market demand occur, these diagrams reveal a *short-run* equilibrium situation. There are no shortages or surpluses in the market to cause price or total quantity to change. Nor can any of the firms in the industry improve its profits by altering output. Note, too, that higher unit and marginal costs or a weaker market demand situation could have created a loss situation similar to Figure 10-4. You are urged to sketch, in Figures 10-7(a) and (b), how higher costs and a less favourable demand could cause short-run losses.

Firm Versus Industry   Figures 10-7(a) and (b) underscore a point made earlier: Product price is a given to the *individual* competitive firm, but, at the same time, the supply plans of all competitive producers *as a group* are a basic determinant of product price. If we recall the fallacy of composition, we find there is no inconsistency here. Though each firm, supplying a negligible fraction of total supply, cannot affect price, the sum of the supply curves of all the many firms in the industry constitutes the industry supply curve, and this curve does have an important bearing on price. *Under competition, equilibrium price is a given to the individual firm and simultaneously is the result of the production (supply) decisions of all firms taken as a group.*

PROFIT MAXIMIZATION IN THE LONG RUN

In the short run there are a given number of firms in an industry, each of which has a fixed, unalterable plant. By contrast, in the long run firms already in an industry have sufficient time either to expand or to contract their plant capacities. More importantly, the number of firms in the industry may either increase or decrease as new firms enter or existing firms leave. We now examine how these long-run adjustments modify our conclusions about short-run output and price determination.

Assumptions and Goal

We will make certain simplifying assumptions, none of which will impair the general validity of our conclusions.

1. Entry and Exodus We assume that the only long-run adjustment is the entry and exodus of firms. Furthermore, we ignore the short-run adjustments already analysed, to grasp more clearly the nature of long-run competitive adjustments.

2. Identical Costs We also assume that all firms in the industry have identical cost curves. This lets us discuss an "average," or "representative," firm knowing that all other firms in the industry are similarly affected by any long-run adjustments that occur.

3. Constant-Cost Industry We assume for the moment that the industry under discussion is a constant-cost industry. This means that the entry and exodus of firms will *not* affect resource prices or, therefore, the locations of the unit-cost schedules of individual firms.

We will describe long-run competitive adjustments both verbally and through graphic analysis. The basic conclusion we seek to explain is as follows: *After all long-run adjustments are completed — that is, when long-run equilibrium is achieved — product price will be exactly equal to, and production will occur at, each firm's point of minimum average total cost.*

This conclusion follows from two basic facts: (1) firms seek profits and shun losses, and (2) under competition, firms are free to enter and leave industries. If price initially exceeds average total costs, the resulting economic profits will attract new firms to the industry. But this expansion of the industry will increase product supply until price is brought back down into equality with average total cost. Conversely, if price is initially less than average total cost, resulting losses will cause firms to leave the industry. As they leave, total product supply will decline, bringing price back up into equality with average total cost.

Zero Profit Model

Our conclusion can best be demonstrated, and its significance evaluated, by assuming that a representative firm in a purely competitive industry is initially in long-run equilibrium. This is shown in Figure 10-8(a), where price and minimum average total cost are

equal at $50. Economic profits here are zero; the industry is in equilibrium, or "at rest," because there is no tendency for firms to enter or leave the industry. The going market price is determined by total, or industry, demand and supply, as shown by D_0 and S_0 in Figure 10-8(b). By examining the quantity axes of the two graphs, we note that if all firms are identical, there must be 1,000 firms in the industry, each producing 100 units, to achieve the industry's equilibrium output of 100,000 units.

Entry of Firms Eliminates Profits

Let's upset the long-run equilibrium in Figure 10-8 and trace the subsequent adjustments. Suppose a change in consumer tastes increases product demand from D_0 to D_1. This shift in demand makes production profitable; the new price of $60 exceeds average total cost of $50. *These economic profits will lure new firms into the industry.* Some of the entrants will be newly created firms; others will shift from less prosperous industries.

As the firms enter, the market supply of the product will increase, causing product price to gravitate downward from $60 towards the original $50 level. Economic profits will persist and entry will therefore continue until short-run market supply has increased to S_1. At this point, price is again equal to minimum average total cost at $50. The economic profits caused by the boost in demand have been competed away to zero and as a result, the previous incentive for more firms to enter the industry has disappeared. Long-run equilibrium is restored.

Figure 10-8 tells us that on the re-establishment of long-run equilibrium, industry output is 110,000 units, and that each firm in the now expanded industry is producing 100 units. We can conclude that the industry is now composed of 1,100 firms; that is, 100 new firms have entered the industry.

Exodus of Firms Eliminates Losses

Now let's suppose the consumer demand falls from D_0 to D_2 in Figures 10-9(a) and (b). This forces price down to $40, making production unprofitable. *In time, resulting losses will induce firms to leave the industry.* Owners can realize a better return elsewhere. As capital equipment wears out and contractual obligations expire, some firms will simply fold.

As this exodus of firms proceeds, however, industry supply will decrease, moving from S_0 toward S_1. Price will begin to rise from $40 back toward $50. Losses will force firms to leave the industry until supply has declined to S_1, at which point price is again

FIGURE 10-8   Temporary profits and the re-establishment of long-run equilibrium in (a) a representative firm and (b) the industry

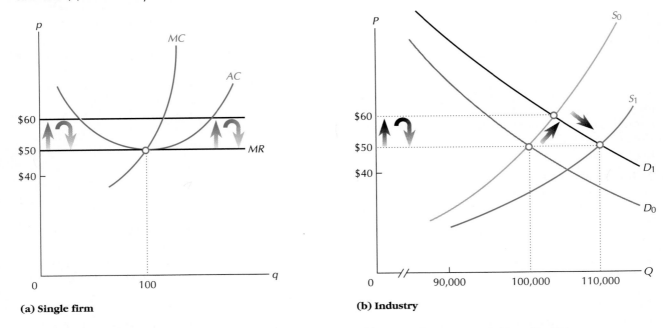

(a) Single firm

(b) Industry

A favourable shift in demand (D_0 to D_1) will upset the original equilibrium and cause economic profits. But profits will cause new firms to enter the industry, increasing supply (S_0 to S) and lowering product price until economic profits are once again zero.

exactly $50, barely consistent with minimum average total cost. The exodus of firms has continued until losses have been eliminated and long-run equilibrium has once again been restored.

Observe in Figures 10-9(a) and (b) that total quantity supplied is now 90,000 units and each firm is producing 100 units. This means that the industry is now populated by only 900 firms, rather than the original 1,000.

Long-Run Supply for a Constant-Cost Industry

What is the character of the **long-run supply curve** that evolves from this analysis of the expansion or contraction of a competitive industry? Although our discussion is concerned with the long run, we have noted that the market supply curves of Figures 10-8(b) and 10-9(b) are short-run industry supply curves. However, the analysis itself permits us to sketch the nature of the long-run supply curve for this competitive industry. The crucial factor in determining the shape of the industry's long-run supply curve is the effect, if any, that changes in the number

of firms in the industry will have on the costs of the individual firms in the industry.

Constant-Cost Industry   In the foregoing analysis of long-run competitive equilibrium, we assumed the industry under discussion was a **constant-cost industry**. This means that industry expansion through the entry of new firms will not affect resource prices or, therefore, production costs. Graphically, the entry of new firms does *not* change the position of the long-run average-cost curves of the individual firms in the industry.

When will this be the case? For the most part, when the industry's demand for resources is small in relation to the total demand for those resources. This is most likely to occur when the industry employs unspecialized resources that are being demanded by many other industries.

Perfectly-Elastic Supply   What will the long-run supply curve for a constant-cost industry look like? The answer is contained in our previous discussion of the long-run adjustments toward equilibrium. Here we assumed that entrance or departure of firms would not affect costs. The result was that entry or

FIGURE 10-9 **Temporary losses and the re-establishment of long-run equilibrium in (a) a representative firm and (b) the industry**

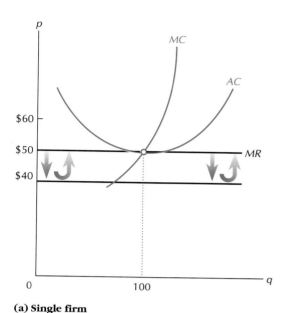

(a) Single firm

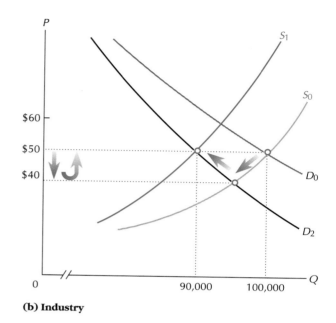

(b) Industry

An unfavourable shift in demand (D_0 to D_2) will upset the original equilibrium and cause losses. But losses will cause firms to leave the industry, decreasing supply (S_0 to S_1) and increasing product price until all losses have disappeared.

exodus of firms would alter industry output but always bring product price back to the original $50 level, where it is just consistent with the unchanging minimum average total cost of production. Specifically, we discovered that the industry would supply 90,000, 100,000, or 110,000 units of output, all at a price of $50 per unit. *The long-run supply curve of a constant-cost industry is perfectly elastic.*

This is demonstrated graphically in Figure 10-10, where the data from Figures 10-8 and 10-9, are retained. Suppose that industry demand is originally D_0, industry output is Q_0 (100,000), and product price is Q_0P_0 ($50). Now assume that demand increases to D_1, upsetting this equilibrium. The resulting economic profits will attract new firms. Because this is a constant-cost industry, entry will continue and industry output will expand until price is driven back down to the unchanged minimum average-total-cost level. This will be at price Q_1P_1 ($50) and output Q_1 (110,000).

This analysis is reversible. A decline in short-run industry demand from D_0 to D_2 will cause an exodus of firms and, ultimately, a restoration of equilibrium at price Q_2P_2 ($50) and output Q_2 (90,000). A line that

FIGURE 10-10 **The long-run supply curve for a constant-cost industry is perfectly elastic**

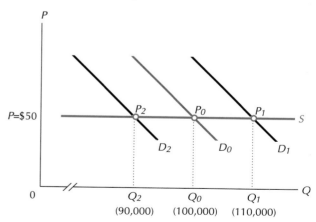

Because the entry or exodus of firms does not affect resource prices or therefore unit costs, an increase in demand (D_0 to D_1) will cause an expansion in industry output (Q_0 to Q_1) but no alteration in price ($Q_0P_0 = Q_1P_1$). Similarly, a decrease in demand (D_0 to D_2) will cause a contraction of output (Q_0 to Q_2) but no change in price ($Q_0P_0 = Q_2P_2$). This means that the long-run industry supply curve (S) will be perfectly elastic.

connects all points, such as these three, shows the various price-quantity supplied combinations that would be most profitable for the industry when it has had sufficient time to make *all* desired adjustments to assumed changes in industry demand. By definition, this line is the industry's long-run supply curve. In the case of a constant-cost industry, we note that this line, *S* in Figure 10-10, is perfectly elastic.

Long-Run Supply for an Increasing-Cost Industry

But constant-cost industries are a special case. Usually, the entry of new firms will bid up resource prices and therefore unit costs for individual firms in the industry. When an industry is using a significant portion of some resource whose total supply is not readily increased, the entry of new firms will increase resource demand in relation to supply and increase resource prices. This is particularly so in industries using specialized resources whose initial supply is not readily increased. Higher resource prices will result in higher long-run average costs for firms in the industry. These higher costs take the form of an upward shift in the long-run average-cost curve for the representative firm.

Two-Way Profit Squeeze   The net result is that when an increase in product demand causes economic profits and attracts new firms to the industry, a two-way squeeze on profits will occur to eliminate those profits. On the one hand, the entry of new firms will increase market supply and lower product price and, on the other, the entire average-total-cost curve of the representative firm will shift upward. The equilibrium price will now be higher than it was originally. The industry will only produce a larger output at a higher price because industry expansion has increased average total costs and, in the long run, product price must cover these costs. A greater industry output will be forthcoming at a higher price, thus the industry supply curve for an increasing-cost industry will be upsloping. Instead of getting either 90,000, 100,000, or 110,000 units at the same price of $50, in an increasing-cost industry 90,000 units might be forthcoming at $45; 100,000 at $50; and 110,000 at $55. The higher price is required to induce more production because costs per unit of output increase as the industry expands.

This can be seen graphically in Figure 10-11. Original market demand, industry output, and price are D_0, Q_0 (100,000) and $Q_0 P_0$ ($50) respectively. An increase in demand to D_1 will upset this equilibrium

FIGURE 10-11   **The long-run supply curve for an increasing-cost industry is upsloping**

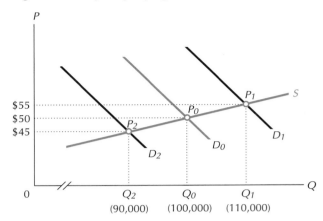

In an increasing-cost industry, the entry of new firms in response to increases in demand (D_2 to D_0 to D_1) will bid up resource prices and thereby increase unit costs. As a result, an increased industry output (Q_2 to Q_0 to Q_1) will be forthcoming only at higher prices ($Q_1 P_1 > Q_0 P_0 > Q_2 P_2$). The long-run industry supply curve (S) is therefore upsloping.

and lead to economic profits. As new firms enter, (1) industry supply will increase, tending to drive product price down, and (2) resource prices will rise, causing the average total costs of production to rise. Because of these average-total-cost increases, the new long-run equilibrium price will be established at some level *above* the original price, such as $Q_1 P_1$ ($55).

Conversely, a decline in demand from D_0 to D_2 will make production unprofitable and cause firms to leave the industry. The new equilibrium price will be established at some level *below* the original price, such as $Q_2 P_2$ ($45). Connecting these three equilibrium positions, we derive an upsloping long-run supply curve shown by S in Figure 10-11.

Long-Run Supply for a Decreasing-Cost Industry

In some industries firms may experience lower costs as the industry expands. Such industries are *decreasing-cost industries*. Classic example: As more mines are established in a given locality, each firm's costs in pumping out water seepage may decline. With more mines pumping, seepage into each is less, and pumping costs are therefore reduced. Furthermore, with only a few mines in an area, industry output might be so small that only relatively primitive and therefore costly transportation facilities are available. But as the number of firms and industry output expand, a railroad might build a spur into the area and thereby significantly reduce transportation costs.

You are urged to replicate the analysis underlying Figure 10-11 to show that the long-run supply curve of a decreasing-cost industry will be *downsloping*.

PURE COMPETITION AND EFFICIENCY

Whether a purely competitive industry is one of constant or increasing costs, the final long-run equilibrium position for each firm will have the same basic characteristics. As shown in **Figure 10-12 (Key Graph)**, price (and marginal revenue) will settle where they are equal to minimum average cost. However, we discovered in Chapter 9 that the marginal-cost curve intersects, and is therefore equal to, average cost at the point of minimum average cost. In the long-run equilibrium position, "everything is equal." MR ($= P$) = AC = MC.

FIGURE 10-12 For the competitive firm in long-run equilibrium, $P = AC = MC$

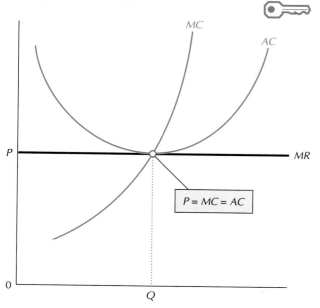

The equality of price and minimum average cost indicates that the firm is using the most efficient known technology and is charging the lowest price, *P*, and producing the greatest output, *Q*, consistent with its costs. The equality of price and marginal cost indicates that resources are being allocated in accordance with consumer preferences.

This triple equality tells us that although a competitive firm may realize economic profits or losses in the short run, it will break even by producing in accordance with the MR ($= P$) = MC rule in the long run. Also, this triple equality suggests certain conclusions of great social significance concerning the efficiency of a purely competitive economy. Subject to certain limitations and exceptions, a purely competitive economy will lead to the most efficient use of society's scarce resources. ***A competitive economy will allocate the limited amounts of resources available to society so as to maximize the satisfactions of consumers.*** The efficient use of limited resources requires that two conditions — which we will call allocative efficiency and productive efficiency — be fulfilled.

First, to achieve **allocative efficiency** resources must be apportioned among firms and industries to obtain the particular mix of products that is most desired by society (consumers). Allocative efficiency is realized when it is impossible to change the composition of total output to achieve a net gain for society.

Second, **productive efficiency** requires that each good in this optimum product mix be produced in the least costly way. To facilitate our discussion of how these conditions would be achieved under purely competitive conditions, let's examine the second point first.

1 Productive Efficiency: P = Minimum AC We know that in the long run, competition forces firms to produce at the point of minimum average total cost of production and to charge that price that is just consistent with these costs. This is a most desirable situation from the consumer's point of view. It means that firms must use the best available (least-cost) technology or they will not survive.

For example, glance back at the final equilibrium position shown in Figure 10-9(a). Each firm in the industry is producing 100 units of output by using $5,000 (equal to average cost of $50 *times* 100 units) worth of resources. If that same output had been produced at a total cost of $7,000, resources would be being used inefficiently. Society would be faced with the net loss of $2,000 worth of alternative products. Note too that consumers benefit from the lowest product price possible under the cost conditions currently prevailing.

2 Allocative Efficiency: P = MC Production must not only be technologically efficient, but must also be goods consumers want most. The competi-

Box 10-1

THE THEORY OF CONTESTABLE MARKETS

The concept of contestable markets suggests that the market power of imperfectly competitive producers may be severely constrained by potential industry entrants.

As noted in this chapter, the outcomes of purely competitive markets set standards of efficiency by which imperfectly competitive markets are judged. Both allocative and productive efficiency are realized when an industry is purely competitive. Princeton's William Baumol argues that the *potential* entry of firms to industries that are *not* purely competitive may also bring about the efficient results associated with pure competition.

Baumol has developed the notion of a *contestable market,* which means a market in which firm entry and exit are costless or virtually so. Envision a contestable market that is oligopolistic, that is, comprised of three or four large firms. The contestability of the market means that it is subject to "hit and run" entry by other firms because they can enter and leave virtually without cost. It follows that any economic profits or production inefficiencies on the part of the several firms in the industry will attract new entrants. (Productive inefficiencies imply that profits are being forgone by existing producers and new entrants can realize such profits by producing efficiently.) Hence, in contestable markets the mere presence of potential competition will force existing firms to produce efficiently and to charge prices that yield only a normal profit. Stated differently, incumbent firms are forced to behave as would purely competitive firms in order to forestall entry of other firms. We thus realize the socially desirable outcomes of purely competitive markets in contestable markets even though the latter are populated by only a few firms. The important factor that promotes these outcomes is not the number of firms in the industry, but costless entry and exit.

The most cited example of a contestable market is the airline industry. Assume there are just two airlines flying the Toronto–Vancouver route. If entry and exit were costly, the market would *not* be contestable and the two incumbent airlines might realize substantial economic profits from their protected market position. But in fact additional airlines can enter and leave this particular segment of the air transportation market with minimal cost. The reason is that the relevant capital equipment — the airplanes themselves — are highly mobile. Hence, if an additional airline were to enter and find the Toronto–Vancouver route to be unprofitable, it could simply pull out by flying its equipment to some other route. The important point is that the awareness of the possibility of costless entry will compel the two airlines currently flying the Toronto–Vancouver route to provide their transportation services efficiently and at prices that yield only a normal profit.

The main policy implication of contestable markets is that the focus of anti-monopoly policy should shift from the current structure or competitive conditions within an industry to the conditions of entry. The primary criticism of contestable market theory is that its applicability is extremely limited. Critics contend that there are few, if any, industries — including the aforementioned airline industry — in which entry and exit are costless.

tive market system functions so that resources are allocated to produce a total output whose composition best fits consumer preferences.

We must first grasp the social meaning of competitive product and resource prices. *The money price of any product — product X — is society's measure of the relative worth of that product at the margin.* Similarly, recalling the notion of opportunity costs, *the marginal cost of producing X measures the value of the other goods that the resources used in the production of an extra unit of X could otherwise have pro-*

duced. In short, product price measures the benefit, or satisfaction, that society gets from additional units of X, and the marginal cost of an additional unit of X measures the sacrifice, or cost to society, of other goods in using resources to produce more of X.

Under-Allocation: $P > MC$ Now, under competition, the production of each product will occur up to that precise point at which price is equal to marginal cost (Figure 10-12). The profit-seeking competitor will realize the maximum possible profit only by equating price and marginal cost. To produce short of the MR (= *P*) = MC point will mean less than maximum profits to the individual firm and an *under-allocation* of resources to this product from society's standpoint. The fact that price exceeds marginal cost indicates that society values additional units of X more highly than the alternative products the appropriate resources could otherwise produce.

Over-Allocation: P < MC   For similar reasons, the production of X should not go beyond the output at which price equals marginal cost. To do so means less than maximum profits for producers and an *over-allocation* of resources to X from the standpoint of society. To produce X at some point at which marginal cost exceeds price means that resources are being used in the production of X at the sacrifice of alternative goods that society values more highly than the added units of X.

Our conclusion is that **under pure competition, producers will produce each commodity up to that precise point at which price and marginal cost are equal. This means that resources are efficiently allocated under competition.** Each good is produced to the point at which the value of the last unit is equal to the value of the alternative goods sacrificed by its production.

It is the presumption of allocative efficiency that makes most economists hesitant to advocate governmental interference with, or regulations of, *free* markets, unless the reasons for such interference are clear and quite compelling.

Dynamic Adjustments   A further attribute of purely competitive markets is their ability to restore efficiency in the use of resources when disrupted by dynamic changes in the economy. In a competitive economy, any changes in consumer tastes, resource supplies, or technology will automatically set in motion appropriate realignments of resources.

As we have already explained, an increase in consumer demand for product X will increase its price. Disequilibrium will occur in that at its present output, the price of X will now exceed its marginal cost. This will create economic profits in industry X and stimulate its expansion. Its profitability will permit the industry to bid resources away from now less pressing uses. Expansion in this industry will end only when the price of X again equals its marginal cost, that is, when the value of the last unit produced once again equals the value of the alternative goods society forgoes in producing the last unit of X.

QUALIFICATIONS

Our conclusion that a purely competitive market system results in both productive and allocative efficiency must be qualified in several important respects.

The Income Distribution Problem   The contention that pure competition will allocate resources efficiently is predicated on some given distribution of money income resulting in a certain structure of demand. The competitive market system then brings about an efficient allocation of resources or, stated differently, an output of goods and services whose composition maximizes fulfilment of these particular consumer demands.

But if the distribution of money income is altered so that the structure of demand changes, would the competitive market system negotiate a new allocation of resources? The answer is yes; the market system would reallocate resources and therefore change the composition of output to maximize the fulfilment of this new pattern of consumer wants.

The problem, then, is which of these two "efficient" allocations of resources is the "most efficient"? Which allocation of resources yields the greatest level of satisfaction to society? There is no *scientific* answer to this question because we cannot measure and compare the satisfaction derived by various individuals from goods and services.

If all people were alike in their capacities to obtain satisfaction from income, economists could recommend that income be distributed equally and that the allocation of resources appropriate to *that* distribution would be the "best" or "most efficient" of all. But people differ in their education, experiences, and environment, as well as their inherited mental and physical characteristics. Such differences can be used to argue for an unequal distribution of income.

The market system does not provide for social or **public goods**. To better understand this concept consider the characteristics of *private goods*, which are produced through the market system. These goods are *divisible*, in that they come in units small enough to be afforded by individual buyers. Furthermore, private goods are subject to the **exclusion principle**, in that those who are willing and able to pay the equilibrium price get the product, but those who are unable or unwilling to pay are excluded from the benefits provided by the product.

Public goods would not be produced at all by the market system because their characteristics are essentially the opposite of those of private goods. Public goods are *indivisible*, involving such large units that they cannot be sold to individual buyers. More importantly, the exclusion principle does *not* apply; that is, there is no effective way of excluding individuals from the benefits of public goods once those goods come into existence. Obtaining the benefits of private goods is predicated on *purchase*; the benefits from public goods accrue to society from the *production* of such goods.

The distribution of income associated with the working of the competitive market system is quite unequal and therefore may lead to the production of luxury items for the rich while denying the basic needs of the poor. Many economists believe that the distribution of income that pure competition provides should be modified by public action. They maintain that allocative efficiency is hardly a virtue if it is a response to an income distribution that offends prevailing standards of equity.

Market Failure: Externalities and Public Goods The conclusion that competitive markets automatically bring about allocative efficiency rests on the assumption that there is no **market failure**, that all the benefits and costs associated with the production and consumption of each product are fully reflected in the market demand and supply curves respectively. Stated differently, it is assumed that there are no **spillovers** or **externalities** associated with the production or consumption of any good or service. *Externalities* or *spillovers*[2] occur when some

of the benefits or costs associated with the production or consumption of a good "spill over" on to third parties, that is, to parties other than the immediate buyer or seller.

The profit-seeking activities of producers will bring about an allocation of resources that is efficient from society's point of view only if marginal cost embodies *all* the costs that production entails and product price accurately reflects *all* the benefits that society gets from a good's production. Only in this case will competitive production at the MR ($= P$) = MC point balance the *total* sacrifices and satisfactions of society and result in an efficient allocation of resources. To the extent that price and marginal cost are not accurate indexes of sacrifices and satisfactions — to the extent that spillover costs and benefits exist — production at the MR ($= P$) = MC point will *not* signify an efficient allocation of resources (see Figure 19-1 and 19-2). Despite its other virtues, the competitive market system ignores this important class of goods and services — national defence, flood-control programs, and so forth — that can and do yield satisfaction to consumers but cannot be priced and sold through the market system.

Productive Techniques Purely competitive markets may not always entail the use of the most efficient productive techniques or encourage development of improved techniques. There are both a static (or "right now") aspect and a dynamic (or "over time") aspect of this criticism.

Natural Monopolies The static aspect involves the *natural monopoly* problem introduced in Chapter 9. In certain lines of production, existing technology may be such that a firm must be a large-scale producer to realize the lowest unit costs of production. Given consumer demand, this suggests that a relatively small number of large-scale producers is needed if production is to be carried on efficiently. Existing mass-production economies might be lost if such an industry were populated by the large number of small-scale producers that pure competition requires.

Technological Progress The dynamic aspect of this criticism concerns the willingness and ability of purely competitive firms to undertake technological advance. The progressiveness of pure competition is debated by economists. Some authorities believe that a purely competitive economy would *not* foster a very rapid rate of technological progress. They argue, first, that the incentive for technological advance may be weak under pure competition

---

[2] Spillovers or externalities may go by other names — for example, external economies and diseconomies, neighbourhood effects, and social benefits and costs. For a detailed treatment of externalities see Chapter 19.

because the profit rewards accruing to an innovating firm from a cost-reducing technological improvement will be quickly competed away by rival firms adopting the new technique. Second, the small size of the typical competitive firm and the fact that it tends to "break even" in the long run raise serious questions whether such producers could finance substantial programs of organized research. We will return to this controversy in Chapter 13.

Range of Consumer Choice   A purely competitive economy might not provide a sufficient range of consumer choice or foster development of new products. This criticism, like the previous one, has both a static and a dynamic aspect. Pure competition, it is contended, means product standardization, whereas other market structures — for example, monopolistic competition and, frequently, oligopoly — encom-

pass a wide range of types, styles, and quality gradations of any product. This product differentiation widens the consumer's range of free choice and simultaneously allows the buyer's preferences to be more completely fulfilled. Similarly, critics of pure competition point out that, just as pure competition is not likely to be progressive in developing new productive techniques, neither is this market structure conducive to improving existing products or creating completely new ones.

The question of the progressiveness of various market structures in terms of both productive techniques and product development will recur in the following three chapters.[3]

_____

[3] Instructors who want to consider agriculture as a case study in pure competition should insert Chapter 22 at this point.

CHAPTER SUMMARY

1. The market structures of *a.* pure competition, *b.* pure monopoly, *c.* monopolistic competition, and *d.* oligopoly are classifications into which most industries can be fitted with reasonable accuracy.

2. A purely competitive industry comprises a large number of independent firms producing a standardized product. Pure competition assumes that firms and resources are mobile among different industries.

3. No single firm can influence market price in a competitive industry; the firm's demand curve is perfectly elastic and price therefore equals marginal revenue.

4. Short-run profit maximization by a competitive firm can be analysed by a comparison of total revenue and total cost or through marginal analysis. A firm will maximize profits by producing that output at which total revenue exceeds total cost by the greatest amount. Losses will be minimized by producing where the excess of total cost over total revenue is at a minimum and less than total fixed costs.

5. Provided price exceeds minimum average variable cost, a competitive firm will maximize profits or minimize losses in the short run by producing at that output at which price or marginal revenue equals marginal cost. If price is less than average variable cost, the firm will minimize its losses by closing down. If price is greater than average variable cost but less than average total cost, the firm will minimize its losses by producing the $P = MC$ output. If price exceeds average total cost, the $P = MC$ output will provide maximum economic profits for the firm.

6. Applying the MR $(= P) = MC$ rule at various possible market prices leads to the conclusion that the segment of the firm's short-run marginal-cost curve lying above average variable cost is its short-run supply curve.

7. In the long run, competitive price will equal the minimum average cost of production because economic profits will cause firms to enter a competitive industry until those profits have been competed away. Conversely, losses will force the exodus of firms from the industry until product price once again barely covers unit costs.

8. The long-run supply curve is perfectly elastic for a constant-cost industry, upsloping for an increasing-cost industry, and downsloping for a decreasing cost industry.

9. The long-run equality of price and minimum average cost means that competitive firms will use the most efficient known (least-cost) technology and charge the lowest price consistent with their production costs. The equality of price and marginal cost implies that resources will be allocated in accordance with consumer tastes. The competitive price system will reallocate resources in response to a change in consumer tastes, technology, or resource supplies to maintain allocative efficiency over time.

10. The equality of price and marginal cost implies that resources will be allocated in accordance with consumer tastes. The competitive price system will reallocate resources in response to a change in consumer tastes, technology, or resource supplies to maintain allocative efficiency over time.

11. Economists recognize four possible deterrents to allocative efficiency in a competitive economy. *a.* There is no reason why the competitive market system will result in an optimal distribution of income. *b.* In allocating resources, the competitive model does not allow for spillover costs and benefits or for the production of public goods. *c.* A purely competitive industry may preclude the use of the best-known productive techniques and foster a slow rate of technological advance. *d.* A competitive system provides neither a wide range of product choice nor an environment conducive to the development of new products.

TERMS AND CONCEPTS

allocative efficiency (p. 163)
average, total, and marginal revenue (pp. 146–7)
break-even point (p. 148)
close-down case (p. 149)
constant-cost industry (p. 160)
exclusion principle (p. 166)
externalities (p. 166)
imperfect competition (p. 145)
long-run supply curve (p. 160)
loss-minimizing case (p. 152)
market failure (p. 166)

monopolistic competition (p. 144)
MR (= *P*) = MC rule (p. 151)
nonprice competition (p. 145)
oligopoly (p. 145)
productive efficiency (p. 163)
profit-maximizing case (p. 151)
public goods (p. 166)
pure competition (p. 144)
pure monopoly (p. 144)
short-run supply curve (p. 156)
spillover costs and benefits (p. 166)

QUESTIONS AND STUDY SUGGESTIONS

1. Briefly indicate the basic characteristics of pure competition, pure monopoly, monopolistic competition, and oligopoly. Under which of these market structures does each of the following most accurately fit: *a.* a supermarket in your home town; *b.* the steel industry; *c.* Manitoba wheat farm; *d.* the chartered bank

in which you or your family has an account; e. the automobile industry. In each case justify your classification.

2. Strictly speaking, pure competition never has existed and probably never will. Then why study it?

3. Use the following demand schedule to determine total and marginal revenues for each possible level of sales.

Product price	Quantity demanded	Total revenue	Marginal revenue
$2	0	$_____	
2	1	_____	$_____
2	2	_____	_____
2	3	_____	_____
2	4	_____	_____
2	5	_____	_____

a. What can you conclude about the structure of the industry in which this firm is operating? Explain.

b. Graph the demand, total-revenue, and marginal-revenue curves for this firm.

c. Why do the demand and marginal-revenue curves coincide?

d. "Marginal revenue is the change in total revenue." Do you agree? Explain verbally and graphically, using the above data.

4. Why is the equality of marginal revenue and marginal cost essential for profit maximization in all market structures? Explain why price can be substituted for marginal revenue in the MR = MC rule when an industry is purely competitive.

5. Explain: "A competitive producer must look to average variable cost in determining whether or not to produce in the short run, to marginal cost in deciding upon the best volume of production, and to average total cost to calculate profits or losses." Why might a firm produce at a loss in the short run rather than close down?

6. Assume the following unit-cost data for a purely competitive producer:

Total product	Average fixed cost	Average variable cost	Average total cost	Marginal cost
0				
1	$60.00	$45.00	$105.00	$45
2	30.00	42.50	72.50	40
3	20.00	40.00	60.00	35
4	15.00	37.50	52.50	30
5	12.00	37.00	49.00	35
6	10.00	37.50	47.50	40
7	8.57	38.57	47.14	45
8	7.50	40.63	48.13	55
9	6.67	43.33	50.00	65
10	6.00	46.50	52.50	75

a. At a product price of $32, will this firm produce in the short run? Why or why not? If it does produce, what will be the profit-maximizing or loss-minimizing output? Explain. Specify the amount of economic profit or loss per unit of output.

b. Answer the questions of 6a assuming product price is $41.

c. Answer the questions of 6a assuming product price is $56.

d. Complete the short-run supply schedule shown below for the firm, and indicate the profit or loss incurred at each output (columns 1 to 3).

(1) Price	(2) Quantity supplied, single firm	(3) Profit (+) or loss (−)	(4) Quantity supplied, 1,500 firms
$26	_____	$_____	_____
32	_____	_____	_____
38	_____	_____	_____
41	_____	_____	_____
46	_____	_____	_____
56	_____	_____	_____
66	_____	_____	_____

e. Explain: "That segment of a competitive firm's marginal-cost curve that lies above its average-variable-cost curve constitutes the short-run supply curve for the firm." Illustrate graphically.

f. Now assume there are 1,500 identical firms in this competitive industry; that is, there are 1,500 firms, each of which has the same cost data as shown here. Calculate the industry supply schedule (column 4).

g. Suppose the market demand for the product are as follows:

Price	Total quantity demanded
$26	17,000
32	15,000
38	13,500
41	12,000
46	10,500
56	9,500
66	8,000

What will equilibrium price be? What will equilibrium output be for the industry? For each firm? What will profit or loss be per unit? Per firm? Will this industry expand or contract in the long run?

7. Using diagrams for both the industry and a representative firm, illustrate competitive long-run equilibrium. Employing these diagrams, show how a. an

increase, and *b.* a decrease in market demand will upset this long-run equilibrium. Trace graphically and describe verbally the adjustment processes by which the long-run equilibrium is restored. Assume the industry is one of constant costs.

8. Distinguish carefully between constant-cost, increasing-cost, and decreasing-cost industries. Answer question *7.* assuming the industry is one of increasing costs. Compare the long-run supply curves of constant-cost, increasing-cost, and decreasing-cost industries.

9. Suppose a decrease in demand occurs in a competitive increasing-cost industry. Contrast the product price and industry output existing after all long-run adjustments are completed with those that originally prevailed.

10. In long-run equilibrium, $P = AC = MC$. Of what significance for the allocation of resources is the equality of P and AC? The equality of P and MC? Distinguish between productive and allocative efficiency in your answer.

11. Explain why some economists believe that an unequal distribution of income might impair the efficiency with which a competitive market system allocates resources. What other criticisms can be made of a purely competitive economy?

11

Price and Output Determination: Pure Monopoly

We deal with monopolies — sole sellers of various products and services — on a daily basis. When we mail a letter, we are using the services of Canada Post, a government-sponsored monopoly. Similarly, when we use the telephone, turn on the lights, or subscribe to cable TV, we are patronizing monopolies.

We now jump to the opposite end of the industry spectrum and examine the characteristics, price–output behaviour, and social desirability of pure monopoly. How is a pure monopoly defined? What conditions underlie its existence? How does a monopolist's price–output behaviour compare with that of a purely competitive industry? Do monopolists achieve the allocative and productive efficiency associated with pure competition? If not, can government policies improve the price–output behaviour of a pure monopolist?

PURE MONOPOLY: AN INTRODUCTION

Absolute or **pure monopoly** *exists when a single firm is the sole producer of a product or provider of a service for which there are no close substitutes.* Let's first examine the characteristics of pure monopoly and then discuss a few examples.

Characteristics

1 Single Seller   A pure, or absolute, monopolist is a one-firm industry. A single firm is the only producer of a given product or the sole supplier of a service; the firm and the industry are synonymous.

2 No Close Substitutes   Thus, the monopolist's product is unique in the sense that there are no close substitutes available. From the buyer's viewpoint, there are no reasonable alternatives. The buyer must buy the product or service from the monopolist or do without it.

3 "Price Maker"   We saw that the individual firm operating under pure competition exercises no influence over product price; it is a "price taker." This is so because it contributes only a negligible portion of total supply. In contrast, the pure monopolist is a **price maker**; the firm exercises considerable control over price because it controls the total quantity supplied. Given a downsloping demand curve for its product, the monopolist can change product price by manipulating the quantity of the product supplied. If it is advantageous, the monopolist will use this power.

4 Blocked Entry   A pure monopolist has no immediate competitors because there are **barriers to entry**. Economic, technological, legal, or other, obstacles must exist to keep new competitors from coming into the industry if monopoly is to persist. Entry under conditions of pure monopoly is totally blocked.

5 Advertising   The fact there are no close substitutes for the monopolized product has interesting implications for advertising. Depending on the type of product or service involved, a monopolist may or may not engage in extensive advertising and sales promotion. For example, a pure monopolist selling a luxury good such as diamonds might advertise heavily to increase the demand for the product. The result may be that more people will buy diamonds rather than take vacations. Local public utilities, on the other hand, normally do not make large expenditures for advertising, since people wanting water, gas, and electric power already know from whom they must buy these necessities.

Examples

In most cities government owned or regulated public utilities — gas and electric companies, the water company, the telephone company, the cable TV company, and the public transit system — are all monopolies or virtually so. There are no close substitutes for goods and services provided by these public utilities. Candles or kerosene lights are very imperfect substitutes for electricity; telegrams, letters, and courier services can be substituted for the telephone. But such substitutes are costly and inconvenient.

There are also a number of private, unregulated monopolies. On the international scene, the classic example is the DeBeers diamond syndicate, which effectively controls 80% to 90% of the world's supply of diamonds. But in Canada major manufacturing monopolies are rare and frequently transient because in time new competitors emerge to erode their single-producer status.

Professional sports leagues also embody monopoly power by granting member clubs franchises to be the sole suppliers of their services in designated geographic areas. The larger Canadian cities are served by a single professional baseball, football, or hockey team. If you want to see a live major-league professional hockey game in Calgary or Montreal, you have no choice but to patronize the Flames and *les Canadiens*, respectively.

Monopoly may also have a geographic dimension. A small town may be served by only one airline or railway. The local bank branch, movie theatre, or bookstore may approximate a monopoly in a small and isolated community.

Importance

Analysis of pure monopoly is important for at least two reasons.

1. A not insignificant amount of economic activity — perhaps 6% of the GDP — is carried out under conditions approaching pure monopoly.

2. A study of pure monopoly yields valuable insights into monopolistic competition and oligopoly, which will be discussed in Chapters 12 and 13. These two market structures combine in differing degrees characteristics of pure competition and pure monopoly.

BARRIERS TO ENTRY

The absence of competitors characterizing pure monopoly is largely explainable in terms of factors that prohibit firms from entering an industry. These barriers to entry are also pertinent in explaining the existence of oligopoly and monopolistic competition between the market extremes of pure competition and pure monopoly. In pure monopoly, entry barriers effectively block all potential competition.

What forms do these entry barriers assume?

Economies of Scale

Modern technology in some industries is such that efficient, low-cost production can be achieved only if producers are extremely large both absolutely and in relation to the market. Where economies of scale are very significant, a firm's long-run average-cost schedule will decline over a wide range of output (Figure 9-9(b)). Given market demand, achieving low unit costs depends on the existence of a small number of firms or, in the extreme case, only one firm.

The automobile, aluminum, and basic steel industries are a few of many heavy industries that reflect such conditions. If three firms currently enjoy all available economies of scale and each has roughly one-third of a market, it is easy to see why new competitors may find it extremely difficult to enter this industry.

New firms entering the market as small-scale producers will have little or no chance to survive and expand. As small-scale entrants, they cannot realize the cost economies enjoyed by the existing "Big Three" and therefore will be unable to realize the profits necessary for survival and growth. New competitors in the automobile and basic steel industries will not come from the successful operation and expansion of small "backyard" producers. They simply will not be efficient enough to survive.

The other option is to enter the industry as a large-scale producer. In practice, this is extremely difficult. It is very difficult for a new and untried enterprise to secure the money capital needed to obtain capital facilities comparable to those of the Big Three in the automobile industry. The financial obstacles in the way of starting big are so great, in many cases, as to be prohibitive.

Public Utilities: Natural Monopolies

In a few industries, economies of scale are particularly pronounced *and*, at the same time, competition is impractical, inconvenient, or simply unworkable.

Such industries are called **natural monopolies**. Most public utilities — the electric and gas companies, bus and railway firms, cable television, and water and communication facilities — fit into this category. These industries are generally given exclusive franchises by government. In return for this sole right to supply electricity, water, or bus service to a given geographic area, government reserves the right to regulate the operations of such monopolies to prevent abuses of the monopoly power it has granted. Sometimes, especially in the provision of electricity, governments achieve this by setting up Crown corporations.

As an example, it would be exceedingly wasteful for a community to have a number of firms supplying water or electricity. Technology is such in these industries that large-scale and extensive capital costs on generators, pumping and purification equipment, water mains, and transmission lines are required. This problem is aggravated because capital equipment must be sufficient to meet peak demands that occur on hot summer days when lawns are being watered and air conditioners operated, or, in the case of electricity, during the supper hours in the middle of a blizzard. The point is that unit costs of production decline with the number of cubic metres of water or kilowatt hours of electricity supplied by each firm. Unit costs thus fall as firm size increases.

The presence of several water and electricity suppliers would divide the total market and reduce the sales of each competitor. Each firm would be pushed back up its declining long-run average-cost curve, and therefore electricity and water rates would be unnecessarily high. In addition, competition could be highly inconvenient. The presence of a half-dozen telephone companies in an area could mean the inconvenience of having six telephones and six telephone books — not to mention six telephone bills — to ensure communications with all other residents in the same area.

Since natural monopolies can lower their average costs by expanding output, they try to increase sales by price cutting. As a result, cutthroat price competition breaks out when a number of firms exist in these public utilities industries. The result will be losses, the bankruptcy of weaker rivals, and the eventual merger of the survivors. The evolving pure monopoly may be anxious to recoup past losses and to profit fully from its new position of market dominance by charging monopoly prices for its goods or services.

To spare society such disadvantageous results, government will usually grant an exclusive franchise to a single firm to supply water, natural gas, electricity, telephone service, or train or bus transportation. In return, government reserves the right to designate the monopolist's geographic area of operation, to regulate the quality of its services, and to control the prices it can charge. The result is a regulated, or government-sponsored, monopoly — monopoly designed to achieve low unit costs but regulated so that consumers will benefit from these cost economies. Some of the problems associated with regulation will be examined later in this chapter and in Chapter 14.

Legal Barriers: Patents and Licences

We have already noted that government frequently gives exclusive franchises to natural monopolies. Government also creates legal entry barriers in awarding patents and licences.

Patents   By granting an inventor the exclusive right to produce or license a product for seventeen years, Canadian patent laws are aimed at protecting the inventor from having the product or process usurped by rival enterprises that have not shared in the time, effort, and money outlays that have gone into its development. By the same token, patents may provide the inventor with a monopoly position for the life of the patent. Patent control figured prominently in the growth of many modern-day industrial giants — National Cash Register, General Motors, Xerox, Polaroid, General Electric, and Du Pont. The United Shoe Machinery Company in the United States is a notable example of how patent control can be abused to achieve monopoly power. In this case, United Shoe became the exclusive supplier of certain essential shoemaking machinery by requiring all lessees of its patented machine to sign a "tying agreement" in which shoe manufacturers agreed also to lease all other shoemaking machinery from United Shoe. This allowed United Shoe to monopolize the market until partially effective anti-trust action was taken by the United States government in 1955.

Research underlies the development of patentable products. Firms that gain a measure of monopoly power by their own research or by purchasing the patents of others are in a strategic position to consolidate and strengthen their market position. The profits from one important patent can finance the research required to develop new patentable products. The pharmaceutical industry is a case in point. Patents on prescription drugs have produced large monopoly profits that have helped finance the discovery of new patentable medicines. Monopoly power achieved through patents may well be cumulative.

Licences   Entry into an industry or occupation may be limited by government through the issuing of licences. At the national level the Canadian Radio-Television and Telecommunications Commission licenses radio and television stations. In many large cities one must obtain a municipal licence to drive a taxicab. The restriction of the supply of cabs creates monopoly earnings for cab owners and drivers. In a few instances government might license itself to provide some product and thereby create a public monopoly. For example, the sale of liquor in each province is exclusively through provincially owned retail outlets. Many provinces have "licensed" themselves to run lotteries.

Ownership of Essential Inputs

A firm owning or controlling a resource that is essential in production can prohibit the creation of rival firms. The Aluminum Company of America retained its monopoly position in the aluminum industry for many years by virtue of its control of all basic sources of bauxite, the major ore used in aluminum fabrication. The International Nickel Company of Canada (Inco) used to control approximately 90% of the world's known nickel reserves. Most of the world's diamond mines are owned or effectively controlled by the De Beers Company of South Africa. Similarly, it is very difficult for new professional sports leagues to evolve when existing leagues have contracts with the best players and leases on the major stadiums and arenas.

Two Implications

Our discussion of barriers to entry suggests two noteworthy points about monopoly.

1 Relatively Rare   Barriers to entry are rarely complete. This is simply another way of stating our earlier point, that pure monopoly is relatively rare. Although, research and technological advance may strengthen the market position of a firm, technology may also undermine existing monopoly power. Existing patent advantages may be circumvented by the development of new and distinct, yet substitutable, products. New sources of strategic raw materials may be found. In the long run monopoly persists only with the sanction or aid of government — for example, Canada Post's monopoly on the delivery of first-class mail.

2 Desirability? It is implied in our discussion that monopolies may be desirable or undesirable from the standpoint of economic efficiency. The public-utilities and economies-of-scale arguments suggest that market demand and technology may be such that efficient, low-cost production presupposes the existence of monopoly. On the other hand, our comments on inputs ownership, patents, and licensing as sources of monopoly imply undesirable connotations of monopoly.

MONOPOLY DEMAND

Let's begin our analysis of the price-output behaviour of a pure monopolist by making three assumptions.

1. Our monopolist's status is secured by patents, economies of scale, or resource ownership.

2. The firm is *not* regulated by government.

3. The firm is a single-price monopolist; it charges the same price for all units of output.

The crucial difference between a pure monopolist and a purely competitive seller lies on the demand side of the market. We recall from Chapter 10 that the purely competitive seller faces a perfectly elastic demand schedule at the market price determined by industry supply and demand. The competitive firm is a "price taker" that can sell as much or as little as it wants at the going market price. The monopolist's demand curve — indeed, the demand curve of *any* imperfectly competitive seller — is much different. Because the pure monopolist is the industry, its demand curve is the industry demand curve.[1] And the industry demand curve is not perfectly elastic; it is downsloping. This is illustrated by columns 1 and 2 of Table 11-1. There are three implications of a downsloping demand curve that must be understood.

1 Price Exceeds Marginal Revenue A downsloping demand curve means that a pure monopoly can increase its sales only by charging a lower unit price for its product. *Since the monopolist must lower price to boost sales, marginal revenue is less than price (average revenue) for every level of output except the first.* The reason? Price cuts will apply not only to the extra output sold but also to *all* other units of output.

In Figure 11-1 we have extracted two price–quantity combinations — $142–3 and $132–4 — from the monopolist's demand curve. By lowering price from $142 to $132, the monopolist can sell one more unit and thus gain as revenue the fourth unit's price of $132. This gain is designated as the coloured rectangle in Figure 11-1. But to sell this fourth unit for $132, the monopolist must lower price on the first three units from $142 to $132. This $10 price reduction on 3 units results in a $30 revenue loss as indicated by the gray rectangle in Figure 11-1. The *net* change in total revenue or, in other words, marginal revenue, from selling the fourth unit is $102 — the $132 gain minus the $30 loss.

FIGURE 11-1 Price and marginal revenue under pure monopoly

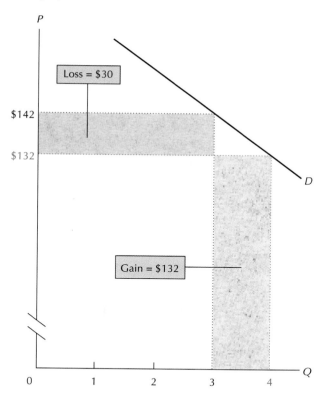

A pure monopolist — or, in fact, any imperfect competitor with a downsloping demand curve — must reduce price to sell more output. As a consequence, marginal revenue will be less than price. In our example, by reducing price from $142 to $132 the monopolist gains $132 from the sale of the fourth unit. But from this gain must be subtracted $30, which reflects the $10 price cut that has been made on each of the first three units. Hence, the fourth unit's marginal revenue is $102 (= $132 − $30), considerably less than its $132 price.

---

[1] Recall in Chapter 10 that we presented separate diagrams for the purely competitive industry *and* for a single firm in that industry. Because with pure monopoly the firm and the industry are one and the same, we need only a single diagram.

TABLE 11-1   Revenue and cost data of a pure monopolist (*hypothetical data*)

Revenue data				Cost data			
(1) Quantity of output	(2) Price (average revenue)	(3) Total revenue	(4) Marginal revenue	(5) Average total cost	(6) Total cost	(7) Marginal cost	(8) Profit (+) or loss (−)
0	$172	$ 0			$ 100		$ −100
1	162	162	$162	$190.00	190	$ 90	− 28
2	152	304	142	135.00	270	80	+ 34
3	142	426	122	113.33	340	70	+ 86
4	132	528	102	100.00	400	60	+128
5	122	610	82	94.00	470	70	+140
6	112	672	62	91.67	550	80	+122
7	102	714	42	91.43	640	90	+ 74
8	92	736	22	93.73	750	110	− 14
9	82	738	2	97.78	880	130	−142
10	72	720	− 18	103.00	1030	150	−310

This same point is evident in Table 11-1 where we observe that marginal revenue of the second unit of output is $142 rather than its $152 price because a $10 price cut must be taken on the first unit to increase sales from 1 to 2 units. Similarly, to sell 3 units, the firm must lower price from $152 to $142. The resulting marginal revenue will be just $122 — the $142 addition to total revenue the third unit of sales provides less $10 price cuts on the first 2 units of output. It is this rationale that explains why the marginal-revenue data of column 4 of Table 11-1 fall short of product price in column 2 for all levels of output except the first. Because marginal revenue is by definition the increase in total revenue associated with each additional unit of output, the declining marginal revenue figures mean that total revenue will increase at a diminishing rate, as shown in column 3 of Table 11-1.

The relationships between the demand, marginal revenue, and total revenue curves are portrayed graphically in Figure 11-2(a) and (b). In drawing this diagram we have extended the demand and revenue data of columns 1 to 4 of Table 11-1 by continuing to assume that successive $10 price cuts will each elicit one additional unit of sales. That is, 11 units can be sold at $62, 12 at $52, and so forth.

In addition to the fact that the marginal revenue curve lies *below* the demand curve, note the special relationship between total revenue and marginal revenue. Because marginal revenue is by definition the change in total revenue, we observe that so long as total revenue is increasing, marginal revenue is positive. When total revenue reaches its maximum, marginal revenue is zero. When total revenue is diminishing marginal revenue is negative.

2 Price Maker   In all imperfectly competitive markets in which downsloping demand curves are relevant — purely monopolistic, oligopolistic, and monopolistically competitive markets — firms have a price policy. By virtue of their ability to influence total supply, the output decisions of these firms necessarily affect product price. This is most evident in pure monopoly, where one firm controls total output. Faced with a downsloping demand curve in which each output is associated with some unique price, the monopolist unavoidably determines price in deciding what volume of output to produce.

The monopolist simultaneously chooses both price and output. In columns 1 and 2 of Table 11-1, we find that the monopolist can sell only an output of 1 unit at a price of $162, only an output of 2 units at a price of $152, and so forth.

This does not mean that the monopolist is "free" of market forces in establishing price and output, or that the consumer is completely at the monopolist's mercy. The monopolist's downsloping demand curve means that it cannot raise price without losing sales or gain sales without charging a lower price.

3 Price Elasticity   The total-revenue test for price elasticity of demand is the basis for our third conclusion. Recall from Chapter 5 that the total-revenue test

FIGURE 11-2   Demand, marginal revenue, and total revenue of an imperfectly competitive firm

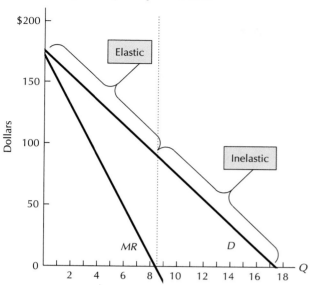

(a) Demand and marginal-revenue curves

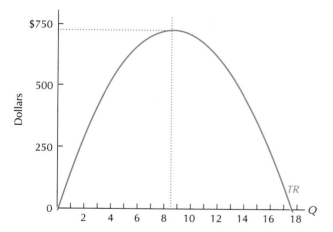

(b) Total-revenue curve

Because it must lower price to increase its sales, an imperfectly competitive firm's marginal-revenue curve (*MR*) lies below its downsloping demand curve (*D*). Total revenue (*TR*) increases at a decreasing rate, reaches a maximum, and then declines. Note that because *MR* is the change in *TR*, a unique relationship exists between *MR* and *TR*. In moving down the elastic segment of the demand curve, *TR* is increasing and hence *MR* is positive. When *TR* reaches its maximum, *MR* is zero. In moving down the inelastic segment of the demand curve, *TR* is declining, so *MR* is negative. A monopolist or other imperfectly competitive seller will never choose to lower price into the inelastic segment of its demand curve because by doing so, it will simultaneously reduce total revenue and increase production costs, thereby lowering profits.

tells us that when demand is elastic (inelastic), a decline in price will increase (decrease) total revenue. Beginning at the top of the demand curve in Figure 11-2(a), observe that for all price reductions from $172 down to approximately $82, total revenue increases (and marginal revenue therefore is positive). This means that demand is elastic in this price range. Conversely, for price reductions below $82, total revenue decreases (marginal revenue is negative), which indicates the demand is inelastic.

Our generalization is that a monopolist will never choose a price–quantity combination where total revenue is decreasing (marginal revenue is negative). ***The profit-maximizing monopolist will always want to avoid the inelastic segment of its demand curve in favour of some price–quantity combination in the elastic segment.*** By lowering price into the inelastic range, total revenue will decline. But the lower price is associated with a larger output and therefore increased total costs. Lower revenue and higher costs mean diminished profits.

QUICK REVIEW (11-1)

1. A pure monopolist is the sole supplier of a product or service for which there are no close substitutes.

2. Monopolies exist because of entry barriers such as economies of scale, patents and licences, and the ownership of essential resources.

3. The monopolist's demand curve is downsloping, causing the marginal revenue curve to lie below it.

4. Price declines in the elastic range of the monopolist's demand curve will increase total revenue, and marginal revenue will be positive; in the inelastic portion of the demand curve price declines will decrease total revenue, and marginal revenue will be negative.

OUTPUT AND PRICE DETERMINATION

What specific price–quantity combination on its demand curve will a profit-maximizing monopolist choose? To answer this question we need to add production costs to our understanding of monopoly demand.

Cost Data

On the cost side, we will assume that although the firm is a monopolist in the product market, it hires resources competitively and employs the same technology as our competitive firm in the preceding chapter. This allows us to use the cost data developed in Chapter 9 and applied in Chapter 10, to compare the price–output decisions of a pure monopoly with those of a pure competitor. Columns 5 to 7 of Table 11-1 restate the pertinent cost concepts of Table 9-2.

MR = MC Rule

A profit-seeking monopolist will employ the same rationale as a profit-seeking firm in a competitive industry. A monopolist will produce each successive unit of output so long as it adds more to total revenue than it does to total costs. The firm will produce up to that output at which marginal revenue equals marginal cost.

A comparison of columns 4 and 7 in Table 11-1 indicates that the profit-maximizing output is 5 units; the fifth unit is the last unit of output whose marginal revenue exceeds its marginal cost. What price will the monopolist charge? The downsloping demand curve of columns 1 and 2 of the table indicates that there is only one price at which 5 units can be sold: $122.

This analysis is presented graphically in **Figure 11-3 (Key Graph)**, where the demand, marginal-revenue, average-total-cost, and marginal-cost data of Table 11-1 have been drawn. Comparing marginal revenue and marginal cost confirms that the profit-maximizing output is 5 units or, more generally, Q_m. The indicated price is P_m. To charge a price higher than P_m, the monopolist must move up the demand curve, meaning that sales will fall short of the profit-maximizing level Q_m. If the monopolist charges less, it would involve a sales volume in excess of the profit-maximizing output.

Columns 2 and 5 of Table 11-1 indicate that at 5 units of output, product price of $122 exceeds average total cost of $94. Economic profits are therefore $28 per unit; total economic profits are then $140 (= 5 × $28). In Figure 11-3, per unit profit is indicated by the distance AP_m, and total economic profits — the shaded area — are found by multiplying this unit profit by the profit-maximizing output, Q_m.

No Monopoly Supply Curve

Recall that the supply curve of a purely competitive firm is that portion of its marginal cost curve lying

---

FIGURE 11-3   The profit-maximizing position of a pure monopolist

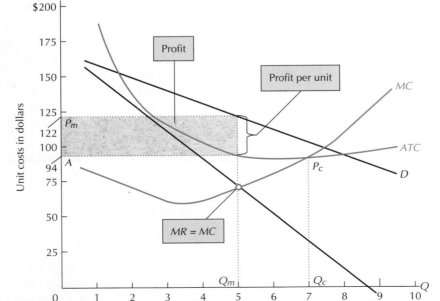

The pure monopolist maximizes profits by producing the *MR* = *MC* output. In this instance, profit is AP_m per unit; total profits are measured by the shaded rectangle.

above average variable costs (Figure 10-6). At first glance we would suspect that the pure monopolist's marginal cost curve would also be its supply curve. But this is *not* the case. ***The pure monopolist has no supply curve.*** The reason is that there is no unique relationship between price and quantity supplied. The price and amount supplied depend on the location of the demand (and therefore marginal revenue) curves. Like the competitive firm, the monopolist equates marginal revenue and marginal cost, but for the monopolist marginal revenue is less than price. Because the monopolist does *not* equate marginal cost to price, it is possible for different demand conditions to bring about different profit-maximizing prices for the same output. To convince yourself of this, go back to Figure 11-3 and pencil in a steeper (less elastic) demand curve, drawing its corresponding marginal revenue curve so that it intersects marginal cost at the same point as does the present marginal revenue curve. With the steeper demand curve this new MR = MC output will yield a higher price. Thus, our conclusion is that no single, unique price is associated with output level Q_m, and therefore there is no supply curve for the pure monopolist.

Misconceptions Concerning Monopoly Pricing

Our analysis explodes some popular fallacies about monopoly behaviour.

1 Not Highest Price Because a monopolist can manipulate output and price, it is often alleged that a monopolist "will charge the highest price it can get." This is wrong. There are many prices above P_m in Figure 11-3, but the monopolist shuns them because they entail a smaller-than-maximum profit. *Total* profits are the difference between *total* revenue and *total* costs, and each of these two determinants of profits depends on quantity sold as much as on price and unit cost.

2 Total, Not Unit, Profits The monopolist seeks maximum total profits, not maximum *unit* profits. In Figure 11-3, a careful comparison of the vertical distance between average cost and price at various possible outputs indicates that per-unit profits are greater at a point slightly to the left of the profit-maximizing output, Q_m. This is seen in Table 11-1, where unit profits are $32 at 4 units of output as compared with $28 at the profit-maximizing output of 5 units. Here the monopolist is accepting a lower-than-maximum per-unit profit because the additional sales more than compensate for the lower unit profits. A

profit-seeking monopolist would rather sell 5 units at a profit of $28 per unit (for a total profit of $140) than 4 units at a profit of $32 per unit (for a total profit of only $128).

3 Losses Pure monopoly does *not* guarantee economic profits. True, the likelihood of economic profits is greater for a pure monopolist than for a purely competitive producer. In the long run, a competitive firm can only make a normal profit; barriers to entry permit the monopolist to perpetuate economic profits in the long run.

Like a purely competitive producer, the monopolist will not persistently operate at a loss. Thus we can expect the monopolist to realize a normal profit or better in the long run. However, if the demand-and-cost situation faced by the monopolist is sufficiently less favourable than the one shown in Figure 11-3, short-run losses will be realized. Despite its dominance in the market, the monopolist shown in Figure 11-4 (p. 183) realizes a loss (of an amount shown by the shaded area) by virtue of weak demand and relatively high costs.

ECONOMIC EFFECTS OF MONOPOLY

Let's now evaluate pure monopoly from the standpoint of society as a whole. We will examine (1) price, output, and resource allocation; (2) some uncertainties caused by difficulties in making cost comparisons between competitive firms and a monopolist; (3) technological progress; and (4) income distribution.

Price, Output, and Resource Allocation

In Chapter 10, we concluded that pure competition would result in both "productive efficiency" and "allocative efficiency." Productive efficiency is realized because in the long run, the free entry and exodus of firms would force firms to operate at the optimum rate of output where unit costs of production would be at a minimum. Product price would be at the lowest level consistent with average total costs. In Figure 11-3, in long-run equilibrium, the competitive firm would sell Q_c units of output at a price of Q_cP_c.

Allocative efficiency is reflected in the fact that production under competition would occur up to the point at which price (the measure of a product's value to society) would equal marginal cost (the measure of the alternative products forgone by society in producing any given commodity).

Figure 11-3 indicates that, *given the same costs*, a pure monopoly will produce much less desirable results. As we have already discovered, the pure monopolist will maximize profits by producing an output of Q_m and charging a price of P_m. ***The monopolist will find it profitable to sell a smaller output and to charge a higher price than would a competitive producer.*** [2] Output Q_m is short of the Q_c point where average total costs are minimized (the intersection of MC and ATC). Looking back at column 5 of Table 11-1, ATC at the monopolist's 5 units of output is $94.00, as compared to the $91.43 that would result under pure competition. Also, at Q_m

units of output, product price is considerably greater than marginal cost. This means that society values additional units of this monopolized product more highly than it does the alternative products that resources could otherwise produce. The monopolist's profit-maximizing output results in an underallocation of resources; the monopolist finds it profitable to restrict output and therefore employ fewer resources than are justified from society's standpoint.

Income Distribution

Business monopoly probably contributes to inequality in income distribution. By virtue of their market power, monopolists charge a higher price than would a purely competitive firm with the same costs; monopolists in effect can levy a "private tax" on consumers and thereby realize substantial economic profits. These monopoly profits, it should be noted, are not widely distributed because corporate stock ownership is largely concentrated in the hands of upper income groups. The owners of a monopoly firm tend to be enriched at the expense of the rest of society.

Cost Complications

Our evaluation of pure monopoly has led us to conclude that, *given identical costs*, a purely monopolistic firm will find it profitable to charge a higher price, produce a smaller output, and foster an allocation of economic resources inferior to that of a purely competitive industry. These contrasting consequences are rooted in the entry barriers characterizing monopoly.

Now we must recognize that costs may *not* be the same for purely competitive and monopolistic producers. Unit costs incurred by a monopolist may be either larger or smaller than those facing a purely competitive firm. Several potentially conflicting considerations are involved: (1) economies of scale, (2) the notion of "X-inefficiency," (3) monopoly-preserving expenditures, and (4) the "very long run" perspective that allows for technological progress. We examine the first three issues in this section, and technological progress in the ensuing section.

Economies of Scale Revisited The assumption that unit costs available to the competitive firm and a monopoly are the same may not hold in practice. Given production techniques and therefore production costs, consumer demand may not be sufficient to support a large number of competing firms pro-

---

[2] In Figure 11-3, the price–quantity comparison of monopoly and pure competition is from the vantage point of the single purely competitive *firm* of Figure 10-7(a). An equally illuminating approach is to start with the purely competitive *industry* of Figure 10-7(b), reproduced below. Recall that the competitive industry's supply curve, *S*, is the horizontal sum of the marginal-cost curves of all the firms in the industry. Comparing this with industry demand, *D*, we get the purely competitive price and output of P_c and Q_c. Now suppose that this industry becomes a pure monopoly as a result of a wholesale merger or one firm's somehow buying out all its competitors. Assume, too, that no changes in costs or market demand result from this dramatic change in the industry's structure. What were formerly, say, 100 competing firms are now a pure monopolist, consisting of 100 branch plants.

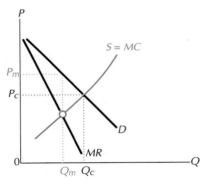

The industry supply curve is now the marginal-cost curve of the monopolist, the sum of the MC curves of its many branch plants. The important change, however, is on the market-demand side. From the viewpoint of each individual competitive firm, demand was perfectly elastic, and marginal revenue was therefore equal to price. Each firm equated MC to MR (and therefore to *P*) in maximizing profits (Chapter 10). But industry demand and individual demand are the same to the pure monopolist; the firm *is* the industry, and thus the monopolist correctly envisions a downsloping demand curve, *D*. This means that marginal revenue, MR, will be less than price; graphically, the MR curve lies below the demand curve. In choosing the profit-maximizing MC = MR position, the monopolist selects an output Q_m that is smaller, and a price P_m that is greater, than if the industry were organized competitively.

FIGURE 11-4 **The loss-minimizing position of a pure monopolist**

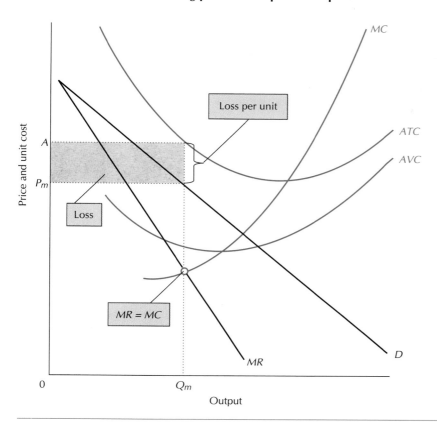

If demand, *D*, is weak and costs are high, the pure monopolist may be unable to make a profit. Because P_m exceeds *AVC* at Q_m, it will minimize losses in the short run by producing at that output where *MR* = *MC*. Loss per unit is AP_m, and total losses are indicated by the shaded rectangle.

ducing at an output that permits each one to realize all *existing* economies of scale. In such instances, a firm must be large in relation to the market — it must be a monopoly — to produce efficiently (at low unit cost).

This is shown diagrammatically in Figure 11-5. The argument is that with pure competition each firm would have only a small share of the market, such as Q_c. This small share forces each firm back up the long-run average cost curve so that unit costs are high (AC_c). Economies of scale are *not* being realized, and average costs are therefore high.

But with monopoly the single firm can achieve existing scale economies and lower unit costs. A monopolist may realize output Q_m with the consequent lower average cost of AC_m. Presumably these lower costs — even after allowing for an economic profit — translate into a lower product price than competitive firms could charge.

How important is this exception? Most economists believe that it applies mostly to public utilities and is not significant enough to undermine our general conclusions about the restrictive nature of monop-

oly. Evidence suggests that the large corporations in many manufacturing industries now have more monopoly power than can be justified on the grounds that these firms are merely availing themselves of existing economies of scale.

X-Inefficiency While economies of scale *might* argue for monopoly in a few cases, the notion of X-inefficiency tends to suggest that monopoly costs might be *higher* than those associated with more competitive industries. What is X-inefficiency? Why might it plague monopolists more than competitive firms?

All of the average cost curves used in this and other chapters are based on the assumption that the firm chooses technologies that permit the firm to achieve the minimum average cost for each level of output. **X-inefficiency** occurs when a firm's actual costs of producing any output are greater than the minimum possible costs. In Figure 11-5, X-inefficiency is represented by unit costs of AC_x (as opposed to AC_c) for output Q_c and average costs of AC'_x (rather than AC_m) for output Q_m. Any point

FIGURE 11-5   Economies of scale and x-inefficiency

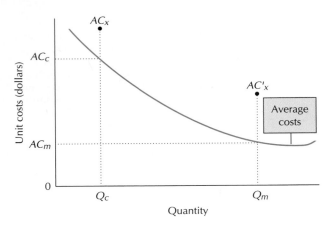

This diagram serves to demonstate two unrelated points. First, given the existence of extensive economies of scale, we note that a monopolist can achieve low unit costs of AC_m at Q_m units of output. In contrast, if the market were divided among a number of competing firms so that each produced only Q_c, then scale economies would be unrealized and unit costs of AC_c would be high. The second point is that X-inefficiency — the inefficient internal operation of a firm — results in higher-than-necessary costs. For example, unit costs might be AC_x, rather than AC_c for Q_c units of output and AC'_x rather than AC_m for the Q_m level of output.

above the average cost curve in Figure 11-5 is attainable but reflects internal inefficiency or "bad management."

Why does X-inefficiency occur? Managers may often have goals — for example, firm growth, an easier work life, the avoidance of business risk, providing jobs for incompetent friends and relatives — that conflict with cost minimization. Or X-inefficiency may arise because a firm's workers are poorly motivated.

Rent-Seeking Expenditures   Economists use the term **rent-seeking behaviour** in referring to activities designed to transfer income or wealth to a particular firm or resource supplier at someone else's or society's expense. We have seen that a monopolist can earn economic profits even in the long run. Therefore, it is no surprise a firm may go to considerable expense to acquire or maintain monopoly privileges granted by government. A monopolist's barrier to entry may depend on legislation or an exclusive licence provided by government, as in radio and television broadcasting. To sustain or enhance the consequent economic profits, the

monopolist may spend large amounts on legal fees, lobbying, and public relations advertising to persuade government to grant or sustain its privileged position. These expenditures add nothing to the firm's output, but increase its costs. Rent-seeking expenditures mean that monopoly might entail higher costs and a greater efficiency loss than suggested by Figures 11-3 and 11-5.

Technological Progress: Dynamic Efficiency

We have noted that our condemnation of monopoly must be qualified where *existing* mass-production economies might be lost if an industry comprises a large number of small, competing firms. Now we must consider the issue of **dynamic efficiency**, or whether monopolists are more likely to develop more efficient production techniques over time than competitive firms. Are monopolists more likely to improve productive technology, thereby lowering (shifting downward) their average-cost curves, than are competitive producers? Although we will concentrate on changes in productive techniques, the same question applies to product improvement. Do monopolists have greater means and incentives to improve their products and thus enhance consumer satisfaction? This is fertile ground for honest differences of opinion.

The Competitive Model   Competitive firms certainly have the incentive to employ the most efficient *known* productive techniques. Their very survival depends on being efficient. But competition deprives firms of economic profit — an important means and a major incentive to develop *new* improved productive techniques or *new* products. The profits from technological innovation may be short-lived to the innovating competitor. An innovating firm in a competitive industry will find that its many rivals will soon duplicate or imitate any technological advance it may achieve; rivals will share the rewards but not the costs of successful technological research.

The Monopoly Model   In contrast — thanks to entry barriers — a monopolist may persistently realize substantial economic profits. Hence the pure monopolist will have greater financial resources for technological innovation than will competitive firms. But what about the monopolist's incentives for technological advance? Here the picture is clouded.

There is one imposing argument suggesting that the monopolist's incentives to develop new techniques or products will be weak: the absence of com-

Box 11-1

In the Media

The accompanying article highlights the disagreement regarding monopoly power. Established pharmaceutical companies want to extend the length of time that their products enjoy a monopoly on the market through patent protection. They claim that they need an extended period of patent protection to make the required profits that allow large research and development costs. The generic drug manufacturers disagree with this line of reasoning, presumably arguing that such monopoly profits are not required for an even longer period. An extended period of patent protection would be detrimental to the generic drug manufacturers.

BIG DRUG COMPANIES TO GET ADDED PATENT PROTECTION

Ottawa's move a tough pill to swallow for generic industry

The federal government has endorsed an international trade proposal that would increase patent protection for multinational pharmaceutical manufacturers at the expense of Canada's generic drug industry. . . .

Barry Sherman, president of Canada's largest generic drug manufacturer, **Apotex Inc.**, reacted furiously to the news.

"I can't believe it. It's bizarre," Mr. Sherman said. "It's a complete capitulation to American pressure and it will destroy our industry."

The Pharmaceutical Manufacturers Association of Canada, which represents the large brand-name manufacturers, hailed [the trade minister's] action, saying that the move will lead to about $230-million in extra investment in Canada in the next few years.

About $180-million of that would be in capital investment and the other $50-million would be in additional research and development.

"This is a step in the right direction," said PMAC president Judy Erola. "It would mean an enormous amount of investment for Canada."

Wayne Schnarr, research director for the Canadian Drug Manufacturers Association, said it is unlikely that Apotex now will proceed with the second stage of a proposed $50-million expansion in Winnipeg.

Apotex has said it is committed to building the $20-million pilot phase of the chemical manufacturing plant, but the rest of the project is contingent on the current system remaining in effect.

Mr. Sherman was too angry to even deal with that issue yesterday.

"They put a nail in our coffin in 1987 [with Bill C-22]. Then they put another nail in and say, 'Oh, it's just one more nail.' Well, it's completely shut the lid on us. We're gasping for air."

Mr. Schnarr added that the generic industry will now begin to stagnate. "There will be no money for major new investments."

The Globe and Mail, "Report on Business," January 15, 1992.

petitors. Because of its sheltered market position, the pure monopolist can afford to be inefficient and lethargic. The monopolist has every reason to be satisfied with the status quo, to become complacent. It might well pay the monopolist to withhold or "file" technological improvements in both productive techniques and products to exploit existing capital equipment fully.

And even when improved techniques are belatedly introduced by monopolists, the accompanying cost reductions will accrue to the monopolist as increases in profits and only partially, if at all, to con-

sumers in the form of lower prices and an increased output. Proponents of this view point out that in a number of industries that approximate monopoly the interest in research has been minimal. Such advances as have been realized have come largely from outside the industry or from the smaller firms making up the competitive fringe of the industry.

Basically, there are at least two counterarguments:

1. Technological advance lowers unit costs and expands profits. As our analysis of Figure 11-3 implies, lower costs will give rise to a profit-maximizing position that involves a larger output and a lower price. Any expansion of profits will not be of a transitory nature; barriers to entry protect the monopolist from profit encroachment by rivals. Thus, technological progress is profitable to the monopolist, and therefore will be undertaken.

2. Research and technological advance may be one of the monopolist's barriers to entry; hence the monopolist must persist and succeed in these areas or eventually fall prey to new competitors, including those located abroad. Technological progress, it is argued, is essential to the maintenance of monopoly.

A Mixed Picture What can be offered by way of a summarizing generalization on the economic efficiency of pure monopoly? In a static economy where economies of scale are equally accessible to a monopolist and purely competitive firms, pure competition will be superior in that it forces use of the best-known technology and allocates resources according to the wants of society. However, when economies of scale available to the monopolist are not attainable by small competitive producers, the inefficiencies of pure monopoly are less evident.

QUICK REVIEW (11-2)

1. **The monopolist maximizes profits (or minimizes losses) at the MR = MC output and charges the price on its demand curve that corresponds to this output.**

2. **Given identical costs, a monopolist will be less efficient than a purely competitive firm because it produces less output and charges a higher price.**

3. **The inefficiencies of monopoly may be offset by economies of scale and technological progress, but intensified by the presence of X-inefficiency and rent-seeking expenditures.**

PRICE DISCRIMINATION

Up to now we have assumed that the monopolist charges a uniform price to all buyers. Under certain conditions, the monopolist can exploit its market position more fully and thereby increase profits by charging different prices to different buyers. In so doing, the seller is engaging in price discrimination. **Price discrimination** *occurs when a given product is sold at more than one price and these price differences are not justified by cost differences.*

Conditions

The opportunity to engage in price discrimination is not readily available to all sellers. In general, price discrimination is workable when three conditions are realized.

1 Monopoly Power The seller must be a monopolist or at least possess some degree of monopoly power, that is, some ability to control output and price.

2 Market Segregation The seller must be able to segregate buyers into separate classes, where each group has a different willingness or ability to pay for the product. This separation of buyers is usually based on different elasticities of demand, as later illustrations will make clear.

3 No Resale The original purchaser cannot resell the product or service. If buyers in the low-price segment of the market can easily resell in the high-price segment, the resulting decline in supply would increase price in the low-price segment and the increase in supply would lower price in the high-price segment. The price discrimination policy would thereby be undermined. This correctly suggests that service industries, such as the transportation industry or legal and medical services, are especially susceptible to price discrimination.

Illustrations

Price discrimination is widely practised in our economy. The sales representative who must communicate important information to corporate headquarters has a highly inelastic demand for long-distance telephone service and pays the high daytime rate. The university student making a periodic "reporting in" phone call home has an elastic demand and defers the call to take advantage of lower evening or weekend rates. Electric utilities frequently segment their markets by end uses, such as lighting and heating. The absence of reasonable substitutes means that the demand for electricity for illumination is inelastic and the price per kilowatt hour for this use is high. But the availability of natural gas and petroleum as alternatives to electrical heating makes the demand for electricity elastic for this purpose, and the price charged is therefore lower. Similarly, industrial users of electricity are typically charged lower rates than residential users because the former may have the alternative of constructing their own generating equipment while the individual household does not.

Movie theatres and golf courses vary their charges on the basis of time (higher rates in the evening and on weekends when demand is strong) and age (ability to pay). Railways vary the freight rate charged according to the market value of the product being shipped; the shipper of 10 tonnes of television sets or costume jewellery will be charged more than the shipper of 10 tonnes of gravel or coal. Airlines charge high fares to travelling executives, whose demand for travel is inelastic, and offer a variety of lower fares in the guise of "family rates" and "standby fares" to attract vacationers and others whose demands are more elastic.

Consequences

The economic consequences of price discrimination are twofold.

1. It is not surprising that a monopolist will be able to increase its profits by practising price discrimination.

2. Other things being equal, a discriminating monopolist will produce a larger output than a non-discriminating monopolist.

1 More Profits   The simplest way to understand why price discrimination can yield additional profits is to look again at our monopolist's downsloping demand curve, in Figure 11-3. We note that, although the profit-maximizing uniform price is $122, the segment of the demand curve lying above the profit area in Figure 11-3 tells us there are buyers who would be willing to pay *more than* P_m ($122) rather than forgo the product.

If the monopolist can identify and segregate each of these buyers and charge the maximum price each would pay, the sale of any given level of output will be more profitable. In columns 1 and 2 of Table 11-1, we note that the buyers of the first 4 units of output would be willing to pay more than the equilibrium price of $122. If the seller could practise perfect price discrimination by extracting the maximum price each buyer would pay, total revenue would increase from $610 (= $122 × 5) to $710 (= $122 + $132 + $142 + $152 + $162) and profits would increase from $140 (= $610 − $470) to $240 (= $710 − $470).

2 More Production   Other things being the same, the discriminating monopolist will in fact choose to produce a larger output than the nondiscriminating monopolist. Recall that when the nondiscriminating monopolist lowers price to sell additional output, the lower price will apply not only to the additional sales but also to *all* prior units of output. But when a perfectly discriminating monopolist lowers price, the reduced price applies *only* to the additional unit sold and *not* to prior units. Hence, price and marginal revenue are equal for any unit of output.

As indicated in Table 11-1, because marginal revenue now equals price, the monopolist will find that it is profitable to produce 7, rather than 5, units of output. The additional revenue beyond the 5 units level is $214 (= $112 + $102). Thus total revenue for 7 units is $924 (= $710 + $214). Total cost for 7 units is $640 (= 7 × $91.43), so profits are $284.

Ironically, although price discrimination increases the monopolist's profit compared to a nondiscriminating monopolist, it also results in greater output and thus less allocative inefficiency. In our example, the output level of 7 units matches that which would occur in pure competition. That is, allocative efficiency (P = MC = ATC) is achieved. Questions 5 and 6 at the end of this chapter may be helpful in comparing the price and output decisions of a nondiscriminating and discriminating monopolist.

REGULATED MONOPOLY

Most purely monopolistic industries are "natural monopolies" and subject to regulation. In particular, the prices or rates public utilities — railways, airlines, telephone companies, natural gas and electricity suppliers — can charge are determined by a federal, provincial, or local regulatory commission or board.

Figure 11-6 shows the demand and cost conditions of a natural monopoly. Because of the advantages of larger firm size, demand cuts the average cost curve at a point where long-run average cost is still falling. It would be inefficient to have many firms in such an industry because, by dividing the market, each firm would move further to the left on its average cost curve so unit costs would be substantially higher. The relationship between market demand and costs is such that the attainment of low unit costs presumes only one producer.

We know by application of the MR = MC rule that P_m and Q_m are the profit-maximizing price and output that the unregulated monopolist would choose. Because price exceeds average total cost at Q_m, the monopolist enjoys a substantial economic profit. Furthermore, price exceeds marginal cost, which indicates an underallocation of resources to this product or service. Can government regulation bring about better results from society's point of view?

FIGURE 11-6   Regulated monopoly

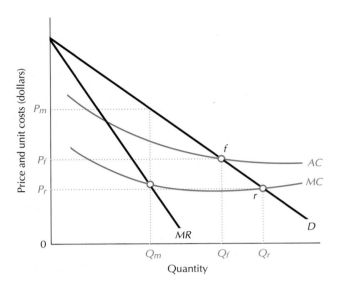

Price regulation can improve the social consequences of a natural monopoly. The optimum social price, P_r, will result in an efficient allocation of resources, but is likely to entail losses and therefore call for permanent public subsidies. The "fair-return" price, P_f, will allow the monopolist to break even, but will not fully correct the underallocation of resources.

Optimal Social Price: $P = MC$

If the objective of our regulatory commission is to achieve allocative efficiency, it should attempt to establish a ceiling price for the monopolist that is equal to *marginal cost*. Since each point on the market demand curve designates a price–quantity combination, and noting that marginal cost cuts the demand curve only at point r, it is clear the P_r is the only price equal to marginal cost. The imposition of this maximum or ceiling price causes the monopolist's effective demand curve to become P_rrD; the demand curve becomes perfectly elastic, and therefore $P_r = MR$, out to point r, where the regulated price ceases to be effective.

By imposing the fixed price P_r and letting the monopolist choose its profit-maximizing or loss-minimizing output, the allocative results of pure competition can be simulated. Production takes place where $P_r = MC$, and this equality indicates an efficient allocation of resources to this product or serv-

ice.[3] This price, which achieves allocative efficiency, is called the **optimal social price**.

"Fair-Return" Price: $P = AC$

But the optimal social price, P_r, may pose a problem of losses for the regulated firm. The price that equals marginal cost is likely to be so low that average total costs are not covered, as is shown in Figure 11-6. The inevitable result is losses. The reason for this lies in the basic character of public utilities. Because they are required to meet peak demands (both daily and seasonally) for their product or service, they tend to have substantial excess productive capacity when demand is relatively normal. This high level of investment in capital facilities means that unit costs of production are likely to decline over a wide range of output.

The market demand curve in Figure 11-6 cuts marginal cost at a point to the left of the marginal-cost–average-total-cost intersection, so the optimal social price is necessarily below AC. Therefore, to enforce an optimal social price on the regulated monopolist would mean short-run losses and, in the long run, bankruptcy for the utility.

What to do? One option would be a public subsidy sufficient to cover the loss marginal-cost pricing would entail. Another possibility is to condone price discrimination, in the hope that the additional revenue gained will permit the firm to cover costs.

In practice, regulatory commissions have pursued a third option: they have tended to back away from the objective of allocative efficiency and marginal-cost pricing. Most regulatory agencies in Canada are concerned with establishing a **"fair-return" price**. This is so because an optimal social price would lead to losses and eventual bankruptcy.

We see that the fair or fair-return price in Figure 11-6 would be P_f, where price equals *average* cost. Because the demand curve cuts average cost only at point f, clearly P_f is the only price that permits a fair return. The corresponding output at regulated price P_f will be Q_f.

---

[3] While "allocative efficiency" is achieved, "productive efficiency" would only be achieved by chance. In Figure 11-6 we note that production takes place at Q_r, which is less than the output at which average costs are minimized. Can you redraw Figure 11-6 to show those special conditions where both allocative and productive efficiency are realized?

Dilemma of Regulation

Comparing the results of the optimal social price (P = MC) and the fair-return price (P = AC) suggests a policy dilemma. When price is set to achieve the most efficient allocation of resources (P = MC), the regulated utility is likely to suffer losses. Survival of the firm would depend on permanent public subsidies out of tax revenues. On the other hand, although a fair-return price (P = AC) allows the monopolist to cover costs, it only partially resolves the underallocation of resources that the unregulated monopoly would foster. The fair-return price would only increase output from Q_m to Q_f, while the optimal social output is Q_r. Despite this problem, regulation can improve on the results of monopoly from the social point of view. Price regulation can simultaneously reduce price, increase output, and reduce the economic profits of monopolies.

QUICK REVIEW (11-3)

1. **Price discrimination occurs when a seller charges different prices that are not based on cost differentials.**

2. **The conditions necessary for price discrimination are: (a) monopoly power; (b) the segregation of buyers on the basis of different demand elasticities; and (c) the inability of buyers to resell the product.**

3. **Monopoly price can be reduced and output increased through government regulation.**

4. **The optimal social price (P = MC) achieves allocative efficiency but may result in losses; the fair-return price (P = AC) yields a normal profit but falls short of allocative efficiency.**

CHAPTER SUMMARY

1. A pure monopolist is the sole producer of a commodity for which there are no close substitutes.

2. Barriers to entry, in the form of *a.* economies of scale, *b.* natural monopolies, *c.* patent ownership and research, and *d.* ownership or control of essential inputs, help explain the existence of pure monopoly and other imperfectly competitive market structures. Barriers to entry that are formidable in the short run may prove to be surmountable in the long run.

3. The pure monopolist's market situation differs from a competitive firm in that the monopolist's demand curve is downsloping, causing the marginal-revenue curve to lie below the demand curve. Like the competitive seller, the pure monopolist will maximize profits by equating marginal revenue and marginal cost. Barriers to entry may permit a monopolist to acquire economic profits even in the long run. Note, however, that *a.* the monopolist does not charge "the highest price it can get"; *b.* the maximum total profit sought by the monopolist rarely coincides with maximum unit profits; *c.* high costs and a weak demand may prevent the monopolist from realizing any profit at all; *d.* the monopolist will want to avoid the inelastic range of its demand curve.

4. Given the same costs, the pure monopolist will find it more profitable to restrict output and charge a higher price than would a competitive seller. This restriction of output causes resources to be misallocated, as is evidenced by the fact that price exceeds marginal costs in monopolized markets.

5. Monopoly also tends to increase income inequality.

6. However, the costs of monopolists and competitive producers may not be the same. On the one hand, economies of scale may make lower unit costs accessible to monopolists but not to competitors. On the other hand, there is evidence that X-inefficiency — the failure to produce with the least-costly combination of inputs — is more common to monopolists than it is to competitive firms and that monopolists may make sizable expenditures to maintain monopoly privileges conferred by government.

7. Economists disagree as to how conducive pure monopoly is to technological advance. Some believe pure monopoly is more progressive than pure competition, because its ability to realize economic profits helps finance technological research. Others, however, argue that the absence of rival firms and the monopolist's desire to exploit fully its existing capital facilities weaken the monopolist's incentive to innovate.

8. A monopolist can increase its profits by practising price discrimination, provided it can segregate buyers on the basis of different elasticities of demand and the product or service cannot be readily transferred between the segmented markets. Other things being equal, the discriminating monopolist will produce a larger output than will the nondiscriminating monopolist.

9. Price regulation can be invoked to eliminate wholly or partially the tendency of monopolists to underallocate resources and to earn economic profits. The "optimal social" price is determined where the demand and marginal cost curves intersect; the "fair-return" price is determined where the demand and average-cost curves intersect.

TERMS AND CONCEPTS

barriers to entry (p. 174)
dilemma of regulation (p. 189)
dynamic efficiency (p. 184)
"fair-return" price (p. 188)
natural monopoly (p. 175)
optimal social price (p. 188)

price discrimination (p. 186)
price maker (p. 174)
pure monopoly (p. 174)
rent-seeking behaviour (p. 184)
X-inefficiency (p. 183)

QUESTIONS AND STUDY SUGGESTIONS

1. "No firm is completely sheltered from rivals; all firms compete for consumers' dollars. Pure monopoly, therefore, does not exist." Do you agree? Explain.

2. Discuss the major barriers to entry. Explain how each barrier can foster monopoly or oligopoly. Which barriers, if any, do you think give rise to monopoly that is socially justifiable?

3. How does the demand curve faced by a purely monopolistic seller differ from that confronting a purely competitive firm? Why does it differ? Of what significance is the difference? Why is the pure monopolist's demand curve not perfectly inelastic?

4. Use the demand schedule below to calculate total revenue and marginal revenue. Plot the demand, total revenue, and marginal revenue curves and carefully explain the relationships between them. Explain why the marginal revenue of the fourth unit of output is $3.50, even though its price is $5.00. Use Chapter 5's total-revenue test for price elasticity to designate the elastic and inelastic segments of your graphed demand curve. What generalization can you make regarding the relationship between marginal revenue and elasticity of demand? Suppose that somehow the marginal cost of successive units of output was zero. What output would the profit-seeking firm produce? Finally, use your analysis to explain why a monopolist would never produce in the inelastic range of its demand curve.

Price	Quantity demanded	Price	Quantity demanded
$7.00	0	$4.50	5
6.50	1	4.00	6
6.00	2	3.50	7
5.50	3	3.00	8
5.00	4	2.50	9

5. Suppose a pure monopolist is faced with the demand schedule shown below and the same cost data as the competitive producer discussed in question 6 at the end of Chapter 10. Calculate total and marginal revenue and determine the profit-maximizing price and output for this monopolist. What is the level of profits? Verify your answer graphically and by comparing total revenue and total cost. If this firm could engage in perfect price discrimination, what would be the level of output? Of profits?

Price	Quantity demanded	Total revenue	Marginal revenue
$115	0	$_____	
100	1	_____	$_____
83	2	_____	_____
71	3	_____	_____
63	4	_____	_____
55	5	_____	_____
48	6	_____	_____
42	7	_____	_____
37	8	_____	_____
33	9	_____	_____
29	10	_____	_____

6. Draw a diagram showing the relevant-demand, marginal-revenue, average-cost, and marginal-cost curves and the equilibrium price and output for a nondiscriminating monopolist. Use the same diagram to show the equilibrium position of a monopolist able to practise perfect price discrimination. Compare equilibrium outputs, total revenues, and economic profits in the two cases. Comment upon the economic desirability of price discrimination.

7. Assume a pure monopolist and a purely competitive firm have the same unit costs. Contrast the two with respect to *a.* price, *b.* output, *c.* profits, *d.* allocation of resources, and *e.* impact upon the distribution of income. Since both monopolists and competitive firms follow the MC = MR rule in maximizing profits, how do you account for the different results? Why might the costs of a purely competitive firm and monopolist *not* be the same? What are the implications of such cost differences?

8. "A monopolist is not likely to bring about technological progress." Justify why you agree or disagree.

9. Critically evaluate and explain:

   a. "Because they can control product price, monopolists are always assured of profitable production by simply charging the highest price consumers will pay."

   b. "The pure monopolist seeks that output that will yield the greatest per-unit profit."

   c. "An excess of price over marginal cost is the market's way of signalling the need for more production of a good."

   d. "The more profitable a firm, the greater its monopoly power."

   e. "The monopolist has a price policy; the competitive producer does not."

   f. "With respect to resource allocation, the interests of the seller and of society coincide in a purely competitive market but conflict in a monopolized market."

   g. "In a sense, the monopolist makes a profit for not producing: the monopolist produces profits more than it does goods."

10. Assume a monopolistic publisher has agreed to pay an author 15% of the total revenue from the sales of a text. Will the author and the publisher want to charge the same price for the text? Explain.

11. Suppose a firm's demand curve lies below its average-total-cost curve at all levels of output. Can you conceive of any circumstances by which production might be profitable?

12. Are community colleges and universities engaging in price discrimination when they charge full tuition to some students and provide financial aid to others? What are the advantages and disadvantages of this practice?

13. Explain verbally and graphically how price (rate) regulation may improve the performance of monopolies. In your answer distinguish between *a.* optimal social (marginal cost) pricing and *b.* fair-return (average cost) pricing. What is the "dilemma of regulation"?

14. It has been proposed that natural monopolists should be allowed to determine their profit-maximizing outputs and prices and then government should tax their profits away and distribute them to consumers in proportion to their purchases from the monopoly. Is this proposal as socially desirable as requiring monopolists to equate price with marginal cost or average cost?

12

Price and Output Determination: Monopolistic Competition

A consumer living in a sizable town or city will have an array of choices when buying many products. Take the purchase of a sweater. You could go to a discount store and buy an imported acrylic sweater for about $15; or purchase a fleece pullover with your school's logo and colours for $30. Alternatively, you could choose a cotton knit from a mail-order catalogue for about $45, or go to an upscale clothier to purchase a top-of-the-line wool sweater for over $100. The product choices reflect monopolistic competition: a market structure in which competition occurs not only on the basis of price, but also product quality, service, and advertising.

Pure competition and pure monopoly are the exception, not the rule, in our economy. Most market structures fall somewhere between these two extremes. In the present chapter, we examine monopolistic competition. This market structure is a blending of a considerable amount of competition with a small dose of monopoly power.

Our objectives in this chapter are to:

1. Examine the nature and prevalence of monopolistic competition.

2. Analyse and evaluate the price–output behaviour of monopolistically competitive firms.

3. Explain and assess the role of nonprice competition, based on product quality, service, and advertising, in monopolistically competitive industries.

MONOPOLISTIC COMPETITION: CONCEPT AND OCCURRENCE

Let's expand on the definition of monopolistic competition.

Relatively Large Numbers

Monopolistic competition refers to a market structure in which a relatively large number of firms offer similar but not identical products. The contrasts between this and pure competition are important. Monopolistic competition does not require the presence of hundreds of thousands of firms, but only a fairly large number — say, 25, 35, 60, or 70.

Several important characteristics of monopolistic competition follow from the presence of relatively large numbers.

1. Small Market Share   Each firm has a comparatively small percentage of the total market, which implies a limited amount of control over market price.

2. No Collusion   The presence of a relatively large number of firms also ensures that collusion — concerted action by firms to restrict output and rig price — is all but impossible.

3. Independent Action   With numerous firms in the industry, there is no mutual interdependence among them. Each firm determines its policies without considering the possible reactions of rival firms. This is a very reasonable way to act in a market in which one's rivals are numerous. After all, the 15% increase in sales that firm X may realize by cutting price will be spread so thinly over its 20, 40, or 60 rivals that for all practical purposes, the impact on their sales will be imperceptible.

Product Differentiation

In contrast to pure competition, monopolistic competition has the fundamental feature of **product differentiation**. Purely competitive firms produce a standardized or homogeneous product such as

wheat or corn; monopolistically competitive producers turn out variations of a given product. Product differentiation may take a number of different forms.

1 Product Quality   Product differentiation may take the form of physical or qualitative differences in products themselves. Personal computers, for example, differ in terms of hardware capacity, software, graphics, and the degree to which they are user-friendly. There are scores of competing principles of economics texts that differ in terms of content, organization, presentation and readability, pedagogical aids, graphics and design. Any medium-sized city will have a variety of retail stores selling men's and women's clothing that vary greatly in terms of styling, materials, and quality of workmanship. Similarly, one fast-food hamburger chain may feature lean beef while a competitor stresses the juiciness of its hamburgers.

2 Services   Services and conditions surrounding the sale of a product are important aspects of product differentiation. One grocery store may stress the helpfulness of its clerks who bag your groceries and carry them to your car. A "warehouse" competitor may leave bagging and carrying to its customers but feature lower prices. One-day clothes cleaning may be preferred to cleaning of equal quality that takes three days. The snob appeal of a store, the courteousness and helpfulness of clerks, the firm's reputation for service or exchanging its products, and credit availability are all service aspects of product differentiation.

3 Location   Products may also be differentiated by location and accessibility. Small mini-groceries or convenience stores successfully compete with large supermarkets, even though they have a much more limited range of products and charge significantly higher prices. They compete on the basis of being close to customers and situated on much-travelled streets — and by staying open twenty-four hours a day. For example, a gas station's close proximity to the Trans-Canada highway gives it a locational advantage that allows it to sell gasoline at a higher price than the same brand sells for in a town located 2 or 3 kilometres from the highway.

4 Promotion and Packaging   Product differentiation also arises from perceived differences created through advertising, packaging, and the use of brand names and trademarks. A celebrity's name associated with such products as jeans or perfume may enhance those products in the minds of buyers. Many consumers prefer a toothpaste packaged in a pump container to the same toothpaste in a conventional tube. While there are many aspirin-type products, product promotion and advertising may convince many consumers that Bayer or Anacin is superior, and worth a higher price than a generic substitute.

One important implication of product differentiation is that producers do have a degree of control over the prices of their products. Consumers have preferences for the products of specific sellers and *within limits* will pay more to satisfy those preferences.

Nonprice Competition

Under monopolistic competition economic rivalry centres not only on price, but also on nonprice factors such as product quality, advertising, and conditions associated with the sale of a product. Great emphasis is placed on trademarks and brand names to convince consumers, through advertising and other forms of sales promotion, that a firm's product is better than its rivals.

Easy Entry

Entry into monopolistically competitive industries tends to be relatively easy. The fact that monopolistically competitive firms are typically small-sized suggests that economies of scale and capital requirements are few. Compared with pure competition, however, added financial barriers may result

from the need to develop a product different from that of one's rivals and to advertise it. Existing firms may hold patents on their products and copyrights on their brand names and trademarks, making it more difficult and costly to successfully imitate them.

Illustrations

Table 12-1 lists a group of industries that approximate monopolistic competition. Also, grocery stores, gasoline stations, barber shops, dry cleaners, clothing stores, and so forth, operate under conditions similar to those just described.

PRICE AND OUTPUT DETERMINATION

We now analyse the price–output behaviour of a monopolistically competitive firm. We assume initially that the firms in the industry are producing *given* products and engaging in a *given* amount of promotional activity. Later in the chapter, we will note how product variation and advertising modify our discussion.

The Firm's Demand Curve

Our explanation is couched in terms of **Figure 12-1(a) (Key Graph)**. The basic feature of this diagram, which distinguishes it from our analyses of pure competition and pure monopoly, is the elasticity of the

FIGURE 12-1 Monopolistically competitive firms tend to realize a normal profit in the long run

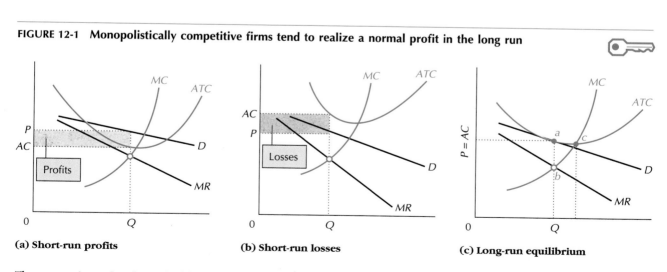

(a) Short-run profits (b) Short-run losses (c) Long-run equilibrium

The economic profits shown in (a) will induce new firms to enter, causing the profits to be competed away. The losses indicated in (b) will cause an exodus of firms until normal profits are restored. Thus in (c), where price just covers unit costs at the *MR = MC* output, the firm's long-run equilibrium position is portrayed.

TABLE 12-1 **Percentage of output[1] produced by firms in selected low-concentration manufacturing industries**

Industry	Four largest firms	Eight largest firms	Twenty largest firms
Hosiery	34.4	51.6	79.6
Knitted fabric manufacturers	25.3	42.9	73.6
Footwear	24.9[2]	40.7	61.7
Feed industry	23.1	32.5	48.3
Boatbuilding and repair	22.8	35.3	52.0
Concrete products	22.7	35.2	51.1
Miscellaneous furniture and fixtures	18.1	32.4	57.0
Children's clothing industry	16.2	27.4	51.1
Kitchen cabinets	15.2[2]	24.3	37.6
Wooden household furniture	12.5	20.7	37.3
Miscellaneous metal fabricating	12.2	21.9	42.5
Men's and boys' clothing contractors	11.8	20.4	41.0
Platemaking, typesetting, etc.	11.8	18.7	31.4
Metal dies, moulds, patterns	8.5	15.5	31.9
Women's clothing contractors	7.3	11.8	21.1

[1] As measured by value of shipments. Data for 1985.
[2] Data for 1984.
Source: Statistics Canada, *Industrial Organization and Concentration in the Manufacturing, Mining and Logging Industries,* 1985 (Ottawa, June 1989).

firm's individual demand curve. ***The demand curve faced by a monopolistically competitive seller is highly, but not perfectly, elastic.*** It is much more elastic than the demand curve of the pure monopolist, because the monopolistically competitive seller is faced with a relatively large number of rivals producing close-substitute goods. Yet for two reasons, the monopolistically competitive seller's sales curve is not perfectly elastic. First, the monopolistically competitive firm has fewer rivals; second, the products of these rivals are close but not perfect substitutes.

Box 12-1

THE MARKET FOR PRINCIPLES OF ECONOMICS TEXTBOOKS*

The market for principles texts embraces a number of the characteristics of monopolistic competition.

There are many more economics texts that could be used in the principles course. If you undertook the arduous task of comparing a number of them, you would find considerable differences. While there is some variation in subject matter, most leading texts cover the same core topics. Books do vary considerably as to the rigour and detail with which material is presented. They also vary as to reading level. Some books have a one-colour format, others a multicolour presentation. Books vary greatly in the use of such pedagogical devices as photos, "boxed features," cartoons, learning objectives, intrachapter summaries, and glossaries. Publishers seek the mix of these features that will be most appealing to instructors and students.

Texts are also differentiated by their accompanying "packages" of ancillary materials. These include study guides, videos, and computer tutorial and simulation programs to aid student understanding. Instructor manuals, test banks, and overhead transparencies are designed to save instructor time and enhance teacher productivity. Were you to trace the introduction and development of these various pedagogical aids and instructional materials, you would find that when any one of them was introduced and proved attractive to adopters, that feature would be quickly incorporated into future editions of most other old and new books.

Product differentiation is accompanied by considerable nonprice competition. Texts are advertised by direct mail and in widely read economics journals. Publishers provide potential adopters with free copies and use "trade fair" booths at economics conventions to publicize their wares. Sales representatives of the various publishers — who receive bonuses for exceeding sales quotas — prowl the halls of academia to make professors aware of the distinguishing features and alleged advantages of their particular text. Over 1 million students take principles course each year so the battle for market shares is vigorous.[1]

Price competition probably plays a secondary role in the textbook market. First, unlike most markets, the product is chosen for the consumer by a second party. Your instructor — who gets a free text from the publisher and may not even be aware of its retail price — decides the text you must read for the course. Second, instructors usually put textbook quality above price. It would prove very costly to students to use an inaccurate, poorly written text that might impair the teaching-learning process. The significant exception is that over the years more and more instructors have opted for lower-priced paperbacks that split micro and macro components of the course. Thus, a student taking only one semester of economics can avoid the higher cost of a two-semester hardback.

While there are no artificial barriers to entering the market, the widespread use of multicolour formats and the obligation to provide an array of student-instructor ancillary items poses a significant financial barrier. It may take an investment of $1 million or more for a publisher to enter the market with a text and ancillaries comparable to those already on the market. Even so, it is not uncommon to find two or three new entries in the market every year.

In summary, the economics textbook market is characterized by product differentiation and nonprice competition. Price competition is muted and the only entry barrier is financial.

[1] In Canada over 65,000 students take principles courses each year, less than 10% of the U.S. market. However, the price of entry for Canadian publishers into this market runs between $100,000 and $300,000, considerably higher than 10% of the average U.S. investment per text.

* Based on Timothy Tregarthen, "The Market for Principles of Economics Texts," *The Margin*, March 1987, pp. 14–15; and Joseph E. Stiglitz, "On the Market for Principles of Economics Textbooks: Innovation and Product Differentiation," *Journal of Economic Education*, Spring 1988, pp. 171–177.

The precise degree of elasticity in the monopolistically competitive firm's demand curve will depend on the number of rivals and the degree of product differentiation. The larger the number of rivals and the weaker the product differentiation, the greater will be the elasticity of each seller's demand curve; that is, the closer the situation will be to pure competition.

The Short Run: Profits or Losses

The firm will maximize its profits or minimize its losses in the short run by producing that output designated by the intersection of marginal cost and marginal revenue, for reasons with which we are now familiar. The representative firm of Figure 12-1(a) produces output Q, charges price P, and realizes a total profit of the size indicated by the shaded area. But a less favourable cost-and-demand situation may exist, putting the monopolistically competitive firm in the position of realizing losses in the short run. This is illustrated by the shaded area in Figure 12-1(b). In the short run, the monopolistically competitive firm may either realize an economic profit or be faced with losses.

The Long Run: Normal Profits

In the long run, however, the *tendency* is for the monopolistically competitive firms to earn a normal profit.

Profits: Firms Enter   In the short-run profits case, in Figure 12-1 (a), economic profits will attract new rivals because entry is relatively easy. As new firms enter, the demand curve faced by the typical firm will fall (shift to the left) and become more elastic. Why? Because each firm has a smaller share of the total demand and now faces a larger number of close-substitute products. This in turn tends to make economic profits disappear. When the demand curve is tangent to the average-cost curve at the profit-maximizing output, as shown in Figure 12-1(c), the firm is just making normal profits. Output Q is the equilibrium output for the firm. As Figure 12-1(c) indicates, any deviation from that output will entail average costs that exceed product price and, therefore, losses for the firm. Furthermore, economic profits have been competed away and there is no incentive for additional firms to enter.

Losses: Firms Leave   In the short-run losses case, in Figure 12-1(b), an exodus of firms would occur in the long run. Faced with fewer substitute products and an expanded share of total demand, surviving firms will find that their losses disappear and gradually give way to approximately normal profits. (For simplicity's sake, we have assumed constant costs; shifts in the cost curve as firms enter or leave would complicate our discussion slightly, but would not alter the conclusions.)

Complications   We have been very careful to say that the representative firm in a monopolistically competitive market *tends* to earn a normal profit in the long run. Certain complicating factors prevent us from being more definitive than this.

1. Some firms may achieve a measure of product differentiation that cannot be duplicated by rivals even over a long span of time. A given gasoline station may have the only available location at the busiest intersection in town. Or a firm may hold a patent that gives it a slight — and more or less permanent — advantage over imitators. Such firms may realize some economic profits even in the long run.

2. Remember that entry is not completely unrestricted. Because of product differentiation, there are likely to be greater financial barriers to entry than otherwise would be the case. This again suggests that some economic profits may persist even in the long run.

3. A final consideration may work in the opposite direction, causing losses — below-normal profits — to persist in the long run. For example, the proprietors of a corner delicatessen persistently accept a return less than they could earn elsewhere because their business is a way of life to them. The suburban barber ekes out a meager existence because cutting hair is all the barber wants to do. All things considered, however, the long-run normal profit equilibrium of Figure 12-1(c) is probably a reasonable portrayal of reality.

WASTES OF MONOPOLISTIC COMPETITION

We know that economic efficiency requires the triple equality of price, marginal cost, and average cost. The equality of price and marginal cost is necessary for *allocative efficiency*: the allocation of the right amount of resources to the product. The equality of price with minimum average total cost results in *productive efficiency*: production where ATC is at a minimum. This equality means consumers will enjoy the largest volume of the product and the lowest price that least-cost conditions allow.

Excess Capacity

In monopolistically competitive markets, neither allocative nor productive efficiency is realized. An examination of Figure 12-2, which enlarges the relevant portion of Figure 12-1(c) and adds detail, shows that the monopolistic element in monopolistic competition causes a modest underallocation of resources to goods produced. Price exceeds marginal cost in long-run equilibrium.

FIGURE 12-2   The efficiency aspects of monopolistic competition

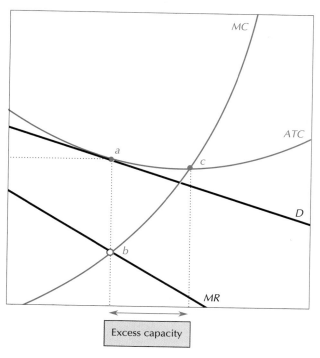

Excess capacity

In long-run equilibrium a monopolistically competitive firm achieves neither allocative nor productive efficiency. An underallocation of resources is reflected in the fact that the product price of *a* exceeds the marginal cost of *b*. Productive efficiency is not realized because production occurs where unit costs of *a* exceed the minimum attainable cost of *c*.

We also observe in Figure 12-1(c) that the monopolistically competitive firms produce short of the most efficient (least unit cost) output. There is a higher unit cost than the minimum attainable. This means a higher price than would result under pure competition. Consumers do *not* benefit from the largest output and lowest price that cost conditions permit. Indeed, the monopolistically competitive firms must charge a higher than competitive price in the long run in order to achieve a normal profit.

Monopolistically competitive industries tend to be overcrowded with firms, each of which is underutilized, or operating short of optimum capacity. That is typified by many kinds of retail establishments; for example, the thirty or forty gasoline stations, all operating with excess capacity, that populate a medium-sized city. These are the so-called **wastes of**

monopolistic competition, the underutilized plants and consumers penalized through higher than competitive prices for this underutilization.

Redeeming Features

In many monopolistically competitive industries, however, the price and output results are not drastically different from those of pure competition. The highly elastic nature of each firm's demand curve guarantees that the results are nearly the same. Furthermore, the product differentiation that characterizes monopolistic competition means buyers can select from many variations of the same general product. This will fulfil the diverse tastes of consumers. In fact, there is a trade-off between product differentiation and the production of a given product at the minimum average cost. The stronger the product differentiation (the less elastic the demand curve), the further to the left of the minimum average costs will production take place. But the greater the product differentiation, the more likely that diverse consumer tastes will be fully satisfied.

QUICK REVIEW (12-1)

1. Monopolistic competition refers to industries that are comprised of a relatively large number of firms, operating noncollusively, in the production of differentiated products.

2. In the short run a monopolistically competitive firm will maximize profits or minimize losses at an output at which marginal revenue equals marginal cost.

3. In the long run easy entry and exodus of firms leads to firms making a normal profit.

4. A monopolistically competitive firm's equilibrium output is such that price exceeds marginal cost (indicating that resources are underallocated to the product) and price exceeds minimum average total cost (consumers do not get the product at the lowest unit cost and price attainable).

NONPRICE COMPETITION

It is not very satisfying to the monopolistically competitive firm to barely capture a normal profit for its efforts. We can therefore expect firms to take steps to improve on the long-run equilibrium position. How can this be accomplished? The answer lies in product differentiation. Each firm has a product distinguishable, in some more or less tangible way, from those of its rivals. The product is presumably subject to further differentiation through product development. The emphasis on real product differences and the creation of perceived differences may also be achieved through advertising and related sales promotion. In this way it might prevent the long-run tendency of Figure 12-1(c) from becoming a reality.

Product development and advertising will add to the firm's costs. But they can also be expected to increase the demand for the product. If demand increases by more than enough to compensate for development and promotional costs, the firm will have improved its profit position. As Figure 12-1(c) suggests, the firm may have little or no prospect of increasing profits by price cutting. So why not practise **nonprice competition**?

Product Differentiation and Product Development

The likelihood that easy entry will promote product variety and product improvement is a redeeming feature of monopolistic competition that may offset, wholly or in part, the "wastes" associated with this market structure. There are two distinct considerations here: (1) product differentiation at a point in time, and (2) product improvement over a period of time.

1 Differentiation Product differentiation means that the consumer will be offered a wide range of types, styles, brands, and quality gradations of any given product. Compared with the situation of pure competition, this is an advantage to the consumer. The range of choice is widened, and variations and shadings of consumer tastes are met by producers. But sceptics warn that product differentiation is not an unmixed blessing. Product proliferation may reach the point where the consumer becomes confused and rational choice is rendered time-consuming and difficult.

2 Development Competition is an important avenue of technological innovation and product improvement over time. Product development may be cumulative in two different senses. First, a successful product improvement by one firm obligates rivals to imitate or improve on a competitor's temporary market advantage, or suffer losses. Second, profits realized from a successful product improvement can be used to finance further improvements.

However, there are notable criticisms of the product development that may occur under monopolistic competition. Critics point out that many product alterations are more apparent than real, consisting of frivolous and superficial changes in the product that do *not* improve its durability, efficiency, or usefulness. A more exotic container, bright packaging, or "shuffling the chrome" is frequently the focal point for product development.

Do the advantages of product differentiation, properly discounted, outweigh the "wastes" of monopolistic competition? It is difficult to say without examining specific cases, and even then, concrete conclusions are difficult to make.

THE ECONOMICS OF ADVERTISING

A monopolistically competitive firm may gain at least a temporary edge on rivals by altering its product. It may also seek the same result by attempting to influence consumer preferences through advertising and sales promotion. Advertising *may* be a mechanism through which a firm can increase its share of the market and enhance consumer loyalty to its particular product.

Controversy and Scope

In fact, there is considerable disagreement as to the economic and social desirability of advertising. Advertising and promotional expenditures in Canada are estimated to be almost $10 billion. Thus, if advertising is generally wasteful, any potential virtues of monopolistically competitive markets are thereby dimmed, and the need for corrective public policies is indicated.

Two Views

The controversy over advertising has generated two rather diametrically opposed views.[1] In outlining these two positions, bear in mind that advertising is not confined to monopolistic competition. Product differentiation and heavy advertising are also characteristic of many oligopolistic industries (Chapter 13). Thus, our comments are equally germane to these industries.

The **traditional view** sees advertising as a redundant and economically wasteful expenditure that

---

[1] The ensuing discussion draws on Robert B. Eklund, Jr. and David S. Saurman, *Advertising and the Market Process* (San Francisco: Pacific Research Institute for Public Policy, 1988).

Box 12-2

DO FIRMS ADVERTISE TOO MUCH?

It is debatable whether advertising is excessive from the consumer's point of view. But simple analysis suggests that advertising may often be excessive from the vantage point of individual firms.

Imperfectly competitive firms face a dilemma when it comes to advertising and other forms of nonprice competition. Let us consider this dilemma in terms of Acme and Ajax corporations, which are rivals in the manufacture and sale of blue jeans.

The four cells in the accompanying figure show what daily profits would be with either "large" or "small" advertising budgets. The figures in the cells are such that the number above the diagonal indicates Ajax's profits and the number below the diagonal shows Acme's profits. For example, if Acme chooses a large advertising budget and Ajax a small one (cell B), Acme will gain market share at Ajax's expense, and as a result Acme's profits will be $1,200 and Ajax's only $600. Cell C portrays the opposite set of circumstances. Because their advertising efforts are about equal in cells A and D, both firms realize one-half of the market and thereby receive equal profits. But profits are greater in cell D because advertising expenditures are smaller than in cell A; that is, the lower expenditures on advertising in cell A more than compensate for any lost revenue the firms may experience because of reduced sales.

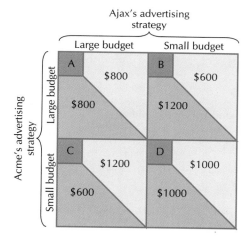

A dilemma arises because the dynamics of the situation leads to an outcome at cell A, where advertising expenditures are large. To illustrate, assume both firms initially have small advertising budgets and are each realizing $1,000 profits. But Acme now recognizes that if it increases its advertising expenditures *and Ajax does not*, then Acme's profits will increase to $1,200 (cell D to B). However, this move by Acme will cause Ajax's profits to fall to $600. Ajax can increase its profits by also shifting to a large advertising budget (cell B to A). Ajax's profits are now $800, rather than $600. Ajax's large advertising budget strategy has taken some sales from Acme and lowered its profits from $1,200 to $800. An identical scenario evolves if we begin again with cell D and assume Ajax (rather than Acme) takes the initiative to increase its advertising budget.

In short, cells B and C are not stable or equilibrium outcomes and, assuming there is no collusion between the two firms, the dynamics of the situation moves the outcome to cell A, where advertising budgets are large and profits are less than with smaller advertising budgets (cell D). Because much advertising is in response to the advertising of one's rivals, firms may end up with larger advertising budgets and smaller profits than are otherwise attainable. In a word, there is too much advertising, from the seller's perspective.

generates economic concentration and monopoly power. The **new perspective** on advertising sees it as an efficient means for both providing information to consumers and enhancing competition. Let us contrast these two views in three critical areas.

1 Persuasion or Information? The traditional view holds that the main purpose of advertising is to manipulate or persuade consumers to alter their preferences in favour of the advertiser's product. A television beer commercial conveys little or no useful information to consumers. Advertising is often based on misleading and extravagant claims that confuse and frequently insult the intelligence of consumers, not enlighten them. Indeed, advertising may well persuade consumers in some cases to pay high prices for much-acclaimed but inferior products, forgoing better but unadvertised products selling at lower prices.

The new perspective contends that consumers need extensive information about product characteristics and prices in order to make rational decisions. Advertising is alleged to be a low-cost means of providing that information. Suppose you are in the market for a CD player and there was no newspaper or magazine advertising of this product. To make a rational choice you might have to spend several days visiting electronics stores to determine the prices and features of various brands. This entails both direct costs (gasoline, parking fees) and indirect costs (the

value of your time). Advertising, it is argued, reduces your "search time" and minimizes these costs.

2 Concentration or Competition? Does advertising generate monopoly or stimulate competition? The traditional view envisions some firms as being more successful than others in establishing "brand loyalty" through advertising. As a consequence, such firms are able to increase their sales, expand their market share, and enjoy enlarged profits. Enhanced profits permit still more advertising and further enlargement of the firm's market share and profits. Successful advertising can lead to the expansion of some firms at the expense of others and therefore to increased industrial concentration. Consumers eventually lose all the advantages of competitive markets. Furthermore, potential new entrants to the industry will be faced with the need to incur large advertising expenditures to establish their product in the marketplace; hence, advertising expenditures may be a formidable barrier to entry.

The traditional view is portrayed graphically in Figure 12-3(a). By successfully generating brand loyalty through advertising, the firm's demand curve

FIGURE 12-3   Advertising and a firm's demand curve: two views

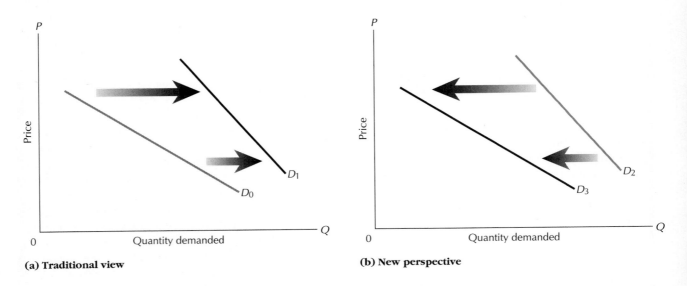

(a) Traditional view

(b) New perspective

The traditional view of advertising sees advertising as a device that increases the successful advertiser's market share and enhances brand loyalty. The result is greater market concentration as the demand curve of the successful advertiser shifts rightward and becomes more inelastic as shown by the D_0 to D_1 movement in panel (a). The new perspective regards advertising as a means of increasing consumer awareness of substitute products, thereby enhancing competition. Consequently, advertising in an industry will cause a firm's demand curve to shift leftward and become more elastic as portrayed by the movement from D_2 to D_3 in panel (b).

shifts rightward from D_0 to D_1, implying a larger market share. The fact that curve D_1 is less elastic than D_0 indicates a lessening of competition; successful advertising has convinced consumers that there exist fewer good substitutes for this firm's product. The less elastic demand curve also means that the producer can charge higher prices with less loss of sales.

The new perspective sees advertising as a force that enhances competition. By providing information about the wide variety of substitute products available to buyers, advertising diminishes monopoly power. In fact, advertising is frequently associated with the introduction of new products designed to compete with existing brands. Could the Hyundai and Isuzu automobiles have gained a foothold in the North American market without advertising?

In terms of Figure 12-3(b) advertising, in a world of costly and imperfect knowledge, makes consumers more aware of the range of substitutable products available to them and provides them with valuable information on the prices and characteristics of these goods. Before advertising consumers may have only been aware that products B and C were good substitutes for A. But advertising provides them with the knowledge that D, E, and F are also substitutable for A. As a consequence of the advertising of all firms in the industry, the demand curve of each firm shifts leftward as from D_2 to D_3 in Figure 12-3(b) and becomes more elastic. Both of these changes reflect enhanced competition.

3 Wasteful or Efficient? The traditional view contends that advertising is wasteful. First, it makes markets less competitive and therefore obstructs the realization of either allocative or productive efficiency. Second, advertising allegedly diverts resources from higher-valued uses. For example, timber, which is sorely needed in the production of housing, is squandered on unsightly billboards and on producing the paper used for the ubiquitous advertising supplements in local newspapers. Advertising allegedly constitutes an inefficient use of scarce resources. Finally, advertising expenditures contribute to higher costs, ultimately reflected in higher prices to consumers.

The new perspective views advertising as an efficiency-enhancing activity. It is an inexpensive means of providing useful information to consumers and thus lowers search costs. By enhancing competition, advertising is conducive to both greater allocative and productive efficiency. Finally, by facilitating the successful introduction of new products, advertising is conducive to technological progress.

Empirical Evidence

Evidence on the economic effects of advertising is mixed because studies are usually plagued by data problems and difficulties in determining cause and effect. For example, suppose it is found that firms that do a great deal of advertising seem to have considerable monopoly power and large profits. Does this mean that advertising creates barriers to entry that in turn generate monopoly power and profits? Or do entry barriers associated with factors remote from advertising cause monopoly profits that in turn allow firms to spend lavishly in advertising their products? In any event, at this time there is simply no consensus on the economic implications of advertising.[2]

QUICK REVIEW (12-2)

1. **Monopolistically competitive firms may seek economic profits through product differentiation, product development, and advertising.**

2. **The traditional view of advertising alleges that it is a persuasive rather than informative activity; it promotes economic concentration and monopoly power; and it is a source of economic waste and inefficiency.**

3. **According to the new perspective, advertising is a low-cost source of information for consumers; a means of increasing competition by making consumers aware of substitutable products; and a source of greater efficiency in the use of resources.**

Monopolistic Competition and Economic Analysis

Our discussion of nonprice competition correctly implies that the equilibrium situation of a monopolistically competitive firm is actually more complex than the previous graphic analysis indicates. Figure 12-1(a), (b), and (c) *assumes* a given product and a given level of advertising expenditures. The monopolistically competitive firm, however, must actually juggle three variable factors — price, product, and promotion — in seeking maximum profits. What specific variety of product, selling at what price and supplemented by what level of promotional activity, will

---

[2] The reader who wishes to pursue this topic should consult Mark S. Albion and Paul W. Farris, *The Advertising Controversy: Evidence on the Economic Effects of Advertising* (Boston, Mass.: Auburn House Publishing Company, 1981).

result in the greatest level of profits? There is no simple answer.

At best, we can note that each possible combination of price, product, and promotion poses a different demand and cost (production plus promotion) structure for the firm, some of which will allow it maximum profits. This optimum combination cannot be readily forecast but must be sought by trial and error. Even here, certain limitations may be imposed by the actions of rivals. A firm may not eliminate advertising expenditures for fear its share of the market will decline sharply, benefiting rivals who do advertise. Similarly, patents held by rivals will rule out certain desirable product variations.

CHAPTER SUMMARY

1. The distinguishing features of monopolistic competition are: *a.* there are enough firms so that each has little control over price, mutual interdependence is absent, and collusion is virtually impossible; *b.* products are characterized by real and perceived differences and by varying conditions surrounding their sale; *c.* economic rivalry entails both price and nonprice competition; and *d.* entry to the industry is relatively easy. Many aspects of retailing, and some industries where economies of scale are few, approximate monopolistic competition.

2. Monopolistically competitive firms may earn economic profits or incur losses in the short run. The easy entry and exodus of firms gives rise to a tendency for them to earn a normal profit in the long run.

3. The long-run equilibrium position of the monopolistically competitive producer is less socially desirable than that of a purely competitive firm. Under monopolistic competition, price exceeds marginal cost, resulting in an underallocation of resources to the product, and price exceeds minimum average total cost, indicating that consumers do not get the product at the lowest price cost conditions would allow. However, because the firm's demand curve can be highly elastic, these "wastes" of monopolistic competition should not be overemphasized.

4. Product differentiation provides a means by which monopolistically competitive firms can offset the long-run tendency for economic profits to approximate zero. Through product development and advertising outlays, a firm may strive to increase the demand for its product more than nonprice competition increases its costs.

5. Although subject to certain dangers and problems, product differentiation affords the consumer a greater variety of products at any point in time, and improved products over time. Whether these features fully compensate for the "wastes" of monopolistic competition is an unresolved question.

6. The traditional and new perspective views of advertising differ as to whether advertising *a.* is persuasive or informative, *b.* promotes monopoly or competition, and *c.* impairs or improves efficiency in resource use. Empirical evidence reveals no consensus about whether advertising is an anti- or pro-competitive force.

7. In practice, the monopolistic competitor seeks that specific combination of price, product, and promotion that will maximize its profits.

TERMS AND CONCEPTS

monopolistic competition (p. 194)
nonprice competition (p. 199)
product differentiation (p. 194)

traditional and new perspective on advertising (pp. 200–201)
wastes of monopolistic competition (p. 199)

QUESTIONS AND STUDY SUGGESTIONS

1. How does monopolistic competition differ from pure competition? From pure monopoly? Explain fully what product differentiation entails.

2. Compare the elasticity of the monopolistically competitive producer's demand curve with that of *a.* a pure competitor, and *b.* a pure monopolist. Assuming identical long-run costs, compare graphically the prices and output that would result under pure competition and monopolistic competition. Contrast the two market structures in terms of allocative and productive efficiency. Explain: "Monopolistically competitive industries are characterized by too many firms, each of which produces too little."

3. "Monopolistic competition is monopoly up to the point at which consumers become willing to buy close substitute products and competitive beyond that point." Explain.

4. "Competition in quality and in service may be quite as effective in giving buyers more for their money as is price competition." Do you agree? Explain why monopolistically competitive firms frequently prefer nonprice to price competition.

5. Critically evaluate and explain:

   a. "In monopolistically competitive industries, economic profits are competed away in the long run; hence there is no valid reason to criticize the performance and efficiency of such industries."

   b. "In the long run, monopolistic competition leads to a monopolistic price but not to monopolistic profits."

6. Do you agree or disagree with the following statements? Why?

   a. "The amount of advertising a firm does is likely to vary inversely with the real differences in its product."

   b. "If each firm's advertising expenditures merely tend to cancel the effects of its rivals' advertising, it is clearly irrational for these firms to maintain large advertising budgets."

7. Carefully evaluate the two views expressed in the following statements:

   a. "It happens every day. Advertising builds mass demand. Production goes up — costs come down. More people can buy — more jobs are created. These are the ingredients of economic growth. Each stimulates the next in a cycle of productivity and plenty that constantly creates a better life for you."

   b. "Advertising constitutes 'inverted education' — a costly effort to induce people to buy without sufficient thought and deliberation and therefore to buy things they don't need. Furthermore, advertising intensifies economic instability because advertising outlays vary directly with the level of consumer spending."
      Which view do you think is more accurate? Justify your position.

8. Compare the traditional and new perspective views of advertising. Which do you think is more accurate?

CHAPTER

13

Price and Output Determination: Oligopoly

U p to now we have studied three market structures: pure competition, monopoly, and monopolistic competition. The remaining market structure to be investigated is oligopoly: a market structure in which a few firms are dominant. Such is the case in some of our manufacturing, mining, and distribution sectors. We first define oligopoly, then we note its occurrence and reasons for its existence. Our main goal is to study models that try to explain the possible courses of price–output behaviour of oligopolies. We will note that nonprice competition — product development and advertising — is significant in this market structure. We will assess the economic efficiency and social desirability of oligopoly, and end with a brief case study of the automobile industry.

OLIGOPOLY: CONCEPT AND OCCURRENCE

What are the basic characteristics of oligopoly? How frequently is it encountered in our economy?

Oligopoly Defined

Oligopoly exists when a few large firms, producing a homogeneous or differentiated product, dominate a market. "Fewness" means that the firms are mutually interdependent in that each must consider the possible reactions of its rivals to its price, advertising, and product development decisions.

But what specifically is meant by "a few" firms? This is necessarily vague, because the market model of oligopoly covers much ground. Thus oligopoly encompasses the tin can industry, in which two firms dominate an entire national market, and the situation in which ten or fifteen gasoline stations may enjoy roughly equal shares of the petroleum products market in a medium-sized town. Generally, when we hear of the "Big Three," "Big Four" or "Big Six," we can be relatively certain that the industry has an oligopoly market structure.

Homogeneous or Differentiated Products Firms in an oligopoly may produce **homogeneous** (standardized) or **differentiated** products. Many industrial products — steel, zinc, copper, aluminum, lead, cement, and industrial alcohol — are virtually standardized products in the physical sense and are produced under oligopolistic conditions. On the other hand, many consumer goods — automobiles, tires, detergents, greeting cards, breakfast cereals, cigarettes, and a host of household appliances — are differentiated but also produced by oligopolies.

Concentration Ratios Economists often use **concentration ratios** as an approximate measure of the structure of an industry. The data in Table 13-1 show the four-firm concentration ratios — the percentage of total industry sales accounted for by the four largest firms — for a number of industries. Note, for example, that almost 100% of tobacco products and about 70% of the batteries produced in Canada are manufactured by the four largest firms in each industry.

Generally, when the largest four firms control 40% or more of the total market, the industry is oligopolistic. Using this benchmark, more than one-half of Canada's manufacturing industries are oligopolies.

While concentration ratios provide useful insights on the competitiveness or monopolization of various industries, they are subject to several shortcomings.

1 Localized Markets Concentration ratios pertain to the nation as a whole, while relevant markets for some products are actually highly localized because of high transportation costs. For example, the concentration ratio for ready-mix concrete (Table 12-1) suggests a competitive industry. But the sheer bulk of this product limits the relevant market to a given town or metropolitan area and in such localized markets we typically find oligopolistic suppliers. We have already suggested that at the local level, some aspects of the retail trade — particularly in small- and medium-sized towns — are characterized by oligopoly.

2 Interindustry Competition Definitions of industries are somewhat arbitrary and we must be aware of **interindustry competition**, that is, competition between two products associated with different industries. Table 13-1's high concentration ratios for the aluminum and copper industries understate the degree of competition because aluminum and copper compete in many applications — for example, in the market for electrical transmission lines.

3 World Trade The data are for Canadian products and therefore often overstate monopoly power because they do not take into account the **import competition** of foreign suppliers. The automobile industry is a highly relevant illustration. While Table 13-1 tells us that four firms account for 95% of the domestic production of motor vehicles, it ignores the fact that about 30% of the automobiles purchased in Canada are imports.

4 Herfindahl Index Another problem associated with concentration ratios is that they fail to measure accurately the distribution of market power among the several dominant firms. For example, suppose that in the long-distance telephone industry one firm controlled all service. In a second industry — say, the automobile industry — assume four firms exist and each has 25% of the market. For both industries the four-firm concentration ratio would be 100%. But the telecommunications industry would be a pure monopoly, while the auto industry would be an oligopoly characterized perhaps by significant rivalry. The market power would be substantially greater in the telecommunications than in the auto industry, a fact not reflected in the identical 100% concentration ratios.

The **Herfindahl Index** deals with this problem. This index is *the sum of the squared market shares of each firm in the industry*. By squaring

TABLE 13-1   Percentage of output[1] produced by firms in selected high-concentration manufacturing industries

Industry	Percent of industry output produced by first four firms
Glass[2]	100.0
Cane and beet sugar processors[2]	100.0
Tobacco products	99.4
Breweries	97.7
Motor vehicles	95.1
Abrasives[2]	91.0
Aluminum rolling and casting	88.8
Asphalt roofing	86.1
Major appliances	85.0
Copper rolling	82.4
Cement	81.7
Fibre and filament yarn	79.4
Railroad rolling stock	78.8
Leather tanneries	77.4
Distilleries	77.0
Lubricating oils and greases	76.4
Shipbuilding and repair	71.4
Batteries	69.4
Wood preservation industry	68.9
Wire and wire rope industry	68.2
Petroleum products	64.0
Steel pipe and tubes	63.7

[1] As measured by value of shipments. Data for 1985.
[2] First eight firms.

Source: Statistics Canada, *Industrial Organization and Concentration in the Manufacturing, Mining and Logging Industries, 1985* (Ottawa, June 1989).

tical four-firm concentration ratios of 85%. Industry X may be characterized by vigorous price competition and technological progress, evidenced by improved product and production techniques. In contrast, firms of industry Y may price their products collusively and be technologically stagnant. From society's viewpoint the "competitive" performance of industry X is clearly superior to the "monopolistic" performance of Y, a fact concealed by the identical concentration ratios. Nevertheless, used with caution, concentration ratios serve as helpful indicators of the degree of monopoly power embodied in various industries.

Underlying Causes

Why are certain industries composed of only a few firms? The answer lies primarily in cost economies, other barriers to entry, and mergers.

Economies of Scale   We saw in Chapter 9, that where economies of scale are substantial (see Figure 9-9(b)), reasonably efficient production will be possible only with a small number of producers. In other words, efficiency requires that the productive capacity of each firm be large relative to the total market. Indeed, it is an unstable situation for an industry to have a large number of high-cost firms, each of which is failing to realize existing economies of scale.

In Figure 9-7, for example, a firm currently operating with the small and inefficient plant size indicated by ATC-1 will recognize that this short-run position is unsatisfactory; it can realize substantially lower unit costs and a larger profit by expanding its plant to ATC-2. The same can be said for the move to ATC-3. However, given a reasonably stable market demand, all the many firms with small (ATC-1) plant sizes cannot now survive. Profitable expansion to large plant sizes by some will necessarily come at the expense of rivals. The realization of economies of scale by some firms implies that the number of rival producers is simultaneously being reduced through failure or merger.

Historically, in many industries technological progress has made more and more economies of scale attainable over time. Many industries started out with a primitive technology, few economies of scale, and many competitors. But as technology improved and economies of scale became increasingly pronounced, the less aggressive firms fell by the wayside and a few producers emerged.

For example, estimates suggest that as many as seventy to eighty firms populated the Canadian automobile industry in its infancy. Over the years, the

the market shares, much greater weight is given to larger firms than smaller ones. In the hypothetical case of the single-firm telecommunications industry the index would be 100^2 or 10,000. For the four-firm auto industry the index would be $25^2 + 25^2 + 25^2 + 25^2$ or 2,500. To generalize, the larger the Herfindahl Index, the greater the degree of market power within an industry.

5 Performance   Finally, concentration ratios tell us nothing about the actual market performance of various industries. Industries X and Y may have iden-

development of mass-production techniques reduced the field through failure and combination. Now the Big Three — General Motors, Ford, and Chrysler — account for over 70% of the Canadian-produced automobile market. The same trend has been at work with a vengeance in the snowmobile field where, as recently as fifteen or so years ago, there were fifty or sixty manufacturers. Now, in Canada there is only *one*: Bombardier Inc.

But why aren't new firms created to enter the automobile industry? The answer is that to achieve the low unit costs essential to survival, any new entrants must necessarily start out as large producers. This may require several billion dollars' worth of investment in machinery and equipment alone. Economies of scale can prove a formidable barrier to entry. They explain not only the evolution of oligopoly in many industries, but also why such industries are not likely to become more competitive.

Other Barriers   The development or persistence of some oligopolies can be traced, at least in part, to other entry barriers. In the electronics, chemical, and aluminum industries, ownership of patents and control of strategic raw materials have been important. And prodigious advertising outlays may be an added financial barrier to entry.

The Urge To Merge   The final factor in explaining oligopoly or fewness is merger. The motivation for merger has diverse roots. Of immediate relevance is the fact that the combining of two or more formerly competing firms by merger may increase their market share substantially, enabling the new and larger production unit to achieve greater economies of scale.

Another significant motive underlying the "urge to merge" is the market power that may accompany merger. A firm that is larger both absolutely and relative to the market may have greater ability to control the market for and the price of its product than does a smaller, more competitive producer. Also, the large size that merger entails may give the firm the advantage of being a "big buyer" and permit it to demand and obtain lower prices (costs) from input suppliers than previously.

OLIGOPOLY BEHAVIOUR: A GAME THEORY OVERVIEW

Oligopoly pricing behaviour has the characteristics of a game of strategy such as poker, chess, or bridge. The best way to play your hand in a poker game depends on the way rivals play theirs. Players must pattern their actions according to the actions and expected reactions of rivals. Let's use a simple **game theory model** to grasp the basics of oligopolistic pricing behaviour. To simplify we assume a **duopoly** — a two-firm oligopoly — exists.

Consider Figure 13-1, which shows the price-profit or profits-payoff matrix for two firms that produce athletic shows. Pricing strategies for the firms — say, Leapers and Jumpers — are shown along the left and top margins respectively. Entries in the matrix show the profit payoffs to the two firms associated with any given combination of pricing strategies. Leapers' profit (in millions) is shown in the northeast portion of each cell and Jumpers' profit is in the southwest portion. For example, if both firms adopt a high-price strategy (cell A), each will realize a $12 million profit. Alternatively, if Jumpers follows a high-price policy and Leapers a low-price policy (cell B), Jumpers' profit will be only $6 million and Leapers' will be $15 million.

Although the data of Figure 13-1 are hypothetical, the profit figures are not arbitrarily chosen. In reality, if Jumpers committed itself to a high price and did not vary from it, Leapers could increase its profits by choosing a low price and gaining market share at Jumpers' expense. The same rationale applies if Leapers commits to a high price and Jumpers opts for a low price.

Mutual Interdependence

The most evident point demonstrated by Figure 13-1 is the **mutual interdependence** of oligopolists. Each firm's profits will depend not only on its own pricing strategy, but also on that of its rivals. As we have just observed, if Jumpers adopts a high-price policy, its profit will be $12 million *provided* Leapers also employs a high-price strategy (cell A). But if Leapers uses a low-price strategy against Jumpers' high-price strategy (cell B), Leapers will increase its market share and thereby its profits from $12 to $15 million. Leapers' higher profits come at the expense of Jumpers' whose profits fall from $12 to $6 million. Jumpers' high-price strategy is only a "good" strategy *if* Leapers employs the same strategy. Indeed, a good, workable definition of oligopoly is that *oligopoly exists when the number of firms in an industry is so small that each must consider the reactions of rivals in formulating its price policy*.

Collusive Tendencies

A second point is that oligopoly often leads to **collusion**, meaning some sort of formal or informal

FIGURE 13-1   The profit-payoffs for a two-firm oligopoly

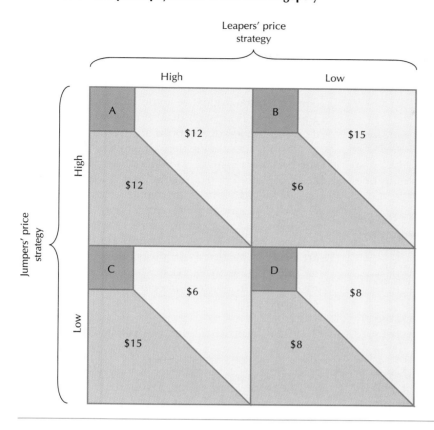

Both firms would realize the largest profit of $12 million if each adhered to a high-price policy (cell A). But if they are acting independently or competitively, each might achieve a higher profit of $15 million by adopting a low-price policy against its rival's high-price policy (cells B and C). Such independent pricing causes the outcome to gravitate to cell D where profits are only $8 million. Collusion can be used to establish mutual high prices and increase each firm's profits from $8 million (cell D) to $12 million (cell A). But cells B and C remind us of the temptation to cheat on a collusive agreement.

arrangement to coordinate pricing strategies or fix prices. To illustrate in terms of Figure 13-1, suppose that initially both firms are independently following high-price strategies. Each realizes a $12 million profit (cell A).

Observe that *either* Leapers or Jumpers could increase its profits by switching to a low-price strategy (cell B or C). If Leapers uses a low-price strategy against Jumpers' high-price strategy, its profits will increase to $15 million and Jumpers' will fall to $6 million. But by comparing cells B and D, we note that when Leapers shifts to a low-price policy, Jumpers would be better off if it also adopted a low-price policy. By doing so its profit would increase from $6 million (cell B) to $8 million (cell D).

Similarly, starting again at cell A, if Jumpers switched to a low-price policy against Leapers' high-price strategy, Jumpers' profit would increase to $15 million and Leapers' would fall to $6 million (cell C). And, again, Leapers could increase its profit from $6 million (cell C) to $8 million (cell D) by also switching to a low-price policy.

What we find is that independent action by oligopolists will likely lead to mutual "competitive" low-price strategies. Independent oligopolists compete with respect to price and this leads to lower prices and lower profits. This is clearly beneficial to consumers, but not to the oligopolists.

How can oligopolists avoid the low-profit outcome of cell D? The answer is *not* to establish prices competitively or independently, but rather to collude. The two firms must agree to establish and maintain a high-price policy. Each firm will thus increase its profits from $8 million (cell D) to $12 million (cell A). Momentarily we will discuss a variety of specific collusive practices.

Incentive to Cheat

The payoff matrix also explains why an oligopolist might be strongly tempted to cheat on a collusive agreement. Suppose that as a result of collusion Jumpers and Leapers both agree to high-price policies with each earning $12 million in profits (cell A).

The temptation to cheat on this pricing agreement arises because either firm can increase its profits to $15 million by lowering its price (cell B or C). If Jumpers agrees to a high-price policy but secretly "cheats" on that agreement by actually charging low prices, the outcome moves from cell A to cell C. Result? Jumpers' profit rises to $15 million and Leapers' falls to $6 million.

FOUR OLIGOPOLY MODELS

To gain further insights on oligopolistic price–output behaviour, we will examine four distinct models (1) the kinked demand curve, (2) collusive pricing, (3) price leadership, and (4) cost-plus pricing.

Why not a single model as in our discussions of the other market structures? There is no standard portrait of oligopoly for two major reasons.

1. Oligopoly encompasses a greater range and diversity than other market structures. It includes "tight oligopoly" in which two or three firms dominate an entire market, as well as "loose oligopoly" in which six or seven firms share, say, 70 or 80% of a market while a "competitive fringe" of firms share the remainder. It includes both product differentiation and standardization. It encompasses cases where firms act in collusion and those where they act independently. It embodies situations in which barriers to entry are very strong and those in which they are less so. In short, the diversity of oligopoly pre-

cludes development of a simple market model that provides a general explanation of oligopolistic behaviour.

2. The element of mutual interdependence added by fewness is a significant complication. The inability of a firm to predict with certainty the reactions of its rivals makes it virtually impossible to estimate the demand and marginal-revenue data faced by an oligopolist. Without such data, firms cannot determine their profit-maximizing price and output.

Despite these analytical difficulties, two interrelated characteristics of oligopolistic pricing have been observed. First, oligopolistic prices are inflexible, or "sticky." Prices change less frequently in oligopoly than under pure competition, monopolistic competition, and, in some instances, pure monopoly. Second, when oligopolistic prices do change, firms are likely to change their prices together; oligopolistic price behaviour suggests the presence of incentives to act in concert or collusively in setting and changing prices.

Kinked Demand: Noncollusive Oligopoly

Imagine an oligopolistic industry comprised of just three firms, A, B, and C, each having about one-third of the total market for a differentiated product. Assume the firms are "independent" in that they do not engage in collusive practices in setting prices. Suppose, too, that the going price for firm A's product is PQ and its current sales are Q, as shown in Figure 13-2(a).

Now the question is, "What does the firm's demand, or sales, curve look like?" Mutual interdependence, and the uncertainty of rivals' reactions that interdependence entails, make this question difficult to answer. The location and shape of an oligopolist's demand curve depend on how the firm's rivals will react to a price change introduced by A. There are two plausible assumptions about the reactions of A's rivals.

Match Price Changes   One possibility is that firms B and C will exactly match any price change initiated by A. In this case, A's demand and marginal-revenue curves will look like D_1 and MR_1 in Figure 13-2(a). If A cuts price, its sales will increase very modestly, because its two rivals will follow suit to prevent A from gaining any price advantage over them. The small increase in sales that A (and its two rivals) will realize is at the expense of other industries; A will gain no sales from B and C. If A raises the going price, its sales will fall only modestly, because B and C match its price increase, so A does not price itself out

FIGURE 13-2   The kinked demand curve

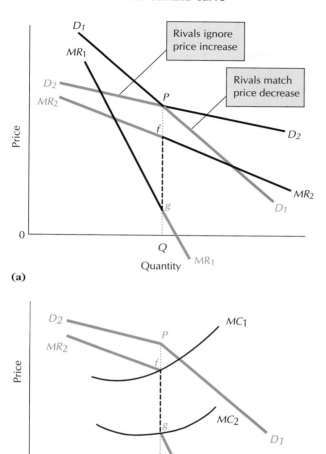

(a)

(b)

The nature of a noncollusive oligopolist's demand and marginal-revenue curves as shown in (a) will depend upon whether its rivals will match (D_1D_1 and MR_1MR_1) or ignore (D_2D_2 and MR_2MR_2) any price changes that it may initiate from the current price, PQ. In all likelihood, an oligopolist's rivals will ignore a price increase but follow a price cut. This causes the oligopolist's demand curve to be kinked (D_2PD_1) and its marginal-revenue curve to have a vertical break, or gap (MR_2MR_1) as shown in (b). Furthermore, because any shift in marginal costs between MC_1 and MC_2 will cut the vertical (dashed) segment of the marginal-revenue curve, no change in either price, PQ, or output, Q, will occur.

of the market. The industry now loses some sales to other industries, but A loses no customers to B and C.

Ignore Price Changes   The other possibility is that firms B and C will ignore any price change invoked

by A. In this case, the demand and marginal-revenue curves faced by A will resemble D_2 and MR_2 in Figure 13-2(a). The demand curve in this case is considerably more elastic than under the assumption that B and C will match A's price changes. The reasons are clear. If A lowers its price and its rivals do not, A will gain sales significantly at the expense of its two rivals because it will be underselling them. Conversely, if A raises its price and its rivals do not, A will lose many customers to B and C. Because of product differentiation, however, A's sales do not fall to zero when it raises its price; some of A's customers will pay the higher price because they have strong preferences for A's product.

A Mixed Strategy   Which is the most logical assumption for A to make on how its rivals will react to any price change it might initiate? Common sense and observation of oligopolistic industries suggest that price declines will be matched as a firm's competitors act to prevent the price cutter from taking their customers, but that price increases will be ignored, because rivals of the price-increasing firm stand to gain the business lost by the price booster. In other words, the coloured D_2P segment of the "rivals ignore" demand curve seems relevant for price increases, and the coloured PD_1 segment of the "rivals match" demand curve is more realistic for price cuts. It is logical, or at least a good guess, that an oligopolist faces a **"kinked" demand curve** on the order of D_2PD_1 as shown in Figure 13-2(b) (Ignore the MC_1 and MC_2 curves for now.) The curve is highly elastic above the going price, but much less elastic or even inelastic below the current price.

Note, also, that if it is correct to suppose that rivals will follow a price cut but ignore an increase, the marginal-revenue curve of the oligopolist will also have an odd shape. It, too, will be made up of two segments — the MR_2f part of the marginal-revenue curve appropriate to D_2 and the gMR_1 part appropriate to D_1D_1 in Figure 13-2(a). Because of the sharp differences in elasticity of demand above and below the going price, there is a gap, or what we can treat as a vertical segment, in the marginal-revenue curve. In Figure 13-2(b), the marginal-revenue curve is shown by the two coloured lines connected by the dashed vertical segment, or gap.

Price Inflexibility   This analysis goes far to explain why price changes may be infrequent in noncollusive oligopolistic industries.

1. The kinked demand schedule gives each oligopolist good reason to believe that any change in price will be for the worse. Many customers will desert the firm if it raises price. If it lowers price, its sales at best will increase very modestly. Even if a price cut increases its total revenue somewhat, the oligopolist's costs may well increase by a more-than-offsetting amount. Should the coloured PD_1 segment of its sales schedule be *inelastic*, in that E_d is less than 1, the firm's profit will surely fall.

A price decrease will lower the firm's total receipts, and the production of a somewhat larger output will increase total costs. Worse yet, a price cut by A may be *more* than met by B and C, leading to a **price war**; the amount sold by A may actually decline as its rival firms charge still lower prices. These are all good reasons, on the demand side of the picture, that noncollusive oligopolies might seek the quiet life and follow live-and-let-live price policies.

2. The other reason for price inflexibility under noncollusive oligopoly works from the cost side of the picture. The broken marginal-revenue curve that accompanies the kinked demand curve suggests that within limits, substantial cost changes will have no effect on output and price. Any shift in marginal cost between MC_1 and MC_2 in Figure 13-2(b) will result in no change in price or output; MR will continue to equal MC at output Q at which price PQ will be charged.

Shortcomings   The kinked demand analysis has two major criticisms. First, the analysis *does not explain how the going price gets to be at PQ (Figure 13-2) in the first place*. Rather, it only helps to explain why oligopolists may be reluctant to deviate from an existing price that yields them a "satisfactory" or "reasonable" profit. The kinked demand curve explains price inflexibility but not price itself.

Second, oligopoly prices may not be as rigid — particularly in an upward direction — as the kinked demand theory implies. During inflationary periods such as the 1970s and early 1980s, producers in oligopolistic industries raised their prices substantially. Such price increases might be better explained in terms of collusive oligopoly.

Collusion and Cartels

Our game theory model has suggested oligopoly is conducive to collusion. Collusion occurs when firms in an industry reach an overt or covert agreement to fix prices, divide or share the market, and otherwise restrict competition among themselves. The disadvantages and uncertainties of the noncollusive, kinked-demand model to producers are obvious.

There is always the danger of a price war. In particular, in a general business recession, each firm will find itself with excess capacity, and it can reduce per-unit costs by increasing its market share. Then, too, a new firm may surmount entry barriers and initiate aggressive price cutting to gain a foothold in the market. In addition, the rigid prices suggested by the kinked demand curve may adversely affect profits if general inflationary pressures increase costs. Thus, collusive control over price may permit oligopolists to reduce uncertainty, increase profits, and perhaps even prohibit the entry of new rivals.

Price and Output   Where will price and output be established under **collusive oligopoly**? Assume once again there are three firms — A, B, and C — producing, in this instance, homogeneous products. Each firm has identical cost curves. Each firm's demand curve is indeterminate unless we know how its rivals will react to any price change. Therefore, suppose each firm assumes its two rivals will match either a price cut or a price increase. In other words, each firm's demand curve is of the D_1 type in Figure 13-2(a). Assume further that the demand curve for each firm is identical. Given identical cost, demand, and marginal-revenue data, we can say that Figure 13-3 represents the position of each of our three oligopolistic firms.

What price–output combination should each firm choose? If firm A were a pure monopolist, the answer would be clear: Establish output at Q, where marginal revenue equals marginal cost, charge the corresponding price, PQ, and enjoy the maximum profit attainable. However, firm A *does* have two rivals selling identical products, and if A's assumption that its rivals will match its price proves to be incorrect, the consequences could be disastrous for A. If B and C actually charge prices below PQ, then firm A's demand curve will shift sharply to the left as its potential customers turn to its rivals, who are now selling the same product at a lower price. Of course, A can retaliate by cutting its price too, but this will move all three firms down their demand curves, lowering their profits, and perhaps even driving them to some point where average cost exceeds price and losses are incurred.

So the question becomes, "Will B and C want to charge a price below PQ?" Under our assumptions, and recognizing that A will have little choice except to match any price they may set below PQ, the answer is no. Faced with the same demand and cost circumstances, B and C will find it in their interest to produce Q and charge PQ. This is a curious situation;

FIGURE 13-3   Collusion and the tendency toward joint-profit maximization

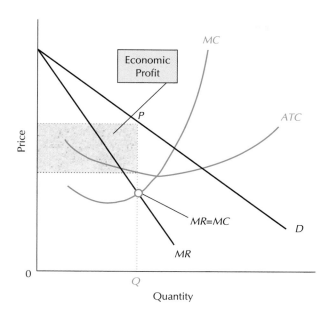

If oligopolistic firms are faced with identical or highly similar demand and cost conditions, they will tend to behave collusively and maximize joint profits. The price and output results are essentially the same as those of pure (unregulated) monopoly; each oligopolist charges price *PQ* and produces output *Q*.

each firm finds it most profitable to charge the same price, *PQ*, but only if its rivals will actually do so!

How can the three firms realize the *PQ*-price and *Q*-quantity solution in which each is keenly interested? The answer is evident: The firms will all be motivated to collude — to get together and talk it over — and agree to charge the same price, *PQ*. In addition to reducing the omnipresent possibility of a price war, each firm will realize the maximum profit. And for society, the result is likely to be about the same as if the industry were a pure monopoly composed of three identical plants (Chapter 11).

Overt Collusion: The OPEC Cartel   Collusion may assume a variety of forms. The most comprehensive form of collusion is the **cartel**, which typically involves a formal written agreement with respect to both price and production. Output must be controlled — the market must be shared — to maintain the agreed-upon price.

The most spectacularly successful international cartel of recent years has been OPEC (the Organization of Petroleum Exporting Countries). Comprised of thirteen nations, OPEC was very effective in the 1970s in restricting oil supply and raising prices. The cartel was able to raise world oil prices from U.S. $2.50 to $11.00 per barrel within a six-month period in 1973–74. By early 1980, price hikes had brought the per barrel price into the U.S. $32 to $34 range. The result was enormous profits for cartel members, greater world-wide inflation, and serious international trade deficits for oil importers.

OPEC was highly effective in the 1970s for several reasons. First, OPEC dominated the world market for oil. If a nation imported oil, it was almost obligated to do business with OPEC. Second, the world demand for oil was strong and expanding in the 1970s. Finally, the short-run demand for oil was highly inelastic, which meant that a small restriction of output by OPEC would result in a relatively large price increase. Thus, as shown in Figure 13-4, in 1973–74 and again in 1979–80 OPEC was able to achieve dramatic oil price increases and only incur a

FIGURE 13-4   The OPEC cartel and the world oil market

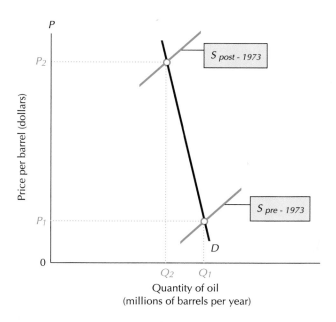

Because of the inelasticity of the demand for oil, in 1973–74 and again in 1979–80 the OPEC cartel was able to obtain a dramatic increase in the price of oil (P_1 to P_2) accompanied by only a very modest decline in production and sales (Q_1 to Q_2).

very modest decline in sales. Given this inelastic demand, higher prices translated into greatly increased total revenues for OPEC members. The accompanying smaller output meant lower total costs. The combination of more total revenue and lower total costs resulted in greatly expanded profits.

Covert Collusion: The Electrical Equipment Conspiracy   Cartels are illegal in both Canada and the United States; collusion has been covert or secret. For example, in 1960 an extensive price-fixing and market-sharing scheme involving heavy electrical equipment, such as transformers, turbines, circuit breakers, and switchgear, was uncovered in the United States. Elaborate secret schemes were developed by such participants as General Electric, Westinghouse, and Allis-Chalmers to rig prices and divide the market. Twenty-nine manufacturers and forty-six company officials were indicted in this "great electrical conspiracy," which violated United States antitrust laws. Substantial fines, jail penalties, and lawsuits by victimized buyers were the final outcome. In contrast, no one has ever gone to jail for breaches of Canada's Combines Investigation Act (renamed the Competition Act in mid-1986).

In innumerable other instances, collusion is even more subtle. **Gentlemen's agreements** frequently are struck at cocktail parties, on the golf course, or at trade association meetings. Competing firms reach a verbal agreement on product price, leaving market shares to the ingenuity of each seller as reflected in nonprice competition. Although they collide with the Competition Act, the elusive character of gentlemen's agreements makes them more difficult to detect and prosecute successfully.

Obstacles to Collusion   Cartels and similar collusive arrangements are often difficult to establish and maintain. Let us briefly consider several important barriers to collusion.

1 Demand and Cost Differences   When oligopolists' costs and product demands differ, it is more difficult to agree on price, especially where products are differentiated and changing frequently over time. Indeed, even with highly standardized products, we would expect that firms might have somewhat different market shares and would operate with differing degrees of productive efficiency, thus they would have different demand and cost curves.

In either event, differences in costs and demand will mean that the profit-maximizing price for each firm will differ; there will be no single price that is readily acceptable to all. Price collusion therefore depends on the ability to achieve compromises and concessions — to arrive at a degree of "understanding" that in practice is often difficult to attain. For example, the MR = MC positions of firms A, B, and C may call for them to charge $12, $11, and $10 respectively, but this price cluster or range may be unsatisfactory to one or more of the firms.

2 Number of Firms   Other things being equal, the larger the number of firms, the more difficult it is to achieve a cartel or other form of price collusion. Agreement on price by three or four producers that control an entire market is much more readily accomplished than it is when ten firms each have roughly 10% of the market.

3 Cheating   As our game theory made clear, there is also a more-or-less persistent temptation for collusive oligopolists to make secret price concessions in order to get additional business.

The difficulty with cheating is that buyers who are paying a high price may get wind of the lower-priced sales and demand similar treatment. Or buyers receiving price concessions from one oligopolist may use this concession as a wedge to get even larger price concessions from the firm's rivals. The attempt of buyers to play sellers against one another may precipitate a price war among the firms. Although it is potentially profitable, secret price concessions threaten the maintenance of collusive oligopoly over time. Collusion is more likely to persist when cheating is easy to detect and punish.

4 Recession   Recession is usually an enemy of collusion because slumping markets cause the oligopolists' demand and marginal-revenue curves to shift to the left and each firm moves back to a higher point on its average-cost curve. Firms find they have substantial excess productive capacity, sales are down, unit costs are up, and profits are being squeezed. Under these conditions, businesses may feel they can better avoid serious profit reductions by price cutting in the hope of gaining sales at the expense of rivals.

5 Potential Entry   The enhanced prices and profits that result from collusion may attract new entrants, including foreign firms. Such entry would increase market supply and reduce prices and profits. Therefore, successful collusion requires that the colluding oligopolists can block entry of new producers.

6 Legal Obstacles: Anti-combines   Our Competition Act prohibits cartels and the kind of price-fixing collusion we have been discussing. Thus, less obvious means of price rigging — such as price leadership — have evolved in Canada.

OPEC in Disarray

The highly successful OPEC oil cartel of the 1970s fell into disarray in the 1980s. The reasons for OPEC's decline relate closely to the obstacles to collusion we have just enumerated.

First, the dramatic increase in oil prices in the 1970s stimulated the search for new oil reserves, and soon non-OPEC nations, which OPEC could not block from entering world markets, became part of the world oil industry. Great Britain, Norway, and Mexico have become major world oil suppliers. As a result, OPEC's share of world oil production fell sharply.

Second, on the demand side, oil conservation, a world-wide recession in the early 1980s, and the expanded use of alternative energy sources (such as coal, natural gas, and nuclear power) reduced the demand for oil. The combination of greater production by non-OPEC nations and a decline in world demand generated an oil glut that seriously impaired OPEC's ability to control world oil prices.

Third, OPEC has had a serious cheating problem stemming from the relatively large number of members (thirteen) and the diversity of their economic circumstances. Saudi Arabia is the dominant cartel member; it has the largest oil reserves and is probably the lowest-cost producer. It has favoured a "moderate" pricing policy because it has feared that very high oil prices would hasten the development of alternative energy sources (such as solar power and synthetic fuels) and increase the attractiveness of existing substitutes such as coal and natural gas. Such developments would greatly reduce the value of its vast oil reserves. Saudi Arabia also has a small population and a very high per capita GDP. But other members — for example, Nigeria and Venezuela — are very poor, have large populations, and are burdened with large external debts. Others — Iran, Iraq, and Libya — have had large military commitments. All of these members have had immediate needs for cash. Thus, there has been substantial cheating. Some members have exceeded assigned production quotas and have sold oil at prices below those agreed to by the cartel.

Price Leadership: Tacit Collusion

Price leadership is a type of gentlemen's agreement by which oligopolists can coordinate their price behaviour without engaging in outright collusion. Formal agreements and clandestine meetings are not involved. Rather, a practice evolves whereby the "dominant" firm — usually the largest or the most

efficient in the industry — initiates price changes, and all other firms more or less automatically follow. The importance of price leadership is evidenced in the fact that such industries as farm machinery, anthracite coal, cement, copper, gasoline, newsprint, tin cans, lead, sulphur, rayon, fertilizer, glass containers, steel, automobiles, and nonferrous metals are practising, or have in the recent past practised, price leadership.

Cigarette Pricing   Consider the case of the cigarette industry, which provides a classic example of tight price leadership. In this instance, the American Big Three, producing from 68% to 90% of total output, evolved a highly profitable practice of price leadership, which resulted in virtually identical prices over the entire 1923–41 period.

Since 1946, cigarette pricing has been somewhat less rigid, reflecting both successful anti-combines action and the development of increasingly heterogeneous product lines. But overall, there has been little evidence of enhanced price rivalry.

Leadership Tactics   The examination of price leadership in a variety of industries suggests that the price leader is likely to observe several tactics.

1. Because price changes always entail some risk that rivals will not follow, price adjustments will be made infrequently. The price leader will *not* change prices in response to tiny day-to-day changes in cost and demand conditions. Price will be changed only when cost and demand conditions have been altered significantly and on an industry-wide basis. For example, in response to industry-wide wage increases, an increase in taxes, or an increase in the price of some basic input such as energy. In the automobile industry, price adjustments have traditionally been made when new models are introduced each fall.

2. Impending price adjustments are often communicated by the price leader to the industry through speeches by major executives, trade publication interviews, and so forth. By publicizing "the need to raise prices," the price leader can elicit a consensus among its competitors for the actual increase.

3. The price leader does not necessarily choose the price that maximizes short-run profits for the industry. The industry may want to discourage new firms from entering. If barriers to entry are based on cost advantages (economies of scale) or existing firms, these cost barriers may be surmounted by new entrants *if* product price is set high enough. New firms that are relatively inefficient because of their small size may survive and grow if the industry's price is very high. To discourage new competitors and thereby maintain the current oligopolistic structure of the industry, price may be established below the profit-maximizing level.

Cost-Plus Pricing

Another model of oligopolistic price behaviour centres on what is variously known as *markup, rule-of-thumb*, or **cost-plus pricing**. The oligopolist estimates cost per unit of output and a markup is applied to cost to determine price. Unit costs, however, vary with output and therefore the firm must assume some typical or target level of output. For example, the firm's average-cost figure may be that which is realized when the firm is operating at, say, 75% or 80% of capacity. A markup, usually in the form of a percentage, is applied to average cost in determining price. For example, an appliance manufacturer may estimate unit costs of dishwashers to be $250, to which a 50% markup is applied. This yields a $375 price to retailers.

But why is the markup 50%, rather than 25% or 100%? The answer is that the firm is seeking some target profit or rate of return on its investment. To illustrate, consider the pricing techniques used by General Motors for over four decades prior to the advent of aggressive foreign competition in the mid-1970s:

> GM started with the goal of earning, on the average over the years, a return of approximately 15 percent after taxes on total invested capital. Not knowing how many autos would be sold and hence unit costs (including prorated fixed costs), it calculated costs on the assumption of operation at 80 percent of conservatively rated capacity. A standard price was calculated by adding to unit cost a sufficient profit margin to yield the desired 15 percent after-tax return. The rule would be adjusted across the product line to take account of actual and potential competition, business conditions, long-run strategic goals, and other factors. Actual profit then depended on the number of vehicles sold. Between 1960 and 1979, GM's actual return on stockholders' equity fell below 15 percent in only four years, all marked by recession and/or OPEC-induced gasoline price shocks. The average return was 17.6 percent. After 1979, recession and intensifying import competition caused GM frequently to fall short of its target.[1]

[1] F.M. Scherer and David Rose, *Industrial Market Structure and Economic Performance*, 3rd ed. (Boston: Houghton Mifflin Company, 1990), p. 262.

Two final points: First, this method of pricing is *not* inconsistent with outright collusion or price leadership. If the several producers in an industry have roughly similar costs, adherence to a common pricing formula will result in highly similar prices and price changes. As we will find in a case study later in this chapter, General Motors uses cost-plus pricing *and* is the price leader in the automobile industry. Second, cost-plus pricing has obvious advantages for multi-product firms, which would otherwise be faced with the difficult and costly process of estimating demand and cost conditions for perhaps hundreds of different products. In practice, it is virtually impossible to allocate correctly certain common overhead costs such as power, lighting, insurance, and taxes to specific products.

ROLE OF NONPRICE COMPETITION

We have noted that, for several reasons, oligopolists have an aversion to price competition. This aversion may lead to some more or less informal type of collusion on price. In North America, however, price collusion is usually accompanied by nonprice competition. It is typically through nonprice competition that each firm's share of total market is determined. This emphasis on nonprice competition has its roots in two basic facts.

1 Less Easily Duplicated Price cuts can be quickly and easily met by a firm's rivals. Thus, the possibility of significantly increasing one's share of the market through price competition is small. And of course the risk is always present that price competition will precipitate a disastrous price war. Nonprice competition is less likely to get out of hand. Oligopolists seem to feel that more permanent advantages can be gained over rivals through nonprice competition because product variations, improvements in productive techniques, and successful advertising gimmicks cannot be duplicated as easily as price reductions.

2 Greater Financial Resources There is a more evident reason for the tremendous emphasis on nonprice competition: Manufacturing oligopolists typically have substantial financial resources with which to support advertising and product development. Thus, although nonprice competition is a basic characteristic of both monopolistically competitive and oligopolistic industries, the latter are typically in a financial position to indulge more fully in nonprice competition.

OLIGOPOLY AND ECONOMIC EFFICIENCY

Is oligopoly an "efficient" market structure from society's standpoint? How does the price–output behaviour of the oligopolist compare with that of a purely competitive firm? Because there are a variety of oligopoly models — kinked demand, collusion, price leadership, and cost-plus pricing — it is difficult to make such a comparison.

Allocative and Productive Efficiency

Many economists believe that the outcome of oligopolistic markets is approximately that shown in Figure 13-3. Note that, as compared to the benchmark of pure competition (Figure 10-12), production occurs where price exceeds marginal cost and short of that output where average total cost is minimized. In terms of the terminology of Chapters 10 and 11, neither allocative efficiency ($P = MC$) nor productive efficiency ($P = $ minimum ATC) is likely to occur under oligopoly.

One may even argue that oligopoly is actually less desirable than pure monopoly simply because pure monopoly in Canada is frequently subject to government regulation to mitigate abuses of market power. Informal collusion among oligopolists may yield price and output results similar to pure monopoly, yet at the same time maintain the outward appearance of several independent and "competing" firms.

Two qualifications are relevant. First, in recent years foreign competition has generated more rivalry in a number of oligopolistic markets — autos and steel come immediately to mind — and has undermined such cozy arrangements as price leadership and cost-plus pricing and stimulated more competitive pricing. Second, recall that oligopolistic firms may purposely keep prices below the short-run profit-maximizing level to deter entry where entry barriers are less formidable.

Dynamic Efficiency

What about the "very long-run" perspective where we allow for innovation in terms of improvements in product quality and more efficient production methods?

Competitive View   One view is that competition provides a compelling incentive to be technologically progressive. If a given firm does not seize the initiative, one or more rivals will introduce an improved product or a cost-reducing production technique that may drive it from the market. Both the desire of short-term profits and long-term survival provide competitive firms with the persistent pressure to improve products and lower costs through innovation.

Some adherents to this competitive view allege that oligopolists may often have a strong incentive to impede innovation and restrain technological progress. The larger corporation wants to maximize profits by exploiting fully all its capital assets. Why rush to develop and introduce a new product (for example, fluorescent lights) when that product's success will render obsolete all equipment designed to produce an existing product (incandescent bulbs)? Furthermore, it is not difficult to cite oligopolistic industries in which interest in research and development has been modest at best: The steel, cigarette, and aluminum industries are cases in point.

Schumpeter–Galbraith View   In contrast the Schumpeter–Galbraith view holds that large oligopolistic firms with market power are necessary for rapid technological progress.

High R&D Costs   It is argued, first, that modern research to develop new products and new productive techniques is very expensive. Therefore, only large oligopolistic firms can finance extensive research and development (R & D) activities.

Barriers and Profits   Second, the existence of barriers to entry gives the oligopolist some assurance that it will realize any profit rewards from successful R & D endeavours. Small competitive firms have neither the *means* nor the *incentives* to be technologically progressive; large oligopolists do.[2]

If the Schumpeter–Galbraith view is correct, it suggests that over time oligopolistic industries will foster rapid product improvement, lower unit production costs, lower prices, and perhaps a greater output and more employment than would the same industry organized competitively. There is anecdotal and case-study evidence suggesting that many oligopolistic manufacturing industries — television and other electronics products, home appliances, automobile tires — have been characterized by substantial improvements in product quality, falling relative prices, and expanding levels of output and employment.

---

[2] John Kenneth Galbraith, *American Capitalism*, rev. ed. (Boston: Houghton Mifflin Company, 1956), pp. 86–88. Also see Joseph Schumpeter, *Capitalism, Socialism and Democracy* (New York: Harper & Row Publishers, Inc., 1942).

Technological Progress: The Evidence

Which view is correct? Empirical studies have yielded ambiguous results. The consensus, however, seems to be that giant oligopolies are probably *not* a fountainhead of technological progress. A pioneering study[3] of sixty-one important inventions made from 1880 to 1965 indicates that over half were the work of independent inventors disassociated from corporate industrial research laboratories. Such substantial advances as air conditioning, power steering, the ballpoint pen, cellophane, the jet engine, insulin, xerography, the helicopter, and the catalytic cracking of petroleum have this individualistic heritage. Other equally important advances have come from small- and medium-sized firms.

According to this study, about two-thirds — forty out of sixty-one — of the basic inventions of this century have been fathered by independent inventors or the research activities of relatively small firms.

This is not to deny that in a number of oligopolistic industries — for example, the steel, aluminum, and nickel industries — research activity has been vigorously and fruitfully pursued. The Big Two in Canadian steel — Dofasco and Stelco — decided a long time ago that research and development were essential to their survival in the face of competition from U.S. Steel. Since then, the research activity of U.S. Steel (now named USX) has declined markedly, while it has remained at a substantial level in the Canadian industry.

Some leading researchers in this field have tentatively concluded that technological progress in an industry may be determined more by the industry's scientific character and "technological opportunities" than by its market structure. There may simply be more opportunities for progress in the computer and electronics industries than in the brickmaking and cigarette industries, regardless of market structure.

QUICK REVIEW (13-2)

1. The kinked-demand curve model is based on the assumption that an oligopolist's rivals will match a price cut but ignore a price increase. This model is consistent with observed price rigidity found in some oligopolistic industries.

2. A cartel is a collusive association of firms that establishes a formal agreement to determine price and to divide the market among participants.

3. Price leadership occurs when one firm — usually the largest or most efficient — determines price, and rival firms establish identical or highly similar prices.

4. Cost-plus pricing means that a firm establishes price by adding a percentage markup to the average cost of its product.

5. Oligopoly is conducive to neither allocative nor productive efficiency. There is disagreement as to whether oligopoly is conducive to technological progress.

AUTOMOBILES: A CASE STUDY[4]

The North American automobile industry provides an informative case study of oligopoly, illustrating many of the points made in this chapter. It also indicates that market structure is not permanent and, in particular, that foreign competition can upset the oligopolists' "quiet life."

Market Structure Although there were more than eighty auto manufacturers in the early 1920s in the United States and almost as many in Canada, a number of mergers (most notably the combining of Chevrolet, Pontiac, Oldsmobile, Buick, and Cadillac into General Motors), many failures during the Great Depression of the 1930s, and the increasing importance of entry barriers all reduced numbers in the industry. Currently, three large firms — General Motors (GM), Ford, and Chrysler — dominate the North American market for domestically produced automobiles.

These firms are gigantic in size: according to *The Report on Business Magazine*, in 1991, ranked by sales, GM was second, Ford third and Chrysler sixteenth. Furthermore, all three firms are leading truck manufacturers, produce a variety of household appliances, are involved in U.S. defence contracting, and have extensive overseas interests.

---

[3] John Jewkes, David Sawers, and Richard Stillerman, *The Sources of Invention*, rev. ed. (New York: St. Martin's Press, Inc., 1968).

[4] This section draws heavily on Walter Adams and James W. Brock, "The Automobile Industry," in Walter Adams (ed.), *The Structure of American Industry*, 7th ed. (New York: Macmillan Publishing Co., Inc., 1986), pp. 126–171.

Entry Barriers   Entry barriers are substantial, as is evidenced by the fact that it has been about six decades since a North American firm successfully entered the automobile industry. The primary barrier is economies of scale. It is estimated that the minimum efficient scale for a producer is about 300,000 units of output per year. However, given the uncertainties of consumer tastes, experts believe a truly viable firm must produce at least two different models. Hence to have a reasonable prospect of success, a new firm would have to produce about 600,000 autos per year.

The estimated cost of an integrated plant (involving the production of engines, transmissions, other components, and product assembly) might be as much as $1.2 to $1.4 billion. Other entry barriers include the need for extensive advertising and a far-flung dealer network (GM has over 16,000 dealers; Chrysler has over 11,000) that provide spare parts and repair service. A newcomer would also face the expensive task of overcoming existing brand loyalties. Given that the North American automobile industry spent over $3 billion per year on advertising in each of the past five years, this is no small matter.

Price Leadership and Profits   The indicated industry structure — a few firms with high entry barriers — has been fertile ground for collusive or coordinated pricing. GM has traditionally been the price leader. Each fall, with the introduction of new models, GM would establish prices for its basic models, and Ford and Chrysler would set the prices of their comparable models accordingly. (Details of how GM established its prices were outlined in the earlier section on cost-plus pricing.)

In the past several decades automobile prices have moved up steadily and at a rate exceeding the overall rate of inflation. And despite large periodic declines in demand and sales, automobile prices have displayed considerable downward rigidity, although import competition and recession have caused rebates and financing subsidies to become common in recent years.

Over the years, price leadership has proven to be very profitable. In the 1947–77 period the Big Three earned an average profit rate significantly greater than that of all manufacturing corporations taken as a whole.

Styling and Technology   In addition to advertising, nonprice competition has centred on styling and technological advance. In practice, the former has been stressed over the latter. As early as the 1920s,

GM recognized that the replacement market was becoming increasingly important compared to the market for first-time purchasers. Therefore, its strategy — later adopted by other manufacturers — became one of annual styling changes accompanied by model proliferation. The purpose is to achieve higher sales and profits by encouraging consumers to replace their autos with greater frequency and to encourage buyers to shift their purchases from basic to "upscale" models.

Technological progress in the industry presents a mixed picture. With respect to manufacturing processes, the industry has not altered its basic production techniques since Ford's introduction of the moving assembly line some seventy years ago. Overwhelming consumer survey evidence and prices suggest that the North American industry still lags behind offshore producers in both quality of product and efficiency of production. Thus the industry has done at best only a fair job of adapting and improving upon new production technologies that others have pioneered.

Foreign Competition   In the last two decades the automobile market in North America has become more competitive than the tight oligopolistic structure of the two domestic industries would suggest. GM, Ford, and Chrysler have been challenged by foreign (particularly Japanese) producers.

The reasons for the growth of foreign competition are many.

1 Rising Gas Prices   The OPEC-inspired increases in gasoline prices in the 1970s prompted a shift in consumer demand toward smaller, fuel-efficient imports from Japan and Germany. Many analysts contend that North American producers seriously misjudged the scope and apparent permanence of this shift.

2 Quality   In addition, many consumers perceived that imports had quality advantages. A 1990 consumer survey with respect to perceived automobile quality found seven Japanese models, two German models, and only one North American-made car in the top ten. The North American car ranked fifth.

3 Costs   Finally, lower overseas wages and higher labour productivity have given the Japanese and Koreans a substantial cost advantage on compact cars.

The response of the domestic automobile industry to enhanced foreign competition has been essentially twofold.

Box 13-1

In the Media

The auto industry is in a state of flux brought on by foreign competition and excess supply. As this book goes to press, Canada, the U.S., and Mexico are engaged in discussions to bring about a North American free trade agreement (NAFTA). The table below sets out cost comparisons between North American and some major countries producing autos.

FREE TRADE / *Canada appears to have little choice but to get involved in auto trade talks to make sure Mexico and the U.S. don't benefit at its expense*

150,000 CANADIANS WATCHING

BY TIMOTHY PRITCHARD
Auto Industry Reporter

Next month, negotiators from Canada, the United States and Mexico are to hold their first meeting on how to structure trade in autos and parts under a North American free-trade agreement.

The net result will be of vital interest to the almost 150,000 Canadians who work in auto assembly and parts plants, and who have already seen wrenching changes over the past few years.

Japanese penetration of the North American industry has dramatically altered consumer buying habits — and reshaped the way parts makers and assemblers do business.

While Japan is not a participant in the talks, the negotiators are aware of that country's $31-billion (U.S.) auto trade surplus with the United States (76 per cent of the total trade surplus). The Americans have since won concessions from Japanese car makers to double their purchases of U.S. parts.

The three countries engaged in NAFTA talks have different objectives, as do industry groups. Canada's auto industry is not only worried about the outcome, but also about trade developments in general.

Massive recessionary restructuring has cost Canada 24,000 auto jobs since 1989, and seen the flight of some companies to the United States.

With free trade, Mexico expects investment and jobs. Canada seems to have little choice but to make sure that Mexican and U.S. gains are not at Canada's expense.

Detroit's Big Three want any new trade structure to give them advantages for existing investment in Mexico, as in Canada, and to meet demands of the U.S. Corporate Average Fuel Economy Act. CAFE sets higher fuel efficiency standards for cars with less than 75-percent U.S. content. (The content rules are different than those for auto pact trade.)

Comparing the costs of an auto part

Typical North American part's cost breakout	Mexico	Japan	Brazil, S. Korea or Taiwan	Spain
Labour 10 to 30%	8 to 24% less	Same	8 to 24% less	2 to 10% less
Material 60%	6% less	Same	6% less	Same
Depreciation 2 to 6%	Same	Same	Same	Same
Other Inventory Transport Duty	6 to 9% more	10 to 15% more	10 to 15% more	5 to 10% more
Overall	5 to 24% less	10 to 20% more	1% more to 20% less	Equal to 9% more

Table *source:* Booz, Allen and Hamilton information

The Globe and Mail, "Report on Business," December 30, 1991.

1 Protection   The industry — with the support of organized labour — successfully lobbied government for protection. The result, beginning in 1981, was "voluntary" import quotas on Japanese cars that effectively restrained competition. Reduced foreign competition allowed domestic manufacturers to boost their prices to consumers. For example, one authoritative estimate suggests that the import quotas strengthened the domestic oligopoly to the extent that on the average domestic producers earned an additional $400 in profits on each car sold in 1983. Given that the output of North American producers was about 8 million cars in 1983, the aggregate increase in profits of domestic manufacturers was $2.8 billion.[5] These estimates clearly indicate that North American consumers have a great stake in free international trade and the competition it generates.

But the Japanese have responded to import quotas and the uncertainties inherent in the changing dollar–yen exchange rate by building automobile plants in North America. These so-called "transplants" now produce about 10% of the cars sold in North America. The success of Japanese production here is reflected in the fact that they built ten new factories in North America in the 1980s, precisely the number closed by the Big Three in the 1987–1989 period. It is significant that the Japanese have not sacrificed their production cost advantage by producing in North America. The transplants embody state-of-the-art equipment and Japanese industrial relations techniques. The result is an automobile built for $500 to $800 less than in most of the Big Three's plants.

The second response of domestic producers has been to coopt and mitigate foreign competition by initiating an elaborate network of joint ownership arrangements and joint ventures with foreign producers. Chrysler owns about one-fourth of Mitsubishi and imports both compact cars and parts from the latter. Mitsubishi in turn is a part owner of Korea's Hyundai Motor Company. General Motors has a joint production arrangement with Toyota in California and Ontario, and has significant ownership shares in other lesser-known Japanese auto manufacturers. Ford owns about one-fourth of Mazda. These arrangements cast a cloud of doubt on the contention that foreign competition has had an important "disciplining" effect on North American auto manufacturers. Adams and Brock, two astute observers of the industry, point out that ". . . a decade of joint ventures in the automotive industry has secured an interlocking system of mutually acceptable accords, and may well have forged the groundwork for cartelizing the world automobile industry."[6]

Another effect of Japanese competition has been to alter the GM price leadership pattern that characterized the industry for many decades. In 1977–1978 both the U.S. and Canadian dollars significantly declined in value relative to the yen, meaning that each dollar earned by the Japanese on auto sales in North America translated into smaller yen profits. Led by Toyota, the Japanese raised their prices in four steps during the 1978 model year. North American producers generally followed these increases. Again in 1985–1988 a depreciating dollar further increased Japanese car prices but, perhaps alarmed by declining market shares, the Big Three only boosted prices by about one-third of the Japanese increases. In short, the price leadership role of GM has been clouded by a new group of foreign rivals.

We have now finished our analysis of the four basic product market models — pure competition, pure monopoly, monopolistic competition, and oligopoly. You should examine Table 10-1 to ensure that the main characteristics of each of these models are clearly understood.

CHAPTER SUMMARY

1. Oligopolistic industries are characterized by the presence of a few firms, each of which has a significant fraction of the market. Firms thus situated are mutually interdependent; the behaviour of any one firm directly affects, and is affected by, the actions of rivals. Products may be virtually uniform or signifi-

[5] "Carving Up the Car Buyer," *Newsweek*, March 5, 1984, pp. 72–73. The estimates are those of Robert Crandall of The Brookings Institute. The import quotas further hurt North American consumers by restricting the supply and increasing the prices of Japanese cars.

[6] Walter Adams and James W. Brock, "Joint Ventures, Antitrust, and Transnational Cartelization," *Northwestern Journal of International Law & Business*, Winter 1991, p. 465.

cantly differentiated. Underlying reasons for the evolution of oligopoly are economies of scale, other entry barriers, and the advantages of merger.

2. Concentration ratios can be used as a measure of oligopoly and market power. The Herfindahl Index, which gives more weight to larger firms, is designed to measure market dominance in an industry.

3. Game theory shows the mutual interdependence of oligopolists' price policies; reveals the tendency to act collusively; and explains the temptation to cheat on collusive agreements.

4. Important models of oligopoly include: *a.* the kinked-demand model, *b.* collusive oligopoly, *c.* price leadership, and *d.* cost-plus pricing.

5. Noncollusive oligopolists may face a kinked demand curve. This curve and the accompanying marginal-revenue curve help explain the price rigidity that characterizes such markets; they do not, however, explain the level of price.

6. The uncertainties inherent in noncollusive pricing are conducive to collusion. There is a tendency for collusive oligopolists to maximize joint profits — that is, to behave somewhat like pure monopolists. Demand and cost differences, the presence of a "large" number of firms, "cheating" through secret price concessions, recessions, and the Competition Act are all obstacles to collusive oligopoly.

7. Price leadership is a less formal means of collusion whereby the largest or most efficient firm in the industry initiates price changes and the other firms follow.

8. With cost-plus or markup pricing, oligopolists estimate their unit costs at some target level of output and add a percentage "markup" to determine price.

9. Market shares in oligopolistic industries are usually determined on the basis of nonprice competition. Oligopolists emphasize nonprice competition because *a.* advertising and product variations are less easy for rivals to match, and *b.* oligopolists frequently have ample resources to finance nonprice competition.

10. It is unlikely that either allocative or productive efficiency is realized in oligopolistic markets. The competitive view envisions oligopoly as being inferior to more competitive market structures in promoting product improvement and cost-decreasing innovations. The Schumpeter–Galbraith view is that oligopolists have both the incentive and financial resources to be technologically progressive.

TERMS AND CONCEPTS

cartel (p. 215)
collusion (p. 210)
collusive oligopoly (p. 214)
concentration ratio (p. 208)
cost-plus pricing (p. 218)
duopoly (p. 210)
game theory model (p. 210)
gentlemen's agreement (p. 216)
Herfindahl Index (p. 208)
homogeneous and differentiated oligopoly (p. 208)

import competition (p. 208)
interindustry competition (p. 208)
kinked demand curve (p. 213)
mutual interdependence (p. 210)
oligopoly (p. 208)
price leadership (p. 217)
price war (p. 214)
traditional and Schumpeter–Galbraith views (p. 219)

QUESTIONS AND STUDY SUGGESTIONS

1. Why do oligopolies exist? List five or six oligopolists whose products you own or regularly purchase. What distinguishes oligopoly from monopolistic competition?

2. "Fewness of rivals means mutual interdependence, and mutual interdependence means uncertainty as to how those few rivals will react to a price change by any one firm." Explain. Of what significance is this for determining demand and marginal revenue? Other things being equal, would you expect mutual interdependence to vary directly or inversely with the degree of product differentiation? With the number of firms? Explain.

3. What is the meaning of a four-firm concentration ratio of 60%? 90%? What are the shortcomings of concentration ratios as measures of market power?

4. Suppose that in industry A five firms have annual sales of 30, 30, 20, 10, and 10% of total industry sales. For the five firms in industry B the figures are 60, 25, 5, 5, and 5%. Calculate the Herfindahl Index for each industry and compare their likely competitiveness.

5. Explain the general character of the data in the following profits-payoff matrix for oligopolists C and D. All profit figures are in thousands.

	C's price →	
	$40	$35
D's price ↓		
$40	$57 / $60	$59 / $55
$35	$50 / $69	$55 / $58

   a. Use the table to explain the mutual interdependence that characterizes oligopolistic industries.

   b. Assuming no collusion, what is the likely outcome of this game?

   c. Given your answer to question *b.*, explain why price collusion is mutually profitable. Why might there be a temptation to cheat on the collusive agreement?

6. What assumptions concerning a rival's responses to price changes underlie the kinked demand curve? Why is there a gap in the marginal-revenue curve? How does the kinked demand curve help explain oligopolistic price rigidity? What are the shortcomings of the kinked-demand model?

7. Why might price collusion occur in oligopolistic industries? Assess the economic desirability of collusive pricing. Explain: "If each firm knows that the price of each of its few rivals depends on its own price, how can the prices be determined?" What are the main obstacles to collusion? Apply these obstacles to the weakening of OPEC in the 1980s.

8. Assume the demand curve shown in question 4 in Chapter 11 applies to a pure monopolist that has a constant marginal cost of $4. What price and output will be most profitable for the monopolist? Now assume the demand curve applies to a two-firm industry (a "duopoly") and that each firm has a constant marginal cost of $4. If the firms collude, what price and quantity will maximize their joint profits? Demonstrate why it might be profitable for one of the firms to cheat. If the other firm becomes aware of this cheating, what will happen?

9. Explain how price leadership might evolve and function in an oligopolistic industry. Is cost-plus pricing compatible with collusion?

10. "Oligopolistic industries have both the means and the inclination for technological progress." Do you agree? Explain.

11. "If oligopolists really want to compete, they should do so by cutting their prices rather than by squandering millions of dollars on advertising and other forms of sales promotion." Do you agree? Why don't oligopolists usually compete by cutting prices?

12. Using Figure 13-3, explain how a collusive oligopolist might increase its profits by offering secret price concessions to buyers. On the diagram, indicate the amount of additional profits that the firm may realize. What are the risks involved in such a policy?

13. Review the case study of the automobile industry and identify aspects of industry structure and behaviour that are oligopolistic. What responses have domestic producers made to increasing foreign competition?

14

Government Competition Policy and Regulation of Monopolies

How are electricity, natural gas, local phone calls, and railroad service related? This question is easy; all are "utilities" and subject to **industrial regulation** — government regulation of prices (rates) within selected industries. Governments also encourage competition by enforcing **anti-combines** laws that make it illegal for firms to collude to affect the market price of their output.

And what do workplace safety standards, infant seats, acid rain, affirmative action, and auto fuel economy have in common? All are the objects or results of **social regulation** — government regulation of the conditions under which goods are produced, their physical characteristics, and the impact of their production on society.

Anti-combines, industrial, and social regulation — government interventions in the marketplace — are the central topics of this chapter. Specifically, our discussion unfolds as follows. First, we clarify some terms and summarize the debate over the desirability of industrial concentration. Next, government policy toward monopoly and anti-competitive business practices is examined, considering both anti-combines legislation and the regulation of industries that are natural monopolies. We follow this discussion with a case study of deregulation of the airline industry. Finally, the more recent and controversial social regulation of industry is discussed.

INDUSTRIAL CONCENTRATION: DEFINITIONS

Before considering the pros and cons of industrial concentration, let's define our terminology.

In Chapter 11 we developed and applied a strict definition of monopoly. A *pure*, or *absolute*, monopoly, we said, is a one-firm industry — a situation where a unique product is being produced entirely by a single firm, entry to the industry being blocked by insurmountable barriers.

In this chapter we will use the term *industrial concentration* to include pure monopoly and markets in which there is much potential monopoly power. **Industrial concentration** *exists whenever a single firm or a small number of firms control the major portion of the output of an important industry*. One, two, or three firms dominate the particular industry, presumably resulting in higher than competitive prices and economic profits. This definition, which is closer to how most people understand the "monopoly problem," includes a large number of industries that we previously designated as oligopolies.

In using the term "industrial concentration," we refer to those industries in which firms are large in absolute terms *and* in relation to the total market. Examples are the electric equipment industry, in which Northern Telecom, Canadian General Electric, and Westinghouse Canada, large by any absolute standard, dominate the market; the automobile industry, where General Motors of Canada, Ford of Canada, and Chrysler Canada are similarly situated; the petroleum industry, dominated by Petro-Canada, Imperial Oil (Exxon), and Shell Canada; the aluminum industry, where industrial giant Alcan Aluminum reigns supreme; and the steel industry, where the two giant firms of Dominion Foundries & Steel (Dofasco) and Steel Company of Canada (Stelco) command the lion's share of this large market.

INDUSTRIAL CONCENTRATION: BENEFICIAL OR HARMFUL?

It is not at all clear whether industrial concentration is, on balance, advantageous or disadvantageous to the working of our economy.

The Case Against Industrial Concentration

The essence of the case against monopoly and oligopoly was stated in previous chapters. Let's summarize and extend those arguments.

1 Inefficient Resource Allocation Monopolists and oligopolists find it possible and profitable to restrict output and charge higher prices than if the given industry were organized competitively. Recall that with pure competition production occurs at the point where $P = MC$. This equality specifies an efficient allocation of resources because price measures the value to society of an extra unit of output, while marginal cost reflects the sacrifice of alternative goods. In maximizing profits a business monopolist equates not price, but marginal revenue with marginal cost. At this $MR = MC$ point, price will exceed marginal cost, designating an underallocation of resources to the monopolized product. As a result, the economic well-being of society is less than it would be with pure competition.

2 Unprogressive Critics hold that industrial concentration is neither essential for achieving existing mass-production economies nor conducive to technological progress.

Empirical studies suggest that in some manufacturing industries, "fewness" is not essential for achieving economies of scale. In these industries, firms need only realize a small percentage — in many cases less than 2 or 3% — of the total market to achieve low-cost production; industrial concentration is *not* a prerequisite of productive efficiency.

Furthermore, the basic unit for technological efficiency is not the firm, but the individual plant. Thus, one can correctly argue that productive efficiency calls for, say, a large-scale, integrated auto-manufacturing plant. But it is perfectly consistent to argue that there is no technological justification for the existence of General Motors, which is essentially a giant business corporation composed of a number of geographically distinct plants.

Nor does technological progress depend on huge corporations with substantial monopoly power. The evidence does *not* support the view that large size and market power correlate closely with technological progress. Indeed, the sheltered position of firms in highly concentrated industries is conducive to inefficiency and lethargy; there is no competitive spur to productive efficiency. Furthermore, monopolists and oligopolists tend to resist or suppress technological advances that may cause sudden obsolescence of their existing machinery and equipment.

3 Income Inequality   Industrial concentration is also criticized as a contributor to income inequality. Because of entry barriers, monopolists and oligopolists can charge a price above average cost and consistently realize economic profits. These profits are realized by corporate stockholders and executives who are generally among the upper income groups.

4 Political Clout   A final criticism is based on the assumption that economic power and political clout go hand in hand. It is argued that giant corporations exert undue influence over government, and this is reflected in legislation and government policies that are congenial, not to the public interest, but rather, to the preservation and growth of these industrial giants. Big businesses allegedly have exerted political power to become primary beneficiaries of tax loopholes, patent policy, tariff and quota protection, and other subsidies and privileges.

Defence of Industrial Concentration

Industrial concentration *does* have supporters. Defence of industrial concentration includes the following:

1 Superior Products   One defence is the contention that monopolists and oligopolists have gained their positions of market dominance by offering superior products. Business monopolists do not coerce consumers to buy, say, Colgate or Crest toothpaste, soft drinks from Coca-Cola and Pepsi, mainframe computers from IBM, ketchup from Heinz, or soup from Campbell. Consumers have collectively decided that these products are more desirable than those offered by other producers. Monopoly profits and large market shares therefore have been "earned" through superior performance.

2 Underestimating Competition   A second defence of industrial concentration is that economists may view competition too narrowly. For example, while there may be only a few firms producing a given product, those firms may be faced with severe **interindustry competition** — competition from other firms producing distinct but highly substitutable products. The fact that a handful of firms are responsible for the nation's output of steel belies the competition that steel faces in specific markets from aluminum, copper, wood, plastics, and a host of other products.

   Foreign competition must also be taken into account. While General Motors dominates domestic automobile production, strong import competition constrains its pricing and output decisions.

Furthermore, the large profits resulting from full exploitation of a monopolist's market power is an inducement to potential competitors to enter the industry. Thus, **potential competition** acts as a restraint on the price and output decisions of firms now possessing market power.

3 Economies of Scale   Where existing technology is highly advanced, only large producers — firms that are large both absolutely and in relation to the market — can realize low unit costs and therefore sell to consumers at relatively low prices. The traditional anti-monopoly contention that industrial concentration means less output, higher prices, and an inefficient allocation of resources assumes that cost economies would be equally available to firms whether the industry's structure was highly competitive or quite monopolistic. In fact, this is frequently not the case; economies of scale may be accessible only if competition — in the sense of a large number of firms — is absent.

4 Technological Progress   Recall the *Schumpeter-Galbraith view* that monopolistic industries — in particular, three- and four-firm oligopolies — are conducive to a high rate of technological progress. Oligopolistic firms have both the financial resources *and* the incentives to undertake technological research.

ANTI-COMBINES LEGISLATION

In view of the sharp conflict of opinion over the relative merits of industrial concentration, it is not surprising that government policy toward concentration has been less than clear-cut and consistent. Although the major thrust of federal legislation and policy has been to maintain and promote competition, we will examine later certain policies and acts that have furthered the development of monopoly and oligopoly.

Historical Background

Historically, our economy has been a fertile ground for development of a suspicious, fearful public attitude toward industrial concentration. Though relatively dormant in the nation's early years, this fundamental distrust of big business came into full bloom in the decades following Confederation. The widening of local markets into national markets as transportation facilities improved, the ever-increasing mechanization of production, and the increasingly widespread adoption of the corporate form of business enterprise were important forces causing development of industrial concentration between the 1880s and World War I.

Not only were questionable tactics employed in the concentration of various industries, but the resulting market power was almost invariably exerted to the detriment of all who did business with these monopolies. Farmers and small businesses, being particularly vulnerable to the growth of monopoly power, were among the first to criticize its development. Consumers and labour unions were not far behind in voicing their disapproval.

Because of development of industries in which market forces no longer provided adequate control to ensure socially tolerable behaviour, two techniques of control have been adopted as substitutes for, or supplements to, the market.

1. In those few markets where economic realities preclude the effective working of the market — that is, where there is "natural monopoly" — we have established public **regulatory agencies** to control economic behaviour.

2. In most other markets in which economic and technological conditions have not made monopoly essential, social control has taken the form of **anti-combines legislation** designed to inhibit or prevent the growth of monopoly.

First, we will consider the major pieces of anti-combines legislation which, as refined and extended by various amendments, constitute the basic law of the land with respect to corporate size and concentration. Before we do, let's examine merger types.

Merger Types Mergers are of three basic types, as shown in Figure 14-1. This diagram shows two stages of production, one the input stage, the other the final-good stage of two distinct final-good industries: autos and beer. Each rectangle represents a particular firm.

A **horizontal merger** *is a merger between two competitors selling similar products in the same market*. In Figure 14-1 this type of merger is shown as a combination of glass producers T and U. Other hypothetical examples of horizontal mergers would be Ford Motor Company merging with General Motors or Molson merging with Labatts.

A **vertical merger** — *the merging of firms at different stages of the production process in the same industry* — is shown in Figure 14-1 as a merger between firm Z, a hops producer, and firm F, a brewery. Vertical mergers involve firms having buyer-seller relationships. Examples of mergers of this type are Pepsico's mergers with Pizza Hut, Taco Bell, and Kentucky Fried Chicken. Pepsico supplies soft drinks to each of these fast-food operations.

A **conglomerate merger** *is the merger of a firm in one industry by a firm in another unrelated industry*. In Figure 14-1 a merger between firm C, an auto manufacturer, and firm D, a brewery, fits this description.

The Act of 1889

Canadian anti-combines legislation began in 1889 with the passage of an Act that made it a misdemeanour to conspire to either restrict trade or output, or competition. Three years later, the Act of 1889 became a section of the Criminal Code and the offence became an indictable one. In the first ten years of this century there were *six* prosecutions under the section, resulting in four convictions. Apparently, securing evidence was particularly difficult, and further changes became necessary.

Combines Investigation Act, 1910

The result was the passing of the **Combines Investigation Act** in 1910, an Act whose name was with us in successive Acts until June 1986, when it became the Competition Act. The 1910 Act authorized a judge, on receiving an application by six persons, to order an investigation into an alleged combine.

The 1910 Act was hardly a success, for two reasons: (1) Rarely could six private citizens be found willing to bear the publicity and expense of initiating an investigation. (2) Each investigation, if and when ordered by a judge, started afresh; there was no per-

FIGURE 14-1 Types of mergers

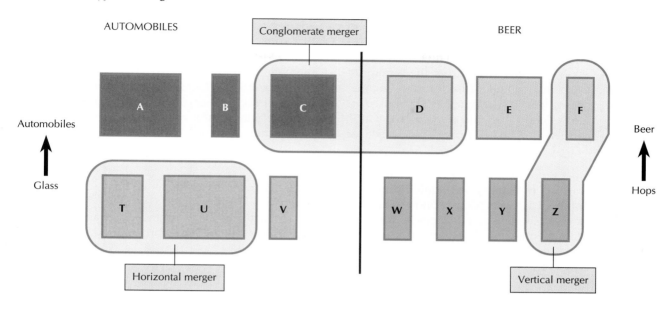

Horizontal mergers (T + U) bring together firms selling similar products; vertical mergers (F + Z) connect firms having a buyer-seller relationship; and conglomerate mergers (C + D) join unrelated firms.

son or body to administer the Act continuously. Thus, there was only *one* investigation under the Act before World War I.

The next fifty years saw no fundamental change. Of note were the 1952 amendments to the Act, which split the duties of the combines commissioner and assigned them to two separate agencies — one for investigation and research, the other for appraisal and report. Thus were established a director of investigation and research and a Restrictive Trade Practices Commission, the latter being superseded in June 1986 by the Competition Tribunal (see below).

In 1960, the Combines Investigation Act was at last amended to include the provisions relating to combinations that had been laid down in the Criminal Code since 1892. As well, mergers and monopolies now were deemed unlawful only if a "detriment or against the interest of the public."

In 1967, the newly formed Department of Consumer and Corporate Affairs took over responsibility for combines, mergers, monopolies, and restraint of trade. Shortly thereafter, in 1969, the Economic Council of Canada reported that the provisions of the Combines Investigation Act making mergers and monopolies criminal offences were "all but inoperative" because a criminal offence had to be proved "beyond a shadow of a doubt" — a very difficult task.

However, the Economic Council did *not* recommend barriers be placed in the way of a company achieving dominance through internal growth or superior efficiency. The Economic Council's whole approach then was based on the goal of economic efficiency. It was this same approach that led the Economic Council to recommend that competition policy be extended to services.

On January 1, 1976, new amendments to the Combines Investigation Act became effective, with the result that it became applicable to services as well.

The Competition Act, 1986

Successive governments in Ottawa have attempted to bring about substantial changes to Canada's law governing monopolies. Three attempts, Bills brought before Parliament in 1971, 1977, and 1977–79, met with organized opposition from business. Extensive consultations with the private sector and provincial governments preceded the introduction of yet another Bill in 1984. The 1984 election intervened and this Bill, too, was not enacted.

Finally, in June 1986, Parliament passed the Competition Tribunal Act and the **Competition Act**, the latter being the new name for the Combines Investigation Act. Some of the major changes are worth noting.

Civil Law Framework   Mergers and monopolies are no longer subject to the sanctions of the criminal law, thus it is easier to prosecute those mergers and monopolies that are not in the public interest. Henceforth, a **Competition Tribunal** adjudicates under a civil law framework that will permit the issuing of remedial orders that will maintain or restore competition in the market. The tribunal is composed of judges of the Federal Court and lay persons, with a judge as chairperson. The Restrictive Trade Practices Commission is abolished as a result.

Merger   Only those mergers that result in an unacceptable lessening of competition could be prohibited or modified by the Competition Tribunal. Mergers that result in gains in efficiency — through, for example, economies of scale — that more than offset the costs stemming from the lessening of competition are allowed.

Abuse of Dominant Position   The abuse-of-dominance provision is designed to ensure that dominant firms compete with other firms on merit, not through the abuse of their market power.

Conspiracy   The conspiracy provision that existed in the Combines Investigation Act is considerably tightened by adding that the existence of a conspiracy may be proven from circumstantial evidence with or without direct evidence of communication among the parties. The maximum fine has been increased from $1 million to $10 million.

Export Agreements   Export consortia — combines — are permitted, provided they relate only to the export of products from Canada, even should they have the unintended, ancillary effect of lessening domestic competition.

Specialization Agreements   Many of our industries are composed of firms with short production runs of several different products. Efficiency could be gained through greater specialization and longer production runs. Hence the Competition Tribunal may approve a specialization agreement if the promised gains in efficiency are likely to more than offset the costs caused by the lessening of competition.

Banks   Banking agreements and bank mergers are subject to the Competition Act.

Crown Corporations   All Crown corporations, both federal and provincial, that engage in commercial activity in competition with other firms are subject to the Act.

The thrust of the latest version of the Competition Act is the surveillance of all firms providing goods and services in our economy, but the Act recognizes that some mergers may be warranted from an efficiency viewpoint. This is especially important since the coming of the Canadian–U.S. Free Trade Agreement (FTA) in 1989. Our firms now must increasingly compete with American firms; any advantage that may be gained through mergers that increase efficiency should not be forgone.

Exemptions to Anti-Combines Legislation

Over the years, government has enacted certain laws that have either exempted certain specific industries or, alternatively, have excluded certain trade practices from anti-combines prosecution. In doing so, the government has fostered the growth of monopoly power.

It should be noted that labour unions, cooperatives, **caisses populaires**, and credit unions have been exempt — subject to limitations — from the competition law. We will see in Chapter 22 that legislation and policy have provided some measure of monopolistic power for agriculture and kept agricultural prices above competitive levels. Since 1945, federal and provincial legislation, on balance, has generally promoted the growth of labour unions. The government-sponsored growth has resulted, according to some authorities, in the development of union monopolies, whose goal is above-competitive wage rates. At provincial and local levels, a wide variety of occupational groups have been successful in establishing licensing requirements that arbitrarily restrict entry to certain occupations, thereby keeping wages and earnings above competitive levels (Chapter 16). Finally, as we saw in Chapter 11, **patent laws** may encourage monopolies into research and development.

QUICK REVIEW (14-2)

1. **There are three types of mergers: horizontal, vertical, and conglomerate.**

2. **The first Canadian anti-combines legislation was passed in 1889. Its purpose was to make it unlawful to restrict competition unduly.**

3. **The original anti-combines legislation subsequently came under the Criminal Code, making successful prosecution difficult.**

4. **The Competition Act, passed in 1986, removed anti-combines activity from the Criminal Code, making prosecution easier. This Act also stressed that even if some mergers lessened competition, they should be allowed if such mergers bring about significant efficiency gains.**

5. **Some government legislation lessens competitive forces, for example, patent laws. But patent laws may encourage research and development.**

NATURAL MONOPOLIES AND THEIR REGULATION

Anti-combines legislation is based on the assumption that society will benefit by preventing monopoly from evolving and by preventing oligopolists from acting collusively and thus forming a *de facto* monopoly. We now consider a special case, wherein there is an economic rationale for an industry to be organized monopolistically.

Theory of Natural Monopoly

A **natural monopoly** exists when economies of scale are so extensive that a single firm can supply the entire market at lower unit cost than could a number of competing firms. Such conditions exist for the so-called **public utilities**, such as electricity, water, gas, telephone service, and so on (Chapter 11). In these cases, the economies of scale in producing and distributing the product are very large, so that large-scale operations are necessary if low unit costs — and a low price — are to be realized (see Figure 9-9(b)). In this situation, competition is simply uneconomic. If the market were divided among many producers, economies of scale would not be realized, unit costs would be high, and high prices would be necessary to cover those costs.

Alternatives that present themselves as possible means of promoting socially acceptable behaviour on the part of a natural monopoly are public ownership and public regulation.

Public ownership has been established in several instances; Canada Post, Canadian National Rail, Air Canada — partially privatized in 1988 — and the St. Lawrence Seaway come to mind at the national level. All the provinces except Alberta and Prince Edward Island have Crown corporations producing their electricity, while mass-transit, the water system,

and garbage collection are typically public enterprises at the local level.

Public regulation is also an option extensively pursued in Canada; the transportation, energy, telecommunications, broadcasting, insurance, securities, financial, and pharmaceuticals industries are all subject to public regulation. Table 14-1 lists the major federal regulatory agencies.

As this table reveals, however, not all the regulatory agencies are concerned with natural monopolies; the agricultural agencies, in particular, are concerned with *creating* monopolies where none previously existed, to increase farmers' revenues. All of the provinces also have such regulatory bodies.

The intent of "natural monopoly" legislation is embodied in the **public interest theory of regulation**. This theory envisions that such industries will be regulated for the benefit of the public, so that consumers may be ensured good service at reasonable rates. The rationale is this: If competition is inappropriate, *regulated* monopolies should be established to avoid possible abuses of uncontrolled monopoly power. Regulation should guarantee that consumers benefit from the economies of scale — that is, the lower per-unit costs. In practice, regulators seek to establish rates that will cover production costs and yield a "fair" or "reasonable" return to the enterprise. The goal is to set price equal to average total cost. (You might want to review the "Regulated Monopoly" section of Chapter 11 at this point.)

Problems

There is considerable disagreement about the effectiveness of regulation in practice. Let's briefly examine three major criticisms of regulation.

TABLE 14-1   **The main federal regulatory agencies**

Agricultural Stabilization Board
Atomic Energy Control Board
Canadian Dairy Commission
Canadian Egg Marketing Agency
Canadian Radio-television and Telecommunications Commission
Canadian Transport Commission
Canadian Wheat Board
National Harbours Board
National Energy Board

1 Costs and Efficiency Regulatory experience suggests that there are a number of interrelated problems associated with cost containment and efficiency in the use of resources.

1. A major goal of regulation is to establish prices so regulated firms will receive a "normal" or "fair" return above their production costs. But this means in effect that firms are operating on the basis of cost-plus pricing and therefore have no incentive to contain costs. Higher costs will mean larger total profits, so why develop or accept cost-cutting innovations if your "reward" will be a reduction in price? Stated technically, regulation tends to foster considerable *X-inefficiency* (see Chapter 11).

2. A regulated firm may resort to accounting trickery to overstate its costs and obtain a higher unjustified profit. Furthermore, in many instances prices are set by the commission so that the firm will receive a stipulated rate of return based on the value of its real capital. This poses a special problem. To increase profits, the regulated firm might make an uneconomic substitution of capital for labour, thereby contributing to an inefficient allocation of resources within the firm (X-inefficiency).

2 Commission Deficiencies Another criticism is that the regulatory commissions function inadequately because they are frequently "captured" or controlled by the industries they are supposed to regulate. Commission members often were executives in these very industries. Therefore, regulation is *not* in the public interest, but rather it protects and nurtures the comfortable position of the natural monopolist. It is alleged that regulation typically becomes a means of guaranteeing profits and protecting the regulated industry from potential new competition that technological change might create.

3 Regulating Competitive Industries Perhaps the most profound criticism of industrial regulation is that it has sometimes been applied to industries that are *not* natural monopolies and that, in the absence of regulation, would be quite competitive. Regulation has been used in industries such as trucking and airlines, where economies of scale are not great and entry barriers are relatively weak. In such instances it is alleged that regulation itself, by limiting entry, creates the monopoly rather than the conditions portrayed in Figure 11-4. The result is higher prices and less output than would have been the case without regulation. Contrary to the public interest theory of regulation, the beneficiaries of regulation are the regulated firms and their employees. The losers are the public and potential competitors barred from entering the industry.

Example: Regulation of the railways by the Canadian Transport Commission may have been justifiable in the late 1800s and the early decades of this century. But by the 1930s the nation had developed a network of highways and the trucking industry had seriously undermined the monopoly power of the railways. At this point it would have been desirable to dismantle the CTC and let the railways and truckers, along with barges and airlines, compete with one another. Instead, the regulatory net of the CTC was cast wider in the 1930s to include the airlines, while each province created its own trucking oligopoly.

Legal Cartel Theory

The regulation of potentially competitive industries has given rise to the **legal cartel theory of regulation**. In the place of socially minded officials *forcing* regulation on natural monopolies to protect consumers, this view sees practical politicians as supplying the "service" of regulation to firms that *want* to be regulated. Regulation is desired because it constitutes a kind of legal cartel that can be highly profitable to the regulated firms. The regulatory commission performs such functions as dividing up the market (for example, the CTC, before deregulation, assigning routes to specific airlines) and restricting potential competition by enlarging the cartel (for example, adding the interprovincial trucking industry to the CTCs domain). While private cartels tend to be unstable and subject to breakdown, the special attraction of the government-sponsored cartel under the guise of regulation is that it endures.

Proponents of the legal cartel theory point to occupational licensing (Chapter 16) as the labour market manifestation of their theory. Certain occupational groups — lawyers, physicians, dentists, engineers, barbers, hairdressers, dietitians, among many others — demand licensing on the grounds that it is necessary to protect the public from charlatans and quacks. But at least part of the reason may be to limit occupational entry so that practitioners may receive monopoly incomes.

DEREGULATION: THE CASE OF THE AIRLINES

The legal cartel theory, increasing evidence of inefficiency in regulated industries, and the contention that government was in fact regulating potentially competitive industries, all contributed to the deregulation movement of the 1970s and 1980s in both the United States and Canada. Important legislation has been passed in both countries in the past several years that deregulates in varying degrees the airline, trucking, banking, and railroad industries.

Controversy

Deregulation has been controversial, and the nature of the controversy is quite predictable. Basing their arguments on the legal cartel theory, proponents of deregulation contend it will result in lower prices and more output, and will eliminate bureaucratic inefficiencies. Some critics of deregulation, embracing the public interest theory, argue that deregulation will result in gradual monopolization of the industry by one or two firms, in turn leading to higher prices and diminished output or service. Other critics contend that deregulation may lead to excessive competition and industry instability and that vital services (for example, transportation) may be withdrawn from smaller communities. Still others stress that, as increased competition reduces each firm's revenues, firms may lower their safety standards as they try to reduce costs and remain profitable.

Perhaps the most publicized case of deregulation involves the airlines. The United States Airline Deregulation Act (ADA) was passed in 1978. Prior to ADA the airlines were regulated by the Civil Aeronautics Board (CAB). The CAB controlled airline fares and allocated interstate routes among the airlines. By controlling the allocation of routes the CAB was also able to control industry entry. And, in fact, no new carriers were permitted to enter the major interstate routes from the CAB's creation in 1938 until deregulation began in the late 1970s. In Canada, the 1980s saw similar deregulation of the airlines.

Effects of American Airline Deregulation

What have been the effects of airline deregulation? Determining the impacts of deregulation has been complicated by such factors as fluctuating airplane fuel costs, the 1981–82 and 1990–91 recessions, and the significant expansion of national income between 1982 and 1990. Moreover, deregulation is still only about a decade old and adjustments are still incomplete. Nevertheless, some of the effects of deregulation have become clear.

Fares Deregulation has exerted substantial downward pressure on fares. Air fares overall have risen less than the general price level. Discount air tickets,

in particular, have dramatically increased in availability and declined in price.

Fare reductions have slowed since 1988, but, in general, fares remain about 20% lower in real terms than before deregulation. Of course, the benefits of fare reductions have not been spread uniformly among all airline markets; passengers flying between large cities have enjoyed greater decreases.

There are two reasons deregulation has produced lower air fares.

1. Competition among air carriers has driven ticket prices downward, closer to the average cost of service than under the legal-cartel form of regulation.

2. Competition has greatly pressured firms to reduce their costs. For example, the industry has adopted a "hub-and-spoke" routing system analogous to a bicycle wheel. Passengers are flown from smaller cities along "spokes" into major "hub" airports, where they change planes and then fly to their more distant destinations. This system has reduced unit costs by allowing airlines to use smaller planes on the spoke routes and to make use of wide-bodied craft between the major hub airports. Wide-body aircraft cost less to operate per seat-kilometre than smaller aircraft. Some airlines have established a two-tier wage system in which new workers are paid substantially less for a given job than are current employees. In many instances, union work rules have been made more flexible to increase worker productivity and reduce wage costs. In short, some of the major cost reductions *and* adjustment problems associated with deregulation have occurred in relevant labour markets.

Service and Safety Although critics of airline deregulation predicted that airline service — particularly to smaller communities — would be curtailed or abandoned, this fear has turned out to be exaggerated. While some major airlines have withdrawn from a few smaller cities, commuter airlines have often filled the resulting void. The hub-and-spoke system has increased flight frequencies at most airports. It also has reduced the amount of airline-switching required of passengers.

On the negative side, the more frequent stopovers now required in hub cities have increased the average travel time between cities. Also, by increasing the volume of air traffic, deregulation has contributed to greater airport congestion, resulting in more frequent and longer flight delays.

Has deregulation reduced the "safety margin" of air transportation, as some critics charge? There is mixed evidence on this question. On the one hand, the increased volume of air traffic has resulted in more reported instances of near collisions in the skies. On the other hand, the accident and fatal-accident rates of airlines are lower today than they were before deregulation. Furthermore, because lower air fares have caused people to substitute air travel for more dangerous automobile travel, deregulation has prevented many deaths annually on North American highways.

Industry Structure Airline deregulation initially brought with it entry of numerous new carriers. In the past few years, however, the industry has gone through a "shakeout" in which many firms have failed and others have merged with stronger competitors. In 1991 eight airlines accounted for 90% of domestic air traffic in the United States, whereas in Canada Air Canada and Canadian Airlines accounted for a similar high percentage.

Growing concentration in the airline industry is of considerable concern. As this book goes to press, there is persistent talk in the industry that Air Canada will soon merge with Canadian Airlines International, leaving only one major airline in this country. Some think consolidation of the industry may be detrimental to the very goals of deregulation itself. In the U.S. single carriers control 75% or more of departures at six large "fortress" hubs. The General Accounting Office found that in 1990 fares at 15 American airports dominated by one or two airlines were about 20% higher than at 22 airports where competition was more brisk. Moreover, two factors make entry of new carriers into lucrative hubs difficult.

1 Lack of Airport Capacity The lack of airport capacity — at least in the short term — means that airline markets are far from being perfectly contestable. A firm wishing to enter a market because existing carriers are earning economic profits cannot do so if long-term leases allow existing carriers to control the airline gates at the profitable airports. It is alleged that some gates, in fact, go unused because dominant carriers refuse to release them to competitors.

2 Airline Practices Several tactics make it difficult for new firms to enter the airline industry successfully. Airline reservation systems developed by the major carriers give their own flights priority listings on the computers used by travel agents. Also, frequent flyer programs — discounts based on accumulated flight mileage — encourage passengers to use dominant existing carriers rather than new entrants. Finally, price matching by existing carriers makes it exceedingly difficult for new entrants to lure

customers through lower ticket prices. When Wardair was transformed from a charter operation to a scheduled airline to compete with the two existing airlines it was not able to survive for very long in what became a rough competitive environment in which price cuts were quickly matched by other competitors.

Although it is too soon for a definitive assessment of airline deregulation, most economists view the outcome to date as positive. In the U.S. the federal government has estimated that airline deregulation produced a $100 billion net benefit to society during the 1980s. The tight oligopoly that seems to be emerging in the industry, however, is a mixed blessing. While it may lead to a handful of financially strong airlines, each having cost-minimizing route structures, it predictably will lead to price leadership and other business practices associated with oligopoly. At a minimum, strict enforcement against anticompetitive mergers and business tactics may be needed to preserve the gains from deregulation. Another pro-competitive option would be to repeal laws that bar foreign airlines from flying domestic routes in both the United States and Canada.

QUICK REVIEW (14-3)

1. **Natural monopoly occurs where economies of scale are so extensive that only a single firm can produce the product at minimum cost.**

2. **The public interest theory of regulation holds that government must regulate business to prevent allocative inefficiency arising from monopoly power.**

3. **The legal cartel theory of regulation suggests that firms seek government regulation to reduce price competition and ensure stable profits.**

4. **Although deregulation of the airline industry has reduced fares and produced net social benefits, it has also created growing industry concentration.**

SOCIAL REGULATION

The "old" regulation just discussed has been labelled economic or **industrial regulation**. Here government is concerned with the overall economic performance of a few specific industries, and concern focuses on pricing and service to the public. Begin-

Box 14-1

In The Media

Deregulation in both Canada and the United States is leading to an "open sky policy," in which both countries' airlines can compete on each other's turf. Only those airlines that can successfully compete will survive. As the article below points out, our airlines' costs are moving down closer to those prevailing south of the border. But more improvement is required if our domestic airlines are to compete successfully with the three giant U.S. airlines.

OUR AIRLINES CLOSE TO U.S. IN COSTS

OTTAWA (CP) — Canadian airlines aren't quite as efficient as United States carriers but are doing better than many European and Asian airlines, a study done for the federal government says.

And when Canadian ownership rules, fuel taxes and landing fees are discounted, Canadian airlines are coming close to U.S. airlines in cost competitiveness, says the study.

The report was commissioned for a special federal inquiry into international air policy which has released a five-volume report.

The study says that in terms of labor costs and productivity per employee, Canadian Airlines International is doing better than most U.S. airlines.

Air Canada is less efficient than most U.S. airlines, because it has a low employee productivity level, the study says.

Air Canada spokesperson Denis Couture said the study's conclusions on efficiency are based on 1989 data and a lot has changed since then. Couture says the Persian Gulf war and the ensuing recession forced Air Canada to lay off 4,000 employees and trim the number of routes it flies.

But Canadian Airlines spokesperson Gerry Goodridge says his company's figures show it remains 16 per cent more efficient than Air Canada but 20 per cent behind the average of the three giants of U.S. airlines — American, Delta and United.

The study says that Canadian airlines pay 21 per cent less per employee in wages than U.S. companies but pay 16 per cent more for fuel as well as higher airport landing fees.

They also get less favourable tax treatment than U.S. airlines and cannot be more than 25 per cent foreign-owned, which makes it harder to raise money through the sale of shares.

"On most measures, the two Canadian airlines have higher average costs when compared with major U.S. carriers but lower costs than European carriers," the report says.

The two Canadian airlines have worked hard on improving their cost competitiveness through "more efficient work rules, have kept their labor costs in line and are in the process of modernizing their aircraft fleet."

"Continuing attention to their cost structure will be of critical importance to their competitive positions in the future."

The report says that in terms of return on equity, Air Canada managed a steady improvement through the late 1980s but results at Canadian slipped after it bought Wardair in 1988.

In terms of passenger revenue for every kilometre flown, Air Canada ranks with the top American airlines while Canadian is in the middle of the pack.

From Canadian Press. Appeared in *The Toronto Star*, January 29, 1992

---

ning largely in the early 1960s, government regulation of a new type evolved and grew quickly. This relatively new **social regulation** has been called "health, safety, and environmental regulation." It controls the conditions under which goods and services are produced, the impact of production on society, and the physical characteristics of the goods themselves. Thus, for example, the Food and Drugs Act and Regulations list chemical additives that may be used in foods; the Canada Labour (Safety) Code and its provincial counterparts attempt to protect workers against occupational injuries; the Hazardous Products Act specifies minimum standards for potentially unsafe products; regulations promulgated under the Fisheries Act restrict the amount of effluents an industry can discharge into waters inhabited by aquatic life; the Environmental Protection Service of the federal Ministry of the Environment develops and enforces environmental protection regulations.

Distinguishing Features

Social regulation differs from economic regulation in several ways.

1. Social regulation is often applied across the board to virtually all industries, and directly affects far more people. While the Air Transport Committee of the Canadian Transport Commission controls only the air transport industry, the rules and regulations of the Canada Labour (Safety) Code and its provincial counterparts apply to every employer.

2. The nature of social regulation involves government in the very details of the production process. For example, rather than simply specify safety standards for vehicles, the 1970 federal Motor Vehicle Safety Act includes, among many others, six standards limiting motor vehicle exhaust, evaporative, and noise emissions.

3. A final distinguishing feature of social regulation is its rapid expansion. Of the 140 federal statutes enacted since Confederation to regulate business, twenty-five came into being between 1970 and 1978. In the same nine years, the provinces enacted 262 of the 1,608 statutes passed since Confederation.

This recitation of a few of the better-known regulatory statutes suggests the basic reason for their creation and growth: much of society had achieved a reasonably affluent level of living by the 1960s, and attention shifted to improvements in the quality of life. This improvement called for safer and better products, less pollution, better working conditions, and greater equality of opportunity.

Costs and Criticisms

It is generally agreed that the overall objectives of social regulation are laudable. But there is great controversy as to whether the benefits of these regulatory efforts justify the costs. Regulatory activities, it is claimed, have been carried to the point where the marginal costs of regulation exceed the marginal benefits. Why might this be the case? Why is social regulation allegedly inefficient?

Uneconomic Goals   It is contended that many of the social regulation laws are poorly drawn so that regulators are virtually prohibited from making economically rational decisions and rules. Regulatory objectives and standards are often stated in legal, political, or engineering terms that result in the pursuit of goals beyond the point at which marginal benefits equal marginal costs. Businesses complain that regulators press for small increments of improvements, unmindful of costs.

Inadequate Information   Decisions must often be made and rules promulgated on the basis of inadequate information. The federal Health Protection Branch, for example, may make sweeping decisions about the use of suspected carcinogens in products on the basis of very limited experiments with laboratory animals.

Overzealous Personnel   It is contended that the regulatory agencies may tend to attract overzealous personnel who "believe" in regulation. It is argued that the bureaucrats of the new statutory regulatory agencies may sometimes be overly sensitive to criticism by some special interest group — for example, environmentalists. The result is bureaucratic inflexibility and the establishment of extreme or nonsensical regulations so that no watchdog group will question the agency's commitment to its given social goal.

Economic Implications

If overregulation does exist, what are its consequences?

1 Higher Prices   Social regulation directly increases product prices because compliance costs normally get passed on to consumers. Furthermore, social regulation indirectly contributes to higher product prices to the extent that it reduces labour productivity. Resources invested in anti-pollution equipment are not available for investment in new machinery to increase output per worker. Where wage rates are inflexible downward, declines in labour productivity increase marginal and average costs of production. In effect, product-supply curves shift leftward, causing product prices to rise.

2 Slower Innovation   The new regulation may have a negative impact on the rate of innovation. The fear that a new, technologically superior plant will not meet environmental protection regulations or that a new product may run into difficulties with the Hazardous Products Act may be enough to persuade

Box 14-2

DOES CANADA NEED AN INDUSTRIAL POLICY?

Should government be more actively involved in determining the structure of industry?

There has been a growing concern in recent years that Canada's industries have been seriously eroded. Our domestic markets have been flooded with foreign motorcycles, cameras, watches, and electronics equipment, suggesting that our competitive edge has been lost.

Noting apparent Japanese successes, many political, union, and business leaders — but only a limited number of economists — feel that Canada needs an industrial policy to reverse our alleged industrial decline. It is argued that government should undertake a more active and direct role in determining the structure and composition of Canadian industry. Government, it is held, should use low-interest loans, loan guarantees, special tax treatment, research and development subsidies, anti-combines immunity, and even foreign trade protection to accelerate the development of "high-tech" industries and to revitalize certain core manufacturing industries such as steel. Conversely, it should hasten the movement of resources out of declining "sunset" industries. Presumably the net result will be that the Canadian economy will enjoy a higher average level of productivity and be more competitive in world markets.

Opponents of industrial policy make a number of points.

1 Deindustrialization?

Has Canada in fact deindustrialized? Has our manufacturing sector experienced serious decline? Statistics show that manufacturing in the aggregate accounts for a falling percentage of domestic output in 1991, dropping from about 30% in 1950 to about 20% today. Employment in manufacturing has declined from over 30% to 17% of total employment in the 1950–1991 period, but that reflects the growth of labour productivity rather than industrial demise.

2 Foreign Experience

Advocates of an industrial policy typically cite Japan as a model. In the post-World War II era Japan has achieved rapid economic growth; it has been highly successful in penetrating world markets; and it has had a much-publicized industrial policy. Yet the overall role of industrial policy as a causal factor in Japanese industrial success is not clear. The picture is mixed.

Japanese industrial policy has had both successes and failures. Some targeted industries, including semi-conductor and machine tools, are almost certainly stronger than they would have been without government support and can be claimed as successes for Japanese industrial policy. Other industries, such as shipbuilding and steel, probably grow more quickly because of government aid, but undoubtedly would have developed without any government intervention. However, the Japanese government has also picked losers. Aluminum smelting and petrochemicals were favoured industries some years ago, but the public and private investments have paid off very poorly and now their capacity is being reduced. There are also several examples of successful industries that did not receive government assistance, including motorcycles and consumer electronics.

3 Markets and Politics

While a proposal to create an industrial policy that subsidizes "sunrise" industries and hastens the phasing out of "sunset" industries sounds appealing, critics question the government's ability to identify future industrial "winners" and "losers." The issue here is whether private investors using capital markets have better foresight than public officials in determining industrial winners and losers. Critics argue that private investors have a greater incentive in investing their own funds to obtain accurate information on the future prospects of various industries than might government bureaucrats in investing the *taxpayers'* funds.

Furthermore, might not government use its power to allocate investment funds to buy the political support of various industries? Might not the economic goal of enhanced industrial efficiency be subverted to the political goal of getting re-elected? It is feared that the creation of a new industrial policy may lead to "lemon socialism," that is, government support or ownership of declining industries and dying companies.

Those who are sceptical of industrial policy contend that government can best stimulate Canadian industry by (1) using monetary and fiscal policy to create a favourable macroeconomic environment (high employment, low inflation, low interest rates) and (2) adjusting tax and regulatory systems to enhance incentives for investment and technological advance.

a firm to produce the same old product in the same old way.

3 Reduced Competition   Social regulation may have an anti-competitive effect, since it tends to be a relatively greater economic burden for small firms than for large firms. The costs of complying with the new regulations are, in effect, fixed costs. Smaller firms produce less output over which to distribute their costs, thus their compliance costs per unit of output set them at a competitive disadvantage with their larger rivals. The burden of social regulation is more likely to put small firms out of business and thereby contribute to the increased concentration of industry.

In Support of Social Regulation

Social regulation is not without its defenders. The problems with which social regulation contends are serious and substantial. But after years of relative neglect, society cannot expect to cleanse the environment, enhance the safety of the workplace, and improve economic opportunity without incurring substantial costs. Furthermore, cost calculations may paint too dim a picture of social regulation. Benefits tend to be taken for granted, are more difficult than costs to measure, and may accrue to society only over an extended period of time.

QUICK REVIEW (14-4)

1. Social regulation is concerned with conditions under which goods and services are produced, the effect of production on society, and physical characteristics of goods themselves.

2. Critics of social regulation say that uneconomic policy goals, inadequate information, unintended side effects, and overzealous personnel combine to create regulatory costs that exceed regulatory benefits.

3. Defenders of social regulation point to the large benefits arising from policies that keep dangerous products from the marketplace, reduce workplace injuries and death, contribute to clean air and water, and reduce employment discrimination.

CHAPTER SUMMARY

1. The case against industrial concentration centres on contentions that it *a.* causes a misallocation of resources; *b.* retards the rate of technological advance; *c.* promotes income inequality; and *d.* may result in some interest groups having more political clout.

2. The defence of industrial concentration is built around the following points: *a.* firms have obtained their large market shares by offering superior products; *b.* interindustry and foreign competition, along with potential competition from new industry entrants, make Canadian industries more competitive than generally believed; *c.* some degree of monopoly may be essential to realize economies of scale; and *d.* monopolies and oligopolies may be technologically progressive.

3. Mergers can be of three types: horizontal, vertical, and conglomerate.

4. The cornerstone of anti-combines policy consists of amendments to the Criminal Code in 1892 and the Combines Investigation Acts of 1910 and 1923, as subsequently frequently amended. On the fifth attempt since 1971, the Competition Act was finally passed in mid-1986, supplanting the Combines Investigation Act.

5. Government, however, has also done much to promote, both directly and indirectly, the concentration of economic power and the growth of monopoly. Industrial exceptions to the competition law include the exemption of unions, cooperatives, credit unions, and *caisses populaires*. Government continues to sponsor the growth of monopoly power in agriculture through the setting up of marketing boards. Occupational licensing, patent laws, and protective tariffs also constitute bases for the development of industrial concentration.

6. The objective of industrial regulation is to protect the public from the market power of natural monopolies by regulating prices and quality of service. Critics contend that industrial regulation is conducive to inefficiency and rising costs and that, in many instances, it constitutes a legal cartel for the regulated firms. Legislation passed in the last decade brought about varying degrees of deregulation in the airline, trucking, banking, and railroad industries.

7. Airline deregulation in North America has lowered fares and increased the efficiency of the industry, producing a sizable net benefit to society. It has also resulted in growing concentration in the industry.

8. Social regulation has to do with product safety, safer working conditions, less pollution, and greater economic opportunity. Critics contend that businesses are overregulated since marginal costs of regulation exceed its marginal benefits, while its defenders dispute that contention.

TERMS AND CONCEPTS

anti-combines legislation (p. 227)
Combines Investigation Act (p. 230)
Competition Act (p. 231)
Competition Tribunal (p. 232)
conglomerate merger (p. 230)
foreign competition (p. 229)
horizontal merger (p. 230)
industrial concentration (p. 228)
industrial regulation (p. 236)
interindustry competition (p. 229)
legal cartel theory of regulation (p. 234)

natural monopoly (p. 233)
patent laws (p. 232)
potential competition (p. 229)
public interest theory of regulation (p. 233)
public ownership (p. 233)
public regulation (p. 233)
public utility (p. 233)
regulatory agencies (p. 230)
social regulation (p. 237)
vertical merger (p. 230)

QUESTIONS AND STUDY SUGGESTIONS

1. You are president of one of the Big Three automobile producers. Discuss critically the case against industrial concentration. Now suppose you are a representative for a farm organization and are attempting to convince a parliamentary committee that the presence of industrial concentration is a significant factor contributing to the farm problem. Critically evaluate the case for industrial concentration.

2. Suppose a proposed merger of firms will simultaneously lessen competition and reduce unit costs through economies of scale. Should such a merger be allowed?

3. "The competition law serves to penalize efficiently managed firms." Do you agree?

4. What types of industries should be subjected to industrial regulation? What specific problems does industrial regulation entail? Why might an inefficient combination of capital and labour be employed by a regulated natural monopoly?

5. Briefly explain the three types of mergers.

6. In view of the problems in regulating natural monopolies, compare optimal social (marginal-cost) pricing and fair-return pricing by referring again to Figure 11-4. Assuming a government subsidy might be used to cover any loss entailed by marginal-cost pricing, which pricing policy would you favour? What problems might the subsidy entail?

7. How does social regulation differ from industrial regulation? What types of costs and benefits are associated with social regulation?

4

Factor Markets and the Distribution of Income

15

Production and the Demand for Resources

In the preceding section we explored the pricing and output of goods and services under a variety of product market structures. The purely competitive cucumber farmer considers the market price and decides how many acres to plant. The monopolistically competitive local restaurant decides on the best combination of price, quality, and advertising to maximize its profits. The automobile manufacturer pays close attention to the business strategies of rivals and sets its price and production plans accordingly. The provincial natural gas monopoly files requests for rate increases before the provincial utility board, and then provides service to all customers.

Although firms and market structures differ greatly, firms in general have something in common. In producing their product — be it cucumbers, sandwiches, automobiles, or natural gas — they must hire productive resources. Among other resources, the cucumber farmer needs land, tractors, fertilizer, and labourers to harvest the crop. The restaurant buys kitchen equipment and hires cooks and waiters. The auto manufacturer purchases production materials and hires executives, accountants, engineers, and assembly-line workers. The gas company leases land, builds pipeline and storage tanks, and hires billing clerks.

In this chapter we turn from the pricing and production of goods to the pricing and employment of resources needed in production. Land, labour, capital, and entrepreneurial resources directly, or indirectly, are owned and supplied by households. In terms of our circular flow model of the economy (Chapter 3), we now shift attention from the bottom loop of the diagram, where firms supply and households demand products, to the top loop, where households supply and businesses demand resources. This reversal of roles, in part, necessitates a separate discussion of resource pricing.

SIGNIFICANCE OF RESOURCE PRICING

There are several related reasons to study resource pricing.

1 Money Incomes   Resource prices constitute a major determinant of money incomes. The expenditures businesses make in acquiring economic resources flow as wage, rent, interest, and profit incomes to those households that supply the resources at their disposal.

2 Resource Allocation   Just as product prices ration finished goods and services to consumers, so resource prices allocate scarce resources among various industries and firms. An understanding of how resource prices affect resource allocation is particularly significant since, in a dynamic economy, the efficient allocation of resources over time calls for continuing shifts in resources among alternative uses.

3 Cost Minimization   To the firm, resource prices are costs, and to realize maximum profits, a firm must produce the profit-maximizing output with the most efficient (least costly) combination of resources. Given technology, resource prices play the major role in determining the quantities of land, labour, capital, and entrepreneurial ability that are to be combined in the productive process.

4 Policy Issues   Finally, there are numerous ethical questions and public policy issues surrounding the resource market. The functioning of resource markets can result in considerable inequality in the personal distribution of income. To alleviate such inequality should a special tax be levied on "excess" profits? Is it desirable for government to establish a wage floor in the form of a minimum-wage law? What

about ceilings on interest rates? Are current government subsidies to farmers justifiable? Chapter 18 will explore the facts and ethics of income distribution.

COMPLEXITIES OF RESOURCE PRICING

Economists generally agree about the basic principles that determine resource pricing. Yet there is considerable disagreement as to the variations in these principles that must be made as they are applied to specific resources and particular markets. While economists generally agree that the pricing and employment of economic resources (factors of production) are a supply and demand phenomenon, they also recognize that in particular markets resource supply and demand may assume unique and often complex dimensions. This is further complicated when the operation of supply and demand forces are altered or even largely supplanted by the policies and practices of government, firms, or labour unions — not to mention a host of other institutional considerations.

Our major objective in this chapter is to explain the basic factors underlying the demand for economic resources. We will couch our discussion in terms of labour, recognizing that the principles outlined also generally apply to land, capital, and entrepreneurial ability. In Chapter 16, we combine our understanding of resource demand with a discussion of labour supply in analysing wage rates. Then in Chapter 17, we incorporate the supply side of the markets for resources to analyse the prices of, and returns to, land, capital, and entrepreneurial ability.

MARGINAL PRODUCTIVITY THEORY OF RESOURCE DEMAND

Let's first examine resource demand by a firm that is hiring some specific resource in a competitive market and, in turn, is selling its product in a competitive market. The simplicity of this situation lies in the fact that under competition the firm, as a price taker, can dispose of as little or as much output as it chooses at the going market price. The firm is selling such a negligible fraction of total output that it exerts no influence on product price. Similarly, in the resource market, competition means that the firm is hiring such a small fraction of the total supply of the resource that its price is unaffected by the quantity the firm purchases.

Resource Demand as a Derived Demand

The demand for resources is a **derived demand**; it is derived from the finished goods and services that resources help produce. Resources do not directly satisfy consumer wants, but do so indirectly by producing goods and services. No one wants to consume a hectare of land, a tractor, or the labour services of a farmer, but households do want to consume the various food and fibre products these resources help produce.

Marginal Revenue Product (MRP)

The derived nature of resource demand implies that the strength of the demand for any resource will depend on (1) the productivity of the resource in helping to create a good, and (2) the market price of the good it is producing. A resource that is highly productive in turning out a commodity highly valued by society will be in great demand. On the other hand, demand will be very weak for a relatively unproductive resource that is only capable of producing some good not in great demand by households.

Productivity   The roles of productivity and product price in determining resource demand can be clearly seen in Table 15-1. Here we assume a firm adds one variable resource — labour — to its fixed plant. Columns 1 to 3 remind us that the law of diminishing returns will apply in this situation, causing the **marginal product (MP)** of labour to fall beyond some point. (It might be helpful to review the subsection entitled "Law of Diminishing Returns" in Chap-

ter 9 at this point.) For simplicity, assume diminishing marginal productivity sets in with the first worker hired.

Product Price   But the derived demand for a resource also depends on the price of the commodity it produces. Column 4 adds this price information. Note that product price is constant, in this case $2, because we are supposing a competitive product market. Multiplying column 2 by column 4, we get the total-revenue data of column 5. From these total-revenue data we can compute **marginal revenue product** (**MRP**) — *the increase in total revenue resulting from the use of each additional variable input (labour, in this case)*. This is indicated in column 6.

Rule for Employing Resources: MRP = MRC

The MRP schedule — columns 1 and 6 — constitutes the firm's demand schedule for labour. To explain this, we must first discuss the rule that guides a profit-seeking firm in hiring any resource. *To maximize profits, a firm should hire additional units of any given resource so long as each successive unit adds more to the firm's total revenue than it does to its total costs.*

The amount each additional unit of a resource adds to the firm's total (resource) cost is called **marginal resource cost** (**MRC**). Thus we can restate our rule for hiring resources as follows: *It will be profitable for a firm to hire additional units of a resource up to the point at which the re-*

TABLE 15-1   The demand for a resource: pure competition in the sale of the product (*hypothetical data*)

(1) Units of resource	(2) Total product	(3) Marginal product (MP), or $\triangle$(2)	(4) Product price	(5) Total revenue, or (2) × (4)	(6) Marginal revenue product (MRP), or $\triangle$(5)
0	0		$2	$ 0	
1	7	7	2	14	$14
2	13	6	2	26	12
3	18	5	2	36	10
4	22	4	2	44	8
5	25	3	2	50	6
6	27	2	2	54	4
7	28	1	2	56	2

source's MRP is equal to its MRC. If the number of workers a firm is currently hiring is such that the MRP of the last worker exceeds his or her MRC, the firm can clearly profit by hiring more workers. But if the number being hired is such that the MRC of the last worker exceeds the MRP, the firm is hiring workers who are not paying their way, and it can thereby increase its profits by laying off some workers. You may have recognized that this **MRP = MRC rule** is very similar to the MR = MC profit-maximizing rule employed throughout our discussion of price and output determination. The rationale of the two rules is the same, but the point of reference is now *inputs* of resources rather than *outputs* of product.

MRP Is a Demand Schedule

Just as product price and marginal revenue are equal in a purely competitive product market, so *resource price and marginal resource cost are equal when a firm is hiring a resource in a competitive market*. In a purely competitive labour market, the wage rate is set by the total supply and demand for labour. Because it hires such a small fraction of the total supply of labour, a single firm cannot influence this wage rate. This means that total resource cost increases by exactly the amount of the going wage rate for each additional worker hired; the wage rate and MRC are equal. It follows that so long as it is hiring labour in a competitive labour market, *the firm will hire workers to the point at which their wage rate (or MRC) is equal to their MRP.*[1]

The data in column 6 of Table 15-1 shows that if the wage rate is $13.95 the firm will hire only one worker. This is so because the first worker adds $14 to total revenue and slightly less — $13.95 — to total costs. For each successive worker, however, MRC exceeds MRP, indicating that it will not be profitable to hire another worker. If the wage rate is $11.95, we apply the same reasoning and discover that it will pay the firm to hire both the first and second workers. Similarly, if the wage rate is $9.95, three will be hired. If $7.95, four. If $5.95, then five. And so forth. It is evident that *the MRP schedule constitutes the firm's demand for labour, because each point on this schedule (curve) indicates the number of workers the firm would hire at each possible wage rate that might exist.* This is shown graphically in Figure 15-1.

---

[1] The logic here is the same as that which allowed us to change the MR = MC profit-maximization rule to P = MC for the purely competitive seller of Chapter 10.

FIGURE 15-1   The purely competitive seller's demand for a resource

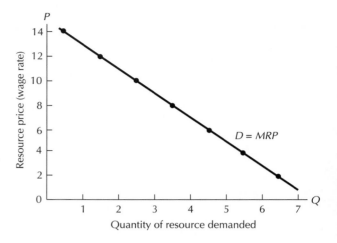

The *MRP* curve is the resource demand curve. The location of the curve depends upon the marginal productivity of the resource and the price of the product. Under pure competition, product price is constant; therefore, it is solely because of diminishing marginal productivity that the resource demand curve is downsloping.

The rationale employed here is familiar to us. Recall that in Chapter 10 we applied the price-equals-marginal-cost or P = MC rule for the profit-maximizing *output* to discover that the portion of the competitive firm's short-run marginal-cost curve lying above average variable cost is the short-run *product* supply curve (Figure 10-6). Now we are applying the MRP = MRC rule for the profit-maximizing *input* to the firm's MRP curve and determining that this curve is the input or *resource* demand curve.

Resource Demand Under Imperfect Competition

Our analysis of labour demand becomes more complex when we assume that the firm is selling its product in an imperfectly competitive market. Pure monopoly, oligopoly, and monopolistic competition in the product market all mean that the firm's product demand curve is downsloping; the firm must accept a lower price in order to increase its sales.

Table 15-2 takes this into account. The productivity data of Table 15-1 are retained in columns 1 to 3, but now assume, in column 4, that product price must be lowered to sell the marginal product of each successive worker. The MRP of the purely competitive seller falls for one reason: marginal product

TABLE 15-2   The demand for a resource: imperfect competition in the sale of the product (*hypothetical data*)

(1) Units of resource	(2) Total product	(3) Marginal product (MP), or △(2)	(4) Product price	(5) Total revenue, or (2) × (4)	(6) Marginal revenue product (MRP), or △(5)
0	0		$2.80	$ 0	
		7			$18.20
1	7		2.60	18.20	
		6			13.00
2	13		2.40	31.20	
		5			8.40
3	18		2.20	39.60	
		4			4.40
4	22		2.00	44.00	
		3			2.25
5	25		1.85	46.25	
		2			1.00
6	27		1.75	47.25	
		1			−1.05
7	28		1.65	46.20	

diminishes. But the MRP of the imperfectly competitive seller falls for two reasons: marginal product diminishes *and* product price falls as output increases.

The net result is that the MRP curve — the resource demand curve — of the imperfectly competitive producer is less elastic than that of a purely competitive producer. At a wage rate or MRC of $11.95, both the purely competitive and the imperfectly competitive seller will hire two workers. But at $9.95, the competitive firm will hire three and the imperfectly competitive firm only two. And at $7.95, the purely competitive firm will take on four employees and the imperfect competitor only three. This difference in elasticity can be readily visualized by graphing the MRP data of Table 15-2, as in Figure 15-2, and comparing them with Figure 15-1.[2]

It is not surprising that the imperfectly competitive producer is less responsive to wage cuts in terms of workers employed than is the purely competitive producer. The reluctance of the imperfect competitor to employ more resources and thereby produce more output when resource prices fall reflects the imperfect competitor's tendency to restrict output in the

product market. Other things being equal, the imperfectly competitive seller will produce less of a product than would a purely competitive seller. In producing this smaller output, the seller will demand fewer resources.

FIGURE 15-2   The imperfectly competitive seller's demand for a resource

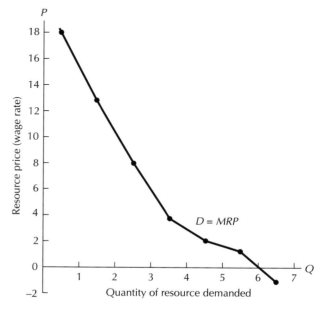

An imperfectly competitive seller's resource demand curve slopes downward because marginal product diminishes and product price falls as output increases.

[2] Note that the points in Figures 15-1 and 15-2 are plotted halfway between each number of workers because MRP is associated with the *addition* of one more worker. Thus in Figure 15-2, for example, the MRP of the second worker ($13.00) is plotted not at 1 or 2, but rather at 1½. This "smoothing" technique also allows us to present a continuously downsloping curve rather than one that moves downward in discrete steps as each worker is hired.

Market Demand for a Resource

We can now derive the market demand curve for a resource. You will recall that the total, or market, demand curve for a product is developed by summing up the demand curves of all individual buyers in the market. Similarly, the market demand curve for a particular resource can be derived in essentially the same way: adding up MRP curves for all firms hiring that resource.

DETERMINANTS OF RESOURCE DEMAND

What are the determinants of resource demand? The very derivation of resource demand suggests three related factors — the resource's productivity, the market price of the product it is producing, and changes in the prices of other resources.

Changes in Product Demand

Because resource demand is a derived demand, any change in the demand for the product will affect product price and therefore the MRP of the resource. Other things being equal, *a change in the demand for the product that a particular type of labour is producing will shift labour demand in the same direction*. In Table 15-1, assume an increase in product demand that boosts product price from $2 to $3. If you calculate the new labour demand curve and plot it in Figure 15-1, you will find it lies to the right of the old curve. Similarly, a drop in product demand and price will shift the labour demand curve to the left.

A few examples will help you understand changes in resource demand. The 1987 stock-market crash entailed a decline in the demand for stocks and a consequent decline in the demand for stockbrokers, causing widespread layoffs on Toronto's Bay Street as well as on other stock exchanges. Similarly, the increases in the prices of oil, natural gas, and electricity that have occurred since the mid-1970s increased the demand for wood-burning stoves. An interesting labour market impact was an increase in the demand for chimney sweeps. Finally, in late 1987 McDonald's used television commercials to attract homemakers and retirees to work in its company-owned restaurants. Why did this recruitment campaign begin in 1987 rather than a decade or two earlier? A major reason was that more and more women were working outside the home and thus had less time for meal preparation. The result was an increase in the demand for restaurant meals and an increase in the demand for fast-food workers that could not be entirely filled by teenagers, the traditional source of labour for fast-food restaurants.

Productivity Changes

Other things held constant, *a change in the productivity of labour will shift the labour demand curve in the same direction*. If we were to double the MP data of column 3 in Table 15-1 we would find that the MRP data would also double, indicating an increase in labour demand.

Productivity of any resource can be altered in several ways:

1. The marginal productivity data for labour will depend on the quantities of other resources with which it is combined. The greater the amount of capital and land resources with which labour is combined, the greater will be the marginal productivity and the demand for labour.

2. Technological improvements will have the same effect. The better the quality of the capital, the greater the productivity of labour. Steelworkers employed with a given amount of real capital in the form of modern oxygen furnaces are more productive than when employed with the same amount of real capital in the old open-hearth furnaces.

3. Improvements in the quality of the variable resource itself — labour — will increase marginal productivity, and therefore the demand for labour. In effect, we have a new demand curve for a different, more skilled, kind of labour.

Box 15-1

In the Media

The increasing efficiency of automobiles has meant that demand for gasoline has remained flat, even if the number of cars in Canada has increased by almost 50% since the 1970s. Moreover, oil companies now have to cater to the fuel requirement of new vehicles that use environmentally friendly fuels.

DRIVERS WILL PAY TAB FOR NEW TECHNOLOGY

BY TIMOTHY PRITCHARD
Auto Industry Reporter

Today, oil companies are paying a price for the development of increasingly fuel-efficient cars, but more changes lie ahead and drivers will soon begin paying for them.

Refiners will have to invest to keep up with new vehicle and environmental technology — and they will have to be profitable to do it.

So as refinery and service station capacity is cut back, prices at the pump will go up, say investment analysts who follow the industry.

Canada's car population of 13 million is almost 50 per cent higher than it was in the mid-1970s, but gasoline consumption is no greater than it was 15 years ago. Great efficiencies have been achieved by building smaller and lighter cars.

In 1975, the average passenger car in Ontario burned 18.6 litres to travel 100 kilometres in combined city and highway driving, according to calculations by DesRosiers Automotive Consultants of Toronto. The comparable figure for 1989 was 9.6 litres for 100 kilometres, and a better performance is likely as older cars are replaced.

But flat gasoline sales are only one challenge facing the oil companies.

They soon will have to refit stations to sell a greater variety of fuels, including ethanol, methanol and natural gas.

By permission of *The Globe and Mail*, January 30, 1992.

All these considerations are important in explaining why the average level of (real) wages is higher in Canada than in most other countries. Canadian workers are usually healthier and better trained than those of other nations, and in most industries they work with a larger and more efficient stock of capital goods and much more abundant natural resources. This translates into a strong demand for labour. On the supply side of the market, labour is *relatively* scarce as compared with most other nations. A strong demand and a relatively scarce supply result in high wage rates. This will be discussed further in Chapter 16.

Prices of Other Resources

Just as changes in the prices of other products will change the demand for a specific commodity, so changes in the prices of other resources can be expected to alter the demand for a particular resource. And just as the effect of a change in the price of product X upon the demand for product Y depends upon whether X and Y are substitute or complementary goods (Chapter 4), so the effect of a change in the price of resource A upon the demand for resource B will depend upon their substitutability or their degree of complementarity.

Substitute Resources Suppose that in a certain production process technology is such that labour and capital are substitutable for one another. Now assume a decline occurs in the price of machinery. The resulting impact on the demand for labour will be the net result of two opposed effects: the substitution effect and the output effect.

Substitution Effect The decline in the price of machinery will prompt the firm to substitute machinery for labour. At given wage rates, smaller quantities of labour will now be employed. This decrease in the demand for labour is referred to as the **substitution effect**.

Output Effect Because the price of machinery has fallen, the costs of producing various outputs will also decline. With lower costs, the firm will find it profitable to produce and sell a larger output. This greater output, which is referred to as the **output effect**, will increase the demand for all resources, including labour.

The substitution and output effects are working in opposite directions. For a decline in the price of machinery, the substitution effect decreases and the output effect increases the demand for labour. The net impact on labour demand will depend on the relative sizes of the two opposed effects. *If the substitution effect outweighs the output effect, a change in the price of a substitute resource will change the demand for labour in the same direction. If the output effect exceeds the substitution effect, a change in the price of a substitute resource will change the demand for labour in the opposite direction.*

Complementary Resources Recall from Chapter 4 that certain products, such as cameras and film or computers and software, are complementary goods in that they go together and are jointly demanded. Resources may also be complementary in that an increase (decrease) in the quantity of one of them employed in the production process will require an increase (decrease) in the amount used of the other as well.

When labour and capital are complementary, for example, a decline in the price of machinery will increase the demand for labour through the output effect. Conversely, in the case of an *increase* in the price of capital, the output effect will reduce the demand for labour. *A change in the price of a complementary resource will cause the demand for labour to change in the opposite direction.*

Recapitulation: The demand curve for labour will *increase* (shift rightward) when:

1. the demand for (and therefore the price of) the product produced by that labour increases;

2. the productivity (MP) of labour increases;

3. the price of a substitute input decreases, provided the output effect is greater than the substitution effect;

4. the price of a substitute input increases, provided the substitution effect exceeds the output effect;

5. the price of a complementary input decreases.

ELASTICITY OF RESOURCE DEMAND

What determines the sensitivity of producers to changes in resource prices? Or, more technically, what determines the elasticity of resource demand? Several generalizations provide important insights in answering this question.

1 Rate of MP Decline A purely technical consideration — the rate at which the marginal product of the variable resource declines — is crucial. *If the marginal product of labour declines slowly as it is added to a fixed amount of capital, the MRP, or demand curve for labour, will decline slowly and tend to be highly elastic.* A small decline in the price of such a resource will yield a relatively large increase in the amount demanded. Conversely, if the marginal productivity of labour declines sharply, the MRP, or labour demand curve, will decline rapidly. This means that a relatively large decline in the wage rate will be accompanied by a very modest increase in the amount of labour hired; resource demand will be inelastic.

2 Ease of Resource Substitutability The degree to which resources are substitutable is also a determinant of elasticity. *The larger the number of good substitute resources available, the greater will be the elasticity of demand for a particular resource.* If a furniture manufacturer finds that five or six different types of wood are equally satisfactory in making coffee tables, a rise in the price of any one type of wood may cause a very sharp drop in the amount demanded, as the producer substitutes other woods. At the other extreme, it may be impossible to substitute: bauxite is absolutely essential in the production of aluminum ingots. Thus, the demand for bauxite by aluminum producers is very inelastic.

Note that *time* can play an important role in the input substitution process. For example, a firm's truck drivers may obtain a substantial wage increase with little or no immediate decline in employment. But over time, as the firm's trucks wear out and are replaced, the company may purchase larger trucks and thereby be able to deliver the same total output with fewer drivers. Alternatively, as the firm's trucks depreciate, it might turn to entirely different means of transportation.

3 Elasticity of Product Demand The elasticity of demand for any resource will depend on the elasticity of demand for the product it helps to produce. *The greater the elasticity of product demand, the* greater the elasticity of resource demand. The derived nature of resource demand would lead us to expect this relationship. A small rise in the price of a product with great elasticity of demand will sharply reduce output, and therefore bring about a relatively large decline in the amounts of various resources demanded. This implies that the demand for the resource is elastic.

4 Labour Cost/Total Cost Ratio   *The larger the proportion of total production costs accounted for by a resource, the greater will be the elasticity of demand for that resource.* For example, if labour costs were the only production cost, then a 20% increase in wage rates would shift the firm's cost curves upward by 20%. Given the elasticity of product demand, this substantial increase in costs would cause a relatively large decline in sales and a sharp decline in the amount of labour demanded. Labour demand would be elastic. But if labour costs were only 50% of production costs, then a 20% increase in wage rates would only increase costs by 10%. Given the same elasticity of product demand, a relatively small decline in sales, and therefore in the amount of labour, would result. The demand for labour would be inelastic.

QUICK REVIEW (15-2)

1. **A resource demand curve will shift because of changes in product demand, changes in the productivity of the resource, and changes in the prices of other inputs.**

2. **If resources A and B are substitutable, a decline in the price of A will decrease the demand for B if the substitution effect exceeds the output effect. But if the output effect exceeds the substitution effect, the demand for B will increase.**

3. **If resources C and D are complements, a decline in the price of C will increase the demand for D.**

4. **The elasticity of demand for a resource will be less (a) the more rapid the decline in marginal product; (b) the smaller the number of substitutes; (c) the smaller the elasticity of product demand; and (d) the smaller the proportion of total cost accounted for by the resource.**

OPTIMAL COMBINATION OF RESOURCES

So far, we have centred our discussion on one variable input — labour. But in the long run, firms can vary the amounts of *all* the resources they use. It is therefore important to consider what combination of resources a firm will choose when all are variable. While our analysis will be based on two resources, it can readily be extended to any number one chooses to consider.

We will consider two interrelated questions:

1. What is the least-cost combination of resources to use in producing *any* given level of output?

2. What combination of resources will maximize a firm's profits?

The Least-Cost Rule

A firm is producing *any* given output with the **least-cost combination of resources** when the last dollar spent on each resource entails the same marginal product. That is, *the cost of any output is minimized when the marginal product per dollar's worth of each resource used is the same.* In terms of two resources, labour and capital, the cost-minimizing position occurs where:

$$\frac{\text{MP of labour}}{\text{price of labour}} = \frac{\text{MP of capital}}{\text{price of capital}} \qquad (1)$$

You can see why fulfilling this condition means least-cost production. Suppose that the prices of capital and labour are both \$1 per unit, but that capital and labour are being employed in such amounts that the marginal product of labour is 10 and the marginal product of capital is 5. Our equation tells us that this is clearly *not* the least costly combination of resources: MP_L/P_L is 10/1 and MP_C/P_C is 5/1.

If the firm spends a dollar less on capital and shifts that dollar to labour, it will lose the 5 units of output produced by the marginal dollar's worth of capital, but will gain the 10 units of output from the employment of an extra dollar's worth of labour. *Net* output will increase by 5 (= 10 − 5) units for the same total cost. This shifting of dollars from capital to labour will push the firm down its MP curve for labour and back up its MP curve for capital, moving the firm toward a position of equilibrium wherein equation (1) is fulfilled. At that point, the MP of both labour and capital might be, for example, 7.

Whenever the same total cost results in a greater total output, the cost per unit — and therefore the total cost of any given level of output — is being reduced. To be able to produce a *larger* output with a *given* total-cost outlay is the same thing as being able to produce a *given* output with a *smaller* total-cost outlay. And as we have seen, the cost of producing any given output can be reduced so long as $MP_L/P_L \neq MP_C/P_C$.

The Profit-Maximizing Rule

Simply minimizing cost is not sufficient for maximizing profit. There are many different levels of output that a firm can produce in the least costly way. But there is only one unique output that will maximize profits. Recalling our earlier analysis of product markets, this profit-maximizing *output* is where marginal revenue equals marginal cost (MR = MC). Let us now derive a comparable rule from the standpoint of resource *inputs*.

In deriving the demand schedule for labour early in this chapter, we determined that the profit-maximizing quantity of labour to employ is that quantity at which the wage rate, or price of labour, (P_L), equals the marginal *revenue* product of labour (MRP_L) or, more simply, $P_L = MRP_L$.

The same rationale applies to any other resource — for example, capital. Capital will also be employed in the profit-maximizing amount when its price equals its marginal revenue product, or $P_C = MRP_C$. Thus in general, we can say that when hiring resources *in competitive markets*, a firm will realize the **profit-maximizing combination of resources** when each input is employed up to the point at which its price equals its marginal revenue product:

$$P_L = MRP_L$$
$$P_C = MRP_C$$

Dividing both sides of the equation by their respective prices, we have:

$$\frac{MRP_L}{P_L} = \frac{MRP_C}{P_C} = 1 \qquad (2)$$

Note in equation (2) that it is not sufficient that the MRPs of the two resources be *proportionate* to their prices: the MRPs must be *equal to* their prices, and the ratios therefore equal to 1. For example, if MRP_L = \$15, P_L = \$5, MRP_C = \$9, and P_C = \$3, the firm would be underemploying both capital and labour, even though the ratios of MRP to resource price were identical for both resources. The firm could expand its profits by hiring additional amounts of both capital and labour until it had moved down their downsloping MRP curves to the points at which MRP_L was

equal to \$5 and MRP_C was \$3. The ratios would now be 5/5 and 3/3, and equal to 1.[3]

A subtle but significant point must be added: Although we have separated the two for discussion purposes, the profit-maximizing position of equation (2) subsumes the least-cost position of equation (1). [Note that if we divide the MRP numerators in equation (2) by product price, we would obtain equation (1).] A firm that is maximizing its profits *must* be producing the profit-maximizing output with the least costly combination of resources. If it is *not* using the least costly combination of labour and capital, then it could produce the same output at a smaller total cost and realize a larger profit. Thus, a necessary condition for profit-maximization is the fulfilment of equation (1). But equation (1) is not a sufficient condition for profit maximization. It is quite possible for a firm to produce the "wrong" output, an output that does not maximize profits, but to produce that output with the least costly combination of resources.

Numerical Illustration

A numerical illustration may help us to grasp the least-cost and profit-maximizing rules. In columns 2,

---

[3] It is not difficult to demonstrate that equation (2) is consistent with (indeed, the equivalent of) the P = MC rule for determining the profit-maximizing output of Chapter 10. We begin by taking the reciprocal of equation (2):

$$\frac{P_L}{MRP_L} = \frac{P_C}{MRP_C} = 1$$

Recall that, assuming pure competition in the product market, marginal revenue product, MRP, is found by multiplying marginal product, MP, by product price, P_x. Thus we can write:

$$\frac{P_L}{MP_L \times P_x} = \frac{P_C}{MP_C \times P_x} = 1$$

Multiplying through by product price, P_x, we get:

$$\frac{P_L}{MP_L} = \frac{P_C}{MP_C} = P_x$$

The two ratios measure marginal cost. That is, if we divide the cost of an additional input of labour or capital by the associated marginal product, we have the addition to total cost, that is, the *marginal* cost, of each additional unit of output. For example, if the price of an extra worker (P_L) is \$10 and that worker's marginal product (MP_L) is, say, 5 units, then the marginal cost of each of those 5 units is \$2. The same reasoning applies to capital. We thus obtain:

$$MC_x = P_x$$

Our conclusion is that equation (2) in the text, showing the profit-maximizing combination of *inputs*, is the equivalent of our earlier P = MC rule, which identified the profit-maximizing *output*.

3, 2', and 3' of Table 15-3 we show the total products and marginal physical products for various amounts of labour and capital that are assumed to be the only inputs needed in producing product X. Both inputs are subject to the law of diminishing returns.

We also assume that labour and capital are supplied in competitive resource markets at $8 and $12 respectively and that product X is sold competitively at $2 per unit. For both labour and capital we can determine the total revenue associated with each input level by multiplying total product by the $2 product price. These data are shown in columns 4 and 4'. This allows us to calculate the marginal revenue product of each successive input of labour and capital as shown in columns 5 and 5'.

Producing at Least-Cost   What is the least-cost combination of labour and capital to use in producing, say, 50 units of output? Answer: 3 units of labour and 2 units of capital. Note from columns 3 and 3' that in hiring 3 units of labour $MP_L/P_L = 6/8 = 3/4$ and for 2 units of capital $MP_C/P_C = 9/12 = 3/4$, so equation (1) is fulfilled. And columns 2 and 2' indicate that this combination of labour and capital does, indeed, result in the specified 50 ($= 28 + 22$) units of output. How can we verify that costs are actually minimized? First, note that the total cost of employing 3 units of labour and 2 of capital is $48 [$= (3 \times \$8) + (2 \times \$12)$] or, alternatively stated, cost per unit of output is $0.96 ($= \$48/50$).

Observe, too, that there are other combinations of labour and capital that will yield 50 units of output. For example, 5 units of labour and 1 unit of capital will produce 50 ($= 37 + 13$) units, but we find that total cost is now higher at $52 [$= (5 \times \$8) + (1 \times \$12)$], meaning that average unit cost has risen to $1.04 ($= \$52/50$). Note that by employing 5 units of labour and 1 of capital the least-cost rule would be violated in that $MP_L/P_L = 4/8$ is less than $MP_C/P_C = 13/12$, indicating that more capital and less labour should be employed to produce this output.

Similarly, 50 units of output also could be produced with 2 units of labour and 3 of capital. The total cost of the 50 units of output would again be $52 [$= (2 \times \$8) + (3 \times \$12)$], or $1.04 per unit. Here equation (1) is not fulfilled in that $MP_L/P_L = 10/8$, which exceeds $MP_C/P_C = 6/12$. This inequality suggests that the firm should use more labour and less capital.

Maximizing Profits   Will 50 units of output maximize the firm's profits? Answer: No, because the profit-maximizing rule stated in equation (2) is *not* fulfilled when employing 3 units of labour and 2 of capital. We know that to maximize profits any given input should be employed until its price equals its marginal revenue product ($P_L = MRP_L$ and $P_C = MRP_C$). But for 3 units of labour we find in column 5 that labour's MRP is $12 while its price is only $8. This means it is profitable to hire more labour. Simi-

TABLE 15-3   The least-cost and profit-maximizing combinations of labour and capital (*hypothetical data*)*

Labour (price = $8)					Capital (price = $12)				
(1)	(2)	(3)	(4)	(5)	(1')	(2')	(3')	(4')	(5')
				Marginal					Marginal
	Total	Marginal	Total	revenue		Total	Marginal	Total	revenue
Quantity	product	product	revenue	product	Quantity	product	product	revenue	product
0	0	0	$ 0	$ 0	0	0	0	$ 0	$ 0
1	12	12	24	24	1	13	13	26	26
2	22	10	44	20	2	22	9	44	18
3	28	6	56	12	3	28	6	56	12
4	33	5	66	10	4	32	4	64	8
5	37	4	74	8	5	35	3	70	6
6	40	3	80	6	6	37	2	74	4
7	42	2	84	4	7	38	1	76	2

*To simplify, it is assumed in this table that the productivity of each resource is independent of the quantity of the other. For example, the total and marginal product of labour is assumed not to vary with the quantity of capital employed.

Box 15-2

INPUT SUBSTITUTION: THE CASE OF CABOOSES

Substituting among inputs — particularly when jobs are at stake — can be controversial.

A firm will achieve the least-cost combination of inputs when the last dollar spent on each makes the same contribution to total output. This rule also implies that a firm is unimpeded in changing its input mix in response to technological changes or changes in input prices. Unfortunately, in the real world the substitution of new capital for old capital and the substitution of capital for labour may be controversial and difficult to achieve.

Consider the case of railway cabooses. The railways claim that technological advance has made the caboose obsolete. In particular, railways want to substitute a "trainlink" that can be attached to the coupler of the last car of a train. This small black box contains a revolving strobe light and instruments that monitor train speed, air-brake pressure, and other relevant data, which it transmits to the locomotive engineer. The trainlink costs only $4,000, compared with $80,000 for a new caboose. And, of course, the trainlink replaces one member of the train crew.

The railways cite substantial cost economies from this rearrangement of capital and labour inputs. But the union that represents railway conductors and brakemen knows that the demise of the caboose means a decline in the demand for its members. The union therefore made a concerted, but unsuccessful, effort to halt the elimination of cabooses on trains. The union argued that the elimination of cabooses would reduce railway safety.

The union contended that, unlike humans, trainlinks cannot detect broken wheels or axles nor overheated bearings. From the vantage point of the railways this looked like featherbedding — the protection of unnecessary jobs. The railways contended that available data showed no safety differences between trains using and those not using cabooses. Indeed, safety may be enhanced without cabooses because many injuries are incurred by crew who are riding in cabooses.

While cabooses are virtually extinct in Europe, they were the rule in Canada until 1988. In the United States, the railway unions have lobbied successfully for legislation in four states that makes cabooses mandatory. In all other states, the use of cabooses remains a matter of collective bargaining negotiations.

---

larly, for 2 units of capital we observe in column 5′ that MRP is $18 and capital's price is only $12, indicating that more capital should be employed.

When hiring 3 units of labour and 2 of capital to produce 50 units of output, the firm is underemploying both inputs. Labour and capital are both being used in less than profit-maximizing amounts. The marginal revenue products of labour and capital are equal to their prices and equation (2) is fulfilled when the firm is employing 5 units of labour and 3 units of capital. This is therefore the profit-maximizing combination of outputs.[4] The firm's total cost will

be $76, which is made up of $40 ($= 5 \times \$8$) worth of labour and $36 ($= 3 \times \$12$) worth of capital.

Total revenue of $130 is determined by multiplying total output of 65 ($= 37 + 28$) by the $2 product price or, alternatively, by simply summing the total revenue attributable to labour ($74) and to capital ($56). The difference between total revenue and total cost is, of course, the firm's economic profit, which in this instance is $54 ($= \$130 - \$76$). Equation (2) is fulfilled when 5 units of labour and 3 of capital are employed: $MRP_L/P_L = 8/8 = MRP_C/P_C = 12/12 = 1$. You should experiment with other combinations of labour and capital to demonstrate that they will yield an economic profit less than $54.

Our example also verifies our earlier assertion that a firm using the profit-maximizing combination of inputs is also necessarily producing the resulting output with the least cost. In fulfilling equation (2) the firm is automatically fulfilling equation (1). In this case, for 5 units of labour and 3 of capital we observe

---

[4] Given that we are dealing with discrete (nonfractional) increases in the two outputs, you should also be aware that in fact the employment of 4 units of labour and 2 of capital are equally profitable. The fifth unit of labour's MRP and its price are equal (at $8), so that the fifth unit neither adds to, nor subtracts from, the firm's profits. The same reasoning applies to the third unit of labour.

that $MP_L/P_L = 4/8 = MP_C/P_C = 6/12$. Questions 5 and 7 at the end of this chapter are recommended to further your understanding of the least-cost and profit-maximizing combination of inputs.[5]

CRITICISM OF MARGINAL PRODUCTIVITY THEORY

Our discussion of resource pricing is the cornerstone of the controversial view that economic justice is one of the outcomes of a competitive market economy. Table 15-1 tells us in effect that labour receives an income payment equal to the marginal contribution it makes to the firm's revenue. Bluntly stated, labour is paid what it is worth. Therefore, if we accept the proposition that we are paid according to what we produce, the marginal productivity theory seems to provide a fair and equitable distribution of income. Because the marginal productivity theory equally applies to capital and land, the distribution of all incomes can be held as equitable.

At first glance, an income distribution whereby workers and owners of property resources are paid in accordance with their contribution to output sounds eminently fair. But there are serious criticisms of the **marginal productivity theory of income distribution**.

---

[5] Footnote 1 in Chapter 16 modifies our least-cost and profit-maximizing rules for the situation in which a firm is hiring resources under imperfectly competitive conditions. Where there is imperfect competition in the resource market, the marginal resource cost (MRC) — the cost of an extra input — exceeds the resource price (P). Hence, we must substitute MRC for P in the denominators of equations (1) and (2).

1 Inequality   Critics argue that the distribution of income resulting from payment according to marginal productivity may be highly unequal because productive resources are very unequally distributed in the first place. Aside from differences in genetic endowments, individuals encounter substantially different opportunities to enhance their productivity through education and training. Some may not be able to participate in production at all, because of mental or physical handicaps, and would obtain no income under a system of distribution based solely on marginal productivity. Ownership of resources is also highly unequal. Many landlords obtain their property by inheritance rather than through their own productive effort. Hence income from inherited property conflicts with the "To each according to what one creates" proposition. This reasoning can lead one to advocate government policies to modify the income distribution resulting from payments made strictly according to marginal productivity.

2 Monopsony and Monopoly   The marginal productivity theory rests on the assumption of competitive markets. We will find in Chapter 16 that labour markets, for example, are riddled with imperfections. Some employers exert monopsony power in hiring workers. And some workers, through labour unions and professional associations, wield monopoly power in selling their services. Indeed, the process of collective bargaining over wages suggests a power struggle over the division of income. In this struggle, market forces — and income shares based on marginal productivity — are pushed into the background. In short, we will find that because of market imperfections, wage rates and other resource prices frequently do *not* measure contributions to a nation's domestic output.

CHAPTER SUMMARY

1. Resource prices are a major determinant of money incomes; simultaneously, they perform the function of rationing resources to various industries and firms.

2. The fact that the demand for any resource is derived from the product it helps produce means that the demand for a resource will depend on its productivity and the market value (price) of the good it is producing.

3. The marginal revenue product schedule of any resource is the demand schedule for that resource. This follows from an application of the rule that a firm hiring under competitive conditions will find it most profitable to hire a resource up to the point where the price of the resource equals its marginal revenue product.

4. The demand curve for a resource is downsloping, because the marginal product of additional inputs of any resource declines in accordance with the law of diminishing returns. When a firm is selling in an imperfectly competitive market, the resource demand curve will fall for a second reason: product price must be reduced to permit the firm to sell a larger output. The market demand for a resource can be derived by summing the demand curves of all firms hiring that resource.

5. The demand for a resource will shift as a result of a. a change in the demand for, and therefore the price of, the product the resource is producing; b. changes in the productivity of the resource; c. changes in prices of other resources.

6. If resources A and B are substitutable, a decline in the price of A will decrease the demand for B, provided the substitution effect is greater than the output effect. But if the output effect exceeds the substitution effect, a decline in the price of A will increase the demand for B.

7. If resources C and D are complementary or jointly demanded there is only an output effect, and a change in the price of C will change the demand for D in the opposite direction.

8. The elasticity of resource demand will be greater a. the slower the rate at which the marginal product of the resource declines, b. the larger the number of good substitute resources available, c. the greater the elasticity of demand for the product, and d. the larger the proportion of total production costs attributable to the resource.

9. Any level of output will be produced with the least costly combination of resources when the marginal product, per dollar's worth of each input, is the same, that is, when

$$\frac{\text{MP of labour}}{\text{price of labour}} = \frac{\text{MP of capital}}{\text{price of capital}}$$

10. A firm will employ the profit-maximizing combination of resources when the price of each resource is equal to its marginal *revenue* product or, algebraically, when

$$\frac{\text{MRP of labour}}{\text{price of labour}} = \frac{\text{MRP of capital}}{\text{price of capital}} = 1$$

TERMS AND CONCEPTS

derived demand (p. 247)
least-cost combination of resources (p. 253)
marginal product (p. 247)
marginal productivity theory of income distribution (p. 257)

marginal resource cost (p. 247)
marginal revenue product (p. 247)
MRP = MRC rule (p. 248)
profit-maximizing combination of resources (p. 254)
substitution and output effects (p. 252)

QUESTIONS AND STUDY SUGGESTIONS

1. What is the significance of resource pricing? Explain in detail how the factors determining resource demand differ from those underlying product demand. Explain the meaning and significance of the notion that the demand for a resource is a *derived* demand. Why do resource demand curves slope downward?

2. Complete the following labour demand table for a firm that is hiring labour competitively and selling its product in a competitive market.

Units of labour	Total product	Marginal product	Product price	Total revenue	Marginal revenue product
1	17	$_____	$2	$_____	$_____
2	31		2		
3	43	_____	2	_____	_____
4	53	_____	2	_____	_____
5	60	_____	2	_____	_____
6	65	_____	2	_____	_____

a. How many workers will the firm hire if the going rate is $27.95? $19.95? Explain why the firm will not hire a larger or smaller number of workers at each of these wage rates.

b. Show, in schedule form and graphically, the labour demand curve for this firm.

c. Redetermine the firm's demand curve for labour on the assumption that it is selling in an imperfectly competitive market and that, although it can sell 17 units at $2.20 per unit, it must lower product price by 5¢ in order to sell the marginal product of each successive worker. Compare this demand curve with that derived in question 2b. Which curve is more elastic? Explain any differences.

3. Distinguish between a change in resource demand and a change in the quantity of a resource demanded. What specific factors might lead to a change in resource demand? A change in the quantity of a resource demanded?

4. What factors determine the elasticity of resource demand? What effect will each of the following have on the elasticity or the location of the demand for resource C that is being used in the production of commodity X? Where there is any uncertainty as to the outcome, specify the causes of that uncertainty.

a. An increase in the demand for product X.

b. An increase in the price of substitute resource D.

c. An increase in the number of resources substitutable for C in producing X.

d. A technological improvement in the capital equipment with which resource C is combined.

e. A decline in the price of complementary resource E.

f. A decline in the elasticity of demand for product X, due to a decline in the competitiveness of the product market.

5. Suppose the productivity of labour and capital are as shown below. The output of these resources sells in a purely competitive market for $1 per unit. Both labour and capital are hired under purely competitive conditions at $1 and $3 respectively.

Units of capital	MP of capital	Units of labour	MP of labour
1	24	1	11
2	21	2	9
3	18	3	8
4	15	4	7
5	9	5	6
6	6	6	4
7	3	7	1
8	1	8	$1/2$

a. What is the least-cost combination of labour and capital to employ in producing 80 units of output? Explain.

b. What is the profit-maximizing combination of labour and capital for the firm to employ? Explain. What is the resulting level of output? What is the economic profit?

c. When the firm employs the profit-maximizing combination of labour and capital determined in *5b*, is this combination also the least costly way of producing the profit-maximizing output? Explain.

6. Using the substitution and output effects, explain how a decline in the price of resource A *might* cause an increase in the demand for substitute resource B. If resources C and D are complementary and used in fixed proportions, what will be the impact of an increase in the price of C upon the demand for D?

7. In each of the following four cases MRP_L and MRP_C refer to the marginal revenue products of labour and capital, respectively, and P_L and P_C refer to their prices. Indicate in each case whether the conditions are consistent with maximum profits for the firm. If not, state which resource(s) should be used in larger amounts and which resource(s) should be used in smaller amounts.

a. $MRP_L = \$8$; $P_L = \$4$; $MRP_C = \$8$; $P_C = \$4$.

b. $MRP_L = \$10$; $P_L = \$12$; $MRP_C = \$14$; $P_C = \$9$.

c. $MRP_L = \$6$; $P_L = \$6$; $MRP_C = \$12$; $P_C = \$12$.

d. $MRP_L = \$22$; $P_L = \$26$; $MRP_C = \$16$; $P_C = \$19$.

8. Demonstrate algebraically that the condition for the profit-maximizing level of output is the equivalent of the condition for the profit-maximizing combination of inputs.

9. If each input is paid in accordance with its marginal revenue product, will the resulting distribution of income be ethically just?

The Pricing and Employment of Resources: Wage Determination

I n all probability the most important price you will encounter in your lifetime will be your wage rate. It will be critical in determining the economic well-being of you and your family. Hence, the following facts and questions may be of more than casual interest.

Real wages, and therefore living standards, have increased historically in Canada. What forces account for these increases?

Union workers generally receive higher wages than nonunion workers. How are unions able to accomplish this wage advantage?

The average salary for major league baseball players in 1991 was about $1,000,000 as compared to about $45,000 for schoolteachers. What causes differences in wages and incomes?

Most people are paid an hourly wage rate. But some workers are paid by the number of units produced or receive commissions and royalties. What is the rationale for various compensation schemes?

Having explored the strategic factors underlying resource demand, we now introduce supply as it characterizes the markets for labour, land, capital, and entrepreneurial ability to understand how wages, rents, interest, and profits are determined.

We discuss wages prior to other resource prices because to the vast majority of households, the wage rate is the most important price in the economy; it is their sole or basic source of income. About three-quarters of the national income is in the form of wages and salaries.

Our objectives in discussing wage determination are to: (1) understand the forces underlying the general level of wage rates in Canada; (2) see how wage rates are determined in particular labour markets; (3) analyse the impact of unions on the structure and level of wages; (4) discuss the economic effects of the minimum wage; (5) explain wage differentials; and (6) survey a number of compensation schemes that link pay to worker performance.

Throughout this chapter, we rely on the marginal productivity theory of Chapter 15 as an explanation of labour demand.

MEANING OF WAGES

Wages, or wage rates, are the price paid for the use of labour. Economists often use the term "wages" broadly to apply to the payments received by (1) blue- and white-collar workers of almost infinite variety; (2) professionals — physicians, lawyers, dentists, teachers; (3) owners of small businesses — barbers, plumbers, and a host of retailers — for the labour services they provide in operating their own businesses.

Wages may take the form of bonuses, royalties, commissions, and monthly salaries, but for the most part we use the term "wages" to mean wage rates per unit of time — per hour, per day, and so forth. This designation will remind us that the wage rate is a price paid for the use of units of labour service. It also lets us distinguish between "wages" and "earnings," the latter depending on wage rates *and* the number of hours or weeks of labour service supplied in the market.

We also distinguish between money or nominal wages and real wages. **Nominal wages** are the amount of money received per hour, per day, per week, and so forth. **Real wages**, however, are the quantity of goods and services one can obtain with one's nominal wages.

One's real wages depend on one's nominal wages and the prices of the goods and services one buys. The percentage change in real wages can be determined by subtracting the percentage change in the price level from the percentage change in nominal wages. Thus an 8% increase in nominal wages during a year when the price level increases by 5% yields a 3% increase in real wages. Unless otherwise indicated, our discussion will be in terms of real wage rates by assuming that the level of product prices is constant.

GENERAL LEVEL OF WAGES

Wages differ among nations, regions, various occupations, and individuals. Wage rates are vastly higher in Canada than in China or India; they are generally higher in British Columbia, Ontario, and Alberta than in Quebec and the Atlantic provinces; plumbers are paid more than general labourers; lawyer A may earn twice as much as lawyer B for the same number of hours of work. Wage rates also differ according to gender and age.

The general or average level of wages is a composite of a wide range of different specific wage rates. This admittedly vague concept is a useful point of departure in making and explaining international and interregional wage comparisons. Data indicate that the general level of real wages in Canada is among the highest in the world. The simplest explanation is that the demand for labour in Canada has been great in relation to supply.

Role of Productivity

We know that the demand for labour — or any other resource — depends on its productivity. The greater the productivity of labour, the greater the demand for it. And given the total supply of labour, the stronger the demand, the greater the average level of real wages. The demand for Canadian labour has been strong because Canadian labour is highly productive. But why the high productivity? The reasons are several.

1 Capital Canadian workers are employed in conjunction with large amounts of capital equipment. For example, the average Canadian worker is assisted by some $80,000 worth of machinery and equipment — more than any other worker in the world.

2 Natural Resources Natural resources are very abundant in relation to the size of the labour force.

Canada is richly endowed with arable land, basic mineral resources, and ample sources of industrial power. The fact that Canadian workers have large amounts of high-quality natural resources to work with is perhaps most evident in agriculture, where historically the growth of productivity has been dramatic.

3 Technology   Canadian workers in many industries not only use more capital equipment but technologically superior equipment than do most foreign workers. Similarly, work methods are steadily being improved through detailed scientific study and research.

4 Labour Quality   The health, education, and training of Canadian workers have been generally superior to that of the labour of most other nations. This means that even with the same quantity and quality of natural and capital resources, Canadian workers would be more efficient than many of their foreign counterparts.

5 Other Factors   Less tangible yet important items underlying the high productivity of Canadian labour are (*a*) the efficiency and flexibility of Canadian management; (*b*) a business, social, and political environment that puts great emphasis on production and productivity; (*c*) generally, an adequately sized market that provides the opportunity for firms to realize mass-production economies.

Real Wages and Productivity

The dependence of real hourly wages on the productivity level is indicated in Figure 16-1. Note the close long-run relationship between real hourly wages and output per person-hour. Since real income and real output are two ways of viewing the same thing, it is no surprise that **real income (earnings) per worker can increase only at about the same rate as output per worker**. More real output per hour means more real income to distribute for each hour worked. The simplest case is the classic one of Robinson Crusoe on the desert island. The number of coconuts he can pick or fish he can catch per hour *is* his real wage per hour.

Secular Growth

But simple supply and demand analysis suggests that even if the demand for labour is strong in Canada, increases in the supply of labour will reduce the general level of wages over time. It is true that the Canadian population and the labour force have grown

FIGURE 16-1   Output per hour and real average hourly earnings, all business-sector industries

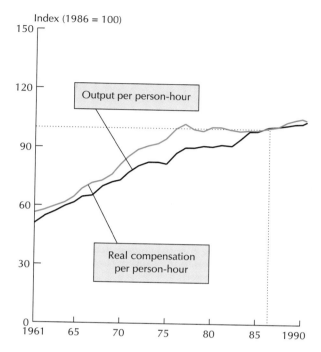

Over a period of years, there has been a close relationship between real hourly wages and output per person-hour. As a result of large nominal wage increases between 1974 and 1977, real wages rose considerably above output per person-hour. Note that real wages have not increased since then, while output per person-hour has caught up. (*Source:* Statistics Canada, *Aggregate Productivity Measures*, 1990–91 (Ottawa, 1992) Table 1.

significantly over the decades. However, increases in the supply of labour have usually been more than offset by increases in the demand for labour, stemming from the productivity-increasing factors discussed above. The result has been a long-run, or secular, increase in wage rates and employment, as suggested by Figure 16-2.

WAGES IN PARTICULAR LABOUR MARKETS

We now turn from the general level of wages to specific wage rates. What determines the wage rate received by a specific type of worker? Demand and supply analysis again provides a revealing approach. Our analysis covers some half-dozen basic market models.

FIGURE 16-2   The secular trend of real wages in Canada

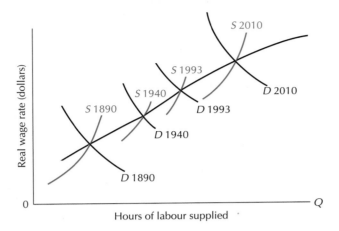

Real wage rate (dollars)

Hours of labour supplied

The productivity of Canadian labour has increased substantially in the long run, causing the demand for labour to increase in relation to the supply. The result has been increases in real wages.

Competitive Model

A purely **competitive labour market** has the following characteristics:

1. Many firms are competing with one another in hiring a specific type of labour;

2. Numerous qualified workers with identical skills are independently supplying this type of labour service;

3. Neither firms nor workers can exert control over the market wage rate.

Market Demand   Suppose that there are many — two hundred — firms demanding a particular type of semiskilled or skilled labour. The total, or market, demand for this labour can be determined by adding up the labour demand curves (the MRP curves) of the individual firms, as suggested in **Figure 16-3 (a)** and **(b) (Key Graph)**.

Market Supply   On the supply side, we assume there is no union; workers compete individually for available jobs. The supply curve for a particular type of labour will be upsloping, reflecting the fact that in the absence of unemployment, hiring firms as a group will be forced to pay higher wage rates to obtain more workers. This is so because the firms must bid these workers away from other industries, occupations, and localities. Within limits, workers have alternative job opportunities; they may work in

other industries in the same locality, or they may work in their present occupations in different cities or provinces. In a full-employment economy, the group of firms in this particular labour market must pay higher and higher wage rates to attract this type of labour away from these alternative job opportunities. Similarly, higher wages are necessary to induce individuals not currently in the labour force to seek employment.

Market Equilibrium   The equilibrium wage rate and the equilibrium level of employment for this type of labour are determined at the intersection of the labour demand and labour supply curves. In Figure 16-3 (b), the equilibrium wage rate is W_c ($6), and the number of workers hired is Q_c (1,000). To the individual firm, the wage rate W_c is given. Each of the many hiring firms employs such a small fraction of the total available supply of this type of labour that none can influence the wage rate. The supply of labour is perfectly elastic to the individual firm, as shown by S in Figure 16-3 (a). Each individual firm will find it profitable to hire workers up to the point at which the going wage rate is equal to labour's MRP. This is merely an application of the MRP = MRC rule developed in Chapter 15. (Indeed, the demand curve in Figure 16-3 (a) is based upon Table 15-1.)

As Table 16-1 indicates, *because resource price is given to the individual competitive firm, the marginal cost of that resource (MRC) will be constant and equal to resource price (the wage rate).* In this case, the wage rate and hence the marginal cost of labour are constant to the individual firm. Each additional worker hired adds precisely his or her wage

TABLE 16-1   The supply of labour: pure competition in the hire of labour (hypothetical data)

(1) Units of labour	(2) Wage rate	(3) Total labour cost (wage bill)	(4) Marginal resource (labour) cost
0	$6	$ 0	
1	6	6	$6
2	6	12	6
3	6	18	6
4	6	24	6
5	6	30	6
6	6	36	6

FIGURE 16-3   **The supply of, and the demand for, labour in (a) a single competitive firm and (b) a competitive market**

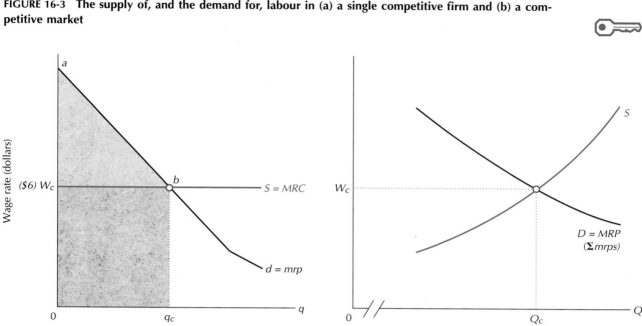

(a) Individual firm

(b) Market

In a competitive labour market, the equilibrium wage rate, W_c, and number of workers employed, Q_c, are determined by supply, S, and demand, D, as shown in (b). Because this wage rate is given to the individual firm hiring in the market, its labour supply curve, $S = MRC$, is perfectly elastic, as in (a). The firm finds it most profitable to hire workers up to the $MRP = MRC$ point. The area $0abq_c$ represents the firm's total revenue, of which $0W_cbq_c$ is its total wage cost; the remaining area W_cab is available for paying nonlabour resources.

rate ($6 in this case) to the firm's total resource cost. The firm, then, will maximize its profits by hiring workers to the point at which their wage rate, and therefore marginal resource cost, equals their marginal revenue product. In Figure 16-3 (a), the "typical" firm will hire q_c (5) workers.

Note that the firm's total revenue from hiring q_c workers can be found by summing their MRPs. In this case the total revenue from the five workers is indicated by the area $0abq_c$ in Figure 16-3 (a). Of this total revenue, the area $0W_cbq_c$ is the firm's total wage cost and the triangular area W_cab represents additional revenue available to reward other inputs such as capital, land, and entrepreneurship.

Monopsony Model

Characteristics   Let's now consider the case of a **monopsonist**, an employer with monopolistic buy-

ing (hiring) power. Monopsony has the following characteristics.

1. The given firm's employment is a large portion of the total employment of a particular kind of labour.

2. This type of labour is relatively immobile either geographically or in the sense that, if workers sought alternative employment, they would have to acquire new skills.

3. The firm is a "wage maker" in that the wage rate it must pay varies directly with the number of workers it employs.

In some instances, the monopsonistic power of employers is virtually complete, in the sense that there is only one major employer in a labour market. For example, the economies of some towns and cities depend almost entirely on one major firm. A copper-mining company may be the basic source of employment in a remote British Columbia town. A textile mill in Quebec's Eastern Townships, a Gatineau paper mill, or a Newfoundland fish processor may provide a large proportion of the employment in its locality.

In other cases, *oligopsony* may prevail: three or four firms may each hire a large portion of the supply of labour in a particular market. Our study of oligopoly suggests that there is a strong tendency for oligopsonists to act in concert — much like a monopsonist — in hiring labour.

Upsloping Supply to Firm When a firm hires a considerable portion of the total available supply of a particular type of labour, its decisions to employ more or fewer workers will affect the wage rate. Specifically, *if a firm is large in relation to the labour market, it will have to pay a higher wage rate to obtain more labour.* For simplicity's sake, suppose there is only one employer of a particular type of labour in a specified geographic area.

In this polar case the labour supply curve to that firm and the total supply curve for the labour market are identical. This supply curve, for reasons already made clear, is upsloping, indicating that the firm must pay a higher wage rate to attract more workers. This is shown by S in Figure 16-4. The supply curve is, in

effect, the average-cost-of-labour curve from the firm's point of view; each point on it indicates the wage rate (cost) per worker that must be paid to attract the corresponding number of workers.

MRC Exceeds Wage Rate But the higher wages involved in attracting *additional* workers will also have to be paid to *all* workers currently employed at lower wage rates. The payment of a uniform wage to all workers will mean that the cost of an extra worker — the marginal resource (labour) cost (MRC) — will exceed the wage rate by the amount necessary to bring the wage rate of all workers currently employed up to the new wage level.

Table 16-2 illustrates this point. One worker can be hired at a wage rate of $6. But hiring a second worker forces the firm to pay a higher wage rate of $7. Marginal resource (labour) cost is $8 — the $7 paid the second worker plus a $1 raise for the first worker. Stated differently, total labour cost is $14 (= 2 × $7), rather than the $13 that would be the case if the first worker were paid $6 and the second paid $7. Hence, the MRC of the second worker is $8 (= $14 − $6), not the $7 wage rate paid the second worker. Similarly, the marginal labour cost of the third worker is $10 — the $8 that must be paid to attract this worker from alternative employments plus $1 raises for the first two workers.

The important point is that *to the monopsonist, marginal resource (labour) cost will exceed the wage rate*. Graphically, the MRC curve (columns 1 and 4 in Table 16-2) will lie above the average cost, or supply, curve of labour (columns 1 and 2). This is shown in Figure 16-4.

FIGURE 16-4 **The wage rate and level of employment in a monopsonistic labour market**

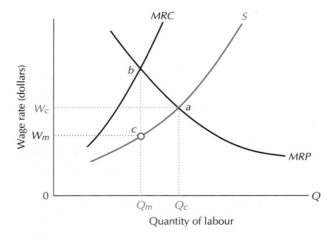

In a monopsonistic labour market, the employer's marginal resource (labour) cost curve (*MRC*) lies above the labour supply curve (*S*). Equating *MRC* with labour demand *MRP* at point *b*, the monopsonist will hire *Q_m* workers (as compared with *Q_c* under competition) and pay the wage rate *W_m* (as compared with the competitive wage *W_c*).

TABLE 16-2 **The supply of labour: monopsony in the hire of labour (*hypothetical data*)**

(1) Units of labour	(2) Wage rate	(3) Total labour cost (wage bill)	(4) Marginal resource (labour) cost
0	$5	$ 0	
1	6	6	$6
2	7	14	8
3	8	24	10
4	9	36	12
5	10	50	14
6	11	66	16

Equilibrium To maximize profits, the firm will equate marginal resource (labour) cost with the MRP.[1] The number of workers hired by the monopsonist is indicated by Q_m, and the wage rate paid, W_m, is indicated by the corresponding point on the resource supply, or average-cost-of-labour, curve.

It is particularly important to contrast these results with those a competitive labour market would yield. With competition in the hire of labour, the level of employment would have been greater (Q_c) and the wage rate would have been higher (W_c). It simply does not pay the monopsonist to hire workers up to the point at which the wage rate and labour's MRP are equal. *Other things being equal, the monopsonist maximizes its profits by hiring a smaller number of workers and thereby paying a less-than-competitive wage rate.* In the process, society gets a smaller output,[2] and workers get a wage rate less by bc than their marginal revenue product.

Just as a monopolistic seller finds it profitable to restrict product output to realize an above-competitive price for goods, so the monopsonistic employer of resources finds it profitable to restrict employment to realize below-competitive wage rates.[3]

---

[1] The fact that MRC exceeds resource price when resources are hired or purchased under imperfectly competitive (monopsonistic) conditions calls for appropriate adjustments in Chapter 15's least-cost and profit-maximizing rules for hiring resources. (See equations (1) and (2) in the "Optimal Combination of Resources" section of Chapter 15.) Specifically, we must substitute MRC for resource price in the denominators of our two equations. That is, with imperfect competition in the hiring of both labour and capital, equation (1) becomes

$$\frac{MP_L}{MRC_L} = \frac{MP_C}{MRC_C} \qquad (1')$$

and equation (2) is restated as

$$\frac{MRP_L}{MRC_L} = \frac{MRP_C}{MRC_C} = 1 \qquad (2')$$

In fact, equations (1) and (2) can be regarded as special cases of $(1')$ and $(2')$, wherein firms happen to be hiring under purely competitive conditions and resource price is therefore equal to, and can be substituted for, marginal resource cost.

[2] This is analogous to the monopolist's restricting output as it sets product price and output on the basis of marginal revenue, not product demand. In this instance, resource price is set on the basis of marginal labour (resource) cost, not resource supply.

[3] Will a monopsonistic employer also be a monopolistic seller in the product market? Not necessarily. The Eastern Townships textile mill may be a monopsonistic employer, yet face severe domestic and foreign competition in selling its product. In other cases — for example, the automobile and steel industries — firms have both monopsonistic and monopolistic (oligopolistic) power.

Illustrations Monopsonistic labour market outcomes are not common in our economy. There are typically many potential employers for most workers, particularly when these workers are occupationally and geographically mobile. Also, unions often counteract monopsony power in labour markets. Nevertheless, there is evidence of monopsony in such diverse labour markets as those for nurses, professional athletes, public school teachers, newspaper employees, and some building trade workers.

In the case of nurses, the major employers in most localities are a relatively small number of hospitals. Furthermore, the highly specialized skills of nurses are not readily transferable to other occupations. It has been found in accordance with the monopsony model that, other things being equal, the smaller the number of hospitals in a town or city (that is, the greater the degree of monopsony), the lower the starting salaries of nurses.

The market for professional athletes is also of interest. Although *potential* employers are quite numerous, the market is characterized by ingenious collusive devices by which employers have attempted, with considerable success, to limit competition. The National Hockey League and the Canadian Football League have established systems of rules that tie a player to one team and prevent him from selling his talents to the highest bidder on the open (competitive) market. In particular, through the new player draft, the team that selects or "drafts" a player has the exclusive right to bargain a contract with that player. Furthermore, the so-called "reserve clause" in each player's contract gives his team the exclusive right to purchase his services for the next season. Though players' associations and collective bargaining agreements that stipulate "free agency" for experienced players have made the labour markets for professional athletes in recent years more competitive, collusive monopsony persists.

Empirical studies have shown that, prior to 1976, baseball players (despite very high salaries) were paid substantially less than their estimated MRPs, which is consistent with Figure 16-4. (See Box 16-1.) However, beginning in 1976, players were allowed to become "free agents" — they became free to sell their services to any interested team — after their sixth season of play. A comparison of the salaries of the first group of free agents with their estimated MRPs indicates that the competitive bidding of teams for free agents brought their salaries and MRPs into close accord, as our competitive model suggests.

Box 16-1

PAY AND PERFORMANCE IN PROFESSIONAL BASEBALL

Professional baseball has provided an interesting "laboratory" in which the predictions of wage theory have been empirically tested.

Until 1976 professional baseball players were bound to a single team through the so-called "reserve clause" that prevented players from selling their talents on the open (competitive) market. Stated differently, the reserve clause conferred monopsony power upon the team that originally drafted a player. As we have seen in the present chapter, labour market theory would lead us to predict that this monopsony power would permit teams to pay wages less than a player's marginal revenue product (MRP). However, since 1976 major league players have been able to become "free agents" at the end of their sixth season of play and at that time can sell their services to any team. Orthodox theory suggests that free agents should be able to increase their salaries and bring them more closely into accord with their MRPs. Research tends to confirm both of the indicated predictions.

Scully[1] found that before baseball players could become free agents their salaries were substantially below their MRPs. Scully estimated a player's MRP as follows. First, he determined the relationship between a team's winning percentage and its revenue. Then he estimated the relationship between various possible measures of player productivity and a team's winning percentage. He found the ratio of strikeouts to walks for pitchers and the slugging averages for hitters (all nonpitchers) to be the best indicators of a player's contribution to the winning percentage. These two estimates were combined to calculate the contribution of a player to a team's total revenue.

TABLE 1　Marginal revenue products and salaries of professional baseball pitchers in the U.S., 1968–1969 (in U.S. dollars)

(1) Performance*	(2) Marginal revenue product	(3) Salary
1.60	$ 57,600	$31,100
1.80	80,900	34,200
2.00	104,100	37,200
2.20	127,400	40,200
2.40	150,600	43,100
2.60	173,900	46,000
2.80	197,100	48,800
3.00	220,300	51,600
3.20	243,600	54,400
3.40	266,800	57,100
3.60	290,100	59,800

*Strikeout-to-walk ratio.
Source: Scully, op. cit., p. 923.

As noted, Scully calculated that prior to free agency the estimated MRPs of both pitchers and hitters were substantially greater than player salaries. Table 1 shows the relevant data for pitchers. Column 1 indicates pitcher performance as measured by lifetime strikeout-to-walk ratio. A higher ratio indicates a better pitcher. Column 2 indicates MRP after player training costs are taken into account and column 3 shows actual average salary for pitchers in each quality class. As expected, salaries were far less than MRPs. Even the lowest quality pitchers (those with a 1.60 strikeout-to-walk ratio) received on the average salaries amounting to only about 54% of their MRPs. Observe, too, that the gap between MRP and average salary widens as player quality improves. "Star" players were exploited more than other players. The best pitchers received salaries that were only about 21% of their MRPs. The same general results apply to hitters. For example, the least productive hitters on the average received a salary equal to about 37% of their MRPs.

Sommers and Quinton[2] have assessed the economic fortunes of fourteen players who constituted the "first family" of free agents. In accordance with the predictions of labour market theory, their research indicates that the competitive bidding of free agency has brought the salaries of free agents more closely into accord with their estimated MRPs. The data for the five free-agent pitchers are shown in Table 2 where we find a surprisingly close correspondence between estimated MRPs and salaries. Although MRP and salary differences are larger for hitters, Sommers and Quinton conclude that the overturn of the monopsonistic reserve clause "has forced owners into a situation where there is a greater tendency to pay players in relation to their contribution to team revenues."

TABLE 2   Estimated marginal revenue products and player costs, 1977 (in U.S. dollars)

(1) Pitcher	(2) Marginal revenue product	(3) Annual contract cost*
Garland	$282,091	$230,000
Gullett	340,846	349,333
Fingers	303,511	332,000
Campbell	205,639	210,000
Alexander	166,203	166,667

*Includes annual salary, bonuses, the value of insurance policies and deferred payments, etc.
Source: Sommers and Quinton, op. cit., p. 432.

How have baseball team owners reacted to the escalating salaries under free agency? In early 1986 the players' union filed a grievance charging that the twenty-six professional baseball clubs had acted in concert against signing any of the players who became free agents in 1985. In fact, of the sixty-two players who became free agents in 1985, only two had signed contracts with a different team before the season began. In effect, the players charged that owners had attempted to restore some of the monopsony power they previously possessed. Such collusive action is illegal because it violates the collective bargaining agreement that exists between players and owners. In the fall of 1987 an arbitrator ruled that baseball owners had conspired to "destroy" the free-agent market, and in 1990 the courts in the U.S. ordered club owners to pay $102.5 million (U.S.) in lost salaries to players.

[1]Gerald W. Scully, "Pay and Performance in Major League Baseball," *American Economic Review*, December 1974, pp. 915-930.

[2]Paul M. Sommers and Noel Quinton, "Pay and Performance in Major League Baseball: The Case of the First Family of Free Agents," *Journal of Human Resources*, Summer 1982, pp. 426-435.

QUICK REVIEW (16-1)

1. **Real wages have increased historically in Canada because labour demand has increased relative to labour supply.**

2. **Real wages per worker have increased at approximately the same rate as worker productivity.**

3. **The competitive employer is a "wage taker" and employs workers at the point where the wage rate or MRC equals MRP.**

4. **The labour supply curve to a monopsonist is upsloping, causing MRC to exceed the wage rate for each worker. Other things being equal, the monopsonist will hire fewer workers and pay a lower wage rate than would a purely competitive employer.**

Some Union Models

Thus far, we have assumed that workers actively compete in the sale of their labour services. In some markets, workers collectively "sell" their labour services through unions. To see the economic impact of unions in the simplest context, let us first suppose a union is formed in an otherwise competitive labour market. A union is now bargaining with a relatively large number of employers.

Unions seek many goals. The basic economic objective, however, is to raise wage rates. The union can pursue this objective in several different ways.

Increasing the Demand for Labour   From the unions' viewpoint, the most desirable technique for raising wage rates is to increase the demand for labour. As shown in Figure 16-5, an increase in the demand for labour will result in *both* higher wage rates and more jobs. The relative size of these

FIGURE 16-5   Unions and the demand for labour

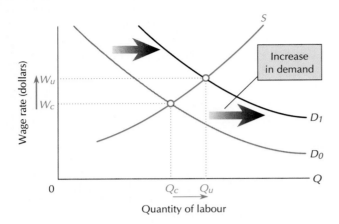

When unions can increase the demand for labour (D_0 to D_1), higher wage rates (W_c to W_u) and a larger number of jobs (Q_c to Q_u) can be realized.

increases will depend on the elasticity of labour supply.

A union might increase labour demand by altering one or more of the determinants of labour demand (Chapter 15). Specifically, a union can attempt to (1) increase the demand for the product or service it is producing, (2) enhance labour productivity, or (3) alter the prices of other inputs.

1 Increase Product Demand   Unions may attempt to increase the demand for the products they help produce — and hence increase the derived demand for their own labour services — by advertising or by political lobbying. Union television ads urging consumers to "buy the union label" are relevant. Historically, the International Ladies Garment Workers Union (ILGWU) has joined with its employers to finance advertising campaigns to bolster the demand for their products.

On the political front we see construction unions lobbying for new highway or urban renewal projects. Similarly, teachers' unions and associations push for increased public spending on education. And it is no accident that some unions have vigorously supported their employers in seeking protective tariffs or import quotas designed to exclude competing foreign products. The automobile workers have sought such protection. Thus, a decline in the supply of imported cars through tariffs or negotiated agreements between nations will increase their prices, thereby increasing the demand for North American–

made autos and boosting the derived demand for North American auto workers.

Some unions have sought to expand the demand for labour by forcing "make-work," or "featherbedding," rules on employers. It took a Canada-wide strike back in the 1950s before the railways were able to drop firemen from freight-yard diesels — firemen who had no fire to tend since the days of the steam locomotives.

2 Increase Productivity   While many decisions affecting labour productivity — for example, decisions concerning quantity and quality of real capital — are made unilaterally by management, there is a growing interest in establishing joint labour–management committees designed to increase labour productivity.

3 Increase Prices of Substitutes   Unions might enhance the demand for their own labour by increasing the prices of substitute resources. A good example is that unions — whose workers are generally paid significantly more than the minimum wage — strongly support increases in the minimum wage. An alleged reason for this position is that unions want to increase the price of potentially substitutable low-wage, nonunion labour. A higher minimum wage for nonunion workers will deter employers from substituting them for union workers, thereby bolstering the demand for union workers.

Unions can also increase the demand for their labour by supporting public actions that *reduce* the price of a complementary resource. For example, unions in industries that use large amounts of energy might actively oppose rate increases proposed by electric or natural gas utilities. Where labour and energy are complementary, energy price increases might reduce the demand for labour through the output effect.

Unions recognize that their capacity to influence the demand for labour is difficult and uncertain. As many of our illustrations imply, unions are frequently trying to forestall *declines* in labour demand rather than actually increasing it. In view of these considerations, it is not surprising that union efforts to increase wage rates have concentrated on the supply side of the market.

Exclusive, or Craft, Unionism   Unions may boost wage rates by reducing the supply of labour. Historically, organized labour has favoured policies designed to restrict the supply of labour to the economy as a whole to bolster the general level of wages. Labour unions have supported legislation that has (1) reduced child labour, (2) encouraged compulsory retirement, and (3) enforced a shorter work week. Labour unions have never been as enthusiastic about immigration as the Canadian Manufacturers Association and the Chamber of Commerce.

More relevant for present purposes is that specific types of workers have adopted, through unions, techniques designed to restrict their numbers. This is especially true of *craft unions* — unions that comprise workers of a given skill, such as electricians, carpenters, bricklayers, plumbers, and printers. These unions have frequently forced employers to agree to hire only union workers, giving the union virtually complete control of the supply of labour. Then, by following restrictive membership policies — long apprenticeships, exorbitant initiation fees, the limitation or flat prohibition of new members — the union causes an artificial restriction of the labour supply. As shown in Figure 16-6, this results in higher wage rates. This approach to achieving wage increases is called **exclusive unionism**. Higher wages are the result of excluding workers from the union and therefore from the supply of labour.

Occupational licensing is another widely used means of restricting the supplies of specific kinds of labour. Here a group of workers in an occupation will pressure provincial or municipal governments to pass a law to provide that, say, barbers (or physicians, lawyers, dentists, plumbers, beauticians, opticians, cinema projectionists) can practise their trade only if they meet certain specified requirements. These requirements might specify the level of education, amount of work experience, passing of an examination, and personal characteristics ("the practitioner must be of good moral character").

The licensing board administering the law is typically dominated by members of the licensed occupation. The result is self-regulation, conducive to policies that reflect self-interest. In short, imposing arbitrary and irrelevant entrance requirements or setting an unnecessarily stringent examination can restrict entrants to the occupation. Ostensibly, the purpose of licensing is to protect consumers from incompetent practitioners. But in fact, licensing laws are frequently abused in that the number of qualified workers is artificially restricted, resulting in above-competitive wages and earnings for those in the occupation (Figure 16-6). Furthermore, licensing requirements often specify a residency requirement that tends to inhibit the interprovincial movement of qualified workers. It is estimated that over two hundred occupations are now licensed in Canada.

FIGURE 16-6   Exclusive, or craft, unionism

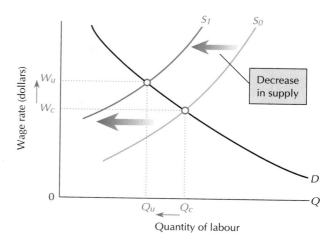

By reducing the supply of labour (S_0 to S_1) through the use of restrictive membership policies, exclusive unions achieve higher wage rates (W_c to W_u). However, the restriction of labour supply also reduces the number of workers employed (Q_c to Q_u).

Inclusive, or Industrial, Unionism   Most unions, however, do not attempt to limit their membership. On the contrary, they seek to organize all available or potential workers. This is characteristic of the so-called *industrial unions* — unions such as the automobile workers and steelworkers that seek as members all unskilled, semiskilled, and skilled workers in a given industry. A union can afford to be exclusive when its members are so highly skilled that substitute workers are not readily available in quantity. But a union that comprises largely unskilled and semi-skilled workers will undermine its own existence by limiting its membership, causing numerous highly substitutable nonunion workers to be readily available for employment.

If an industrial union includes virtually all workers in its membership, firms will be under great pressure to agree to the wage rate demanded by the union, because by going on strike, the union can deprive the firm of its entire labour supply.

Inclusive unionism is illustrated in Figure 16-7. Initially, the competitive equilibrium wage rate is W_c and the level of employment is Q_c. Now suppose an industrial union is formed, and it imposes a higher, above-equilibrium wage rate of, say, W_u. This wage rate changes the supply curve of labour to the firms from the pre-union S curve to the post-union $W_u aS$

FIGURE 16-7   Inclusive, or industrial, unionism

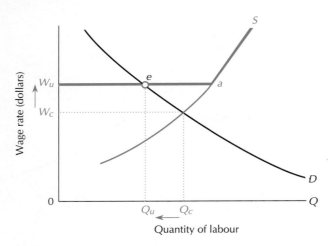

By organizing virtually all available workers and thereby controlling the supply of labour, inclusive industrial unions may impose a wage rate, such as W_u that is above the competitive wage rate, W_c. The effect is to change the labour supply curve from S to $W_u aS$. At the W_u wage rate, employers will cut employment from Q_c to Q_u.

curve, shown by the heavy line.[4] No workers will be forthcoming at a wage rate less than that demanded by the union. If employers decide it is better to pay this higher wage rate than to suffer a strike, they will cut back on employment from Q_c to Q_u.

By agreeing to the union's W_u wage demand, individual employers become "wage takers" at this wage and therefore face a perfectly elastic labour supply curve over the $W_u a$ range. Because labour supply is perfectly elastic, MRC is equal to the W_u wage over this range. The Q_u level of employment results from employers equating MRC ($= W_u$) with MRP, as embodied in the labour demand curve.

Note that at W_u there is an excess supply or surplus of labour in the amount ea. Without the union — in a purely competitive labour market — we expect these unemployed workers to accept lower wages and the wage rate would as a result fall to the

W_c competitive equilibrium level. But this doesn't happen, because workers are acting collectively through their union. Workers cannot individually offer to work for less than W_u; nor can employers contractually pay less.

Wage Increases and Unemployment

As Figures 16-6 and 16-7 suggest, the wage-raising actions of both exclusive and inclusive unionism cause employment to decline. A union's success in achieving above-equilibrium wage rates is tempered by the consequent decline in the number of workers employed. This unemployment effect can act as a restraining influence on union wage demands. A union cannot expect to maintain solidarity within its ranks if it seeks a wage rate so high that joblessness will result for, say, 20% or 30% of its members.

The unemployment impact of wage increases might be mitigated from the union's standpoint in two ways.

1. Growth   The normal growth of the economy increases the demand for most kinds of labour through time. Thus a rightward shift of the labour demand curves in Figures 16-6 and 16-7 could offset, or more than offset, any unemployment effects that would otherwise be associated with the indicated wage increases.

2. Elasticity   The size of the unemployment effect depends on the elasticity of demand for labour. The more inelastic the demand, the smaller will be the unemployment accompanying a given wage-rate increase. If unions have sufficient bargaining strength, they *may* obtain provisions in their collective bargaining agreements that reduce the substitutability of other inputs for labour and thereby reduce the elasticity of demand for union labour. For example, a union may force employer acceptance of rules blocking the introduction of new machinery and equipment. Or the union may bargain successfully for severance or layoff pay that increases the cost to the firm of substituting capital for labour when wage rates are increased. Similarly, the union might gain a contract provision that prohibits the firm from subcontracting production to nonunion (lower-wage) firms, effectively restricting the substitution of less expensive labour for union workers. For these and other reasons, the unemployment restraint on union wage demands may be less pressing than our exclusive and inclusive union models suggest.

---

[4] Technically, the wage rate W_u makes the labour supply curve perfectly elastic over the $W_u a$ range in Figure 16-7. If employers hire any number of workers in this range, the union-imposed wage rate is effective and must be paid, or the union will supply no labour at all — the employers will be faced with a strike. If employers want a number of workers over $W_u a$, they will have to bid up wages above the union's minimum. This will only occur if the market demand curve for labour shifts rightward so that it intersects the aS range of the labour supply curve.

Bilateral Monopoly Model

Suppose now that a strong industrial union is formed in a labour market that is monopsonistic, rather than competitive. In other words, we combine the monopsony model with the inclusive unionism model. The result is **bilateral monopoly**. The union is a monopolistic "seller" of labour, in that it controls the labour supply and can exert an influence over wage rates. It faces a monopsonistic employer (or combination of oligopsonistic employers) of labour, who can also affect wages by altering their employment. This is not an extreme or special case. In such important industries as steel, automobiles, meat-packing, and farm machinery, "big labour" — one huge industrial union — bargains with "big business" — a few huge industrial giants.

Indeterminant Outcome This situation is shown in Figure 16-8, which merely superimposes Figure 16-7 on 16-4. The monopsonistic employer will seek the below-competitive equilibrium wage rate W_m, and the union presumably will press for some above-competitive equilibrium wage rate such as W_u. Which of these two possibilities will result? We cannot say with certainty. The outcome is indeterminate, since economic theory does not explain what the resulting wage rate will be. We should expect the resulting wage to lie somewhere between W_m and W_u. Beyond that, all we can say is that the party with the most bargaining power and the most effective bargaining strategy will be able to get its opponent to agree to a wage close to the one it seeks.

Desirability These comments suggest another important feature of the bilateral monopoly model. It is possible that the wage and employment outcomes might be more socially desirable than the term bilateral monopoly would imply. Monopoly on one side of the market *might* in effect cancel out the monopoly on the other side of the market, yielding competitive or near-competitive results. If either the union or management prevailed in this market — if the actual wage rate were determined at either W_u or W_m — employment would be restricted to Q_m (where MRP = MRC), which is below the competitive level. But now suppose that the countervailing power of the union roughly offsets the original monopsony power of management, and that a bargained wage rate of about W_c, which is the competitive wage, is agreed upon. Once management agrees to this wage rate, its incentive to restrict employment disappears; no longer can the employer depress wage rates by restricting employment. Thus management equates

FIGURE 16-8 Bilateral monopoly in the labour market

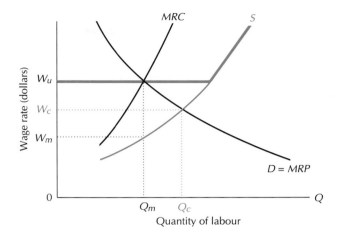

When a monopsonistic employer seeks the wage rate W_m and the inclusive union it faces seeks an above-equilibrium wage rate such as W_u, the actual outcome is logically indeterminate.

the bargained wage rate W_c (= MRC) with MRP and finds it most profitable to hire Q_c workers.

The Minimum-Wage Controversy

Both the federal and provincial governments have enacted **minimum wage** legislation. In 1992 the minimum wage was $4.00 an hour at the federal level. Roughly 80% of all nonsupervisory workers are covered. Our analysis of the effects of union wage-fixing raises the much-debated question of how effective minimum-wage legislation is as an anti-poverty device.

Case Against the Minimum Wage Critics, reasoning in terms of Figure 16-7, contend that the imposition of effective (above-equilibrium) minimum wages will simply push employers back up their MRP or labour demand curves because it is now profitable to hire fewer workers. The higher wage costs may even force some firms out of business. The result is that some of the poor, low-wage workers, whom the minimum wage was designed to help, will now find themselves out of work. Critics say that a worker who is unemployed at a minimum wage of $4.50 per hour is clearly worse off than if he or she were employed at the market wage rate of $4.00 per hour.

Case For the Minimum Wage Advocates allege that critics have analysed the impact of the minimum wage in an unrealistic context. Figure 16-7 presumes a competitive and static market. The imposition of a minimum wage in a monopsonistic labour market (Figure 16-8) suggests that the minimum wage can increase wage rates without causing unemployment. Indeed, higher minimum wages may even result in more jobs by eliminating the monopsonistic employer's motive to restrict employment. Furthermore, the imposition of an effective minimum wage may increase labour productivity, shifting the labour demand curve to the right and offsetting any unemployment effects the minimum wage might otherwise induce.

But how might a minimum wage increase productivity? First, a minimum wage may have a *shock effect* on employers. Firms using low-wage workers may be inefficient in the use of labour; the higher wage rates imposed by the minimum wage will presumably shock these firms into using labour more efficiently, and so the productivity of labour rises. Second, it is argued that higher wages will increase the incomes, and therefore the health and motivation of workers, making them more productive.

Evidence Which view is correct? The consensus from the many research studies of the minimum wage is that it does cause some unemployment, particularly among teenage workers (16–19 years of age). It is estimated that the minimum wage reduced teenage employment opportunities by 15% in Canada. Young adults (age 20–24) are also adversely affected; a 10% increase in the minimum wage increased unemployment by 2.5 to 3.5 percentage points for young men and 1.5 to 3.0 percentage points for young women. Older women, who are disproportionately represented in low-wage occupations, suffer larger declines in employment than do men. The other side of the coin is that those who remain employed receive higher incomes and tend to escape poverty. The overall anti-poverty effect of the minimum wage may thus be a mixed, ambivalent one. Those who lose their jobs are forced into the unemployment and social assistance systems; those who remain employed tend to escape poverty.

WAGE DIFFERENTIALS

We now consider differences that persist between different occupations and different individuals in the same occupations. Why does a corporate executive or professional athlete receive $300,000, $500,000, or even $1,000,000 a year while laundry workers get a paltry $14,000 a year? Why is the average annual salary $891,000 for major-league baseball players, as compared with $43,000 for acute-care nurses and $45,000 for school teachers? What rationale lies behind Chrysler Corporation paying its chairman, Lee Iacocca, total compensation of over $23 million in 1987? Table 16-3 shows the substantial **wage differentials** that exist among certain common occupation groups. Our objective is to gain some insight as to why these differentials exist.

Once again, the forces of supply and demand provide a general answer. If the supply of a particular type of labour is very great in relation to the demand for it, the wage rate will be low. But if demand is great and the supply relatively small, wages will be very high. But we want to discover *why* supply and demand conditions differ in various labour markets. To do this, we must probe those factors that lie behind the supply and demand of particular types of labour.

If (1) all workers were homogeneous, (2) all jobs were equally attractive to workers, and (3) labour markets were perfectly competitive, all workers would receive precisely the same wage rate. This is not a particularly startling statement. It suggests that in an economy having one type of labour and, in effect, one type of job, competition would result in a single wage rate for all workers. The statement is important in that it suggests reasons wage rates do differ in practice. (1) Workers are not homogeneous. They differ in innate abilities and in training and, as a result, they fall into noncompeting occupational groups. (2) Jobs vary in attractiveness; the nonmonetary aspects of various jobs are not the same. (3) Labour markets are typically characterized by imperfections.

Noncompeting Groups

Workers are not homogeneous; they differ significantly in their mental and physical capacities *and* in their education and training. At any point in time the labour force can be thought of as falling into many **noncompeting groups**, each of which may be composed of one or several occupations for which the members of this group qualify.

Ability A relatively small number of people have the inherent abilities to be brain surgeons, concert violinists, research chemists, or professional athletes. The result is that the supplies of these particular types

TABLE 16-3   Average hourly wages in selected industries, April 1992

Industry	Average hourly earnings (paid by the hour)
Goods producing industries	$16.49
Service producing industries	12.27
Logging & forestry	20.11
Mining, quarrying, & oil wells	21.95
Manufacturing	15.54
Construction	17.74
Transportation, communication, & other utilities	17.32
Trade	10.62
Finance, insurance, & real estate	11.26
Community business, & personal service	12.55
Industrial aggregate	13.84

Source: Statistics Canada, *Employment, Earnings, and Hours, April 1992* (Ottawa, July 1992).

of labour are very small in relation to the demand for them and consequently wages and salaries are high. These and similar groups do not compete with one another nor with other skilled or semiskilled workers. The violinist does not compete with the surgeon, nor does the laundry worker compete with either the violinist or the surgeon.

The concept of noncompeting groups is a flexible one; it can be applied to various subgroups and even to specific individuals in a given group. Some especially skilled lawyers are able to command fees considerably in excess of their run-of-the-mill colleagues. Wayne Gretzky and a few others demand and get salaries many times higher than the average professional hockey player. In each instance their less-talented colleagues are only imperfect substitutes.

Investing in Human Capital: Education
Noncompeting groups — and therefore wage differentials — also exist because of differing amounts of investment in human capital. A **human capital investment** refers to expenditures on education and training that improve the skills or, in other words, the productivity, of workers. Like business purchases of machinery and equipment, expenditures that increase one's productivity can be regarded as investments because *current* expenditures or costs are incurred with the intention that these costs will

be more than compensated for by an enhanced *future* flow of earnings.

Figure 16-9 indicates, first, that individuals with larger investments in education do achieve higher incomes during their work careers than those who have made smaller education investments. A second point is that the earnings of more-educated workers rise more rapidly than those of less-educated workers. The primary reason for this is that more-educated workers usually get more on-the-job training.

Although education yields higher incomes, it also entails costs. For example, a university education entails not only direct costs (tuition, fees, books) but also indirect or opportunity costs (forgone earnings). Question: Does the higher pay received by more-educated workers compensate for these costs? The answer is "yes." Rates of return have recently been estimated to be 10 to 13% for investing in a secondary education and 8 to 10% for higher education.

Equalizing Differences

If a group of workers in a particular noncompeting group is equally capable of performing several different jobs, one might expect that the wage rate would be identical for each of these jobs. But this is not the case. A group of high school graduates may be equally capable of becoming bank clerks or unskilled construction workers. But these jobs pay

FIGURE 16-9   Educational levels and family income, 1987

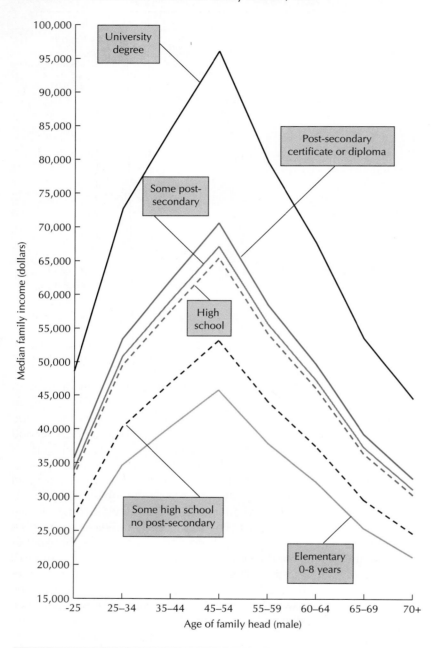

Investment in education yields a return in the form of an income differential enjoyed throughout one's work life. *Source:* Statistics Canada, *Income Distribution by Size in Canada, 1990* (Ottawa, 1991).

different wages. In virtually all localities, construction labourers receive higher wages than do bank clerks.

These differences can be explained on the basis of the *nonmonetary aspects* of the two jobs. The construction job involves dirty hands, a potentially sore back, the hazard of accidents, and irregular employment, both seasonally and cyclically. The banking job usually means physical comfort, pleasant air-conditioned surroundings, and little fear of injury or layoff. Other things being equal, it is easy to see why workers would rather pick up a deposit slip than a shovel. The result is that construction contractors must pay higher wages than banks to compensate for the unattractive, nonmonetary aspects of construction jobs. These wage differentials are called **equal-**

Box 16-2

In the Media

Earlier it was noted that salaries of baseball players increased significantly after players were able to become "free agents." The following article argues that in the NHL the breaking of the ranks by one of the owners (in effect, the disintegration of a monopsony situation) set the stage for rapidly escalating salaries for the top stars, probably to be followed by similar increases for ordinary rank and file players.

NHL OWNERS HAVE SEEN ONLY TIP OF SPIRALING SALARY ICEBERG

Al Strachan
Calgary

Any reader of the sports pages knows that salary levels have skyrocketed lately in both hockey and baseball.

But it would be wrong to simply assume that, as a result, players of both sports are vastly overpaid. Each game has followed a different line of development and the two should not be equated.

In baseball, the mega-salaries are little more than the continuation of a trend that began in the mid-seventies when Andy Messersmith and Dave McNally defeated the owners in court. (Curt Flood was the first to successfully challenge the reserve clause, but it was McNally and Messersmith who used their legal triumphs to exact substantial salary increases.)

Since then, the power of the owners has been consistently eroded by the lawyers, and player salaries have leap-frogged into the stratosphere.

Hockey, however, is a different story. It was not until 1989 that the top-line players suddenly began to be granted large salary increases and the development came about not because of legal challenges, but because one of the owners broke ranks and actually told the truth.

When Los Angeles Kings owner Bruce McNall bought Wayne Gretzky from the Edmonton Oilers for $15 million (U.S.), he was quick to announce that he felt he had picked up a bargain. Once the early returns proved his prescience, he immediately rewarded Gretzky with a new salary.

In keeping with hockey precedent, Gretzky said he felt he was already earning enough, thank you very much. McNall begged to differ and boosted Gretzky's salary by about 33 per cent into the $3-million range.

Suddenly, the price of quality hockey players went up. Many stars saw their salaries double. Others saw them triple. Some did better still. Brett Hull's salary was increased tenfold as he went from $125,000 in 1989-90 to $1.166 million (plus a $600,000 signing bonus) in 1990-91. This year, Hull will earn $1.5-million.

Others whose salaries increased by at least 100 per cent around the same time included Brian Bellows, Ray Bourque, Paul Coffey, Kevin Hatcher, Steve Larmer, Al MacInnis, Cam Neely, James Patrick, Patrick Roy, Scott Stevens and Rick Tocchet.

By permission of *The Globe & Mail*, December 27, 1991.

izing differences, because they must be paid to compensate for nonmonetary differences in various jobs.

Market Imperfections

Market imperfections, in the form of various immobilities, help explain wage differences paid on identical jobs. These imperfections can be divided into the following categories.

1 Geographic Immobilities   Workers are generally reluctant to leave friends, relatives, and associates, to force their children to change schools, and to incur the costs and inconveniences of adjusting to a new job and a new community. Geographic mobility is likely to be particularly low for older workers with seniority rights and substantial claims to pension payments on retirement. Similarly, an optometrist or dental hygienist who is qualified to practise in one province may not meet the licensing requirements of other provinces, and therefore his or her ability to move geographically is impeded. Language can be a barrier into and out of Quebec. Also, workers who may be willing to move may simply be ignorant of job opportunities and wage rates in other areas. As Adam Smith noted more than two centuries ago, "A man is of all sorts of luggage the most difficult to be transported." The reluctance or inability of workers to move slows down the rate at which geographic wage differentials for the same occupations narrow.

2 Institutional Immobilities   Geographic immobilities may be reinforced by artificial restrictions on mobility imposed by institutions. We have noted that craft unions find it to their advantage to restrict membership. After all, if carpenters and bricklayers become plentiful, the wages they can command will decline. Thus the low-paid, nonunion carpenter of Epsom, Ontario, may be willing to move to Edmonton in the pursuit of higher wages. But his chances of successfully doing so are slim. He will probably be unable to get a union card — and no card, no job. The professions impose similar artificial restraints. For example, at most universities individuals lacking advanced degrees are simply not considered for employment as professors.

3 Sociological Immobilities   Finally, we must acknowledge sociological immobilities. Despite regulatory legislation to the contrary, women workers frequently receive less pay than men on the same job. The consequence of racial discrimination is that recent immigrants historically have been forced to accept lower wages on given jobs than native-born Canadians. The economic effects of discrimination will be analysed below in the context of the "crowding hypothesis."

A final point: Usually all three of these considerations — noncompeting groups, equalizing differences, and market imperfections — will play a role in the explanation of actual wage differentials. For example, the differential between the wages of a physician and a construction worker is largely explainable on the basis of noncompeting groups. Physicians fall into a noncompeting group where, because of certain abilities and financial requisites to entry, the supply of labour is small in relation to demand, and wages are therefore high. In construction work, where intellectual and financial prerequisites are much less significant, the supply of labour is great in relation to demand, and wages are low compared to those of physicians. However, were it not for certain unattractive features of the construction

worker's job and the fact that craft unions pursue restrictive membership policies, the differential would probably be even greater.

QUICK REVIEW (16-2)

1. **Unions may achieve above-equilibrium wage rates by increasing labour demand, restricting supply (exclusive unionism), or by bargaining (inclusive unionism).**

2. **Bilateral monopoly occurs where a monopsonist bargains with an inclusive union. Wages and employment are indeterminant in this situation.**

3. **Proponents of the minimum wage argue that it is an effective means of assisting the working poor; critics contend that it is poorly targeted and causes unemployment.**

4. **Wage differentials are attributable in part to differences in worker abilities and education, nonmonetary differences in jobs, and market imperfections.**

PAY AND PERFORMANCE

The models of wage determination presented in this chapter presume that worker compensation is always in the form of a standard hourly wage rate. In fact, pay schemes are often more complex in composition and purpose. For example, many workers receive annual salaries rather than hourly pay. Also, pay plans are frequently designed by employers to elicit some desired level of performance by workers.

The Principal–Agent Problem

Firms hire workers because they help produce goods or services that firms can sell for a profit. Workers may be thought of as the firm's *agents* — hired to advance the interests of the firm. Similarly, firms may be regarded as *principals* or parties who hire others (agents) to help them achieve their goals. Principals and their agents have a common interest. The principal's (firm's) objective is profits, and agents (workers) are willing to help firms earn profits in return for payments of wage income.

But the interests of firms and workers are not identical. When these interests diverge, a so-called **principal–agent problem** arises. Agents might increase their utility by **shirking** on the job — providing less than agreed-upon worker effort or by taking unau-thorized work breaks. The security guard in a ware-house may leave work early or spend time reading a novel as opposed to making the assigned rounds. A salaried manager may spend much time out of the office, looking after personal interests, rather than attending to urgent company business.

Firms (principals) have a profit incentive to reduce or eliminate shirking. There are essentially two means of accomplishing this. One option is to moni-tor workers. But monitoring is often difficult and costly. Hiring another worker to monitor our security guard might double the costs of having a secure warehouse. The other means of resolving a princi-pal–agent problem is through the creation of some sort of **incentive pay plan** that ties worker compen-sation more closely to worker output or perform-ance. Such incentive pay schemes include piece rates, commissions and royalties, and bonuses and profit sharing.

Piece Rates   *Piece rates* are compensation paid in proportion to the number of units an individual pro-duces. By paying fruit pickers by the bushel and typ-ists by the page, the principal need not be concerned with shirking or monitoring costs.

Commissions and Royalties   Commissions and royalties tie pay to the *value* of sales. Realtors, insur-ance agents, stockbrokers, and retail salespersons commonly receive *commissions* based on the mone-tary value of their sales. *Royalties* are paid to record-ing artists and authors based on a certain percentage of sales revenue.

Bonuses and Profit-sharing   *Bonuses* are pay-ments beyond one's annual salary based on some factor such as individual or firm performance. A pro-fessional baseball player may receive bonuses for a high batting average, the number of home runs, or the number of runs batted in. A manager may receive bonuses based on the profit performance of his or her unit. *Profit-sharing* allocates a specified percent-age of a firm's profits to its employees.

Seniority Pay   It is widely observed that wages and earnings increase with job tenure. One recent expla-nation of this is that it is advantageous to both work-ers and employers to pay junior workers less than their MRPs and senior workers more than their MRPs. This theory of *seniority pay* may be an inexpensive way of reducing shirking when monitoring costs are high. Workers are discouraged from shirking because detection will mean forgoing the high seniority pay

accruing in later years of employment. From the firm's standpoint, turnover is reduced because work-ers who quit will forfeit the high seniority pay. The increased productivity of workers is the source of extra sales revenue from which the firm and the workers, respectively, enhance their profits and life-time pay. Young workers accept wages that are ini-tially less than their MRPs for the opportunity to participate in a labour market where in time the reverse will be true. The increased work effort and higher average productivity are appealing to the workers because they are the source of higher life-time earnings.

Efficiency Wages   The notion of *efficiency wages* suggests that employers might get greater effort from their workers by paying them relatively high, above-equilibrium wage rates. Glance back at Figure 16-3 for a competitive labour market where the equilib-rium wage rate is $6. What if an employer decided to pay an above-equilibrium wage of $7 per hour? Rather than put the firm at a cost disadvantage in comparison to rival firms that are paying only $6, the higher wage *might* improve worker effort and pro-ductivity so that unit labour costs actually fall. For example, if each worker produces 10 units of output per hour at the $7 wage rate as compared to only 6 units at the $6 wage rate, unit labour costs will be only $.70 (= $7 ÷ 10) for the high-wage firm as opposed to $1.00 (= $6 ÷ 6) for firms paying the equilibrium wage.

An above-equilibrium wage might enhance worker efficiency in several ways. The higher wage permits the firm to attract higher quality workers. Worker morale should be higher. Turnover will be reduced, resulting in both a more experienced work-force and lower recruitment and training costs. Because the opportunity cost of losing a high-wage job is greater, workers are likely to put forth their best efforts with less supervision and monitoring.

Equilibrium Revisited

Labour market equilibrium is often more complex than the simple determination of wage rates and employment (Figures 16-3 through 16-8). When prin-cipal–agent problems involving shirking and moni-toring costs arise, decisions must also be made with respect to the most effective compensation scheme. When we recognize that work effort and productivity are related to the form of worker compensation, the choice of pay plan is not a matter of indifference to either employer or employee.

MORE ON THE ECONOMIC EFFECTS OF UNIONS

Are the economic effects of labour unions positive or negative? We will address this important issue by examining several questions: Do unions raise wages? Do they increase or diminish economic efficiency? Do they make the distribution of earnings more or less equal? There is considerable uncertainty and debate about the answers to these questions.

The Union Wage Advantage

Our union models (Figure 16-5, 16-6, and 16-7) all imply that unions have the capacity to raise wage rates. Has unionization in fact caused wage rates to be higher than otherwise?

Empirical research quite overwhelmingly suggests that *unions do raise the wages of their members relative to comparable nonunion workers*, although the size of the union wage advantage varies according to occupation, industry, race, and sex. There is also evidence to suggest that the union wage advantage increased in the 1970s. Thus, research suggests that over the 1923–58 period the average union–nonunion pay difference was about 10% to 15%. More recent studies indicate that the difference widened to 20% to 30% in the 1970s. Note that these are average differentials and that there is considerable variation among industries and occupations. Furthermore, recent wage freezes and pay cuts ("givebacks") may have diminished the 20% to 30% advantage in the early 1980s. Labour economists have speculated that the union wage advantage may have returned to the 10%–15% range by the end of the 1980s.

These estimates of the union wage advantage are understated because union workers enjoy substantially larger *fringe benefits* than do nonunion workers. Union workers are more likely to have private pensions, dental insurance, and paid vacations and sick leaves than are nonunion workers. Moreover, unionized workers have the company paying their public health insurance premiums in the provinces that charge them. Where such benefits are available to both union and nonunion workers, their magnitude is greater for the union workers. Thus the total compensation (wage rates plus fringe benefits) advantage of union workers is greater than the previously indicated 10% to 15%.

There is also general agreement that **unions have probably had little or no impact on the average level of real wages received by labour — both organized and unorganized — taken as a whole**. At first glance these two conclusions — that unions gain a wage advantage but do not affect the average level of real wages — may seem inconsistent. But they need not be if the wage gains of organized workers are at the expense of unorganized workers. Higher wages in unionized labour markets may cause employers to move back up their labour demand curves and hire fewer workers. These unemployed workers may seek employment in nonunion labour markets. The resulting increase in the supply of labour will depress wage rates in these nonunion markets. The net result may well be no change in the average level of wages. Indeed, the tight relationship between productivity and the average level of real wages, shown in Figure 16-1, correctly suggests that unions have little power to raise real wage rates for labour as a whole. But Figure 16-1 is an average relationship and is therefore compatible with certain groups of (union) workers getting higher relative wages if other (nonunion) workers are simultaneously getting lower real wages.

Efficiency and Productivity

Are unions a positive or a negative force insofar as economic efficiency and productivity are concerned? How do unions affect the allocation of resources? While there is much disagreement about the efficiency aspects of unions, it is instructive to consider some of the ways unions might affect efficiency both negatively and positively. We will consider the negative view first.

Negative View   There are essentially three basic means by which unions might exert a negative impact on efficiency.

1 Featherbedding and Work Rules   Some unions have undoubtedly diminished productivity growth by engaging in make-work or featherbedding practices and resisting the introduction of output-increasing machinery and equipment. These productivity-reducing practices often come into being against a backdrop of technological change. Labour and management may agree to a team size that is reasonable and appropriate at the time the agreement is concluded, but labour-saving technology may then emerge that renders the team too large. The union is likely to resist the potential loss of jobs. For example, union painters sometimes refused to use spray guns and in some instances limited the width of paint brushes. In more recent years, the typographer unions resisted the introduction of computers in setting type. Historically, the musicians' union insisted on oversized orchestras for musical shows and required that a union standby orchestra be paid by employers using nonunion orchestras.

More generally, one can argue that unions are responsible for the establishment of work rules and practices that are inimical to efficient production. For example, under seniority rules workers may be promoted in accordance with their employment tenure, rather than in terms of who can perform the available job with the greatest efficiency. Also, unions may impose jurisdictional restrictions on the kinds of jobs workers may perform. For example, sheet-metal workers or bricklayers may be prohibited from performing the simple carpentry work that is often associated with their jobs. Observance of such rules means, in this instance, that unneeded and underutilized carpenters must be available. Finally, it is often contended that unions constrain managerial prerogatives to establish work schedules, determine production targets, and to make freely the decisions contributing to productive efficiency.

2 Strikes A second means by which unions may adversely affect efficiency is through strikes. If union and management reach an impasse in their negotiations, a strike will result and the firm's production will cease for the strike's duration. The firm will forgo sales and profits and workers will sacrifice income.

Statistics on strike activity suggest that strikes are relatively rare and that the associated aggregate economic losses are relatively minimal. While currently an estimated 9,000 collective bargaining agreements are in effect, the number of main work stoppages (more than 500 employees) in 1989 was 67. Furthermore, most of these strikes lasted only a few days. The average amount of work-time lost each year because of strikes is only about one-fifth of 1% of total work-time. This loss is the equivalent of four hours per worker per year, which is less than five minutes per worker per week!

3 Labour Misallocation A third and more subtle avenue through which unions might adversely affect efficiency is the union wage advantage itself. Figure 16-10 is instructive. Here we have drawn (for simplicity's sake) identical labour demand curves for the unionized and nonunion sectors of the labour market for some particular kind of labour. Our discussion assumes pure competition in both product and resource markets. If there were no union present initially, then the wage rate that would result from the competitive hire of labour would be, say, W_n. We now assume a union comes into being in sector 1 and succeeds in increasing the wage rate from W_n to W_u. As a consequence, N_1N_2 workers lose their jobs in the

union sector. Assume they all move to nonunion sector 2 where they secure employment. This increase in labour supply in the nonunion sector depresses the wage rate from W_n to W_s.

Recall that the labour demand curves reflect the marginal revenue products (MRPs) of workers or, in other words, the contributions that workers make to the domestic output. This means that the coloured area $A + B + C$ in the union sector represents the *decrease* in domestic output caused by the N_1N_2 employment decline in that sector. This $A + B + C$ area is the sum of the MRPs — the total contribution to domestic output — of the workers displaced by the W_n to W_u wage increase achieved by the union. Similarly, the re-employment of these workers in nonunion sector 2 results in an *increase* in domestic output indicated by the coloured area $D + E$. Because area $A + B + C$ exceeds area $D + E$, there is a net loss of domestic output. More precisely, because $A = D$ and $C = E$, the *net* loss attributable to the union wage advantage is equal to area B. Since the same amount of employed labour is now producing a smaller output, labour is clearly being misallocated and inefficiently used.

Attempts to estimate the output loss due to the allocative inefficiency associated with union wage gains suggest that the loss is relatively small. A pioneering study, assumed a 15% union wage advantage and estimated that approximately 0.14% — only about one-seventh of 1% — of the domestic output was lost! A more recent estimate indicates that union monopoly wage gains cost the United States economy 0.2% to 0.4% of gross domestic product. In Canadian terms, in 1991 this amounted to $1.35 billion to $2.7 billion, or $50 to $100 per person.

Positive View Others take the position that, on balance, unions make a positive contribution to productivity and efficiency.

1 Managerial Performance: The Shock Effect The *shock effect* is the idea that a wage increase, imposed by a union in this instance, may induce affected firms to adopt improved production and personnel methods and thereby become more efficient. One may carry Figure 16-10's analysis of labour misallocation one step further and argue that the union wage advantage will prompt union firms to *accelerate* the substitution of capital for labour and *hasten* the search for cost-reducing (productivity-increasing) technologies. When faced with higher production costs due to the union wage advantage, employers will be pushed to reduce costs by using more machinery and by seeking improved produc-

FIGURE 16-10 **The effect of the union wage advantage on the allocation of labour**

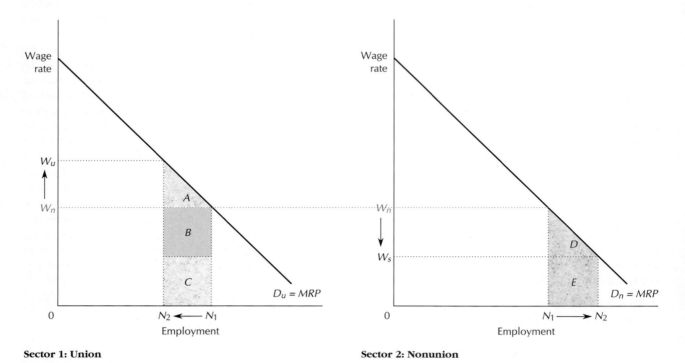

Sector 1: Union   **Sector 2: Nonunion**

The higher wage W_u that the union achieves in sector 1 causes the displacement of N_1N_2 workers. The re-employment of these workers in nonunion sector 2 reduces the wage rate there from W_n to W_s. The associated loss of output in the union sector is area $A + B + C$, while the gain in the nonunion sector is only area $D + E$. Hence, the net loss of output is equal to area B. The union wage advantage has obviously resulted in the misallocation of labour and a decline in economic efficiency.

tion techniques using less of both labour and capital per unit of output. In fact, if the product market is reasonably competitive, a unionized firm with labour costs that are, say, 10% to 15% higher than those of nonunion competitors will simply not survive unless productivity can be raised. Thus, union wage pressure may inadvertently generate managerial actions that increase national productivity.

2 Reduced Worker Turnover Unions may also contribute to rising productivity within firms through their effects on worker turnover and worker security. Unions function as a **collective voice** for members in resolving disputes and improving working conditions. If a group of workers is dissatisfied with its conditions of employment, it has two potential means of response. These are the "exit mechanism" and the "voice mechanism."

The **exit mechanism** simply refers to the use of the labour market — leave or exit your present job in search of a better one — as a means of reacting to

"bad" employers and "bad" working conditions.

In contrast, the **voice mechanism** entails communication by workers with the employer to improve working conditions and resolve worker grievances. It might be risky for *individual* workers to express their dissatisfaction to employers because employers may retaliate by firing them as "troublemakers." But unions can provide workers with a *collective* voice to communicate problems and grievances to management and to press for their satisfactory resolution.

More specifically, unions may help reduce worker turnover in two ways.

1. Unions provide the voice mechanism as a substitute for the exit mechanism. Unions are effective in correcting job dissatisfactions that would otherwise be "resolved" by workers through the exit mechanism of changing jobs.

2. The union wage advantage is a deterrent to job changes. Higher wages make unionized firms more attractive places to work. Several studies suggest that the decline in quit rates attributable to unionism is substantial, ranging from 31% to 65%.

A lower quit rate increases efficiency in several ways. First, lower turnover means a more experienced and, hence, more productive labour force. Second, fewer quits reduce the firm's recruitment, screening, and hiring costs. Finally, reduced turnover makes employers more willing to invest in the training (and therefore the productivity) of their workers. If a worker quits or "exits" at the end of, say, a year's training, the employer will get no return from the higher worker productivity attributable to that training. Lower turnover increases the likelihood that employers will receive a return on any training they provide, thereby making them more willing to upgrade their labour forces.

3 Seniority and Informal Training   Much productivity-increasing training is transmitted informally. More-skilled workers may explain their functions to less-skilled workers on the job, during lunch, or during a coffee break. However, a more-skilled senior worker may want to conceal his or her knowledge from less-skilled junior workers *if* the latter can become competitive for the former's job. Because of union insistence on the primacy of seniority in such matters as promotion and layoff, worker security is enhanced. Given this security, senior workers will be more willing to pass on their job knowledge and skills to new or subordinate workers. This informal training enhances the quality and productivity of the firm's work force.

Mixed Research Findings   A relatively large number of studies have measured the impact of unionization on productivity. These studies attempt to control for differences in labour quality, the amount of capital equipment used per worker, and other factors aside from unionization that might contribute to productivity differences. Unfortunately, the evidence from the studies is inconclusive. For every study that finds a positive union effect on productivity, another study concludes that there is a negative effect. All we can say is that at present there is no generally accepted conclusion regarding the overall impact of unions on labour productivity.

Distribution of Earnings

Labour unions envision themselves as institutions that enhance economic equality. Do unions in fact reduce the inequality with which earnings are distributed? The most convincing evidence suggests that unions do reduce earnings inequality.

Increasing Inequality   Some economists use Figure 16-10's analysis of labour misallocation to conclude that unions increase earnings inequality. They contend that in the absence of the union, competition would bring wages into equality at W_n in these two sectors or submarkets. But the higher union wage realized in sector 1 displaces workers who seek re-employment in the nonunion sector. In so doing they depress nonunion wages. Instead of wage equality at W_m, we have higher wage rates of W_u for union workers and lower wages of W_s for nonunion workers. The impact of the union is clearly to increase earnings inequality. Furthermore, the fact that unionization is more extensive among the more highly skilled, higher-paid blue-collar workers than among less-skilled, lower-paid blue-collar workers also suggests that the obtaining of a wage advantage by unions increases dispersion of earnings.

Promoting Equality   There are other aspects of union wage policies that suggest that unionism promotes greater, not less, equality in the distribution of earnings.

1 Uniform Wages Within Firms   In the absence of unions, employers are apt to pay different wages to individual workers on the same job. These wage differences are based on perceived differences in job performance, length of job tenure, and, perhaps, favouritism. Unions traditionally seek uniform wage rates for all workers performing a particular job. While nonunion firms tend to assign wage rates to *individual workers*, unions — in the interest of worker allegiance and solidarity — seek to assign wage rates to *jobs*. To the extent that unions are successful, wage and earnings differentials based upon supervisory judgments of individual worker performance are eliminated. An important side effect of this standard-wage policy is that wage discrimination against minorities and women is likely to be less when a union is present.

2 Uniform Wages Among Firms   In addition to seeking standard wage rates for given occupational classes *within* firms, unions also seek standard wage rates *among* firms. The rationale is that the existence of substantial wage differences among competing firms may undermine the ability of unions to sustain and enhance wage advantages.

For example, if one firm in a four-firm oligopoly is allowed to pay significantly lower wages to its union workers, the union is likely to find it difficult to maintain the union wage advantage in the other three firms. In particular, during a recession the high-wage firms are likely to put great pressure on the union to lower wages to the level of the low-wage firm. To avoid this kind of problem, unions seek to "take wages out of competition" by standardizing wage rates among firms, thereby reducing the degree of wage dispersion.

What is the *net* effect of unions on the distribution of earnings? Although the issue remains controversial, one authoritative study concluded that the wage effects indicated in Figure 16-10 *increase* earnings inequality by about 1%, but the standardization of wage rates within and among firms *decreases* inequality by about 4%. The net result is a 3% decline in earnings inequality due to unions. Because about a third of the labour force is unionized, this 3% reduction in inequality is substantial.

QUICK REVIEW (16-3)

1. **Union workers receive wage rates 10 to 15% higher than comparable nonunion workers.**

2. **Union work rules, strikes, and the misallocation of labour associated with the union wage advantage are means by which unions may reduce efficiency.**

3. **Unions may enhance productivity through the shock effect, by reducing worker turnover, and by providing the worker security prerequisite to informal on-the-job training.**

4. **On balance, unions probably reduce wage inequality by achieving wage uniformity within and among firms.**

THE ECONOMICS OF DISCRIMINATION

Discrimination — gender, ethnic, and racial — is a market imperfection that contributes to wage differentials. A society ought to eliminate all types of discrimination not only for reasons of moral justice, but for efficiency as well.

Occupational Segregation: The Crowding Model

Studies of **occupational discrimination** against women single out the importance of job segregation — male–female occupational differences that reflect deeply ingrained attitudes about the labour market

characteristics and capabilities of women. More specifically, the **crowding model** asserts that occupational discrimination has crowded women workers into a limited number of occupations, causing labour supply to be great relative to demand and therefore wage rates and incomes to be low.

Though racial and ethnic discrimination also exists in Canada, our stress here is on discrimination against women because of their already very great and continuously growing importance in the labour force. As Table 16-4 reveals, women make up almost 45% of our labour force, the **female participation rate** having doubled to 58% since 1961.

Crowding: A Simple Model The character and consequences of occupational discrimination can be revealed through a simple supply and demand model. We make three simplifying assumptions.

1. The labour force is equally divided between male and female workers. Let's say there are six million male and six million female workers.

2. The economy comprises three occupations, each having identical labour demand curves, as shown in Figure 16-11.

3. Men and women have identical labour force characteristics; each of the three occupations could be filled equally well by men or women.

TABLE 16-4 Women in the labour force, 1901–1991

Year	Women in labour force (thousands)	Women in labour force as percent of	
		Total labour force	All women aged 15* and older
1901	239	13.4%	16%
1911	360	13.2	19
1921	487	15.4	20
1931	706	17.0	22
1941	889	19.9	23
1951	1,149	22.0	24
1961	1,780	27.3	29
1971	2,961	34.3	40
1981	4,812	40.6	52
1986	5,523	42.9	55
1991	6,188	44.9	58

*For 1901 to 1961, the minimum age was 14.

Source: Gail C.A. Cook (ed.), *Opportunity for Choice* (Ottawa: Information Canada, 1976), p. 97; Statistics Canada, *Labour Force Annual Averages 1991* (Ottawa: February 1992).

FIGURE 16-11   The simple economics of occupational discrimination

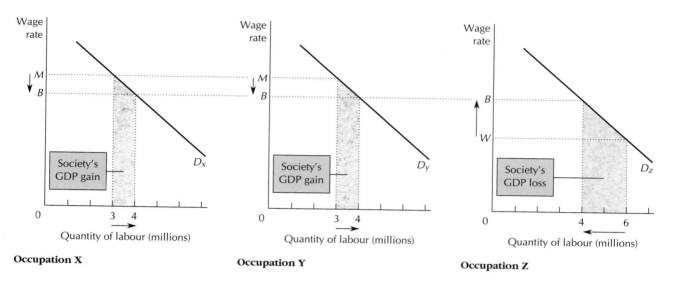

By crowding women into one occupation, men enjoy high wage rates of 0*M* in occupations X and Y, while women receive low wages of 0*W* in occupation Z. The abandonment of discrimination will equalize wage rates at 0*B* and result in a net income increase (real domestic output), or a net gain for society.

Suppose now that as a consequence of irrational discrimination, the six million women are excluded from occupations X and Y and crowded into occupation Z. Men distribute themselves equally among occupations X and Y, so there are three million male workers in each occupation and the resulting common wage rate for men is 0*M*. (Assuming no barriers to mobility, any initially different distribution of males between X and Y would result in a wage differential that would prompt labour shifts from low- to high-wage industry until wage equality was realized.) Note that women, on the other hand, are crowded into occupation Z and because of this occupational segregation, receive a much lower wage rate, 0*W*. Given the reality of discrimination, this is an "equilibrium" situation. Women *cannot*, because of discrimination, reallocate themselves to occupations X and Y in the pursuit of higher wage rates.

Eliminating   Discrimination   Assume   that through legislation or sweeping changes in social attitudes,   discrimination   disappears.   Women, attracted by higher wage rates, will shift from Z to X and Y. Specifically, one million women will shift into X and another one million into Y, leaving four million workers in Z. At this point, four million workers will be in each occupation and wage rates will be equal

to 0*B* in all three occupations. Wage equality eliminates the incentive for further reallocations of labour.

This new, nondiscriminatory equilibrium is to the obvious advantage of women who now receive higher wages and to the disadvantage of men who now get lower wages. Women were initially exploited through discrimination to the benefit of men; the ending of discrimination corrects that situation.

There is also a net gain to society. Recall that the labour demand curve reflects labour's marginal revenue product (Chapter 15) or, in other words, labour's contribution to the domestic output.[5] Hence the "society's gain" for occupations X and Y shows the *increases* in domestic output — the market value of the marginal or extra output — realized by adding one million women workers in each of those two occupations. Similarly, the "society's loss" for occupation Z shows the *decline* in domestic output caused by the shifting of the two million women workers from occupation Z. Note that the sum of the two additions to domestic output exceeds the subtraction from domestic output when discrimination is

---

[5] Technical note: This assumes pure competition in product and resource markets.

Box 16-3

In the Media

Despite some improvements, women's wages are on average still below those of men, suggesting discrimination still prevails in the labour market. Note that wages of women that never married are closer to those of men, giving credence to some research that points to higher wages for women that do not interrupt careers and thus have more experience in the labour force.

WOMEN'S WAGES EDGING UP, BUT REAL GAINS STILL NOT SEEN

Canadian Press

OTTAWA — Women who work full time have crept closer to earning what men do, but it is still not clear that women are making real gains.

Full-time female workers earned 67.6 per cent of what men did in 1990 — $24,923 compared with $36,863, Statistics Canada reported yesterday. That is up from 65.8 per cent in 1989.

Women's wages have never been closer to men's earnings — 25 years ago women made 58.4 per cent of what men did. But the figures do not necessarily mean that women are taking even tiny steps forward, labour experts said.

The main reasons:

- More women have lower-paid, part-time jobs or work from their homes — jobs that were not taken into account in the statistics.
- Women may be catching up only as men fare worse.

"We're not looking at women at the bottom of the labour market; we're looking at women who are lucky enough to have full-time jobs," said Judy Fudge, who heads the employment committee of the National Action Committee on the Status of Women.

Women made 59.9 per cent of what men did in 1990 when part-time and temporary wage earners are considered. But Statistics Canada says comparing full-time workers more accurately reflects the male-female wage gap.

Ms. Fudge said even full-time women workers are not necessarily getting paid much more — the wage gap is narrowing because the average male wage is falling.

Men earned 6.9 per cent less in 1990 than 15 years earlier in real terms, Statscan figures show. Women's earnings rose 6.4 per cent in the same period.

Jeffrey Reitz, a University of Toronto industrial relations professor, said a U.S. study showed that only some women are making gains. Those in traditionally male jobs are earning more, but that is offset by large numbers of women entering the work force and vying for traditionally female occupations where real wages have fallen, Prof. Reitz said.

The Statscan figures also show:

- Women with university degrees earned 72.8 per cent of what similarly educated men did. Women with Grade 8 or less made 62.4 per cent of what men in the same group did.
- Women's earnings were 87.6 per cent of men's in the 15-to-24 age group, but 61.9 per cent for those aged 45 to 54.
- Wages of women who had never married were 89.8 per cent of those of men in the same category; married women's wages were 62.6 per cent of those of married men.

By permission of *The Globe and Mail*, January 28, 1992. Courtesy of Press News Limited.

ended. This is to be expected. After all, women workers are reallocating themselves from occupation Z, where their contribution to domestic output (their MRP) is relatively low, to alternative employments in X and Y, where their contributions to domestic output (their MRPs) are relatively high. Conclusion: *Society gains from a more efficient allocation of resources when discrimination is abandoned.* Discrimination places the nation on a point inside its production possibilities frontier (Chapter 2).

Addenda

Two important comments must be appended to our discussion of discrimination.

Comparable Worth Doctrine   The first involves public policy. The reality of pervasive occupational segregation has given rise to the issue of comparable worth. Legislation that forced employers to pay equal wages to men and women performing the same jobs was of no help to many women because occupational segregation limited their access to the jobs held by men. The essence of the **comparable worth doctrine — equal pay for work of equal value —** is that female secretaries, nurses, and clerks should receive the same salaries as male truck drivers or construction workers if the levels of skill, effort, and responsibility in these disparate jobs are comparable. The basic advantage of comparable worth is that it is a means of quickly correcting perceived pay inequities.

While the concept of comparable worth has considerable appeal, there are a number of important objections. For example, any comparison of the relative worth of various jobs is necessarily subjective and therefore arbitrary, opening the door to endless controversies and lawsuits. Second, wage-setting by administrative or bureaucratic judgment, rather than supply and demand, does not bode well for long-run efficiency. To the extent that the calculated worth of specific jobs varies from their market or equilibrium values, worker shortages or surpluses will develop. Furthermore, increasing the wages of women could attract even more females to traditionally "women's jobs" and thereby prolong occupational segregation. The comparable worth doctrine promises to be a key issue in antidiscrimination policy in the years ahead.

Nondiscriminatory Factors   Not all of the average income differentials found between males and females are necessarily due to discrimination. Most researchers agree that some part of the male–female earnings differential is attributable to factors other than discrimination. For example, the typical work-life cycle of married women who have children involves a continuous period of work until birth of the first child, then a five- to ten-year period of non-participation or partial participation in the labour force related to childbearing and child care, followed by a more continuous period of work experience when the mother is in her late thirties or early forties. The net result is that, on the average, married women have accumulated much less labour force experience than men in the same age group. Thus, on average, women are paid a lower average wage rate. (See Box 16-3.)

Furthermore, family ties apparently provide married women with less geographical mobility in job choice than is the case with men. In fact, married women may give up good positions to move with husbands who decide to accept jobs located elsewhere. Some married women may put convenience of job location and flexibility of working hours ahead of occupational choice. Thus, women may have purposely crowded into such occupations as nursing and elementary school teaching because such occupations have the greatest carry-over value for productive activity within the home.

All this implies that some part of the male–female earnings differential is due to considerations other than sex discrimination. It also suggests that the male–female wage gap will narrow in the future, now that a greater number of women are attending university, maintaining employment through their childbearing years, and pursuing higher-paying professional jobs. In this regard, a recent StatsCan study reveals that the income of women in the labour force who have never married is at about 90% of the male level.

QUICK REVIEW (16-4)

1. The crowding model demonstrates how *(a)* men can increase their wages at the expense of women and *(b)* occupational segregation diminishes the domestic output.

2. Comparable worth is the notion that females in one occupation should receive the same wages as males in another occupation if the levels of skill, effort, responsibility, and working conditions are comparable.

CHAPTER SUMMARY

1. Wages are the price paid per unit of time for the services of labour.

2. The general level of wages is higher in Canada than in most foreign nations because the demand for labour is great in relation to the supply. The strong demand for Canadian labour is based on its high productivity. Over time, various productivity-increasing factors have caused the demand for labour to increase in relation to the supply, accounting for the long-run rise of real wages in Canada.

3. The determination of specific wage rates depends on the structure of the particular labour market. In a competitive market, the equilibrium wage rate and level of employment are determined at the intersection of labour supply and demand.

4. Under monopsony, however, the marginal-resource-cost curve will lie above the resource supply curve, because the monopsonist must bid up wage rates in hiring extra workers and pay that higher wage to *all* workers. The monopsonist will hire fewer workers than under competitive conditions to achieve less-than-competitive wage rates (costs) and thereby greater profits.

5. A union may raise competitive wage rates by *a.* increasing the derived demand for labour, *b.* restricting the supply of labour through exclusive unionism, and *c.* directly enforcing an above-equilibrium wage rate through inclusive unionism.

6. In many important industries, the labour market takes the form of bilateral monopoly wherein a strong union "sells" labour to a monopsonistic employer. The wage rate outcome of this labour market model is logically indeterminate.

7. Economists disagree about the desirability of the minimum wage as an antipoverty mechanism. While it causes unemployment for some low-income workers, it raises the incomes of others who retain their jobs.

8. Union workers currently enjoy wages that are 10 to 15% higher than comparable nonunion workers. There is little evidence to suggest that unions have been able to raise the average level of real wages for labour as a whole.

9. Wage differentials are largely explainable in terms of *a.* noncompeting groups arising from differences in the capacities and education of different groups of workers; *b.* equalizing differences, that is, wage differences that must be paid to offset nonmonetary differences in jobs; *c.* market imperfections in the form of geographic, artificial, and sociological immobilities.

10. The principal–agent problem arises when workers shirk — provide less-than-expected work effort. Firms may combat this problem by monitoring workers or by creating incentive pay schemes that link worker compensation to work effort.

11. There is disagreement as to whether the net effect of unions on allocative efficiency and productivity is positive or negative. The negative view cites *a.* inefficiencies associated with featherbedding and union-imposed work rules; *b.* loss of output through strikes; and *c.* the misallocation of labour to which the union wage advantage gives rise. The positive view holds that *a.* through the shock effect, union wage pressure spurs technological advance and mechanization of the production process; *b.* as collective voice institutions, unions contribute to rising productivity by reducing labour turnover; and *c.* the enhanced security of union workers increases their willingness to teach their skills to less-experienced workers.

12. Those who contend that unions increase earnings inequality argue that *a.* unionization increases the wages of union workers but lowers the wages of nonunion workers and *b.* unions are strongest among highly paid skilled blue-collar workers but relatively weak among low-paid unskilled blue-collar workers. But other economists contend that unions contribute to greater earnings equality because unions *a.* seek uniform wages for given jobs within firms and *b.* seek uniform wages among firms.

13. Historically, an increasing percentage of all working-age women has entered the labour market, and women constitute a rising percentage of the total labour force.

14. The average income of full-time female workers is about 60% that of males. This differential is partially the result of discrimination and, in particular, job segregation.

15. The crowding model of occupational segregation indicates how men may gain higher earnings at the expense of women. The model also shows that discrimination involves a net loss of domestic output.

Terms and Concepts

bilateral monopoly (p. 273)
collective voice (p. 282)
comparable worth doctrine — equal pay for work of equal value (p. 287)
competitive labour market (p. 264)
crowding model of occupational segregation (p. 284)
equalizing differences (p. 277)
exclusive and inclusive unionism (pp. 270, 271)
exit and voice mechanisms (p. 282)
female participation rate (p. 284)

human capital investment (p. 275)
incentive pay plan (p. 279)
monopsonist (p. 265)
nominal and real wage rates (p. 262)
noncompeting groups (p. 274)
occupational discrimination (p. 284)
occupational licensing (p. 271)
principal–agent problem (p. 278)
shirking (p. 278)
the minimum wage (p. 273)
wage differentials (p. 274)

Questions and Study Suggestions

1. Explain why the general level of wages is higher in Canada than in most foreign nations. What is the most important single factor underlying the long-run increase in the average real wage rates in Canada? What, if anything, does this suggest concerning the ability of unions to raise real wages?

2. a. Describe wage determination in a labour market in which workers are unorganized and many firms actively compete for the services of labour. Show this situation graphically, using W_1 to indicate the equilibrium wage rate and Q_1 to show the number of workers hired by the firms as a group. Compare the labour supply curve of the individual firm with that of the total market and explain any differences. Identify total revenue, total wage cost, and revenue available for the payment of nonlabour resources in the firm's diagram.

   b. Suppose now that the formerly competing firms form an employers' association that hires labour as a monopsonist would. Describe verbally the impact upon wage rates and employment. Adjust the market graph drawn for question *2a*, showing the monopsonistic wage rate and employment level as W_2 and Q_2 respectively.

c. Using the monopsony model, explain why hospital administrators frequently complain about a "shortage" of nurses. Do you have suggestions for correcting this shortage?

3. Describe the techniques unions might employ to raise wages. Evaluate the desirability of each from the viewpoint of *a.* the union, and *b.* society as a whole. Explain: "Craft unionism directly restricts the supply of labour; industrial unionism relies upon the market to restrict the number of jobs."

4. Assume a monopsonistic employer is paying a wage rate of W_m and hiring Q_m workers, as is indicated in Figure 16-8. Now suppose that an industrial union is formed and that it forces the employer to accept a wage rate of W_c. Explain verbally and graphically why, in this instance, the higher wage rate will be accompanied by an *increase* in the number of workers hired.

5. Complete the following labour supply table for a firm hiring labour competitively.

Units of labour	Wage rate	Total labour cost (wage bill)	Marginal resource (labour) cost
1	$14	$_____	$_____
2	14	_____	_____
3	14	_____	_____
4	14	_____	_____
5	14	_____	_____
6	14	_____	_____

a. Show graphically the labour supply and marginal revenue (labour) cost curves for this firm. Explain the relationships of these curves to one another.

b. Compare these data with the labour demand data of question 2 in Chapter 15. What will the equilibrium wage rate and level of employment be? Explain.

c. Now redetermine this firm's supply schedule for labour on the assumption that it is a monopsonist and that, although it can hire the first worker for $6, it must increase the wage rate by $3 to attract each successive worker. Show the new labour-supply and marginal labour cost curves graphically and explain their relationships to one another. Compare these new data with those of question 2 in Chapter 15. What will be the equilibrium wage rate and the level of employment? Why does this differ from your answer to question *5b*?

6. A critic of the minimum wage has contended, "The effects of minimum wage legislation are precisely the opposite of those predicted by those who support it. Government can legislate a minimum wage, but cannot force employers to hire unprofitable workers. In fact, minimum wages cause unemployment among low-wage workers who can least afford to give up their small incomes." Do you agree? What bearing does the elasticity of labour demand have upon this assessment? What factors might possibly offset the potential unemployment effects of a minimum wage?

7. What is the estimated size of the union wage advantage? Explain: "Although union workers get higher wages than nonunion workers, unions have not been successful in raising the average real wage of the Canadian labour force."

8. What are the basic considerations that help explain wage differentials? What long-run effect would a substantial increase in safety for underground coal miners have on their wage rates in comparison with those of other workers?

9. Comment on each of the following statements:

   a. "By constraining the decisions of management, unions inhibit efficiency and productivity growth."

   b. "As collective voice institutions, unions increase productivity by reducing worker turnover, inducing managerial efficiency, and enhancing worker security."

10. What is meant by investment in human capital? Use this concept to explain a. wage differentials, and b. the long-run rise in real wage rates in Canada.

11. What is meant by the principal–agent problem? Have you ever worked in a setting where this problem has arisen? If so, do you think increased monitoring would have eliminated the problem? Why don't firms simply hire more supervisors to eliminate shirking?

12. The notion of efficiency wages suggests that an above-equilibrium wage rate will elicit a more-than-offsetting increase in worker productivity. By what specific means might the higher wage cause worker productivity to rise? Why might young workers accept a seniority pay plan under which they are initially paid less than their MRPs?

13. "There is an inherent cost to society that accompanies any union wage gain. That cost is the diminished efficiency with which labour resources are allocated." Explain this contention. Are you in agreement?

14. Describe the various avenues through which unions might alter the distribution of earnings. Evaluate: "Unions purport to be egalitarian institutions, but their effect is to increase earnings inequality among Canadian workers."

15. "Many of the lowest-paid people in society — for example, short-order cooks — also have relatively poor working conditions. Hence, the notion of compensating wage differentials is disproved." Do you agree? Explain.

16. Use supply-and-demand analysis to explain the impact of occupational segregation or "crowding" on the relative wage rates and earnings of men and women. Who gains and who loses as a consequence of eliminating occupational segregation? Is there a net gain or loss to society as a whole? "Wage differences between men and women do not reflect discrimination, but rather differences in job continuity and rational decisions with respect to education and training." Do you agree?

CHAPTER

17

The Pricing and Employment of Resources: Rent, Interest, and Profits

Emphasis in the previous two chapters was on labour markets because wages and salaries account for about three-fourths of our domestic income. In the present chapter we focus on three other sources of income — rent, interest, and profits — comprising the remaining one-fourth of domestic income.

You undoubtedly are aware of these income sources. We read stories of incredibly high land rents in urban areas such as Tokyo, where an acre of land may sell for more than $100 million. An acre of desert may cost $780 million along the Las Vegas casino strip; meanwhile, an acre of desert just 50 km away can be bought for about $72. *How are land prices and rents determined?*

If you put money in a one year Guaranteed Investment Certificate (GIC) in 1991, you probably received an annual interest rate of about 10%. One year later the same GIC paid only about 6%. *What factors determine interest rates and explain changes in rates?*

The news media continuously document the profit and loss performance of various firms and industries. The maker of Nintendo video games has reaped large profits. And the firm producing AZT, a drug that prolongs the life of AIDS patients, doubled its profits over a three-year period. Meanwhile, some automakers and airlines have recently suffered record losses. *What are the sources and functions of profits and losses?*

ECONOMIC RENT

To most people, the term "rent" means the sum one must pay for a two-bedroom apartment or a dormitory room. To the business executive, "rent" is a payment made for use of a factory building, machinery, or warehouse facilities. Closer examination finds these commonsense definitions of rent to be confusing and ambiguous. Dormitory room rent, for example, includes interest on the money capital the university has borrowed to finance the dormitory's construction, wages for custodial service, utility payments, and so forth.

Economists use the term "rent" in a narrower, but less ambiguous, sense. **Economic rent *is the price paid for the use of land and other natural resources that are completely fixed in total supply***. The unique supply conditions of land and other natural resources — their fixed supply — make rental payments distinguishable from wage, interest, and profit payments.

Let's examine this feature and some of its implications through supply and demand analysis. To avoid complications, assume first that all land is of the same grade or equally productive. Suppose too that all land has just one use, being capable of producing just one product — say, wheat. And assume that land is being rented in a competitive market.

In Figure 17-1, S indicates the supply of arable farmland available in the economy as a whole and D_1 the demand of farmers for use of that land. As with all economic resources, demand is a derived demand. It is downsloping because of the law of diminishing returns and the fact that product price must be reduced to sell additional units of output.

Perfectly Inelastic Supply

The unique feature of our analysis is on the supply side. For all practical purposes, the supply of land is perfectly inelastic, as reflected in S. Land has no production cost; it is a "free and nonreproducible gift of nature." The economy has only a limited amount of land. It is true that within limits, existing land can be made more usable by clearing, drainage, and irrigation. But these programs are capital improvements and not changes in the amount of land. Furthermore, such variations in the usability of land are a very small fraction of the total amount of land in existence and do not undermine the basic argument that land

FIGURE 17-1 **The determination of land rent**

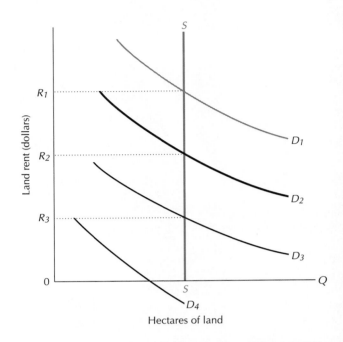

Because the supply of land and other natural resources is perfectly inelastic (S), demand is the sole active determinant of land rent. An increase (D_2 to D_1) or decrease (D_2 to D_3) in demand will cause considerable changes in rent (R_2 to R_1 and R_2 to R_3). If demand is very small (D_4) relative to supply, land will be a "free good."

and other natural resources are in virtually fixed supply. Note, however, that their supply to particular uses, such as agriculture or housing, is not fixed, since a higher price can induce people to shift land from other uses.

Changes in Demand

The fixed nature of the supply of land means that demand is the only active determinant of land rent; supply is passive. And what determines the demand for land? Those factors discussed in Chapter 15 — the price of the product grown on the land, the productivity of land (which depends, in part, on the quantity and quality of the resources with which land is combined), and the prices of those other resources that are combined with land. If, in Figure 17-1, the demand for land should increase from D_2 to D_1 or decline from D_2 to D_3, land rent would change from R_2 to R_1 or R_3, but the amount of land supplied would remain unchanged at $0S$. Note that changes in economic rent will have no impact on the amount of land available. In technical terms, there is a large price effect and no quantity effect when the demand for land changes. If the demand for land is only D_4, land rent will be zero — land will be a "free good," because it is not scarce enough in relation to the demand for it to command a price.

Land Rent Is a Surplus

The completely inelastic supply of land must be contrasted with the relative elasticity of such property resources as apartment buildings, machinery, and warehouses. These resources are not fixed in total supply. A higher price will give entrepreneurs the incentive to construct and offer larger quantities of these resources. Conversely, a decline in their prices will induce suppliers to allow existing facilities to depreciate and not be replaced. The same general reasoning applies to the total supply of labour. Within limits, a higher average level of wages will induce more workers to enter the labour force and lower wages will cause them to drop out of the labour force. In other words, the supplies of non-land resources are upsloping — the prices paid to such resources perform an **incentive function.** A high price provides an incentive to offer more; a low price, to offer less.

Not so with land. Rent serves no incentive function, because the total supply of land is fixed. If rent is $10,000, $500, $1, or $0 a hectare, the same amount of land will be available to society. Rent, in other words, could be eliminated without affecting the productive potential of the economy. For this reason, economists consider ***rent to be a surplus,*** a payment that is not necessary to ensure that land will be available to the economy as a whole.[1]

A Single Tax on Land?

If land is a free gift of nature, costs nothing to produce, and would be available even in the absence of rental payments, why should rent be paid to those who, by historical accident or inheritance, happen to be landowners? Socialists have long argued that all land rents are unearned incomes. Therefore, land should be nationalized — owned by the state — so that any payments for its use can be used by the state to further the well-being of the entire population rather than being utilized by a landowning minority.

Henry George's Proposal   In the United States, criticism of rental payments took the form of a **single-tax movement,** which gained much support in the late 1800s. Spearheaded by Henry George's provocative book *Progress and Poverty* (1879), this reform movement maintained that economic rent could be completely taxed away without impairing the available supply of land or, therefore, the productive potential of the economy as a whole.

George observed that as population grew and the geographic frontier closed, landowners enjoyed larger and larger rents from their landholdings. These increments in rent were the result of a growing demand for a resource whose supply was perfectly inelastic; some landlords were receiving high incomes, not through rendering any productive effort, but solely from holding advantageously located land. George maintained that these increases in land rent belonged to the economy as a whole, and that land rents should be taxed away and spent for public uses.

Indeed, George held that there was no reason to tax away only 50% of the landowner's unearned rental income. Why not take 70% or 90% or 99%? In seeking popular support for his ideas on land taxation, Henry Geroge proposed that taxes on rental incomes be the *only* tax levied by government.

George's case for taxing land was based not only on fairness, but also on efficiency grounds. Unlike virtually every other tax, a tax on land does *not* alter or distort the allocation of resources. For example, a tax on wages will reduce after-tax wages and might weaken incentives to work. But no such reallocations of resources occur when land is taxed. The most profitable use for land before it is taxed remains the most profitable use after the tax is imposed. Of course, a landlord could withdraw land from production when a tax is imposed, but this would mean no rental income at all.

Criticisms   Critics of the single tax on land make four points.

1. Current levels of government spending are such that a land tax alone would not bring in enough revenue.

2. As noted earlier, in practice most income payments combine elements of interest, rent, wages, and

---

[1] A portion — in some instances a major portion — of wage and salary incomes may be surplus, in that these incomes exceed the minimum amount necessary to keep individuals in their current line of work. For example, a hockey superstar may receive $1 million a year, while his next best occupational option, as, say, a high school coach, would earn him only $40,000 or $45,000 per year. Most of his current income is therefore a surplus. Observe that in the twilight of their careers, professional athletes sometimes accept sizable salary reductions rather than seek employment in alternative occupations.

profits. Land is typically improved in some manner by productive effort, and economic rent cannot be readily disentangled from payments for capital improvements.

3. The question of unearned income goes beyond land and land ownership. One can argue that many individuals and groups other than landowners benefit from receipt of "unearned" income associated with the overall advance of the economy. For example, consider the capital gains income received by someone who, twenty or twenty-five years ago, purchased (or inherited) stock in a firm that has experienced rapid growth (say, IBM or Xerox). How is this income different from the rental income of the landowner?

4. Finally, a piece of land is likely to have changed ownership many times. *Former* owners may have been the beneficiaries of past increases in land rent. It is hardly fair to tax *current* owners who paid the competitive market price for land.

Productivity Differences

Thus far we have assumed that all units of land are of the same grade. In practice, this is not so. Different hectares vary greatly in productivity. These productivity diferences stem primarily from dfferences in soil fertility and such climatic factors as rainfall and temperature. It is these factors that explain why southeastern Saskatchewan soil is excellently suited to wheat production, the Palliser Triangle is much less so, and northern muskeg is incapable of wheat production. These productivity differences will be reflected in resource demand. Competitive bidding by farmers will establish a high rent for the very productive Saskatchewan land. The less-productive Palliser Triangle will command a lower rent, and northern muskeg no rent at all.

Location is equally important in explaining differences in land rent. Other things being equal, renters will pay more for a unit of land strategically located with respect to materials, labour, and customers than for a unit of land whose location is remote from these markets. Witness the high land rents in large metropolitan areas.

The rent differentials to which quality differences in land would give rise can be seen by looking at Figure 17-1 from a slightly different point of view. Suppose, as before, that only one agricultural product, say wheat, can be produced on four grades of land, *each* of which is available in the fixed amount, 0S. When combined with identical amounts of capi-

tal, labour, and other cooperating resources, the productivity of each grade of land is reflected in demand curves D_1, D_2, D_3, and D_4. Grade 1 land is the most productive, as reflected in D_1, whereas D_4 represents grade 4 the least productive. The resulting rents for grades 1, 2, and 3 land will be R_1, R_2, and R_3 respectively, rent differentials mirroring the diferences in the productivity of the three grades of land. Grade 4 land is so poor in quality that it would not pay farmers to bring it fully into production; it would be a "free" and only partially used resource.

Alternative Uses and Costs

We have also supposed thus far that land has only one use. Actually, we know that land normally has a number of alternative uses. A hectare of southeast Saskatchewan farmland may be useful in raising not only wheat, but also canola, barley, oats, and cattle, or it may be useful as a site for a house or factory.

What is the importance of this obvious point? It indicates that although land is a free gift of nature and has no production cost from the viewpoint of society as a whole, the rental payments of individual producers are *costs*. The total supply of land will be available to society even if no rent at all is paid for its use, but from the standpoint of individual firms and industries, land has alternative uses, and therefore payment must be made by specific firms and industries to attract that land from those other uses. Such payments by definition are costs. Again, the fallacy of composition (Chapter 1) has entered our discussion. From the standpoint of society, there is no alternative but for land to be used by society. Therefore, to society, rents are a surplus, not a cost. But because land has alternative uses, the rental payments of wheat farmers or any other individual user are a cost; such payments are required to attract land from alternative uses.

QUICK REVIEW (17-1)

1. **Economic rent is the price paid for resources such as land whose supply is perfectly inelastic.**

2. **Land rent is a surplus in that land would be available to society even if rent were not paid.**

3. **The surplus nature of land rent was the basis for Henry George's single-tax movement.**

4. **Differential rents allocate land among alternative uses.**

INTEREST

The interest rate is the price paid for the use of money. It is the amount of money one must pay for the use of one dollar for a year. Two aspects of this income payment are noteworthy.

1 Stated as Percentage   Interest is typically stated as a percentage of the amount of money being borrowed rather than as an absolute amount. Stating interest as a percentage facilitates comparison of interest paid on loans of much different absolute amounts. We can immediately compare an interest payment of, say, $432 per year per $2,880 and one of $1,800 per year per $12,000. In this case, both interest payments are 15% — a fact not at all obvious from the absolute figures. Provincial laws call for the uniform statement of interest costs so that borrowers will understand the interest rate they are paying.

2 Money Not a Resource   Money is *not* an economic resource. As such, money cannot produce goods and services. However, money can be used to acquire capital goods — factory buildings, machinery, warehouses, and so forth. These facilities do contribute to production. Thus in hiring the use of money capital, businesses are ultimately buying the use of real capital goods.

Loanable Funds Theory of Interest

The **loanable funds theory of interest** explains the interest rate in terms of the demand for and supply of loanable funds. The equilibrium interest rate equates the quantities of loanable funds demanded and supplied.

Supply of Loanable Funds   Let's first consider the loanable funds theory in a simplified form, in which we assume that households are the sole suppliers and businesses are the only demanders of loanable funds. In Figure 17-2 the supply of loanable funds is shown as an upsloping curve; a larger quantity of funds will be made available at high interest rates than at low interest rates. The explanation of this is that most individuals prefer present consumption to future consumption because, given the uncertainties of life, present consumption seems more tangible and therefore more valuable. It follows that a consumer must be compensated by an interest payment to defer consumption or, in other words, to save. The upsloping supply of loanable funds curve indicates that, the larger the interest rate, the more households

FIGURE 17-2   The loanable funds theory of interest

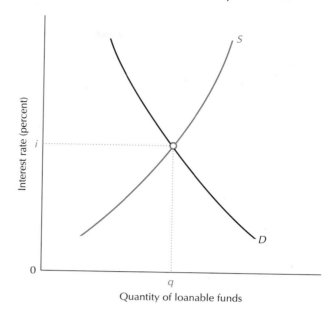

The loanable funds theory of interest envisions the equilibrium interest rate as being determined by the intersection of the demand for, and the supply of, loanable funds. The supply curve is upsloping because, the higher the interest rate, the more willing households are to save. The demand curve is downsloping because businesses are more willing to borrow and invest loanable funds the lower the interest rate.

are willing to save (or, alternatively, the less of their incomes they consume).

Demand for Loanable Funds   Demand for loanable funds comes primarily from businesses that want to replace or add to their stocks of capital goods. Firms demand loanable funds to build new plants or warehouses, to purchase machinery and equipment, and so forth.

Consider in simplified fashion the character of such investment decisions. Suppose a firm is contemplating the purchase of a machine that will increase its output and sales to the extent that its total revenue will rise by $110 for the year. Also assume the machine costs $100 and has a useful life of just one year. Comparing the $10 earned above the cost of the machine with that cost, we find the **rate of return** on this investment is 10% (= $10/$100).

The firm must now compare the interest rate — the price of loanable funds — with the 10% rate of

Box 17-1

DETERMINING THE PRICE OF CREDIT

There are a variety of lending practices that can cause the effective interest rate to be quite different than what it appears to be.

Borrowing and lending — receiving and granting credit — are a way of life. Individuals receive credit when they negotiate a mortgage loan and when they use their credit cards. Conversely, individuals make loans when they open a savings account at a chartered bank or buy a government saving bond.

It remains difficult, however, to determine exactly how much interest one pays and receives in borrowing and lending. A few illustrations will be helpful. Let us suppose that you borrow $10,000 that you agree to repay plus $1,000 of interest at the end of the year. In this instance the interest rate is 10%. To determine the interest rate (r) one merely compares interest paid with the amount borrowed:

$$r = \frac{\$1,000}{\$10,000} = 10\%$$

But in some cases a lender, say, a bank, will *discount* the interest payment at the time the loan is made. Thus, instead of giving the borrower $10,000, the bank discounts the $1,000 interest payment in advance, giving the borrower only $9,000. This increases the interest rate:

$$r = \frac{\$1,000}{\$9,000} = 11\%$$

While the absolute amount of interest paid is the same, in this second case the borrower has only $9,000 available for the year.

An even more subtle point is that, in order to simplify their calculations, many financial institutions assume a 360-day year (twelve 30-day months). This means the borrower has the use of the lender's funds for five days less than the normal year. This use of a "short year" also increases the interest rate paid by the borrower.

The interest rate paid can change dramatically if a loan is repaid in installments. Suppose a bank lends you $10,000 and charges interest in the amount of $1,000 to be paid at the end of the year. But the loan contract requires you to repay the $10,000 loan in 12 equal monthly installments. The effect of this is that the *average* amount of the loan outstanding during the year is only $5,000. Hence:

$$r = \frac{\$1,000}{\$5,000} = 20\%$$

Here interest is paid on the total amount of the loan ($10,000) rather than the outstanding balance (which averages $5,000 for the year), making for a much higher interest rate.

Another fact that influences the effective interest rate is whether or not interest is *compounded*. Suppose you deposit $10,000 in a savings account that pays a 10% interest rate compounded semiannually. In other words, interest is paid on your "loan" to the bank twice a year. At the end of the first six months, $500 of interest (10% of $10,000 for one-half a year) is added to your account. At the end of the year, interest is calculated on $10,500 so that the second interest payment is $525 (10% of $10,500 for one-half a year). Hence:

$$r = \frac{\$1,025}{\$10,000} = 10.25\%$$

This means that a bank advertising a 10% interest rate compounded semiannually is actually paying more interest to its customers than a competitor paying a simple (noncompounded) interest rate of 10.20%.

"Let the borrower beware" is a fitting motto in the world of credit.

return to determine whether the investment is profitable and therefore should be made. For example, if funds can be borrowed at some rate less than the rate of return, say 6%, then the investment is profitable and should be undertaken. But if funds are available at a 14% rate of interest, this investment is unprofitable and should not be made.

Why is the demand for loanable funds downsloping, as shown in Figure 17-2? At higher interest rates, fewer investment projects will be profitable to businesses and hence a small quantity of loanable funds will be demanded. Conversely, more investment projects will be profitable and therefore more loanable funds will be demanded at lower interest rates. Indeed, we have just seen in our example that it is profitable to purchase the $100 machine if funds can be borrowed at 6%, but it is not profitable if the firm must borrow at 14%.

Extending the Model   We now want to make our portrayal of the loanable funds market more realistic in two different ways.

Shifting Curves   The first extension of the model considers factors that might cause the supply and demand curves of loanable funds to shift and thereby change the equilibrium interest rate.

Changes in Supply   Consider the supply side. Anything that causes households to be more thrifty will prompt them to save more at each interest rate, shifting the supply curve rightward. For example, if the tax laws were changed to exempt interest earned on savings from taxation, we would expect the supply of loanable funds to increase and the equilibrium interest rate to decrease. Conversely, a decline in thriftiness would shift the curve leftward and increase the equilibrium interest rate.

Changes in Demand   On the demand side, anything that increases the rates of return on potential investments will increase the demand for loanable funds. Let's return to our earlier example, wherein a firm would receive additional revenues of $110 by purchasing a $100 machine and, hence, realize a 10% return on the investment. What factors might increase or decrease that rate of return? Suppose a technological advance raises the productivity of the machine so that it produces still more output and thereby increases the firm's total revenue by $120 rather than $110. The rate of return will now be 20%, rather than 10%. Before the technological advance the firm would demand no loanable funds at, say, a

14% interest rate. But now it would demand $100, implying a rightward shift of the demand for loanable funds curve.

Similarly, an increase in consumer demand for the firm's product — reflecting perhaps the movement of the economy from recession to prosperity — will increase product price. Even though we assume the productivity of the machine is unchanged, the firm's additional total revenue might again rise from $110 to $120, which increases the rate of return to 20%. This implies that the demand for loanable funds has shifted rightward. Conversely, we would expect a decline in the price of the firm's product to decrease the demand for loanable funds.

Other Transactors   We must also recognize that there are more transactors on both the demand and supply side of the loanable funds market. For example, while households are suppliers of loanable funds, many also demand those same funds. Households borrow to finance large purchases such as housing, automobiles, and furniture and household appliances. Governments are also on the demand side when they borrow to finance budgetary deficits. On the supply side, businesses that have revenues in excess of their current costs or expenditures may make the consequent business saving available in the market for loanable funds. Note that households and businesses are on both the supply and demand sides of the market.

Finally, in studying macroeconomics you will find that chartered banks and other financial institutions not only gather and make available the savings of households and businesses, but also create loanable funds when they lend. Hence, financial institutions are another source of loanable funds.

Range of Rates

Although it is convenient to think in terms of a single interest rate, in fact there are a whole cluster or range of interest rates. Table 17-1 lists many interest rates frequently referred to in the media. Note that these rates range from 7.69% to 18%. Why the differences?

1 Risk   The greater the chance the borrower will not repay the loan, the more interest the lender will charge to compensate for this risk.

2 Maturity   Other things being equal, long-term loans usually command higher rates of interest than do short-term loans, because the long-term lender suffers the inconvenience and possible financial sac-

TABLE 17-1 Selected interest rates, September, 1992

Type of interest rate	Annual percentage
10-year Government of Canada bond	7.69
10-year New Brunswick bond	8.36
30-year B.C. Telephone bond	9.09
9-year Canadian Pacific bond	9.03
5-year closed mortgage	8.50
91-day Treasury bill (Government of Canada)	5.48
Prime rate (rate charged by banks to their best corporate customers)	6.25
Visa interest rate	18.00

rifice of forgoing alternative uses for his or her money for a greater period of time.

3 Loan Size Given two loans of equal length and risk, the interest rate usually will be somewhat higher on the smaller of the two loans. This is because administrative costs of a large and a small loan are about the same.

4 Market Imperfections Market imperfections are also important in explaining some interest rate differentials. The small-town bank branch that monopolizes the local money market may charge high interest rates on loans to consumers because households find it inconvenient to "shop around" at bank branches in somewhat distant cities, where they might have been able to negotiate a demand loan at a lower interest rate than a consumer loan. The large corporation, on the other hand, can survey a number of rival investment houses in floating a new bond issue, securing the lowest obtainable rate.

To circumvent the difficulties involved in discussing the whole structure of interest rates, economists talk of "the" interest rate or the **pure rate of interest**. This pure rate is best approximated by the interest paid on long-term, virtually riskless bonds, such as the long-term bonds of the Government of Canada. This interest payment can be thought of as being made solely for the use of money over an extended time period, because the risk factor and administrative costs are negligible and the interest on such securities is not distorted by market imperfections. The pure interest rate in mid-1989 was about 9.5%.

Role of the Interest Rate

The interest rate is an extremely important price since it simultaneously affects both the *level* and *composition* of investment goods production.

Interest and Domestic Output The level of the interest rate affects the aggregate levels of domestic output and employment in the economy. Other things being equal, a high interest rate tends to depress, while a low interest rate will stimulate domestic output and employment. When businesses can borrow at low interest rates, a larger volume of investments in capital equipment and plant facilities will be profitable. This means a higher volume of economic activity and, consequently, more output and more jobs. Similarly, low interest rates stimulate interest-sensitive expenditures by consumers in such goods as automobiles and housing. Conversely, high interest rates curtail investment and consumer spending and reduce both domestic output and employment.

Interest and the Allocation of Capital Prices are rationing devices. The interest rate is no exception; it performs the function of allocating money capital, and therefore physical capital, to various firms and investment projects. It rations the available supply of money or liquidity to investment projects whose expected profitability is sufficiently high to warrant payment of the going interest rate.

If the expected rate of net profits of additional physical capital in the computer industry is 14% and the required funds can be secured at an interest rate of 10%, the computer industry will be able to borrow and expand its capital facilities. If the rate of net profits of capital in the steel industry is expected to be only 8%, it may be unprofitable for this industry to accumulate more capital goods at the 10% interest rate. *The interest rate allocates money, and ultimately physical capital, to those industries in which it will be most productive and therefore most profitable. Such an allocation of capital goods is in the interest of society as a whole.*

QUICK REVIEW (17-2)

1. **Interest is the price paid for the use of money.**

2. **The equilibrium interest rate is determined by the demand for and the supply of loanable funds.**

3. **There exists a range of interest rates that is influenced by risk, maturity, loan size, and market imperfections.**

4. **The equilibrium real interest rate affects the aggregate level of investment and therefore the level of domestic output; it also allocates money and real capital to specific industries and firms.**

ECONOMIC PROFITS

As with rent, economists find it advantageous to define profits more narrowly than do accountants. To accountants, "profit" is what remains of a firm's total revenue after it has paid individuals and other firms for materials, capital, and labour supplied to the firm. To the economist, this conception is too broad and ambiguous. The difficulty is that this view of profits takes into account only **explicit costs**: payments made by the firm to outsiders. It ignores **implicit costs**: payments to similar resources owned and self-employed by a firm. In other words, the accountant's concept of profits fails to allow for implicit wage, rent, and interest costs. **Economic**, or **pure, profits** are what remain after *all* opportunity costs — both explicit and implicit wage, rent, and interest costs and a normal profit — have been subtracted from a firm's total revenue (Chapter 9). Economic profits may be either positive or negative (losses).

For example, farmers who own their land and equipment and provide all their own labour grossly overstate their economic profits if they subtract only their payments to outsiders for seed, insecticides, fertilizer, and gasoline, from their total receipts. Actually, much or possibly all of what remains is the implicit rent, interest, and wage costs that the farmers forgo in deciding to self-employ the resources they own rather than make them available in alternative employments. Interest on the capital or wages for the labour contributed by the farmers are no more profits than are the payments that would be made if outsiders had supplied these resources. Economic profits are a residual — the total revenue remaining after *all* costs are taken into account.

Role of the Entrepreneur

The economist views profits as the return to a very special type of resource — enterpreneurial ability. The functions of the entrepreneur were summarized

in Chapter 2. They entail (1) taking the initiative to combine other resources in producing a good or service; (2) making basic, nonroutine policy decisions for the firm; (3) introducing innovations in the form of new products or production processes; (4) bearing the economic risks associated with all of these functions.

Part of the entrepreneur's return is called a **normal profit**. This is the minimum return or payment necessary to keep the entrepreneur in some specific line of business activity. This normal profit payment is a cost (Chapter 9). However, we know that a firm's total revenue may exceed its total costs (explicit and implicit, the latter inclusive of a normal profit). This extra or excess revenue above all costs is an economic profit. This residual — which is *not* a cost, because it is in excess of the normal profit required to retain the entrepreneur in the industry — accrues to the entrepreneur. The entrepreneur is the residual claimant.

Economists offer several theories to explain why this residual of economic profit might occur. As we will see in a moment, these explanations relate to:

1. The *risks* the entrepreneur bears by functioning in a dynamic and uncertain environment, or by undertaking innovational activity.

2. The possibility of attaining *monopoly power*.

Sources of Economic Profit

Our understanding of economic profits and the entrepreneur's functions can be enhanced by describing an artificial economic environment, within which pure profits would be zero. Then by noting real-world deviations from this environment, we can lay bare the sources of economic profit.

In a purely competitive, static economy, pure profits would be zero. By a **static economy** we mean one in which all the basic data — resource supplies, technological knowledge, and consumer tastes — are constant and unchanging. A static economy is one in which all determinants of cost and supply, and demand and revenue, are constant.

In such an economic environment economic uncertainty is nonexistent. The outcome of price and production policies is accurately predictable. Furthermore, the static nature of such a society precludes innovation. Under pure competition, any pure profits (positive or negative) that might have existed initially in various industries will disappear with the entry or exodus of firms in the long run. All costs —

Box 17-2

In the Media

William Gates, founder of the computer software firm Microsoft, recently became the richest citizen in the U.S., at least on paper. He was able to amass such wealth primarily on the strength of his entrepreneurial ability.

MICROSOFT CHIEF RICHEST IN U.S. WITH $6.5 BILLION

SEATTLE (Reuter) — Microsoft Corp. chairman and founder William Gates appears to have become America's wealthiest individual, with his stock in the world's largest software maker worth nearly $6.5 billion (U.S.).

Microsoft shares surged $2.75 Thursday to close at $114 in the first day of trading in 1992.

The company's stock has risen more than 1,200 per cent since Microsoft went public in the mid-1980s, and the latest surge brings Gates's 56.7 million shares to a value of $6.46 billion.

"It's going through the ceiling," one analyst said of the stock price.

Analysts estimate Microsoft shares will jump as high as $130 over the next 12 months, which would bring 35-year-old Gates's wealth on paper to nearly $7.4 billion.

The latest surge surpasses the $5.9 billion attributed to John Warner Kluge in *Forbes* magazine's annual ranking of the wealthiest people in the United States, published in October. Kluge owns Metromedia, a communications company.

No updated estimates were available for the value of Kluge's holdings in Metromedia, but *Forbes* estimates that he has about $2.5 billion in cash. This might rise by $100 million to $200 million over the next year at present interest rates.

Gates was not available for comment and Microsoft had no comment. Most Wall Street analysts expressed more interest in the company's financials than the fortunes of its founder and largest shareholder.

But an analyst noted that Gates's personal fortune remains locked into Microsoft. Gates has few other investments aside from a minority stake in the Seattle-based start-up biotechnology company Icos Corp.

"What would happen if he tried to sell all that stock?" the analyst asked. "It would push the price down to half, probably, and then he'd have to pay taxes on it, so it's kind of a meaningless number."

Microsoft said Gates had 56,700,930 shares of Microsoft as of the end of October. A spokesperson said Microsoft released no news Thursday that would account for the day's stock activity.

The Toronto Star, January 4, 1992. Copyright © 1992 by Reuters. Reprinted with permission.

both explicit and implicit — will therefore be precisely covered in the long run, leaving no residual in the form of economic profits (Figure 10-12).

The notion of zero economic profits in a static, competitive economy enhances our understanding of profits by suggesting that the presence of profits is linked to the dynamic nature of market economy and its accompanying uncertainty. Furthermore, it indicates that economic profits may arise from a source apart from the directing, innovating, risk-bearing functions of the entrepreneur. And that source is the presence of some degree of monopoly power.

Uncertainty, Risk, and Profits In a dynamic economy, the future is always uncertain. This means that the entrepreneur necessarily assumes risks. Prof-

its can be thought of, in part, as a reward for taking risks.

In linking pure profits with uncertainty and risk-bearing, we must distinguish between risks that are insurable and those that are not. Some types of risks — fires, floods, theft, and accidents to employees — are measurable, in that actuaries can accurately estimate their average occurrence. As a result, these are typically insurable risks. Firms can avoid or at least provide for them by incurring a known cost in the form of an insurance premium. It is the bearing of **uninsurable risks**, that is a potential source of economic profits.

Uninsurable risks, are uncontrollable and unpredictable changes in demand (revenue) and supply (cost) conditions facing the firm. Some of these uninsurable risks stem from unpredictable changes in the general economic environment or, more specifically, from the business cycle. Prosperity brings substantial windfall profits to most firms, whereas severe recessions mean widespread losses. In addition, changes are constantly taking place in the structure of the domestic and world economy.

Even in a full-employment, noninflationary economy, changes are always occurring in consumer tastes, technology, and resource supplies. Example: Technological change has been such that vinyl long-play records have given way to cassettes and the latter in turn have lost their market to compact discs. Digital audio tapes may soon challenge compact discs.

Such changes continually alter the revenue and cost data faced by individual firms and industries, leading to structural changes as favourably affected industries expand and adversely affected industries contract. The point is that profits and losses can be associated with taking on uninsurable risks stemming from both cyclical and structural changes in the economy.

Uncertainty, Innovations, and Profits The uncertainties just discussed are external to the firm; they are beyond the control of the individual firm or industry. One other very important dynamic feature of a market economy — innovation — occurs at the initiative of the entrepreneur. Firms deliberately introduce new methods of production and distribution to reduce costs, introduce new products, and increase their revenue. The entrepreneur purposely undertakes to upset existing cost and revenue data in a way that is hoped will be profitable.

But once again, uncertainty enters the picture. Despite exhaustive market surveys, new products may prove to be economic failures. Three-dimensional movies and disk cameras come readily to mind as product failures. Similarly, of the many new novels, textbooks, records, and tapes that appear every year, only a handful garner large profits. Nor is it known with certainty whether a new machine will actually provide the cost economies predicted for it while it is still in the blueprint stage. Innovations purposely undertaken by entrepreneurs bring with them uncertainty, just as do those changes in the economic environment over which an individual enterprise has no control. In a sense, innovation as a source of profits is merely a special case of risk-bearing.

Under competition and in the absence of patent laws, profits from innovations will be temporary. Rival firms will imitate successful (profitable) inno-

vations, competing away all economic profits. Nevertheless, such profits may always exist in a progressive economy as new successful innovations replace older ones whose associated profits have been competed away.

Monopoly Profits The existence of monopoly in some form or another is a final source of economic profits. Because of its ability to restrict output and deter entry, a monopolist may persistently enjoy economic profits, provided demand is strong relative to cost (Figure 11-3).

There are both a causal relationship and a notable distinction between uncertainty and monopoly as sources of profits. The causal relationship involves the fact that an entrepreneur can reduce uncertainty by achieving monopoly power. The competitive firm is exposed to the vagaries of the market; the monopolist, however, can partially control the market and minimize the adverse effects of uncertainty. Furthermore, innovation is an important source of monopoly power; the short-run uncertainty associated with the introduction of new techniques or products may have been carried out for the purpose of achieving a measure of monopoly power.

Functions of Profits

Profit is the prime mover of a market economy. As such, profits influence both the level of resource utilization and the allocation of resources among alternative uses.

Investment and Domestic Output It is profit — or the *expectation* of profit — that induces firms to innovate. Innovation stimulates investment, total output, and employment. Innovation is a fundamental aspect of the process of economic growth, and it is the pursuit of profit that underlies most innovation. However, profit expectations are volatile, with the result that investment, employment, and the rate of growth have been unstable.

Profits and Resource Allocation Recall from Chapters 9 and 10 that entrepreneurs seek profits and shun losses. Economic profits are a signal that society wants that particular industry to expand. Profit rewards are more than an inducement for an industry to expand; they also are the financial means by which firms in such industries can add to their productive capacities.

Losses, on the other hand, signal society's desire for the afflicted industries to contract; losses penalize firms that fail to adjust their productive efforts to those goods and services most preferred by consumers.

INCOME SHARES

Our discussion in this and the previous chapter would be incomplete without a brief empirical summary as to the importance of wages, rent, interest, and profits as proportions or relative shares of the domestic income. Table 17-2 sets out income shares in terms of the income categories since 1926. Although these accounting conceptions of income do not neatly fit the economist's definitions of wages, rent, interest, and profits, they do yield some usable insights about the relative size and trends of income shares.

Current Shares

The most recent figures in the table, reveal the dominant role of labour income. Defining labour income as "wages, salaries and supplementary labour income" (fringe benefits), labour currently receives about 75% of the domestic income. But some economists argue that since proprietors' income (the sum of columns 5 and 6) is largely comprised of wages and salaries, it should be added to the official "wages and salaries" category to determine labour income. When we use this broad definition, labour's share rises to over 80% of domestic income. Interestingly, although we label our system a "capitalist economy," the capitalist share of domestic income — which we will define as the sum of "corporation profits," and "interest and miscellaneous investment income," less "inventory valuation adjustment" — is less than 20% of the domestic income.

Historical Trends

What historical trends can be deduced from Table 17-2? Let's concentrate on the dominant wage share.

Using the narrow definition of labour's share as simply "wages and salaries," we note an increase from about 60% in the late 1920s to over 70% in the past decade.

Structural Changes   Although there are several tentative explanations of these data, one prominent theory stresses the structural changes that have occurred in our economy. Two specific points are made.

1. *Corporate Growth*   Noting the constancy of the capitalist share (the sum of columns 3, 4, and 7) — which was roughly 17% in both the late 1920s and in the past decade — we find that the expansion of labour's share of the economy has come at the expense of the share going to proprietors (columns 5 and 6). This suggests that the evolution of the corporation as the dominant form of business enterprise may be an important explanatory factor. Individuals who would have operated their own corner grocery in the 1920s are the hired managers of corporate supermarkets in the 1980s or 1990s.

2. *Changing Industry Mix*   The changing output mix, and therefore the industry mix, that have occurred, have tended to increase labour's share. Overall, there has been a long-term change in the composition of output and industry. There has been a reallocation of labour from agriculture to both manufacturing and service sectors. These shifts account for much of the growth of labour's share, reflected in column 2 of Table 17-2.

Unions?   It is tempting to explain an expanding wage share in terms of the growth of labour unions. But there are difficulties with this approach.

First, the growth of the labour movement in Canada does not fit well chronologically with the growth of labour's share of domestic income. Most of the growth of "wages and salaries" occurred after 1952, while much of the growth in the labour movement came between 1900 and 1950.

Second, recall from Chapter 16 the possibility that wage increases for union members may come at the expense of the wages of unorganized workers. In obtaining higher wages, unions restrict employment opportunities (Figure 16-6 and 16-7) in organized industries. Unemployed workers and new entrants to the labour force therefore seek jobs in the nonunion sectors. The resulting increases in labour supply tend to depress wage rates in nonunion jobs. If this scenario is correct, then higher wages for union workers may be achieved not at the expense of the capitalist

TABLE 17-2   Relative shares of domestic income, 1926–1991 (*selected years or period averages of shares for individual years*)

(1) Year or period	(2) Wages, salaries, and supplementary labour income	(3) Corporation profits before taxes	(4) Interest and miscellaneous investment income	(5) Accrued net income of farmers from farm production	(6) Net income of nonfarm unincorporated business including rent	(7) Inventory valuation adjustment	(8) Net domestic income at factor cost
1926	55.3%	11.4%	3.2%	14.1%	14.9%	1.1%	100%
1927–28	55.5	12.5	3.4	13.1	15.2	0.3	100
1929	60.0	12.9	3.7	8.0	15.7	−0.3	100
1932	69.3	4.1	4.5	3.6	14.7	3.8	100
1933	70.2	9.7	4.3	2.6	14.1	−0.9	100
1937	62.6	15.6	3.1	6.9	13.9	−2.1	100
1941	61.9	18.1	2.8	7.0	12.6	−2.4	100
1945	63.4	13.1	2.7	9.2	12.0	−0.4	100
1951	60.7	17.9	2.5	10.5	12.0	−3.6	100
1952	60.5	15.4	2.5	9.4	11.6	0.6	100
1957–60	67.0	13.7	3.9	3.6	12.0	−0.2	100
1961–65	67.7	14.2	4.3	3.6	10.6	−0.3	100
1966–70	70.9	13.5	4.7	2.7	8.8	−0.6	100
1971	73.0	12.2	5.5	2.0	8.2	−0.9	100
1973	70.6	16.0	5.7	3.0	7.2	−2.5	100
1975	71.2	14.8	7.1	2.9	6.0	−2.0	100
1976	71.9	13.4	8.0	2.2	5.9	−1.4	100
1979	69.3	16.4	10.7	1.7	5.4	−3.5	100
1982	72.7	9.2	12.2	1.2	5.8	−1.1	100
1990	72.6	8.7	11.1	0.6	7.0	−0.0	100
1991	74.8	6.2	10.7	0.7	7.2	0.4	100

Source: 1926–1986: Statistics Canada, *National Income and Expenditure Accounts, Annual estimates 1926–86*, Table 70; Statistics Canada, *National Income and Expenditure Accounts, First Quarter*, 1992, Table 1.

share, but rather at the expense of the nonunion wage share. Overall, the total labour share — union plus nonunion — could well be unaffected by unions.

Finally, if domestic income is disaggregated into industry sectors and the historical trend of the wage share in each sector is examined, we reach a curious conclusion. Generally, labour's share has grown more rapidly in those sectors where unions are weak than in sectors that are highly unionized.

CHAPTER SUMMARY

1. Economic rent is the price paid for the use of land and other natural resources whose total supplies are fixed.

2. Rent is a surplus since land would be available to the economy as a whole even in the absence of all rental payments. The notion of land rent as a surplus gave rise to the single-tax movement of the late 1800s.

3. Differences in land rent are explainable in terms of differences in productivity due to the fertility and climatic features of land and in its location.

4. Land rent is a surplus rather than a cost to the economy as a whole; however, because land has alternative uses from the standpoint of individual firms and industries, rental payments of firms and industries are correctly regarded as costs.

5. Interest is the price paid for the use of money. The equilibrium interest rate is determined by the demand for and supply of loanable funds.

6. The equilibrium interest rate influences the level of investment and helps ration financial and physical capital to specific firms and industries.

7. Economic, or pure, profits are the difference between a firm's total revenue and its total costs, the latter defined to include implicit costs, which include a normal profit. Profits accrue to enterpreneurs for assuming the uninsurable risks associated with organizing and directing economic resources and innovating. Profits also result from monopoly.

8. Profit expectations influence innovating and investment activities, and therefore the level of employment. The basic function of profits and losses, however, is to induce that allocation of resources that is in general accord with the tastes of consumers.

9. The largest share of domestic income goes to labour. Narrowly defined as "wages and salaries," labour's relative share has increased through time. When more broadly defined to include "proprietor's income," labour's share has been about 80% and the capitalist share about 20% of domestic income since 1926.

TERMS AND CONCEPTS

economic or pure profit (p. 301)
economic rent (p. 294)
explicit and implicit costs (p. 301)
incentive function (p. 295)
loanable funds theory of interest (p. 297)
normal profit (p. 301)

pure rate of interest (p. 300)
rate of return (p. 297)
single-tax movement (p. 295)
static economy (p. 301)
uninsurable risks (p. 302)

QUESTIONS AND STUDY SUGGESTIONS

1. How does the economist's usage of the term "rent" differ from everyday usage? "Though rent need not be paid by society to make land available, rental payments are very useful in guiding land into the most productive uses." Explain.

2. Explain why economic rent is a surplus to the economy as a whole but a cost of production from the standpoint of individual firms and industries. Explain: "Rent performs no 'incentive function' in the economy." What arguments can be made for and against a heavy tax on land?

3. If money capital is not an economic resource, why is interest paid and received for its use? What considerations account for the fact that interest rates differ greatly on various types of loans? Use these considerations to explain the relative size of the interest rates charged on the following: a. a ten-year, $1,000 government bond; b. a $20 pawnshop loan; c. an NHA mortgage loan on a $120,000 house; d. a 36-month, $12,000 chartered bank loan to finance an automobile; e. a 60-day, $100 loan from a personal finance company.

4. Why is the supply of loanable funds upsloping? Why is the demand for loanable funds downsloping? Explain the equilibrium interest rate and indicate factors that might cause it to change.

5. What are the major economic functions of the interest rate? Of economic profits? How might the fact that more and more firms are financing their investment activities internally affect the efficiency with which the interest rate performs its functions?

6. How do the concepts of accounting profits and economic profits differ? Why are economic profits smaller than accounting profits? What are the three basic sources of economic profits? Classify each of the following in accordance with these sources: *a.* a firm's profit from developing and patenting a ballpoint pen containing a permanent ink cartridge; *b.* a restaurant's profit that results from construction of a new highway past its door; *c.* the profit received by a firm benefiting from an unanticipated change in consumer tastes.

7. Why is the distinction between insurable and uninsurable risks significant for the theory of profits? Carefully evaluate: "All economic profits can be traced to either uncertainty or the desire to avoid it."

8. Explain the absence of economic profit in a purely competitive, static economy. Realizing that the major function of profits is to allocate resources in accordance with consumer preferences, evaluate the allocation of resources in such an economy.

9. What has happened to wage, profit, interest, and rent shares of domestic income over time? Explain the alleged growth of labour's share in terms of structural changes in the economy.

18

Income Inequality and Poverty

There is significant income inequality in Canada, and the incidence of poverty rose in the first two years of the 1990s as a deep recession persisted.

The issue of income inequality has come to the fore as the after-tax real family income stagnated over the course of the 1980s, having increased a meagre 0.5% compared with a 22% increase during the 1970s, 34% in the 1960s, and 27% in the 1950s.

Even more troubling is the fact that child poverty is on the rise, particularly in the "have" provinces of Ontario and British Columbia. Statistics Canada estimated that in 1990 17.4% of the nation's children under 16 were poor, an almost 15% increase over 1989.

How income should be distributed has a long and controversial history in both economics and philosophy. Should our national income and wealth be more, or less, equally distributed than is now the case? Or, is society making the proper response to the question "For whom?"

We begin by surveying some basic facts concerning the distribution of income in Canada. Next, the major causes of income inequality are considered. We then examine the trade-off between equality and efficiency. We will look at the poverty problem and consider existing income-maintenance programs, and the possibility of introducing a negative income tax to alleviate poverty.

INCOME INEQUALITY: THE FACTS

How equally — or unequally — is income distributed in Canada? How wide is the gulf between rich and poor? Has the degree of income inequality increased or lessened over time?

Personal Income Distribution

Average income in Canada is among the highest in the world. The average income for all families was about $51,600 in 1990. In Table 18-1 we find that 2.6% of all families received less than $10,000 a year in 1990; 6.7% of all families received less than $20,000 per year. At the top of the income pyramid, we find that 18.2% of the families received incomes of $75,000 or more per year. These figures suggest *there is considerable* **income inequality** *in Canada.*

Trends in Income Inequality

Over time economic growth has raised incomes. In *absolute* terms, the entire distribution of income has been moving upward over time. Has this changed the *relative* distribution of income — that is, the income of one group compared to another? Incomes can move up in absolute terms and the degree of relative inequality may or may not be affected. Table 18-2 shows the relative distribution of income. Here we divide the total number of income receivers into five numerically equal groups, or *quintiles*, and show the percentage of total personal (before tax) income received by each in selected years.

The relative distribution of income has been basically stable since 1951, when Statistics Canada began its detailed family-income surveys. Note that since 1951 the richest fifth of all families has received nine or ten times as much income as the poorest fifth.

The Lorenz Curve

The degree of income inequality can be seen through a **Lorenz curve**, as shown in Figure 18-1. Here we *cumulate* the "percent of families" on the horizontal axis and the "percent of income" on the vertical axis. The possibility of a completely equal distribution of income is represented by the diagonal line because such a line indicates that any given percentage of families receives that same percentage of income.

FIGURE 18-1   The Lorenz curve

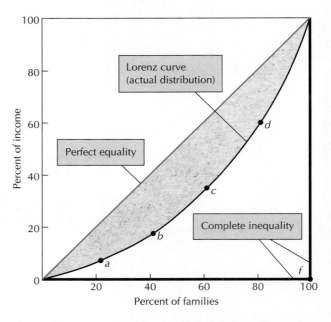

The Lorenz curve is a convenient means of visualizing the degree of income inequality. Specifically, the shaded area between the line of perfect equality and the Lorenz curve reflects the degree of income inequality.

That is, if 20% of all families receives 20% of total income, 40% receives 40%, 60% receives 60%, and so on, all of these points will fall on the diagonal line.

By plotting the 1990 data from Table 18-2, we locate the Lorenz curve to visualize the actual distribution of income. Observe that the bottom 20% of all families received 4.7% of the income, shown by point *a*; the bottom 40% received 15.1% (= 4.7 + 10.4), shown by point *b*; and so forth. The shaded area, determined by the extent to which the resulting Lorenz curve deviates from the line of perfect equality, indicates the degree of income inequality. The larger this area, the greater the degree of income inequality.

If the actual income distribution were perfectly equal, the Lorenz curve and the diagonal would coincide and the gap would disappear. At the opposite extreme is the situation of complete inequality, where 1% of families has 100% of the income and the rest have none. In that case, the Lorenz curve would coincide with the horizontal and right vertical axes of the graph, forming a right angle at point *f*, as indicated by the heavy lines. This extreme degree of inequality would be indicated by the entire area southeast of the diagonal.

TABLE 18-1   The distribution of personal income by families and unattached individuals, 1990

(a) (1) Personal income class	(2) Percent of all families in this class	(3) Percent of all unattached individuals in this class	(4) Percent of all families and unattached individuals in this class	(5) Percent of all families in this class and all lower classes	(6) Percent of all unattached individuals in this class and all lower classes	(7) Percent of all families and unattached individuals in this class and all lower classes
Under $10,000	2.6	20.5	8.2	2.6	20.5	8.2
$10,000 to $14,999	4.1	23.4	10.2	6.5	43.9	18.4
$15,000 to $19,999	6.7	11.7	8.3	13.2	55.6	26.7
$20,000 to $29,999	13.4	18.9	15.1	26.6	74.5	41.8
$30,000 to $49,999	28.7	18.9	25.6	55.3	93.4	67.4
$50,000 to $74,999	26.4	} 6.5	19.6	81.7	} 100.0	87.0
$75,000 and over	18.2		12.9	100.0		100.0
	100.0	100.0	100.0			

(b)	Families	Unattached individuals	Families & unattached individuals
Average 1990 income	$ $51,633	$ $22,615	$ 42,525
Median 1990 income	$ $46,069	$ $17,458	$ 35,795
1990 population	7,201,000	3,294,000	10,495,000

Source: Statistics Canada, *Income Distributions by Size in Canada, 1990* (Ottawa, December 1991), Tables 1, 24, and 34.

The Lorenz curve can be used to contrast the distribution of income at different points in time, among different groups (for example, native-born and

TABLE 18-2   Percentage of total before-tax and after-tax income received by each one-fifth of families and unattached individuals

	Before tax				After tax
Quintile	1951	1965	1989	1990	1990
Lowest 20%	4.4	4.4	4.8	4.7	5.6
Second 20%	11.2	11.8	10.5	10.4	11.5
Third 20%	18.3	18.0	16.9	16.9	17.5
Fourth 20%	23.3	24.5	24.6	24.8	24.7
Highest 20%	42.8	41.4	43.2	43.3	40.6
	100.0	100.0	100.0	100.0	100.0

Source: Statistics Canada, *Income Distributions: Incomes of Non-Farm Families and Individuals in Canada, 1951–1965* (Ottawa, 1969); *Income Distributions by Size in Canada, 1990* (Ottawa, 1991); and *Income After Taxes, Distributions by Size in Canada, 1990* (Ottawa, 1992), Table 26.

recent immigrants), before and after taxes and transfer payments are taken into account, or between different countries. As already observed, the Lorenz curve has not shifted significantly since World War II. Comparisons with other countries suggest that the distribution of income in Canada is quite similar to most other industrially advanced countries.

ALTERNATIVE INTERPRETATIONS

The perceptive reader may raise several objections to our data.

Taxes

Is after-tax income much more equally distributed? The answer is no, as the last column of Table 18-2 reveals. ***In Canada, the before-tax and after-tax distributions of income are not much different.*** The overall tax system is only slightly progressive. Hence, because of taxes, the poor person's income is increased by a somewhat higher percentage than the

Box 18-1

In the Media

Every year as soon as the latest statistics are released, the media report the country's top income earners. In the last few decades doctors, dentists, and lawyers have topped the list. Using the explanations of income inequality given in this chapter try to identify some of the reasons the professions allow their members to earn a high income. The other point raised by the article below is that some people with high incomes do not pay enough taxes. Explain the trade-off between equality and efficiency in connection with the discussion on taxes.

DOCTORS, DENTISTS TOP INCOMES LIST

Taxman Scores Biggest Gains

BY ALAN FREEMAN
Parliamentary Bureau

OTTAWA — Doctors, dentists, lawyers and accountants top the income lists, according to statistics released by Revenue Canada yesterday.

The leaders, by far, remain self-employed physicians and surgeons, whose average income in 1989 was $120,499, up 5.9 per cent from $113,810 in 1988. No. 2 spot was held by self-employed dentists with average incomes of $98,867, a gain of 4.4 per cent from $94,666 in 1988.

Self-employed lawyers and notaries came in third with average incomes of $96,967, a rise of 6.4 per cent from $91,142. By contrast, self-employed farmers reported average income of only $19,448, a gain of 6.3 per cent from $18,298 a year earlier.

Self-employed accountants also had a good year in 1989 as their average income soared 16.6 per cent to an average of $76,487 from $65,600 a year earlier. But they remained in fourth place among professionals in their average income.

Teachers and professors declared average income of $42,033, up 2.8 per cent from $40,869 in 1988, the statistics show.

While the self-employed professionals showed healthy gains in their income, the taxman did even better. The average federal income tax paid by accountants jumped 28.8 per cent to $13,833 from $10,740 in 1988.

Federal taxes paid by doctors increased 13.2 per cent, dentists 10 per cent and lawyers 12.3 per cent.

Among larger cities, West Vancouver reported the highest average income at $48,506 for all tax returns and an average of $57,510 for taxable returns. But Westmount, a Montreal neighbourhood, was tops if smaller municipal units are also included.

Of the 11,200 returns filed with Westmount addresses, average income was $66,621, and of 9,240 taxable returns from the municipality, average income was $79,041.

Steven Langdon, NDP finance critic, said the taxation statistics on capital gains deductions prove the income tax system favours the rich.

Canadians claimed a total of $7.3-billion in capital gains deductions in 1989, with more than half of the deductions claimed by individuals who had incomes of $100,000 or more.

"It gives us a picture of how unfair and vicious this particular tax benefit is in terms of income distribution," Mr. Langdon said in an interview.

According to the figures, a total of 595,490 Canadians claimed capital gains deductions in 1989. But the lion's share, or $3.9-billion, was claimed by 74,350 tax filers with income of more than $100,000.

A total of 18.1 million Canadians filed tax returns for 1989, of which 13.4 million were taxable.

Mr. Langdon also noted that 7,010 tax filers with income of $50,000 or more paid no income tax at all in 1989, including 180 with incomes of $250,000 and more. Those numbers are up from 2,910 and 100 for the two categories in 1987, Mr. Langdon said, proving that many wealthy Canadians still escape income tax.

But a spokesman for Finance Minister Donald Mazankowski said the percentage of high-income Canadians who don't pay income tax continues to fall from 1.6 per cent in 1984 to 0.5 per cent in 1989.

"We're getting at the problem," he said. "We feel that we have taken measures that are starting to pay off to make sure that a greater percentage of high-income individuals are paying their fair share of income tax."

By permission of *The Globe and Mail*, January 11, 1992.

rich person's is reduced; as a result, relative incomes are little changed.

Lifetime Income

Another objection to the Statistics Canada data is that they portray the distribution of income in a single year and thereby conceal the possibility that the *lifetime earnings* of families might be more equal. Suppose Jacobs earns $1,000 in year 1 and $100,000 in year 2, while Kendall earns $100,000 in year 1 and only $1,000 in year 2. Do we have income inequality? The answer depends on the period of measurement. Annual data would reveal great income inequality; but for the two-year period we have complete equality.

This is important because there is evidence to suggest that there is a considerable "churning around" in the distribution of income over time. In fact, most workers follow an age-earnings profile whereby their income starts at relatively low levels, reaches a peak during middle age, and then declines. A glance back at Figure 16-11 reveals this general pattern. It follows that even if people received the same stream of income over their lifetimes, there would still exist considerable income inequality in any given year because of age differences. In any year, the young and old would receive low incomes while the middle-aged would receive high incomes. This would occur despite complete equality of lifetime incomes.

It has been argued that Canadians are staying longer in school and that some of the "statistical poor" undoubtedly include people whose increased education and prospects permit them to drop out of the workaday world for a while. Moreover, the bottom 20% of income earners, besides the genuinely poor, also includes retired families living comfortably off assets.

INCOME INEQUALITY: CAUSES

Why does Canada have the degree of income inequality shown in Tables 18-1 and 18-2? In general, we note that the market system is an impersonal mechanism. It has no conscience and it does not cater to ethical standards of an "equitable," or "just" distribution of income. Some of the more specific factors contributing to income inequality include:

1 Ability Differences People have different intellectual and physical abilities. Some are equipped to enter the relatively highly paid fields of medicine and law. Others have the talent and drive necessary to become great artists or musicians. On the other hand, some people can only get menial, low-paying jobs or are unable to work at all. Some are blessed with the physical ability and coordination to become highly paid professional athletes. Differences in ability mean that some individuals can make contributions to total output that command very high incomes, others cannot.

2 Education and Training Individuals differ significantly in the amounts of education and training they have obtained and, therefore, in their capacities to earn income. In part, these differences are a matter of voluntary choice. Smith chooses to enter the labour force upon high school graduation, while Jones decides to attend university. On the other hand, such differences may be involuntary: Smith's family may simply be unable to finance a university education or even to provide the necessary nutrition, shelter, or study conditions for Smith to do well in primary school.

3 Job Tastes and Risk Incomes differ because of differences in "job tastes." Those willing to take arduous, unpleasant jobs — for example, underground mining and garbage collecting — and work long hours with great intensity will tend to earn more. Some people boost their income by "moonlighting" — by holding two jobs. Individuals also differ in their willingness to assume risk. We refer here not only to the racing car driver, but to a person who takes an entrepreneurial risk. Though most fail, the fortunate few who gamble successfully on the introduction of a new product or service may realize very substantial incomes.

4 Property Ownership   Ownership of property resources, and therefore the receipt of property incomes, is very unequal. The vast majority of households own little or no resources, while some supply very great quantities of machinery, real estate, farmland, and so forth. Basically, property incomes account for the position of these family units at the very pinnacle of the income pyramid. The right of inheritance and the fact that "wealth begets wealth" reinforce the role played by unequal ownership of resources in determining income inequality.

5 Market Power   Ability to "rig the market" on one's own behalf is undoubtedly a major factor in accounting for income inequality. Certain unions and professional groups have adopted policies that limit the supplies of their productive services, thereby boosting the incomes of their members. Legislation that provides for occupational licensing, as in the case of lawyers, doctors, and accountants, can also be a basis for exerting market power in favour of the licensed group.

6 Discrimination   Simple supply and demand analysis suggests how discrimination — in this case labour market discrimination — generates income inequality. Suppose that gender discrimination restricts women to a few "female" occupations (secretaries, nurses, teachers). This means that the supplies of female workers will be great relative to demand in these few occupations so that wages and incomes will be low. Conversely, discrimination means males do not have to compete with women in "male" occupations. Supply is artificially limited relative to demand in these occupations with the result that wages and incomes are high.

7 Luck, Connections, Misfortune   Luck, chance, and being in the right place at the right time have all caused individuals to stumble into fortunes. Discovering oil on a run-down farm or meeting the right press agent have accounted for some high incomes. Nor can personal contacts and political influence be discounted as means of attaining the higher income brackets. On the other hand, a host of misfortunes, such as prolonged illness, serious accident, death of the family breadwinner, and unemployment may plunge a family into relative poverty. The burden of such misfortunes is borne very unevenly by the population and thus contributes to the degree of income inequality.

QUICK REVIEW (18-1)

1. **Income inequality has remained largely unchanged in the last decade; currently the top fifth of all families receive about 43% of before-tax income and the bottom fifth receive under 5%.**

2. **The Lorenz curve portrays income inequality graphically.**

3. **Differences in ability, education, job tastes, property ownership, and market power — along with discrimination and luck — help explain income inequality.**

EQUALITY VERSUS EFFICIENCY

Society ought to strive to eliminate, or at least minimize, income inequality. Unfortunately, there is a trade-off between equality and efficiency. Let's explore the case for and against greater equality to understand the nature of the trade-off.

The Case for Equality: Maximizing Utility

The basic argument for an equal distribution of income is that income equality is necessary if consumer satisfaction (utility) is to be maximized. The rationale for this argument is shown in Figure 18-2, where it is assumed that the money incomes of two individuals, Anderson and Brooks, are subject to diminishing marginal utility (Chapter 7). In any time period, income receivers spend the first dollars received on those products they value most — on products whose marginal utility is high. As their most pressing wants become satisfied, consumers then spend additional dollars of income on less important, lower marginal utility, goods. The identical diminishing "marginal utility from income" curves reflect the assumption that Anderson and Brooks have the same capacity to derive utility from income.

Now suppose there is $10,000 worth of income (output) to be distributed between Anderson and Brooks. The best or optimal distribution would be an equal distribution, which causes the marginal utility of the last dollar to be the same for both persons. We can prove this by demonstrating that for an initially unequal distribution of income, the combined total utility of the two individuals can be increased by moving towards equality.

FIGURE 18-2   The utility-maximizing distribution of a given income

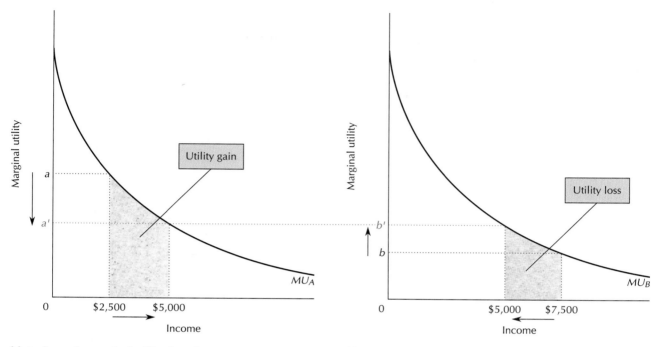

(a) Anderson's marginal utility from income   **(b) Brooks' marginal utility from income**

Proponents of income equality argue that given identical "marginal utility from income" curves, Anderson and Brooks will maximize their combined utility when any given income (say $10,000) is equally distributed. If income is unequally distributed ($2,500 to Anderson and $7,500 to Brooks), the marginal utility derived from the last dollar will be greater for Anderson ($0a$) than for Brooks ($0b$) and hence a redistribution toward equality will result in a net increase in total utility. The utility gain shown by the colour area in panel (*a*) exceeds the utility loss indicated by the gray area in panel (*b*). When equality is achieved, the marginal utility derived from the last dollar of income will be equal for both consumers ($0a' = 0b'$); therefore, there is no further redistribution of income that will increase total utility.

For example, suppose that initially the $10,000 of income is distributed unequally so that Anderson gets only $2,500 and Brooks receives $7,500. We observe that the marginal utility from the last dollar received by Anderson is high ($0a$) and the marginal utility from Brooks's last dollar of income is low ($0b$). The redistribution of a dollar's worth of income from Brooks to Anderson — that is, toward greater equality — would increase (by $0a - 0b$) the combined total utility of the two consumers. Anderson's utility gain exceeds Brooks's loss. This will continue to be the case until income is equally distributed with each person receiving $5,000. At this point, the marginal utility of the last dollar is identical for Anderson and Brooks ($0a' = 0b'$) and hence further redistribution cannot increase total utility.

The Case for Inequality: Incentives and Efficiency

Although the logic of the argument for equality is sound, critics attack its fundamental assumption that there exists some fixed amount of income to be distributed. Critics of income equality argue that *the way in which income is distributed is an important determinant of economic growth — the amount of income produced and available for distribution.*

Suppose, in Figure 18-2, that Anderson earns $2,500 and Brooks $7,500. In moving toward equality, society (government) must *tax* away some of Brooks's income and *transfer* it to Anderson. This tax-transfer process will diminish the income rewards of high-income Brooks and raise the income rewards of low-income Anderson and, in so doing, reduce the incentives of both to *earn* high incomes. Why should Brooks work hard, save and invest, or undertake entrepreneurial risks, when the rewards from such activities will be reduced by taxation? And why should Anderson be motivated to increase his income when government stands ready to transfer income to him?

In the extreme, imagine a situation in which government levies a 100% tax on income and distributes the tax revenue equally to its citizens. Why work hard? Indeed, why work at all? Why assume business risks? Why save — that is, forgo current consumption — to invest? The economic incentives to get ahead will have been removed and the productive efficiency of the economy — and hence the amount of income to be distributed — will diminish. The way the income pie is distributed affects the size of that pie!

The Equality–Efficiency Trade-Off

The essence of the income (in)equality debate is that there exists a fundamental **trade-off between equality and efficiency**. Thus the problem for a society inclined toward social economic justice is how to achieve a more equal redistribution of income so as to minimize the adverse effects on economic efficiency. Consider this *leaky-bucket analogy*. Assume society agrees to shift income from the rich to the poor. But the money must be transferred from affluent to indigent in a leaky bucket. The leak represents an efficiency loss — the loss of output and income — due to the harmful effects of the tax-transfer process on incentives to work, to save and invest, and to accept entrepreneurial risk. It also reflects the fact that resources must be diverted to the bureaucracies that administer the tax-transfer system.

How much leakage will society accept and continue to endorse the redistribution? If cutting the income pie in more equal slices tends to shrink the pie, what amount of shrinkage will society tolerate? Is a loss of one cent on each redistributed dollar acceptable? Five cents? Twenty-five cents? Forty cents? This is a critical, value-laden question that will permeate future political debates over extensions and modifications of our income maintenance programs.

THE DISMAL ECONOMICS OF POVERTY

Many people are less concerned with the larger question of income distribution than they are with the more specific issue of inadequate income. Therefore, armed with some background information on income inequality, let's now turn to the poverty problem. How extensive is poverty in Canada? What are the characteristics of the poor? And what is the best strategy to lessen poverty?

Defining Poverty

Poverty does not lend itself to precise definition. But it helps to distinguish between absolute and relative poverty. **Absolute poverty** occurs when the basic material needs — food, clothing, and shelter — of an individual or family are not met. **Relative poverty** refers to an individual's or family's low income relative to others in society. Thus, while a family's basic material needs may be met, it would still be considered poor if its income relative to others is much lower.

While it is possible to eradicate absolute poverty, relative poverty will probably always be around, at least in a market economy, where some individuals are able to earn much more than others (Chapter 16).

A family's needs have many determinants: its size, its health, the ages of its members, and so forth. Its means include currently earned income, transfer payments, past savings, property owned, and so on. Statistics Canada uses a (revised) "low income cut-off": families that spend 56.2% or more of their income on food, shelter, and clothing (almost 25 percentage points above the 32.5% of the average Canadian household) are considered to be in straitened circumstances and therefore below the cut-off. The cut-off or "poverty line" is related both to family size and to the size of the area of residence: the bigger the city, the higher the cut-off. Hence in 1990 an unattached person living in a rural area on less than $9,637 a year was poor, while a big-city (500,000 and more people) cousin was poor on less than $14,155. For a family of four, the rural poverty line was $19,117; the big-city one, $28,081. For a family of six, rural poverty started below $22,672 and in the big city at $33,303. Applying these definitions to 1990 income data for Canada, it was found that *12.1% of families and 34.1% of unattached individuals lived in poverty.*

Who Are the Poor?

Who are these 3.8 million souls — 14.1% of the population — who live in poverty? Unfortunately for purposes of public policy, the poor are heterogeneous: they can be found in all geographic regions; they are whites and native peoples; they include large num-

Box 18-2

In the Media

Much of the confusion and controversy surrounding the subject of poverty in Canada centres around the failure to distinguish between absolute and relative poverty. In the following editorial from The Globe and Mail, *the authors consider this important distinction and conclude that on average the poor are better off today than they were some 30 years earlier. However, in relative terms the poor continue to receive a small percentage of the income generated in Canada.*

THE MEANING OF POVERTY IN CANADA

JESUS said the poor are always with us. Are they?

In 1961, Statistics Canada estimated that 29 per cent of the Canadian population was living below the poverty line, more precisely called the low-income cut-off. In 1967, the federal agency estimated that 24 per cent of Canadians were poor. Although by 1990 this had been reduced to only 14.6 per cent of the population, the Canadian Council on Social Development, which uses a different calculation of poverty, still classified 25.5 per cent of households as poor in 1987.

Has the degree of income inequality changed since the Woodstock generation? In 1970, the bottom 20 per cent of the population received 5.23 per cent of society's total income. In 1986, the poorest 20 per cent were still pulling in exactly 5.23 per cent of that year's total income. In 1970, slightly more than 41 cents out of every dollar earned went to the top 20 per cent of the population. Sixteen years later, the top fifth of Canadians were still earning slightly more than 41 per cent of total income.

So the poor are still with us, and they are still as impoverished as they were 30 years ago. Right?

Well, not exactly. It depends on how you define "poor." Take for example Statistics Canada's calculation of the low-income cutoff. In 1959, researchers estimated that the average Canadian family spent 50 per cent of its gross income on food, clothing and shelter. Any family spending more than this amount on the essentials would be living in "straitened circumstances." Arbitrarily adding 20 per cent to that number, they decided to classify anyone who would have to spend more than 70 per cent of income on the basics as low-income.

As real incomes grew, Canadians spent a smaller proportion of their income on the essentials. Statistics Canada accordingly adjusted its definition of the poverty line. By 1969, surveys showed that Canadian families were spending only 42 per cent of income on the three essentials. Statistics Canada once again added a 20 per cent mark-up to this, giving a new poverty cut-off of 62 per cent of expenditure on the basics. In 1978, the 62 per cent standard yielded to one of 58.5 per cent, to be replaced in 1986 by a 56.2 per cent standard — not much more than the average family spent a generation before.

The result is that there is a substantial difference between the 1961 and the 1991 definitions of poverty. In 1961, Statistics Canada classified as low-income any family of three with an annual income of less than $3,000. By our calculations, $3,000 in 1961 dollars is equivalent to $14,969 in 1990 dollars. Yet the StatsCan low-income cut-off for a family of three living in a big city in 1990 was $24,255; the poverty line for a three-person household developed by the Canadian Council on Social Development for 1990 was $24,956.

So are things improving, or aren't they? The confusion lies in the difference between relative and absolute measures of poverty. There is no absolute definition of poverty — nor can there be, for poverty in a poor nation such as India means something very different from poverty in Canada. Therefore, measures of poverty in Canada are primarily measures of income inequality: a relative term. As Canadians' average incomes have risen, so has the poverty threshold. Without trying to be callous, the truth is that Canadians — including low-income Canadians — are wealthier today than they were in 1961.

The pie has gotten bigger. The poor are still getting a relatively smaller slice than anyone else — but they are getting a bigger piece than their counterparts from 1961.

By permission of *The Globe and Mail*, Monday, January 13, 1992.

bers of both rural and urban people; they are both old and young.

Yet, despite this pervasiveness, poverty is far from randomly distributed, as Table 18-3 demonstrates. An aging widow with four years of schooling living in an Atlantic town and prevented from seeking paid work by her four under-16 children still at home — well, she is likely to be poor. And when her children have left home and she is over 70, her fortunes look no brighter. The strong correlation shown in Table 18-3 between working few weeks in the year and being poor is expected. However, note that 5.4% of families

and 12.2% of unattached individuals who worked 49 to 52 weeks were still poor.

The high poverty rates for children are especially disturbing because in a very real sense poverty breeds poverty. Poor children are at greater risk for a range of long-term problems, including poor health and inadequate education, crime, drugs, and teenage pregnancy. Many of today's impoverished will reach adulthood unhealthy, illiterate, and unemployable. The increased concentration of poverty among children bodes poorly for reducing poverty in the near future.

TABLE 18-3   Incidence of low income by selected characteristics, 1990

	Estimated percentage below low income cut-off*	
	Families	Unattached individuals
All families and unattached individuals	12.1%	34.1%
By region — Atlantic provinces	12.7	31.8
— Quebec	14.5	44.0
By age of household head — 24 and under	38.4	52.6
— 25 to 34 years	15.2	21.1
— 65 and over	8.2	43.6
By sex of household head — female	40.2	39.3
By marital status of household head — neither married nor single†	31.8	37.0
By weeks worked — none	24.4	52.2
— 1–9 weeks	48.9	78.1
— 10–19 weeks	34.1	69.0
— 20–29 weeks	22.6	46.4
— 30–39 weeks	14.5	37.9
— 40–48 weeks	13.2	27.8
— 49–52 weeks	5.4	12.2
By education of household head — 0–8 years of school	16.5	55.1
— some secondary	16.6	39.8
By origin of household head — Canadian born	11.4	33.5
— non-Canadian born	15.1	37.4
By number of children younger than 16 years — none	8.1	34.1
— 1	17.3	—
— 2	15.0	—
— 3 or more	20.9	—

*As defined on p. 36 of the source, families that on average spent 56.2% or more of their income on food, shelter, and clothing were considered to be in straitened circumstances and, therefore, below the new 1986 low income cut-off. According to this criterion, it is estimated that 3.8 million persons — 2,804,000 in families and 1,023,000 unattached individuals — were below the low income cut-off in 1990.

†Divorced, separated, widowed.

Source: Statistics Canada, *Income Distribution by Size in Canada, 1990* (Ottawa, 1991), Table 67 and Appendix Table 2.

Recalling our previous discussion of movement or "churning" within the income distribution, we also note that there is considerable movement in and out of poverty. Just over half of those who are in poverty one year will remain below the poverty line the next year. On the other hand, poverty is much more persistent for some groups, in particular families headed by women.

The "Invisible" Poor

These facts and figures on the extent and character of poverty may be difficult to accept. After all, ours is an affluent society. How does one square the depressing statistics on poverty with everyday observations of abundance? The answer lies mainly in the fact that much Canadian poverty is hidden; it is largely invisible.

There are three major reasons for this invisibility. First, a sizable proportion of the people in the poverty pool change from year to year. Research has shown that as many as one-half of those in poverty are poor for only one or two years before successfully climbing out of poverty. Hence, many of these people are not visible to us as being permanently downtrodden and needy. Second, the "permanently poor" are increasingly isolated. Poverty persists in the slums and ghettos of large cities and is not readily visible from the expressway or commuter train. Similarly, rural poverty and the chronically depressed areas of eastern Quebec and the Atlantic provinces are also off the beaten path. Third, and perhaps most important, the poor are politically invisible. They often do not have interest groups fighting the various levels of governments for their rights.

THE INCOME MAINTENANCE SYSTEM

The existence of a wide variety of income-maintenance programs is evidence that alleviation of poverty has been accepted as a legitimate goal of public policy. In recent years, income-maintenance programs have involved substantial monetary outlays and large numbers of beneficiaries. About two-thirds of the federal government's 1992–3 expenditures (*not* counting the interest paid on the national debt) were transfer payments. The government estimated these $84 billion of expenditures would be disbursed as shown in Table 18-4. It should be noted, however, that the bulk of these transfers go to the non-poor,

and only a few of these programs are specifically targeted at the poor.

In addition to all these programs, there is the **Canada Pension Plan (CPP)** — funded by obligatory employee and employer contributions.[1] The maximum pension payable in 1992 was $636.11 a month. It increases each year, in January, by the percentage increase in the cost of living in the previous year.

The **Old Age Security (OAS)** pension is paid on application at age 65 to everyone resident in Canada for forty years or for at least ten years immediately before attaining the age of 65. The **Guaranteed Income Supplement (GIS)** is paid on application, subject to a means test, to those receiving the OAS pension but who have an income below a certain level. Considerably more than half of Canadians over 65 draw the GIS. Both the OAS pension and the GIS are increased every three months by the percentage increase in the cost of living in the previous three months. **Family allowances**, like OAS payments, are universal. Having one or more children younger than 18 qualifies each and every mother for the baby bonus. Since the baby bonus and the OAS and CPP pensions are all taxable, the poor keep a higher proportion of these transfers than do the better-off. Thus these schemes reduce income inequality.

Unemployment insurance (UI) was started in 1940 to insure *workers* against the hazards of losing their jobs. Certainly it has lessened the misery of the very large number of involuntarily unemployed during recessionary periods. In the early 1970s, unemployment insurance benefits were greatly increased so that there was created a positive incentive for *marginal* workers to enter the labour force, not to work, but to qualify for benefits. In 1977, benefits were decreased slightly while qualifying for them was made more difficult.

"The Welfare Mess"

There is no doubt that the social insurance system — not to mention local welfare, public housing, rent subsidies, minimum-wage legislation, agricultural subsidies, free dental treatment and drugs for those on welfare, private transfers through charities, veterans' benefits, and pensions — provides important means of alleviating poverty. On the other hand, the system, broadly defined, has been subject to a wide variety of criticisms.

---

[1] The Quebec Pension Plan, for residents of that province, is similar.

TABLE 18-4   Federal government transfer payments

Program	Estimated expenditures, fiscal year ending March 31, 1993, millions of dollars
Unemployment insurance	$20,189[1]
Old age security, guaranteed income supplement, and spouses' allowances	19,505
Family allowances	2,910
Established Programs Financing to support provision by the provinces of:	
health services	6,185[2]
post-secondary education	1,899
Canada Assistance Plan to bear 50% of cost to provinces of such welfare as child and family support services, as well as payments under the Vocational Rehabilitation of Disabled Persons Act	6,285[3]
Veterans' pensions and allowances	1,493
Transfers to other governments for Human Resource Development Programs	1,168
Housing programs for low-income families	1,981
Indian and Inuit affairs: improved housing, social and medical services, education and training, economic and employment development, and community infrastructures	2,760
Transfers to the territorial governments	1,045
Other transfers (mostly to the provinces)	18,551
Total	$83,971

[1]Entirely funded by the contributions of employers and employees.

[2]Provincial transfer payments to hospitals including federal transfers for that purpose were $22.9 billion in 1991.

[3]Provincial transfer payments to persons including federal transfers for that purpose were $31.4 billion in 1991.

Source: Government of Canada, *1992–1993 Estimates, Part I: The Government Expenditure Plan and Part II: The Main Estimates* (Ottawa: Supply and Services Canada, 1992).

1 Work Incentives   It is argued that many programs impair incentives to work. For example, many people on welfare would actually lose money by going to work. Since $1 of benefits is often lost for every $1 earned, there is no incentive to become a productive member of society. Moreover, a family going off welfare loses its right to free dental care and free medicine. Thus, the individual or family can be worse off by working.

Similarly, unemployment insurance benefits allow unemployed workers to seek a new job at a more leisurely pace, contributing to both the volume and duration of unemployment. Also, growing welfare benefits are financed by higher and higher taxes on the more productive, higher-income members of society, thereby weakening their incentives to work, take risks, and invest.

2 Abuses and Inequities   Many income-maintenance programs often benefit those who are *not* needy. This is particularly the case with unemployment insurance. The extension of coverage has induced many secondary income earners — those not primarily responsible for the family's income — to enter the labour force. Some of these people, as mentioned above, work barely long enough to qualify for unemployment insurance benefits. Other secondary income earners, while having an honest attachment to the labour force, on losing their jobs involuntarily, have no need of unemployment insurance benefits because of the continuing high income of the primary income earner. However, it is true that there are many families where the earnings of each spouse are so low that both must work to have a decent living standard for the family. But it is precisely those people who work, pay taxes, and make unemployment insurance contributions on their minimum wage incomes who are most victimized by someone's spouse drawing more in unneeded benefits than these working poor make in their unpleasant jobs.

3 Administrative Costs and Problems Critics charge that the growth of our welfare programs has created a clumsy and inefficient system, characterized by red tape and dependent on a huge bureaucracy for its administration. As such, administration costs can be a significant part of the total cost of many programs.

QUICK REVIEW (18-2)

1. **The fundamental argument for income equality is that it maximizes consumer utility; the basic argument for income inequality is that it is necessary to stimulate economic incentives.**

2. **Absolute poverty occurs when the basic material needs are not met. Relative poverty refers to an individual or family's low income relative to the rest of society.**

3. **By government standards some 3.8 million people or 14.1% of the population live in poverty.**

4. **Our income maintenance system is composed of both social insurance programs and public assistance ("welfare") programs.**

REFORM PROPOSALS

Negative Income Tax (NIT)

This criticism has led to support for a new approach to income maintenance. The contention is that the entire patchwork of existing income maintenance programs should be replaced by a **negative income tax (NIT)**. The term NIT suggests that the government should subsidize households with NIT payments when household incomes fall *below* a certain level.

Comparing Plans

Let's examine the two critical elements of any NIT plan. First, a NIT plan specifies a **guaranteed annual income** below which family incomes would not be allowed to fall. Second, the plan embodies a **benefit-loss rate** (sometimes called a **marginal transfer rate**), which indicates the rate at which

subsidy benefits — transfer payments — are reduced or "lost" as a consequence of earned income.

Consider Plan One of the three plans shown in Table 18-5. In Plan One, guaranteed annual income is $8,000 and the benefit loss rate is 50%. If the family earns no income, it will receive a NIT subsidy of $8,000. If it earns $4,000, it will lose $2,000 ($4,000 of earnings *times* the 50% benefit-loss rate) of subsidy benefits and total income will be $10,000 (= $4,000 of earnings *plus* $6,000 of subsidy). If $8,000 is earned, the subsidy will fall to $4,000, and so on. Note that at $16,000 the NIT subsidy becomes zero. The level of earned income at which the subsidy disappears and at which normal (positive) income tax applies on *further* increases in earned income is called the **break-even income**.

One might criticize Plan One on the grounds that a 50% benefit-loss rate is too high and therefore does not provide sufficient incentives to work. Hence in Plan Two, the $8,000 guaranteed income is retained, but the benefit-loss rate is reduced to 25%. We note, however, that the break-even level of income increases to $32,000 and many more families would now qualify for NIT subsidies. Furthermore, a family with any given earned income will now receive a larger NIT subsidy. For both of these reasons, a reduction of the benefit-loss rate to enhance work incentives will raise the cost of a NIT plan.

Examining Plans One and Two, still another critic might argue that the guaranteed income is too low, in that it does not get families out of poverty. Plan Three raises the guaranteed income to $16,000 and retains the 50% benefit-loss rate of Plan One. While Plan Three does a better job of raising the incomes of the poor, it too yields a higher break-even income and would therefore be more costly than Plan One. Furthermore, if the $16,000 income guarantee of Plan Three were coupled with Plan Two's 25% benefit-loss rate to strengthen work incentives, the break-even income level would shoot up to $64,000 and add even more to NIT costs.[2]

Goals and Conflicts

By comparing these three plans we find that there are trade-offs among the goals of an "ideal" income

---

[2] You may have sensed the generalization that, given the guaranteed income, the break-even level of income varies *inversely* with the benefit-loss rate. Specifically, the break-even income can be found by dividing the guaranteed income by the benefit-loss rate. Hence for Plan One, $8,000/0.50 = $16,000. Can you also demonstrate that given the benefit-loss rate, the break-even level of income varies *directly* with the guaranteed income?

TABLE 18-5   The negative income tax: three plans (*hypothetical data for a family of four*)

Plan One ($8,000 guaranteed annual income and 50% benefit-loss rate)			Plan Two ($8,000 guaranteed annual income and 25% benefit-loss rate)			Plan Three ($16,000 guaranteed annual income and 50% benefit-loss rate)		
(1) Earned income	(2) NIT subsidy	(3) Total income	(1) Earned income	(2) NIT subsidy	(3) Total income	(1) Earned income	(2) NIT subsidy	(3) Total income
$ 0	$8,000	$ 8,000	$ 0	$8,000	$ 8,000	$ 0	$16,000	$16,000
4,000	6,000	10,000	8,000	6,000	14,000	8,000	12,000	20,000
8,000	4,000	12,000	16,000	4,000	20,000	16,000	8,000	24,000
12,000	2,000	14,000	24,000	2,000	26,000	24,000	4,000	28,000
16,000*	0	16,000	32,000*	0	32,000	32,000*	0	32,000

*Indicates break-even income. Determined by dividing the guaranteed income by the benefit-loss rate.

maintenance plan. First, a plan should be effective in getting families out of poverty. Second, it should provide adequate incentives to work. Third, the plan's costs must not be high. Table 18-5 tells us that these three objectives conflict with one another and that compromises or trade-offs are necessary.

Plan One, with a low guaranteed income and a high benefit-loss rate, keeps costs down. But the low-income guarantee means it is not very effective in eliminating poverty and the high benefit-loss rate weakens work incentives. In comparison, Plan Two has a lower benefit-loss rate and therefore stronger work incentives. But it is more costly, because it involves a higher break-even income and therefore pays benefits to more families.

Compared to Plan One, Plan Three entails a higher guaranteed income and is clearly more effective in eliminating poverty. While work incentives are the same as with Plan One, the higher guaranteed income makes the plan more costly. The problem is to find the magic numbers that will provide a "decent" guaranteed income, maintain "reasonable" incentives to work, and entail "acceptable" costs.

CHAPTER SUMMARY

1. The distribution of personal income in Canada reflects considerable inequality. Little change has occurred in the postwar period. The Lorenz curve shows the degree of income inequality graphically.

2. Causes of income inequality include discrimination and differences in abilities, education and training, job tastes, property ownership, and market power.

3. The basic argument for income equality is that it maximizes consumer satisfaction from a given income. The main argument against income equality is that equality undermines incentives to work, invest, and assume risks, thereby tending to reduce the amount of income available for distribution.

4. Absolute poverty occurs when the basic material needs are not met. Relative poverty refers to an individual or family's low income relative to the rest of society. Absolute poverty can be eradicated, but relative poverty is much more difficult to resolve.

5. Current statistics suggest that about 14% of the country lives in poverty. Poverty is concentrated among the poorly educated, the aged, and families headed by women.

6. Our present income maintenance system is comprised of social insurance programs (Canada Pension Plan and unemployment insurance benefits), universal programs (Old Age Security Pension and Family Allowances), and public assistance or welfare programs. The present welfare programs have been criticized as being administratively inefficient, fraught with inequities, and detrimental to work incentives. Some economists believe that a negative income tax would provide a superior income maintenance system.

TERMS AND CONCEPTS

absolute poverty (p. 316)
benefit-loss rate (marginal transfer rate) (p. 321)
break-even income (p. 321)
Canada Pension Plan (p. 319)
equality–efficiency trade-off (p. 316)
family allowance (p. 319)
guaranteed annual income (p. 321)

Guaranteed Income Supplement (p. 319)
income inequality (p. 310)
Lorenz curve (p. 310)
negative income tax (p. 321)
Old Age Security (p. 319)
relative poverty (p. 316)
unemployment insurance benefits (p. 319)

QUESTIONS AND STUDY SUGGESTIONS

1. Assume Al, Beth, Carol, David, and Ed receive incomes of $500, $250, $125, $75, and $50 respectively. Construct and interpret a Lorenz curve for this five-person economy.

2. Briefly discuss the major causes of income inequality. With respect to income inequality, is there any difference between inheriting property and inheriting a high IQ? Explain.

3. Use the "leaky-bucket analogy" to discuss the equality–efficiency trade-off. Compared to our present income maintenance system, do you believe that a negative income tax would reduce the leak?

4. Should a nation's income be distributed to its members according to their contributions to the production of that total income or to the members' needs? Should society attempt to equalize income *or* economic opportunities? Are the issues of "equity" and "equality" in the distribution of income synonymous? To what degree, if any, is income inequality equitable?

5. Analyse in detail: "There need be no trade-off between equality and efficiency. An 'efficient' economy that yields an income distribution that many regard as unfair may cause those with meagre income rewards to become discouraged and stop trying. Hence, efficiency is undermined. A fairer distribution of rewards may generate a higher average productive effort on the part of the population, thereby enhancing efficiency. If people think they are playing a fair economic game and this belief causes them to try harder, an economy with an equitable income distribution may be efficient as well."

6. Comment upon or explain:

   a. "To endow everyone with equal income will certainly make for very unequal enjoyment and satisfaction."

   b. "Equality is a 'superior good': the richer we become, the more of it we can afford."

   c. "The mob goes in search of bread, and the means it employs is generally to wreck the bakeries."

   d. "Under our welfare system we have foolishly clung to the notion that employment and receipt of assistance must be mutually exclusive."

   e. "Some freedoms may be more important in the long run than freedom from want on the part of every individual."

   f. "Capitalism and democracy are really a most improbable mixture. Maybe that is why they need each other — to put some rationality into equality and some humanity into efficiency."

7. What are the major criticisms of our present income maintenance system?

8. The following table contains three illustrative negative income tax (NIT) plans.

Plan One			Plan Two			Plan Three		
Earned income	NIT subsidy	Total income	Earned income	NIT subsidy	Total income	Earned income	NIT subsidy	Total income
$ 0	$4,000	$4,000	$ 0	$4,000	$ 4,000	$ 0	$8,000	$ 8,000
2,000	3,000	5,000	4,000	3,000	7,000	4,000	6,000	10,000
4,000	2,000	6,000	8,000	2,000	10,000	8,000	4,000	12,000
6,000	1,000	7,000	12,000	1,000	13,000	12,000	2,000	14,000

   a. Determine the basic benefit, the benefit-loss rate, and the break-even income for each plan.

   b. Which plan is the most costly? The least costly? Which plan is the most effective in reducing poverty? The least effective? Which plan embodies the strongest disincentive to work? The weakest disincentive to work?

   c. Use your answers in part *b* to explain the following statement: "The dilemma of the negative income tax is that you cannot bring families up to the poverty level on the one hand, and simultaneously preserve work incentives and minimize program costs on the other."

Government and Current Economic Problems

19

Government and Market Failure

There are five economic functions of government: (1) providing the legal foundation and social environment conducive to the effective operation of the market system, (2) maintaining competition, (3) redistributing income and wealth, (4) adjusting the allocation of resources to provide public goods and correct for externalities, and (5) stabilizing the economy. In this and the next chapter we discuss these functions, extend and deepen our understanding of government, and identify some of the problems it faces in carrying out its economic functions.

In the present chapter, the topic of *market failure* is introduced. Our recently acquired tools of marginal analysis permit us to provide a fuller discussion of public goods and externalities.

ECONOMIC FUNCTIONS OF GOVERNMENT

The economic functions of government are many and varied. The economic role of government is so broad in scope that it is difficult to establish an all-inclusive list of its economic functions. We will employ the following breakdown of government's economic activities as a pattern for our discussion, recognizing that some overlapping is unavoidable.

Some of the economic functions of government strengthen and facilitate the operation of the market system. The two major activities of government in this area are:

1. Providing the legal foundation and a social environment conducive to the effective operation of the market system.

2. Maintaining competition.

Through a second group of functions, government supplements and modifies the operation of the market system. There are three major functions of government here. They involve:

3. Redistributing income and wealth.

4. Adjusting the allocation of resources to alter the composition of the nation's output.

5. Promoting growth and stabilizing the economy by controlling unemployment and inflation caused by business fluctuations.

In reality most government activities and policies have *some* impact in all these areas. For example, a program to redistribute income to the poor affects the allocation of resources to the extent that the poor buy somewhat different goods and services than do wealthier members of society.

LEGAL AND SOCIAL FRAMEWORK

Government undertakes the task of providing the legal framework and certain basic services requisite to the effective operation of a market economy. The necessary legal framework involves such things as providing for the legal status of business enterprises, defining the rights of private ownership, and providing for the enforcement of contracts. Government also establishes legal rules of the game to govern the relationships of businesses, resource suppliers, and consumers with one another. Through legislation, government is enabled to referee economic relationships, detect foul play, and exercise authority in imposing appropriate penalties. The basic services provided by government include police powers to

maintain internal order, a system of standards for measuring the weight and quality of products, and a monetary system to facilitate the exchange of goods and services.

The Food and Drug Act and Regulations of 1920 and the various amendments provide an example of how government has strengthened the operation of the market system. Under this Act, the Food Directorate of the Ministry of Health and Welfare of Canada conducts research on nutrition, food composition, food additives, pesticides, veterinary drugs, and environmental contaminants in foods; updates and promulgates food standards and regulations; and evaluates submissions from food manufacturers. The Drugs Directorate is responsible for programs relating to the safety, purity, and effectiveness of drugs on the market. All these measures are designed to prevent fraudulent activities by producers and increase the public's confidence in the integrity of the market system. The necessity for the Food and Drugs Act can be judged from the fact that back in 1877 in the first report under a predecessor Act, the commissioner reported that 51.7% of all food products analysed were found to be adulterated.

The presumption is that this type of government activity will improve resource allocation. Supplying a medium of exchange, ensuring the quality of products, defining ownership rights, and enforcing contracts tend to increase the volume of exchange. This widens markets and permits greater specialization in the use of resources. Such specialization, we saw in Chapter 2, means a more efficient allocation of resources. However, note that there is the argument that government has overregulated the interactions of businesses, consumers, and workers, thereby stifling economic incentives and impairing productive efficiency.

MAINTAINING COMPETITION

In a market economy it is the supply and demand decisions of *many* sellers and buyers that determine market prices. Profits and survival await the competitive producers who obey the market system; losses and eventual bankruptcy are the lot of those who deviate from it. With competition, buyers are the boss, the market is their agent, and businesses are their servant.

On the other hand, monopolists can artificially restrict the output of products and thereby enjoy higher prices and, very frequently, persistent economic profits. Monopolists are not regulated by the will of society as competitive sellers are. Producer sovereignty supplants consumer sovereignty to the degree that monopoly supplants competition. The result is that resources are allocated in terms of the profit-seeking interests of monopolistic sellers rather than in terms of the wants of society as a whole. Thus, monopoly causes a misallocation of economic resources.

In Canada, governments — federal and provincial — have attempted to control monopoly in two ways.

1. In the case of "natural monopolies" — that is, in industries where technological and economic realities rule out the possibility of competitive markets — governments have created public commissions to regulate prices and service standards.

2. The federal government has also enacted a series of anti-monopoly or anti-combines laws, beginning with an Act in 1889, for the purpose of maintaining and strengthening competition. These regulatory commissions and anti-combines laws were examined in Chapter 14. *The market economy has certain biases and shortcomings that compel government to supplement and modify its operation.*

REDISTRIBUTION OF INCOME

The market system is an impersonal mechanism that can bring about a distribution of income that may be more unequal than society desires. Government has assumed the responsibility for ameliorating income inequality in our society. This responsibility is reflected in a variety of policies and programs.

1. *Transfer payments* provide aid to the destitute, to the aged and handicapped, and to dependent families.

2. Governments sponsor *insurance plans*: the compulsory federal unemployment insurance and the provincial health insurance plans (with federal subsidy).

3. Governments also alter the distribution by *market intervention*, that is, by modifying the prices established by market forces. Price supports for farmers and minimum-wage legislation are illustrations of government price-fixing designed to raise the incomes of specific groups.

4. Finally, the federal *income tax* is designed to take a greater proportion of the incomes of the rich than of the poor and therefore has a kind of Robin Hood effect upon income distribution.

In seeking to reduce income inequality between persons, the federal government also attempts to lessen *regional* inequality through, among other pro-

grams, *equalization grants*, which the federal government makes to all the provinces except the three most affluent — Ontario, Alberta, and British Columbia.

REALLOCATION OF RESOURCES

While the market system has many virtues it ceases to function under certain circumstances. Economists are cognizant of two major cases of *market failure*, that is, situations in which the competitive market system would either (1) produce the "wrong" amounts of certain goods and services, or (2) fail to allocate any resources to the production of certain goods and services whose output is economically justified. The first case involves "spillovers" or "externalities" and the second "public" or "social" goods. When market failure occurs, government intervention is required. This and the next chapter deal in some detail with the issue of market failure and its remedy.

STABILIZATION

One of the most important functions of government is that of stabilizing the economy — assisting the private economy to achieve both the full employment of resources and a stable price level. Macroeconomics examines in detail the determinants of employment and the price level in a market economy. At this point we pause only to outline briefly the stabilization function of government.

The key point is that the level of output depends directly on total or aggregate expenditures. A high level of total spending means it will be profitable for the various industries to produce large outputs; this condition in turn will necessitate that resources be close to fully employed. But there are no mechanisms in a market system to ensure that aggregate expenditures will be at a level that will provide for full employment. Two unhappy possibilities might arise.

1 Unemployment The level of total spending in the private sector may be too low for full employment. The government's obligation in this case is to increase private spending so that total spending — private *and* public — will be sufficient to generate full employment.

2 Inflation The second possibility is that spending will be in excess of productive capacity. Excessive aggregate expenditure is inflationary. Government's obligation is to eliminate the excess spending.

MARKET FAILURE AND THE REALLOCATION OF RESOURCES

Let's turn our attention to the main topic of this chapter: market failure and ways government deals with it. We first look at externalities, and then turn to the issue of public goods.

Spillovers or Externalities

One of the virtues of a competitive market system is that it results in an efficient allocation of resources. But this conclusion assumes that there are no **spillovers** or **externalities** associated with the production or consumption of any good or service. A *spillover*[1] occurs when some of the benefits or costs associated with the production or consumption of a good "spill over" on to third parties, that is, to parties other than the immediate buyer or seller. Spillovers are also termed externalities because they are benefits and costs accruing to some individual or group external to the market transaction.

Spillover Costs   When the production or consumption of a commodity inflicts costs on some third party without compensation, there exists a **spillover cost**. The most obvious examples of spillover costs involve environmental pollution. When a chemical manufacturer, pulp and paper maker, or meat-packing plant dumps its wastes into a lake or river, swimmers, anglers, and boaters — not to mention communities that seek a usable water supply — suffer spillover costs.

Figure 19-1(a) tells the story of how spillover or social costs affect the allocation of resources. When spillover costs occur — when producers shift some of their costs onto the community — their production costs are lower than would otherwise be the case. The supply curve does not include or "capture" all the costs that can be legitimately associated with the production of the good. Hence the producer's supply curve, S, understates the total cost of production and therefore lies to the right of the supply curve that would include all costs, S_t. The result, shown in Figure 19-1(a), is that the equilibrium output Q_e is larger than the optimum output Q_o and the price charged in

the market, P_e, is less than the actual cost to society, P_o, of producing the last unit of output. Resources are *overallocated* to the production of this commodity.

Correcting for Spillover Costs   What actions might government take to correct the overallocation of resources associated with spillover costs? How might government "internalize" the external costs? Two basic types of corrective action are common: legislative action and specific taxes.

1 Direct Controls   Looking at our examples of air and water pollution, the most direct action is to pass legislation that prohibits or limits pollution. Such legislation forces potential polluters to bear the costs of directly controlling their industrial wastes. For example, firms must buy and install smoke-abatement equipment or facilities to purify water that has been contaminated by manufacturing processes. Such action forces potential offenders, under the threat of legal action, to bear *all* the costs associated with their production. Legislation can shift the supply curve S toward S_t in Figure 19-1(b), tending to bring the equilibrium and optimum outputs into equality.

2 Specific Taxes   Government might levy a specific tax that approximates the spillover costs per unit of output. Through this tax, government attempts to shove back onto the offending firms those external or spillover costs that private industry would otherwise avoid. A specific tax equal to T per unit in Figure 19-1(b) will increase the firms' costs, shifting the supply curve from S to S_t. The result is that the equilibrium output Q_e will decline so that it corresponds with the optimum output Q_o, and the overallocation of resources will be eliminated.

Spillover Benefits   Spillovers may also take the form of benefits. The production or consumption of certain goods and services may confer social, external, or **spillover benefits** on third parties or the community at large, for which payment or compensation is not required. For example, measles and polio immunization shots result in direct benefits to the immediate consumer. But immunization against these contagious diseases yields widespread and substantial spillover benefits to the entire community.

Education is another standard example of spillover benefits. Education entails benefits to individual consumers: well-educated people generally achieve higher incomes than do less-educated people. But education also confers sizable benefits on society; for example, the economy as a whole benefits from a

---

[1] Spillovers may go by other names — for example, external economies and diseconomies, neighbourhood effects, and social benefits and costs.

FIGURE 19-1   Spillover costs and the overallocation of resources

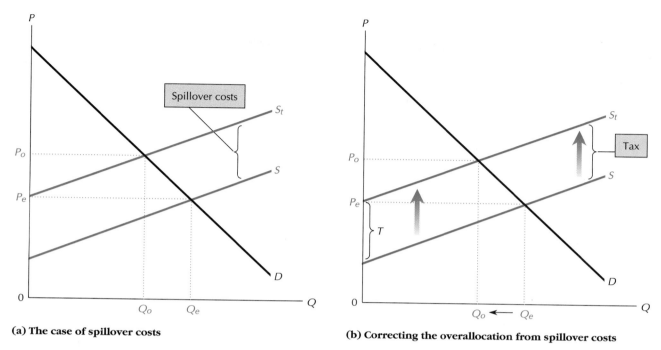

(a) The case of spillover costs

(b) Correcting the overallocation from spillover costs

With spillover costs in (a) we find that the lower costs borne by businesses, as reflected in S, fail to reflect all costs, as embodied in S_t. Consequently, the equilibrium output Q_e is greater than the efficient or optimum output Q_o. This overallocation of resources can be corrected by legislation or, as shown in (b), by imposing a specific tax T, which raises the firm's costs and supply curve from S to S_t.

more versatile and more productive labour force on the one hand, and smaller outlays in the areas of crime prevention, law enforcement, and welfare programs on the other. Significant, too, is the fact that political participation correlates positively with the level of education.

Figure 19-2(a) shows the impact of spillover benefits on resource allocation. The existence of spillover benefits means that the market demand curve, which reflects only private benefits, understates total benefits. The market demand curve fails to capture all the benefits associated with the provision and consumption of goods and services that entail spillover benefits. Thus D in Figure 19-2(a) indicates the benefits that private individuals derive from education; D_t is drawn to include these private benefits *plus* the additional spillover benefits accruing to society at large. While market demand D and supply S_t would yield an equilibrium output of Q_e, this output would be less than the optimum output Q_o. The market system would not produce enough education; the market system would not produce enough education;

resources would be *underallocated* to education.

What policies are appropriate for the case of spillover benefits? Assuming that the spillover or social benefits are not inordinately large when compared with the benefits received by individual purchasers, government can either encourage the consumption of the resource through a subsidy to consumers or its production through a subsidy to producers. In Figure 19-2(b), the subsidy to consumers increases demand from D to D_t, resulting in an increase in output from Q_e to the optimum level Q_o. In Figure 19-2(c), the subsidy to producers moves the supply curve downward from S_t to S'_t. As a result, output will increase from Q_e to the optimal level Q_o. Thus, the underallocation of resources will be corrected.

A third policy option arises if spillover benefits are extremely large: Government may simply choose to finance or, in the extreme, to own and operate such industries.

It will be helpful to extend our discussion of the various options to solving the externality problem.

FIGURE 19-2   Spillover benefits and the underallocation of resources

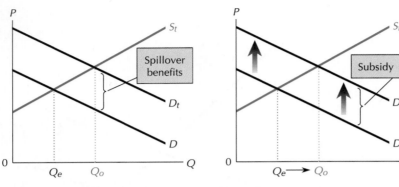 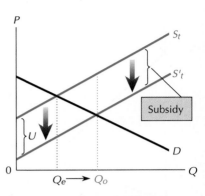

(a) The case of spillover benefits   (b) Correcting the underallocation of resources: demand side   (c) Correcting the underallocation of resources: supply side

Spillover benefits in (a) cause society's total benefits from a product, as shown by D_t, to be understated by D in the market. As a result, the equilibrium output Q_e is less than the optimum output Q_o. This can be corrected by a subsidy to consumers, as shown in (b), which increases market demand from D to D_t. Alternatively, the underallocation can be eliminated by providing producers with a subsidy of U, which increases their supply curve from S_t'.

Individual Bargaining

In many situations externalities do not require government intervention; they can be solved through individual bargaining.

Coase Theorem   According to the **Coase theorem**, named after its originator Ronald Coase, negative or positive spillovers do *not* require government intervention where (1) property ownership is clearly defined, (2) the number of people involved is small, and (3) bargaining costs are negligible. Government should confine its role under these circumstances to encouraging bargaining between affected individuals or groups. Because the economic self-interests of the parties are at stake, bargaining with one another will enable them to find an acceptable solution to the externality. Property rights place a price tag on an externality, creating an opportunity cost for both parties. Hence, a compelling incentive emerges for the parties to find ways to solve the externality problem.

Extended Example   Suppose an owner of a large parcel of forest land is considering contracting with a logging company to clear-cut (totally cut) thousands of hectares of old-growth fir trees. The complication is that the forest surrounds a lake with a nationally known resort on its shore. The resort is on land owned by the resort owner. The unspoiled beauty of the general area attracts vacationers from all over the

nation to the resort. Should provincial or municipal government intervene to prevent the tree cutting?

According to the Coase theorem, the forest owner and the resort owner can resolve this situation without government intervention. As long as *one* of the parties to the dispute has property rights to what is at issue, an incentive will exist for *both* parties to negotiate a solution acceptable to each. In our example, the owner of the timberlands holds the property rights to the land to be logged. The owner of the resort therefore has an incentive to negotiate with the forest owner to reduce the logging impact. Clearly, excessive logging of the forest surrounding the resort will reduce tourism and therefore revenues to the resort owner.

Less obvious, but equally strong, is the economic incentive of the forest owner to explore the possibility of an agreement with the resort owner. Why? The answer draws directly on the idea of opportunity cost. One important cost incurred by the owner in logging the forest is the forgone payment that the forest owner could obtain from the resort owner for agreeing *not* to clear-cut the fir trees. The resort owner should be willing to make a lump-sum or annual payment to the owner of the forest to avoid or minimize the spillover cost. Or, perhaps the resort owner will be willing to buy the forested land at a relatively high price to prevent the logging. As viewed by the forest owner, a payment to preclude logging or a purchase price above the value of the land as a tree farm are *opportunity costs* of logging the land.

We would predict a negotiated agreement that both parties would regard as better than clear-cutting the firs. According to the Coase theorem, government intervention would not be needed to correct this potential externality.

Alternative Assignment of Property Right A surprising facet of the Coase theorem is that an efficient outcome is independent of which of the two parties is assigned the property right. As an extreme example, suppose government had in advance assigned to the resort owner a "property" right consisting of a legal prohibition of tree cutting within several kilometres of the resort without permission of the resort owner.

Now, we would expect the owner of the forest land to seek out the resort owner to discuss the situation. And the resort owner would discover a new opportunity cost. Under the new arrangement of property rights, the resort owner could secure a payment from the owner of the timberland in exchange for allowing, say, selective cutting of some of the older trees on an annual basis. This potential payment is an opportunity cost of *not* allowing tree cutting, as viewed by the resort owner.

Once again the two parties would have an economic incentive to negotiate a mutually acceptable agreement. In so doing they would eliminate or lessen the externality.

Limitations Unfortunately, many negative externalities involve large numbers of affected parties, high bargaining costs, and community property such as air and water. Private bargaining in these situations will not remedy the spillover costs. As just one example, the acid rain problem involving Canada and the United States affects millions of people spread out over two nations. The vast number of affected parties could not independently negotiate an agreement to remedy this problem. In these circumstances, we must rely on government or governments to find acceptable solutions.

Nevertheless, the Coase theorem reminds us that clearly defined property rights can be a positive factor in remedying some externalities.

Liability Rules and Lawsuits

Although private negotiation may not be a realistic solution to most externality problems, clearly established property rights may be helpful in another way.

Government has established a framework of laws that define private property and protect it from damage done by other parties. These laws — and the legal tort (wrongful act) system to which they give rise — permit those suffering spillover costs to sue for damages.

Consider the following case. Suppose the Ajax Degreaser Company regularly dumps leaky barrels containing solvents into a nearby canyon owned by Bar Q Ranch. Bar Q eventually discovers this dump site, and after tracing the drums to Ajax, immediately contacts its lawyer. Ajax gets sued! Not only will Ajax have to pay for the clean up, it may well have to pay Bar Q additional damages for despoiling its property.

Clearly defined property rights and government specified liability rules thus provide an avenue for remedying some externality problems. They do so directly by forcing the perpetrator of the externality to pay damages to those injured. They do so indirectly by discouraging firms and individuals from initially generating negative externalities, for fear of being sued. Thus, it is not surprising that many significant externalities do *not* involve private property, but rather property held in common. It is the *public* bodies of water, the *public* lands, and the *public* air, where ownership is less clear, that often bear the brunt of negative externalities.

Caveat: Like private negotiations, private lawsuits to resolve externalities have their own limitations. Lawsuits are expensive, time consuming, and have uncertain outcomes. Large legal fees and major time delays in the court system are commonplace. Also, the uncertainty associated with the court outcome reduces the effectiveness of this approach. Will the court accept your claim that your emphysema has resulted from the smoke emitted by the factory next door, or will it conclude that your ailment is unrelated to the plant's pollution? Can you prove that a specific firm in the area is the source of the contamination of your well? What are Bar Q's options if Ajax Degreaser goes out of business during the litigation?

A Market for Externality Rights

One of the more novel policy approaches suggested to remedy negative externalities is to create a **market for externality rights**. We confine our discussion to pollution, although other externalities might also lend themselves to this approach.

The rationale for creating a market for pollution rights is that the air, rivers, lakes, oceans, and public lands, such as parks and streets, are all primary objects for pollution because the *rights* to use these resources are either held "in common" by society or are unspecified by law. As a result, no specific private individual or institution has an incentive to restrict the use or maintain the purity or quality of these resources because no one has the right to realize a monetary return from doing so. We maintain the property we own — we periodically paint and repair our homes — in part because we will gain the value of these improvements at the time of resale. But, as long as "rights" to air, water, and certain land resources are commonly held and these resources made freely available, there will be no incentive to maintain them or restrict their use. Hence, these natural resources are "overconsumed" and thereby polluted.

Creating a Market   The proposal is therefore made that an appropriate pollution-control agency should determine the amount of pollutants that can be discharged into the water or air of a given region each year and still maintain the quality of the water or air at some acceptable standard. For example, the agency may determine that 500 tonnes of pollutants can be discharged into Metropolitan Lake and "recycled" by Nature. Hence, 500 pollution rights, each entitling the owner to dump 1 tonne of pollutants into the lake in the given year, are made available for sale each year. The resulting supply of pollution rights is fixed and therefore perfectly inelastic, as shown in Figure 19-3.

The demand for pollution rights will take the same downsloping form as will the demand for any other input. At high prices, polluters either will stop polluting or will pollute less by acquiring pollution-abatement equipment. Thus, an equilibrium market price for pollution rights — in this case $100 — will be determined at which an environment-preserving quantity of pollution rights will be rationed to polluters. Note that without this market — that is, if the use of the lake as a dump site for pollutants were free — 750 tonnes of pollutants would be discharged into the lake and it would be "overconsumed," or polluted, in the amount of 250 tonnes.

Over time, as human and business populations expand, demand will increase, as from D_{1993} to D_{2003}. *Without* a market for pollution rights, pollution would occur in 2003 in the amount of 500 tonnes beyond that which can be assimilated by Nature. *With* the market for pollution rights, price will rise from $100 to $200 and the amount of pollutants will remain at 500 tonnes — the amount that the lake can recycle.

FIGURE 19-3   The market for pollution rights

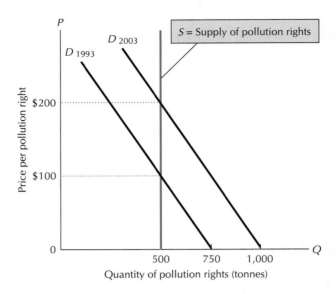

Pollution can be controlled by having a public body determine the amount of pollution the atmosphere or a body of water can safely recycle, and then sell these limited rights to polluters. The effect is to make the environment a scarce resource with a positive price. Economic and population growth will increase the demand for pollution rights over time, but the consequence will be an increase in the price of pollution rights rather than more pollution.

Advantages   This proposal has several advantages relative to direct controls. Most importantly, it reduces society's costs because pollution rights can be bought and sold. Suppose that it costs Acme Pulp Mill $20 a year to reduce a particular noxious water-borne discharge by 1 tonne while it costs Zemo Chemicals $8000 a year to accomplish this same reduction. Also, assume that Zemo increases its output such that it needs to reduce its pollution discharge by 1 tonne.

Without the sale of pollution rights, the cost of reducing the pollution by 1 tonne would be $8000. But Zemo will find it cheaper to buy 1 tonne of pollution rights for the $100 price shown in Figure 19-3 rather than cut pollution at a cost of $8000. Acme, on the other hand, will be willing to sell 1 tonne of pollution rights for $100 to Zemo, incurring the $20 expense of reducing its own discharge by 1 tonne. The total economic cost of reducing the 1 tonne of discharge will therefore be $20 rather than $8000.

Market-based plans have other advantages. Potential polluters are confronted with an explicit monetary incentive not to pollute: They must buy pollution rights to do so. Conservation groups can fight pollution by buying up and withholding pollution rights, reducing actual pollution below governmentally determined standards. As the demand for pollution rights increases over time, the growing revenue from the sale of the given quantity of pollution rights could be devoted to environment improvement. Similarly, with time the rising price of pollution rights should stimulate the search for improved techniques to control pollution.

Society's Optimal Amount of Externality Reduction

As distinct from economic goods, negative externalities such as pollution are "economic bads"; they reduce the recipient's utility rather than increase it. If something is bad, shouldn't society eliminate it entirely? Why should society allow firms or municipalities to discharge *any* impure waste into public waterways or emit *any* pollution into our air?

The answer is that reducing a negative spillover will come at a "price" and therefore society must decide on how much of a reduction it wants to "buy." Totally eliminating pollution may not be desirable, even if it were technologically feasible. Because of the law of diminishing returns, cleaning up the last 1% of effluents from an industrial smokestack normally is far more costly than cleaning up the previous 10%. Eliminating that 10% is most likely more costly than cleaning up the prior 10%, and so on.

Stated technically, the marginal cost (MC) to the firm and hence to society — the opportunity cost of the extra resources used — rises as more and more pollution is reduced. At some point MC may rise so high that it exceeds society's marginal benefit (MB) of further pollution abatement (reduction). Additional actions to reduce pollution will therefore lower society's well-being; total cost will rise by more than total benefit.

MC, MB, and Equilibrium Quantity Figure 19-4 helps demonstrate this point. Observe the rising marginal cost curve, MC, and the downward sloping marginal benefit curve, MB. Society's marginal benefits of pollution abatement decline because of the law of diminishing marginal utility; the benefits from reducing pollution are utility based, and marginal utility (not total utility) falls as greater amounts of pollution abatement are achieved.

Stated generally, the **optimal amount of externality reduction** occurs where society's marginal cost and marginal benefit of reducing an externality

FIGURE 19-4 Society's optimal amount of pollution abatement

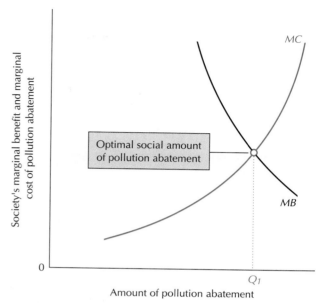

The optimal amount of externality reduction — in this case pollution abatement — occurs at Q_1 where society's marginal cost and marginal benefit of reducing the externality are equal. Reductions of pollution beyond Q_1 will reduce allocative efficiency by overallocating resources to pollution control.

are equal (MB = MC). In Figure 19-4 this amount of pollution abatement is Q_1. When MB exceeds MC, additional abatement moves society toward allocative efficiency; the added benefit of cleaner air or water exceeds the benefit of any alternative use of the required resources. When MC exceeds MB, further abatement reduces allocative efficiency; the benefits from using resources alternatively are greater than using them to further reduce pollution.

In reality, it is difficult to measure the marginal costs and benefits of pollution control. Nevertheless, Figure 19-4 is useful in demonstrating that some pollution may be socially efficient. This is so, not because pollution is desirable, per se, but because beyond some level of control, further abatement may reduce our well-being.

Shifts in Locations of Curves The locations of the marginal cost and marginal benefit curves in Figure 19-4 are not forever fixed; they can, and probably do, shift over time. For example, suppose the technology of pollution control equipment dramatically improves. We would expect the cost of pollution abatement to fall, society's MC curve to shift rightward, and the optimal level of abatement to rise. As another example, suppose society increases its desire for cleaner air and water because of new information about adverse health effects of pollution. The MB curve in Figure 19-4 would shift rightward, and again, the optimal level of pollution control would increase beyond Q_1. You are urged to test your understanding of these statements by drawing new MC and MB curves in Figure 19-4.

QUICK REVIEW (19-1)

1. **Government enhances the operation of the market system by providing an appropriate legal foundation, promoting competition, redistributing income and wealth, adjusting the allocation of resources to provide public goods and correct for externalities, and stabilizing the economy.**

2. **Government can correct the overallocation of resources associated with spillover costs through direct control or specific taxes; the underallocation of resources associated with spillover benefits can be offset by subsidies.**

3. **Policies for coping with negative externalities include (a) private bargaining, (b) liability rules and lawsuits, (c) direct controls, (d) specific taxes, and (e) markets for externality rights.**

4. **The optimal amount of externality reduction occurs where society's marginal cost and marginal benefit of reducing the externality are equal.**

PUBLIC GOODS

The second type of failure is when the market fails to allocate any resources to the production of certain goods whose output is economically justified.

Consider the characteristics of *private goods*, which are produced through the market system. These goods are *divisible*, in that they come in units small enough to be afforded by individual buyers. Furthermore, private goods are subject to the **exclusion principle**: those who are willing and able to pay the market price get the product, but those who are unable or unwilling to pay are excluded from the benefits provided by the product.

There are certain kinds of goods and services — called **public** or **social goods** — that would not be produced at all by the market system because their characteristics are essentially the opposite of those of private goods. Public goods are *indivisible*, involving such large units that they cannot be sold to individual buyers. Individuals can buy hamburgers, computers, and automobiles through the market, but not anti-tank missiles, highways, and air-traffic control.

More importantly, the exclusion principle does *not* apply; there is no effective way of excluding individuals from the benefits of public goods once those goods come into existence. Obtaining the benefits of private goods is predicated on *purchase*; the benefits from public goods accrue to society from the *production* of such goods.

Illustrations　The classic public goods example is a lighthouse on a treacherous coast or harbour. The construction of a lighthouse would be economically justified if the benefits (fewer shipwrecks) exceeded production costs. But the benefit accruing to each individual user would not justify the purchase of such a large and indivisible product. In any event, once in operation, its warning light is a guide to *all* ships. There is no practical way to exclude certain ships from its benefits. Therefore, why should any ship owner voluntarily pay for the benefits received from the light? The light is there for all to see, and a ship captain cannot be excluded from seeing it if the ship owner chooses not to pay. Economists call this the **free-rider problem**: people can receive benefits from a good without contributing to its costs.

Given that the exclusion principle cannot be applied, there is no economic incentive for private enterprises to supply lighthouses. Here is a service that yields substantial benefits but for which the market would allocate no resources. National defence, flood-control, public health, and insect-abatement programs are other public goods. If society is to enjoy such goods and services, they must be provided by the public sector and financed by compulsory charges in the form of taxes.

Large Spillover Benefits　While the exclusion principle distinguishes public from private goods, a variety of other goods and services are provided by government even though the exclusion principle *could* be applied. In particular, such goods and services as education, streets and highways, police and fire protection, libraries and museums, preventive medicine, and sewage disposal could be subject to the exclusion principle; that is, they could be priced and provided by private producers through the market system. But, as noted earlier, these are all services that entail substantial spillover benefits and therefore would be underproduced by the market system.

Therefore, government undertakes or sponsors their provision to avoid the underallocation of resources that would otherwise occur. Such goods and services are sometimes called *quasi-public goods*. One can readily understand the longstanding controversies surrounding the status of medical care and housing. Are these private goods to be provided through the market system, or are they quasi-public goods to be provided by government? It is generally agreed in Canada that medical care is a quasi-public good, with taxes paying most of the bills.

PUBLIC GOODS: EXTENDING THE ANALYSIS

A *private* good is divisible and is also subject to the exclusion principle — those unable or unwilling to pay are excluded from the benefits provided by the product.

A market demand curve for a private good is the horizontal summation of demand curves representing each individual buyer (review Table 7-2 and Figure 7-2). If Adams wants to buy 3 hot dogs at $1 each; Benson, 1 hot dog; and Conrad, 2 hot dogs; the market demand will reflect that 6 hot dogs (= 3 + 1 + 2) are demanded at a $1 price. The market demand resulting from the sum of the desires of each potential individual buyer creates a possibility for sellers to gain revenue and make a profit. The equilibrium amount of a private good produced and purchased is dictated by product price, which is jointly determined by market demand and supply. This equilibrium output is optimal in that it maximizes the combined well-being of the buyers and sellers, the only people affected by the transactions.

A serious snag develops, however, if we apply this same line of thinking to a public good. Once the good is provided, the producer cannot exclude nonpayers from receiving its indivisible benefits. Because they will obtain the benefit from a public good whether or not they pay for it, potential buyers will *not* reveal their true preferences for it. In other words, they will become free-riders who will *not* voluntarily pay for the public good in the marketplace. *Thus, the market demand curve for a public good will be either nonexistent or significantly understated.* The demand for the product expressed in the marketplace will not generate enough revenue to cover the costs of production, even though the collective benefits of the good may exceed the relevant economic costs.

Demand for Public Goods

How might we determine society's optimal (allocatively efficient) amount of a public good in view of this problem? For simplicity, suppose Adams and Benson are the only people in the economy and their true demand schedules for a particular public good, say, national defence, are those shown as columns 1 and 2 and columns 1 and 3 of Table 19-1. These demand schedules are "phantom" demand curves since the two people will not actually reveal them in the marketplace. Instead, we assume that this information has been discovered through a survey indicating Adams's and Benson's willingness to pay for each added unit of the public good, rather than go without it.

Suppose government decides to produce 1 unit of this public good. Because the exclusion principle does not apply, neither Adams nor Benson will voluntarily offer to pay for this unit because each can consume it without paying. Adams' consumption of the good does not preclude Benson from also consuming it. But the combined amount of money these two citizens are willing to pay, rather than each not having this one unit of the good, can be determined through the information in Table 19-1. Columns 1 and 2 show that Adams would be willing to pay $4 for the first unit of the public good; columns 1 and 3

TABLE 19-1   Demand for a public good, two individuals (*hypothetical data*)

(1) Quantity	(2) Adams's willingness to pay (price)		(3) Benson's willingness to pay (price)		(4) Collective willingness to pay (price)
1	$4	+	$5	=	$9
2	3	+	4	=	7
3	2	+	3	=	5
4	1	+	2	=	3
5	0	+	1	=	1

show that Benson would be willing to pay $5 for it. The $9 price (column 4) these two are jointly willing to pay is the sum of the amounts each is willing to pay. Similarly, the collective price they are willing to pay for the second unit of the public good is $7 (= $3 by Adams plus $4 by Benson).

We could then employ this same procedure for the third unit, and so on. Looking at the collective willingness to pay (column 4), for each additional unit, we construct a collective demand schedule for a public good. Rather than adding the *quantities demanded* at each price as when determining the market demand for a private good, we are adding the *prices* people collectively are willing to pay for the last unit of the public good at each quantity demanded.

Figure 19-3 shows the same summing procedure graphically, using data from Table 19-1 to illustrate the adding-up process. Observe that we are summing Adams' and Benson's demand curves for the public good *vertically* to derive the collective demand curve. The height of the collective demand curve D_c at 2 units of output, for example, is $7 — the sum of the amount that Adams and Benson together are willing to pay for the second unit (= $3 + $4). Likewise, the height of the collective demand curve at 4 units of the public good is $3 (= $1 + $2).

Our collective demand curve D_c is based on the monetary value of the perceived benefits of the various extra units that are equally available to both persons for simultaneous consumption. The curve predictably slopes downward because of the law of diminishing marginal utility: Successive units of the public good will yield less added satisfaction than the previous units.

Optimal Quantity of a Public Good

The optimal quantity of the public good alluded to in Figure 19-5 can now be determined. In Figure 19-5(c) the supply curve for the public good is upsloping in the usual sense. The short-run law of diminishing returns, which gives rise to the upsloping supply curve, applies whether making missiles (public goods) or mufflers (private goods). In this case, the optimal quantity of the public good will be 3 units, shown by the intersection of the collective demand and supply curves.

Recalling that a supply curve reflects marginal costs, if 2 units are produced, the collective willingness to pay for that second unit (= $7) will exceed the good's marginal cost of production (= $3). This situation illustrates an underproduction of the good

FIGURE 19-5   The optimal amount of a public good

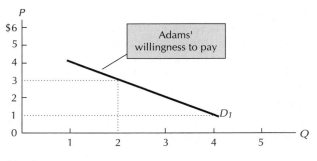

(a) Adams

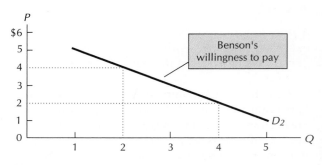

(b) Benson

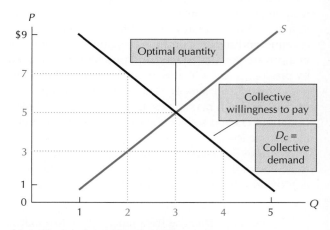

(c) Collective demand and supply

Graphically, the collective demand curve D_c for the public good shown in (c) is found by summing vertically the individual demand curves D_1 and D_2 exhibited in (a) and (b). Government should provide 3 units of the public good because at that quantity the combined marginal benefit, as measured by the citizens' willingness to pay for the last unit (shown by D_c), equals the good's marginal cost (shown by S).

and therefore an *underallocation* of resources to this use.

On the other hand, the sum of the amount these two people are willing to pay for the fourth unit (= $3) of the public good is less than that unit's marginal cost (= $7). Hence, the fourth unit entails an overproduction of the good and an *overallocation* of resources to this use.

The optimal quantity of the public good is 3 units, where the combined willingness to pay for the extra unit — the combined marginal benefit to the two consumers — just matches the marginal cost of that unit ($5 = $5). This "marginal benefit equals marginal cost" principle is analogous to the MR = MC output rule and the MRP = MRC input rule for maximizing profit.

Benefit-Cost Analysis

Economic theory therefore provides some guidance to efficient decision making in the public sector. This guidance can be helpful in understanding **benefit-cost analysis**.

Concept   Suppose government is contemplating a specific project, for example, a flood-control project. The basic nature of the economizing problem tells us that any decision to use more resources in the public sector will involve both a benefit and a cost. The benefit is the extra satisfaction resulting from the output of more public goods; the cost is the loss of satisfaction associated with the accompanying decline in the production of private goods (or some alternative public good). Should the resources under consideration be shifted from the private to the public sector? The answer is "Yes" *if* the benefits from the extra public goods exceed the cost resulting from having fewer private goods. The answer is "No" *if* the value or cost of the forgone private goods is greater than the benefits associated with the extra public goods.

But benefit-cost analysis can do more than indicate whether a public program is worth undertaking. It can also provide guidance as to the extent to which a given project should be pursued. Economic questions, after all, are not simply questions to be answered by "Yes" or "No," but rather, matters of "how much" or "how little." In the case of flood control we note first that a flood-control project is a public good in that the exclusion principle is not readily applicable. Now, should government undertake a flood-control project in a given river valley? And, if so, what is the proper size or scope for the project?

Illustration   Table 19-2 lists a series of increasingly ambitious and increasingly costly flood-control plans. To what extent, if at all, should government undertake flood control? The answers depend on costs and benefits. Costs in this case are largely the capital costs of constructing and maintaining levees and reservoirs; benefits are reduced flood damage.

A quick glance at all the plans shows that for each plan total benefits (column 4) exceed total costs (column 2), indicating that a flood-control project on this river is economically justifiable. This can be seen directly in column 6 where total annual costs (column 2) are subtracted from total annual benefits (column 4). But the question of the optimal size or scope for this project remains. This answer is determined by comparing the additional, or *marginal*, costs and the additional, or *marginal* benefits associated with each plan. The guideline is the one we established when discussing the optimal amount of a public good: Pursue an activity or project as long as the marginal benefits (column 5) exceed the marginal costs (column 3). Stop the activity or project at, or as close as possible to, that point at which marginal benefits equal marginal costs.

TABLE 19-2   Benefit-cost analysis for a flood-control project

(1) Plan	(2) Total annual cost of project	(3) Marginal cost	(4) Total annual benefit (reduction in damage)	(5) Marginal benefit	(6) Net benefit, or (4) − (2)
Without protection	$ 0		$ 0		$ 0
A: Levees	3,000	$ 3,000	6,000	$ 6,000	3,000
B: Small reservoir	10,000	7,000	16,000	10,000	6,000
C: Medium reservoir	18,000	8,000	25,000	9,000	7,000
D: Large reservoir	30,000	12,000	32,000	7,000	2,000

Source: Adapted from Otto Eckstein, *Public Finance*, 3rd ed. (Englewood Cliffs, N.J.: Prentice-Hall, Inc., 1973), p. 23. Used with permission.

In this case Plan C — the medium-sized reservoir — is the best plan. Plans A and B are too modest; in both cases marginal benefits exceed marginal costs. Plan D's marginal costs ($12,000) exceed marginal benefits ($7000) and therefore cannot be justified. Plan D isn't economically justifiable; it overallocates resources to this project. Plan C is closest to the optimum; it expands flood control so long as marginal benefits exceed marginal costs.

Regarded from a slightly different vantage point, the **marginal benefit = marginal cost rule** will determine which plan entails the maximum excess of total benefits (column 4) over total costs (column 2) or, in other words, the plan that yields the maximum *net* benefit to society. We confirm directly in column 6 that the maximum net benefit (of $7000) is associated with Plan C.

Benefit-cost analysis shatters the myth that "economy in government" and "reduced government spending" are synonymous. "Economy" is concerned with efficiency in resource use. If a government program yields marginal benefits that are less than the marginal benefits attainable from alternative private uses — that is, if costs exceed benefits — then the proposed public program should *not* be undertaken. But if benefits exceed costs, then it would be uneconomical or "wasteful" *not* to spend on that governmental program. Economy in government does *not* mean minimization of public spending; rather, it means allocating resources between the private and public sectors until no net benefits can be realized from further reallocations.

Measurement Problems

Benefit-cost analysis is helpful in promoting clear thinking about the public sector and is useful in actual studies of projects such as flood control, pollution cleanup, and highway construction. But the benefits and costs associated with public goods are partially externalities that are difficult to measure.

Consider the possible benefits and costs associated with construction of a new expressway in a major metropolitan area. In addition to estimating the obvious costs — land purchase and construction costs — the responsible agency must also estimate the spillover cost of additional air pollution resulting from an enlarged flow of traffic. Furthermore, more traffic may call for increased expenditures for traffic police.

What about benefits? Improved transportation means a widening of markets, more competition, and a greater opportunity for the community to specialize and improve economic efficiency. But what is the monetary value of this benefit? The expressway also may make more jobs accessible to the central-city poor. Again, what is the dollar value of these benefits?

The point is that the full costs and benefits associated with government programs are not easily calculated, and benefit-cost analysis is frequently difficult to apply.

QUICK REVIEW (19-2)

1. **Government must provide public goods because such goods are indivisible and entail benefits from which nonpaying consumers cannot be excluded.**

2. **The demand for a public good is found by vertically adding the prices that members of the society are willing to pay for each unit of output at various output levels.**

3. **The optimal social amount of a public good is that at which the marginal benefit and marginal cost of the good are equal.**

4. **Benefit-cost analysis is the method of evaluating alternative projects or sizes of projects by comparing marginal benefits and marginal costs.**

THE CIRCULAR FLOW REVISITED

Government is thoroughly integrated into the real and monetary flows that make up the economy. It is informative to re-examine the redistributional, allocative, and stabilization functions of government in terms of Chapter 2's circular flow model. In Figure 19-6, flows (1) through (4) merely restate Figure 3-2. Flows (1) and (2) show business expenditures for the resources provided by households. Recall that these expenditures are costs to businesses, but represent wage, rent, interest, and profit income to households. Flows (3) and (4) portray households making consumer expenditures for the goods and services produced by businesses.

Now carefully consider the numerous modifications that stem from the addition of government. Flows (5) through (8) tell us that government makes purchases in both product and resource markets. Specifically, flows (5) and (6) represent government purchasing such things as paperclips, computers, and military equipment from private businesses.

FIGURE 19-6   The circular flow and the public sector

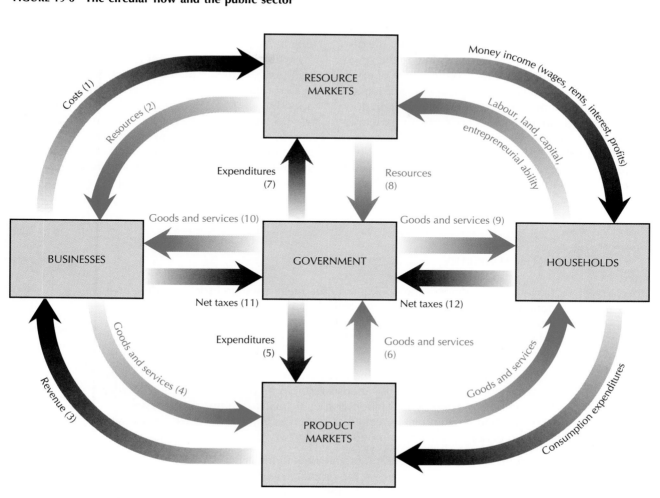

Government expenditures, taxes, and transfer payments affect the distribution of income, the allocation of resources, and the level of economic activity.

Flows (7) and (8) reflect government purchases of resources. The federal government employs and pays salaries to members of Parliament, senators, the armed forces, Department of Justice lawyers, a multitude of bureaucrats, and so on. Provincial and municipal governments hire teachers, bus drivers, and police officers and firefighters. The federal government might lease or purchase land to expand a Canadian Forces base; a city may buy land to build a new elementary school.

Government then provides public goods and services to both households and businesses as shown by flows (9) and (10). The financing of public goods and services requires tax payments by households and businesses as reflected in flows (11) and (12). We

have labelled these flows as *net* taxes to acknowledge that they also include negative taxes in the form of transfer payments to households and subsidies to businesses. Thus flow (11) entails not merely corporation income, sales, and excise taxes flowing from businesses to government, but also various subsidies to farmers, shipbuilders, and the railways.[2] Similarly, government also collects taxes (personal income taxes, social insurance levies) directly from households and makes available transfer payments (for

---

[2] Most business subsidies are "concealed" in the form of low-interest loans, loan guarantees, tax concessions, or the public provisions of facilities free or at price less than costs.

example, welfare payments and social insurance benefits) as shown by flow (12).

Our expanded circular flow model allows us to grasp more clearly how government can alter the distribution of income, reallocate resources, and change the level of economic activity. The structure of taxes and transfer payments can have a significant impact upon the distribution of income. To illustrate, in flow (12) a tax structure that draws tax revenues primarily from well-to-do households combined with a system of transfer payments to low-income households will result in greater equality in the distribution of income. Flows (6) and (8) imply an allocation of

resources that differs from that of a purely private economy. Government buys goods and labour services that differ from those purchased by households. Finally, all of the governmental flows suggest means by which government might attempt to stabilize the economy. For example, if the economy was experiencing unemployment, an increase in government spending with taxes and transfers held constant would increase aggregate spending, output, and employment. Similarly, given the level of government expenditures, a decline in taxes or an increase in transfer payments would increase spendable incomes and boost private spending.

CHAPTER SUMMARY

1. Government enhances the operation of the market system by a. providing an appropriate legal and social framework; b. acting to maintain competition; c. redistributing income and wealth; d. adjusting the allocation of resources to provide public goods and correct for externalities; and e. promoting growth and stabilizing the economy.

2. Spillovers or externalities cause the equilibrium output of certain goods to vary from the optimal output. Spillover costs result in an overallocation of resources that can be corrected by legislation or specific taxes. Spillover benefits are accompanied by an underallocation of resources that can be corrected by subsidies to either consumers or producers.

3. According to the Coase theorem, private bargaining is capable of solving potential externality problems where a. the property rights are clearly defined, b. the number of people involved is small, and c. bargaining costs are negligible.

4. Clearly established property rights and liability rules permit some spillover costs to be prevented or remedied through private lawsuits. Lawsuits, however, are costly, time consuming, and uncertain as to their results.

5. Direct controls and specific taxes can improve resource allocation in situations where externalities affect many people and involve community resources. Both direct controls (smokestack emission standards) and specific taxes (taxes on firms producing toxic chemicals) increase production costs and hence product price. As product price rises, the externality is reduced since less of the output is bought and sold.

6. Markets for pollution rights, in which people can buy and sell the rights to a fixed amount of pollution place a price tag on pollution and encourage firms to reduce or eliminate it.

7. The optimal social amount of externality abatement occurs where society's marginal cost and marginal benefit of reducing the externality are equal. This optimal amount of pollution abatement is likely to be less than a 100% reduction. Changes in technology or changes in society's attitudes about pollution can affect the optimal amount of pollution abatement.

8. Graphically, the collective demand curve for a particular public good can be found by summing *vertically* each of the individual demand curves for that good. The demand curve that results from this process indicates the collective willingness to pay for the last unit of any given amount of the public good.

9. The optimal quantity of a public good occurs where the combined willingness to pay for the last unit — the marginal benefit of the good — equals the good's marginal cost.

10. Benefit-cost analysis can provide useful guidance of the economic desirability and most efficient scope of public goods output. The major difficulty in applying benefit-cost analysis is that the full costs and benefits of a public good or service are not easily calculated.

11. The circular flow model is a useful means for envisioning how government performs its redistributional, allocative, and stabilizing functions.

Terms and concepts

benefit-cost analysis (p. 339)
Coase theorem (p. 332)
exclusion principle (p. 336)
free-rider problem (p. 336)
marginal benefit = marginal cost rule
    (p. 340)

market for externality rights (p. 333)
optimal amount of externality reduction
    (p. 335)
public or social goods (p. 336)
spillover costs and spillover benefits (p. 330)
spillovers or externalities (p. 330)

Questions and study suggestions

1. Enumerate and briefly discuss the main economic functions of government.

2. Explain why, in the absence of spillovers, equilibrium and optimal outputs are identical in competitive markets. What divergences arise between equilibrium and optimal output when *a.* spillover costs and *b.* spillover benefits are present? How might government correct for these discrepancies? "The presence of spillover costs suggests an underallocation of resources to that product and the need for governmental subsidies." Do you agree? Explain how zoning and seat belt laws might be used to deal with a problem of spillover costs.

3. What are the basic characteristics of public goods? Explain the significance of the exclusion principle. By what means does government provide public goods?

4. Use your understanding of the characteristics of private and public goods to determine whether the following should be produced through the market system or provided by government: *a.* bread; *b.* street lighting; *c.* bridges *d.* parks; *e.* swimming pools; *f.* medical care; *g.* mail delivery; *h.* housing; *i.* air traffic control; *j.* libraries.

5. Draw a production possibilities curve with public goods on the vertical axis and private goods on the horizontal axis. Assuming the economy is initially operating on the curve, indicate the means by which the production of public goods might be increased. How might the output of public goods be increased if the economy is initially functioning at a point inside of the curve?

6. Given the following three individual demand schedules for a particular good, and assuming these three people are the only ones in the society, determine *a.* the market demand schedule on the assumption that the good is a private good, and *b.* the collective demand schedule on the assumption that the good is a public good. Explain the differences, if any, in your schedules.

Individual 1		Individual 2		Individual 3	
P	Q_d	P	Q_d	P	Q_d
$8	0	$8	1	$8	0
7	0	7	2	7	0
6	0	6	3	6	1
5	1	5	4	5	2
4	2	4	5	4	3
3	3	3	6	3	4
2	4	2	7	2	5
1	5	1	8	1	6

7. Use your demand schedule for a public good determined in question 6 and the following supply schedule to ascertain the optimal quantity of this public good. Explain why this is the optimal quantity.

P	Q_s
$19	10
16	8
13	6
10	4
7	2
4	1

8. The following table shows the total costs and total benefits in billions for four different antipollution programs of increasing scope. Which program should be undertaken? Why?

Program	Total cost	Total benefit
A	$ 3	$ 7
B	7	12
C	12	16
D	18	19

9. An apple-grower's orchard provides nectar to a neighbour's bees, while a bee-keeper's bees help the apple grower by pollinating the apple blossoms. Use Figure 19-2 to explain why this situation might lead to an underallocation of resources to apple growing and to beekeeping. How might this underallocation get resolved via the means suggested by the Coase theorem?

10. Explain: "Without a market for pollution rights, dumping pollutants into the air or water is costless; in the presence of the right to buy and sell pollution rights, dumping pollution creates an opportunity cost for the polluter." What is the significance of this fact to the search for better technology to reduce pollution?

11. Manipulate the MB curve in Figure 19-4 to explain the following statement: "The optimal amount of pollution abatement for some substances, say, water from storm drains, is very low; the optimal amount of abatement for other substances, say, cyanide poison, is close to 100%." Explain.

12. "Most governmental actions have simultaneous impacts on the distribution of income, the allocation of resources, and the levels of unemployment and prices." Use the circular flow model to confirm this assertion for each of the following: *a.* the construction of a new high school in Uxbridge township; *b.* a 2% reduction in the corporation income tax; *c.* increased public funding of day care for children; *d.* a $5 billion increase in defence spending; *e.* the levying of a tax on air polluters; and *f.* an increase in the minimum wage from $4.50 to $5.50.

20

Market Failure: Environmental Pollution and Information

I n the 1990s the issue of environmental pollution is likely to be even more at the forefront of public concerns than it was in the 1980s. We are bombarded with environmental issues: the expanding hole in our ozone layer, the greenhouse effect, nuclear waste, lakes containing traces of dozens of chemicals known to be harmful to humans, and a dearth of dump sites in which to dispose of our mounting garbage. In this chapter we take a closer look at the problem of pollution and how governments ought to deal with it.

But there is a more subtle form of market failure: when either buyers or sellers have incomplete or inaccurate information and the cost of attaining that information is prohibitive. Consider for example, the purchase of a chocolate bar. If government did not force producers of chocolate bars to list the ingredients, people with allergies could be at great risk. Those people could have each brand of chocolate bar analysed at a laboratory to determine each and every ingredient, but the costs would be high. Under such circumstances government ought to increase the data available to market participants so that society's resources will be allocated more efficiently. We investigate the situation when there is inadequate information both about sellers and buyers.

THE ECONOMICS OF POLLUTION

Pollution, the most acute negative externality facing industrial society, provides a relevant illustration of several of the concepts and public policies discussed in the last chapter. This spillover takes several forms, including air, water, and solid-waste (garbage) pollution. What are the dimensions of these problems? What are their causes? What public policies are in place to reduce them?

Dimensions of the Problem

The extent and seriousness of the pollution problem has been well documented in the popular press, and needs only a review here. We know that some rivers, lakes, and bays have turned into municipal and industrial sewers. A significant percentage of our population drinks water of dubious quality. There are an estimated 27,000 major industrial and utility sources of air pollution in North America, which contibute to lung cancer, emphysema, pneumonia, and other respiratory diseases. Almost one billion kilograms of toxic chemicals, some of them carcinogens, are released into the air each year in North America. Solid waste disposal has become an acute problem for many cities as the most readily available dump sites have been filled and citizens resist the establishment of dumps or incinerators near them.

The nations of Eastern Europe are so polluted that it will take several decades, at best, for them to be cleaned up. Governments have identified numerous dangerous toxic-waste disposal sites in Canada. Recent giant oil spills in Alaska and the Persian Gulf have seriously damaged those two important ecosystems. Passive cigarette smoke has been found to cause cancer in nonsmokers.

Possible global consequences of environmental pollution are equally disturbing. Some scientists contend that the concentrations of industry, people structures, and cement that constitute cities might create air and heat pollution sufficient to cause irreversible and potentially disastrous changes in the earth's climate and weather patterns through the so-called greenhouse effect. Headlines warn us that our continued use of CFCs has contributed to a rising rate of skin cancer by depleting the earth's stratospheric ozone layer.

Causes: The Law of Conservation of Matter and Energy

The root of the pollution problem can best be envisioned through the **law of conservation of matter and energy**. This law holds that matter can be transformed into other matter or into energy but can never vanish. All inputs (fuels, raw materials, water, and so forth) used in the economy's production processes will ultimately result in an equivalent residual of waste. For example, unless it is continuously recycled, the cotton found in a T-shirt ultimately will be abandoned in a closet, buried in a dump, or burned in an incinerator. Even if burned it will not truly vanish; instead, it will be transformed into heat and smoke.

Fortunately, the ecological system — Nature, if you are over fifty — has the self-regenerating capacity that allows it, within limits, to absorb or recycle such wastes. But the volume of such residuals has tended to outrun this absorptive capacity.

Why has this happened? Why do we have a pollution problem? Causes are manifold, but perhaps four are paramount.

1 Population Density   There is the simple matter of population growth. An ecological system that may accommodate 50 or 100 million people may begin to break down under the pressures of billions of people.

2 Rising Incomes   Economic growth means that each person consumes and disposes of more output. Paradoxically, the affluent society helps to spawn the effluent society. A rising GDP (gross domestic product) means rising GDG (gross domestic garbage). Thus a high standard of living permits Canadians to own millions of motor vehicles. But autos and trucks are a primary source of air pollution and, concommitantly, give rise to the hard problem of disposing of hundreds of thousands of junked vehicles each year. Additionally, millions of tires hit the nation's scrapheap each year.

3 Technology   Technological change is another contributor to pollution. For example, the addition of lead to gasoline posed a serious threat to human health, leading to the government requirement of unleaded fuel. The development and widespread use of "throw-away" containers made of virtually indestructible aluminum or plastic add substantially to the solid-waste crisis. Some detergent soap products have been highly resistant to sanitary treatment and recycling.

4 Incentives   Profit-seeking manufacturers will choose the least-cost combination of inputs and will find it advantageous to bear only unavoidable costs. If they can dump waste chemicals into rivers and lakes rather than pay for expensive treatment and proper disposal, businesses will be inclined to do so. If manufacturers can discharge smoke and the hot water used to cool machinery rather than purchase expensive abatement and cooling facilities, they will do so. The result is air and water pollution — both chemical and thermal — and, in the economist's jargon, the shifting of certain costs to the community at large as external or spillover costs. Enjoying lower "internal" costs than if they had not polluted the environment, the producers can sell their products at a lower price, expand their production, and realize larger profits.

But it is neither just nor accurate to lay the entire blame for pollution at the door of industry. On the one hand, a well-intentioned firm that wants to operate in a socially responsible way with respect to pollution may find itself in an untenable position. If an individual firm "internalizes" all its external or spillover costs by installing, say, water-treatment and smoke-abatement equipment, the firm will find itself at a cost disadvantage in comparison to its polluting competitors. The socially responsible firm will have higher costs and will be forced to raise its product price. The "reward" for the pollution-conscious firm is a declining market for its product, diminished profits, and, in the extreme, the prospect of bankruptcy. This means that effective action to combat pollution must be undertaken collectively through government.

On the other hand, given that an important function of government is to correct the misallocation of resources that accompanies spillover costs, it is ironic that most major cities are heavy contributors to the pollution problem. Power plants located in various municipalities are frequently major contributors to air pollution; many cities discharge inadequately treated sewage into rivers or lakes because it is inexpensive and convenient to do so.

Similarly, individuals avoid the costs of proper refuse pickup and disposal by burning their garbage. We also find it easier to use throw-away containers rather than recycle "return" containers. The majority of families with babies opt for the convenience of disposable diapers, which glut landfills, rather than using reusable cloth diapers (Box 20-1). Smoke from woodstoves, fireplaces, and outdoor grills has become a major pollution problem in some towns and cities.

Direct Controls and Taxes

Alternative approaches for achieving allocative efficiency are needed when large numbers of people are affected by a negative externality, such as pollution, and community resources are being harmed. In Chapter 19 we addressed direct controls and specific taxes as two policy options. A brief review of these approaches as they relate to pollution will be useful.

1 Direct Controls   The most direct approach to reducing negative externalities is to pass legislation placing limits on the amount of the activity that can take place. To date, this approach has dominated public policy in Canada. Clean air legislation has been enacted in many provinces to limit the amounts of nitrogen oxide, particulates, and other substances that plants can emit into the air. Clean water legislation has specified the amount of heavy metals, detergents, and other pollutants firms can discharge into rivers and bays. Toxic waste laws specify special procedures and dump sites for disposing of contaminated soil and solvents. Violation of these laws brings with it fines and, occasionally, imprisonment.

The effect of direct controls is to force offending firms to incur costs associated with pollution control. Thus, the private marginal costs of producing these goods and services rise. In Figure 19-1(b), the supply curve — which we now know reflects private marginal costs — shifts upward from S to S_t. Product price increases, equilibrium output falls from Q_e to Q_o, and the initial Q_eQ_o overallocation of resources is corrected.

2 Specific Taxes   A second policy approach to significant and widespread spillover costs is to levy specific taxes or emission charges on the perpetrators. For example, a government can place an excise tax on manufacturers of chlorofluorocarbons (CFCs), which have been found to deplete the stratospheric ozone layer protecting the earth from excessive solar ultraviolet radiation. This substance is used widely as a coolant in refrigeration, blowing agent for foam, and solvent for electronics. Facing such a tax, manufacturers must decide whether to pay it or expend additional funds to purchase or develop substitute products. In either case, the marginal cost of producing CFCs will rise, ideally shifting the private suppy curve in Figure 19-1(b) leftward from S to S_t. Equilibrium price will therefore increase and equilibrium output will decline from Q_e to the allocatively efficient level Q_0.

Trading of Pollution Rights

Although it has not yet been tried in Canada, in the United States legislation in the last decade has allowed for trading of air pollution rights. The Clean

Air Act of 1990 strengthened and extended such pro-visions. The American Environmental Protection Agency (EPA) now permits firms to exchange pollution rights internally and externally.

Polluters are allowed to transfer air pollution rights internally between individual sources within their plants. That is, as long as they meet the overall pollution standard assigned to them, firms may increase one source of pollution by offsetting it with reduced pollution from another part of their operations.

The EPA also permits external trading of pollution rights. It has set targets for reducing air pollution in regions where the minimum standards ae not being met. Previously, new pollution sources could not enter these regions unless existing polluters went out of business. In the last decade or so, the EPA has allowed firms that reduce their pollution below set standards to sell pollution rights to new or existing firms. Thus, a new firm desiring to locate in a partic-ular urban area might be able to buy rights to emit 20 tonnes of nitrous oxide annually from an existing firm that has reduced its emissions below its allowa-ble limit. The price of these emission rights will depend on their supply and demand.

A small, but growing market for such rights has recently emerged and appears to be working well. The acid rain provisions of the U.S. Clean Air Act of 1990 will greatly expand this market.

Solid Waste Disposal and Recycling

Nowhere is the law of conservation of matter and energy more apparent than in solid waste disposal. The 180 million tonnes of garbage that accumulate annually in North American landfills have become a growing externality problem. Landfills in southern Ontario, in particular, are either completely full or rapidly filling up. On the receiving end, many people in rural areas near newly expanding dumps are understandably upset about the increased truck traf-fic on their highways and growing mounds of smelly garbage in local dumps. Also, some landfills are pro-ducing serious ground water pollution.

The high opportunity cost of urban and suburban land, and the negative externalities created by dumps, make the landfill solution to solid waste increasingly expensive. An alternative garbage pol-icy is to incinerate it in plants that produce electricity. But, people object to having garbage incinerators — a source of truck traffic and air pollution — close to their homes. So where do we turn for a solution to the growing problem of solid waste?

Although garbage dumps and incinerators are likely to remain the mainstays of garbage disposal, recycling is receiving increased attention.

Market for Recyclable Items   The incentives for recycling can be shown through our basic supply and demand analysis. In Figure 20-1(a) we have drawn a

---

FIGURE 20-1   The economics of recycling

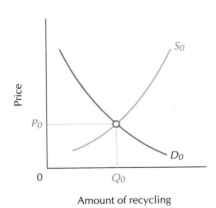
(a) Equilibrium price and quantity

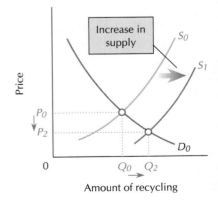
(b) Incentives to buy recyclable items

(c) Incentives to sell recyclable items

The equilibrium price and amount of materials recycled are determined by supply and demand, as shown in (a). In (b), policies that increase the incentives for producers to buy recyclable items shift the demand curve rightward and raise both equilibrium price and the amount of recycling. In (c), policies that encourage households to recycle expand the equilibrium amount of recycling but also reduce the equilibrium price of recyclable items.

Box 20-1

In the Media

Recycling is the mantra of the 1990s. The following article reports how the Ontario government has provided grants to recycle disposable diapers, estimated to account for about 2% of municipal garbage. Government intervention, through subsidies, is required to induce private firms to take up the task of recycling disposable diapers, which, at least initially, would not be sufficiently profitable for a private firm to undertake.

DISPOSABLE DIAPERS TO BE RECYCLED

Partly funded by Ontario, pilot plant to start this month

BY MARTIN MITTELSTAEDT

Used disposable diapers, long a symbol of the throw-away society, will be recycled at a plant in Mississauga partly funded by the Ontario government.

Knowaste Technologies Inc. said it will process used disposable diapers from four Toronto hospitals into their component parts in a pilot project starting this month.

The main product from the recycling venture will be kraft wood pulp, which represents about 80 per cent of the material used in a diaper. Once recovered and sanitized, the pulp can be used in new diapers, Knowaste said.

Plastic film and fibre account for about 15 per cent of a diaper and will be converted into a low-cost oil sorbent. Knowaste is testing the super absorbent polymer from the remaining 5 per cent of the diaper as a composting aid.

Human wastes in the diapers will be processed by municipal sewage plants.

If the venture is successful, the program will be expanded to 30 to 40 hospitals, day-care centres and institutions for the elderly as early as this June when a $1.2-million commercial recycling plant is expected to open.

The Ontario Ministry of the Environment has provided grants of $546,000 for the project, which is also sponsored by Procter & Gamble Inc., Du Pont Canada Inc., Hercules Canada Inc., and Kendall Canada Inc., all diaper makers or industry suppliers.

Disposable diapers account for about 2 per cent of municipal garbage, and have been attacked as wasteful by environmentalists and suppliers of reusable cloth products.

Marlene Conway, Knowaste president, said recycling will give those institutions wishing to use disposables "freedom of choice" while eliminating the burden placed on urban landfills from the product. Ms. Conway is the majority shareholder of Knowaste, a private company with no connections to corporations that make diapers or their suppliers.

The recycling venture was attacked by cloth diaper proponents. "I feel resentful that the government is pouring $500,000 into it," said Michael Brigham, director of Absolutely Diapers Inc. of Toronto.

The provincial govenment is spending $186,000 on 23 projects promoting reusable cloth diapers.

By permission of *The Globe and Mail*, December 31, 1991.

demand and supply curve for some recyclable product, say, glass.

The demand for recyclable glass derives from manufacturers of glass who use it as a resource in producing new glass. Just as a firm has a demand for labour and capital, it has a demand for raw materials useful in producing its product, and recyclable materials may be one such input. The demand curve for recycled glass slopes downward, telling us that man-

ufacturers will increase their purchases of recyclable glass as its price falls.

The location of the resource demand curve in Figure 20-1(a) depends partly on the demand for the product that the recycled glass is being used to produce. The greater the demand for the product, the greater is the demand for recycled inputs. The location also depends on the technology and, thus, the cost of using original raw materials rather than recycled glass in the production process. The more costly it is to use original materials relative to recycled glass, the further to the right will be the demand curve for recyclable glass.

The supply curve for recyclable glass slopes upward in the typical fashion in that higher prices increase the incentive for households to recycle. The location of the supply curve depends on such factors as the attitudes of households toward recycling and the cost to them of alternative disposal.

The equilibrium price P_0 and quantity Q_0 in Figure 20-1(a) are determined at the intersection of the supply and demand curves. At price P_0 the market clears; there is neither a shortage nor a surplus of recyclable glass.

Policy Suppose that government wishes to encourage recycling as an alternative to land dumps or incineration. It could do this in one of two basic ways.

1 Demand Incentives Government could increase recycling by increasing the demand for recycled products. If the demand curve in Figure 20-1(b) shifts from D_0 rightward to D_1, equilibrium price and quantity will increase to P_1 and Q_1. An example of a specific policy that might accomplish this goal would be to place specific taxes on the inputs substitutable for recycled glass in the production process. Such taxes would encourage firms to use more of the untaxed recycled glass and less of the original taxed inputs. Alternatively, government could shift its purchases toward goods produced with recycled inputs and require that its contractors do the same.

We might also mention that environmental awareness by the public itself can contribute to rightward shifts of the demand curve for recycled resources. Fearing negative consumer backlashes against their products, firms such as Procter and Gamble (disposable diapers) and McDonald's (packaging of fast foods) have undertaken multi-million dollar campaigns to use recycled plastic and paper.

2 Supply Incentives As shown in Figure 20-1(c), government can also increase recycling by shifting the supply curve rightward, as from S_0 to S_1. Equilibrium price would fall from P_0 to P_2 and equilibrium quantity — in this case, recyclable glass — would rise from Q_0 to Q_2. Many local governments have implemented specific policies that fit within this framework. For example, they encourage recycling by providing curbside pickup of recyclable goods at a lower monthly fee than for pickup of normal garbage.

In a few cases, supply incentives for recycling have been so effective that the prices of some recyclable items have fallen to zero. You can envision this outcome by shifting the supply curve in Figure 20-1(c) further and further rightward. In fact, some cities now are *paying* manufacturers to truck away certain recyclable products, such as mixed paper (negative price), rather than charging them a price. This may or may not promote allocative efficiency. On the one hand, the cost of paying firms to take away recyclable products may be lower than that of alternative disposal, particularly in view of the negative externalities of dumps and incinerators. If so, recycling will promote allocative efficiency.

On the other hand, a policy of paying firms to take away recyclable items need not always be economical. In some cases it may be more costly to recycle goods than to bury or incinerate them, even when externalities are considered. If so, recycling will *reduce* efficiency rather than increase it.

Government's task is to find the optimal amount of recycling compared to alternative disposal of garbage. It can do this by estimating and comparing the marginal benefit and marginal cost of recycling. And, incidentally, consumers as a group can reduce the initial accumulation of garbage by steering purchases away from products having excessive packaging.

QUICK REVIEW (20-1)

1. **The ultimate cause of pollution is the law of conservation of matter and resources, which holds that matter can be transformed into other matter or into energy, but cannot vanish.**

2. **Environmental pollution problems can be alleviated either through direct control, via legislated standards, or levying taxes.**

3. **Trading in air-pollution rights is being tried in the U.S. Initial assessments suggest it is working well.**

INFORMATION FAILURES

Thus far we have added new details and insights concerning two types of market failure: public goods and externalities. But there is another, more subtle, market failure that also merits elaboration. This inefficiency results when either buyers or sellers have incomplete or inaccurate information and the cost of obtaining better information is prohibitive.

Market information normally is sufficient to ensure that goods and services are produced and purchased in allocatively efficient quantities. But in some instances, inadequate information precludes sorting out legitimate from illegitimate sellers, or legitimate from illegitimate buyers. In these markets, society's scarce resources will not be allocated efficiently, implying that government should intervene by increasing the information available to the market participants. Under rare circumstances government may itself supply a good for which information problems have prohibited profitable production.

Inadequate Information About Sellers

We begin by asking how inadequate information about *sellers* and their products can cause market failure. Examining the market for gasoline and for the services of surgeons will give us an answer.

Gasoline Market   First, we consider the market for gasoline and assume an absurd situation. Suppose there is no system of weights and measures established by law, no government inspection of gasoline pumps, and no laws against false advertising. Each gas station therefore can use whatever measure it chooses; it can define a litre of gas as it pleases. A station can advertise that its gas is 87 octane when in fact it is only 75. It can rig its pumps to indicate it is providing more gas than the amount being delivered.

The consumer's cost of obtaining reliable information under these conditions is exceptionally high, if not prohibitive. Each consumer will have to buy samples of gas from various gas stations, have them tested for octane level, and pour gas into a measuring device to see how the station has calibrated the pump. Also, the consumer will need to use a calculator to ascertain if the machine is correctly multiplying the price per litre by the number of litres. And these activities will need to be repeated regularly, since the station owner can alter the product quality and the accuracy of the pump at will.

Because of the high costs of obtaining information about the seller, many customers will opt out of this chaotic market. One tankful of a 50% solution of gasoline and water will be enough to discourage many motorists from further driving. More realistically, the conditions described in this market will encourage consumers to vote for political candidates who promise to provide a governmental solution. The oil companies and honest gasoline suppliers will not object to this government intervention. They will realize that, by enabling this market to work, accurate information will expand their total sales.

Government has intervened in the market for gasoline and other markets having similar information difficulties. It has established a system of weights and measures, employed inspectors to check accuracy of gasoline pumps, and passed laws against fraudulent claims and misleading advertising. There can be no doubt that these government activities have produced net benefits for society.

Licensing of Surgeons   Let's now look at a second example of how inadequate information about sellers can create market failure. Suppose that anyone can hang out a shingle and claim to be a surgeon in much the same way that anyone can become a house painter. The market will eventually sort out the true surgeons from those who are learning by doing or are fly-by-night operators who move into and out of an area. As people die from unsuccessful surgery, law suits for malpractice eventually will eliminate the medical imposters. People needing surgery for themselves or their loved ones can glean information from newspaper reports and solicit information from people — or their relatives — who have undergone similar operations.

But this process of generating information for those needing surgery will take considerable time and will impose unacceptably high human and economic costs. There is a fundamental difference between an amateurish paint job on one's house and being on the receiving end of heart surgery by a bogus physician. The marginal cost of obtaining information about sellers in this market is excessively high. The high risk of getting surgery done without good information will result in an underallocation of resources to surgery.

Government has remedied this market failure through a system of qualifying tests and licensing. This licensing enables consumers to obtain inexpensive information about a service they only infrequently buy. Government has taken a similar role in several other areas of the economy. For example, it approves new medicines, regulates the securities industry, and requires warnings on containers of potentially hazardous substances. It also requires warning labels on cigarette packages and disseminates information about communicable diseases. It issues warnings about unsafe toys and inspects restaurants for health-related violations.

Inadequate Information About Buyers

Just as inadequate information about sellers can keep markets from achieving allocative efficiency, so can inadequate information about *buyers*. These buyers can either be consumers buying products or firms buying resources.

Moral Hazard Problem Private markets may underallocate resources to a particular good or service for which there is a severe **moral-hazard problem**. *The moral hazard problem is the tendency of one party to a contract to alter her or his behaviour in ways that are costly to the other party.* A contract will not be profitable to a seller, for example, if the seller must incur large costs to identify those buyers most likely to alter their behaviour in cost-imposing ways.

To understand this point, suppose a firm offers an insurance policy that pays a set amount of money per month to people who suffer divorces. The attraction of this insurance is that it pools the economic risk of divorce among thousands of people and, in particular, protects nonworking spouses and children from the economic hardship that divorce often brings. Unfortunately, the moral hazard problem reduces the likelihood that insurance companies can profitably provide this type of insurance contract.

After taking out this insurance, some people will alter their behaviour in ways that impose heavy costs on the insurer. Specifically, married couples will have less of an incentive to get along and to iron out marital difficulties. At the extreme, some people might be motivated to obtain a divorce, collect the insurance, and then live together. The problem is that the insurance promotes *more* divorces, the very outcome it protects against. The moral hazard difficulty will force the insurer to charge such high premiums for this insurance that few policies will be bought. If the insurer could identify in advance those people most prone to alter their behaviour, the firm could exclude them from buying it. But the firm's marginal cost of getting this information is too high compared to the marginal benefit. Thus, this market fails.

Divorce insurance is not available in the marketplace, but society recognizes the benefits of insuring against the hardships of divorce. It has corrected for this underallocation of "hardship insurance" through child-support laws that dictate payments — when the economic circumstances so warrant — to the spouse who retains the children. Alimony laws also play a role.

Finally, government provides "divorce insurance" of sorts through Mothers' Allowance payments. If a divorce leaves a spouse with children destitute, the family is eligible for Mothers' Allowance payments. Government intervention does not eliminate the moral hazard problem; instead, it overcomes or offsets it. Unlike private firms, government need not earn a profit to continue the insurance.

The moral hazard concept has numerous applications. We mention them only in passing, to reinforce your understanding of the basic principle.

1. Drivers may be less cautious because they have car insurance.

2. Medical malpractice insurance may increase the amount of malpractice.

3. Guaranteed contracts for professional athletes may reduce their performance.

4. Unemployment insurance may lead some workers to shirk.

5. Government insurance on bank deposits may encourage banks to make risky loans.

Adverse Selection Problem Another information problem resulting from inadequate information about buyers is the **adverse selection problem**. *The adverse selection problem arises when information known by the first party to a contract is not known by the second, and, as a result, the second party incurs major costs.* Unlike the moral hazard problem, which arises *after* a person signs a contract, the adverse selection problem arises *at the time* a person signs the contract.

In insurance, the adverse selection problem is that people most likely to receive insurance payouts are those who will buy insurance. For example, those in poorest health will seek to buy the most generous health insurance policies. Or, at the extreme, a person planning to hire an arsonist to "torch" his failing business has an incentive to buy fire insurance.

Our example of hypothetical divorce insurance sheds further light on the adverse selection problem. If the insurance firm sets the premiums on the basis of the average rate of divorce, many of the married couples about to get a divorce will buy insurance. An insurance premium based on average probabilities will make for a great insurance buy for those about to get divorced. Meanwhile, those in highly stable marriages will opt against buying it. In summary, the adverse selection problem will eliminate the pooling of risk that is the basis for profitable insurance. The insurance rates needed to cover payouts will be so high that few people will wish or be able to buy this insurance.

Where private firms underprovide insurance because of information problems, government often establishes some type of social insurance. Government can require everyone in a particualr group to enter the insurance pool and thereby can overcome

Box 20-2

USED CARS: THE MARKET FOR "LEMONS"

Inadequate product information can result in markets where sellers offer only defective goods.

A new car loses much of its market value as the buyer drives it off the sales lot. Physical depreciation alone cannot explain this large loss of value. The same new car can sit on the dealer's lot for weeks, or even months, and retain its value.

One explanation of this paradox rests on the idea of inadequate information about *used* cars.* Auto owners have much more knowledge about the mechanical conditions of their vehicles than do potential buyers of used cars. At the time of the purchase, individual buyers of used cars find it difficult to distinguish between so-called "lemons" — defective cars — and vehicles of the same car make and model that operate perfectly. Therefore, a single price emerges for used cars of the same year, make, and model whether they are lemons or high-quality vehicles. This price roughly reflects the average quality of the vehicles, influenced by the proportion of lemons to high-quality cars. The higher the proportion of lemons, the lower are prices of used cars.

An adverse selection problem now becomes evident. Owners of lemons have an incentive to sell their cars to unsuspecting buyers, while owners of high-quality autos will wish to keep their cars. Therefore, most used cars on the market will be of lower quality than the same car models that are *not* for sale. As people become aware of this, the demand for used cars will decline and prices of used cars will fall. These lower prices will further reduce the incentive of owners of high-quality used cars to offer them for sale. At the extreme, only lemons will appear on the market; *poor-quality products will drive out high-quality products*.

We thus have a solution to our paradox. Once a buyer drives a new car away from the dealership, the auto's value becomes the value set in the lemons' market. This is true even though the probability is high that the new car is of high quality.

The instantaneous loss of new car value would be even greater were it not for several factors. Because new-car warranties are transferable to used-car buyers, purchasers of low-mileage late-model cars are protected against costly repairs. Thus, the demand for these vehicles rises. Also, prospective buyers can distinguish good cars from lemons by hiring mechanics to perform inspections. Moreover, sellers can signal potential buyers that their cars are not lemons through ads such as "Must sell, transferred abroad," "Divorce forces sale." Of course, the buyer must determine the truth of these claims. Additionally, auto rental companies routinely sell high-quality, late-model cars, increasing the ratio of good cars to lemons in the used-car market.

Government also plays a role in solving the market failure evident in the lemons' market. Many states in the U.S. have "lemon laws" that force auto dealers to take back defective new cars. Supposedly, dealers do not offer these lemons for sale in the used-car market until completing all needed repairs. Also, some American states require dealers to either offer warranties on used cars or explicitly state that a car is offered "as is." The latter designation gives the buyer a good clue that the car may be defective.

In brief, both private and governmental initiatives temper the lemons' problem. Nevertheless, this principle is applicable to a wide variety of used products such as autos, computers, and cameras, which are complex and occasionally defective. Buying any of these used products remains a somewhat risky transaction.

*The classical article on this topic is George A. Akerlof, "The Market for 'Lemons': Qualitative Uncertainty and the Market Mechanism," *Quarterly Journal of Economics,* August 1970, pp. 488–500.

the adverse selection problem. The social insurance system in Canada is partly an insurance and partly a welfare program. The social insurance systems overcome the adverse selection problem by requiring universal participation. People who are most likely to need the minimum benefits that social insurance automatically provides are participants in the program. So, too, are those not likely to need the benefits.

Workplace Safety The labour market also provides an example of how inadequate information about buyers (employers) can produce market failures.

Let's consider the issue of workplace safety. For several reasons employers have an economic incentive to provide safe workplaces. A safe workplace reduces the amount of disruption of the production process created by job accidents and lowers the costs of recruiting, screening, training, and retraining new workers. It also reduces a firm's worker compensation insurance premiums (legally required insurance against job injuries).

But a safe workplace comes at a cost. Safe equipment, protective gear, and slower paces of work all entail cost. Thus, the firm will compare its marginal cost and marginal benefit of providing a safer workplace in deciding how much safety to provide. Will this amount of job safety achieve allocative efficiency, as well as maximize the firm's profits?

The answer is "yes" if the labour and product markets are competitive and workers are fully aware of job risks at various places of employment. With full information, workers will avoid working for employers having unsafe workplaces. Hence, the supply of labour to these establishments will be greatly restricted, forcing them to boost their wages to attract a work force. These higher wages give the employer an incentive to provide socially desirable levels of workplace safety; safer workplaces will reduce wage expenses. Only firms that find it very costly to provide safer workplaces will choose to pay high compensating wage differentials, rather than reduce workplace hazards.

But a serious problem arises when workers *do not know* that particular occupations or workplaces are unsafe. Because information about the buyer is inadequate — that is, about the employer and the workplace — the firm may *not* need to pay a wage premium to attract its work force. Its incentive to remove safety hazards therefore is diminished and its profit-maximizing level of workplace safety will be less than socially desirable. In brief, the labour market will fail because of inadequate information about buyers (employers).

Government has several options for remedying this information problem.

1 It can directly provide information to workers about the injury experience of various employers.

2 It can mandate that firms provide information to workers about known workplace hazards.

3 It can establish standards of workplace safety and enforce them through inspection and penalties.

The federal government has mainly employed the "standards and enforcement" approach to improve workplace safety, but some contend that an "information" strategy might be less costly and more effective.

QUICK REVIEW (20-2)

1. **Inadequate information can cause markets to fail, causing society's scarce resources to be allocated inefficiently.**

2. **The moral hazard problem is the tendency of some parties to a contract to alter their behaviour in ways that are costly to the other party; for example, a person who buys insurance may incur added risk.**

3. **As it relates to insurance, the adverse selection problem is the tendency of people who are most likely to collect insurance benefits to buy large amounts of insurance.**

Qualification

People have found many ingenious ways to overcome information difficulties short of government intervention. For example, many firms offer product warranties to overcome the lack of information about themselves and their products. Franchising also helps overcome this problem. When you visit McDonald's or Holiday Inn, you know precisely what you are going to get, as opposed to Sam's Hamburger Shop or the Bates Motel.

Also, some private firms and organizations have specialized in providing information to buyers and sellers. *Consumer Reports* provides product information, labour unions collect and disseminate information about job safety, and credit bureaus provide information to insurance companies. Brokers and bonding agencies also provide information to clients.

However, economists agree that the private sector cannot remedy all information problems. In some situations government intervention is desirable to promote an efficient allocation of society's scarce resources.

CHAPTER SUMMARY

1. The law of conservation of matter and energy is at the heart of the pollution problem. Matter can be transformed into other matter or into energy, but does not disappear. If not recycled, all production inputs will ultimately end up as waste.

2. Environmental pollution problems can be alleviated either through direct control, via legislated standards, or levying taxes.

3. Trading in air-pollution rights is being tried in the United States. Initial assessment suggests it is working well.

4. Recycling is a recent response to the growing garbage disposal problem. The equilibrium price and quantity of recycled items depend on their demand and supply. Government can encourage recycling through either demand or supply incentives.

5. Inadequate information about sellers or buyers can cause markets to fail. The moral hazard problem occurs when people alter their behaviour after they sign a contract, imposing costs on the other party. As it relates to insurance, the adverse selection problem occurs when people who are of above-average risk buy large amounts of insurance.

TERMS AND CONCEPTS

adverse selection problem (p. 355)
law of conservation of matter and energy (p. 348)

market for pollution rights (p. 350)
moral hazard problem (p. 354)

QUESTIONS AND STUDY SUGGESTIONS

1. Relate the law of conservation of matter and energy to:

   a. the air pollution problem; and

   b. the solid waste disposal problem.

2. What are the two basic ways government can attempt to rectify externalities created by environmental pollution?

3. Can a market be created for pollution rights? Where has it been tried, and with what kind of results?

4. Explain why there may be insufficient recycling of products when the externalities associated with landfills and garbage incinerators are not considered? What demand and supply incentives might government provide to promote more recycling?

5. Why is it in the interest of new home buyers *and* builders of new homes to have government building codes and building inspectors?

6. Place an *M* beside items in the following list that describe a moral hazard problem; place an *A* beside those that describe an adverse selection problem.

   a. A person with a terminal illness buys several life insurance policies through the mail.

   b. A person drives carelessly because he or she has insurance.

   c. A person who intends to "torch" his warehouse takes out a large fire insurance policy.

   d. A professional athlete who has a guaranteed contract fails to stay in shape during the off-season.

   e. A woman anticipating having a large family takes a job with a firm that offers exceptional child-care benefits.

21

Public Choice Theory and Taxation

I n view of the positive role of government described in Chapter 19, it may seem surprising that government elicits so much public disenchantment and distrust. This anti-government sentiment has diverse roots, but it stems in part from the apparent failure of costly government programs to resolve socioeconomic ills. For example, it is argued that foreign aid programs have contributed little or nothing to the economic growth of the less developed nations. We hear reports that well-financed school enrichment programs have had no perceptible impact on the educational attainment of students. Some programs have allegedly fostered the very problems they were designed to solve: Our farm programs were originally designed to save the small family farm, but in fact have subsidized larger farms.

There are also charges that government agencies have become mired in a blizzard of paperwork. It is alleged that the public bureaucracy embodies great duplication of effort; that obsolete programs persist; that various agencies work at cross purposes; and so on.

Coincident with this popular disenchantment, there has evolved a body of literature that alleges that, just as certain limitations or failures are embodied in the private sector's market system, so there are also more-or-less inherent deficiencies in the political processes, bureaucratic agencies, and tax systems within the public sector.

The goal of this chapter is to examine some of these difficulties. Specifically, we scrutinize the problems that society has in revealing its true preferences through majority voting. This is followed by a closely related discussion of *government failure* — the contention that certain characteristics of the public sector hinder government's ability to assist the market system in achieving an efficient allocation of resources. Next, we turn toward an analytical examination of taxes and tax incidence. We want to learn how taxes are apportioned in Canada and who bears the burden. After examining the Goods and Services Tax (GST) introduced in 1991, we end the chapter with a brief discussion of the conservative and liberal stances on government and economic freedom.

This is a chapter on **public choice theory** — the economic analysis of government decision making; and on selected topics and problems of **public finance** — the study of public expenditures and revenues.

REVEALING PREFERENCES THROUGH MAJORITY VOTING

Which public goods should be produced and in what amounts? In what circumstances and through what methods should government intervene to correct for externalities? How should the tax burden of financing government be apportioned?

These and many other decisions concerning government are made collectively in Canada through a democratic process that relies heavily on majority voting. Political parties offer voters alternative policy packages, and we elect people who we think will make the best decisions on our collective behalf. Voters "retire" officials who do not adequately represent their collective wishes and elect persons who convince them they will better reflect the collective wants of the electorate. Additionally, citizens periodically have opportunities at the provincial and municipal level to vote directly on ballot issues that involve public expenditures or new legislation.

Although this democratic process generally works well at revealing society's true preferences, it is not without its shortcomings. Just as the market fails in some cases to allocate resources efficiently, our system of voting in some instances produces inefficiencies and inconsistencies. We will now explore some of these potential voting difficulties.

Inefficient Voting Outcomes

Providing a public good having a total benefit greater than its total cost will add to society's well-being. Unfortunately, majority voting raises the possibility of voting outcomes that are economically inefficient. Voters may defeat a proposal to provide a public good even though it may yield total benefits exceeding its total cost. Conversely, majority voting raises the possibility that voters may adopt a proposal to provide a public good costing more than the benefits it could yield.

Illustration: Inefficient "No" Vote   Suppose that a public good, say, national defence, can be provided at a total expense of $900. Also, suppose that there are only three individuals — Adams, Benson, and Conrad — in the society and they will equally share the $900 tax expense; each will be taxed $300. Assume, as illustrated in Figure 21-1(a), that Adams is willing to pay $700 to have this good; Benson, $250; and Conrad, $200. What might be the result if a majority vote is determined on whether or not this good will be provided? Although people do not always vote strictly on the basis of their own economic interest, it is entirely likely that Benson and Conrad will vote "No" because they will incur tax expenses of $300 each while gaining benefits of only $250 and $200, respectively. The majority vote in this case will defeat the proposal even though the total benefit of $1150 (= $700 for Adams + $250 for Benson + $200 for Conrad) exceeds the total cost of $900.

Illustration: Inefficient "Yes" Vote   We can easily construct an example illustrating the converse, in which the majority might favour the provision of a public good even though its total cost exceeds its total benefit. Figure 21-1(b) shows the details. Again, Adams, Benson, and Conrad will equally share the $900 cost of the public good; they each will be taxed $300. But, now note that Adams is only willing to pay $100 for the public good, rather than forgo it. Meanwhile, Benson and Conrad are willing to pay $350 dollars each. They will vote for the public good; Adams will vote against it. The election will result in provision of a public good costing $900 that produces total benefits of $800 (= $100 for Adams + $350 for Benson + $350 for Conrad). Society's resources will be inefficiently allocated to this public good.

The point of our examples is that an inefficiency may take the form of either an overproduction or underproduction of a specific public good, and

FIGURE 21-1   Inefficient voting outcomes

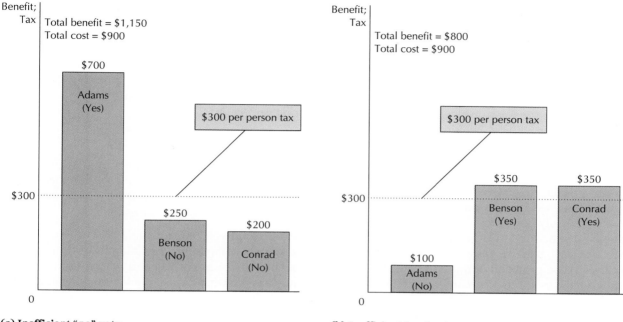

(a) Inefficient "no" vote   (b) Inefficient "yes" vote

Majority voting can produce inefficient decisions. In (a), majority voting leads to rejection of a public good that would entail a greater total benefit than total cost. In (b), majority voting results in provision of a public good having a higher total cost than total benefit.

therefore an overallocation or underallocation of resources for that particular use. In Chapter 19 we saw that government might improve allocative efficiency (resources channelled to their highest valued use) by providing public goods that the market system would not make available. Now we have extended that analysis to reveal that government might fail to provide some public goods whose production is economically justifiable while providing other goods whose creation is not economically warranted.

Our examples illustrate that people have only a single vote no matter how much they might gain or lose from a public good. In both examples shown in Figure 21-1, if buying votes were legal, Adams would be willing to purchase a vote from either Benson or Conrad, paying for it out of prospective personal gain. In the marketplace the consumer can decide *not* to buy a good, even though it is popular with others. Also, specific goods are normally available to people with strong preferences for them even though most consumers conlude that product prices exceed the marginal utilities of these goods. A consumer can buy beef tongues and fresh squid in some supermar-

kets, but it is doubtful these products would be available under a system that used majority voting to stock the shelves. On the other hand, one cannot easily "buy" national defence once the majority has decided it is not worth buying.

To repeat: *Because it fails to incorporate the preferences of the individual voter, majority voting may produce inefficient economic outcomes.*

Interest Groups and Logrolling Ways do exist through which inefficiencies associated with majority voting *may* get resolved. Two examples:

1. Interest Groups Those who have strong preference for a public good may band together into an interest group and use advertisements, mailings, and the like to try to convince others of the merits of a public good. In our first example [Figure 21-1(a)], Adams might make a major effort to convince Benson and Conrad that national defence is actually worth more than the $250 and $200 values they now place on it.

2. Political Logrolling Logrolling — *the trading of votes to secure favourable outcomes on decisions* *that otherwise would be adverse* — can turn an inefficient outcome into an efficient one. In our first example [Figure 21-1(a)], perhaps Benson has a strong preference for a different public good, say, a new road, which Adams and Conrad do not think is worth the tax expense. Now, an opportunity has developed for Adams and Benson to agree to trade votes to ensure provision of *both* national defence and the new road. The majority vote (Adams and Benson) in our three-person society will result in a positive vote for both national defence and the road. Without the logrolling, each would have been rejected. This logrolling will add to society's well-being if, as was true for national defence, the road creates a positive overall net benefit.

Logrolling need not increase economic efficiency. We could easily construct a scenario in which both national defence and the road individually cost more than the total benefits they each provide, and yet both would be provided because of vote trading. All that is necessary for the road and national defence to be provided is that Adams and Benson each secure net gains from their favoured public good.

In other words, the tax cost imposed on Conrad by the expenditures for national defence and the road could exceed Conrad's benefits so much that it swamped the combined net benefit received by Adams and Benson from the public goods. Under conditions of majority voting and logrolling, government will provide each of the public goods and shift a large net burden to Conrad. This scenario is familiar to political scientists who call this practice "pork-barrel politics" (getting public goods for constituents from the public barrel).

Our conclusion is that logrolling can either increase or diminish economic efficiency depending on the circumstances.

The Paradox of Voting

Another difficulty with majority voting is called the **paradox of voting**, which is *a situation where society may not be able to rank its preferences consistently through majority voting.*

Preferences   Consider Table 21-1 where we again assume a community consisting of just three voters: Adams, Benson, and Conrad. Suppose the community has three alternative public goods from which to choose: national defence, a road, and a weather warning system. We would expect each member of the community to arrange the order of the three alternatives according to her or his preferences and then select the preferred option. This implies that each voter will state that they prefer national defence to a

TABLE 21-1   Paradox of voting

	Preferences		
Public good	Adams	Benson	Conrad
National defence	1st choice	3rd choice	2nd choice
Road	2nd choice	1st choice	3rd choice
Weather warning system	3rd choice	2nd choice	1st choice

Election	Voting outcomes Winner
(1) National defence vs. road	National defence (preferred by Adams and Conrad)
(2) Road vs. weather warning system	Road (preferred by Adams and Benson)
(3) National defence vs. weather warning system	Weather warning system (preferred by Benson and Conrad)

road, and a road to a weather warning system, or whatever. We can then attempt to determine the collective preference scale of the community using a majority voting procedure. Specifically, a vote can be held between any two of the public goods and the winner of the contest matched against the third public good.

The three goods and the assumed individual preferences of the three voters are listed in the top portion of Table 21-1. In the lower part of the table, outcomes of various elections are listed. The upper portion indicates that Adams prefers national defence to the road and the road to the weather warning system. This also implies that Adams prefers national defence to the weather warning system. Benson values the road more than the weather warning system and the warning system more than national defence. Benson therefore prefers the road to national defence. Finally, Conrad's first choice is the weather warning system, second choice is national defence, and third choice is the road.

Voting Outcomes   Consider the outcomes of three hypothetical elections decided through majority vote. First, let us match national defence against the road in an election. In Table 21-1 national defence will win this contest because a majority of voters, Adams and Conrad, prefer national defence to a road. This outcome is reported in row (1) of the lower part of the table, where election outcomes are summarized. Next we hold an election to see whether this community wants a road or a weather warning system. A majority of voters, Adams and Benson, prefer the road to the weather warning system, as shown in row (2).

We have determined that the majority in this community prefer national defence to a road *and* prefer a road to a weather warning system. It therefore seems logical to conclude that the community prefers national defence to a weather warning system. But it does not!

To demonstrate this point consider a direct election between national defence and the weather warning system. In row (3) a majority of voters, Benson and Conrad, prefer the weather warning system to national defence. As indicated in Table 21-1, majority voting falsely implies that this community is irrational: it seems to prefer national defence to a road *and* a road to a weather warning system, but would rather have a weather warning system than national defence.

The problem is not one of irrational preferences, but rather one of a flawed procedure for determining

those preferences. Majority voting can yield opposing outcomes depending on how the vote on public expenditures or other public issues is ordered. Majority voting thus fails under some circumstances to make *consistent* choices that reflect the community's underlying preferences. As a consequence, government might find it difficult to provide the "correct" public goods by acting in accordance with majority voting.

Median-Voter Model

One final aspect of majority voting deserves comment because of the insights it reveals into real-world phenomena. The **median-voter model** suggests that *under majority rule the median voter will in a sense determine the outcomes of elections*. The median voter is the person holding the middle position on an issue: One-half of the other voters have stronger preferences for an expenditure on a public good, amount of taxation, or the degree of government regulation; and the remaining one-half have weaker — or negative — preferences.

Illustration   To illustrate this principle again suppose a society composed of Adams, Benson, and Conrad. Now assume that agreement has been reached between the three that as a society they need a weather warning system. Each independently is to submit a total dollar amount that he or she thinks should be spent on the warning system, given the fact that each will be taxed one-third of that amount. An election then will determine the actual size of the system. Because each person can be expected to vote for his or her own proposal, no majority will occur if all the proposals are placed on the ballot at the same time. Thus, the group decides they will first vote between two of the proposals and then match the winner of that vote against the remaining proposal.

The three proposals are as follows: Adams desires a $400 system; Benson wants an $800 system; Conrad opts for a $300 system. Which proposal will win? The median-voter model suggests it will be the $400 proposal submitted by the median voter, Adams. One-half of the other voters favours a more costly system; one-half favours a less costly system. To understand why the $400 system will be the outcome we need to conduct two elections.

First, suppose that the $400 proposal is matched against the $800 proposal. Adams naturally will vote for her $400 proposal, but how will Benson and Conrad vote? Conrad — who proposed a $300 expenditure for the warning system — will vote for the $400 proposal rather than the one for $800. Adam's $400 proposal is selected by a 2-to-1 majority vote. Next, we match the $400 proposal against the $300 proposal. Again the $400 proposal is victorious, because it gets a vote from Adams and one from Benson, who proposed the $800 expenditure and for that reason clearly prefers a $400 expenditure to a $300 one. Adams — the median voter in this case — in a sense is the person who has decided the proper level of expenditure on a weather warning system for this society.

Real-World Applicability Although this is purposely a simple illustration, the idea behind it explains much. We *do* note a tendency for public choices to match up closely with the median view. In fact, we often observe political candidates appealing to the median voter *within the party* to get the nomination. They then shift their views more closely to the political centre when they square off against their opponent from the opposite political party. In effect, they redirect their appeal toward the median voter *within the total population.* They also try to label their opponents as being too liberal, or too conservative, and out of touch with the "mainstream." Additionally, they conduct polls and adjust their positions on issues accordingly.

Implications Two interesting implications of the median voter model merit comment.

1. Many people will be dissatisfied by the extent of government involvement in the economy. The size of government will to a large extent be determined by the median preference, leaving many people desiring a much larger, or a much smaller, public sector. In the marketplace you can buy zero zucchinis, 2 zucchinis, or 200 zucchinis, depending on how much you enjoy zucchinis. In the public sector you get the number of hospitals and provincial highways that the median voter prefers.

2. A related point is that some people may "vote with their feet" by moving into political jurisdictions where the median voter's preferences are closer to their own. Someone may move from the city to a suburb where the level of government services and therefore taxes are lower. Or they may move into an area known for its excellent, but expensive, school system. Demographic changes within political jurisdictions also occur that change the median preference.

For these reasons, and because our personal preferences for government activity are not static, the median preference within political jurisdictions can

and does shift over time. Additionally, information about people's preference is imperfect, leaving much room for politicians to mistake the true median position.

PUBLIC SECTOR FAILURE

Our discussion of the problem of achieving the optimal output of public goods and the problems in voting for that output makes it clear that the economic functions of government are not always performed effectively and efficiently. Just because the economic results of the market are not entirely satisfactory, it does not necessarily follow that the political process will yield superior results. We might agree that government has a legitimate role in dealing with instances of market failure; that is, government should make adjustments for spillover costs and benefits, provide public goods and services, provide information, and so forth. We might also accept benefit-cost analysis as an important guide to efficient decision making in the public sector. But a more fundamental question remains: Are there inherent problems or shortcomings within the public sector that constrain governmental decision making as a mechanism for promoting economic efficiency?

In fact, casual reflection suggests that there may be significant divergence between "sound economics" and "good politics." The former calls for the public sector to pursue various programs so long as marginal benefits exceed marginal costs. Good politics, however, suggests that politicians support those programs and policies that will maximize their chances of getting elected and retained in office.

Let's now briefly consider some reasons given by public choice theorists for **public sector failure** — why the public sector may function inefficiently.

Special Interests and "Rent Seeking"

Ideally, public decisions promote the general welfare or, at least, the interests of the vast majority of the citizenry. But, in fact, government often promotes the goals of small special-interest groups to the detriment of the public at large.

Special-Interest Effect Efficient public decision making is often impaired by a **special-interest effect**. A special-interest issue is a program or policy from which a small number of people individually will receive *large* gains at the expense of a vastly larger number of persons who individually suffer *small* losses.

The small group of potential beneficiaries will be well informed and highly vocal on this issue, pressing politicians for approval. The large numbers who face very small losses will generally be uninformed and indifferent on this issue.

Politicians feel they will lose the support of the small special-interest group that supports the program if they vote against it. But politicians will *not* lose the support of the large group of uninformed voters who will evaluate them on other issues in which these voters have a stronger interest. Furthermore, the politicians' inclination to support special-interest legislation is enhanced by the fact that such groups are often more than willing to help finance the campaigns of "right-minded" politicians. The result is that the politician will support the special-interest program, even though it may *not* be economically desirable from a social point of view.

Rent-Seeking Behaviour   This pursuit through government of a transfer of wealth at someone else's or society's expense is called **rent-seeking behaviour**. As used here the term "rent" means any payment to a resource supplier, business, or other organization above that which would accrue under competitive market conditions. Corporations, trade associations, labour unions, and professional organizations employ a vast amount of resources in their attempt to secure "rent" directly or indirectly dispensed by government. Government provides this "rent" through legislation and policies that increase payments to some groups, leaving others or society at large less well-off.

Examples of special-interest or rent-seeking groups realizing legislation and policies unjustified on the basis of efficiency or equity are manifold: tariffs on foreign products that limit competition and raise prices to consumers; tax loopholes that benefit only the wealthy; public work projects that cost more than the benefits they yield; occupational licensing that goes beyond that needed to protect customers; large subsidies to farmers by taxpayers; and public works programs costing more than the benefits they yield and channelled to constituencies of government MPs.

Clear Benefits, Hidden Costs

The contention is also made that vote-seeking politicians will not *objectively* weigh all costs and benefits of various programs, as economic rationality demands, in deciding which to support and which to reject. Because political officeholders must seek voter support every few years, politicians will favour programs with immediate and clear-cut benefits, on the one hand, and vague, difficult-to-identify, or deferred, costs, on the other. Conversely, politicians will shun programs that embody immediate and easily identifiable costs along with future benefits that are diffuse and vague.

The point here is that such biases in the area of public choice can lead politicians to reject economically justifiable programs and to accept programs that are economically irrational. Example: A proposal to construct and expand mass-transit systems in large metropolitan areas may be economically rational on the basis of objective benefit-cost analysis as illustrated in Table 19-2. But if (1) the program is to be financed by immediate increases in highly visible income or sales taxes *and* (2) benefits will accrue only a decade hence when the project is completed, the vote-seeking politician may decide to oppose the program.

Assume, on the other hand, that a proposed program of increased federal aid to housing is *not* justifiable on the basis of objective benefit-cost analysis. But if costs are concealed and deferred through deficit financing, the program's modest benefits may loom so large that it gains political approval.

Limited Choice

Public choice theorists also argue that the nature of the political process is such that citizens are forced to be less selective in the choice of public goods and services than they are in the choice of private goods and services.

In the private sector, the citizen *as consumer* can reflect personal preferences very precisely by buying certain goods and forgoing others. However, in the public sector the citizen *as voter* is confronted with two or more candidates for office, each of whom represents different "bundles" of programs (public goods and services). In no case is the bundle of public goods represented by any particular candidate likely to fit precisely the wants of the particular voter.

For example, voter Smith's favoured candidate for office may endorse national dental insurance, the development of nuclear energy, subsidies to tobacco farmers, and tariffs on imported automobiles. Citizen Smith votes for this candidate because the bundle of programs she endorses comes closest to matching Smith's preferences, even though Smith may oppose tobacco subsidies and tariffs on foreign cars.

The voter, in short, must take the bad with the good; in the public sector, one is forced to "buy"

Box 21-1

RENT SEEKING AND THE SPECIAL-INTEREST EFFECT

In 1986 there was tax reform in the U.S. It was not easy to get the Tax Reform Act passed through Congress and the Senate, as many interest groups tried to get some sort of special tax treatment. The final Act contains some stark examples of the special-interest effect and rent seeking.

Murray Weidenbaum, chair of President Reagan's Council of Economic Advisers, 1981–1982, looks at the Tax Reform Act of 1986 and points out numerous tax-reducing special-interest clauses.

Despite all the talk about equity, the [Tax Reform] Act [of 1986] contains numerous new special benefits. It would be a breach of legislative etiquette to designate the lucky recipients by name. Congress describes the "goodies" in words like "a paint and glass project which was approved by the management committee of a company on September 11, 1985." That very language was put into the Internal Revenue Code.

Another special benefit goes to "rental property which was assigned FHA [Federal Housing Administration] number 023-36602." That is really neat. It is not considered to be special-purpose legislation, because the benefit covers every taxpayer whose FHA number happens to be 023-36602. Here is my favourite: a project that was "the subject of law suits filed on June 22, 1984 and November 21, 1985." That sets an interesting precedent: getting sued now qualifies some people for being included in the tax code. See [the accompanying] table for other examples of the arbitrary distribution of federal largess in the guise of tax reform.

TABLE 1   Some special favors in the 1986 tax bill language describing the beneficiaries

A "state which ratified the United States Constitution on May 29, 1790."

* * *

A company which entered into a binding contract "on October 3, 1984, for the purchase of 6 semi-submersible units at a cost of $425,000,000."

* * *

"Any taxpayer incorporated on September 7, 1978, which is engaged in the trade or business of manufacturing dolls and accessories."

* * *

Any project "which was the subject of a city ordinance numbered 82-115 and adopted on December 2, 1982."

* * *

Any facility where the developer "was selected on April 26, 1985."

* * *

A project to provide a roof or dome for an existing sports facility if "an 11-member task force was appointed by the county executive in June 1985, to further study the feasibility of the project."

* * *

Any project having one of the following Farmers Home Administration Code numbers:

49284553664
4927742022446
49270742276087
490270742387293
4927074218234
49270742244019
51460742345074

* * *

"Any institution of higher education . . . mandated by a state constitution in 1876."

* * *

"A corporation which was incorporated on December 29, 1969, in the State of Delaware. . . . "

* * *

". . . 10 warehouse buildings built between 1906 and 1910 and purchased under a contract dated February 17, 1926."

* * *

A university established by charter granted by King George II of England on October 31, 1754."

Source: Tax Reform Act of 1986.

Source: Murray Weidenbaum, *Rendezvous with Reality* (New York: Basic Books, Inc., 1988), pp. 95–96. Reprinted with permission.

goods and services one does not want. It is as though, in going to a clothing store, you were forced to buy an unwanted pair of slacks to get a wanted pair of shoes. This is clearly a situation where resources are *not* being allocated efficiently to satisfy consumer wants best. In this sense, the provision of public goods and services is inherently inefficient.

Bureaucracy and Inefficiency

It is often contended that private businesses are innately more efficient than public agencies. The reason for this is *not* that lazy and incompetent workers somehow end up in the public sector, while the ambitious and capable gravitate to the private sector. Rather, it is held that the market system creates incentives and pressures for internal efficiency that are absent in the public sector. The managers of private enterprises have a strong personal incentive — increased profits — to be efficient in their operation. Whether a private firm is in a competitive or monopolistic environment, lower costs through efficient management contribute to enlarged profits. There is no tangible personal gain — a counterpart to profits — for the government bureau chief who achieves efficiency within his or her domain.

There is simply less incentive to be cost-conscious in the public sector. Indeed, in a larger sense the market system imposes an explicit test of performance on private firms — the test of profits and losses. An efficient firm is profitable and therefore successful; it survives, prospers, and grows. An inefficient enterprise is unprofitable and unsuccessful; it declines and in time goes bankrupt and ceases to exist. But there is no similar, clear-cut test by which one can assess efficiency or inefficiency of public agencies. How

can one determine whether the Canadian Broadcasting Corporation, a university, a local fire department, the Ministry of Agriculture, or the Department of Indian Affairs and Northern Development is operating efficiently?

Cynics argue that, in fact, a public agency that uses its resources inefficiently may be in line for a budget increase! In the private sector, inefficiency and monetary losses lead to abandonment of certain activities — the discontinuing of certain products and services. But government, it is contended, is loath to abandon activities in which it has failed. Some suggest that the typical response of government to failure of a program is to double its budget and staff. This means that public sector inefficiency may be sustained on a larger scale.

Furthermore, returning to our earlier comments on special-interest and rent-seeking groups, it has been pointed out that public programs spawn new constituencies of bureaucrats and beneficiaries whose political clout causes programs to be sustained or expanded after they have fulfilled their goals or, alternatively, even if they have failed miserably in their mission. Relevant bureaucrats, school administrators, and teachers may band together to become a highly effective special-interest group for sustaining inefficient programs of provincial funding of education or for causing these programs to be expanded beyond the point at which marginal benefits equal marginal costs.

Some specific suggestions have been offered recently to deal with the problems of bureaucratic inefficiency. Benefit-cost analysis is one suggested approach. It has also been proposed that all legislation establishing new programs contain well-defined performance standards so the public can better judge efficiency. Further, the suggestion has been made that expiration dates — so called "sunset laws" — be written into all new programs, forcing a thorough periodic evaluation that might indicate the need for program abandonment.

QUICK REVIEW (21-1)

1. **Majority voting can produce voting outcomes that are inefficient; projects having greater total benefits than costs can be defeated and projects having greater total costs than total benefits can win.**

2. **The paradox of voting occurs where voting by majority rule fails to provide a consistent ranking of society's preferences for public goods and services.**

3. **The median-voter model suggests that under majority rule the voter having the middle (median) preference will determine the outcome of an election.**

4. **Public-sector failure allegedly occurs because of rent-seeking by special-interest groups, short-sighted political behaviour, limited citizen choices, and bureaucratic inefficiency.**

Imperfect Institutions

One might argue that these criticisms of public sector efficiency are overdrawn and too cynical. Perhaps so. On the other hand, they are sufficiently persuasive to shake one's faith in a simplistic concept of a benevolent government responding with precision and efficiency to the wants of its citizenry. The private sector is by no means perfectly efficient; indeed, government's economic functions are attempts to correct the market system's shortcomings. But the public sector may also be subject to important deficiencies in fulfilling its economic functions.

One of the important implications of the fact that the market system and public agencies are both imperfect institutions is that, in practice, it can be exceedingly difficult to determine whether some particular activity can be performed with greater success in the private or the public sector. It is easy to reach agreement on opposite extremes: National defence must lie in the public sector, whereas wheat production can best be accomplished in the private sector. But what about dental insurance? The provision of

parks and recreation areas? Fire protection? Garbage collection? Housing? Education? Postal services? It is very hard to assess each type of good or service and to say unequivocally that its provision should be assigned to either the public or the private sector. Evidence that this is so is reflected in the fact that all the goods and services mentioned above are provided in part by both private enterprises and public agencies.

APPORTIONING THE TAX BURDEN

Our attention now turns from the difficulties of making collective decisions on the types and amounts of public goods to the difficulties in deciding how those goods should be financed. The characteristics of public goods and services make it difficult to measure precisely the manner in which their benefits are apportioned among individuals and institutions. It is virtually impossible to determine accurately the amount by which John Doe benefits from military installations, a network of highways, a public school system, the national weather bureau, and local police and fire protection.

The situation is a bit different on the taxation side of the picture. Studies reveal with somewhat greater clarity the manner in which the overall tax burden is apportioned. Needless to say, this is a question that affects each of us in an important way. Although the average citizen is concerned with the overall level of taxes, chances are he or she is even more interested in exactly how the tax burden is allocated among individual taxpayers.

Benefits Received Versus Ability To Pay

There are two basic philosophies on how the economy's tax burden should be apportioned.

Benefits-Received Principle   The **benefits-received principle** of taxation asserts that households and businesses should purchase the goods and services of government in basically the same manner in which other commodities are bought. It is reasoned that those who benefit most from government-supplied goods or services should pay the taxes necessary for their financing. A few public goods are financed essentially on the basis of the benefits principle. For example, gasoline taxes are typically earmarked for the financing of highway construction and repairs. Those who benefit from good roads pay the cost of those roads. Difficulties immediately arise, however, when an accurate and widespread application of the benefits principle is considered:

1. How does goverment go about determining the benefits that individual households and businesses receive from national defence, education, and police and fire protection? Recall that public goods entail widespread spillover benefits and that the exclusion principle is inapplicable. Even in the seemingly tangible case of highway finance we find it difficult to measure benefits. Individual car owners benefit in different degrees from the existence of good roads. And those who do not own cars also benefit. Businesses would certainly benefit greatly from any widening of their markets that good roads will encourage.

2. Government efforts to redistribute income would be self-defeating if financed on the basis of the benefits principle. It would be absurd and self-defeating to ask poor families to pay the taxes needed to finance their welfare payments! It would be equally ridiculous to think of taxing only unemployed workers to finance the unemployment insurance payments that they receive.

Ability-To-Pay Principle The **ability-to-pay principle** rests on the idea that the tax burden should be geared directly to one's income and wealth. As the ability-to-pay principle has come to be applied in Canada it contends that individuals and businesses with larger incomes should pay more taxes — both absolutely and relatively — than those with modest incomes.

What is the rationale of ability-to-pay taxation? Proponents argue that each additional dollar of income received by a household will yield smaller and smaller increments of satisfaction, or marginal utility. It is held that, because consumers act rationally, the first dollars of income received in any period of time will be spent on high-urgency goods that yield the greatest marginal utility. Successive dollars of income will go for less urgently needed goods and finally for trivial goods and services. This means that a dollar taken through taxes from a poor person who has few dollars is a greater sacrifice than is a dollar taken by taxes from the rich person. In order to balance the sacrifices that taxes impose on income earners, it is contended that taxes should be apportioned according to the amount of income one receives.

This is appealing, but problems of application exist. Although we might agree that the household earning $100,000 per year has a greater ability to pay taxes than the household receiving a paltry $10,000,

exactly *how much more* ability to pay does the first family have as compared with the second? Should the rich person simply pay the *same percentage* of his or her larger income — and hence a larger absolute amount — as taxes? Or should the rich person be made to pay a *larger fraction* of this income as taxes?

The problem is there is no scientific way of measuring one's ability to pay taxes. Thus, in practice, the answer hinges on guesswork, the tax views of the political party in power, expediency, and how urgently the government needs revenue.

Progressive, Proportional, and Regressive Taxes

Any discussion of the ability-to-pay and the benefits-received principles of taxation ultimately leads to the question of tax rates and the manner in which tax rates change as one's income increases.

Definitions Taxes are classified as being progressive, proportional, or regressive. These designations focus on the relationship between tax rates and *income* simply because all taxes — regardless of whether they are levied on income or on a product or building or parcel of land — are ultimately paid out of someone's income.

1. A tax is **progressive** if its average rate *increases* as income increases. Such a tax claims not only a larger absolute amount, but also a larger fraction or percentage of income as income increases.

2. A **regressive** tax is one whose average rate *declines* as income increases. Such a tax takes a smaller and smaller proportion of income as income increases. A regressive tax may or may not take a larger absolute amount of income as income expands.

3. A tax is **proportional** when its average rate *remains the same*, regardless of the size of income.

We can illustrate these ideas in terms of the personal income tax. Suppose tax rates are such that a household pays 10% of its income in taxes, regardless of the size of its income. This would clearly be a proportional income tax.

Now suppose the rate structure is such that the household with an annual taxable income of less than $10,000 pays 5% in income taxes, the household realizing an income of $10,000 to $20,000 pays 10%, $20,000 to $30,000 pays 15%, and so forth. This, would be a *progressive* income tax.

The final case is where the rates decline as taxable income rises: You pay 15% if you earn less than

$10,000; 10% if you earn $10,000 to $20,000; 5% if you earn $20,000 to $30,000; and so forth. This a regressive income tax. In general, progressive taxes are those that weigh most heavily on the rich; regressive taxes are those that hit the poor hardest.

Applications   What can we say about the progressivity, proportionality, or regressivity of the major kinds of taxes used in Canada.

1. Personal Income Tax   The federal *personal income tax* can be said to be reasonably progressive with marginal tax rates ranging from 15 to 49%.

2. Sales Taxes   At first glance a *general sales tax* with, say, a 3% rate would seem to be proportional. But in fact it is regressive with respect to income. A larger portion of a poor person's income is exposed to the tax than is the case with a rich person; the latter avoids the tax on the part of income that is saved, whereas the former is unable to save. Example: "Poor" Smith has an income of $15,000 and spends it all. "Rich" Jones has an income of $300,000 but spends only $200,000 of it. Assuming a 3% sales tax applies to the expenditures of each individual, we find Smith will pay $450 (3% of $15,000) in sales taxes, and Jones will pay $6,000 (3% of $200,000). Note that whereas *all* of Smith's $15,000 income is subject to the sales tax, only two-thirds of Jones' $300,000 income is taxed. Thus, while Smith pays $450, or 3%, of a $15,000 income as sales taxes, Jones pays $6,000, or just 2%, of a $300,000 income. We conclude that the general sales tax is regressive.

3. Corporate Income Tax   The *corporate income tax* is essentially a flat-rate proportional tax levied by the federal government with a 28% tax rate. But this assumes that corporation owners (shareholders) bear the tax. Some tax experts argue that at least a part of the tax is passed through to consumers in the form of higher product prices. To the extent that this occurs, the tax tends to be regressive, like a sales tax.

4. Property Taxes   Most economists believe that *property taxes* on buildings are regressive for essentially the same reasons as are sales taxes. First, property owners add the tax to the rents that tenants are charged. Second, property taxes, as a percentage of income, are higher for poor families than for rich families because the poor must spend a larger proportion of their incomes for housing.[1] The alleged

regressivity of the property tax may be reinforced by the fact that property-tax rates are not likely to be uniform.

TAX INCIDENCE AND EFFICIENCY LOSS

Determining whether a particular tax is progressive, proportional, or regressive is complicated by the fact that taxes do not always stick where they are levied. It is therefore necessary to locate as best we can the final resting place of a tax, or, more technically, the **tax incidence.** The tools of elasticity of supply and demand are of considerable help in this endeavour. To demonstrate, we focus on a hypothetical excise tax levied on producers of wine. Do producers pay this tax, or do they shift it forward to consumers of wine? This analysis will then provide a logical bridge to a discussion of other aspects of the economic burden of a tax.

Elasticity and Tax Incidence

Suppose that Figure 21-2 shows the market for a certain domestic wine and that the no-tax equilibrium

FIGURE 21-2   The incidence of an excise tax

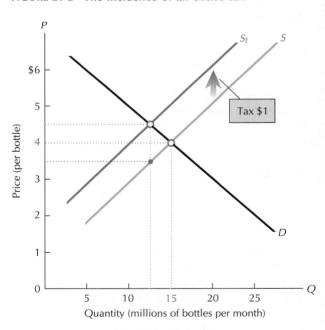

The imposition of an excise tax of a specified amount, say $1 per unit, shifts the supply curve upward by the amount of the tax. This results in a higher price ($4.50) to the consumer and a lower after-tax price ($3.50) to the producer. In this particular case, the burden of the tax is shared equally by consumers and producers.

---

[1] Controversy arises in part because empirical research, that compares the value of housing to lifetime (rather than a single year's) income, suggests that this ratio is approximately the same for all income groups.

price and quantity are $4 per bottle and 15 million bottles. Now assume that government levies a specific sales or excise tax of $1 per bottle on this wine. What is the incidence of this tax?

Division of Burden   Assuming that government imposes the tax on sellers (suppliers), it can be viewed as an addition to the supply price of the product. While sellers were willing to offer, for example, 5 million bottles of untaxed wine at $2 per bottle, they must now receive $3 per bottle — $2 plus the $1 tax — to offer the same 5 million bottles. Sellers must now get $1 more for each quantity supplied to receive the same per unit price they were getting before the tax. The tax thus shifts the supply curve upward as shown in Figure 21-2, where S is the "no-tax" supply curve and S_t is the "after-tax" supply curve.

Careful comparison of after-tax supply and demand with the pretax equilibrium reveals that the new equilibrium price is $4.50 per bottle, compared with the before-tax price of $4.00. In this case, one-half of the tax is paid by consumers in the form of a higher price and the other half by producers in the

form of a lower after-tax price. Consumers pay 50 cents more per bottle and, after remitting the $1 tax per unit to government, producers receive $3.50, or 50 cents less than the $4.00 before-tax price. In this instance, consumers and producers share the burden of the tax equally.

Elasticities   If the elasticities of demand and supply were different from those shown in Figure 21-2, the incidence of the tax would also be different. Two generalizations are relevant.

   1. *Given supply, the more inelastic the demand for the product, the larger the portion of the tax shifted forward to consumers.* The easiest way to verify this is to sketch graphically the extreme cases where demand is perfectly elastic and perfectly inelastic. In the first case the incidence of the tax is entirely on sellers; in the second, the tax shifts entirely to consumers.

   Figure 21-3 contrasts the more likely cases where demand might be relatively elastic (D_e) or relatively inelastic (D_i) in the relevant price range. In the elastic demand case of Figure 21-3(a) a small portion of the tax (PP_e) is shifted forward to consumers and

---

FIGURE 21-3   Demand elasticity and the incidence of an excise tax

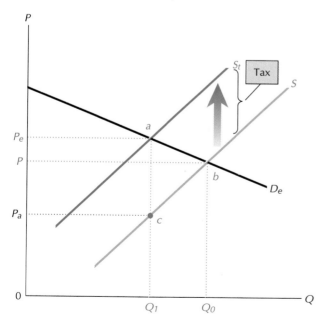

(a) Tax incidence and elastic demand

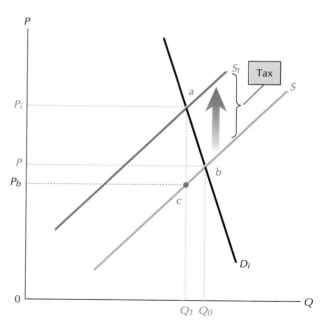

(b) Tax incidence and inelastic demand

In (a) we find that if demand is elastic in the relevant price range, price will rise modestly (*P* to *P*ₑ) when an excise tax is levied. Hence the producer bears most of the tax burden. But if demand is inelastic, as in (b), the price to the buyer will increase substantially (*P* to *P*ᵢ), and most of the tax is thereby shifted to consumers.

most of the tax (PP_a) is borne by producers. In the inelastic demand case of Figure 21-3(b), most of the tax (PP_i) is shifted to consumers and only a small amount (PP_b) is paid by producers.

Note, too, that the decline in equilibrium quantity is smaller, the more inelastic the demand. This recalls one of our previous applications of the elasticity concept: Revenue-seeking legislatures place heavy excise taxes on liquor, cigarettes, automobile tires, and other products whose demand is inelastic.

2. *Given demand, the more inelastic the supply, the larger the portion of the tax borne by producers.* While the demand curves are identical, the supply curve is elastic in Figure 21-4(a) and inelastic in Figure 21-4(b). For the elastic supply curve most of the tax (PP_e) is shifted forward to consumers and only a small portion (PP_a) is borne by producers or sellers. But where supply is inelastic, the reverse is true. The major portion of the tax (PP_b) falls on sellers and a relatively small amount (PP_i) is shifted to buyers. Quantity also declines less with an inelastic supply than it does with an elastic supply.

Gold is an example of a product for which supply is inelastic and therefore for which the burden of an

excise tax would fall mainly on producers. On the other hand, because the supply of baseballs is elastic, much of an excise tax on this product would get passed forward to consumers.

Efficiency Loss of a Tax

We have just observed that an excise tax on producers in a market characterized by typical supply and demand curves is borne partly by producers and partly by consumers. Additional attention to the burden of an excise tax is now warranted. Figure 21-5 is identical to Figure 21-2 but contains additional detail important to our discussion.

Tax Revenue   The $1 excise tax on wine increases the market price from $4 to $4.50 per bottle and reduces the equilibrium quantity from 15 to 12.5 million bottles. Government's tax revenue is $12.5 million (= $1 × 12.5 million bottles), an amount shown as the rectangle labelled *efac* in Figure 21-5. In this case, the elasticities of supply and demand are such that consumers and producers each pay one-half of this total amount, or $6.25 million apiece (= $.50 × 12.5 million bottles). Government uses this $12.5 mil-

FIGURE 21-4   Supply elasticity and the incidence of an excise tax

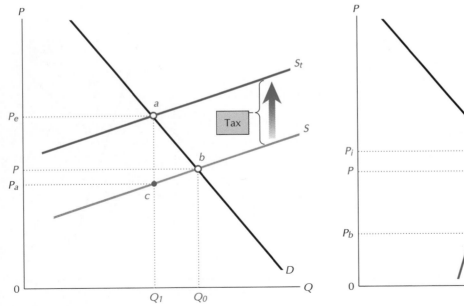

(a) Tax incidence and elastic supply

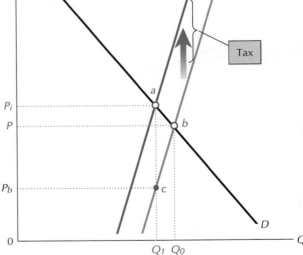

(b) Tax incidence and inelastic supply

Figure (a) indicates that with an elastic supply, an excise tax results in a large price increase (*P* to *P_e*), and the tax is paid largely by consumers. But if supply is inelastic, as in (b), the price rise will be small (*P* to *P_i*) and sellers will have to bear most of the tax.

FIGURE 21-5   Efficiency loss of a tax

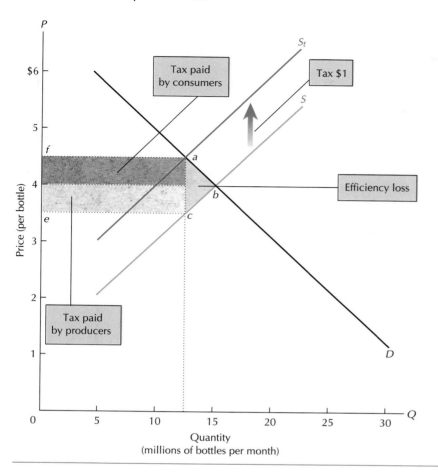

The levy of a $1 excise tax per bottle of wine increases the price per bottle to $4.50 and reduces the equilibrium quantity by 2.5 million bottles. Government's tax revenue is $12.5 million (area *efac*). The efficiency loss of the tax is the amount shown as triangle *abc*.

lion of tax revenue to provide public goods and services of value. Thus there is no loss of well-being to society as a whole from this transfer from consumers and producers to government.

Efficiency Loss   The $1 tax on wine requires consumers and producers to pay $12.5 million of taxes, but also *reduces the equilibrium amount of wine produced and consumed by 2.5 million bottles.* The fact that 2.5 million more bottles of wine were demanded and supplied prior to the tax means they provided benefits in *excess* of their costs of production. We can see this from the following simple analysis.

The *ab* segment of demand curve *D* in Figure 21-5 indicates the willingness to pay — the marginal benefit — associated with each of these 2.5 million bottles consumed prior to the tax. The *cb* segment of supply curve *S*, on the other hand, reflects the marginal cost of each of the bottles of wine. For all but the very last one of these 2.5 million bottles, the marginal benefit (shown by *ab*) exceeds the marginal

cost (shown by *cb*). The reduction of well-being because these 2.5 million bottles are not produced is indicated by the triangle *abc*. This triangle shows the **efficiency loss of the tax**. *This loss is the sacrifice of net benefit accruing to society because consumption and production of the taxed product are reduced below their allocatively efficient levels.*

Role of Elasticities   Most taxes create some degree of efficiency loss, but the amount depends crucially on supply and demand elasticities. Glancing back to Figure 21-3, we observe that the efficiency loss triangle *abc* is greater in Figure 21-3(a), where demand is relatively elastic, than in Figure 21-3(b), where demand is relatively inelastic. Similarly, the area *abc* is greater in Figure 21-4(a) than in Figure 21-4(b), indicating a large efficiency loss where supply is more elastic.

The major principle that our analysis establishes is that the amount of efficiency loss of an excise tax or sales tax varies from market to market depending on the elasticities of supply and demand. *Other things being equal, the greater the elasticities of supply and demand, the greater the efficiency loss of a particular tax.* Two taxes that yield equal revenues do not necessarily entail equal tax burdens for society. This fact complicates government's job of determining the best way to collect its needed tax revenues. Government must consider the efficiency losses of taxes in designing an optimal tax system.

Qualification   We must add an important qualification to our analysis. Other tax goals in many instances may be more important than the goal of minimizing efficiency losses from taxes. Two examples will demonstrate this fact.

1. Government may wish to impose progressive taxes as a way to redistribute income. A 10% excise tax placed on selected luxuries would be a case in point. Because the demand for luxuries is elastic, efficiency losses from this tax could be substantial. However, if the benefits from the redistribution effects of this tax would exceed these efficiency losses then a government would go ahead with such a tax.

2. Government may have intended the $1 tax on wine in Figure 21-2 to reduce consumption of wine by 2.5 million bottles. It may have concluded that consumption of alcoholic beverages produces certain negative externalities. Therefore, it might have levied this tax to adjust the market supply curve for these costs to reduce the amount of resources allocated to wine.

QUICK REVIEW (21-2)

1. **The benefits-received principle holds that government should assess taxes on individuals according to the amount of benefits they receive, regardless of their income; the ability-to-pay tax principle holds that people should be taxed according to their income, regardless of the benefits they receive from government.**

2. **As income increases, the average tax rate rises when a tax is progressive, remains the same when a tax is proportional, and falls when a tax is regressive.**

3. **The more inelastic the demand for a product, the more of an excise tax that is borne by consumers; the more inelastic the supply, the larger the portion borne by producers.**

4. **The efficiency loss of a tax results from the loss of output for which marginal benefits exceed marginal costs.**

RECENT CANADIAN TAX REFORM

The Canadian tax system has undergone two major changes in the last several years. These are (a) the 1987 Tax Reform and (b) the Goods and Services Tax. It must be kept in mind that we refer to the federal government only; each province also levies a number of taxes, some in conjunction with the federal government.

The 1987 Tax Reform

Spurred on by the recent tax reform in the U.S. that significantly lowered marginal tax rates, the Canadian government simplified the personal income tax from 11 categories to only 3. The general implication is to lower the marginal tax rate, which combined with provincial levies was as high as 64%, and at the same time to eliminate tax deductions in favour of tax credits. The top federal marginal tax rate has come down to about 45%.

Subsequent to these reforms the federal surtax was increased and a "claw back" provision was introduced that in effect took back part of the social insurance benefits, primarily unemployment insurance and family allowance, paid to higher income Canadians. Both of these provisions made the income tax system more progressive.

The GST

The controversy surrounding the introduction of the GST was unprecedented. (See Box 21-2.) Much of the dispute arose because of misunderstandings and a concerted and highly publicized effort by the official opposition in Parliament, the Liberal Party, to defeat the legislation.

The GST is similar to a **value-added tax** (VAT). It is much like a sales tax, except that it applies only to the difference between the value of a firm's sales and the value of its purchases from other firms. This is done by allowing firms a tax credit equal to the taxes paid on their inputs.

The GST replaced the federal sales tax, which was levied primarily on manufactured goods and was as high as 13% on some products. The GST at present stands at 7% and is levied on a much broader base that includes both goods and services. The only exemptions are agricultural and fish products, prescription drugs, and medical devices.

An important feature of the GST is that exports are in fact exempt since producers can claim a credit equal to the taxes paid on the inputs used to produce the product. Moreover, imported goods are subject to

Box 21-2

In the Media

The following editorial from The Globe and Mail *attempts to dispel the myths that have surrounded the Goods and Services Tax (GST) since its inception.*

THE GST HORRORS THAT NEVER WERE

THE year just ended was not made seven per cent longer by the GST. The weather is not seven per cent colder for its introduction last New Year's Day, nor is the mail seven per cent slower. The Gulf War, the collapse of the Soviet Union and the unification of Europe are major world events in 1991 that were wholly unrelated to the reform of the federal sales tax. Smallpox has not revived.

That about exhausts the list of consequences that were not foretold with certainty to follow the GST's arrival. Next to free trade, no federal policy initiative attracted more dire prophecies in advance of its implementation. So urgent was it that Canadians be spared this biblical disaster that Liberal Senators felt compelled to refuse it passage, usurping the Commons' centuries-old prerogative in revenue matters. Their desperation could perhaps be understood in another way: for the monsters they saw rising from the GST could survive to scare the children only so long as the tax was not yet in place. They were bound to shrivel in the light of actual experience. After a year with the GST, it is clear the critics were wrong, and wrong in almost every way.

An inflationary tax? Wrong. Instead of the "double-digit" inflation predicted by the president of the Canadian Union of Public Employees, inflation has subsided to less than two per cent on an annualized basis since the spring. The GST's impact, according to separate calculations by the Bank of Canada, the GST Consumer Information Office and Statistics Canada, was to raise prices once-and-for-all by at most 1.5 per cent: almost exactly what the government predicted.

A tax grab? Wrong. This bears repeating: the GST is not a new tax. It replaced an old tax: the 74-year-old manufacturers' sales tax. The difference is reflected in their names. The GST applies to both goods and services; it is imposed not just at the manufacturers' level, but all through the value-added chain. It was always designed to be revenue-neutral: whatever extra revenue it brings in is channeled back in sales tax credits. The government expects gross GST revenues will be within $100-million of the $19.7-billion budgeted.

A regressive tax? Wrong. The information office puts the increase in the cost of living for low-income households at about $200 per year, or 1.1 per cent. But these same households receive sales tax credits of up to $580 a year for a family of four. Meanwhile, those with family income of $48,000 pay 1.15 per cent extra, while the take on families earning $70,000 or more is higher still: about 1.5 per cent. That's because the rich spend more on services, which the GST taxes for the first time. So the GST is a progressive tax: its net effect is to redistribute income to the poor.

An inefficient tax? Wrong. The GST treats manufacturing and services the same; within the manufacturing sector, it applies evenly to all goods; it taxes imports and domestic goods in equal measure, and exempts exports from tax. The GST's input credits ensures firms are not taxed for investing; as a consumption tax, it avoids taxing individuals for saving. It is thus more neutral in its effects on the economy than almost every other tax imaginable.

A complicated tax? Right, partly, though such remedies as the "Quick Method" should spare small businesses much paperwork. The convolutions that remain are more owing to the GST's opponents than its sponsors: the provinces, for refusing to harmonize their own sales taxes, and the opposition in Ottawa, for frightening the federal government off of taxing groceries. Perhaps by this time next year, the tax can be exonerated of these faults too.

By permission of *The Globe and Mail*, December 31, 1991.

the GST, so they are at no particular advantage compared to domestically produced goods.

The GST's implementation on January 1, 1991

coincided with the country being in a recession. Many quickly jumped to the conclusion that the GST at least aggravated, if it was not the cause of, the recession. The government claims the GST will be revenue neutral: it will raise revenues just offset by the elimination of the federal sales tax.

There appears to be a consensus among economists that the GST is an improvement over the old federal sales tax since it introduces less distortions to the price of goods and services. For our exporters it is a definite advantage. Moreover, those in the lower income brackets receive a tax credit. Thus, it is not as regressive as some critics claim.

THE ISSUE OF FREEDOM

We end our discussion of government decision making by considering an important, but elusive, question: What is the nature of the relationship between the role and size of the public sector, on the one hand, and freedom, on the other? Although no attempt is made here to explore this issue in depth, we will outline two divergent views on this question.

The Conservative Position

Many conservative economists believe that, in addition to the economic costs of any expansion of the public sector, there is also a cost in the form of diminished individual freedom. Several related points constitute this position.

First, there is the "power corrupts" argument.[2] "Freedom is a rare and delicate plant . . . history confirms that the great threat to freedom is the concentration of power . . . by concentrating power in political hands, [government] is . . . a threat to freedom."

Second, one can be selective in the market system of the private sector, using one's income to buy precisely what one chooses and rejecting unwanted commodities. But, as noted earlier, in the public sector — even assuming a high level of political democracy — conformity and coercion are inherent. If the majority decides in favour of certain governmental actions — to build a reservoir, to establish dental insurance, to provide a guaranteed annual income — the minority must conform. Hence, the "use of political channels, while inevitable, tends to strain the social cohesion essential for a stable society."[3] To the extent that decisions can be rendered selectively by individuals through markets, the need for conformity

and coercion is lessened and this "strain" reduced. The scope of government should be strictly limited. Finally, the power and activities of government should be dispersed and decentralized.

The Liberal Stance

But liberal economists are sceptical of the conservative position. They hold that the conservative view is based on the **fallacy of limited decisions**. Conservatives implicitly assume that during any particular period there is a limited, or fixed, number of decisions to be made in the operation of the economy. If government makes more of these decisions in performing its stated functions, the private sector of the economy will necessarily have fewer "free" decisions or choices to make. This is held to be fallacious reasoning. By sponsoring the production of public goods, government is, in fact, *extending* the range of free choice by permitting society to enjoy goods and services that would not be available in the absence of governmental provision.

One can cogently argue that it is largely through the economic functions of government that we have freed ourselves in some measure from ignorance, unemployment, poverty, disease, crime, discrimination, and other ills. Note, too, that in providing most public goods, government does not typically undertake production itself, but rather purchases these goods through private enterprise. When government decides to build a highway, private firms are given the responsibility of making many specific decisions and choices in connection with carrying out this decision.

A noted economist has summarized the liberal view in these pointed words:

> Traffic lights coerce me and limit my freedom. Yet in the midst of a traffic jam on the unopen road, was I really "free" before there were lights? And has the algebraic total of freedom, for me or the representative motorist or the group as a whole, been increased or decreased by the introduction of well-engineered stop lights? Stop lights, you know, are also go lights. . . . When we introduce the traffic light, we have, although the arch individualist may not like the new order, by cooperation and coercion created by ourselves greater freedom.[4]

---

[2] Milton Friedman, *Capitalism and Freedom* (Chicago: The University of Chicago Press, 1962), p. 2.

[3] Ibid., p. 23.

[4] Paul A. Samuelson, "Personal Freedoms and Economic Freedoms in the Mixed Economy," in Earl F. Cheit (ed.), *The Business Establishment* (New York: John Wiley & Sons, Inc., 1964), p. 219.

CHAPTER SUMMARY

1. Majority voting creates a possibility of *a.* an underallocation or overallocation of resources to a particular public good, and *b.* inconsistent voting outcomes. The median-voter model predicts that, under majority rule, the person holding the middle position on an issue will in a sense determine the election outcome.

2. Public choice theorists cite a number of reasons why government might be inefficient in providing public goods and services. *a.* There are strong reasons for politicians to support special-interest legislation. *b.* Public choice may be biased in favour of programs with immediate and clear-cut benefits and difficult-to-identify costs *and* against programs with immediate and easily identified costs and vague or deferred benefits. *c.* Citizens as voters have less choice as to public goods and services than they do as consumers in the private sector. *d.* Government bureaucracies have less incentive to operate efficiently than do private businesses.

3. The benefits-received principle of taxation is that those who receive the benefits of goods and services provided by government should pay the taxes required to finance them. The ability-to-pay principle is that those who have greater income should be taxed absolutely and relatively more than those who have less income.

4. The federal personal income tax can be said to be reasonably progressive. The flat-rate federal corporate income tax is regressive. General sales and property taxes tend to be regressive.

5. Excise taxes affect supply and therefore equilibrium price and quantity. The more inelastic the demand for a product, the greater the proportion of the tax shifted to consumers. The greater the inelasticity of supply, the larger the proportion of tax borne by the seller.

6. Taxation involves loss of some output whose marginal benefit exceeds its marginal cost. The more elastic the supply and demand curves, the greater is this efficiency loss of a particular tax.

7. Sales taxes are likely to be shifted; personal income taxes are not. Specific excise taxes may or may not be shifted to consumers, depending on the elasticities of demand and supply. There is disagreement as to whether corporate income taxes are shifted. The incidence of property taxes depends primarily on whether the property is owner- or tenant-occupied.

8. The 1987 federal tax reform simplified income taxes and lowered the marginal tax rate.

9. The GST is similar to a value-added tax. It is more favourable than the federal sales tax it replaced because it introduces less distortions, exports are exempt, and imports will compete on equal footing with domestic goods.

10. There is disagreement as to the relationship between the size of the public sector and individual freedom.

TERMS AND CONCEPTS

ability-to-pay principle (p. 369)
benefits-received principle (p. 368)

efficiency loss of a tax (p. 373)
fallacy of limited decisions (p. 376)

Goods and Services Tax (p. 374)
logrolling (p. 361)
median-voter model (p. 363)
paradox of voting (p. 362)
progressive tax (p. 369)
proportional tax (p. 369)
public choice theory (p. 360)

public finance (p. 360)
public sector failure (p. 364)
regressive tax (p. 369)
rent-seeking behaviour (p. 365)
special-interest effect (p. 364)
tax incidence (p. 370)
value-added tax (p. 374)

QUESTIONS AND STUDY SUGGESTIONS

1. Explain how affirmative and negative majority votes can sometimes lead to inefficient allocations of resources to public goods. Is this problem likely to be greater under a benefits-received or an ability-to-pay tax system? Use the information in Figures 21-1(a) and 21-1(b) to show how society might be better off if Adams were allowed to buy votes.

2. Explain the paradox of voting through reference to the accompanying table that shows the ranking of three public goods by voters Larry, Curley, and Moe.

Public good	Larry	Curley	Moe
Courthouse	2nd choice	1st choice	3rd choice
School	3rd choice	2nd choice	1st choice
Park	1st choice	3rd choice	2nd choice

3. Suppose that there are only five people in a society and that each favours one of the five flood-control options shown in Table 19-2 (include no protection as one of the options). Explain which of these flood-control options will be selected using a majority rule. Will this option be the optimal size of the project from an economic perspective?

4. Carefully evaluate this statement: "The public, as a general rule . . . gets less production in return for a dollar spent by government than from a dollar spent by private enterprise."

5. "To show that a perfectly functioning government can correct some problem in a free economy is not enough to justify governmental intervention, for government itself does not function perfectly." Discuss in detail.

6. How does the problem of nonselectivity in the public sector relate to economic efficiency? Why are public bureaucracies alleged to be less efficient than private enterprises?

7. Explain: "Politicians would make more rational economic decisions if they weren't running for reelection every few years." Do you think this statement has a bearing on the growth of our public debt?

8. Distinguish clearly between the benefits-received and the ability-to-pay principles of taxation. Which philosophy is more evident in our present tax structure? Justify your answer. To which principle of taxation do you subscribe? Why?

9. Precisely what is meant by a progressive tax? A regressive tax? A proportional tax? Comment on the progressivity or regressivity of each of the following taxes, indicating in each case your assumption concerning tax incidence:

a. The federal personal income tax

b. A 7% general sales tax

c. A federal excise tax on automobile tires

d. A municipal property tax on real estate

e. The federal corporate income tax

10. What is the incidence of an excise tax when demand is highly inelastic? Elastic? What effect does the elasticity of supply have on the incidence of an excise tax? What is the efficiency loss of a tax and how does it relate to elasticity of demand and supply?

11. Suppose you are heading a tax commission responsible for establishing a program to raise new revenue through excise taxes. Would elasticity of demand be important to you in determining those products on which excises should be levied? Explain.

12. Briefly explain the federal tax reforms of 1987 and the GST. What are the main advantages of the GST?

13. "The market economy is the only system compatible with political freedom. We therefore should greatly restrain the economic scope of government." Do you agree?

14. *Advanced analysis:* Suppose that the equation for the demand curve for some product X is $P = 8 - .6Q$ and the supply curve is $P = 2 + .4Q$. What is the equilibrium price and quantity? Now suppose that an excise tax is imposed on X such that the new supply equation is $P = 4 + .4Q$. How much tax revenue will this excise tax yield the government? Graph the curves and label the area of the graph that represents the tax collection TC and the area that represents the efficiency loss of the tax EL. Briefly explain why area EL is the efficiency loss of the tax.

22

Agriculture: Economics and Policy

An economic analysis of Canadian agriculture can be justified on a number of grounds. Including the processing, wholesale, and retail sectors, agriculture accounts for approximately 20% of Canada's GDP. Moreover, agriculture employs over 3% of the nation's labour force.

It is a sector that, in the absence of government farm programs, is a real-world example of Chapter 10's purely competitive model. The sector is composed of many firms selling virtually standardized products. Agriculture can be understood by applying the demand and supply tools of competitive markets. As such, agricultural markets can reveal the intended and unintended effects of government policies that interfere with the forces of supply and demand.

As will become evident, agriculture reflects the increasing globalization of markets. In recent decades the economic ups and downs of Canadian agriculture have been closely tied to its ability to gain access to world markets. Farm policies also provide us with excellent illustrations of Chapter 21's special-interest effect and rent-seeking behaviour.

THE ECONOMICS OF AGRICULTURE

Farmers in the past have frequently faced severe problems of fluctuating prices and declining incomes. We distinguish between (1) the **short-run farm problem** of year-to-year fluctuations in farm prices and incomes, and (2) the **long-run farm problem** that relates to those forces causing agriculture to be a declining industry.

Short-Run Problem: Price and Income Instability

The short-run farm problem is the result of (1) an inelastic demand for agriculture products; (2) fluctuations in farm output; and (3) shifts in the demand curve itself.

Inelastic Demand for Agricultural Products   In most developed societies, the price elasticity of demand for agricultural products is low. For farm products in the aggregate, the elasticity coefficient is estimated to be from .20 to .25. These figures suggest that the prices of agricultural products would have to fall by 40 to 50% for consumers to increase their purchases by a mere 10%. Consumers apparently put a low value on additional agricultural output compared with alternative goods.

Why is this so? You will recall that the basic determinant of elasticity of demand is substitutability. When the price of a product falls, the consumer will substitute *that* product for other products whose prices have not fallen. But in wealthy societies this "substitution effect" (Chapter 7) is very modest for food. People do not switch from three to five or six meals each day in response to declines in the relative prices of agricultural products. An individual's capacity to substitute food for other products is subject to very real biological constraints.

The inelastic demand for agricultural products can also be explained in terms of diminishing marginal utility. In a wealthy society, the population by and large is well fed and well clothed; it is relatively saturated with the food and fiber of agriculture. Therefore, additional agricultural output entails rapidly diminishing marginal utility. Thus it takes very large price cuts to induce small increases in consumption. Curve *D* in Figure 22-1 portrays the inelastic demand for agricultural products.

Fluctuations in Output   The inelastic demand for farm products causes small changes in agricultural production to be magnified into relatively larger changes in farm prices and incomes. Farmers possess

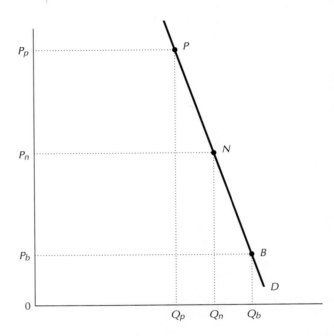

FIGURE 22-1   **The effect of output changes on farm prices and incomes**

Because of the inelasticity of demand for farm products, a relatively small change in output (Q_n to Q_p or Q_b) will cause relatively large changes in farm prices (P_n to P_p or P_b) and incomes $0P_nNQ_n$ to $0P_pPQ_p$ or $0P_bBQ_b$).

only limited control over their production. Floods, droughts, an unexpected frost, insect damage, rust and smut fungi, and similar disasters can mean poor crops. Conversely, an excellent growing season may mean bumper crops. Weather and related factors are beyond the control of farmers, yet they exert an important influence on production.

The highly competitive nature of agriculture makes it virtually impossible for farmers to control production — unless governments authorize and assist in the setting-up of marketing boards, as has happened in Canada. In the absence of such boards, if the hundreds of thousands of widely scattered and independent producers should by chance plant an unusually large or abnormally small portion of their land, very large or small outputs would result, even if the growing season were normal.

Putting the instability of farm production together with the inelastic demand for farm products in Figure 22-1, we can see why farm prices and incomes are highly unstable. Even if we assume that the market demand for agriculture products is stable at *D*, the inelastic nature of demand will magnify small changes in output into relatively large changes in farm prices and income. For example, assume that a "normal" crop of Q_n results in a "normal" price of P_n and a "normal" farm income represented by $0P_nNQ_n$. But a bumper crop or a poor crop will cause large deviations from these normal prices and incomes.

If an unusually good growing season occurs, the resulting bumper crop of Q_b will reduce farm incomes from $0P_nNQ_n$ to $0P_bBQ_b$. When demand is inelastic, an increase in the quantity sold will be accompanied by a *more than* proportionate decline in price. The net result is that total revenue (total farm income) will decline.

Similarly, for farmers as a group, a poor crop caused by drought may boost farm incomes. A poor crop of Q_p will raise total farm income from $0P_nNQ_n$ to $0P_pPQ_p$ because a decline in output will cause a *more than* proportionate increase in price when demand is inelastic. Ironically, for farmers as a group, a poor crop may be a blessing and a bumper crop a hardship. Conclusion: *Given a stable market demand for farm products, inelastic demand will turn relatively small changes in output into relatively larger changes in farm prices and incomes.*

Fluctuations in Domestic Demand   The other aspect of the short-run instability of farm incomes has to do with shifts in the demand curve for agricultural products. Suppose that somehow agricultural output is stabilized at the "normal" level of Q_n in Figure 22-2. Now, because of the inelastic demand for farm products, short-run fluctuations in the demand for these products will cause markedly different prices and incomes to be associated with this level of production that we assume to be constant. A slight drop in demand from D_0 to D_1 will reduce farm incomes from $0P_0aQ_n$ to $0P_1bQ_n$. A relatively small decline in demand gives farmers a drastically reduced money reward for the same amount of production. Conversely, a slight increase in demand — as from D_1 to D_0 — will bring an equally sharp increase in farm incomes for the same volume of output. These large price–income changes are linked to the fact that demand is inelastic.

Unstable Foreign Demand   The essential cause of farm prosperity in the 1970s was booming agricultural exports, while the collapse of export markets was a major cause of the farm crisis of the early 1980s. This dramatic turnabout suggests that Canadian agriculture is heavily dependent on world mar-

FIGURE 22-2   The effect of demand changes on farm prices and incomes

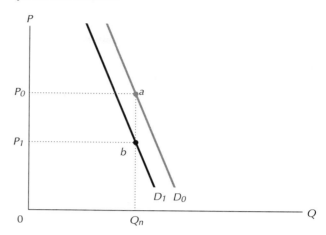

Because of the highly inelastic demand for agricultural products, a small shift in demand (D_0 to D_1) will cause drastically different levels of farm prices (P_0 to P_1) and farm incomes (OP_0aQ_n to OP_1bQ_n) to be associated with a given level of production Q_n.

kets. Such dependency can be a source of demand volatility.

Changes in weather and crop production *in other countries* can affect the demand and, thus, the income of Canadian farmers. Similarly, cyclical fluctuations in incomes in Europe or Japan, for example, can shift the demand for Canadian farm products. So can changes in foreign economic policies. If the nations of Western Europe decide to provide their farmers with greater protection from foreign (Canadian) competition, Canadian farmers will have less access to those markets and export demand will fall. International politics can also add to demand instability. Changes in the international value of the dollar can be critical. The depreciation of the dollar in the 1970s increased the demand for Canadian farm products, while appreciation of the dollar against overseas currencies decreased foreign demand in the early 1980s.

To summarize: The great importance of exports has contributed to the instability of the demand for Canadian farm products. Farm exports are affected, not only by weather, income fluctuations, and economic policies abroad, but also by international politics and fluctuations in the international value of the dollar.

Long-Run Problem: A Declining Industry

Two more characteristics of agricultural markets must be added to price inelastic demand to explain why agriculture has been a declining industry:

1. Over time the supply of agricultural products has increased markedly because of technological progress.

2. Demand for agricultural products has increased slowly over time because demand for them is inelasic with respect to income.

Technology and Supply Increases   When a price inelastic and slowly increasing demand for farm products is accompanied by a rapidly increasing supply, there is inexorable pressure for farm prices and incomes to fall.

A rapid rate of technological advance, particularly since World War I, has caused significant increases in the supply of agricultural products. This technological progress has many roots: the virtually complete electrification and mechanization of farms; improved techniques of land management and soil conservation; irrigation; development of hybrid crops; availability of improved fertilizers and insecticides; and improvements in breeding and care of livestock.

These technological advances have been very significant. The amount of capital used per worker increased tremendously over the 1930–1990 period, permitting approximately a five-fold increase in the amount of land cultivated per farmer. The simplest general index is the increasing number of people a single farmer's output will support. Ninety years ago many Canadian farms were of the subsistence type: the farm kept the family alive and that was about all. By 1946, one farm worker produced enough food and fibre to support fifteen people. By 1991 the number had risen to over eighty! This gives some indication of the extent to which productivity in agriculture has risen. Since World War II productivity in agriculture has increased almost twice as fast as in the non-farm economy.

It is worth noting that most technological advances have *not* been initiated by farmers but are rather the result of government-sponsored programs of research and education and the work of farm machinery producers. Experimental farms, provincial agricultural representatives, educational pamphlets issued by the federal and provincial departments of agriculture, and the research departments of farm machinery, pesticide, and fertilizer producers are the sources of technological advance in Canadian agriculture.

Lagging Demand   Increases in demand for agricultural commodities have failed to keep pace with technologically inspired increases in their supply. The reason lies in the two major determinants of agricultural demand — incomes and population.

Income Inelastic Demand   In less-developed countries, consumers must devote the bulk of their meagre incomes to sustain themselves. But as income expands beyond the subsistence level, consumers will increase their outlays on food at ever-declining rates. Once the stomach is filled, the consumer's thoughts turn to the amenities of life that industry — not agriculture — provides. Economic growth in Canada has boosted average per capita income far beyond the level of bare subsistence. As a result, *increases in the incomes of Canadian consumers lead to less-than-proportionate increases in expenditures on farm products.*

In technical terms, the demand for farm products is *income-inelastic*; it is quite insensitive to increases in income. Estimates indicate that a 10% increase in real per capita disposable income entails at most an increase in the consumption of farm products of only 2%. Certain specific farm products — for example, potatoes and lard — may be inferior goods; that is, as incomes increase, purchases of these products may actually *decrease* (Chapter 4).

Population Growth   Despite the fact that after a minimum income level is reached, each individual consumer's intake of food and fibre will become relatively fixed, more consumers will mean an increase in demand for farm products. In most advanced nations, the demand for farm products increases at a rate roughly corresponding to the rate of population growth. But population increases, added to the relatively small increase in the purchase of farm products that occurs as incomes rise, have not been great enough to match concomitant increases in farm output. Indeed, it is pertinent to note that population growth in Canada has slowed in recent decades.

Graphic Portrayal   When coupled with the inelastic demand for agricultural products, these shifts in supply and demand have tended to reduce farm incomes. This is illustrated in Figure 22-3, where a large increase in supply is shown against a modest increase in demand. Because of the inelastic demand for farm products, these shifts have resulted in a

FIGURE 22-3   A graphic summary of the long-run farm problem

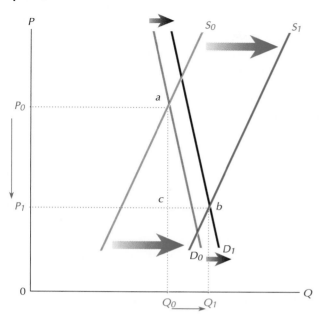

In the long run, increases in the demand for agricultural products (D_0 to D_1) have not kept pace with the increases in supply (S_0 to S_1) that technological advances have permitted. Coupled with the fact that agricultural demand is inelastic, these shifts have tended to depress farm prices (as from P_0 to P_1) and incomes (as from $0P_0aQ_0$ to $0P_1bQ_1$).

process is complicated by the fact that most land remains in agricultural production. Except for the minute portion of total farmland that borders on metropolitan areas, most farmland has no real alternative uses. Farmers leave, but the land they leave is acquired by other farmers and remains in production. Nevertheless, farm and nonfarm incomes have slowly been converging.

TABLE 22-1   The declining farm population, selected years, 1920–1991

Year	Farm population, millions	Percentage of the total population
1920	3.18	36.6
1929	3.26	32.2
1933	3.24	30.3
1941	3.15	27.4
1951	2.91	20.8
1961	2.13	11.7
1971	1.49	6.9
1976	1.26	5.5
1981	1.08	4.4
1991	0.88*	3.3

*Estimate based on size of agricultural labour force.

Source: O.J. Firestone, *Canada's Economic Development 1867–1953* (London: Bowes & Bowes, 1958), p. 60, and Statistics Canada, *Census of Canada, 1931–1991*.

sharp decline in farm prices accompanied by relatively small increases in sales. Farm incomes therefore tend to decline. Diagrammatically, income before the increase in supply occurs (measured by rectangle $0P_0aQ_0$) will exceed farm income after supply increases ($0P_1bQ_1$). The income "loss" of P_1P_0ac is not fully offset by the income "gain" of Q_0cbQ_1. In summary, *given an inelastic demand for farm products, an increase in the supply of farm products relative to the demand for them has created persistent tendencies for farm incomes to fall relative to nonfarm incomes.*

The consequences have been essentially those predicted by the purely competitive model. As farm incomes have historically fallen in comparison to nonfarm incomes, large numbers of farmers have left the industry, as shown in Table 22-1. We would further predict that this exodus would reduce supply relative to demand until farm incomes were roughly equal to nonfarm incomes. However, this adjustment

QUICK REVIEW (22-1)

1. Agricultural prices and incomes are volatile in the short run because an inelastic demand translates small changes in farm output and demand into larger price and income changes.

2. Technological progress has generated large increases in supplies of farm products over time.

3. Increases in demand for farm products have been modest because demand is inelastic with respect to income.

4. The combination of large supply increases and small demand increases has made agriculture a declining industry.

THE ECONOMICS OF FARM POLICY

There is nothing new in governments, both federal and provincial, being involved in farm policy. Land clearing, drainage, production extension, farm management, pest and weed control, research, grading, and inspection services have long been considered proper fields for government involvement. But since the 1930s, detailed "farm programs" to do with (1) farm prices, incomes, and output, (2) farm credit, and (3) crop insurance have come into being and are thriving at both levels of government. There is now more government involvement in agriculture than in any other goods-producing sector. The professed aim of farm policy is to enhance and stabilize farm prices and incomes. Those goals have been achieved through a combination of subsidies, price floors, and marketing boards.

A variety of arguments have been made to justify government involvement in the agricultural sector.

1. Farmers are comparatively poor and should therefore receive higher prices and incomes through public help.

2. Farmers are subject to certain extraordinary hazards — floods, droughts, and invasion by hordes of insects — to which other industries are not exposed and which cannot be fully insured.

3. While farmers are faced with highly competitive markets for their outputs, they typically buy inputs from industries that have considerable market power. In particular, most firms from which farmers buy fertilizer, farm machinery, and gasoline have some capacity to control their prices.

Farmers, in contrast, are at the "mercy of the market" in selling their outputs. Agriculture is the last stronghold of pure competition in an otherwise imperfectly competitive economy; it warrants public aid to offset the disadvantageous terms of trade that result.

Farm Products Marketing Boards

Government involvement in the farm produce marketplace began before the 1930s. With the Great Depression and with farm produce prices and incomes especially depressed, the federal government appointed a Royal Commission on Price Spreads. The commission reported that the hundreds of thousands of primary producers were individually no match for the concentrated agribusiness with which they dealt. With competitive farmers producing and selling and oligopolies buying and processing, market power was one-sided. Faced with a low

offer-to-buy price, one or two farmers, or even a thousand, could not successfully withhold their produce to force up the price, for the oligopolists knew where there were a hundred thousand other farmers who believed they had no option but to sell.

Such considerations and the political pressure of farmers led to the federally enacted Natural Products Marketing Act in 1934, which set up a Federal Marketing Board. This board could delegate its power to local producers' boards, its most important power being to control the sales of a product.

By the end of 1935, about twenty marketing boards were functioning across Canada, but the federal law was declared *ultra vires* by the courts on the grounds that under the BNA Act, regulation of trade *within* a province was reserved exclusively to the provinces.

Several provinces, starting with British Columbia in 1936 and Ontario in 1937, passed laws to allow the already functioning marketing boards to continue under provincial authority. By 1940, all the provinces had farm marketing legislation in force except for Quebec, which brought in such legislation in 1956.

The following is an overview of the major legislation passed with regards to marketing boards and some of the boards and commissions created.

The Canadian Wheat Board   Before this happened, the federal government had more luck with its legislation, notably the Canadian Wheat Board Act of 1935. The Wheat Board is still with us, though under revised legislation. This Crown corporation has complete control over the way western wheat is marketed and the price at which it is sold.

When farmers deliver their wheat to the elevators, they get an initial payment per bushel. This is in effect a floor price and is set low enough that the Wheat Board is confident of being able to meet it out of sales. Later, there may be an interim payment. Almost always there will be a final payment when the wheat is sold, the producers getting the full selling price, less transportation and storage costs, and Wheat Board expenses.

Agricultural Products Marketing Act   This Act was passed by Parliament in 1949. It is the counterpart of the provincial enabling legislation, for this federal law "permits extension of the powers of provincial marketing boards into interprovincial and export trade."

Provincial Farm Products Marketing Acts
Under these provincial umbrella Acts there now exist in Canada about 150 provincial marketing boards for

farm commodities ranging from asparagus to wool. Under these provincial Acts, once a marketing board has been authorized to act at the request of the majority of producers of a specified primary or processed agricultural commodity, then all producers of that commodity are required by law to comply with the marketing board's regulations. The boards go beyond merely negotiating with agribusiness on behalf of the producers. The boards also have the power to allocate quotas, set prices, issue licences, collect fees, and require that the commodity be marketed through them. In a word, the boards create a monopoly. Since the federal government usually prevents the import of food in such quantities as would depress domestic farm prices, the agribusiness pays a marketing board's price or does not buy at all. More than half of the total cash receipts of our farmers are received through marketing boards.

But this does not mean that all farmers make a good living. There are still too many producers of any given commodity, and for many commodities — such as beef, pork, cereals and much of horticulture — no marketing boards exist.

Agricultural Stabilization Board   This is a federal agency established under the Agricultural Stabilization Act in 1958. By law it must support the following commodities at not less than 90% of their average price over the previous five years, with adjustments according to production costs: cattle, hogs, and sheep; industrial milk and cream; and oats and barley not produced on the Prairies (where the Canadian Wheat Board has jurisdiction). The Agricultural Stabilization Board supports prices by buying products outright at the minimum prices set by the law, by granting deficiency payments (see below), or by making direct payments to producers at a fixed rate.

Agricultural Products Board   This federal board — which has the same staff as the Agricultural Stabilization Board — buys, sells, or imports agricultural products and administers food contracts and other commodity operations. It may purchase and hold stocks of agricultural products for later sale, emergency relief in Canada, or assistance programs abroad.

Canadian Dairy Commission   This important federal commission, established in 1966, works with the provincial milk marketing boards to ensure (1) a "fair" return to producers of cream and industrial milk — used in the manufacture of cheese, butter, and powdered milk — and (2) an adequate supply to consumers. The commission supports the market price of major processed products by buying and selling dairy products. In addition, the commission supplements returns from the market by making direct payments of government funds to individual producers under a quota system.

Canadian Livestock Feed Board   Established as a Crown corporation in 1966, this board subsidizes part of the cost of moving feed grains to Eastern Canada and British Columbia to attain, generally, a "fair" equalization of feed grain prices in those parts of Canada. The board may buy, ship, store, handle, and sell feed grains.

National Farm Products Marketing Council   The Act setting up this council in 1972 provided for federal marketing agencies to regulate in interprovincial and export trade any farm product with the exception of those regulated by the Canadian Wheat Board and the Canadian Dairy Commission. Thus, the Canadian Egg Marketing Agency was set up in December 1972, the Canadian Turkey Marketing Agency in 1973, and the Canadian Chicken Marketing Agency in 1978. The Canadian Broiler Hatching Egg Agency completes the list of federal marketing agencies.

How Marketing Boards Work

The aim of marketing boards is to stabilize agricultural prices at a level that insures higher incomes to farmers.

Price Supports

There are two basic methods of supporting prices above their free market equilibrium values: (1) offers to purchase and (2) deficiency payments.

Offers to Purchase   Suppose, in Figure 22-4(a) that the *floor price* — or, as it is commonly called, the **support price** — is P_s as compared with the equilibrium price, P_e. What will be the effect of government making offers to purchase at P_s?

Surplus Output   The most obvious effect is that product surpluses will result. Private consumers will be willing to purchase only $0Q_o$ units at the supported price, while farmers will supply $0Q_s$ units. What happens to the Q_oQ_s surplus that results? The government must buy it to make the above-equilibrium support price effective. Because of such purchases, for example, huge surpluses of butter, skim milk powder, eggs, and pork accumulated in the late

FIGURE 22-4   Price supports and crop restriction

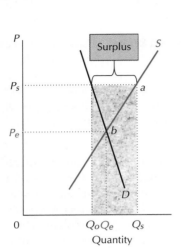

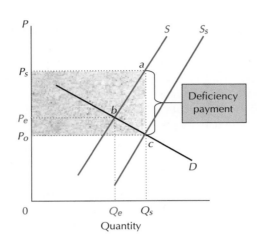

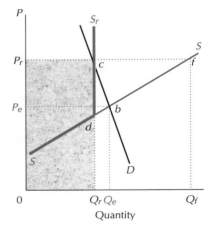

(a) Offers to purchase
Offers to purchase result in surpluses. This method should not be used if demand is elastic.

(b) Deficiency payments
Deficiency payments or subsidies do not result in surpluses. This method should not be used if demand is elastic.

(c) Crop restriction
Crop restriction is the only method with an elastic supply. This method should not be used if demand is elastic. Crop restriction results in neither surpluses nor government payments. All costs (the higher price) are borne by consumers.

1950s. These large accumulated surpluses were economically undesirable on two counts. First, their very existence indicated a misallocation of the economy's resources. Government-held surpluses reflected the fact that the economy was devoting large amounts of resources to the production of commodities that, *at existing supported prices*, were simply not wanted by consumers. Second, the storing of surplus products was expensive, adding to the cost of the farm program and, ultimately, to the consumer's tax bill. By the time the government acted to dispose of its excess butter, it had over one hundred million pounds (forty-five million kilograms) in storage — much of it becoming rancid. The solution was to convert the butter into butter oil, which was then sold abroad at half the butter price.

Consumers Lose   Consumers "lose" in two ways. First, they will pay a higher price (P_s rather than P_e)

and consume less (Q_o rather than Q_e) of the product. Second, they will be paying higher taxes to finance the government's purchase of the surplus. In Figure 22-4(a), this added tax burden will amount to the surplus output Q_oQ_s, multiplied by its price, P_s. Storage costs, of course, add to this tax burden. It is worth noting that the burden of higher food prices falls disproportionately on the poor because they spend a larger proportion of their incomes on food.

Farmers Gain   Farmers gain from price supports. In Figure 22-4(a), gross receipts rise from the free market level of $0P_ebQ_e$ to the supported level of $0P_saQ_s$.

Deficiency Payments   Deficiency payments work as follows: Suppose, in Figure 22-4(b), just as in Figure 22-4(a), that the support price is P_s as compared with the equilibrium price P_e. Also, as before, at price

P_s farmers expand production from Q_e to Q_s. However, with demand as shown by D, consumers will only buy Q_s if the price is P_o. The government arranges for this to be the market price by simply subsidizing production by the amount P_oP_s — the government makes a deficiency payment to each producer equal to P_oP_s times the quantity sold.

The total consumer expenditure is $0P_ocQ_s$, total government expenditure is P_oP_sac = deficiency payment times Q_s. Note that the producers are still on the original supply curve S; that is why they produce Q_s when market demand and deficiency payments combine to present them with a price of P_s. However, S_s is the supply curve as seen by the consumer and is created by the government subsidy or deficiency payment. When we analyse the economic effect of these payments, two considerations arise.

Elasticity of Supply and Demand   Note that the incidence of the subsidy, like the sales tax, is related to the elasticity of the supply and demand curves. In Figure 22-4(b), the combined effects of the elastic demand curve in the price range P_oP_s and the inelastic supply curve result in the incidence of the subsidy being heavily in favour of the producer: the producer gets P_eS_s of the deficiency payment, the consumer only P_eP_o. The effect of elasticity on the incidence of a subsidy is precisely the same as that of a sales tax.

The question of price elasticity of demand does have relevance to Canada's programs. Among agricultural commodities, the demand for butter is relatively elastic — which is why the offer to purchase program of 1958–59 led to such a mountain of it spoiling in storage. Under the subsidies program that replaced it, Canada no longer has butter in storage. This is not to say that the farm-subsidy program works perfectly. After all, the Agricultural Commodity Price Stabilization program cost the taxpayer $90 million in 1989–90, with another $275 million under the Crop Insurance Act. In addition, in 1989–90 the Canadian Dairy Commission (CDC) budgeted for direct subsidy payments to producers of $277 million. In all, the federal government's estimate of transfer payments to farmers in 1989–90 came to $873 million.

Misallocated Resources   It is important to note that there is a more subtle cost embodied in *both* offers to purchase and deficiency payments. Society loses because price supports contribute to economic inefficiency by encouraging an overallocation of resources to agriculture. A price floor or support (P_s)

gives rise to a greater commitment of resources to the agricultural sector than would be generated by the free market (P_e). In terms of Chapter 10's purely competitive model, the market supply curve in Figure 22-4 represents the aggregated marginal costs of all farmers producing this product. An efficient allocation of resources occurs where market price (P_e) is equal to marginal cost at point b. The resulting output of Q_e reflects an efficient allocation of resources. In contrast, the Q_s output associated with the P_s price support clearly represents an overallocation of resources. A misallocation of resources between agriculture and the rest of the economy imposes a cost on society.

Societal Loss   Society at large loses in two important ways. First, taxpayers will pay higher taxes to finance the government's purchase of surplus. In Figure 22-4(a), this added tax burden will amount to the surplus output Q_oQ_s, multiplied by its price P_s — as shown by the shaded area. Storage costs add to this tax burden as do costs of maintaining the elaborate bureaucracy that administers the various farm programs.

International Costs   The costs of farm price supports go beyond those implicit in Figure 22-4. In general, price supports generate economic distortions that transcend national boundaries. For example, above-equilibrium price supports make the Canadian market attractive to foreign producers. But inflows of foreign agricultural products would increase supplies in Canada, aggravating our problem of agricultural surpluses. To prevent this from happening, Canada is likely to impose import barriers in the form of tariffs or quotas. These barriers often restrict the production of more efficient foreign producers, while simultaneously encouraging more production from less efficient Canadian producers. The result is a less efficient use of world agricultural resources.

Similarly, as Canada and other industrially advanced countries with similar agricultural programs dump surplus farm products on world markets, the prices of such products are depressed. Less-developed countries — most of which are heavily dependent on world commodity markets — are hurt because their export earnings are reduced. Thus, Canadian price supports for wheat production have imposed significant costs on Argentina, a major wheat exporter.

Crop Restriction

Another method for increasing prices to farmers is to manage the amount of land devoted to a given crop.

Suppose in Figure 22-4(c), that the government wishes to assure the producers price P_r. Neither offers to purchase nor deficiency payments would be appropriate because of the *elastic supply* with which we are now faced. An offer to purchase at price P_r would result in a surplus of Q_rQ_f, a greater amount than is bought for domestic consumption. A deficiency payment program makes even less sense, for there is simply no demand for quantity $0Q_f$ at any price.

The only sensible way for the government to ensure price P_r in these circumstances is to impose crop restriction. With production restricted to Q_r and with the inelastic demand as shown, price will rise to P_r. The supply curve, in effect, is no longer S, but SdS_r.

Crop or supply restriction is always in effect when marketing boards have the power to allot quotas. Quotas are imposed by the provincial milk marketing boards and the Ontario Flue-Cured Tobacco Growers' Marketing Plan — tobacco being an excellent product both for taxes and crop restriction because of the inelastic demand for it in its present price range.

Operation LIFT (Lower Inventory for Tomorrow) is an example of federal effort at crop restriction. Canada started the 1970–71 crop year with a billion bushels of wheat in storage — some of it still on the farms because of a lack of elevator space — and little prospect of selling it at $1.75 a bushel, let alone the $2.00 figure promised by the federal government in its 1968 election campaign. Under Operation LIFT, a Prairie wheat farmer got $10 for every acre (0.4 hectare) taken out of grain production and put into perennial forage such as hay, or $6 an acre for switching to summer fallow. With up to 1,000 acres (400 hectares) eligible, the maximum a farmer could receive was $10,000. The program cost some $140 million and reduced both the wheat acreage and the crop in the 1970–71 crop year by half. The program was successful though, ironically, crop failures elsewhere — especially in what used to be the USSR — were to give farmers within three years not the long-promised $2 wheat but $5 wheat.

CRITICISM OF FARM POLICY

After more than a half century of experience with government policies designed to stabilize and enhance farm incomes, there is considerable evidence to suggest that these programs are not working well. There is growing belief among economists and political leaders that the traditional goals and techniques of farm policy must be re-examined and revised. Some of the more important criticisms of agricultural policy follow.

Symptoms and Causes   The farm programs have failed to get at the causes of the farm problem. Public policy toward agriculture is designed to treat symptoms and not causes. The root *cause* of the farm problem has been a misallocation of resources between agriculture and the rest of the economy. Historically, the problem has been one of too many farmers. The effect or symptom of this misallocation of resources is relatively low farm incomes. *For the most part, public policy in agriculture has been oriented toward supporting farm prices and incomes rather than toward alleviating the resource allocation problem that is the fundamental cause of these relatively low farm incomes.*

Some critics go further and argue that price–income supports have encouraged people to stay in agriculture when they otherwise would have migrated to some nonfarm occupation. Thus, the price–income orientation of the farm programs have deterred the very reallocation of resources that is necessary to resolve the long-run farm problem.

Misguided Subsidies   Price–income support programs have most benefited those farmers who least need government assistance. Assuming the goal of our farm program is bolstering low farm incomes, it follows that any program of government aid should be aimed at farmers at the bottom of the farm income distribution scale. But the poor, small-output farmer does not produce and sell enough in the market to get much aid from price supports. It is the large farm that reaps the benefits by virtue of its large output. If public policy must be designed to supplement farm incomes, a strong case can be made for targeting those benefits to those farmers in most need.

An income-support program should be geared to *people*, not *commodities*. Many economists contend that, on equity grounds, direct income subsidies to poor farmers are highly preferable to indirect price support subsidies, which go mainly to large and prosperous farmers.

A related point concerns land values. The price and income benefits that various farm programs provide are eventually capitalized into higher farmland values. By making crops more valuable, price supports have made the land itself more valuable. Sometimes this is helpful to farmers, but often it is not. To the extent that farmers rent their farmland, price supports become a subsidy to people who are *not* actively engaged in farming.

The quota system has a similar effect with regard to young would-be farmers. Before they may become dairy farmers, for example, they must buy milk quotas from retiring farmers. An adequate quota can easily cost $100,000. The interest payments on this become a permanent fixed cost that for the young farmer may very well eliminate the benefit of the higher price for milk brought about by the quota system. This applies with even greater force in the poultry business: the average value of an egg quota in Ontario is about $250,000.

Policy Contradictions   The complexity and multiple objectives of farm policy yield a number of conflicts and contradictions. Subsidized research is aimed at increasing farm productivity and increasing the supply of farm products, while quotas reduce supply. Price supports for crops mean increased feed costs for ranchers and high prices for animal products to consumers. Tobacco farmers have been subsidized in the past even though serious health problems are associated with tobacco consumption.

Declining Effectiveness   There is also reason to believe that farm policy has become less effective in accomplishing its goals. In the 1930s many farms were relatively small, semi-isolated units that employed relatively modest amounts of machinery and equipment and provided most of their own inputs. Now, however, farms are large, highly capital-intensive, and closely integrated with both the domestic and international economies.

Farmers now depend on others for such inputs as seed, fertilizers, and insecticides. Agriculture uses more than twice as much physical capital (machinery and buildings) per worker than does the economy as a whole. Farmers now need to borrow large amounts of money to finance the purchases of capital equipment and land *and* for operating capital. Despite an elaborate farm policy designed to enhance farm incomes, high interest rates can easily precipitate losses or bankruptcy for many farmers. Dependence on export markets can also undermine farm policy. A fall in foreign incomes or an increase in the international value of the dollar (which makes Canadian farm products more expensive to foreigners) can unexpectedly reduce Canadian farm exports and wipe out any positive effects of agricultural programs on farm incomes. In short, a much wider range of variables may now alter farm incomes and thereby diminish the effectiveness of farm programs.

The difficult issue being brought into focus by these and similar criticisms is whether an increasingly expensive farm program is economically justifiable. Farm programs entail huge and increasing budgetary costs. The subsidies involved do not benefit the most needy farmers. Farm price supports distort economic incentives, which cause overproduction to persist. Farm programs impose substantial costs on consumers and complicate our international economic policies. Against this web of criticism, a number of economists believe that our farm policy is an example of public sector failure (Chapter 21). They suggest that public policy has not resolved the problems of Canadian agriculture, but rather has become a part of those problems.

THE POLITICS OF FARM POLICY

In view of these criticisms, we may well ask why we have an extensive and costly farm program. Why not abandon price supports and return to free markets? Why do farm programs persist although the farm population — and the farm vote — has declined historically?

Public Choice Theory Revisited

We can respond to these questions in terms of Chapter 21's public choice theory concepts. Recall that *rent-seeking behaviour* involves a group — a labour union, firms in a particular industry, or farmers producing a particular product — pursuing political means to transfer income or wealth to themselves at the expense of another group or society as a whole. The *special-interest effect* refers to a program or policy from which a small group receives *large* benefits at the expense of a much larger group who *individually* suffer *small* losses.

Suppose a specific group of farmers — egg producers or dairy farmers — organize themselves and establish a well-financed political action committee (PAC). The PAC's job is to promote the establishment and perpetuation of government programs that will transfer income to the group (rent-seeking behaviour). Thus the PAC vigorously lobbies Members of Parliament to enact or perpetuate price supports and establish import quotas for eggs or milk. They do this by making political contributions to potentially sympathetic Members of Parliament or political parties. Thus, although egg production is heavily concentrated in a few provinces, the PAC will make contributions to Members of Parliament from other provinces through the political parties to gain support.

But if an interest group is small in number, how can they successfully line their own pockets at the expense of society as a whole? The answer is that, although the aggregate costs of their program might be considerable, the cost imposed on *each individual* taxpayer is small (the special-interest effect). Indeed, citizen-taxpayers at large are likely uninformed about, and indifferent to, the issue at hand because they have little at stake. Civil rights, educational reform, and peace in the Middle East may seem to be much more urgent political issues than a program for a handful of egg producers.

Public choice theory also tells us that politicians are more likely to favour programs having hidden costs. As we have seen, this is often true of farm programs. In discussing Figure 22-4 we found that price supports involve, not simply an explicit transfer from taxpayer to farmer, but also the costs hidden in higher food prices, storage costs for surplus output, bureaucratic costs of administering farm programs, and costs associated with both domestic and international misallocations of resources. While the explicit or direct cost of an egg subsidy program to taxpayers may be small, the price increase provided by such a program carries a hidden subsidy (cost) that is much larger. Because the cost of the subsidy program is largely indirect and hidden, the program is much more acceptable to politicians and the public than if all costs were explicit.

New Directions?

There is reason to predict that farm subsidies may decline in the future.

1 Declining Farm Population   As farm population has declined, its political clout has also diminished. The farm population was about 30% of the total in the 1930s when many of our farm programs were established. That population now is only about 3% of the total. Legislators are critically examining farm programs from the vantage point of their effect on consumers' grocery bills rather than farm incomes.

2 Budget Deficits   Continued pressures to bring under control the federal budget deficit have brought farm subsidies under increased political scrutiny.

3 Policy Conflicts   It is increasingly apparent that domestic farm programs are seriously at odds with

the objective of free world trade. This conflict merits more detailed consideration.

WORLD TRADE AND FARM POLICY

A more critical attitude toward farm subsidies is reflected in the Canadian government's desire to reduce world trade barriers to agricultural products.

Policy Impacts

Consider the impacts of current farm programs on world trade. Virtually every industrialized country — Canada, the United States, Japan, and so forth — intervenes in agriculture by subsidizing and providing protective trade barriers. For example, the European Community (EC) — made up of twelve Western European nations — has established high prices for its domestic agricultural products. These price supports have a number of consequences.

1. To maintain high domestic prices the EC must restrict imports (supplies) of foreign farm products. It does this by imposing import tariffs and quotas, the former being excise taxes and the latter specific quantitative limits on foreign goods.

2. Although the EC was once an importer of food, high price supports have induced European farmers to produce much more output than European consumers want to purchase.

3. To rid itself of these agricultural surpluses the EC has heavily subsidized their export into world markets.

The effects on Canada are that (1) our farmers have great difficulty in selling to EC nations because of their trade barriers; and (2) subsidized exports from the EC depress world prices for agricultural products, making these markets less attractive to our farmers.

Perhaps most important, from an international perspective farm programs such as those of the EC, Canada, and the United States distort world agricultural trade and thereby the international allocation of agricultural resources. Encouraged by artificially high prices, farmers in industrially advanced nations produce more agricultural output than they would otherwise. The resulting surpluses flow into world markets where they depress prices. This means that farmers in countries with no farm programs — often developing countries — face artificially low prices for their exports, which signals them to produce less. In this way farm price distortions alter production away from that based on productive efficiency. For example, price supports cause agricultural resources to be allocated to wheat production, although wheat can perhaps be produced at a lower cost in a developing country.

One estimate suggests that the benefits of free, undistorted agricultural trade to the industrially advanced economies alone would be about $42 billion per year, with Canada, the United States, the EC, and Japan as the major beneficiaries.

Corollary benefits are (1) increased Canadian farm exports; and (2) reduced expenditures on our domestic farm programs, which would help reduce the federal budget deficit. Thus, Canada has compelling economic reasons to favour the liberalization of international agricultural trade.

QUICK REVIEW (22-2)

1. **The main impacts of price supports are to cause surplus production that government must buy and store; raise both farmer incomes and food prices to consumers; and generate an overallocation of resources to agriculture.**

2. **Farm policy has been criticized for delaying the exodus of resources from farming; allocating most subsidies to wealthier farmers; conflicting with other policies such as freer world trade; and being very costly.**

3. **The persistence of farm programs is explainable in terms of rent-seeking behaviour, the special-interest effect, and other aspects of public choice theory.**

4. **The farm programs of Canada, the United States, the European Community, and other industrialized nations have contributed to a misallocation of the world's agricultural resources.**

GATT Negotiations

In fact, Canada — along with a number of food exporting nations known as the Cairns Group (including the U.S., Australia, New Zealand, and Argentina) — has been a leading advocate for elimination of trade barriers on agricultural products and, by implication, the dismantling of price-support programs. Under the aegis of the General Agreement on Tariffs and Trade (GATT) — an international association of over 100 nations dedicated to the promotion of free world trade — Canada, along with the United States, has proposed (1) a ten-year phase out of all agricultural tariffs, (2) elimination of agricultural export subsidies over a five-year period, and (3) a phase out of all domestic farm supports that distort world agricultural trade. Unfortunately, under pressure from their politically powerful farm groups, the EC and Japan have rejected these proposals and negotiations have stalled.

Market-Oriented Income Stabilization

From a long-term perspective, it seems increasingly likely that farm policy will shift from the goal of enhancing to that of stabilizing farm incomes. The goal of *stabilization* is to reduce the sharp year-to-year fluctuations in farm incomes and prices, but to accept the long-run average of farm prices and incomes that free markets would provide. This contrasts with income *enhancement*, which seeks to provide farmers with commodity prices and incomes above those that free markets would yield. Government might moderate the boom and bust character of agricultural markets by supporting prices and accumulating surplus stocks when prices fell significantly below the long-run trend of prices. Conversely, government would augment supply by selling from these stocks when prices rose significantly above the long-run trend.

Proponents believe that **the market-oriented income stabilization policy** has a number of advantages. First, government involvement in agriculture would diminish in that programs of supply management through quotas would be abandoned. Second, prices would reflect long-run equilibrium levels and therefore be conducive to an efficient allocation of resources between agriculture and the rest of the economy. Third, taxpayer costs would be significantly reduced. And, finally, the lower average level of farm prices would stimulate agricultural exports.

GLOBAL VIEW: FEAST OR FAMINE?

The Canadian (and American) farm problem — supply outrunning demand and farm policies that foster surplus production — is not common to most other countries. Many less-developed nations must persistently import foodstuffs. We frequently read of malnutrition, chronic food shortages, and occasionally famine in the nations of Africa and elsewhere. In the future — say, four or five decades from now — will the world be able to feed itself?

While there is no simple answer to this question, it is of interest to summarize some of the pertinent pros and cons.

Pessimists, envisioning impending famine as demand increases ahead of supply, make these arguments.

1. The quantity of arable land is finite and its quality is being seriously impaired by wind and water erosion.

2. Urban sprawl and industrial expansion continue to convert prime land from agriculture to nonagricultural uses.

3. Underground water systems, on which farmers depend for irrigation, are being mined at such a rapid rate that farmlands in some areas will have to be abandoned.

4. World population continues to grow; every day there are hundreds of thousands of new mouths to feed.

5. Some environmentalists suggest that unfavourable long-run climatic changes will undermine future agricultural production.

Optimists offer the following counterarguments.

1. The number of hectares planted to crops has been increasing and the world is far from bringing all of its arable land into production.

2. Agricultural productivity continues to rise and the possibility of dramatic productivity breakthroughs lies ahead as we enter the age of genetic engineering. There is also room for substantial productivity increases in the agricultural sectors of the less-developed countries. For example, improved economic incentives for farm workers in China helped expand agricultural output by about one-third between 1980 and 1985.

3. The rate of growth of world population has been diminishing.

We must also note the adjustment processes elicited by the price system. If food shortages were to develop, food prices would rise. Higher prices would simultaneously induce more production and constrain the amount demanded, and head off the shortages.

Admittedly, the "feast or famine" debate is highly speculative; a clear picture of the world's future production capabilities and consumption needs is not easily discerned. Perhaps the main point to be made is that Canadian agricultural policies should take global considerations into account.

Chapter summary

1. In the short run, the highly inelastic nature of agricultural demand translates small changes in output and small shifts in demand into large fluctuations in prices and incomes.

2. Rapid technological advance, coupled with a highly inelastic and relatively constant demand for agricultural output, has caused agriculture to be a declining industry.

3. The two basic arguments for public assistance to agriculture are *a.* that farmers have borne a disproportionately large share of the costs of economic progress in agriculture, and *b.* that farmers have little market power compared with other sectors of the economy.

4. Historically, agricultural policy has been price-centred. The use of price floors or supports has a number of economic effects: *a.* production is greater than would occur in a free market; *b.* the incomes of farmers are increased; *c.* consumers pay higher prices for farm products; *d.* society at large pays higher taxes either to purchase and store surplus output or to finance deficiency payments, and also bears the cost of an overallocation of resources to agriculture; and *e.* other nations bear the costs associated with import barriers and depressed world farm commodity prices.

5. Government has pursued with limited success a variety of programs to reduce the supply of, and increase the demand for, agricultural products in order to reduce the surpluses associated with price supports.

6. Farm policy has been criticized for *a.* confusing symptoms (low farm incomes) with causes (excess capacity); *b.* providing the largest subsidies to high-income farmers; *c.* contradictions among specific farm programs; *d.* declining effectiveness.

7. The persistence of agricultural subsidies can be explained in terms of public choice theory and, in particular, in terms of rent-seeking behaviour, and the special-interest effect.

8. Canada has unsuccessfully sought through GATT to reduce barriers to international agricultural trade.

9. Canada may be moving toward a policy of stabilizing, but not enhancing, farm incomes.

TERMS AND CONCEPTS

Agricultural Products Board (p. 387)
Agricultural Products Marketing Act (p. 386)
Agricultural Stabilization Board (p. 387)
Canadian Dairy Commission (p. 387)
Canadian Wheat Board (p. 386)
crop restrictions (p. 390)

deficiency payments (p. 389)
long-run farm problem (p. 384)
market-oriented income stabilization (p. 393)
offers to purchase (p. 387)
short-run farm problem (p. 382)

QUESTIONS AND STUDY SUGGESTIONS

1. Explain how each of the following contributes to the farm problem: *a.* inelastic demand for farm products; *b.* rapid technological progress in farming; *c.* the modest long-run growth in demand for farm commodities; *d.* the competitiveness of agriculture; *e.* the relative immobility of agricultural resources. Do exports increase or reduce the instability of demand for farm products?

2. What relationship, if any, can you detect between the fact that the farmer's fixed costs of production are large and the fact that the supply of most agricultural products is generally inelastic? Be specific in your answer.

3. "The supply and demand for agricultural products are such that small changes in agricultural supply will result in drastic changes in prices. However, large changes in farm prices have modest effects on agricultural output." Carefully evaluate. *Hint:* A brief review of the distinction between *supply* and *quantity supplied* may be of assistance.

4. The key to efficient resource allocation is the shifting of resources from low-productivity to high-productivity uses. Given the high and expanding physical productivity of agricultural resources, explain why many economists want to divert resources from farming in the interest of greater allocative efficiency.

5. "Industry complains of the higher taxes it must pay to finance subsidies to agriculture. Yet the fact that the trend of agricultural prices has been downward while industrial prices have been moving upward suggests that on balance agriculture is actually subsidizing industry." Explain and evaluate.

6. "Because consumers as a whole must ultimately pay the total incomes received by farmers, it makes no real difference whether this income is paid through free farm markets or through supported prices supplemented by subsidies financed out of tax revenues." Do you agree?

7. Suppose you are the president of a local district of one of the major farm organizations. You are directed by the district's membership to formulate policy statements for the district that cover the following topics: *a.* anti-combines (competition) policy; *b.* monetary policy; *c.* fiscal policy; and *d.* tariff policy. Briefly outline the policy statements that will best serve the interests of farmers. What is the rationale underlying each statement? Do you see any conflicts or inconsistencies in your policy statements?

8. Carefully demonstrate the economic effects of price supports. On what grounds do economists contend that price supports cause a misallocation of resources?

9. Explain and evaluate the following statements:

   a. "Price supports intensify rather than resolve the farm problem."

   b. "The best farm program is full employment."

   c. "The trouble with support prices in agriculture is that they strip the price mechanism of its ability to allocate resources."

   d. "The problem for current farm policy is that not all farmers are poor."

10. Reconcile these two statements: "The farm problem is one of overproduction." "Despite the great productive capacity of Canadian agriculture, plenty of Canadians are going hungry." What assumptions about the price system are implied in your answer?

11. Compare the economic consequences of *a.* offers to purchase and *b.* deficiency payments for farmers, consumers, taxpayers, and the government. On what grounds do economists contend that offers to purchase and deficiency payments cause a misallocation of resources?

12. How do you reconcile increasingly large aggregate subsidies to agriculture with a declining farm population?

13. Use public choice theory to explain the size and persistence of subsidies to agriculture.

14. What are the effects of farm programs such as those of Canada, the United States, and the European Community on *a.* domestic agricultural prices; *b.* world agricultural prices; and *c.* the international allocation of agricultural resources. Use your responses to explain Canada's proposals in the recent GATT negotiations.

15. What are the major criticisms of farm policy? Do you feel that government should attempt to enhance farm incomes, stabilize farm incomes, or allow farm incomes to be determined by free markets? Justify your position.

Glossary

Ability-to-pay principle — The belief that those who have the greater income (or wealth) should be taxed absolutely and relatively more than those who have less.

Abstraction — Elimination of irrelevant and non-economic facts to obtain an economic principle.

Actual budget — The amount spent by the federal government (to purchase goods and services and for transfer payments) less the amount of tax revenue collected by it in any (fiscal) year; and which can *not* reliably be used to determine whether it is pursuing an expansionary or contractionary fiscal policy. Compare with the Cyclically-adjusted budget (*see*).

Actual cash reserve — The amount a bank has as Vault cash and on deposit at the Bank of Canada.

Actual deficit — The size of the federal government's Budget deficit (*see*) or surplus actually measured or recorded in any given year.

Actual investment — The amount that business Firms do invest; equal to Planned investment plus Unplanned investment.

Adaptive expectations theory — The idea that people determine their expectations about future events (for example, inflation) on the basis of past and present events (rates of inflation) and only change their expectations as events unfold.

Adjustable pegs — The device utilized in the Bretton Woods system (*see*) to change Exchange rates in an orderly way to eliminate persistent Payments deficits and surpluses; each nation defined its monetary unit in terms of (pegged it to) gold or the U.S. dollar, kept the Rate of exchange for its money stable in the short run, and changed (adjusted) it in the long run when faced with International disequilibrium.

Adverse selection problem — A problem that arises when information known to one party to a contract is not known to the other party, causing the latter to incur major costs. Example: Individuals who have the poorest health are more likely to buy health insurance.

Aggregate demand — A schedule or curve that shows the total quantity of goods and services demanded (purchased) at different price levels.

Aggregate demand–aggregate supply model — The macroeconomic model that uses Aggregate demand and Aggregate supply (*see both*) to determine and explain the Price level and the real Domestic output.

Aggregate expenditures — The total amount spent for final goods and services in the economy.

Aggregate expenditures–domestic output approach — Determination of the Equilibrium gross domestic product (*see*) by finding the real GDP at which Aggregate expenditures are equal to the real Domestic output.

Aggregate expenditures schedule — A schedule or curve that shows the total amount spent for final goods and services at different levels of real GDP.

Aggregate supply — A schedule or curve that shows the total quantity of goods and services supplied (produced) at different price levels.

Aggregation — Treating individual units or data as one unit or number. For example, all prices of individual goods and services are combined into a Price level, or all units of output are aggregated into Real GDP.

Agricultural Stabilization Board — The federal agency established in 1958 to support the following commodities at not less than 90% of their average price over the previous five years, with adjustments according to production costs: cattle, hogs, and sheep; industrial milk and cream; and oats and barley not produced on the Prairies [where the Canadian Wheat Board (*see*) has jurisdiction].

Allocative efficiency — The apportionment of resources among firms and industries to obtain the production of the products most wanted by society (consumers): the output of each product at which its Marginal cost and Price are equal.

Allocative factor — The ability of an economy to reallocate resources to achieve the Economic growth that the Supply factors (*see*) make possible.

Annually balanced budget — The equality of government expenditures and tax collections during a year.

Anticipated inflation — Inflation (*see*) at a rate that was equal to the rate expected in that period of time.

Anti-combines — (*See* Combines Investigation Act.)

Anti-Inflation Board — The federal agency established in 1975 (and disbanded in 1979) to administer the government's inflation control program.

Applied economics — (*See* Policy economics.)

Appreciation — An increase in the international price of a currency caused by market forces; not caused by the central bank; the opposite of Depreciation.

Arbitration — The designation of a neutral third party to render a decision in a dispute by which both parties (the employer and the labour union) agree in advance to abide.

Asset — Anything with a monetary value owned by a firm or an individual.

Asset demand for money — The amount of money people want to hold as a Store of value (the amount of their financial assets they wish to have in the form of Money); and which varies inversely with the Rate of interest.

Authoritarian capitalism — An economic system (method of organization) in which property resources are privately owned and government extensively directs and controls the economy.

Authoritarian socialism — (*See* Command economy.)

Average fixed cost — The total Fixed cost (*see*) of a Firm divided by its output (the quantity of product produced).

Average product — The total output produced per unit of a resource employed (total product divided by the quantity of a resource employed).

Average propensity to consume — Fraction of Disposable income that households spend for consumer goods and services; consumption divided by Disposable income.

Average propensity to save — Fraction of Disposable income that households save; Saving divided by Disposable income.

Average revenue — Total revenue from the sale of a product divided by the quantity of the product sold (demanded); equal to the price at which the product is sold so long as all units of the product are sold at the same price.

Average tax rate — Total tax paid divided by total (taxable) income; the tax rate on total (taxable) income.

Average (total) cost — The Total cost of a Firm divided by its output (the quantity of product produced); equal to Average fixed cost (*see*) plus Average variable cost (*see*).

Average variable cost — The total Variable cost (*see*) of a Firm divided by its output (the quantity of product produced).

Balanced budget multiplier — The effect of equal increases (decreases) in government spending for goods and services and in taxes is to increase (decrease) the Equilibrium gross domestic product.

Balance of (international) payments — The annual statement of a nation's international economic dealings showing the Current account (*see*) balance and the Capital account (*see*) balance, the latter including the balance in Official international reserves (*see*).

Balance of payments deficit — When the balance in Official international reserves (*see*) is *positive*.

Balance of payments effect — The inflow of foreign funds that usually accompanies a takeover or the establishment of a new foreign-controlled firm, and the resulting Transfer effect (*see*) outflow of interest and dividends abroad.

Balance of payments surplus — When the balance in Official international reserves (*see*) is *negative*.

Balance of trade — The addition of the balances on goods (merchandise) and services in the Current account (*see*) of the Balance of payments (*see*).

Balance on the capital account — The Capital inflows (*see*) of a nation less its Capital outflows (*see*), both of which include Official international reserves (*see*).

Balance on current account — The exports of goods (merchandise) and services of a nation less its imports of goods (merchandise) and services plus its Net investment income from nonresidents (*see*) and its Net transfers.

Balance on goods and services — The Balance of trade (*see*).

Balance sheet — A statement of the Assets (*see*), Liabilities (*see*), and Net worth (*see*) of a Firm or individual at some given time.

Bank Rate — The interest rate that the Bank of Canada charges on advances (*normally* very short-term loans) made to the chartered banks and other members of the Canadian Payments Association (*see*), equivalent to Discount rate in the United States.

Bankers' bank — The bank that accepts the deposits of and makes loans to chartered banks: the Bank of Canada.

Barrier to entry — Anything that artificially prevents the entry of Firms into an industry.

Barter — The exchange of one good or service for another good or service.

Base year — The year with which prices in other years are compared when a Price index (*see*) is constructed.

Beggar-my-neighbour policy — A government policy that expands a nation's exports or reduces its imports and thereby lessens its Balance-of-payments deficit and increases its rates of employment and economic growth by reducing the exports or expanding imports and worsening the Balance-of-payments position, employment, and economic growth in other nations.

Benefit-cost analysis — Deciding whether to employ resources and the quantity of resources to employ for a project or program (for the production of a good or service) by comparing the marginal benefits with the marginal costs.

Benefit-loss rate — The percentage of any increase in earned income by which subsidy benefits in a Negative income tax (*see*) plan are reduced.

Benefits-received principle — The belief that those who receive the benefits of goods and services provided by government should pay the taxes required to finance them.

Bid rigging — The illegal action of oligopolists who agree either that one or more will not bid on a request for bids or tenders or, alternatively, agree on what bids they will make, and forbidden under the Competition Act (*see*).

Big business — A business Firm that either produces a large percentage of the total output of an industry, is large (in terms of number of employees or stockholders, sales, assets, or profits) compared with other Firms in the economy, or both.

Bilateral monopoly — A market in which there is a single seller (Monopoly) and a single buyer (Monopsony).

Board of Transport Commissioners — The federal agency established by the Railway Act of 1903 to regulate freight rates; superseded by the Canadian Transport Commission (*see*) in 1967.

Brain drain — The emigration of highly educated, highly skilled workers from a country.

Break-even income (1) — The level of Disposable income at which Households plan to consume (spend) all of their income (for consumer goods and services) and to save none of it.

Break-even income (2) — The level of earned income at which Negative income tax (*see*) is reduced to zero and at which normal (positive) income tax applies on further increases in earned income.

Break-even point — Any output that a (competitive) Firm might produce at which its Total cost and Total revenue would be equal; an output at which it has neither a profit nor a loss.

Bretton Woods system — The international monetary system developed after World War II in which Adjustable pegs (*see*) were employed, the International Monetary Fund (*see*) helped to stabilize Foreign exchange rates, and gold and the Key currencies (*see*) were used as Official international reserves (*see*).

Budget deficit — The amount by which the expenditures of the federal government exceed its revenues in any year.

Budget line — A curve that shows the different combinations of two products a consumer can purchase with a given money income.

Budget restraint — The limit imposed upon the ability of an individual consumer to obtain goods and services by the size of the consumer's income (and by the prices that must be paid for the goods and services).

Built-in stability — The effect of Nondiscretionary fiscal policy (*see*) upon the economy; when Net taxes vary directly with the Gross domestic product, the fall (rise) in Net taxes during a recession (inflation) helps to eliminate unemployment (inflationary pressures).

Business cycle — Recurrent ups and downs over a period of years in the level of economic activity.

Business monopoly — A market situation in which a single firm or small number of firms dominate the output of an industry.

Canada Assistance Plan — The federal Act under which the federal government makes funds available to the provinces for their programs of assistance to disabled, handicapped, unemployed (who are not entitled to unemployment insurance benefits), and other needy persons.

Canada Deposit Insurance Corporation — Federal Crown Corporation that, for a fee payable by the chartered banks and federally-chartered trust companies, insures their customers' deposits up to a limit of $60,000 per customer per bank or trust company.

Canada Labour Code — The federal law of 1970 that consolidated previous legislation regulating employment practices, labour standards, and so on, in the federal jurisdiction.

Canada Pension Plan — The compulsory, contributory, earnings-related federal pension plan that covers most employed members of the labour force between the ages of 18 and 65, and payable at the latter age; it came into effect in 1965; there is transferability between the Plan and the Quebec Pension Plan, which applies to the people of that province.

Canada-United States Free Trade Agreement (FTA) — An accord, which came into effect on January 1, 1989, to eliminate all Tariffs (*see*) between the two countries over the following ten years.

Canadian Congress of Labour (CCL) — The Federation of Industrial unions (*see*) formed in 1940 and affiliated with the Congress of Industrial Organizations (*see*); amalgamated into Canadian Labour Congress (*see*) in 1956.

Canadian International Development Agency (CIDA) — The federal agency responsible for the operation and administration of Canada's international development assistance programs of approximately $2.5 billion a year.

Canadian Labour Congress (CLC) — The largest federation of Labour unions (*see*) in Canada, with 3 million members in international and national unions; founded in 1956 on the amalgamation of the Canadian Congress of Labour (*see*) and the Trades and Labour Congress of Canada (*see*).

Canadian Payments Association — The federal agency set up in 1982 to provide for Cheque clearing (*see*).

Canadian Transport Commission — The federal agency set up in 1967 to prevent abuse of monopoly power in the telecommunications and land, water, and air transport industries; on its creation, it took over the Board of Transport Commissioners (*see*), the Air Transport Board, and the Maritime Commission.

Canadian Wheat Board — Federal Crown Corporation established in 1935, which does not own or operate grain-handling facilities but has complete control over the way western wheat is marketed and the price at which it is sold. The Board also acquired complete control of the supplies of all Prairie coarse grains in 1949.

Capacity-creating aspect of investment — The effect of investment spending on the productive capacity (the ability to produce goods and services) of an economy.

Capital — Man-made resources used to produce goods and services; goods that do not directly satisfy human wants; capital goods.

Capital account — That part of the Balance of payments (*see*) that records the net inflows and outflows of liquid capital (money) for direct and portfolio investments at home and abroad, and includes the balance in Official international reserves (*see*).

Capital account deficit — A negative Balance on the capital account (*see*).

Capital account surplus — A positive Balance on the capital account (*see*).

Capital consumption allowances — Estimate of the amount of Capital worn out or used up (consumed) in producing the gross domestic product; depreciation.

Capital flight — The transfer of savings from less developed to industrially advanced countries to avoid government expropriation, taxation, and high rates of inflation or to realize better investment opportunities.

Capital gain — The gain realized when securities or properties are sold for a price greater than the price paid for them.

Capital goods — (*See* Capital.)

Capital inflow — The expenditures made by the residents of foreign nations to purchase equity, shares, and bonds from the residents of a nation.

Capital-intensive commodity — A product that requires a relatively large amount of Capital to produce.

Capital outflow — The expenditures made by the residents of a nation to purchase equity, shares, and bonds from the residents of foreign nations.

Capital-output ratio — The ratio of the stock of Capital to the productive (output) capacity of the economy; and the ratio of a change in the stock of Capital (net investment) to the resulting change in productive capacity.

Capital-saving technological advance — An improvement in technology that permits a greater quantity of a product to be produced with a given amount of Capital (or the same amount of the product to be produced with a smaller amount of Capital).

Capital-using technological advance — An improvement in technology that requires the use of a greater amount of Capital to produce a given quantity of a product.

Cartel — A formal written or oral agreement among Firms to set the price of the product and the outputs of the individual firms or to divide the market for the product geographically.

Cash (primary) reserve — The weighted average of the 10% of their demand (current and personal chequing) account deposits and the 3% of their notice account deposits that the Chartered banks (*see*) must hold as Vault cash (*see*) or on deposit with the Bank of Canada. In August 1989 the average required cash reserve ratio was 4.03%. It is expected that when a Bank Act is passed the reserve requirement will be abolished.

Causation — A cause-and-effect relationship; one or several events bring about or result in another event.

Ceiling price — (*See* Price ceiling.)

Central bank — The bank whose chief function is the control of the nation's money supply: the Bank of Canada.

Central economic planning — Determination of the objectives of the economy and the direction of its resources to the attainment of these objectives by the national government.

Ceteris paribus assumption — (*See* "other things being equal" assumption.)

Change in amount consumed — Increase or decrease in consumption spending that results from an increase or decrease in Disposable income, the Consumption schedule (curve) remaining unchanged; movement from one line (point) to another on the same Consumption schedule (curve).

Change in amount saved — Increase or decrease in Saving that results from an increase or decrease in

Disposable income, the Saving schedule (curve) remaining unchanged; movement from one line (point) to another on the same Saving schedule (curve).

Change in the consumption schedule — An increase or decrease in consumption at each level of Disposable income caused by changes in the Nonincome determinants of consumption and saving (*see*); an upward or downward movement of the Consumption schedule.

Change in the saving schedule — An increase or decrease in Saving at each level of Disposable income caused by changes in the Nonincome determinants of consumption and saving (*see*); an upward or downward movement of the Saving schedule.

Chartered bank — One of the 66 multibranched, Privately owned, commercial, financial intermediaries that have received charters by Act of Parliament and that alone, with Quebec Savings Banks, may call themselves "banks"; and which accept Demand deposits (*see*).

Chartered banking system — All chartered banks as a group.

Checkoff — The deduction by an employer of union dues from the pay of workers and the transfer of the amount deducted to a labour union.

Chequable deposit — Any deposit in a Chartered bank or other financial intermediary (trust company, credit union, etc.) against which a cheque may be written and which deposit, if it is in a bank, is thus part of the M1 (*see*) money supply.

Cheque clearing — The process by which funds are transferred from the chequing accounts of the writers of cheques to the chequing accounts of the recipients of the cheques; also called the "collection" of cheques.

Chequing account — A Demand deposit (*see*) in a chartered bank.

Circuit velocity of money — (*See* Income velocity of money.)

Circular flow of income — The flow of resources from Households to Firms and of products from Firms to Households accompanied in an economy using money by flows of money from Households to Firms and from Firms to Households.

Civilian labour force — Persons fifteen years of age and older who are not residents of the Yukon or the Northwest Territories, who are not in institutions or the armed forces, and who are employed for a wage or salary, seeking such employment, or self-employed for gain.

Classical theory — The Classical theory of employment (*see*).

Classical theory of employment — The macroeconomic generalizations accepted by most economists before the 1930s that led to the conclusion that a capitalistic economy would employ its resources fully.

Closed economy — An economy that neither exports nor imports goods and services.

Close-down case — The circumstance in which a Firm would experience a loss greater than its total fixed cost if it were to produce any output greater than zero; alternatively, a situation in which a firm would cease to operate when the price at which it can sell its product is less than its Average variable cost.

Coase theorem — The idea that Externality problems may be resolved through private negotiations of the affected parties.

Coincidence of wants — The item (good or service) that one trader wishes to obtain is the same item another trader desires to give up and the item the second trader wishes to acquire is the same item the first trader desires to surrender.

COLA — (*See* Cost-of-living adjustment.)

Collection of cheques — (*See* Cheque clearing.)

Collective bargaining — The negotiation of work agreements between Labour unions (*see*) and their employers.

Collective voice — The function a union performs for its members as a group when it communicates their problems and grievances to management and presses management for a satisfactory resolution to them.

Collusion — A situation in which Firms act together and in agreement (collude) to set the price of the product and the output each firm will produce or to determine the geographic area in which each firm will sell.

Collusive oligopoly — Occurs when the few firms composing an oligopolistic industry reach an explicit or unspoken agreement to fix prices, divide a market, or otherwise restrict competition; may take the form of a Cartel (*see*), Gentleman's agreement (*see*), or Price leadership (*see*).

Combined tax-transfer system — The percentage of income collected as taxes less the percentage of income received as transfer payments in different income classes.

Combines Investigation Act — The federal Act, first passed in 1910, whose avowed aim is to prevent agreements to lessen competition unduly; amended and renamed the Competition Act in June 1986.

Command economy — An economic system (method of organization) in which property resources are publicly owned and Central economic planning (*see*) is used to direct and coordinate economic activities.

Commercial bank — (*See* Chartered bank.)

Communism — (*See* Command economy.)

Company union — An organization of employees that is dominated by the employer (the company) and does not engage in genuine collective bargaining with the employer.

Comparable worth doctrine — The belief that women should receive the same salaries (wages) as men when the levels of skill, effort, and responsibility in their different jobs are the same.

Comparative advantage — A lower relative or Comparative cost (*see*) than another producer.

Comparative cost — The amount the production of one product must be reduced to increase the production of another product; Opportunity cost (*see*).

Competing goods — (*See* Substitute goods.)

Competition — The presence in a market of a large number of independent buyers and sellers and the freedom of buyers and sellers to enter and to leave the market.

Competition Act — The Act that amended the Combines Investigation Act (*see*) in June 1986 and, in so doing, renamed it the Competition Act.

Competitive industry's short-run supply curve — The horizontal summation of the short-run supply curves of the Firms in purely competitive industry (*see* Pure competition); a curve that shows the total quantities that will be offered for sale at various prices by the Firms in an industry in the Short run (*see*).

Competitive industry's short-run supply schedule — The summation of the short-run supply schedules of the Firms in a purely competitive industry (*see* Pure competition); a schedule that shows the total quantities that will be offered for sale at various prices by the Firms in an industry in the Short run (*see*).

Competitive labour market — A market in which a large number of (noncolluding) firms demand a particular type of labour from a large number of nonunionized workers.

Complementary goods — Goods or services for which there is an inverse relationship between the price of one and the demand for the other; when the price of one falls (rises) the demand for the other increases (decreases).

Complex multiplier — The Multiplier (*see*) when changes in the Gross domestic product change Net taxes and Imports, as well as Saving.

Concentration ratio — The percentage of the total sales of an industry made by the four (or some other number) largest sellers (Firms) in the industry.

Conditional grant — A transfer to a province by the federal government for a Shared-cost program whereby the federal government undertakes to pay part of the costs (usually half) of programs run by the provinces in accordance with federally set standards; such grants are mostly for health, post-secondary education, and general welfare [mostly under the Canada Assistance Plan (*see*)].

Confederation of National Trade Unions (CNTU) — The Labour union (*see*) federation that represents approximately 20% of Quebec's union members; established in 1921 as the Federation of Catholic Workers of Canada, it was later renamed the Canadian and Catholic Confederation of Labour; it adopted its present name and became nonconfessional in 1956.

Conglomerate combination — A group of Plants (*see*) owned by a single Firm and engaged at one or more stages in the production of different products (of products that do not compete with each other).

Conglomerate merger — The merger of a Firm in one Industry with a Firm in another industry (with a Firm that is neither supplier, customer, nor competitor).

Congress of Industrial Organizations (CIO) — The organization of affiliated Industrial unions formed in the United States in 1936.

Constant-cost industry — An Industry in which the expansion of the Industry by the entry of new Firms has no effect upon the prices the Firms in the industry pay for resources and no effect, therefore, upon their cost schedules (curves).

Consumer goods — Goods and services that satisfy human wants directly.

Consumer sovereignty — Determination by consumers of the types and quantities of goods and services that are produced from the scarce resources of the economy.

Consumption schedule — Schedule that shows the amounts Households plan to spend for Consumer goods at different levels of Disposable income.

Contractionary fiscal policy — A decrease in Aggregate demand brought about by a decrease in Government expenditures for goods and services, an increase in Net taxes, or some combination of the two.

Contractionary monetary policy — Contracting, or restricting the growth of, the nation's Money supply (*see*).

Corporation — A legal entity ("person") chartered by the federal or a provincial government, and distinct and separate from the individuals who own it.

Corporate income tax — A tax levied on the net income (profit) of Corporations.

Correlation — Systematic and dependable association between two sets of data (two kinds of events).

Cost-of-living adjustment (COLA) — An increase in the incomes (wages) of workers that is automatically received by them when there is inflation in the economy and guaranteed by a clause in their labour contracts with their employer.

Cost-plus pricing — A procedure used by (oligopolistic) firms to determine the price they will charge for a product and in which a percentage markup is added to the estimated average cost of producing the product.

Cost-push inflation — Inflation that results from a decrease in Aggregate supply (from higher wage rates and raw material prices) and that is accompanied by decreases in real output and employment (by increases in the Unemployment rate).

Cost ratio — The ratio of the decrease in the production of one product to the increase in the production of another product when resources are shifted from the production of the first to the production of the second product; the amount the production of one product decreases when the production of a second product increases by one unit.

Craft union — A labour union that limits its membership to workers with a particular skill (craft).

Credit — An accounting notation that the value of an asset (such as the foreign money owned by the residents of a nation) has increased.

Credit union — An association of persons who often have a common tie (such as being employees of the same Firm or members of the same Labour union) that sells shares to (accepts deposits from) its members and makes loans to them.

Creeping inflation — A slow rate of inflation; a 2 to 4% annual rise in the price level.

Crop restriction — A method of increasing farm revenue when demand for the product is inelastic. Usually done through a Farm products marketing board (*see*) allotting quotas.

Cross elasticity of demand — The ratio of the percentage change in Quantity demanded of one good to the percentage change in the price of some other good. A negative coefficient indicates the two products are Substitute goods; a positive coefficient indicates Complementary goods.

Crowding model of occupational discrimination — A model of labour markets that assumes Occupational discrimination (*see*) against women and minorities has kept them out of many occupations and forced them into a limited number of other occupations in which the large Supply of labour (relative to the Demand) results in lower wages and incomes.

Crowding-out effect — The rise in interest rates and the resulting decrease in planned investment spending in the economy caused by increased borrowing in the money market by the federal government.

Currency — Coins and Paper money.

Currency appreciation — (*See* Exchange rate appreciation.)

Currency depreciation — (*See* Exchange rate depreciation.)

Current account — That part of the Balance of payments (*see*) that records the total current receipts for merchandise exports, services, investment income from nonresidents, and transfers and the total current payments for merchandise imports, services, investment income to nonresidents, and transfers.

Current account deficit — A negative Balance on current account (*see*).

Current account surplus — A positive Balance on current account (*see*).

Customary economy — (*See* Traditional economy.)

Cyclically-adjusted budget — What the budget balance would be for the total government sector if the economy were operating at an average or cyclically-adjusted level of activity.

Cyclically-adjusted deficit — The budget deficit that would have occurred even though the economy was operating at an average or cyclically-adjusted level of activity.

Cyclically balanced budget — The equality of Government expenditures for goods and services and Net taxes collections over the course of a Business cycle; deficits incurred during periods of recession are offset by surpluses obtained during periods of prosperity (inflation).

Cyclical unemployment — Unemployment caused by insufficient Aggregate expenditures.

Debit — An accounting notation that the value of an asset (such as the foreign money owned by the residents of a nation) has decreased.

Declining economy — An economy in which Net investment (*see*) is less than zero (Gross investment is less than Depreciation).

Declining industry — An industry in which Economic profits are negative (losses are incurred) and which will, therefore, decrease its output as Firms leave the industry.

Decrease in demand — A decrease in the Quantity demanded of a good or service at every price; a shift of the Demand curve to the left.

Decrease in supply — A decrease in the Quantity supplied of a good or service at every price; a shift of the Supply curve to the left.

Deduction — Reasoning from assumption to conclusions; a method of reasoning that tests a hypothesis (an assumption) by comparing the conclusions to which it leads with economic facts.

Deficiency payments — A method of Price support (*see*) whereby the government pays a subsidy to producers when the market price is below the minimum price demand suitable by the government.

Deflating — Finding the Real gross domestic product (*see*) by decreasing the dollar value of the Gross domestic product produced in a year in which prices were higher than in the Base year (*see*).

Deflation — A fall in the general (average) level of prices in the economy.

Demand — A Demand schedule or a Demand curve (*see* both).

Demand curve — A curve that shows the amounts of a good or service buyers wish to purchase at various prices during some period of time.

Demand deposit — A deposit in a Chartered bank against which cheques may be written for immediate payment; bank-created money.

Demand factor — The increase in the level of Aggregate expenditures that brings about the Economic growth made possible by an increase in the productive potential of the economy.

Demand management — The use of Fiscal policy (*see*) and Monetary policy (*see*) to increase or decrease Aggregate expenditures.

Demand-pull inflation — Inflation that is the result of an increase in Aggregate demand.

Demand schedule — A schedule that shows the amounts of a good or service buyers wish to purchase at various prices during some period of time.

Dependent variable — A variable that changes as a consequence of a change in some other (independent) variable; the "effect" or outcome.

Deposit multiplier — (*See* Monetary multiplier.)

Depository institution — A Firm that accepts the deposits of Money of the public (businesses and persons); Chartered banks and other Financial intermediaries (*see*).

Depreciation (1) — (*See* Capital consumption allowances.)

Depreciation (2) — A decrease in the international price of a currency caused by market forces; not caused by the central bank; the opposite of Appreciation.

Derived demand — The demand for a good or service that is dependent upon or related to the demand for some other good or service; the demand for a

resource that depends upon the demand for the products it can be used to produce.

Descriptive economics — The gathering or collection of relevant economic facts (data).

Determinants of aggregate demand — Factors such as consumption, investment, government, and net export spending that, if they change, will shift the aggregate demand curve.

Determinants of aggregate supply — Factors such as input prices, productivity, and the legal-institutional environment that, if they change, will shift the aggregate supply curve.

Determinants of demand — Factors other than its price that determine the quantities demanded of a good or service.

Determinants of supply — Factors other than its price that determine the quantities supplied of a good or service.

Devaluation — A decrease in the defined value of a currency brought about by the central bank; the opposite of Revaluation.

DI — (*See* Disposable income.)

Differentiated oligopoly — An Oligopoly in which the firms produce a Differentiated product (*see*).

Differentiated product — A product that differs physically or in some other way from the similar products produced by other Firms; a product that is similar to but not identical with and, therefore, not a perfect substitute for other products; a product such that buyers are not indifferent to the seller from whom they purchase it so long as the price charged by all sellers is the same.

Dilemma of regulation — When a Regulatory agency (*see*) must establish the maximum price a monopolist may charge, it finds that if it sets the price at the Socially optimum price (*see*), this price is below Average cost (and either bankrupts the Firm or requires that it be subsidized); and if it sets the price at the Fair-return price (*see*), it has failed to eliminate the underallocation of resources that is the consequence of unregulated monopoly.

Direct investment — Investment by nonresidents in a firm they thereby establish or control or come to control through the investment. (*See also* Portfolio investment.)

Directing function of prices — (*See* Guiding function of prices.)

Directly related — Two sets of economic data that change in the same direction; when one variable increases (decreases) the other increases (decreases).

Direct relationship — The relationship between two variables that change in the same direction, for example, product price and quantity supplied.

Discouraged workers — Workers who have left the Civilian labour force (*see*) because they have not been able to find employment.

Discretionary fiscal policy — Deliberate changes in taxes (tax rates) and government spending (spending for goods and services and transfer payment programs) by Parliament for the purpose of achieving a full-employment, noninflationary Gross domestic product and economic growth.

Diseconomies of scale — The forces that increase the Average cost of producing a product as the Firm expands the size of its Plant (its output) in the Long run (*see*).

Disinflation — A reduction in the rate of Inflation (*see*).

Disposable income — Personal income (*see*) less Personal taxes (*see*); income available for Personal consumption expenditures (*see*) and Personal saving (*see*).

Dissaving — Spending for consumer goods and services in excess of Disposable income; the amount by which Personal consumption expenditures (*see*) exceed Disposable income.

Dividend tax credit — A federal government method of reducing the Double taxation (*see*) of corporation income.

Division of labour — Dividing the work required to produce a product into a number of different tasks that are performed by different workers; Specialization (*see*) of workers.

Dollar votes — The "votes" consumers and entrepreneurs in effect cast for the production of the different kinds of consumer and capital goods, respectively, when they purchase them in the markets of the economy.

Domestic economic goal — Assumed to be full employment with little or no inflation.

Domestic income — (*See* Net domestic income.)

Domestic output — Gross domestic product (*see*).

Double counting — Including the value of Intermediate goods (*see*) in the Gross domestic product; counting the same good or service more than once.

Double taxation — Taxation of both corporation net income (profits) and the dividends paid from this net income when they become the Personal income of households.

Dumping — The sale of products below cost in a foreign country.

Duopoly — A market in which there are only two sellers; an Industry in which there are two firms.

Durable good — A consumer good with an expected life (use) of one year or more.

Dynamic progress — The development over time of more efficient (less costly) techniques of producing existing products and of improved products; technological progress.

Earnings — The money income received by a worker; equal to the Wage (rate) multiplied by the quantity of labour supplied (the amount of time worked) by the worker.

Easy money policy — Central bank expanding the Money supply with a view to decreasing interest rates.

Economic analysis — Deriving Economic principles (*see*) from relevant economic facts.

Economic cost — A payment that must be made to obtain and retain the services of a resource; the income a Firm must provide to a resource supplier to attract the resource away from an alternative use; equal to the quantity of other products that cannot be produced when resources are employed to produce a particular product.

Economic efficiency — The relationship between the input of scarce resources and the resulting output of a good or service; production of an output with a given dollar-and-cents value with the smallest total expenditure for resources; obtaining the largest total production of a good or service with resources of a given dollar-and-cents value.

Economic growth — (1) An increase in the Production possibilities schedule or curve that results from an increase in resource supplies or an improvement in Technology; (2) an increase either in real output (Gross domestic product) or in real output per capita.

Economic integration — Cooperation among and the complete or partial unification of the economies of different nations; the elimination of the barriers to trade among these nations; the bringing together of the markets in each of the separate economies to form one large (a common) market.

Economic law — (*See* Economic principle.)

Economic model — A simplified picture of reality; an abstract generalization.

Economic perspective — A viewpoint that envisions individuals and institutions making rational or purposeful decisions based upon a consideration of the benefits and costs associated with one's actions.

Economic policy — Course of action that will correct or avoid a problem.

Economic principle — Generalization of the economic behaviour of individuals and institutions.

Economic profit — The total receipts (revenue) of a firm less all its Economic costs; also called "pure profit" and "above normal profit."

Economic regulation — (*See* Industrial regulation.)

Economic rent — The price paid for the use of land and other natural resources, the supply of which is fixed (perfectly inelastic).

Economics — Social science concerned with using scarce resources to obtain the maximum satisfaction of the unlimited human wants of society.

Economic theory — Deriving Economic principles (*see*) from relevant economic facts; an Economic principle (*see*).

Economies of scale — The forces that reduce the Average cost of producing a product as the Firm expands the size of its Plant (its output) in the Long run (*see*); the economies of mass production.

Economizing problem — Society's human wants are unlimited but the resources available to produce the goods and services that satisfy wants are limited (scarce); the inability of any economy to produce unlimited quantities of goods and services.

EC — European Community — formerly European Economic Community (EEC); (*see* European Common Market).

Efficient allocation of resources — The allocation of the resources of an economy among the production of different products that leads to the maximum satisfaction of the wants of consumers.

Elastic demand — The Elasticity coefficient (*see*) is greater than one; the percentage change in Quantity

demanded is greater than the percentage change in price.

Elasticity coefficient — The number obtained when the percentage change in quantity demanded (or supplied) is divided by the percentage change in the price of the commodity.

Elasticity formula — The price elasticity of demand (supply) is equal to

$$\frac{\text{Percentage change in quantity demanded (supplied)}}{\text{percentage change in price}}$$

which is equal to

$$\frac{\text{change in quantity demanded (supplied)}}{\text{original quantity demanded (supplied)}}$$

$$\text{divided by } \frac{\text{change in price}}{\text{original price}}$$

Elastic supply — The Elasticity coefficient (*see*) is greater than one; the percentage change in Quantity supplied is greater than the percentage change in price.

Emission fees — Special fees that might be levied against those who discharge pollutants into the environment.

Employment rate — The percentage of the Civilian labour force (*see*) employed at any time.

End products — Finished commodities that have attained their final degree of processing, such as commodities used directly for consumption, and machinery.

Entrepreneurial ability — The human resource that combines the other resources to produce a product, makes nonroutine decisions, innovates, and bears risks.

Equality vs. efficiency trade-off — The decrease in Economic efficiency (*see*) that appears to accompany a decrease in Income inequality (*see*); the presumption that an increase in Income inequality is required to increase Economic efficiency.

Equalization payment — An Unconditional grant (*see*) made by the federal government to the seven less wealthy provinces in an attempt to equalize incomes and opportunities across Canada.

Equalizing differences — The differences in the Wages received by workers in different jobs that compensate for nonmonetary differences in the jobs.

Equation of exchange — $MV = PQ$; in which M is the Money supply (*see*), V is the Income velocity of money (*see*), P is the Price level, and Q is the physical volume of final goods and services produced.

Equilibrium domestic output — The real domestic output at which the Aggregate demand curve intersects the Aggregate supply curve.

Equilibrium GDP — The Gross domestic product at which the total quantity of final goods and services produced (the domestic output) is equal to the total quantity of final goods and services purchased (Aggregate expenditures); and at which Leakages (*see*) and Injections (*see*) are equal.

Equilibrium position — The point at which the Budget line (*see*) is tangent to an Indifference curve (*see*) in the indifference curve approach to the theory of consumer behaviour.

Equilibrium price — The price in a competitive market at which the Quantity demanded (*see*) and the Quantity supplied (*see*) are equal; at which there is neither a shortage nor a surplus; and at which there is no tendency for price to rise or fall.

Equilibrium price level — The Price level at which the Aggregate demand curve intersects the Aggregate supply curve.

Equilibrium quantity — The Quantity demanded (*see*) and Quantity supplied (*see*) at the Equilibrium price (*see*) in a competitive market.

Equilibrium real domestic output — The real domestic output that is determined by the equality (intersection) of aggregate demand and aggregate supply; equilibrium GDP.

European Common Market — The association of now twelve Western European nations (with Turkey as an associate member) initiated in 1958 to abolish gradually the Tariffs and Import quotas among them, to establish common Tariffs for goods imported from outside the member nations, to allow the eventual free movement of labour and capital among them, and to create other common economic policies.

European Community — formerly European Economic Community — (*See* European Common Market.)

Excess cash reserve — The amount by which a Chartered bank's Actual cash reserves (*see*) exceeds its Required cash reserve (*see*); Actual cash reserve minus Required cash reserve.

Exchange control — (*See* Foreign exchange control.)

Exchange Fund Account — The account operated by the Bank of Canada on the government's behalf wherein are held Canada's Official international reserves (*see*).

Exchange rate — The Rate of exchange (*see*).

Exchange rate appreciation — An increase in the value of a nation's money in foreign exchange markets caused by free market forces; a decrease in the Rates of exchange for foreign monies.

Exchange rate depreciation — A decrease in the value of a nation's money in foreign exchange markets caused by free market forces; an increase in the Rates of exchange for foreign monies.

Exchange rate determinant — Any factor other than the Rate of exchange (*see*) that determines the demand for and the supply of a currency in the Foreign exchange market (*see*).

Excise tax — A tax levied on the expenditure for a specific product or on the quantity of the product purchased.

Exclusion principle — The exclusion of those who do not pay for a product from the benefits of the product.

Exclusive dealing and tied selling — The illegal action whereby a supplier sells a product only on condition that the buyer acquire other products from the same seller and not from competitors; and forbidden under the Competition Act (*see*).

Exclusive unionism — The policies employed by a Labour union to restrict the supply of labour by excluding potential members in order to increase the Wages received by its members; the policies typically employed by a Craft union (*see*).

Exhaustive expenditure — An expenditure by government that results directly in the employment of economic resources and in the absorption by government of the goods and services these resources produce; Government purchase (*see*).

Exit mechanism — Leaving a job and searching for another one in order to improve the conditions under which a worker is employed.

Expanding economy — An economy in which Net investment (*see*) is greater than zero (Gross investment is greater than Depreciation).

Expanding industry — An industry in which Economic profits are obtained by the firms in the industry and which will, therefore, increase its output as new firms enter the industry.

Expansionary fiscal policy — An increase in Aggregate demand brought about by an increase in Government expenditures for goods and services, a decrease in Net taxes, or some combination of the two.

Expectations — What consumers, business Firms, and others believe will happen or what conditions will be in the future.

Expected rate of net profits — Annual profits a firm anticipates it will obtain by purchasing Capital (by investing) expressed as a percentage of the price (cost) of the Capital.

Expenditure approach — The method that adds all the expenditures made for Final goods and services to measure the Gross domestic product.

Expenditures-output approach — (*See* Aggregate expenditures–domestic output approach.)

Explicit cost — The monetary payment a Firm must make to an outsider to obtain a resource.

Exports — Goods and services produced in a given nation and sold to customers in other nations.

Export subsidies — Government payments that reduce the price of a product to foreign buyers.

Export transaction — A sale of a good or service that increases the amount of foreign money (or of their own money) held by the citizens, firms, and governments of a nation.

External benefit — (*See* Spillover benefit.)

External cost — (*See* Spillover cost.)

External debt — Debt (*see*) owed to foreign citizens, firms, and institutions.

External economies of scale — The reduction in a Firm's cost of producing and marketing that results from the expansion of (the output of or the number of Firms in) the Industry of which the Firm is a member.

Externality — (*See* Spillover.)

Externally held public debt — Public debt (*see*) owed to (Canadian government securities owned by) foreign citizens, firms, and institutions.

Face value — The dollar or cents value stamped on a coin.

Factors of production — Economic resources: Land, Capital, Labour, and Entrepreneurial ability.

Fair-return price — The price of a product that enables its producer to obtain a Normal profit (*see*), and that is equal to the Average cost of producing it.

Fallacy of composition — Incorrectly reasoning that what is true for the individual (or part) is therefore necessarily true for the group (or whole).

Fallacy of limited decisions — The false notion that there are a limited number of economic decisions to be made so that, if government makes more decisions, there will be fewer private decisions to render.

Farm problem — The relatively low income of farmers (compared with incomes in the nonagricultural sectors of the economy) and the tendency for the prices farmers receive and their incomes to fluctuate sharply from year to year.

Farm products marketing boards — The federal and provincial boards, numbering more than 100, that set marketing regulations for commodities ranging from asparagus to turkeys. The boards have the power to allocate quotas, set prices, issue licences, collect fees, and require that the commodity be marketed through them.

Featherbedding — Payment by an employer to a worker for work not actually performed.

Feedback effects — The effects a change in the money supply will have (because it affects the interest rate, planned investment, and the equilibrium GDP) on the demand for money, which is itself directly related to the GDP.

Feedback mechanism — A change in human behaviour that is the result of an actual or predicted undesirable event, and that has the effect of preventing the recurrence or occurrence of the event.

Female participation rate — The percentage of the female population of working age in the Civilian labour force (*see*).

Fewness — A relatively small number of sellers (or buyers) of a good or service.

Fiat money — Anything that is Money because government has decreed it to be Money.

Final goods — Goods that have been purchased for final use and not for resale or further processing or manufacturing (during the year).

Financial capital — (*See* Money capital.)

Financial intermediary — A Chartered bank or other financial institution (trust or mortgage loan company, credit union, *caisse populaire*), which uses the funds (savings) deposited with it to make loans (for consumption or investment).

Financing exports and imports — The use of Foreign exchange markets by exporters and importers to receive and make payments for goods and services they sell and buy in foreign nations.

Firm — An organization that employs resources to produce a good or service for profit and owns and operates one or more Plants (*see*).

(The) firm's short-run supply curve — A curve that shows the quantities of a product a Firm in a purely competitive industry (*see* Pure competition) will offer to sell at various prices in the Short-run (*see*); the portion of the Firm's short-run Marginal cost (*see*) curve that lies above in Average variable cost curve.

Fiscal policy — Changes in government spending and tax collections for the purpose of achieving a full-employment and noninflationary Gross domestic product.

Five fundamental economic questions — The five questions every economy must answer: what to produce, how to produce, how to divide the total output, how to maintain Full employment, and how to assure Economic flexibility (*see*).

Fixed cost — Any cost that in total does not change when the Firm changes its output; the cost of Fixed resources (*see*).

Fixed exchange rate — A Rate of exchange that is prevented from rising or falling by the intervention of government.

Fixed resource — Any resource employed by a Firm the quantity of which the firm cannot change.

Flat-rate income tax — A tax that taxes all incomes at the same rate.

Flexible exchange rate — A Rate of exchange that is determined by the demand for and supply of the foreign money and is free to rise or fall without government interference.

Floating exchange rate — (*See* Flexible exchange rate.)

Floor price — A price set by government that is above the Equilibrium price.

Food and Drugs Act — The federal law enacted in 1920 as outgrowth of legislation dating back to 1875; subsequently amended, the Act and its Regulations now provide for controls over all foods, drugs, cosmetics, and medical devices sold in Canada.

Foreign competition — (*See* Import competition.)

Foreign exchange — (*See* Official international reserves.)

Foreign exchange control — The control a government may exercise over the quantity of foreign money demanded by its citizens and business firms and over the Rates of exchange in order to limit its outpayments to its inpayments (to eliminate a Payments deficit) (*see*).

Foreign exchange market — A market in which the money (currency) used by one nation is used to purchase (is exchanged for) the money used by another nation.

Foreign exchange rate — (*See* Rate of exchange.)

Foreign-trade effect — The inverse relationship between the Net exports (*see*) of an economy and its Price level (*see*) relative to foreign Price levels.

Foreign investment — (*See* Direct investment and Portfolio investment.)

Foreign Investment Review Agency (FIRA) — (*See* Investment Canada.)

45° line — A curve along which the value of the GDP (measured horizontally) is equal to the value of Aggregate expenditures (measured vertically).

Fractional reserve — A Reserve ratio (*see*) that is less than 100% of the deposit liabilities of a Chartered bank.

Freedom of choice — Freedom of owners of property resources and money to employ or dispose of these resources as they see fit, of workers to enter any line of work for which they are qualified, and of consumers to spend their incomes in a manner they deem to be appropriate (best for them).

Freedom of enterprise — Freedom of business Firms to employ economic resources, to use these resources to produce products of the firm's own choosing, and to sell these products in markets of their choice.

Freely floating exchange rates — Rates of exchange (*see*) that are not controlled and that may, therefore, rise and fall; and that are determined by the demand for and the supply of foreign monies.

Free-rider problem — The inability of those who might provide the economy with an economically desirable and indivisible good or service to obtain payment from those who benefit from the good or service because the Exclusion principle (*see*) cannot be applied to it.

Free trade — The absence of artificial (government imposed) barriers to trade among individuals and firms in different nations.

Frictional unemployment — Unemployment caused by workers voluntarily changing jobs and by temporary layoffs; unemployed workers between jobs.

Fringe benefits — The rewards other than Wages that employees receive from their employers and that include pensions, medical and dental insurance, paid vacations, and sick leaves.

Full employment — (1) Using all available economic resources to produce goods and services; (2) when the Unemployment rate is equal to the Full-employment unemployment rate and there is Frictional and Structural but no Cyclical unemployment (and the Real output of the economy is equal to its Potential real output).

Full-employment unemployment rate — The Unemployment rate (*see*) at which there is no Cyclical unemployment (*see*) of the Civilian labour force (*see*) and, because some Frictional and Structural unemployment is unavoidable, equal to from 4% to 6%.

Full production — The maximum amount of goods and services that can be produced from the employed resources of an economy; the absence of Underemployment (*see*).

Functional distribution of income — The manner in which the economy's (the national) income is divided among those who perform different functions (provide the economy with different kinds of resources); the division of Net domestic income (*see*) into wages and salaries, corporation profits, farmers' income, unincorporated business income, interest, and rent.

Functional finance — Use of Fiscal policy to achieve a full-employment, noninflationary Gross domestic product without regard to the effect on the Public debt (*see*).

Game theory — A theory that compares the behaviour of participants in games of strategy, such as poker and chess, with that of a small group of mutually interdependent firms (an Oligopoly).

GATT — (*See* General Agreement on Tariffs and Trade.)

GDP — (*See* Gross domestic product.)

GDP deflator — The Price index (*see*) for all final goods and services used to adjust nominal GDP to derive real GDP.

GDP gap — Potential Real gross domestic product less actual Real gross domestic product.

General Agreement on Tariffs and Trade — The international agreement reached in 1947 by twenty-three nations (including Canada) — and now numbering ninety-six — in which each nation agreed to give equal and nondiscriminatory treatment to the other nations, to reduce tariff rates by multinational negotiations, and to eliminate import quotas.

General equilibrium analysis — A study of the Price system as a whole; of the interrelations among equilibrium prices, outputs, and employments in all the different markets of the economy.

Generalization — Statistical or probability statement; statement of the nature of the relation between two or more sets of facts.

Gentlemen's agreement — An informal understanding on the price to be charged among the firms in an Oligopoly (*see*).

GNP — (*See* Gross national product.)

Gold export point — The Rate of exchange for a foreign money above which — when nations participate in the International gold standard (*see*) — the foreign money will not be purchased and gold will be sent (exported) to the foreign country to make payments there.

Gold flow — The movement of gold into or out of a nation.

Gold import point — The Rate of exchange for a foreign money below which — when nations participate in the International gold standard (*see*) — a nation's own money will not be purchased and gold will be sent (imported) into that country by foreigners to make payments there.

Gold standard — (*See* International gold standard.)

Government current purchases of goods and services — The expenditures of all governments in the economy for Final goods (*see*) and services, less investment goods.

Government purchase — Disbursement of money by government for which government receives a currently produced good or service in return.

Government transfer payment — Disbursement of money (or goods and services) by government for which government receives no currently produced good or service in return.

Gross capital information — (*See* Gross investment.)

Gross domestic product — The total market value of all Final goods (*see*) and services produced in the economy during a year.

Gross investment — Expenditures by business *and by government* for newly produced Capital goods (*see*) — machinery, equipment, tools, and buildings — and for additions to inventories.

Gross national product — Gross domestic product (*see*) plus Net investment income from nonresidents (*see*) (which is always negative in Canada).

Guaranteed annual income — The minimum income a family (or individual) would receive if a Negative income tax (*see*) were to be adopted.

Guaranteed Income Supplement — A 1966 amendment to the Old Age Security Act (*see*) provides for the payment of a full supplement to pensioners with no other income and a partial supplement to those with other, but still low, income.

Guiding function of prices — The ability of price changes to bring about changes in the quantities of products and resources demanded and supplied; (*See* Incentive function of price).

Herfindahl index — A measure of the concentration and competitiveness of an industry; calculated as the sum of the squared market shares of the individual firms.

Homogeneous oligopoly — An Oligopoly (*see*) in which the firms produce a Standardized product (*see*).

Horizontal axis — The "left-right" or "west-east" axis on a graph or grid.

Horizontal combination — A group of Plants (*see*) in the same stage of production and owned by a single Firm (*see*).

Horizontal merger — The merger of one or more Firms producing the same product into a single Firm.

Household — An economic unit (of one or more persons) that provides the economy with resources and uses the money paid to it for these resources to purchase goods and services that satisfy human wants.

Human capital investment — Any action taken to increase the productivity (by improving the skills and abilities) of workers; expenditures made to improve the education, health, or mobility of workers.

Hyperinflation — A very rapid rise in the price level.

IMF — (*See* International Monetary Fund.)

Immobility — The inability or unwillingness of a worker or another resource to move from one geographic area of occupation to another or from a lower-paying to a higher-paying job.

Imperfect competition — All markets except Pure competition (*see*); Monopoly, Monopsony, Monopolistic competition, Monopsonistic competition, Oligopoly, and Oligopsony (*see all*).

Implicit cost — The monetary income a Firm sacrifices when it employs a resource it owns to produce a product rather than supplying the resource in the market; equal to what the resource could have earned in the best-paying alternative employment.

Import competition — Competition that domestic firms encounter from the products and services of foreign suppliers.

Import quota — A limit imposed by a nation on the maximum quantity of a good that may be imported from abroad during some period of time.

Imports — Spending by individuals, Firms, and governments of an economy for goods and services produced in foreign nations.

Import transaction — The purchase of a good or service that decreases the amount of foreign money (or of their own money) held by the citizens, firms, and governments of a nation.

Incentive function of price — The inducement that an increase (a decrease) in the price of a commodity offers to sellers of the commodity to make more (less) of it available; and the inducement an increase (decrease) in price offers to buyers to purchase smaller (larger) quantities; the Guiding function of prices (*see*).

Inclusive unionism — A union that attempts to include all workers employed in an industry as members.

Income approach — The method that adds all the incomes generated by the production of Final goods and services to measure the Gross domestic product.

Income effect — The effect a change in the price of a product has upon the Real income (purchasing power) of a consumer and the resulting effect upon the quantity of that product the consumer would purchase after the consequences of the Substitution effect (*see*) have been taken into account (eliminated).

Income elasticity of demand — The ratio of the percentage change in the Quantity demanded of a good to the percentage change in income; it measures the responsiveness of consumer purchases to income changes.

Income inequality — The unequal distribution of an economy's total income among persons or families in the economy.

Income-maintenance system — The programs designed to eliminate poverty and to reduce the unequal distribution of income.

Incomes policy — Government policy that affects the Money incomes individuals (the wages workers) receive and the prices they pay for goods and services and thereby affects their Real incomes (*see* Wage-price policy.)

Income velocity of money — (*See* Velocity of money.)

Increase in demand — An increase in the Quantity demanded of a good or service at every price; a shift in the Demand curve to the right.

Increase in supply — An increase in the Quantity supplied of a good or service at every price; a shift in the Supply curve to the right.

Increasing-cost industry — An industry in which the expansion of the Industry through the entry of new Firms increases the prices the Firms in the industry must pay for resources and, therefore, increases their cost schedules (moves their cost curves upward).

Increasing returns — An increase in the Marginal product (*see*) of a resource as successive units of the resource are employed.

Independent goods — Goods or services such that there is no relationship between the price of one and the demand for the other; when the price of one rises or falls the demand for the other remains constant.

Independent variable — The variable that causes a change in some other (dependent) variable.

Indifference curve — A curve that shows the different combinations of two products that give a consumer the same satisfaction or Utility (*see*).

Indifference map — A series of indifference curves (*see*), each of which represents a different level of Utility; and which together are the preferences of the consumer.

Indirect taxes — Such taxes as Sales, Excise, and business Property taxes (*see all*), licence fees, and Tariffs (*see*), which Firms treat as costs of producing a product and pass on (in whole or in part) to buyers of the product by charging them higher prices.

Individual demand — The Demand schedule (*see*) or Demand curve (*see*) of a single buyer of a good or service.

Individual supply — The Supply schedule (*see*) or Supply curve (*see*) of a single seller of a good or service.

Induction — A method of reasoning that proceeds from facts to Generalization (*see*).

Industrial Disputes Investigation Act — The 1907 law that marked the beginning of federal labour legislation; it required disputes in the federal jurisdiction to be submitted to a Board of Conciliation and Investigation; replaced by Canada Labour Code (*see*).

Industrial policy — Any policy in which government takes a direct and active role in shaping the structure and composition of industry to promote economic growth.

Industrial regulation — The older and more traditional type of regulation in which government is concerned with the prices charged and the services provided the public in specific industries; in contrast to Social regulation (*see*).

Industrial union — A Labour union that accepts as members all workers employed in a particular industry (or by a particular firm), and that contains largely unskilled or semiskilled workers.

Industrially advanced countries (IACs) — Countries such as Canada, the United States, Japan and the nations of western Europe that have developed Market economies based upon large stocks of technologically advanced capital goods and skilled labour forces.

Industry — The group of (one or more) Firms that produces identical or similar products.

Inelastic demand — The Elasticity coefficient (*see*) is less than one; the percentage change in price is greater than the percentage change in Quantity demanded.

Inelastic supply — The Elasticity coefficient (*see*) is less than one; the percentage change in price is greater than the percentage change in Quantity supplied.

Inferior good — A good or service of which consumers purchase less (more) at every price when their incomes increase (decrease).

Inflating — Finding the Real gross domestic product (*see*) by increasing the dollar value of the Gross domestic product produced in a year in which prices are lower than they were in the Base year (*see*).

Inflation — A rise in the general (average) level of prices in the economy.

Inflationary expectations — The belief of workers, business Firms, and consumers that there will be substantial inflation in the future.

Inflationary gap — The amount by which the Aggregate expenditures schedule (curve) must decrease (shift downward) to decrease the nominal GDP to the full-employment noninflationary level.

Inflationary recession — (*See* Stagflation.)

Infrastructure — For the economy, the capital goods usually provided by the Public sector for the use of its citizens and Firms (*e.g.*, highways, bridges, transit systems, waste-water treatment facilities, municipal water systems, and airports). For the Firm, the services and facilities it must have to produce its products, which would be too costly for it to provide for itself, and which are provided by governments or other Firms (*e.g.*, water, electricity, waste treatment, transportation, research, engineering, finance, and banking).

Injection — An addition of spending to the income-expenditure stream: Investment, Government current purchases of goods and services, and Exports.

Injunction — An order from a court of law that directs a person or organization not to perform a certain act because the act would do irreparable damage to some other person or persons; a restraining order.

In-kind investment — Nonfinancial investment (*see*).

In-kind transfer — The distribution by government of goods and services to individuals and for which the government receives no currently produced good or service in return; a Government transfer payment (*see*) made in goods or services rather than in money.

Innovation — The introduction of a new product, the use of a new method of production, or the employment of a new form of business organization.

Inpayments — The receipts of (its own or foreign) money that the individuals, Firms, and governments of one nation obtain from the sale of goods, services, and investment income, from remittances, government loans and grants, and (liquid) capital inflows from abroad.

Input-output analysis — Using an Input-output table (*see*) to examine interdependencies among different parts (sectors and industries) of the economy and to make economic forecasts and plans.

Input-output table — A table that lists (along the left side) the producing sectors and (along the top) the consuming or using sectors of the economy and that shows quantitatively in each of its rows how the output of a producing sector was distributed among consuming sectors and quantitatively in each of its columns the producing sectors from which a consuming sector obtained its inputs during some period of time (a year).

Insurable risk — An event, the average occurrence of which can be estimated with considerable accuracy, that would result in a loss that can be avoided by purchasing insurance.

Interest — The payment made for the use of money (of borrowed funds).

Interest income — Income of those who supply the economy with Capital (*see*).

Interest rate — The rate of Interest (*see*).

Interest-rate effect — The tendency for increases (decreases) in the Price level to increase (decrease) the demand for money; raise (lower) interest rates; and, as a result, to reduce (expand) total spending in the economy.

Intergovernmental grant — A transfer payment from the federal government to a provincial government or from a provincial to a local government. (*See* Conditional grant and Unconditional grant.)

Interindustry competition — Competition or rivalry between the products produced by Firms in one industry (*see*) and the products produced by Firms in another Industry (or in other Industries).

Interlocking directorate — A situation in which one or more of the members of the board of directors of one Corporation are also on the board of directors of another Corporation; and which is illegal in the United States — but not in Canada — when it tends to reduce competition among the Corporations.

Intermediate goods — Goods that are purchased for resale or further processing or manufacturing during the year.

Internal economic goal — (*See* Domestic economic goal.)

Internal economies — The reduction in the cost of producing or marketing a product that results from an increase in output of the Firm (*see* Economies of (large) scale).

Internally held public debt — Public debt (*see*) owed to (Government of Canada securities owned by) Canadian residents, Firms, and institutions.

International Bank for Reconstruction and Development — (*See* World Bank.)

International economic goal — Assumed to be a current-account balance of zero.

International gold standard — An international monetary system employed in the nineteenth and early twentieth centuries in which each nation defined its money in terms of a quantity of gold, maintained a fixed relationship between its gold stock and money supply, and allowed the free importation and exportation of gold.

International Monetary Fund (IMF) — The international association of nations that was formed after World War II to make loans of foreign monies to nations with temporary Payments deficits (*see*) and to administer the Adjustable pegs (*see*); and which today creates Special Drawing Rights (*see*).

International monetary reserves — The foreign monies — in Canada mostly U.S. dollars — and such other assets as gold and Special Drawing Rights (*see*) that a nation may use to settle a Payments deficit (*see*).

International value of the dollar — The price that must be paid in foreign currency (money) to obtain one Canadian dollar.

Intrinsic value — The value in the market of the metal in a coin.

Inverse relationship — The relationship between two variables that change in opposite directions, for example, product price and quantity demanded.

Investment — Spending for (the production and accumulation of) Capital goods (*see*) and additions to inventories.

Investment Canada — (formerly Foreign Investment Review Agency — FIRA) The federal agency with the professed aim of screening, for benefit to Canada, the setting up in Canada of new firms by nonresidents or the taking over of existing Canadian firms by nonresidents.

Investment curve — A curve that shows the amounts firms plan to invest (along the vertical axis) at different income (Gross domestic product) levels (along the horizontal axis).

Investment-demand curve — A curve that shows real Rates of interest (along the vertical axis) and the amount of Investment (along the horizontal axis) at each Rate of interest.

Investment-demand schedule — Schedule that shows real Rates of interest and the amount of Investment at each Rate of interest.

Investment in human capital — (*See* Human capital investment.)

Investment schedule — A schedule that shows the amounts Firms plan to invest at different income (Gross domestic product) levels.

Invisible hand — The tendency of Firms and resource suppliers seeking to further their self-interests in competitive markets that furthers the best interest of society as a whole (the maximum satisfaction of wants).

Jurisdictional strike — Withholding from an employer the labour services of its members by a Labour union that is engaged in a dispute with another Labour union over which union is to perform a specific kind of work for the employer.

Keynesian economics — The macroeconomic generalizations that are today accepted by most (but not all) economists and that lead to the conclusion that a capitalistic economy does not tend to employ its resources fully and that Fiscal policy (*see*) and Monetary policy (*see*) can be used to promote Full employment (*see*).

Keynesianism — The philosophical, ideological, and analytical views of the prevailing majority of western economists; and their employment theory and stabilization policies.

Keynesian theory — Keynesian economics.

Kinked demand curve — The demand curve a Noncollusive oligopolist (*see*) sees for its output, and which is based on the assumption that rivals will follow a price decrease and will not follow a price increase.

Labour — The physical and mental talents (efforts) of people that can be used to produce goods and services.

Labour force — (*See* Civilian labour force.)

Labour-intensive commodity — A product that requires a relatively large amount of Labour to produce.

Labour productivity — Total output divided by the quantity of labour employed to produce the output; the Average product (*see*) of labour or output per worker per hour or per year.

Labour union — A group of workers organized to advance the interests of the group (to increase wages, shorten the hours worked, improve working conditions, and so on).

Laffer curve — A curve that shows the relationship between tax rates and the tax revenues of government and on which there is a tax rate (between 0 and 100%) at which tax revenues are at a maximum.

Laissez-faire capitalism — (*See* Pure capitalism.)

Land — Natural resources ("free gifts of nature") that can be used to produce goods and services.

Land-intensive commodity — A product that requires a relatively large amount of Land to produce.

Law of conservation of matter and energy — The notion that matter can be changed to other matter or into energy but cannot disappear; all production inputs are ultimately transformed into an equal amount of finished product, energy, and waste (pollution).

Law of demand — The inverse relationship between the price and the Quantity demanded (*see*) of a good or service during some period of time.

Law of diminishing marginal utility — As a consumer increases the consumption of a good or service, the Marginal utility (*see*) obtained from each additional unit of the good or service decreases.

Law of diminishing returns — When successive equal increments of a Variable resource (*see*) are added to the Fixed resources (*see*), beyond some level of employment, the Marginal product (*see*) of the Variable resource will decrease.

Law of increasing opportunity cost — As the amount of a product produced is increased, the Opportunity cost (*see*) — the Marginal cost (*see*) — of producing an additional unit of the product increases.

Law of supply — The direct relationship between the price and the Quantity supplied (*see*) of a good or service during some period of time.

Leakage — (1) a withdrawal of potential spending from the income-expenditures stream: Saving (*see*), tax payment, and Imports (*see*); (2) a withdrawal that reduces the lending potential of the Chartered banking system.

Leakages–injections approach — Determination of the Equilibrium gross domestic product (*see*) by finding the Gross domestic product at which Leakages (*see*) are equal to Injections (*see*).

Least-cost combination rule (of resources) — The quantity of each resource a Firm must employ if it is to produce any output at the lowest total cost; the combination in which the ratio of the Marginal product (*see*) of a resource to its Marginal resource cost (*see*) (to its price if the resource is employed in a competitive market) is the same for all resources employed.

Legal cartel theory of regulation — The hypothesis that industries want to be regulated so that they may form legal Cartels (*see*) and that government officials (the government) provide the regulation in return for their political and financial support.

Legal tender — Anything that government has decreed must be accepted in payment of a debt.

Lending potential of an individual chartered bank — The amount by which a single Chartered bank can safely increase the Money supply by making new loans to (or buying securities from) the public; equal to the Chartered bank's Excess cash reserve (*see*).

Lending potential of the banking system — The amount by which the Chartered banking system (*see*) can increase the Money supply by making new loans to (or buying securities from) the public; equal to the Excess cash reserve (*see*) of the Chartered banking system multiplied by the Money multiplier (*see*).

Less-developed countries (LDCs) — Many countries of Africa, Asia, and Latin America that are characterized by a lack of capital goods, primitive production technologies, low literacy rates, high unemployment, rapid population growth, and labour forces heavily committed to agriculture.

Liability — A debt with a monetary value; an amount owed by a Firm or an individual.

Limited liability — Restriction of the maximum that may be lost to a predetermined amount; the maximum amount that may be lost by the owners (stockholders) of a Corporation is the amount they paid for their shares of stock.

Liquidity — Money or things that can be quickly and easily converted into Money with little or no loss of purchasing power.

Liquidity preference theory of interest — The theory in which the demand for Liquidity (the quantity of Money firms and households wish to possess) and the supply of Liquidity (the quantity of Money available) determine the equilibrium Rate of interest in the economy.

Loaded terminology — Terms that arouse emotions and elicit approval or disapproval.

Loanable funds theory of interest — The concept that the supply of and demand for loanable funds determines the equilibrium rate of interest.

Log-rolling — The trading of votes by legislators to secure favourable outcomes on decisions to provide public goods and services.

Long run — A period of time long enough to enable producers of a product to change the quantities of all the resources they employ; in which all resources and costs are variable and no resources or costs are fixed.

Long-run aggregate supply curve — The aggregate supply curve associated with a time period in which input prices (especially nominal wages) are fully responsive to changes in the price level.

Long-run competitive equilibrium — The price at which the Firms in Pure competition (*see*) neither obtain Economic profit nor suffer losses in the Long run and the total quantity demanded and supplied at that price are equal; a price equal to the minimum long-run average cost of producing the product.

Long-run farm problem — The tendency for the prices of agricultural products and the incomes of farmers to decline relative to prices and incomes in the rest of the economy.

Long-run supply — A schedule or curve that shows the prices at which a Purely competitive industry will make various quantities of the product available in the Long run.

Lorenz curve — A curve that can be used to show the distribution of income in an economy; and when used for this purpose, the cumulated percentage of families (income receivers) is measured along the horizontal axis and the cumulated percentage of income is measured along the vertical axis.

Loss-minimizing case — The circumstances that result in a loss that is less than its Total fixed cost when a competitive Firm produces the output at which total loss is a minimum: when the price at which the firm can sell its product is less than Average total but greater than Average variable cost.

Lump-sum tax — A tax that is a constant amount (the tax revenue of government is the same) at all levels of GDP.

M1 — The narrowly defined Money supply; the Currency (coins and Paper money) and Demand deposits in chartered banks (*see*) not owned by the federal government or banks.

M2 — Includes, in addition to M1, Canadian dollar personal savings deposits and nonpersonal notice deposits at chartered banks.

M2 + — Includes, in addition to M2, deposits at trust and mortgage loan companies, and deposits and shares at *caisses populaires* and credit unions.

M3 — Includes, in addition to M2, Canadian dollar nonpersonal fixed term deposits plus all foreign currency deposits of Canadian residents booked at chartered banks in Canada.

Macroeconomics — The part of economics concerned with the economy as a whole; with such major aggregates as the households, business, international trade, and governmental sectors and with totals for the economy.

Managed floating exchange rate — An Exchange rate that is allowed to change (float) to eliminate persistent Payments deficits and surpluses and is controlled (managed) to eliminate day-to-day fluctuations.

Marginal cost — The extra (additional) cost of producing one more unit of output; equal to the change in Total cost divided by the change in output (and in the short run to the change in total Variable cost divided by the change in output).

Marginal labour cost — The amount by which the total cost of employing Labour increases when a Firm employs one additional unit of Labour (the quantity of other resources employed remaining constant); equal to the change in the total cost of Labour divided by the change in the quantity of Labour employed.

Marginal product — The additional output produced when one additional unit of a resource is employed (the quantity of all other resources employed remaining constant); equal to the change in total product divided by the change in the quantity of a resource employed.

Marginal productivity theory of income distribution — The contention that the distribution of income is equitable when each unit of each resource receives a money payment equal to its marginal contribution to the firm's revenue (its Marginal revenue product).

Marginal propensity to consume — Fraction of any change in Disposable income spent for Consumer goods; equal to the change in consumption divided by the change in Disposable income.

Marginal propensity to import — The fraction of any change in income (Gross domestic product) spent for imported goods and services; equal to the change in Imports (*see*) divided by the change in income.

Marginal propensity to save — Fraction of any change in Disposable income that households save; equal to change in Saving (*see*) divided by the change in Disposable income.

Marginal rate of substitution — The rate (at the margin) at which a consumer is prepared to substitute one good or service for another and remain equally satisfied (have the same total Utility); and equal to the slope of an Indifference curve (*see*).

Marginal resource cost — The amount by which the total cost of employing a resource increases when a Firm employs one additional unit of the resource (the quantity of all other resources employed remaining constant); equal to the change in the total cost of the resource divided by the change in the quantity of the resource employed.

Marginal revenue — The change in the Total revenue of the Firm that results from the sale of one additional unit of its product; equal to the change in Total revenue divided by the change in the quantity of the product sold (demanded).

Marginal-revenue–marginal-cost approach — The method that finds the total output at which Economic profit (*see*) is a maximum (or losses a minimum) by comparing the Marginal revenue (*see*) and the Marginal cost (*see*) of additional units of output.

Marginal revenue product — The change in the Total revenue of the Firm when it employs one additional unit of a resource (the quantity of all other resources employed remaining constant); equal to the change in Total revenue divided by the change in the quantity of the resource employed.

Marginal tax rate — The fraction of additional (taxable) income that must be paid in taxes.

Marginal utility — The extra Utility (*see*) a consumer obtains from the consumption of one additional unit of a good or service; equal to the change in total Utility divided by the change in the quantity consumed.

Market — Any institution or mechanism that brings together the buyers (demanders) and sellers (suppliers) of a particular good or service.

Market demand — (*See* Total demand.)

Market economy — An economy in which only the private decisions of consumers, resource suppliers, and business Firms determine how resources are allocated; the Market system (*see*).

Market failure — The failure of a market to bring about the allocation of resources that best satisfies the wants of society (that maximizes the satisfaction of wants). In particular, the over- or underallocation of resources to the production of a particular good or service (because of Spillovers) and no allocation of resources to the production of Public (social) goods (*see*).

Market for externality rights — A market in which the Perfectly inelastic supply (*see*) of the right to pollute the environment and the demand for the right to pollute would determine the price a polluter would have to pay for the right.

Market period — A period of time in which producers of a product are unable to change the quantity produced in response to a change in its price; in which there is Perfect inelasticity of supply (*see*); and in which all resources are Fixed resources (*see*).

Market policies — Government policies designed to reduce the market power of labour unions and large business firms and to reduce or eliminate imbalances and bottlenecks in labour markets.

Market socialism — An economic system (method of organization) in which property resources are publicly owned and markets and prices are used to direct and coordinate economic activities.

Market system — All the product and resource markets of the economy and the relationships among them; a method that allows the prices determined in these markets to allocate the economy's Scarce resources and to communicate and coordinate the decisions made by consumers, business firms, and resource suppliers.

Median-voter model — The view that under majority rule the median (middle) voter will be in the dominant position to determine the outcome of an election.

Medium of exchange — Money (*see*); a convenient means of exchanging goods and services without engaging in Barter (*see*); what sellers generally accept and buyers generally use to pay for a good or service.

Microeconomics — The part of economics concerned with such individual units within the economy as Industries, Firms, and Households, and with individual markets, particular prices, and specific goods and services.

Minimum wage — The lowest Wage (rate) employers may legally pay for an hour of Labour.

Mixed capitalism — An economy in which both government and private decisions determine how resources are allocated.

Monetarism — An alternative to Keynesianism (*see*); the philosophical, ideological, and analytical views of a minority of North American economists; and their employment theory and stabilization policy, which stress the role of money.

Monetary control instruments — Techniques the Bank of Canada employs to change the size of the nation's Money supply (*see*); Open-market operations (*see*), a change in the Bank Rate (*see*), and Switching Government of Canada deposits (*see*).

Money multiplier — The multiple of its Excess cash reserve (*see*) by which the Chartered banking system (*see*) can expand deposits and the Money supply by making new loans (or buying securities); equal to one divided by the Cash reserve ratio (*see*).

Monetary policy — Changing the Money supply (*see*) in order to assist the economy to achieve a full-employment, noninflationary level of total output.

Monetary rule — The rule suggested by the Monetarists (*see*): the Money supply should be expanded each year at the same annual rate as the potential rate of growth of the Real gross domestic product; the supply of money should be increased steadily at from 3 to 5% per year.

Money — Any item that is generally acceptable to sellers in exchange for goods and services.

Money capital — Money available to purchase Capital goods (*see*).

Money income — (*See* Nominal income.)

Money interest rate — The Nominal interest rate (*see*).

Money market — The market in which the demand for and the supply of money determine the interest rate (or the level of interest rates) in the economy.

Money supply — Narrowly defined: M1 (*see*); more broadly defined: M2, M3, and M2 + (*see*).

Money wage — The amount of money received by a worker per unit of time (hour, day, and so on).

Money wage rate — (*See* Money wage.)

Monopolistic competition — A market in which many Firms sell a Differentiated product (*see*), into which entry is relatively easy, in which the Firm has some control over the price at which the product it produces is sold, and in which there is considerable Nonprice competition (*see*).

Monopoly — (1) A market in which the number of sellers is so few that each seller is able to influence the total supply and the price of the good or service; (2) a major industry in which a small number of Firms control all or a large portion of its output. (*See also* Pure Monopoly.)

Monopsony — A market in which there is only one buyer of the good or service.

Moral hazard problem — The possibility that individuals or institutions will change their behavior in unanticipated ways as the result of a contract or agreement. Example: A bank whose deposits are insured against loss may make riskier loans and investments.

Moral suasion — The statements, pronouncements, and appeals made by the Bank of Canada that are intended to influence the lending policies of Chartered banks.

Most-favoured-nation clause — A clause in a trade agreement between Canada and another nation that provides that the other nation's Imports into Canada will be subjected to the lowest tariff rates levied then or later on any other nation's Imports into Canada.

MR = MC rule — A Firm will maximize its Economic profit (or minimize its losses) by producing the output at which Marginal revenue (*see*) and Marginal cost (*see*) are equal — provided the price at which it can sell its product is equal to or greater than Average variable cost (*see*).

MRP = MRC rule — To maximize Economic profit (or minimize losses), a Firm should employ the quantity of a resource at which its Marginal revenue product (*see*) is equal to its Marginal resource cost (*see*).

Multiplier — The ratio of the change in the Equilibrium GDP to the change in Investment (*see*), or to the change in any other component in the Aggregate-expenditures schedule or to the change in Net taxes; the number by which a change in any component in the Aggregate-expenditures schedule or in Net taxes must be multiplied to find the resulting change in the Equilibrium GDP.

Multiplier effect — The effect upon the Equilibrium gross domestic product of a change in the Aggregate-expenditures schedule (caused by a change in the Consumption schedule, Investment, Net taxes, Government current purchases of goods and services, or Net exports).

Mutual interdependence — Situation in which a change in price (or in some other policy) by one Firm will affect the sales and profits of another Firm (or other Firms) and any Firm that makes such a change can expect the other Firm(s) to react in an unpredictable (uncertain) way.

Mutually exclusive goals — Goals that conflict and cannot be achieved simultaneously.

National income — Total income earned by resource suppliers for their contributions to the production of the Gross national product (*see*); equal to the Gross national product minus the Nonincome charges (*see*).

National income accounting — The techniques employed to measure (estimate) the overall production of the economy and other related totals for the nation as a whole.

National Policy — Sir John A. Macdonald's 1879 policy of high tariff protection for Canadian (Ontario and Quebec) secondary manufacturers.

Natural monopoly — An industry in which the Economies of scale (*see*) are so great that the product can be produced by one Firm at an average cost that is lower than it would be if it were produced by more than one Firm.

Natural rate hypothesis — Contends that the economy is stable in the long run at the natural rate of unemployment; views the long-run Phillips curve (*see*) as being vertical at the natural rate of unemployment.

Natural rate of unemployment — (*See* Full-employment unemployment rate.)

Near-money — Financial assets, the most important of which are savings, term, and notice deposits in Chartered banks, trust companies, credit unions, and other savings institutions, that can be readily converted into Money.

Negative income tax — The proposal to subsidize families and individuals with money payments when their incomes fall below a Guaranteed (annual) income (*see*); the negative tax would decrease as earned income increases (*see* Benefit-loss rate).

Negative relationship — (*See* Inverse relationship.)

Net capital movement — The difference between the real and financial investments and loans made by individuals and Firms of one nation in the other nations of the world and the investments and loans made by individuals and Firms from other nations in a nation.

Net domestic income — The sum of the incomes earned through the production of the Gross domestic product (*see*).

Net exports effect — The notion that the impact of a change in monetary policy will be strengthened by the consequent change in Net exports (*see*). For example a contractionary (expansionary) monetary policy will increase (decrease) domestic interest rates, thereby increasing (decreasing) the foreign demand for dollars. As a result, the dollar appreciates (depreciates) and causes Canadian net exports to decrease (increase).

Net exports — Exports (*see*) minus Imports (*see*).

Net investment — Gross investment (*see*) less Capital consumption allowances (*see*); the addition to the nation's stock of Capital during a year.

Net investment income — The interest and dividend income received by the residents of a nation from residents of other nations less the interest and dividend payments made by the residents of that nation to the residents of other nations. In Canada, always a negative quantity.

Net national income — National income (*see*).

Net national product — Gross national product (*see*) less that part of the output needed to replace the Capital goods worn out in producing the output (Capital consumption allowances [*see*]).

Net taxes — The taxes collected by government less Government transfer payments (*see*).

Net transfers — The personal and government transfer payments made to residents of foreign nations less the personal and government transfer payments received from residents of foreign nations.

Net Worth — The total Assets (*see*) less the total Liabilities (*see*) of a Firm or an individual; the claims of the owners of a firm against its total Assets.

New classical economics — The theory that, although unanticipated price level changes may create macroeconomic instability in the short run, the economy is stable at the full-employment level of domestic output in the long run because of price and wage flexibility.

New International Economic Order — A series of proposals made by the Third World (*see*) for basic changes in its relationships with the advanced industrialized nations that would accelerate the growth of and redistribute world income to the Third World.

NIEO — New International Economic Order (*see*).

NIT — (*See* Negative income tax.)

New perspective view of advertising — Envisions advertising as a low-cost source of consumer information that increases competition by making consumers more aware of substitute products.

NNP — (*See* Net national product.)

Nominal gross domestic output (GDP) — The GDP (*see*) measured in terms of the price level at the time of measurement (unadjusted for changes in the price level).

Nominal income — The number of dollars received by an individual or group during some period of time; the money income.

Nominal interest rate — The rate of interest expressed in dollars of current value (not adjusted for inflation).

Nominal wage rate — The Money wage (*see*).

Noncollusive oligopoly — An Oligopoly (*see*) in which the Firms do not act together and in agreement to determine the price of the product and the output each Firm will produce or to determine the geographic area in which each Firm will sell.

Noncompeting groups — Groups of workers in the economy that do not compete with each other for employment because the skill and training of the workers in one group are substantially different from those of the workers in other groups.

Nondiscretionary fiscal policy — The increases (decreases) in Net taxes (*see*) that occur without Parliamentary action when the Gross domestic product rises (falls) and that tend to stabilize the economy.

Nondurable good — A Consumer good (*see*) such as food, beverages, and tobacco.

Nonexhaustive expenditure — An expenditure by government that does not result directly in the employment of economic resources or the production of goods and services; *see* Government transfer payment.

Nonfinancial investment — An investment that does not require households to save a part of their money incomes; but that uses surplus (unproductive) labour to build Capital goods.

Nonincome charges — Capital consumption allowances (*see*) and Indirect taxes (*see*).

Nonincome determinants of consumption and saving — All influences on consumption spending and saving other than the level of Disposable income.

Noninterest determinants of investment — All influences on the level of investment spending other than the rate of interest.

Noninvestment transaction — An expenditure for stocks, bonds, or second-hand Capital goods.

Nonmarket transactions — The production of goods and services not included in the measurement of the Gross domestic product because the goods and services are not bought and sold.

Nonmerchandise balance — The addition of the balances on services, investment income, and transfers in the Current account (*see*) of the Balance of payments (*see*).

Nonprice competition — The means other than decreasing the prices of their products that Firms employ to attempt to increase the sale of their products; and that includes Quality competition (*see*), advertising, and sales promotion activities.

Nonprice determinant of demand — Factors other than its price that determine the quantities demanded of a good or service.

Nonprice determinant of supply — Factors other than its price that determine the quantities supplied of a good or service.

Nonprice level determinants of aggregate demand — Factors such as consumption, investment, government, and net export spending that, if they change, will shift the aggregate demand curve.

Nonprice level determinants of aggregate supply — Factors such as input prices, productivity, and the legal-institutional environment that, if they change, will shift the aggregate supply curve.

Nonproduction transaction — The purchase and sale of any item that is not a currently produced good or service.

Nontariff barriers (NTBs) — All barriers other than Tariffs (*see*) that nations erect to impede trade among nations; Import quotas (*see*), licensing requirements, unreasonable product-quality standards, unnecessary red tape in customs procedures, and so on.

Nonunion shop — A place of employment at which none of the employees are members of a Labour union (and at which the employer attempts to hire only workers who are not apt to join a union).

Normal good — A good or service of which consumers will purchase more (less) at every price when their incomes increase (decrease).

Normal profit — Payment that must be made by a Firm to obtain and retain Entrepreneurial ability (*see*); the minimum payment (income) Entrepreneurial ability must (expect to) receive to induce it to perform the entrepreneurial functions for a Firm; an Implicit cost (*see*).

Normative economics — That part of economics that pertains to value judgments about what the economy should be like; concerned with economic goals and policies.

Notice, term, and savings deposit — A deposit in a Chartered bank against which cheques may or may not be written but for which the bank has the right to demand notice of withdrawal.

NTBs — (*See* Nontariff barriers.)

Occupational discrimination — The form of discrimination that excludes women from certain occupations and the higher wages paid workers in these occupations.

Occupational licensing — The laws of provincial governments that require a worker to obtain a licence from a provincial board (by satisfying certain specified requirements) before engaging in a particular occupation.

Offers to purchase — A method of Price support (*see*) whereby the government buys the surplus created when it sets the minimum price above the Equilibrium price (*see*).

Official international reserves — The International monetary assets (*see*) owned by the federal government and held in its behalf by the Bank of Canada in the Exchange Fund Account.

Official reserves — Official international reserves (*see*).

Okun's law — The generalization that any one percentage point rise in the Unemployment rate above the Full-employment unemployment rate will increase the GDP gap by 2.5% of the Potential output (GDP) of the economy.

Old Age Security Act — The 1951 federal Act, as subsequently amended, by which a Pension is payable to every person aged 65 and older provided the person has resided in Canada for ten years immediately preceding the approval of an application for pension; in addition a Guaranteed Income Supplement (*see*) may be paid; the Pension is payable in addition to the Canada Pension (*see*).

Oligopoly — A market in which a few Firms sell either a Standardized or Differentiated product, into which entry is difficult, in which the Firm's control over the price at which it sells its product is limited by Mutual interdependence (*see*) (except when there is collusion among firms), and in which there is typically a great deal of Nonprice competition (*see*).

Oligopsony — A market in which there are a few buyers.

OPEC — An acronym for the Organization of Petroleum Exporting Countries (*see*).

Open economy — An economy that both exports and imports goods and services.

Open-economy multiplier — The Multiplier (*see*) in an economy in which some part of any increase in the income (Gross domestic product) of the economy is used to purchase additional goods and services from abroad; and which is equal to the reciprocal of the sum of the Marginal propensity to save (*see*) and the Marginal propensity to import (*see*).

Open-market operations — The buying and selling of Government of Canada securities by the Bank of Canada.

Open shop — A place of employment at which the employer may hire either Labour union members or workers who are not (and need not become) members of the union.

Opportunity cost — The amount of other products that must be forgone or sacrificed to produce a unit of a product.

Optimal amount of externality reduction — That reduction of pollution or other negative externality where society's marginal benefit and marginal cost of reducing the externality are equal.

Optimal distribution of income — The distribution of income that would result in the greatest possible (maximum) satisfaction of consumer wants (Utility) in the economy.

Optimal social price — The price of a product that results in the most efficient allocation of an economy's resources and that is equal to the Marginal cost (*see*) of the last unit of the product produced.

Organization of Petroleum Exporting Countries — The cartel formed in 1960 by thirteen oil-producing countries to control the price at which they sell crude oil to foreign importers and the quantity of oil exported by its members.

"Other things being equal" assumption — Assuming that the factors other than those being considered are constant.

Outpayments — The expenditures of (its own or foreign) money that the individuals, Firms, and governments of one nation make to purchase goods, services, and investment income, for Remittances, for government loans and grants, and (liquid) capital outflows abroad.

Output effect — The impact a change in the price of a resource has upon the output a Firm finds it most profitable to produce and the resulting effect upon the quantity of the resource (and the quantities of other resources) employed by the Firm after the consequences of the Substitution effect (*see*) have been taken into account (eliminated).

Paper-money — Pieces of paper used as a Medium of exchange (*see*); in Canada, Bank of Canada notes.

Paradox of thrift — The attempt of society to save more results in the same amount or less Saving.

Paradox of voting — A situation wherein voting by majority rule fails to provide a consistent ranking of society's preferences for public goods or services.

Partial equilibrium analysis — The study of equilibrium prices and equilibrium outputs or employments in a particular market that assumes prices, outputs, and employments in the other markets of the economy remain unchanged.

Partnership — An unincorporated business Firm owned and operated by two or more persons.

Patent laws — The federal laws that grant to inventors and innovators the exclusive right to produce and sell a new product or machine for a period of seventeen years.

Payments deficit — (*See* Balance of payments deficit.)

Payments surplus — (*See* Balance of payments surplus.)

Peak pricing — Setting the price charged for the use of a facility (the User charge [*see*]) or for a good or service at a higher level when the demand for the use of the facility or for the good or service is greater and at a lower level when the demand for it is less.

Perfect elastic demand — A change in the Quantity demanded requires no change in the price of the commodity; buyers will purchase as much of a commodity as is available at a constant price.

Perfect elastic supply — A change in the Quantity supplied requires no change in the price of the commodity; sellers will make available as much of the commodity as buyers will purchase at a constant price.

Perfect inelastic demand — A change in price results in no change in the Quantity demanded of a commodity; the Quantity demanded is the same at all prices.

Perfect inelastic supply — A change in price results in no change in the Quantity supplied of a commodity; the Quantity supplied is the same at all prices.

Personal consumption expenditures — The expenditures of Households for Durable, semidurable, and nondurable consumer goods and for services.

Personal distribution of income — The manner in which the economy's Personal or Disposable income is divided among different income classes or different households.

Personal income — The income, part of which is earned and the remainder of which is unearned, available to resource suppliers and others before the payment of Personal taxes (*see*).

Personal income tax — A tax levied on the taxable income of individuals (households and unincorporated firms).

Personal saving — The Personal income of households less Personal taxes (*see*) and Personal consumption expenditures (*see*); Disposable income less Personal consumption expenditures; that part of Disposable income not spent for Consumer goods (*see*).

Phillips curve — A curve that shows the relationship between the Unemployment rate (*see*) (on the horizontal axis) and the annual rate of increase in the Price level (on the vertical axis).

Planned economy — An economy in which only government determines how resources are allocated.

Planned investment — The amount that business firms plan or intend to invest.

Plant — A physical establishment (Land and Capital) that performs one or more of the functions in the production (fabrication and distribution) of goods and services.

P = MC rule — A Firm in Pure competition (*see*) will maximize its Economic profit (*see*) or minimize its losses by producing the output at which the price of the product is equal to Marginal cost (*see*), provided that price is equal to or greater than Average variable cost (*see*) in the short run and equal to or greater than Average (total) cost (*see*) in the long run.

Policy economics — The formulation of courses of action to bring about desired results or to prevent undesired occurrences (to control economic events).

Political business cycle — The tendency of Parliament to destabilize the economy by reducing taxes and increasing government expenditures before elections and to raise taxes and lower expenditures after the elections.

Portfolio investment — The buying of bonds and shares by nonresidents, the number of shares bought being insufficient to attain control of the firm. (*See also* Direct Investment.)

Positive economics — The analysis of facts or data for the purpose of establishing scientific generalizations about economic behaviour; compare Normative economics.

Positive relationship — The relationship between two variables that change in the same direction, for example, product price and quantity supplied.

***Post hoc, ergo propter hoc* fallacy** — Incorrectly reasoning that when one event precedes another, the first event necessarily is the cause of the second.

Potential competition — The possibility that new competitors will be induced to enter an industry if firms at present in that industry are realizing large economic profits.

Potential output — The real output (GDP) an economy is able to produce when it fully employs its available resources.

Poverty — An existence in which the basic needs of an individual or family exceed the means available to satisfy them.

Poverty rate — The percentage of the population with incomes below the official poverty income levels established by Statistics Canada.

Predatory pricing — A general, illegal policy of selling at prices unreasonably low with a view to eliminating competition; forbidden under the Competition Act (*see*).

Premature inflation — Inflation (*see*) that occurs before the economy has reached Full employment (*see*).

Price — The quantity of money (or of other goods and services) paid and received for a unit of a good or service.

Price ceiling — A government-fixed maximum price for a good or service.

Price-decreasing effect — The effect in a competitive market of a decrease in Demand or an Increase in Supply upon the Equilibrium price (*see*).

Price discrimination — The selling of a product (at a given time) to different buyers at different prices when the price differences are not justified by differences in the cost of producing the product for the different buyers; an illegal trade practice under the Competition Act (*see*) when it consists in giving a trade purchaser an unfair advantage over its competitors by selling to it at a lower price.

Price elasticity of demand — The ratio of the percentage change in Quantity demanded of a commodity to the percentage change in its price, the responsiveness or sensitivity of the quantity of a commodity buyers demand to a change in the price of the commodity.

Price elasticity of supply — The ratio of the percentage change in the Quantity supplied of a commodity to the percentage change in its price; the responsiveness or sensitivity of the quantity sellers of a commodity supply to a change in the price of the commodity.

Price guidepost — The price charged by an Industry for its product should increase by no more than the increase in the Unit labour cost (*see*) of producing the product.

Price-increasing effect — The effect in a competitive market of an increase in Demand or a decrease in Supply upon the Equilibrium price (*see*).

Price index — An index number that shows how the average price of a "market basket" of goods changes through time. A price index is used to change nominal output (income) into real output (income).

Price leadership — An informal method that the Firms in an Oligopoly (*see*) may employ to set the price of the product they produce: one firm (the leader) is the first to announce a change in price and the other firms (the followers) quickly announce identical (or similar) changes in price.

Price level — The weighted average of the Prices paid for the final goods and services produced in the economy.

Price level surprises — Unanticipated changes in the price level.

Price-maker — A seller (or buyer) of a commodity that is able to affect the price at which the commodity sells by changing the amount it sells (buys).

Price support — The minimum price government allows sellers to receive for a good or service; a price that is the established or maintained minimum price.

Price-taker — A seller (or buyer) of a commodity that is unable to affect the price at which a commodity sells by changing the amount it sells (or buys).

Price-wage flexibility — Changes in the prices of products and in the Wages paid to workers; the ability of prices and Wages to rise or to fall.

Price war — Successive and continued decreases in the prices charged by the firms in an oligopolistic industry by which each firm hopes to increase its sales and revenues and from which firms seldom benefit.

Primary reserve — (*See* Cash reserve.)

Prime rate — The interest rate the Chartered banks (*see*) charge on demand note loans to their best corporate customers.

Principal–agent problem — A conflict of interest that occurs when agents (workers) pursue their own objectives to the detriment of the principal's (employer's) goals.

Private good — A good or service to which the Exclusion principle (*see*) is applicable; and that is provided by privately owned firms to those who are willing to pay for it.

Private property — The right of private persons and Firms to obtain, own, control, employ, dispose of, and bequeath Land, Capital, and other Assets.

Private sector — The Households and business Firms of the economy.

Product differentiation — Physical or other differences between the products produced by different Firms that result in individual buyers preferring (so long as the price charged by all sellers is the same) the product of one Firm to the Products of the other Firms.

Production possibilities curve (frontier) — A curve that shows the different combinations of two goods or services that can be produced in a Full-employment (*see*), Full-production (*see*) economy in which the available supplies of resources and technology are constant.

Production possibilities table — A table that shows the different combinations of two goods or services that can be produced in a Full-employment (*see*), Full-production (*see*) economy in which the available supplies of resources and technology are constant.

Productive efficiency — The production of a good in the least-costly way: employing the minimum quantity of resources needed to produce a given output and producing the output at which Average total cost is a minimum.

Productivity — A measure of average output or real output per unit of input. For example, the productivity of labour may be determined by dividing hours of work into real output.

Productivity slowdown — The recent decline in the rate at which Labour productivity (*see*) in Canada has increased.

Product market — A market in which Households buy and Firms sell the products they have produced.

Profit — (*See*) Economic profit and Normal profit; without an adjective preceding it, the income of those who supply the economy with Entrepreneurial ability (*see*) or Normal profit.

Profit-maximizing case — The circumstances that result in an Economic profit (*see*) for a (competitive) Firm when it produces the output at which Economic profit is a maximum: when the price at which the Firm can sell its product is greater than the Average (total) cost of producing it.

Profit-maximizing rule (combination of resources) — The quantity of each resource a Firm must employ if its Economic profit (*see*) is to be a maximum or its losses a minimum; the combination in which the Marginal revenue product (*see*) of each resource is equal to its Marginal resource cost (*see*) (to its price if the resource is employed in a competitive market).

Program for the Advancement of Industrial Technology — A federal program of providing financial assistance, normally 50%, for the development of new or improved products and processes incorporating advanced technology.

Progressive tax — A tax such that the tax rate increases as the taxpayer's income increases and decreases as income decreases.

Property tax — A tax on the value of property (Capital, Land, stocks and bonds, and other Assets) owned by Firms and Households.

Proportional tax — A tax such that the tax rate remains constant as the taxpayer's income increases and decreases.

Proprietors' income — The net income of the owners of unincorporated Firms (proprietorships and partnerships); the sum of the accrued net income of farm operators from farm production plus the net income of nonfarm unincorporated business, including rent.

Prosperous industry — (*See* Expanding industry.)

Protective tariff — A Tariff (*see*) designed to protect domestic producers of a good from the competition of foreign producers.

Public assistance programs — Programs that pay benefits to those who are unable to earn income (because of permanent handicaps or because they are dependent children), that are financed by general tax revenues, and that are viewed as public charity (rather than earned rights).

Public choice theory — Generalizations that describe how government (the Public sector) makes decisions for the use of economic resources.

Public debt — The amount owed by the Government of Canada to the owners of its securities and equal to the sum of its past Budget deficits (less its Budget surpluses).

Public finance — The branch of economics that analyses government revenues and expenditures.

Public good — A good or service to which the Exclusion principle (*see*) is not applicable; and that is provided by government if it yields substantial benefits to society.

Public interest theory of regulation — The presumption that the purpose of the regulation of an Industry is to protect the public (consumers) from the abuse of the power possessed by Natural monopolies (*see*).

Public sector — The part of the economy that contains all its governments; government.

Public-sector failure — The failure of the Public sector (government) to resolve socioeconomic problems because it performs its functions in an economically inefficient fashion.

Public utility — A Firm that produces an essential good or service, that has obtained from a government the right to be the sole supplier of the good or service in an area, and that is regulated by that government to prevent the abuse of its monopoly power.

Purchasing power parity — The idea that exchange rates between nations equate the purchasing power of various currencies; exchange rates between any two nations adjust to reflect the price level differences between the countries.

Pure capitalism — An economic system (method or organization) in which property resources are privately owned and markets and prices are used to direct and coordinate economic activities.

Pure competition — (1) A market in which a very large number of Firms sells a Standardized product (*see*), into which entry is very easy, in which the individual seller has no control over the price at which the product sells, and in which there is no Nonprice competition (*see*); (2) a market in which there is a very large number of buyers.

Pure monopoly — A market in which one Firm sells a unique product (one for which there are no close substitutes), into which entry is blocked, in which the Firm has considerable control over the price at which the product sells, and in which Nonprice competition (*see*) may or may not be found.

Pure profit — (*See* Economic profit.)

***Pure* rate of interest** — (*See The* Rate of interest.)

Quantity-decreasing effect — The effect in a competitive market of a decrease in Demand or a decrease in Supply upon the Equilibrium quantity (*see*).

Quantity demanded — The amount of a good or service buyers wish (or a buyer wishes) to purchase at a particular price during some period of time.

Quantity-increasing effect — The effect in a competitive market of an increase in Demand or an increase in Supply upon the Equilibrium quantity (*see*).

Quantity supplied — The amount of a good or service sellers offer (or a seller offers) to sell at a particular price during some period of time.

Quasi-public good — A good or service to which the Exclusion principle (*see*) could be applied, but which has such a large Spillover benefit (*see*) that government sponsors its production to prevent an underallocation of resources.

R&D — Research and development; activities undertaken to bring about Technological progress.

Random shock — An event that has a significant effect on an economy but that was unexpected and is not likely to occur again.

Rate of exchange — The price paid in one's own money to acquire one unit of a foreign money; the rate at which the money of one nation is exchanged for the money of another nation.

Rate of interest — Price paid for the use of Money or for the use of Capital; interest rate.

Rational — An adjective that describes the behaviour of an individual who consistently does those things that will enable the achievement of the declared objective of the individual; and that describes the behaviour of a consumer who uses money income to buy the collection of goods and services that yields the maximum amount of Utility (*see*).

Rational expectations theory — The hypothesis that business firms and households expect monetary and fiscal policies to have certain effects upon the economy and, in pursuit of their own self-interests, take actions that make these policies ineffective.

Rationing function of price — The ability of price in a competitive market to equalize Quantity demanded and Quantity supplied and to eliminate shortages and surpluses by rising or falling.

Reaganomics — The policies of the United States Reagan Administration based on Supply-side economics (*see*) and intended to reduce inflation and the Unemployment rate (Stagflation).

Real-balances effect — (*See* Wealth effect.)

Real capital — (*See* Capital.)

Real domestic output (GDP) — The GDP (*see*) measured in terms of a constant price level (adjusted for changes in the price level).

Real gross domestic product — Gross domestic product (*see*) adjusted for changes in the price level; Gross domestic product in a year divided by the GDP deflator (*see*) for that year.

Real income — The amount of goods and services an individual or group can purchase with his, her, or its Nominal income during some period of time; Nominal income adjusted for changes in the Price level.

Real interest rate — The rate of interest expressed in dollars of constant value (adjusted for inflation); and equal to the Nominal interest rate (*see*) less the rate of inflation.

Real rate of interest — The Real interest rate (*see*).

Real wage — The amount of goods and services a worker can purchase with his or her Money wage (*see*); the purchasing power of the Money wage; the Money wage adjusted for changes in the Price level.

Real wage rate — (*See* Real wage.)

Recessionary gap — The amount by which the Aggregate expenditures schedule (curve) must increase (shift upward) to increase the GDP to the full-employment noninflationary level.

Reciprocal selling — The practice in which one Firm agrees to buy a product from a second Firm, and the second Firm agrees, in return, to buy another product from the first Firm.

Reciprocal Trade Agreements Act of 1934 (U.S.) — The federal Act that gave the U.S. President the authority to negotiate agreements with other nations and lower American tariff rates by up to 50% if the other nations would reduce tariff rates on American goods, and which incorporated Most-favoured-nation clauses (*see*) in the agreements reached with these nations.

Refinancing the public debt — Paying owners of maturing Government of Canada securities with money obtained by selling new securities or with new securities.

Regional Development Incentives Act — The federal Act of 1970 designed to create jobs in Canada's slow growth, or "designated" areas.

Regressive tax — A tax such that the tax rate decreases (increases) as the taxpayer's income increases (decreases).

Regulatory agency — An agency (commission or board) established by the federal or a provincial government to control for the benefit of the public the prices charged and the services offered (output produced) by a Natural monopoly (*see*).

Remittance — A gift or grant; a payment for which no good or service is received in return; the funds sent by workers who have legally or illegally entered a foreign nation to their families in the nations from which they have migrated.

Rental income — Income received by those who supply the economy with Land (*see*).

Rent-seeking behaviour — The pursuit through government of a transfer of income or wealth to a resource supplier, business, or consumer at someone else's or society's expense.

Required reserve — [*See* Cash (primary) reserve and Secondary reserve.]

Reserve ratio — [*See* Cash (primary) reserve and Secondary reserve.]

Reserves — [*See* (1) Official international reserves; (2) Cash (primary) reserves and Secondary reserves.]

Resource market — A market in which Households sell and Firms buy the services of resources.

Retiring the public debt — Reducing the size of the Public debt (*see*) by paying money to owners of maturing Government of Canada securities.

Revaluation — An increase in the defined value of a currency brought about by the central bank; the opposite of Devaluation.

Revenue sharing — The distribution by the federal government of some of its tax revenues to provincial governments.

Revenue tariff — A Tariff (*see*) designed to produce income for the (federal) government.

Ricardian equivalence theorem — The idea that an increase in the public debt will have little or no effect on real output and employment because taxpayers will save more in anticipation of future higher taxes to pay the higher interest expense on the debt.

Roundabout production — The construction and use of Capital (*see*) to aid in the production of Consumer goods (*see*).

Rule of 70 — A method by which the number of years it will take for the price level (the increasing variable) to double can be calculated; divide 70 by the annual rate of inflation (the rate of increase).

Sales tax — A tax levied on expenditures for a broad group of products.

Saving — Disposable income not spent for Consumer goods (*see*); not spending for consumption; equal to Disposable income minus Personal consumption expenditures (*see*).

Savings account — A deposit in a financial institution (*see*) that is interest-earning and that can normally be withdrawn by the depositor at any time (though the institution may legally require notice for withdrawal).

Saving schedule — Schedule that shows the amounts Households plan to save (plan not to spend for Consumer goods, *see*) at different levels of Disposable income.

Say's Law — The (discredited) macroeconomic generalization that the production of goods and services (supply) creates an equal demand for these goods and services.

Scarce resources — The fixed (limited) quantities of Land, Capital, Labour, and Entrepreneurial ability (*see all*) that are never sufficient to satisfy the wants of human beings because their wants are unlimited.

Schumpeter-Galbraith view (of oligopoly) — The belief shared by these two economists that large oligopolistic firms are necessary if there is to be a rapid rate of technological progress (because only this kind of firm has both the means and the incentive to introduce technological changes).

SDRs — (*See* Special Drawing Rights.)

Seasonal variation — An increase or decrease during a single year in the level of economic activity caused by a change in the season.

Secondary reserve — The Chartered bank cash in excess of cash reserve requirements, Government of Canada Treasury bills of one year or less, and day-to-day loans to investment dealers who have lines of credit with the Bank of Canada.

Secular trend — The expansion or contraction in the level of economic activity over a long period of years.

Selective controls — The minor techniques used by the Bank of Canada to change the availability of credit: changing the Secondary reserve ratio and Moral suasion (*see both*).

Self-interest — What each Firm, property owner, worker, and consumer believes is best for itself and seeks to obtain.

Semidurable goods — A Consumer good (*see*), other than a Nondurable (*see*), with a life expectancy of less than a year, for example, clothing.

Seniority — The length of time a worker has been employed by an employer relative to the lengths of time the employer's other workers have been employed; the principle that is used to determine which workers will be laid off when there is insufficient work for them all, and which will be rehired when more work becomes available.

Separation of ownership and control — Difference between the group that owns the Corporation (the stockholders) and the group that manages it (the directors and officers) and between the interests (goals) of the two groups.

Service — That which is intangible (invisible) and for which a consumer, firm, or government is willing to exchange something of value.

Shared-cost programs — (*See* Conditional grant.)

Shortage — The result of a price ceiling: a maximum price set by government below the Equilibrium price (*see*).

Short run — A period of time in which producers of a product are able to change the quantity of some but not all of the resources they employ; in which some resources — the Plant (*see*) — are Fixed resources (*see*) and some are Variable resources (*see*); in which some costs are Fixed costs (*see*) and some are Variable costs (*see*); a period of time too brief to allow a Firm (*see*) to vary its plant capacity but long enough to permit it to change the level at which the plant capacity is utilized; a period of time not long enough to enable Firms to enter or to leave an Industry (*see*).

Short-run aggregate supply curve — The aggregate supply curve relevant to a time period in which input prices (particularly nominal wages) remain constant when the price level changes.

Short-run competitive equilibrium — The price at which the total quantity of a product supplied in the Short run (*see*) by a purely competitive industry and the total quantity of the product demanded are equal and which is equal to or greater than the Average variable cost (*see*) of producing the product; and the quantity of the product demanded and supplied at this price.

Short-run farm problem — The sharp year-to-year changes in the prices of agricultural products and in the incomes of farmers.

Simple multiplier — The Multiplier (*see*) in an economy in which government collects no Net taxes (*see*), there are no Imports (*see*), and Investment (*see*) is independent of the level of income (Gross domestic product); equal to one divided by the Marginal propensity to save (*see*).

Single-tax movement — The attempt of a group that followed the teachings of Henry George to eliminate all taxes except one that would tax all Rental income (*see*) at a rate of 100%.

Slope of a line — The ratio of the vertical change (the rise or fall) to the horizontal change (the run) in moving between two points on a line. The slope of an upward sloping line is positive, reflecting a direct relationship between two variables; the slope of a downward sloping line is negative, reflecting an inverse relationship between two variables.

Smoot-Hawley Tariff Act — Passed in 1930, this legislation established some of the highest tariffs in United States history. Its objective was to reduce imports and stimulate the American economy.

Social accounting — (*See* National income accounting.)

Social good — (*See* Public good.)

Social insurance programs — The programs that replace the earnings lost when people retire or are temporarily unemployed, that are financed by pay deductions, and that are viewed as earned rights (rather than charity).

Social regulation — The newer and different type of regulation in which government is concerned with the conditions under which goods and services are produced, their physical characteristics, and the impact of their production upon society; in contrast to Industrial regulation (*see*).

Sole proprietorship — An unincorporated business firm owned and operated by a single person.

Special Drawing Rights — Credit created by the International Monetary Fund (*see*), which a member of the IMF may borrow to finance a Payments deficit (*see*) or to increase its Official international reserves (*see*); "paper gold."

Special-interest effect — Effect on public decision-making and the allocation of resources in the economy when government promotes the interests (goals) of small groups to the detriment of society as a whole.

Specialization — The use of the resources of an individual, a Firm, a region, or a nation to produce one or a few goods and services.

Speculative motive — Keynes' term for the Asset demand for money (*see*).

Spillover — A benefit or cost associated with the consumption or production of a good or service that is obtained by or inflicted without compensation upon a party other than the buyer or seller of the good or service; (*see* Spillover benefit and Spillover cost).

Spillover benefit — The benefit obtained neither by producers nor by consumers of a product but without compensation by a third party (society as a whole).

Spillover cost — The cost of producing a product borne neither by producers not by consumers of the product but without compensation by a third party (society as a whole).

Stabilization funds — International monetary reserves (*see*) and domestic monies used to augment the supply of, or demand for, any currency required to avoid or restrict fluctuations in the rate of exchange; in Canada held in the Exchange Fund Account by the Bank of Canada on behalf of the government.

Stabilization policy dilemma — The use of monetary and fiscal policy to decrease the Unemployment rate increases the rate of inflation, and the use of monetary and fiscal policy to decrease the rate of inflation increases the Unemployment rate; *see* the Phillips curve.

Stagflation — Inflation accompanied by stagnation in the rate of growth of output and a high unemployment rate in the economy; simultaneous increases in both the price level and the Unemployment rate (*see*).

Standardized product — A product such that buyers are indifferent to the seller from whom they purchase it so long as the price charged by all sellers is the same; a product such that all units of the product are perfect substitutes for each other (are identical).

Staple — An exported raw material.

State ownership — The ownership of property (Land and Capital) by government (the state).

Static economy — (1) An economy in which Net investment (*see*) is equal to zero — Gross investment (*see*) is equal to the Capital consumption allowances (*see*); (2) an economy in which the supplies of resources, technology, and the tastes of consumers do not change and in which, therefore, the economic future is perfectly predictable and there is no uncertainty.

Store of value — Any Asset (*see*) or wealth set aside for future use.

Strategic trade policy — The use of trade barriers to reduce the risk of product development by domestic firms, particularly products involving advanced technology.

Strike — The withholding of their labour services by an organized group of workers (a Labour union).

Strikebreaker — A person employed by a Firm when its employees are engaged in a strike against the firm.

Structural unemployment — Unemployment caused by changes in the structure of demand for Consumer goods and in technology; workers who are unemployed either because their skills are not demanded by employers or because they lack sufficient skills to obtain employment.

Subsidy — A payment of funds (or goods and services) by a government, business firm, or household for which it receives no good or service in return. When made by a government, it is a Government transfer payment (*see*) or the reverse of a tax.

Substitutability — The ability of consumers to use one good or service instead of another to satisfy their wants and of Firms to use one resource instead of another to produce products.

Substitute goods — Goods or services such that there is a direct relationship between the price of one and the Demand for the other; when the price of one falls (rises) the Demand for the other decreases (increases).

Substitution effect — (1) The effect a change in the price of a Consumer good would have upon the relative expensiveness of that good and the resulting effect upon the quantity of the good a consumer would purchase if the consumer's Real income (*see*) remained constant; (2) the effect a change in the price of a resource would have upon the quantity of the resource employed by a firm if the firm did not change its output.

Superior good — (*See* Normal good.)

Supplementary labour income — The payments by employers into unemployment insurance, worker's compensation, and a variety of private and public pension and welfare funds for workers: "fringe benefits."

Supply — A Supply schedule or a Supply curve (*see both*).

Supply curve — A curve that shows the amounts of a good or service sellers (a seller) will offer to sell at various prices during some period of time.

Supply factor — An increase in the available quantity of a resource, an improvement in its quality, or an expansion of technological knowledge, which makes it possible for an economy to produce a greater output of goods and services.

Supply schedule — A schedule that shows the amounts of a good or service sellers (a seller) will offer to sell at various prices during some period of time.

Supply shock — One of several events of the 1970s and early 1980s that increased production costs, decreased Aggregate supply, and helped generate Stagflation in Canada.

Supply-side economics — The part of modern Macroeconomics that emphasizes the role of costs and aggregate supply in its explanation of Inflation and unemployed labour.

Supply-side view — The view of fiscal policy held by the advocates of Supply-side economics that emphasizes increasing Aggregate supply (*see*) as a means of reducing the Unemployment rate and Inflation and encouraging Economic Growth.

Support price — (*See* Price support.)

Surplus — The result of a price floor or price support: a minimum price set by government above the Equilibrium price (*see*).

Switching Government of Canada deposits — Action of Bank of Canada to increase (decrease) backing for Money supply (*see*) by switching government deposits from (to) itself to (from) the Chartered banks (*see*).

Tacit collusion — Any method utilized in a Collusive oligopoly (*see*) to set prices and outputs or the market area of each firm that does not involve outright (or overt) collusion (formal agreements or secret meetings); and of which Price leadership (*see*) is a frequent example.

Tangent — The point at which a line touches, but does not intersect, a curve.

Target dilemma — A problem that arises because the central bank cannot simultaneously stabilize both the money supply and the level of interest rates.

Tariff — A tax imposed (only by the federal government in Canada) on an imported good.

Tax — A nonvoluntary payment of money (or goods and services) to a government by a Household or Firm for which the Household or Firm receives no good or service directly in return and which is not a fine imposed by a court for an illegal act.

Tax-based incomes policies (TIP) — An Incomes policy (*see*) that would include special tax penalties for those who do not comply and tax rebates for those who do comply with the Wage-price guide-posts (*see*).

Tax incidence — The income or purchasing power that different persons and groups lose as a result of the imposition of a tax after Tax shifting (*see*) has occurred.

Tax shifting — The transfer to others of all or part of a tax by charging them a higher price or by paying them a lower price for a good or service.

Tax-transfer disincentives — Decreases in the incentives to work, save, invest, innovate, and take risks that allegedly result from high Marginal tax rates and Transfer payment programs.

Tax "wedge" — Such taxes as Indirect taxes (*see*) and pay deductions for Social insurance programs (*see*), which are treated as a cost by business firms and reflected in the prices of the products produced by them; equal to the price of the product less the cost of the resources required to produce it.

Technology — The body of knowledge that can be used to produce goods and services from Economic resources.

Term deposit — A deposit in a Chartered bank or other Financial intermediary against which cheques may not be written; a form of savings account; part of M2, M3, and M2 + (*see all*).

Terms of trade — The rate at which units of one product can be exchanged for units of another product; the Price (*see*) of a good or service; the amount of one good or service that must be given up to obtain one unit of another good or service.

Theory of human capital — Generalization that Wage differentials (*see*) are the result of differences in the amount of Human capital investment (*see*); and that the incomes of lower-paid workers are increased by increasing the amount of such investment.

Theory of public choice — Generalizations that describe how government (the Public sector) makes decisions for the use of economic resources.

***The* rate of interest** — The Rate of Interest (*see*) that is paid solely for the use of Money over an extended period of time and that excludes the charges made for the riskiness of the loan and its administrative costs; and that is approximately equal to the rate of interest paid on the long-term and virtually riskless bonds of the Government of Canada.

Third World — The semideveloped and less-developed nations; nations other than the industrially advanced market economies and the centrally planned economies.

Tied selling — (*See* Exclusive dealing.)

Tight money policy — Increasing the Rate of interest (*see*) by contracting the nation's Money supply (*see*). See also Contractionary monetary policy.

Till money — (*See* Vault cash.)

TIP — (*See* Tax-based incomes policies.)

Token money — Coins that have a Face value (*see*) greater than their Intrinsic value (*see*).

Total cost — The sum of Fixed cost (*see*) and Variable cost (*see*).

Total demand — The Demand schedule (*see*) or the Demand curve (*see*) of all buyers of a good or service.

Total demand for money — The sum of the Transactions demand for money (*see*) and Asset demand for money (*see*); the relationship between the total amount of money demanded and nominal GDP and the Rate of Interest.

Total product — The total output of a particular good or service produced by a firm, a group of firms or the entire economy.

Total revenue — The total number of dollars received by a Firm (or Firms) from the sale of a product; equal to the total expenditures for the product produced by the Firm (or Firms); equal to the quantity sold (demanded) multiplied by the price at which it is sold — by the Average revenue (*see*) from its sale.

Total-revenue test — A test to determine whether Demand is Elastic (*see*), Inelastic (*see*), or of Unitary elasticity (*see*) between any two prices: demand is elastic (inelastic, unit elastic) if the Total revenue (*see*) of sellers of the commodity increases (decreases, remains constant) when the price of the commodity falls; or Total revenue decreases (increases, remains constant) when its price rises.

Total-revenue–total-cost approach — The method that finds the output at which Economic profit (*see*) is a maximum or losses a minimum by comparing the total receipts (revenue) and the total costs of a Firm at different outputs.

Total spending — The total amount buyers of goods and services spend or plan to spend.

Total supply — The Supply schedule (*see*) or the Supply curve (*see*) of all sellers of a good or service.

Trade balance — Balance of trade (*see*).

Trade controls — Tariffs (*see*), export subsidies, Import quotas (*see*), and other means a nation may employ to reduce Imports (*see*) and expand Exports (*see*) in order to eliminate a Balance of payments deficit (*see*).

Trade deficit — The amount by which a nation's imports of merchandise (goods) and services exceed its exports of merchandise (goods) and services.

Trade surplus — The amount by which a nation's exports of merchandise (goods) and services exceed its imports of merchandise (goods) and services.

Trades and Labour Congress of Canada (TLC) — The federation of Craft unions (*see*) formed in 1886 and affiliated with the American Federation of Labour (*see*); amalgamated into the Canadian Labour Congress (*see*) in 1956.

Trading possibilities line — A line that shows the different combinations of two products an economy is able to obtain (consume) when it specializes in the production of one product and trades (exports) this product to obtain the other product.

Traditional economy — An economic system (method of organization) in which traditions and customs determine how the economy will use its scarce resources.

Traditional view of advertising — The position that advertising is persuasive rather than informative; promotes industrial concentration; and is essentially inefficient and wasteful.

Transactions demand for money — The amount of money people want to hold to use as a Medium of exchange (to make payments); and which varies directly with the nominal GDP.

Transfer burden (effect) — The outflow of interest and dividends abroad resulting from foreign investment.

Transfer payment — A payment of money (or goods and services) by a government or a Firm to a Household or Firm for which the payer receives no good or service directly in return.

Tying agreement — A promise made by a buyer when allowed to purchase a patented product from a seller that it will make all of its purchases of certain other (unpatented) products from the same seller.

Unanticipated inflation — Inflation (*see*) at a rate greater than the rate expected in that period of time.

Unconditional grant — A transfer to a province by the federal government that goes into the general revenues of the province to be used as it sees fit; such grants are made for two reasons: (1) as an Equalization payment (*see*) and (2) to make up for the general inadequacy of provincial revenues in relation to provincial responsibilities.

Underemployment — Failure to produce the maximum amount of goods and services that can be produced from the resources employed; failure to achieve Full production (*see*).

Undistributed corporation profits — The after-tax profits of corporations not distributed as dividends to stockholders; corporate or business saving.

Unemployment — Failure to use all available Economic resources to produce goods and services; failure of the economy to employ fully its Civilian labour force (*see*).

Unemployment insurance — The insurance program that in Canada is financed by compulsory contributions from employers and employees and from the general tax revenues of the federal government with benefits (income) made available to insured workers who are unable to find jobs.

Unemployment rate — The percentage of the Civilian labour force (*see*) unemployed at any time.

Unfair competition — Any practice that is employed by a Firm either to eliminate a rival or to block the entry of a new Firm into an Industry and that society (or a rival) believes to be an unacceptable method of achieving these ends.

Uninsurable risk — An event, the occurrence of which is uncontrollable and unpredictable, that would result in a loss that cannot be avoided by purchasing insurance and must be assumed by an entrepreneur (*see* Entrepreneurial ability); sometimes called "uncertainty."

Union shop — A place of employment at which the employer may hire either Labour union members or workers who are not members of the union but who must become members within a specified period of time or lose their jobs.

Unitary elasticity — The Elasticity coefficient (*see*) is equal to one; the percentage change in the quantity (demanded or supplied) is equal to the percentage change in price.

Unit labour cost — Labour costs per unit of output; equal to the Money wage rate (*see*) divided by the Average product (*see*) of labour.

Unlimited liability — Absence of any limit on the maximum amount that may be lost by an individual and that the individual may become legally required to pay; the maximum amount that may be lost and that a sole proprietor or partner may be required to pay.

Unlimited wants — The insatiable desire of consumers (people) for goods and services that will give them pleasure or satisfaction.

Unplanned investment — Actual investment less Planned investment; increases or decreases in the inventories of business firms that result from production greater than or less than sales.

Unprosperous industry — (*See* Declining industry.)

User charge — A price paid by those who use a facility that covers the full cost of using the facility.

Utility — The want-satisfying power of a good or service; the satisfaction or pleasure a consumer obtains from the consumption of a good or service (or from the consumption of a collection of goods and services).

Utility-maximizing rule — To obtain the greatest Utility (*see*) the consumer should allocate Money income so that the last dollar spent on each good or service yields the same Marginal utility (*see*); so that the Marginal utility of each good or service divided by its price is the same for all goods and services.

Value added — The value of the product sold by a Firm less the value of the goods (materials) purchased and used by the Firm to produce the product; and equal to the revenue that can be used for Wages, rent, interest, and profits.

Value-added tax — A tax imposed upon the difference between the value of the goods sold by a firm and the value of the goods purchased by the firm from other firms.

Value judgment — Opinion of what is desirable or undesirable; belief regarding what ought or ought not to be (regarding what is right or just and wrong or unjust).

Value of money — The quantity of goods and services for which a unit of money (a dollar) can be exchanged; the purchasing power of a unit of money; the reciprocal of the Price level.

Variable cost — A cost that, in total, increases (decreases) when the firm increases (decreases) its output; the cost of Variable resources (*see*).

Variable resource — Any resource employed by a firm the quantity of which can be increased or decreased (varied).

VAT — Value-added tax (*see*).

Vault cash — The Currency (*see*) a bank has in its safe (vault) and cash drawers; till money.

Velocity of money — The number of times per year the average dollar in the Money supply (*see*) is spent for Final goods and services (*see*).

VERs — (*See* Voluntary export restrictions.)

Vertical axis — The "up-down" or "north-south" axis on a graph or grid.

Vertical combination — A group of Plants (*see*) engaged in different stages of the production of a final product and owned by a single Firm (*see*).

Vertical intercept — The point at which a line meets the vertical axis of a graph.

Vertical merger — The merger of one or more Firms engaged in different stages of the production of a final product into a single Firm (*see*).

Voluntary export restrictions — The limitation by firms of their exports to particular foreign nations in order to avoid the erection of other trade barriers by the foreign nations.

Wage — The price paid for Labour [for the use or services of Labour (*see*)] per unit of time (per hour, per day, and so on).

Wage differential — The difference between the Wage (*see*) received by one worker or group of workers and that received by another worker or group of workers.

Wage discrimination — The payment to women (or minority groups) of a wage lower than that paid to men (or established groups) for doing the same work.

Wage guidepost — Wages (*see*) in all industries in the economy should increase at an annual rate equal to the rate of increase in the Average product (*see*) of Labour in the economy.

Wage-price controls — A Wage-price policy (*see*) that legally fixes the maximum amounts by which Wages (*see*) and prices may be increased in any period of time.

Wage-price guideposts — A Wage-price policy (*see*) that depends upon the voluntary cooperation of Labour unions and business firms.

Wage-price inflationary spiral — Increases in wage rates that bring about increases in prices, which in turn result in further increases in wage rates and in prices.

Wage-price policy — Government policy that attempts to alter the behaviour of Labour unions and business firms in order to make their Wage and price decisions more nearly compatible with the goals of Full employment and stable prices.

Wage rate — (*See* Wages.)

Wages — The income of those who supply the economy with Labour (*see*).

Wastes of monopolistic competition — The waste of economic resources that is the result of producing an output at which price is greater than marginal cost and average cost is greater than the minimum average cost.

Wealth effect — The tendency for increases (decreases) in the price level to lower (raise) the real value (or purchasing power) of financial assets with fixed money values; and, as a result, to reduce (expand) total spending in the economy.

Welfare programs — (*See* Public assistance programs.)

(The) "will to develop" — Wanting economic growth strongly enough to change from old to new ways of doing things.

World Bank — A bank supported by 151 nations, which lends (and guarantees loans) to less-developed nations to assist them to grow; formally, the International Bank for Reconstruction and Development.

X-inefficiency — Failure to produce any given output at the lowest average (and total) cost possible.

National Income Statistics, 1926–1991

NATIONAL INCOME AND RELATED STATISTICS FOR SELECTED YEARS, 1926–1962
National income statistics are in billions of current dollars

			1926	1929	1933	1937	1939	1940	1942	1944	1945	1946
THE	1	Personal consumption expenditure	$3.508	$4.583	$2.974	$3.878	$3.972	$4.464	$5.466	$6.260	$6.972	$8.012
SUM	2	Government current purchases of goods and services	0.390	0.469	0.392	0.471	0.566	1.048	3.622	4.929	3.576	1.655
OF	3	Gross investment	0.949	1.413	0.208	0.764	0.969	1.097	1.200	0.830	0.890	1.877
	4	Net exports of goods and services	0.368	−0.016	0.234	0.423	0.391	0.460	0.273	0.199	0.855	0.702
	5	Statistical discrepancy	0.139	−0.049	−0.085	−0.059	−0.018	−0.082	−0.064	−0.150	−0.230	−0.079
EQUALS	**6**	**GDP at market prices**	**5.354**	**6.400**	**3.723**	**5.477**	**5.880**	**6.987**	**10.497**	**12.068**	**12.063**	**12.167**
	7	Net investment income from nonresidents	−0.208	−0.261	−0.231	−0.236	−0.259	−0.274	−0.232	−0.220	−0.200	−0.282
EQUALS	**8**	**GNP at market prices**	**5.146**	**6.139**	**3.492**	**5.241**	**5.621**	**6.713**	**10.265**	**11.848**	**11.863**	**11.885**
LESS	9	Indirect taxes less subsidies	0.627	0.711	0.547	0.727	0.759	0.859	1.133	1.167	1.084	1.371
	10	Capital consumption allowances	0.572	0.726	0.532	0.624	0.671	0.786	1.091	1.077	1.042	1.071
	11	Statistical discrepancy	−0.139	0.050	0.085	0.060	−0.019	0.083	0.064	0.151	0.231	0.080
EQUALS	**12**	**Net national income at factor cost**	**4.086**	**4.652**	**2.328**	**3.830**	**4.172**	**4.985**	**7.997**	**9.453**	**9.506**	**9.363**
PLUS	13	Government transfer payments	0.074	0.092	0.180	0.235	0.226	0.204	0.218	0.255	0.542	1.102
	14	Transfers from nonresidents	0.017	0.015	0.013	0.016	0.014	0.013	0.014	0.020	0.036	0.026
	15	Interest on the public debt	0.231	0.235	0.283	0.273	0.275	0.273	0.310	0.423	0.512	0.554
	16	Interest on consumer debt (transfer portion)	0.005	0.006	0.004	0.007	0.007	0.008	0.007	0.004	0.005	0.007
LESS	17	Corporation income taxes	0.034	0.048	0.037	0.101	0.115	0.327	0.629	0.598	0.599	0.654
	18	Undistributed corporation profits	0.189	0.225	−0.045	0.218	0.271	0.168	0.360	0.342	0.367	0.480
	19	Government investment income	0.075	0.076	0.027	0.066	0.064	0.104	0.184	0.273	0.310	0.263
	20	Other earnings not paid out to persons	0.058	−0.014	−0.051	−0.094	−0.106	−0.088	−0.169	−0.074	0.033	−0.232
EQUALS	**21**	**Personal income**	**4.057**	**4.665**	**2.840**	**4.070**	**4.350**	**4.972**	**7.522**	**9.016**	**9.292**	**9.887**
LESS	22	Personal taxes	0.069	0.093	0.088	0.144	0.143	0.174	0.604	0.965	0.938	0.937
EQUALS	**23**	**Personal disposable income**	**3.988**	**4.572**	**2.752**	**3.926**	**4.207**	**4.798**	**6.918**	**8.051**	**8.354**	**8.950**
LESS	24	Personal consumption expenditure	3.508	4.583	2.974	3.878	3.972	4.464	5.466	6.260	6.972	8.012
	25	Interest paid by consumers to corporations	0.005	0.006	0.004	0.007	0.007	0.008	0.007	0.004	0.005	0.007
	26	Current transfers to nonresidents	0.042	0.044	0.016	0.024	0.026	0.026	0.024	0.027	0.026	0.038
EQUALS	**27**	**Personal saving**	**0.433**	**−0.061**	**−0.242**	**0.017**	**0.202**	**0.300**	**1.421**	**1.760**	**1.351**	**0.893**

RELATED STATISTICS			1926	1929	1933	1937	1939	1940	1942	1944	1945	1946
	28	Real GDP (in 1986 dollars)	43.986	52.997	38.331	51.635	56.265	63.722	84.925	91.385	89.170	87.177
	29	Growth rate of real GDP (annual %)	—	0.1	−7.2	8.9	7.5	13.3	17.6	3.7	−2.4	−2.2
	30	Consumer price index† (1986 = 100)	14.0	13.9	10.7	11.6	11.6	12.1	13.4	13.8	13.9	14.4
	31	CPI change (annual %)	1.6	−0.2	−7.1	2.0	0	3.9	5.5	0.5	0.5	3.3
	32	Money supply, M3 less foreign currency (in billions of dollars in December)	2.01	2.27	1.99	2.48	2.90	2.99	3.76	5.19	5.88	6.74
	33	Growth rate of money supply (annual %)	3.9	−2.1	−1.3	3.8	13.3	3.3	13.1	18.9	13.3	14.7
	34	3-month Treasury Bill yield-year's low	—	—	2.00	0.63	0.56	0.64	0.52	0.37	0.36	0.36
	35	3-month Treasury Bill yield-year's high	—	—	2.99	0.80	0.88	0.78	0.55	0.40	0.37	0.40
	36	Unemployment (in thousands)	108	116	826	411	529	423	135	63	73	163
	37	Unemployment as % of civilian labour force	3.0	2.9	19.3	9.1	11.4	9.2	3.0	1.4	1.6	3.4

†The CPI has been converted from a 1981 to a 1986 base by a conversion factor of 1.324, and rounded off.

1947	1949	1950	1951	1952	1953	1954	1955	1956	1957	1958	1959	1960	1961	1962	
$9.427	$11.463	$12.576	$13.973	$15.282	$16.296	$17.078	$18.543	$20.273	$21.699	$23.064	$24.643	$25.780	$26.240	$27.985	1
1.343	1.722	1.928	2.811	3.620	3.824	3.825	4.036	4.426	4.573	4.854	4.976	5.281	6.166	6.567	2
2.820	3.676	4.596	5.515	5.823	6.583	5.773	7.047	9.379	9.228	8.584	9.421	9.253	8.870	9.928	3
0.382	0.506	0.091	−0.137	0.511	−0.137	−0.079	−0.268	−0.866	−0.838	−0.486	−0.765	−0.494	−0.154	−0.038	4
−0.032	−0.020	−0.066	0.118	−0.066	−0.171	−0.066	−0.108	−0.310	−0.195	−0.327	−0.398	−0.372	−0.236	−0.034	5
$13.940	$17.347	$19.125	$22.280	$25.170	$26.395	$26.531	$29.250	$32.902	$34.467	$35.689	$37.877	$39.448	40.886	44.408	6
−0.322	−0.355	−0.425	−0.391	−0.324	−0.301	−0.339	−0.385	−0.461	−0.563	−0.525	−0.609	−0.616	−0.722	−0.771	7
$13.618	$16.992	$18.700	$21.889	$24.846	$26.094	$26.192	$28.865	$32.441	$33.904	$35.164	$37.268	$38.832	40.164	43.637	8
1.678	1.878	2.065	2.548	2.799	2.994	3.042	3.321	3.731	3.975	4.036	4.401	4.587	4.767	5.369	9
1.236	1.657	1.889	2.108	2.347	2.648	2.947	3.366	3.838	4.184	4.155	4.478	4.769	4.919	5.297	10
0.032	0.020	0.067	−0.119	0.066	0.171	0.066	0.109	0.310	0.195	0.327	0.399	0.373	0.237	0.035	11
$10.672	$13.437	$14.679	$17.352	$19.634	$20.281	$20.137	$22.069	$24.562	$25.550	$26.646	$27.990	$29.103	30.241	32.936	12
0.834	0.944	1.025	1.026	1.347	1.452	1.628	1.723	1.760	2.072	2.619	2.732	3.099	2.732	2.934	13
0.017	0.017	0.015	0.018	0.032	0.034	0.034	0.036	0.039	0.039	0.045	0.050	0.052	0.076	0.075	14
0.559	0.572	0.544	0.609	0.651	0.620	0.650	0.664	0.718	0.774	0.826	1.023	1.093	1.184	1.316	15
0.011	0.021	0.029	0.038	0.045	0.058	0.065	0.075	0.087	0.088	0.100	0.110	0.123	0.136	0.146	16
0.702	0.723	0.993	1.431	1.403	1.244	1.115	1.310	1.443	1.378	1.350	1.615	1.588	1.649	1.753	17
0.651	0.738	0.869	1.031	1.009	1.136	1.089	1.531	1.680	1.346	1.511	1.445	1.373	1.440	1.658	18
0.261	0.242	0.280	0.285	0.368	0.378	0.373	0.420	0.537	0.490	0.542	0.604	0.649	0.721	0.795	19
−0.537	−0.222	−0.238	−0.648	0.159	−0.031	0.069	−0.132	−0.217	−0.068	−0.047	−0.120	−0.023	−0.004	−0.087	20
$11.016	$13.510	$14.388	$16.944	$18.770	$19.718	$19.868	$21.438	$23.723	$25.377	$26.880	$28.361	$29.883	30.563	33.288	21
0.962	1.013	0.977	1.356	1.670	1.832	1.849	1.934	2.224	2.456	2.338	2.668	3.028	3.191	3.436	22
$10.054	$12.497	$13.411	$15.588	$17.100	$17.886	$18.019	$19.504	$21.499	$22.921	$24.542	$25.693	$26.855	27.372	29.852	23
9.427	11.463	12.576	13.973	15.282	16.296	17.078	18.543	20.273	21.699	23.064	24.643	25.780	26.240	27.985	24
0.011	0.021	0.029	0.038	0.045	0.058	0.065	0.075	0.087	0.088	0.100	0.110	0.123	0.136	0.146	25
0.047	0.032	0.036	0.044	0.050	0.056	0.065	0.071	0.079	0.087	0.090	0.096	0.098	0.105	0.101	26
$0.569	$0.981	$0.770	$1.533	$1.723	$1.476	$0.811	$0.815	$1.060	$1.047	$1.288	$0.844	$0.854	0.891	1.660	27

1947	1949	1950	1951	1952	1953	1954	1955	1956	1957	1958	1959	1960	1961	1962	
91.665	97.234	104.821	109.492	118.627	124.526	123.163	134.889	146.523	150.179	153.439	159.484	164.126	169.271	181.264	28
5.1	4.5	7.8	4.5	8.3	5.0	−1.1	9.5	8.6	2.5	2.2	3.9	2.9	3.1	7.1	29
15.6	18.4	18.8	21.1	21.5	21.2	21.4	21.4	21.8	22.5	23.1	23.1	23.6	23.9	24.2	30
8.9	3.0	2.0	12.0	1.8	−1.1	1.1	0	1.8	3.1	2.7	0	2.3	1.0	1.3	31
6.97	8.05	8.51	8.68	9.22	9.21	9.99	10.85	11.16	11.38	12.83	12.64	13.22	14.37	14.91	32
3.4	4.8	5.7	2.1	6.2	−0.2	8.5	8.6	2.9	1.9	12.8	−1.5	4.6	8.7	3.8	33
0.40	0.41	0.51	0.63	0.89	1.34	1.06	0.88	2.52	3.62	0.87	3.28	1.70	2.26	3.07	34
0.41	0.51	0.63	0.90	1.30	1.97	1.81	2.56	3.67	4.03	3.49	5.50	4.61	3.28	5.47	35
110	153	186	126	155	162	250	245	197	278	432	372	446	466	390	36
2.2	3.0	3.6	2.4	2.9	3.0	4.6	4.4	3.4	4.6	7.0	6.0	7.0	7.1	5.9	37

NATIONAL INCOME AND RELATED STATISTICS FOR SELECTED YEARS, 1963–1991
National income statistics are in billions of current dollars

			1963	1964	1965	1966	1967	1968	1969	1970	1971	1972	1973	1974
THE	1	Personal consumption expenditure	$29.846	$32.042	$34.714	$37.952	$41.068	$44.842	$49.093	$51.853	$56.271	$63.021	$72.069	$84.231
SUM	2	Government current purchases of goods and services	6.923	7.526	8.269	9.643	11.092	12.685	14.186	16.448	18.228	20.136	22.851	27.480
OF	3	Gross investment	10.673	12.260	14.960	17.200	16.453	17.229	19.621	19.250	21.941	24.660	30.722	39.371
	4	Net exports of goods and services	0.350	0.502	−0.113	−0.020	0.700	0.980	0.139	2.248	1.642	0.958	1.743	0.439
	5	Statistical discrepancy	−0.114	−0.139	−0.307	−0.387	−0.249	−0.318	−0.013	−0.683	−0.792	−0.146	−0.013	0.590
EQUALS	6	**GDP at market prices**	**47.678**	**52.191**	**57.523**	**64.388**	**69.064**	**75.418**	**83.026**	**89.116**	**97.290**	**108.629**	**127.372**	**152.111**
	7	Net investment income from nonresidents	−0.848	−0.908	−0.992	−1.120	−1.240	−1.221	−1.207	−1.351	−1.506	−1.461	−1.730	−2.238
EQUALS	8	**GNP at market prices**	**46.830**	**51.283**	**56.531**	**63.268**	**67.824**	**74.197**	**81.819**	**87.765**	**95.784**	**107.168**	**125.642**	**149.873**
LESS	9	Indirect taxes less subsidies	5.628	6.357	7.181	7.918	8.729	9.520	10.544	11.095	12.053	13.627	15.311	17.867
	10	Capital consumption allowances	5.658	6.148	6.684	7.369	7.881	8.412	9.153	9.948	10.764	11.734	13.628	16.447
	11	Statistical discrepancy	0.115	0.139	0.307	0.388	0.250	0.318	0.013	0.684	0.792	0.147	0.014	−0.590
EQUALS	12	**Net national income at factor cost**	**35.429**	**38.639**	**42.359**	**47.593**	**50.964**	**55.947**	**62.109**	**66.038**	**72.175**	**81.660**	**96.689**	**116.149**
PLUS	13	Government transfer payments	3.007	3.220	3.452	3.781	4.683	5.465	6.123	6.991	8.294	9.981	11.272	13.929
	14	Transfers from nonresidents	0.082	0.089	0.098	0.098	0.109	0.110	0.109	0.123	0.171	0.182	0.215	0.229
	15	Interest on the public debt	1.431	1.546	1.676	1.862	2.080	2.390	2.767	3.252	3.622	4.137	4.788	5.425
	16	Interest on consumer debt (transfer portion)	0.147	0.166	0.198	0.224	0.256	0.364	0.466	0.538	0.553	0.625	0.812	1.176
LESS	17	Corporation income taxes	1.891	2.101	2.197	2.355	2.396	2.852	3.221	3.070	3.346	3.920	5.079	7.051
	18	Undistributed corporation profits	1.894	2.419	2.711	2.802	2.769	3.310	3.396	2.960	3.544	4.449	6.983	8.978
	19	Government investment income	0.899	0.982	1.080	1.226	1.479	1.752	2.276	2.724	3.217	3.739	4.423	6.009
	20	Other earnings not paid out to persons	−0.021	−0.004	−0.323	−0.122	−0.429	−0.626	−0.505	−0.034	−0.569	−1.026	−2.547	−3.898
EQUALS	21	**Personal income**	**35.433**	**38.162**	**42.118**	**47.297**	**51.877**	**56.988**	**63.186**	**68.222**	**75.277**	**85.503**	**99.838**	**118.768**
LESS	22	Personal taxes	3.655	4.226	4.801	6.185	7.445	8.844	10.881	12.606	14.130	15.647	18.091	22.364
EQUALS	23	**Personal disposable income**	**31.778**	**33.936**	**37.317**	**41.112**	**44.432**	**48.144**	**52.305**	**55.616**	**61.147**	**69.856**	**81.747**	**96.404**
LESS	24	Personal consumption expenditure	29.846	32.042	34.714	37.952	41.068	44.842	49.093	51.853	56.271	63.021	72.069	84.231
	25	Interest paid by consumers to corporations	0.147	0.166	0.198	0.224	0.256	0.364	0.466	0.538	0.553	0.625	0.812	1.176
	26	Current transfers to nonresidents	0.110	0.109	0.124	0.128	0.157	0.130	0.185	0.176	0.181	0.215	0.237	0.247
EQUALS	27	**Personal saving**	**1.675**	**1.619**	**2.281**	**2.808**	**2.951**	**2.808**	**2.561**	**3.049**	**4.142**	**5.995**	**8.692**	**10.750**

RELATED STATISTICS			1963	1964	1965	1966	1967	1968	1969	1970	1971	1972	1973	1974
	28	Real GDP (in 1986 dollars)	190.672	203.382	216.802	231.519	238.306	251.064	264.508	271.372	286.998	303.447	326.848	341.235
	29	Growth rate of real GDP (annual %)	5.2	6.7	6.6	6.8	2.9	5.4	5.4	2.6	5.8	5.7	7.7	4.4
	30	Consumer price index (1986 = 100)	24.5	25.0	25.7	26.6	27.6	28.6	30.1	31.0	31.9	33.4	36.0	39.9
	31	CPI change (annual %)	1.6	1.8	3.0	3.2	3.7	3.8	5.0	3.3	2.9	4.7	7.7	10.9
*32		Money supply, M3 (in billions of dollars in December)	15.87	17.03	19.08	20.31	23.59	26.72	27.72*	34.60*	37.72	43.31	52.68	64.09
	33	Growth rate of money supply (annual %)	6.4	7.3	12.0	6.5	16.1	13.3	3.8	10.9†	9.0	14.8	21.6	21.7
	34	3-month Treasury Bill yield–year's low	3.19	3.58	3.62	4.63	4.00	5.48	6.38	4.40	3.00	3.36	3.90	6.07
	35	3-month Treasury Bill yield–year's high	3.78	3.88	4.54	5.19	5.95	6.99	7.81	7.78	4.68	3.73	6.53	9.11
	36	Unemployment (in thousands)	374	324	280	267	315	382	382	495	552	562	520	514
	37	Unemployment as % of civilian labour force	5.5	4.7	3.9	3.6	4.1	4.8	4.7	5.9	6.4	6.3	5.6	5.3

*Prior to 1970, this series *excluded* foreign currency booked in Canada as well as the liabilities of the chartered banks' majority-owned subsidiaries. Thus there is a discontinuity between 1969 and 1970.
†Growth rate of discontinued series.

1975	1976	1977	1978	1979	1980	1981	1982	1983	1984	1985	1986	1987	1988	1989	1990	1991	
$97.566	$111.500	$123.555	$137.427	$153.390	$172.416	$196.191	$210.509	$231.452	$251.645	$274.503	$296.810	$322.769	$349.937	$378.077	398.208	410.413	1
33.266	38.274	43.411	47.386	52.286	59.250	68.792	78.655	84.571	89.089	95.519	100.337	105.836	114.472	123.718	133.781	140.607	2
43.213	49.037	52.090	55.632	68.428	72.624	87.305	71.574	78.329	89.460	96.479	104.122	119.788	136.585	149.898	137.207	131.734	3
−2.408	−1.027	−0.069	1.100	1.794	5.646	3.879	14.053	13.612	15.403	11.531	4.490	4.914	2.925	−1.692	−1.361	−6.503	4
−0.097	0.140	−1.108	0.059	0.198	−0.045	−0.173	−0.349	−2.247	−0.862	−0.044	−1.128	−1.710	1.987	−0.085	0.008	−1.863	5
171.540	197.924	217.879	241.604	276.096	309.891	355.994	374.442	405.717	444.735	477.988	504.631	551.597	605.906	649.916	667.843	674.388	6
−2.538	−3.536	−4.571	−5.950	−7.155	−7.827	−11.337	−12.670	−11.603	−13.486	−14.332	−16.548	−16.444	−18.712	−21.503	−24.256	−22.384	7
169.002	194.388	213.308	235.654	268.941	302.064	344.657	361.772	394.114	431.249	463.656	488.083	535.153	587.194	628.413	643.587	652.004	8
17.087	20.992	23.188	24.819	26.635	27.272	36.457	38.908	40.135	42.714	47.212	53.532	59.719	67.790	75.844	75.231	81.535	9
18.760	21.454	23.798	26.619	30.743	35.527	40.677	44.356	47.060	50.884	55.926	60.214	64.116	68.128	72.411	76.184	79.158	10
0.098	−0.141	1.109	−0.059	−0.199	0.045	0.173	0.350	2.247	0.863	0.045	1.128	1.710	−1.987	0.085	−0.009	1.864	11
133.057	152.083	165.213	184.275	211.762	239.220	267.350	278.158	304.672	336.788	360.473	373.209	409.608	453.263	480.073	492.181	489.447	12
17.259	19.656	22.356	25.185	26.697	30.864	35.307	44.453	51.253	54.180	58.515	62.221	66.438	71.415	77.096	85.260	98.370	13
0.258	0.279	0.331	0.394	0.450	0.519	0.545	0.600	0.610	0.629	0.681	0.774	0.821	0.849	0.853	0.935	0.968	14
6.538	8.101	9.268	11.589	13.810	16.790	22.268	27.072	29.419	34.752	40.183	42.916	45.903	50.410	58.075	63.596	65.592	15
1.351	1.570	1.670	1.918	2.855	3.713	5.362	5.132	3.785	3.791	4.233	4.624	5.268	6.205	8.244	9.036	7.725	16
7.494	7.128	7.238	8.188	10.038	12.078	12.796	11.755	12.320	14.984	15.563	14.383	16.990	17.586	18.518	16.851	13.649	17
8.019	9.863	10.333	12.384	18.522	18.825	11.418	−0.498	11.657	16.971	19.827	15.481	24.172	28.970	22.426	6.660	0.602	18
7.176	8.446	9.978	12.467	14.932	17.940	20.934	22.309	25.267	28.182	29.656	28.833	29.573	32.527	36.208	37.677	37.447	19
−2.804	−1.875	−3.549	−4.841	−7.385	−6.627	−7.531	−2.988	−2.557	−2.236	−1.160	−1.351	−3.888	−2.983	−2.002	0.269	3.050	20
138.578	158.127	174.838	195.163	219.467	248.890	293.215	324.837	343.052	372.239	400.199	426.398	461.191	506.042	549.191	589.551	607.354	21
25.257	29.888	33.464	35.697	39.615	45.237	55.533	61.976	67.039	71.893	78.862	89.244	99.756	111.807	117.951	135.921	140.203	22
113.321	128.239	141.374	159.466	179.852	203.653	237.682	262.861	276.013	300.346	321.337	337.154	361.435	394.235	431.240	453.630	467.151	23
97.566	111.500	123.550	137.427	153.390	172.416	196.191	210.509	231.452	251.645	274.503	296.810	322.769	349.937	378.077	398.208	410.413	24
1.351	1.570	1.670	1.918	2.855	3.713	5.362	5.132	3.785	3.791	4.233	4.624	5.268	6.205	8.244	9.036	7.725	25
0.258	0.269	0.292	0.294	0.347	0.364	0.385	0.443	0.473	0.500	0.554	0.574	0.629	0.709	0.780	0.820	0.860	26
14.146	14.900	15.862	19.827	23.260	27.160	35.744	46.777	40.303	44.410	42.047	35.146	32.769	37.384	44.139	45.566	48.153	27

1975	1976	1977	1978	1979	1980	1981	1982	1983	1984	1985	1986	1987	1988	1989	1990	1991	
350.113	371.688	385.122	402.737	418.328	424.537	440.127	425.970	439.448	467.167	489.437	504.631	526.730	552.958	565.779	563.060	553.457	28
2.6	6.2	3.6	4.6	3.9	1.5	3.7	−3.2	3.2	6.3	4.8	3.1	4.2	5.0	2.3	−0.5	−1.7	29
44.2	47.5	51.3	55.8	61.0	67.1	75.5	83.7	88.6	92.4	96.1	100.0	104.4	108.6	114.0	119.5	126.2	30
10.8	7.5	8.0	8.8	9.2	10.2	12.5	10.8	5.8	4.4	4.0	4.1	4.4	4.0	5.0	4.8	5.6	31
73.66	88.57	101.04	118.87	141.99	162.13	181.15	181.28	178.77	191.03	200.97	218.83	233.637	257.899	291.315	314.243	332.423	32
14.9	20.2	16.5	14.3	19.8	16.3	13.2	4.3	0.7	2.1	5.8	6.5	8.7	7.9	11.2	9.8	7.1	33
6.26	8.14	7.05	7.13	10.78	10.06	14.41	9.80	9.12	9.73	8.53	8.09	6.8	8.29	10.94	11.47	7.25	34
8.64	9.13	8.04	10.46	13.66	17.01	20.82	16.33	9.71	12.73	11.27	11.55	9.58	10.95	12.37	13.80	11.47	35
690	727	850	911	838	867	898	1,305	1,436	1,399	1,328	1,236	1,150	1,031	1,018	1,109	1,417	36
6.9	7.1	8.1	8.4	7.5	7.5	7.6	11.0	11.9	11.3	10.5	9.6	8.8	7.8	7.5	8.1	10.3	37

Sources: Statistics Canada: *National Income and Expenditure Accounts; Bank of Canada Review;* Bank of Canada printouts.

Index

────────────────── *cut here* ──────────────────────────

STUDENT REPLY CARD

In order to improve future editions, we are seeking your comments on

Microeconomics, Sixth Canadian Edition.

Please answer the following questions and return this form via Business Reply Mail. Your opinions matter. Thank you in advance for sharing them with us!

Name of your college or university: _____

Major program of study: _____

Course title: _____

Were you required to buy this book? _____ yes _____ no

Did you buy this book new or used? _____ new _____ used ($_____)

Do you plan to keep or sell this book? _____ keep _____ sell

Is the order of topic coverage consistent with what was taught in your course?

────────────────── *fold here* ──────────────────────────

Are there chapters or sections of this text that were not assigned for your course? Please specify:

Were there topics covered in your course that are not included in the text? Please specify:

What did you like most about this text?

What did you like least?

If you would like to say more, we would appreciate hearing from you. Please write to us at the address shown on the reverse of this page.

cut here

fold here

cut here

7115

Attn.: Sponsoring Editor, Business and Commerce
The College Division

**McGraw-Hill Ryerson Limited
300 Water St.
Whitby, ON
L1N 9Z9**

tape shut